Essentials of Programming in *Mathematica*®

Essentials of Programming in Mathematica provides an introduction suitable for readers with little or no background in the *Mathematica* language, as well as for those with some experience using languages such as C, JAVA, or PERL. The author, an established authority on *Mathematica* programming, has written an example-driven text that covers the language from first principles, as well as including material from natural language processing, bioinformatics, graphs and networks, signal analysis, geometry, computer science, and many other applied areas.

The book is appropriate for self-study or as a text for a course in programming in computational science. Readers will benefit from the author's tips, which provide insight and suggestions on small and large points. He also provides more than 350 exercises from novice through to advanced level, with all of the solutions available online.

- Assumes no formal knowledge of programming
- More than 350 exercises from basic to advanced make the book ideal for teaching or for self-study
- Appeals to a broad readership by using examples derived from a wide variety of fields
- Solutions to exercises are available from www.cambridge.org/wellin_essentials

Paul Wellin worked for Wolfram Research from the mid-1990s through 2011, directing the *Mathematica* training efforts with the Wolfram Education Group. He has taught mathematics both at public schools and at university level for over 12 years. He has given talks, workshops, and seminars around the world on the integration of technical computing and education, and he has served on numerous government advisory panels on these issues. He is the author and co-author of several books on *Mathematica*.

Essentials of Programming in *Mathematica*®

PAUL WELLIN

CAMBRIDGE
UNIVERSITY PRESS

University Printing House, Cambridge CB2 8BS, United Kingdom

Cambridge University Press is part of the University of Cambridge.

It furthers the University's mission by disseminating knowledge in the pursuit of education, learning and research at the highest international levels of excellence.

www.cambridge.org
Information on this title: www.cambridge.org/9781107116665

First published 2016
Reprinted 2022

Printed in the United Kingdom by TJ Books Limited, Padstow Cornwall

A catalogue record for this publication is available from the British Library

Library of Congress Cataloguing in Publication data

ISBN 978-1-107-11666-5 Hardback

Text set in DTL Albertina 11/13; code set in Inconsolata; captions set in Syntax LT Std;
System *Mathematica*®, Version 10.2.
Designed and typeset by the author

Additional resources for this publication at www.cambridge.org/wellin_essentials

To the memory of my father
whose love of books curiously led to this

Contents

Preface

Programming with *Mathematica*

In its brief history, the world of programming has undergone a remarkable evolution. Those of us old enough to remember boxes of punch cards and batch jobs couldn't be happier about some of these changes. One could argue that the limitations, physical and conceptual, of the early programming environments helped to focus that world in a very singular manner. Eventually, efforts to overcome those limitations led to a very visible and broad transformation of the world of computer programming. We now have a plethora of languages, paradigms, and environments to choose from. At times this embarrassment of riches can be a bit overwhelming, but I think most would agree that we are fortunate to have such variety in programming languages with which to do our work.

I learned about *Mathematica* as I suspect many people have – after using several languages over the years, a colleague introduced me to a new and very different tool, *Mathematica*. I soon realized that it was going to help me in my work in ways that previous languages could not. Perhaps the most notable feature was how quickly I could translate the statement of a problem to a working program. This was no doubt due to having a functional style of programming at my fingertips but also being able to think in terms of rules and patterns seemed to fit well with my background in mathematics.

Well, *Mathematica* is no longer a young up-start in the programming world. It has been around now for over 25 years, making it, if not an elder statesman, certainly a mature and familiar player. And one that is used by people in fields as varied as linguistics, bioinformatics, engineering, and information theory. Like myself, many people are first introduced to it in an academic setting. Many more are introduced through a colleague at work. Still others have seen it mentioned in various media and are curious as to what it is all about. After using it to do basic or more advanced computation, most users soon find the need to extend the default set of tools that come with *Mathematica*. Programming is the ticket.

So what makes *Mathematica* such a useful programming tool? First, it is a well-designed language, one whose internal logic will be quite apparent as you get to know it. It is not only easier to use but it also provides an enjoyable programming experience. Second, it is a multi-paradigmatic language, meaning several different styles of programming are available under one roof: functional programming (like LISP or HASKELL), procedural programming (like C, FORTRAN, JAVA, PERL), logic programming (like PROLOG), rule-based programming (SNOBOL and some of PROLOG), and it has a rich string pattern language, including support for regular expressions (like PERL). In no other language can you program in so many styles and mix them at will.

The generality of the *Mathematica* language is in sharp contrast to what are called *domain-specific languages*. As the name implies, these are languages designed to solve problems for a specific application domain. HTML is a classic example – it is a markup language that is only really useful for its intended purpose, marking up web pages. Similarly, TEX, used for page composition of technical material and GRAPHML, for representing, formatting, and operating on graph objects, can both be thought of as domain-specific languages.

Mathematica takes a different approach. The language is general enough that it can be used in a variety of different disciplines to represent and solve computational problems. As for speed, it is fast enough for many problems you will encounter. When the need to increase performance arises, options are available: parallel programming, compilation, connecting to external programs.

Given the generality of *Mathematica* and the fact that you can choose different programming paradigms with which to write your programs, the novice is often left feeling a little bewildered. Which style should you use for a particular problem? Which is fastest? Which approach makes the most sense for your particular domain? In general, although good *Mathematica* programmers rely on a functional style to a great degree, your *Mathematica* programs will contain a combination of styles. They tend to be more compact, easier to read, and easier to debug (although not always) than more traditional procedural implementations. Well, perhaps I am showing my bias. It may be that I chose *Mathematica* because it fit well with how I think; or perhaps my adoption of *Mathematica* has shaped the form of programs I write. Perhaps this is just another instance of the Sapir–Whorf hypothesis in linguistics, which states that a spoken language influences the patterns of thought of the speaker of that language. Rather than go down that rabbit hole, let's just say that you will program differently with *Mathematica*, and, I think, more efficiently and more enjoyably.

Who is this book for?

This book is designed for two overlapping audiences. First, it is intended as a self-contained, self-study book for anyone who wants to learn how to use the *Mathematica* language to solve problems in their domain. Typically, this includes researchers, academics, students, and even hobbyists who are accustomed to picking up and learning about any tools that will help them do what they do better. Comments from users of my previous books have persuaded me that an example-based book, such as this, is appreciated by many.

Second, this book can also be used as a text in a course on *Mathematica* programming such as is used in many schools and universities as part of, or in preparation for, a computational science course. Toward that end, each section includes many exercises to check basic understanding of the concepts in that section, as well as providing extended and (hopefully) interesting examples in their own right. A complete set of solutions in both PDF format and as *Mathematica* notebooks is available at the publisher's website www.cambridge.org/wellin_essentials.

The examples and exercises in this book draw from many different fields, including:

- *Bioinformatics*. Analysis of nucleotide sequences, computing GC ratios, displaying blocks of genetic information, searching for subsequences, protein–protein interaction networks, dot plots, displaying amino acid sequences, space-filling plots.
- *Computer science*. Encoding/encryption, sorting, adjacency structures, Collatz sequences, Hamming numbers, Hamming weight, Tower of Hanoi, Fibonacci numbers, Fibonacci words, Euler numbers, root finders, Horner polynomial representation, inverse permutations, random number algorithms, sieving, associative arrays, Monte Carlo simulations, comparisons with other languages.
- *Data and signal analysis*. Filtering signals (smoothing, clipping, removing spikes), entropy of signals, Benford's law, stem plots, lag plots, statistical analysis of data, random walks, visualizing extent of data, Hamming distance, cluster analysis.
- *Finance and economics*. Time-series analysis of economic and financial data, trend plots, stock screens.
- *Geometry*. Convex hull, diameter of point sets, point-in-polygon problems, traveling salesman-type problems, hypocycloids and epicycloids, area and perimeter problems, boundaries of regions, Heron's formula, triangle medians and centers.
- *Graphs and networks*. Random graphs, regular graphs, bond percolation, connected components, dense graphs, directed acyclic graphs, neighborhood graphs, random walk on graphs.
- *Image processing*. Resizing, filtering, segmentation.
- *Mathematics*. Palindromic numbers, triangular numbers, pyramidal numbers, truth tables, prime gaps, Vandermonde and Jacobian matrices, Mersenne numbers, Venn diagrams, geometric transformations.
- *Solar physics and atmospheric science*. Analyzing and visualizing sunspot activity using time series, analyzing global sea-surface temperature data, solar magnetic field cycles.
- *Textual analysis and natural language processing*. Corpus linguistics, word stemming, stop words, comparative textual analysis, scraping websites for data, sorting strings, bigrams and *n*-grams, word games (anagrams, blanagrams, palindromes), filtering text.

The background necessary to successfully navigate and learn from this book includes some introductory undergraduate mathematics (basic linear algebra, geometry). The science topics and problems introduced in this book are mostly self-contained and, where necessary, they point to available references in the literature. Although no prior experience with programming is assumed, even the most basic experience with writing, running, or debugging programs will be helpful in getting you up and running more quickly.

This book is not a tutorial introduction to *Mathematica*. For that, fortunately, there are many useful resources available, including in-product tutorials, online courses, and many good books. Refer to the Wolfram Research website for a comprehensive listing of these materials.

How to use this book

For those new to *Mathematica*, Chapter 1 will give you a sense of what it means to program, what it means to program in *Mathematica*, and introduces you to some of the basic tools every *Mathematica* user should know about: entering and evaluating expressions, dealing with errors, getting help.

The real meat of the book starts with Chapter 2, which provides a semi-formal description of the *Mathematica* language with a particular focus on expressions. Chapters 3 through 5 (lists, patterns and rules, functions) are the core of the book. Lists are a fundamental data type in *Mathematica* and provide a relatively simple structure for much of what follows. Pattern matching and the use of transformation rules are an essential and somewhat unique aspect that every *Mathematica* programmer must master. Functional programming, introduced in Chapter 5, will likely be new to you, but once you understand it, the speed and efficiency of what you can do will increase dramatically.

Chapter 6 introduces localization constructs, options and messages enabling your programs to look and behave much like the built-in functions. Although you could skip this chapter if you were solely focused on solving particular computational problems, spending some time with these topics will help you to start thinking like a programmer. How will your programs be used by others? How will they likely interact with your programs? What should happen when something goes wrong?

Strings are used of course in linguistics, but they also have broad applicability in computer science, web search, and bioinformatics. They are discussed in Chapter 7, which includes an introduction to regular expressions. If you do little or no work with strings you could safely skim or skip this chapter but there is a lot of useful material there if you do dive in.

Chapter 8 on graphics and visualization gives an introduction to the *Mathematica* graphics language as well as the dynamic expression language as it relates to graphics. Topics on optimizing your graphics code are included.

With all the different approaches available in *Mathematica* to solve problems, it is sometimes difficult to determine the "best" approach. Chapter 9 on program optimization addresses this issue from the point of view of speed and efficiency; that is, which approaches will help your programs run faster and use fewer system resources.

Chapter 10 provides a framework for those who wish to turn their programs into packages that can be shared with colleagues, students, or clients. It includes an extended example, random walks, so that you can begin to see examples of larger programs that include modularization, namespace constructs, messaging, options, testing, and other meta-programming issues that are important to think about as your programming skills advance.

To return to the question about which style of programming you should adopt for a particular problem, I hope that this book will convince you that this is the wrong question to ask. As you become more familiar with the *Mathematica* programming language, you will start to reword and formulate your programs and implement them using all of the tools you have under your belt.

Learning different paradigms does not point to an either/or approach, but allows you to use combinations of programming styles to solve your problems as efficiently as possible.

With that in mind, do not take the formal structure of this book too literally. Although books are pretty linear physical objects – one page or chapter follows another – learning is not linear. It is fine to jump around as the need arises. In fact, you are encouraged to do so. Although, in general, latter material presupposes knowledge of what has come before, several examples and exercises use concepts that are developed later in the book and if you are not already familiar with them, you should feel free to jump ahead.

Numerous references are made throughout the book to tutorials and other help documents that are found in *Mathematica*'s help system, the Wolfram Language and System Documentation Center, referred to as WLDC. This comprehensive help system is available in *Mathematica* under the Help menu and online at reference.wolfram.com.

The exercises (over 350 of them) are an integral part of this book. Some test your knowledge of basic concepts in each section; some extend those concepts; and some use those concepts to solve more substantial and interesting problems. "Life is not a spectator sport" and neither is programming. Try to do as many of the exercises as you can. There is much to learn there.

Resource limitations have prevented the inclusion of the solutions to the exercises with this book (printed, they would stretch over 240 pages). Fortunately, the solutions to the exercises are available online at the publisher's website (www.cambridge.org/wellin_essentials) and the author's website (www.programmingmathematica.com) in both *Mathematica* notebook format as well as PDF. These sites also contain most of the programs and packages developed in this book, the book's bibliography with live clickable references, lists of errata, and some extra material that did not make it into the printed book.

Numerous data files are used throughout this book, many imported from the web and some residing in a project directory for this book. To set up your environment so that import works seamlessly, download the data files from the author's or publisher's website as indicated in the previous paragraph. Then, wherever you put the directory of data files, use something like the following to add that directory to your path. You may find it convenient to put this command in a Kernel/init.m file so that it is evaluated each time you start a new session.

```
PrependTo[$Path,
  ToFileName[{$UserBaseDirectory, "Applications", "EPM", "Data"}]];
```

Finally, a word about *Mathematica* itself. As this book was being developed, a bifurcation occurred and where there was one name, *Mathematica*, now there are two: the *Wolfram Language* and *Mathematica*. The *Wolfram Language* is the name of the underlying language and *Mathematica* is the wider product in which that language occurs. Since I have used both the language and the product throughout the book, in an attempt to simplify, I have opted to refer to the software simply by using the broader term *Mathematica* here.

Acknowledgments

I have been using *Mathematica* for over 25 years now, but I still run into plenty of puzzling things that I would not be able to disentangle without the assistance of others. Thanks are due to Rob Knapp for help in understanding some of the internals of the looping constructs and gaining a deeper understanding of compiling functions. Dan Lichtblau provided some insights into the internals of the Fibonacci computations. Ulises Cervantes-Pimentel helped with region and mesh functionality as well as the structure of the internal representations of these objects. Harry Calkins answered numerous questions on compiling and parallel computation. Charles Pooh provided answers to several of my questions regarding graph functionality and internals. Also, Andre Kuzniarek, Glenn Scholebo, Jeremiah Cunningham, and Larry Adelston helped with a number of production and front end issues. Dennis Coleman provided assistance with some graphic design.

Thanks are also due to Frank E. Blokland, of the Dutch Type Library, for help in working around some OpenType font issues. Frank is the typographer responsible for creating the digital version of the text font used in this book, Albertina (the original design was due to Chris Brand).

David Tranah, my editor at Cambridge University Press, has been extremely helpful in finding the right mix of topics and presentation for such a book. Robert Judkins, in the production department at Cambridge was as efficient and professional as any author could wish. Thanks to Clare Dennison at Cambridge who has quickly and pleasantly handled all those extra little administrative tasks associated with such a project. Thanks are also due to the reviewers of this book, who provided some focused and insightful comments and suggestions on content and style.

The one person who knows better than anyone what it is like to undertake and complete such a project is my wife Sheri. It may have been doable without her patience, support, and love, but it would not have been as enjoyable.

Paul R. Wellin
programmingmathematica@gmail.com

I

Programming with *Mathematica*

Introduction to programming · *Your first Mathematica program* · *Programming paradigms* · *Creating programs* · ***Getting started*** · *Starting and running Mathematica* · *Mathematical expressions* · *Functions* · *Lists* · *Semicolons* · *Alternative input syntax* · *Comments* · ***Getting help*** · *Errors* · *Getting out of trouble* · *Function information* · *Documentation* · ***Notes and further reading***

Mathematica is a large system used across an astonishing array of disciplines – physics, bioinformatics, geo-science, linguistics, network analysis, optics, risk management, software engineering, and many more. It integrates tools for importing, analyzing, simulating, visualizing, reporting, and connecting to other programs. Underlying all of these tools is a modern programming language with which you can extend the things you can do with *Mathematica* almost limitlessly.

This book focuses on the programming language, but before we dive into details of syntax and structure, it will be helpful to look at some of the essential elements of actual programs to give you a better sense of what it means to program with *Mathematica*. So, to start, let us walk through the creation of a short program so you can see how a *Mathematica* programmer might solve a problem. We will not attempt to write the most efficient or shortest code here, but will instead concentrate on the process of programming – things like rewording the problem, finding the right tools and approach, and testing your program. Hopefully, this prelude will give you a better sense of the breadth and depth of the *Mathematica* language and help you answer the question, "Why use *Mathematica* to write programs?"

The second aim of this chapter is to help you become familiar with the *Mathematica* environment, showing you how to get started, how to work with the interface, documentation, and programming tools, and how to start putting them together to do interesting things. The basic syntax used by *Mathematica* is introduced, including functions and lists and several alternate syntaxes that you can use to input expressions. This is followed by information on how to get help when you get stuck or have trouble understanding an error that has occurred. If you are already familiar with these aspects of *Mathematica*, feel free to skim or skip these topics and return to them when the need arises.

1.1 Introduction to programming

Computer programs are detailed and explicit descriptions of the steps to take to accomplish a specific task. The key is converting the original statement of the problem from something you might describe to a colleague in your native natural language into something that a computer can understand and operate on. As an example, suppose you want to write a program for your home's programmable thermostat to control the temperature in your house. A description such as "turn on the heat when it is cold and turn on the air conditioner when it is hot" may be entirely understandable to the humans in your household, but will be of little help in communicating with the thermostat. Instead, imagine formulating the problem as follows: if the ambient temperature drops below 17°C, turn on the heater until the ambient temperature reaches 22°C; if the temperature rises above 29°C, turn on the air conditioner until the temperature drops below 24°C. With this formulation you have enough to translate those instructions into a program.

Let's take this thought experiment one step further. What if you are away at work or school and a door in your house blew open causing the heater to stay on in an attempt to warm the house while cold air rushes in. Although this scenario is atypical, your program could include a conditional check that turns the unit off for one hour say, if it has been on continuously for over two hours.

The task that we commonly think of as "programming" is the set of steps that take a description like the explicit formulation above for the thermostat and actually write code in a language that can be executed on a processor on your computer or on the thermostat itself (with an embedded application). We will pick it up from here with an example that walks through the steps of creating, testing, and refining a program. Using a problem that is simple to describe and does not require a lot of sophisticated programming will help to better focus on these "meta" steps.

Your first Mathematica program

We will create a small program to solve a specific problem – finding and counting palindromic numbers. The process involves stating and then reformulating the problem, implementation, checking typical and atypical input, analyzing and improving efficiency, and performing a post-mortem. There are more aspects that will be discussed throughout this book, such as localization, options, argument checking, and documentation, but at this stage we will keep this initial problem simple. You are not expected to be familiar with all aspects of the program at this point; instead, try to focus on the process here, rather than the details.

As you read through the problem, enter each of the inputs in a *Mathematica* notebook exactly as they appear here, being careful about the syntax. When you have completed each input, press SHIFT+ENTER on your keyboard to evaluate, then go on to the next input (see Section 1.2 for details).

Problem Find all palindromic numbers less than one thousand, then determine how many palindromes there are that are less than one million.

Reformulate the problem A number is a palindrome if it is equal to the number formed by reversing its digits. For example, 1552551 is a palindrome, 1552115 is not. The problem is to create a function that checks if a number is palindromic (returns True if it is, False otherwise); then, from a list of the numbers one through *n*, find all those that pass this palindrome test.

We have restated the problem with an eye toward creating explicit instructions. The ability to do this comes from a knowledge of the constructs and paradigms present in our language, something that is learned over time and experience with that language.

Implementation Given an integer, first we will get a list of its digits, then reverse that list, and finally check that the reversed list is identical to the original list. Start by getting the digits of a number.

```
In[1]:= IntegerDigits[1 552 551]
Out[1]= {1, 5, 5, 2, 5, 5, 1}
```

Function names like `IntegerDigits` are spelled out in full, capitalizing the first letter of each complete word. Arguments to functions, 1552551 in this example, are enclosed in square brackets.

Next, reverse the digits.

```
In[2]:= Reverse[IntegerDigits[1 552 551]]
Out[2]= {1, 5, 5, 2, 5, 5, 1}
```

Check if the list of digits is equal to the list of reversed digits.

```
In[3]:= IntegerDigits[1 552 551] == Reverse[IntegerDigits[1 552 551]]
Out[3]= True
```

Turn this into a program/function that can be run/evaluated for any input.

```
In[4]:= PalindromeQ[n_] := IntegerDigits[n] == Reverse[IntegerDigits[n]]
```

Check a few numbers:

```
In[5]:= PalindromeQ[12 345 678]
Out[5]= False

In[6]:= PalindromeQ[9 991 999]
Out[6]= True
```

Check atypical input Try the function with input for which it was not meant, for example, a symbol.

```
In[7]:= PalindromeQ[f]
Out[7]= True
```

That is not handling bad input correctly. We should try to restrict the function to integer input (Section 6.2 discusses the framework for issuing warning messages when bad input is given).

```
In[8]:= Clear[PalindromeQ];
        PalindromeQ[n_Integer] := IntegerDigits[n] == Reverse[IntegerDigits[n]]
```

Check a few bad inputs:

```
In[10]:= PalindromeQ[f]
Out[10]= PalindromeQ[f]

In[11]:= PalindromeQ[{a, b, c}]
Out[11]= PalindromeQ[{a, b, c}]
```

Solve original problem The original questions were: find all palindromes below one thousand and determine how many there are below one million.

```
In[12]:= Select[Range[10^3], PalindromeQ]
Out[12]= {1, 2, 3, 4, 5, 6, 7, 8, 9, 11, 22, 33, 44, 55, 66, 77, 88, 99, 101, 111, 121, 131, 141,
  151, 161, 171, 181, 191, 202, 212, 222, 232, 242, 252, 262, 272, 282, 292, 303, 313,
  323, 333, 343, 353, 363, 373, 383, 393, 404, 414, 424, 434, 444, 454, 464, 474, 484,
  494, 505, 515, 525, 535, 545, 555, 565, 575, 585, 595, 606, 616, 626, 636, 646, 656,
  666, 676, 686, 696, 707, 717, 727, 737, 747, 757, 767, 777, 787, 797, 808, 818, 828,
  838, 848, 858, 868, 878, 888, 898, 909, 919, 929, 939, 949, 959, 969, 979, 989, 999}

In[13]:= Count[Range[10^6], p_ /; PalindromeQ[p]]
Out[13]= 1998
```

Efficiency How fast is this function for a large list of integers?

```
In[14]:= AbsoluteTiming[
  Select[Range[10^6], PalindromeQ];
 ]
Out[14]= {2.50386, Null}
```

Not too bad, but perhaps we can speed things up. In the definition of `PalindromeQ`, we compute `IntegerDigits[n]` twice, once on each side of the equality check. Instead we can create a local variable `digs` and initialize it with the value of `IntegerDigits[n]`, thus only doing that computation once.

```
In[15]:= Clear[PalindromeQ];

In[16]:= PalindromeQ[n_Integer] := With[{digs = IntegerDigits[n]},
   digs == Reverse[digs]
  ]

In[17]:= AbsoluteTiming[
  Select[Range[10^6], PalindromeQ];
 ]
Out[17]= {2.31562, Null}
```

That didn't help much – probably introducing the scoping construct `With` negated any small gains from reducing the size of the computation. Another strategy might consider using strings which, we know from experience, can be very fast to work with. We will save this approach for Chapter 7 where we discuss strings and compare implementations using lists versus strings.

Actually this problem will parallelize well as the list of numbers to be checked can be distributed across kernels and processors. Any speed improvement will be tied to the number of processors available to run the kernels.

```
In[18]:= LaunchKernels[]
Out[18]= {KernelObject[1, local], KernelObject[2, local],
          KernelObject[3, local], KernelObject[4, local]}

In[19]:= DistributeDefinitions[PalindromeQ]
Out[19]= {PalindromeQ}

In[20]:= AbsoluteTiming[
          Parallelize[Select[Range[10^6], PalindromeQ]];
         ]
Out[20]= {0.887734, Null}
```

Postscript As you work through this example note that the notebook in which the code was developed and tested becomes a documentation of sorts with comments in text cells interspersed here and there to help whoever looks at the code to understand your thinking (including yourself several months or years later). In other words, the notebook interface is your development environment. You could also bundle up your code into a formal package – a platform-independent text file containing *Mathematica* commands – that could be loaded when needed (see Chapter 10).

The code in these examples uses a variety of programming styles and constructs that may be new to you. It is entirely forgivable if you do not understand them at this point – that is what this book is all about! By the time you have worked through a good deal of the book you should be comfortable solving problems using the basic principles of programming – making assignments, defining rules, using conditionals, recursion, and iteration.

Programming paradigms

As you start to write programs in *Mathematica*, it is natural to ask, “How does it compare with programming in other languages?” To start, there are certain details shared by all programming languages and environments. In any language, there is a finite collection of objects that must be put together in a specific order to make statements that are valid in that language. In natural languages, say English, those objects are the alphabet, punctuation symbols, spaces, and so on. The rules of the language describe what are valid statements in that language. In computer languages, those statements are used to communicate instructions to a computer, say to add two integers, or to print a string to the screen, or to iterate a function until a condition is met.

The chief way in which languages differ is in the style of programming that each language uses. Early programming languages, such as FORTRAN and C (and a bit later PERL, PYTHON, and many others), use what is referred to as an *imperative* style of programming. This is one in which a specific sequence of operations are explicitly given and the flow of execution is controlled by the programmer. In other words, the instructions describe *how to perform* each step.

Declarative languages, in contrast, describe the desired result instead of focusing on the underlying machine instructions to get there. That is, they describe *what to do*, rather than how. LISP, SCHEME, HASKELL, and *Mathematica* are mostly declarative languages, although each allows an imperative-style of programming (particularly procedural) to be used as well.

Further distinguishing languages from one another are the steps the programmer takes to try out their programs. In most traditional languages such as FORTRAN, C, and JAVA, you start by writing code in an editor using the constructs of the language. In JAVA, you might write the following source code in an editor:

```
public class HelloWorld {
  public static void main (String[] args) {
    System.out.println ("Hello, World");
  }
}
```

For a similar program in C, you would type:

```
main () {
  printf ("hello, world");
}
```

After saving your code in an appropriately named file, you then run it through a compiler to create an executable file that can be run on your computer. If there is an error somewhere in your program, you go back to your source code and, perhaps with the aid of a debugger, you find and correct any errors and then recompile your program and execute it again.

But there is another way. Some languages, such as LISP, PERL, PYTHON, RUBY, and *Mathematica*, are referred to as *interpreted languages*. What this means is that you use them in an interactive mode: you type in a command, evaluate it in place, and the result is returned. The environment in which you type in the command and see the results is the same; in *Mathematica*, that environment is the notebook.

In PERL, the "Hello World" program is simply:

```
print "Hello World!\n";
```

In *Mathematica*, you type in and then evaluate the following:

```
In[21]:= Print["Hello world"]
         Hello world
```

The advantage of interpreted languages is that you entirely avoid the compile/run/debug cycle of other languages. In addition, these so-called *high-level* interpreted languages contain functions for performing many tasks that you would typically have to implement in a lower-level language (if you are a C programmer, compare Reverse[*lis*] in *Mathematica* with a C program to do the same thing). This saves you time and lets you focus more on the problem at hand and less on the intricacies of memory management, libraries, and registers say.

In the old days, the advantages of compiled languages were speed and access to low-level aspects of your computer. But with advances in hardware, these seeming advantages are much less clear. If a program runs a few tenths of a second faster but takes many more minutes to create, your productivity gains start to evaporate pretty quickly.

Creating programs

In any language, the creation of computer programs involves many different tasks. For our purposes here it is useful to distinguish two broad categories: programming and software development.

Programming involves:

- *Analysis of the problem.* This includes understanding precisely what is being asked and what the answers will look like.
- *Restatement of the problem.* Phrasing the problem in a way that is closer to how you will actually write the program; creating pseudo-code.
- *Formulating a plan of attack.* With what type of data can you prototype the problem? Is the problem one that can be solved using list manipulation? Should you use string functions? Will the computation require extraordinary resources?
- *Implementation.* Translating the problem into code; modularization; if using an interactive language, trying out pieces as you go.

Software development includes:

- *Verification of correctness.* Checking solutions for many types of input; comparing with known solutions; using different algorithms to make comparisons.
- *Debugging.* Finding and correcting errors – from bad syntax or from incorrect algorithms.
- *Robustness.* Checking atypical input that includes special cases, bad input, and generally input that your program was not designed for.
- *Performance and efficiency.* Identifying bottlenecks (possibly through profiling) to improve memory usage and reduce compute time, network bandwidth.
- *Documentation.* Comments and notes about why a specific function or approach was used at a certain step; documenting lightly as you program and then adding more substantial information later.
- *User interface.* What does the user need to know to understand how to use your program? Does it behave like built-in functions or will the user need to learn a new interface element.
- *Portability.* Does your program work on different platforms, environments? Do you need to compile for different operating systems? (Your *Mathematica* programs will run unchanged on any platform that runs *Mathematica*.)

- *Code maintenance.* Periodic checks that your code runs in the latest version of your programming language, on the latest operating system, etc.

Not every program you create will include all of the above pieces, and the order in which you implement them is not so well-defined and discrete as stated here. For example, the `PalindromeQ` program created in the previous section did not include formal documentation outside of comments in the notebook itself. Smaller programs written to solve a basic problem, or programs that you have no intention of sharing with a colleague, student, or client, may not need some of the niceties (such as user interface elements) that another program would have. But the availability of these programming tools and constructs makes *Mathematica* a good choice for both small programs and large-scale applications that will be used by others. This book is designed to give you a good sense of this breadth and depth and to provide a foundational set of tools to use in your *Mathematica* programming.

1.2 Getting started

Let us now turn to some of the basics needed to start using *Mathematica*. If you are not familiar with *Mathematica*, it would be helpful to try out the examples in this section before going further. These examples should give you a sense of what it means to enter, evaluate, and work with some simple computations. If you are already familiar with *Mathematica*, feel free to skim this section lightly.

Starting and running Mathematica

After launching *Mathematica*, parts of it will load into memory and soon a blank window will appear on the screen. This window, called a notebook, is the visual interface to *Mathematica*.

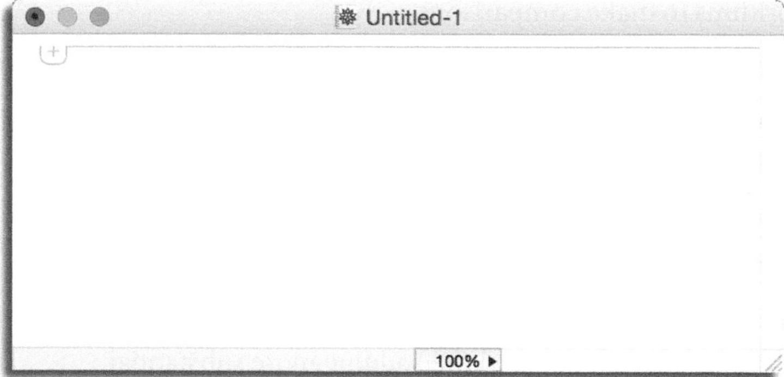

When a blank notebook first appears on the screen, either from just starting *Mathematica* or from selecting New in the File menu, you can start typing immediately. For example, type `N[Pi, 200]` and then press SHIFT+ENTER (hold down the Shift key while pressing the Enter key) to evaluate the expression. *Mathematica* will evaluate the result and print the 200-decimal-digit approximation to π.

When you evaluate an expression in a notebook, *Mathematica* automatically adds input and output prompts *after* you evaluate your input. In the example notebook at the top of the next page, these are denoted In[1]:= and Out[1]=. These prompts can be thought of as markers (or labels) that you can refer to during your *Mathematica* session.

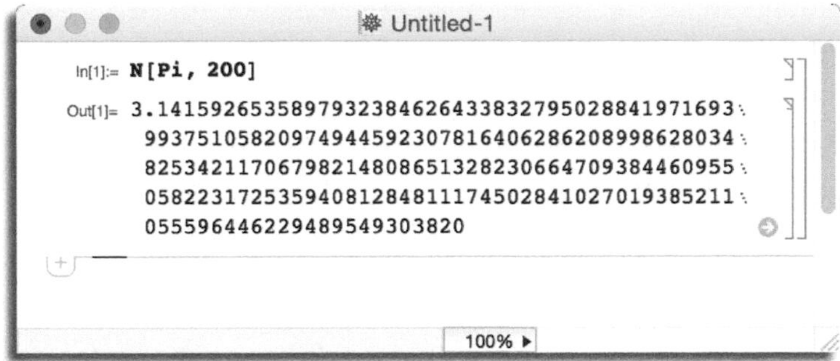

New input can be entered whenever there is a horizontal line that runs across the width of the notebook. If one is not present where you wish to place an input cell, move the cursor up and down until it changes to a horizontal bar and then click the mouse once. A horizontal line should appear across the width of the window. You can immediately start typing and an input cell will be created.

Mathematical expressions can be entered in a traditional-looking two-dimensional format using either palettes for quick entry of template expressions, or keyboard equivalents. For example, the following expression can be entered by using the Basic Math Assistant palette (under the Palettes menu), or through a series of keystrokes as described in the tutorial Entering Two-Dimensional Input in the Wolfram Language Documentation Center (WLDC).

```
In[1]:= 2^100
Out[1]= 1 267 650 600 228 229 401 496 703 205 376
```

To refer to the result of the previous calculation, use the symbol %.

```
In[2]:= % + 1
Out[2]= 1 267 650 600 228 229 401 496 703 205 377
```

To refer to the result of any earlier calculation, use its Out[*i*] label or, equivalently, % *i*.

```
In[3]:= Out[1]
Out[3]= 1 267 650 600 228 229 401 496 703 205 376
```

```
In[4]:= (%1) / 2^90
Out[4]= 1024
```

Mathematical expressions

Mathematical expressions can be entered in a linear syntax using arithmetic operators common to almost all computer languages.

```
In[5]:= 39 / 13
Out[5]= 3
```

Enter this expression in the traditional form by typing 39, CTRL[/], then 13.

```
In[6]:= 39/13
Out[6]= 3
```

The caret (^) is used for exponentiation.

```
In[7]:= 2^5
Out[7]= 32
```

To enter this expression in a more traditional typeset form, type 2, CTRL[^], and then 5.

In[8]:= 2^5

Out[8]= 32

Multiplication can be indicated by putting a space between the two factors, as in mathematical notation. *Mathematica* will automatically display the traditional multiplication sign, ×, between two numbers. The asterisk (*) is also used for that purpose, as is traditional in most computer languages.

```
In[9]:= 2 × 5
Out[9]= 10
```

```
In[10]:= 2 * 5
Out[10]= 10
```

Operations are given the same precedence as in mathematics. In particular, multiplication and division have a higher precedence than addition and subtraction: 3 + 4×5 equals 23 and not 35.

```
In[11]:= 3 + 4 × 5
Out[11]= 23
```

You can enter typeset expressions in several different ways: directly from the keyboard as we did above, using a long (functional) form, or via palettes available from the Palettes menu. Table 1.1 shows some of the more commonly used typeset expressions and how they are entered through the keyboard. Try to become comfortable entering these inputs so that you can easily enter the kinds of expressions used in this book.

TABLE 1.1. *Entering typeset expressions*

Display form	Long (functional) form	Keystrokes
x^2	`Superscript[x,2]`	x, CTRL+6, 2
x_i	`Subscript[x,i]`	x, CTRL+_, i
$\frac{x}{y}$	`FractionBox[x,2]`	x, CTRL+/, y
$\sqrt{x}$	`SqrtBox[x]`	CTRL+2, x
$x \geq y$	`GreaterEqual[x,2]`	x, ESC, >=, ESC, y

Functions

Built-in functions are written as they are in math and science books, except that function names are spelled out, the first letter of each complete word is capitalized, and function arguments are enclosed in square brackets.

```
In[12]:= Factor[x^5 - 1]
Out[12]= (-1 + x) (1 + x + x^2 + x^3 + x^4)
```

Almost all the built-in functions are spelled out in full, as in the above example. The exceptions to this rule are well-known abbreviations such as `D` for differentiation, `Sqrt` for square root, `Log` for logarithm, and `Det` for the determinant of a matrix. The convention of spelling out function names can be quite helpful when you are unsure whether a function exists to perform a particular task. For example, to compute the conjugate of a complex number, an educated guess would be:

```
In[13]:= Conjugate[3 + 4 ⅈ]
Out[13]= 3 - 4 ⅈ
```

Functions of more than one argument separate their arguments with commas, as in traditional mathematical notation. For example, while the following one-argument form of `RandomReal` gives a single random number between zero and ten, the two-argument form can be used to generate a vector or an array of random numbers.

```
In[14]:= RandomReal[10]
Out[14]= 6.62242
```

```
In[15]:= RandomReal[10, 12]
Out[15]= {3.81849, 5.64683, 6.16931, 9.92459, 1.85091, 7.55074,
          1.61231, 4.39048, 2.43564, 2.59877, 1.39747, 2.46044}
```

Lists

Lists are a fundamental data type in *Mathematica* and are used to represent vectors and matrices (and tensors of any dimension), as well as additional arguments to functions such as in `Plot` and `Integrate`. While square brackets `[` and `]` are used to enclose the arguments to functions, curly braces `{` and `}` are used to indicate a list or range of values.

Using lists to represent vectors, the following computes the dot product of two vectors:

```
In[16]:= {a, b, c}.{x, y, z}
Out[16]= a x + b y + c z
```

Lists are used as the arguments to many built-in functions such as `Sum`, `Plot`, and `RandomReal`.

```
In[17]:= sqWave = Sum[1/n Sin[n π x], {n, 1, 9, 2}]
Out[17]= Sin[π x] + 1/3 Sin[3 π x] + 1/5 Sin[5 π x] + 1/7 Sin[7 π x] + 1/9 Sin[9 π x]
```

```
In[18]:= Plot[sqWave, {x, - π, π}]
```

Out[18]=

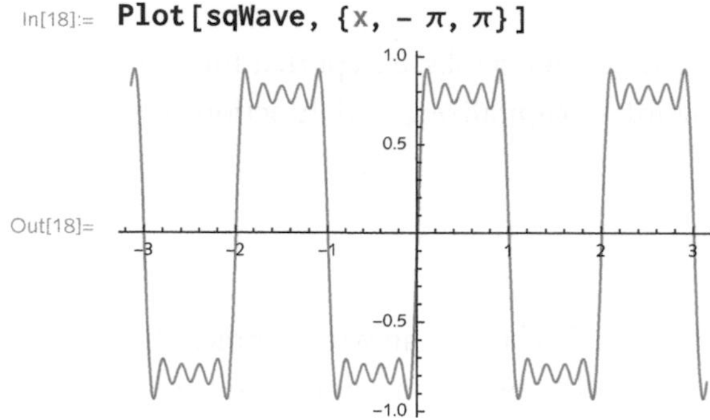

```
In[19]:= RandomReal[{-100, 100}, {4, 4}]
Out[19]= {{78.6216, 64.6651, -81.5924, 36.9842}, {57.6677, -51.265, -59.0191, 86.4116},
          {-86.1984, 89.4375, -15.3311, -32.8491}, {-2.77769, 48.6834, 11.1961, 8.4726}}
```

In the Sum example, the iterator list {i, 1, 9, 2} indicates that the iterator variable i will take on values one through nine in increments of two in each successive iteration. In the Plot example, the list {x, - π, π} indicates that the expression sqWave is to be plotted over an interval as *x* takes on values from $-\pi$ to π. In the last example with RandomReal, the first list specifies the range from which numbers will be chosen and the second list specifies the dimensions, in this case, a 4×4 array.

As you may have noticed, the output of many functions also use lists to display their results.

```
In[20]:= Range[12]
Out[20]= {1, 2, 3, 4, 5, 6, 7, 8, 9, 10, 11, 12}
```

Lists will be discussed in detail in Chapter 3.

Semicolons

When you end an expression with a semicolon (;), the value is computed but it is not displayed. This is quite helpful when the result of the expression would be very long and you do not need to see the output. For example, below we first create a list of the integers from one to ten thousand, suppressing their display with the semicolon; we then compute their sum and average.

```
In[21]:= nums = Range[10000];

In[22]:= Total[nums]
Out[22]= 50005000

In[23]:= % / Length[nums]
Out[23]= 10001/2
```

With the notebook interface, you can input as many lines as you like within an input cell; *Mathematica* will evaluate them all, in order, when you press SHIFT+ENTER.

Alternative input syntax

There are several different ways to write expressions and functions in *Mathematica*. Usually, you will simply use the traditional notation, *fun* [*x*], for example.

```
In[24]:= N[π]
Out[24]= 3.14159
```

But there are alternatives to this syntax that are sometimes used (see Table 1.2). For example, the following syntax uses a prefix operator:

```
In[25]:= N@π
Out[25]= 3.14159
```

Here is the postfix operator notation:

```
In[26]:= π // N
Out[26]= 3.14159
```

For functions with two arguments, you can use an infix notation. The following expression is identical to N[π, 30]:

```
In[27]:= π~N~30
Out[27]= 3.14159265358979323846264338328
```

TABLE 1.2. *Alternative function notation*

Notation	Input syntax
Traditional	N[π]
Prefix	N@π
Postfix	π//N
Infix	π~N~100

Many mathematical functions use traditional symbols and, when available, these can be used instead of the fully spelled-out names. For example, this computes the intersection of two sets using the Intersection function:

```
In[28]:= Intersection[{a, b, d, e}, {b, f, a, z}]
Out[28]= {a, b}
```

Or you can do the same computation using more traditional notation:

```
In[29]:= {a, b, d, e} ⋂ {b, f, a, z}
Out[29]= {a, b}
```

To learn how to enter these and other notations quickly, either from palettes or using keyboard shortcuts, refer to the tutorial Editing and Evaluating Two-Dimensional Expressions (WLDC).

Comments

Input can include *comments* – text that is not evaluated – by enclosing that text with `(*` and `*)`. The comment is inert – it is ignored by the *Mathematica* evaluator.

```
In[30]:= D[Sin[x], {x, 1}] (* first derivative of sin w.r.t. x *)
Out[30]= Cos[x]
```

Exercises

1. Generate a random real number between one and one hundred. Then create a vector of twelve random numbers between one and one hundred. Finally, create a 4×4 array of such numbers and then compute the determinant of that array.
2. Using `Table`, create a 4×4 Hilbert matrix. The entry a_{ij} in row *i*, column *j* of the Hilbert matrix is given by $\frac{1}{i+j-1}$. Check your solution against the built-in `HilbertMatrix`.
3. Add the two lists, `{1, 2, 3, 4, 5}` and `{2, 4, 6, 8, 10}`. Then multiply them element-wise. Finally, multiply the two lists as vectors (dot product).
4. Generate a list of the first twenty-five integers in five different ways.
5. Add the integers one through one thousand in as many different ways as you can.
6. A 2×2 matrix can be created using lists such as $\{\{a, b\}, \{c, d\}\}$. Define a 2×2 numerical matrix and then find its inverse, determinant, transpose, and trace.
7. Create the following matrix using list notation:

   $$\begin{pmatrix} 1 & 1 \\ 1 & 0 \end{pmatrix}$$

   Then find the inverse, determinant, and transpose of the matrix. Finally, compute the fifth matrix power of this matrix (*m.m.m.m.m*).

1.3 Getting help

It was when I found out I could make mistakes that I knew I was on to something.

— Ornette Coleman

Errors

Mistakes may be a learning experience, as Ornette Coleman observed, but you will only learn from them if you can understand them. Some mistakes are easier than others to unravel; some will be quite obvious and some quite subtle. Perhaps the most frequent error you will make is misspelling the name of a function. *Mathematica* uses syntax-coloring to help you identify misspelled symbol names. For example, in the following input, `Sin` is deliberately misspelled. *Mathematica* colors any symbol it does not know about blue. When you evaluate the input, it is returned unchanged because *Mathematica* has no built-in transformation rules for the function `Sine`.

```
In[1]:= Sine[60 Degree]
Out[1]= Sine[60 °]
```

Of course it does have built-in rules for the function `Sin`.

```
In[2]:= Sin[60 Degree]
```

Out[2]= $\frac{\sqrt{3}}{2}$

Giving the wrong number of arguments or the wrong type of arguments to a function will generate a (hopefully useful) message. For example, if you mistakenly give `Sin` two arguments, the input is returned together with a message pointing you at the mistake.

```
In[3]:= Sin[π, 4]
        Sin::argx : Sin called with 2 arguments; 1 argument is expected. ≫
Out[3]= Sin[π, 4]
```

`Interpolation` operates on lists of numbers only and so the following causes the error condition.

```
In[4]:= Interpolation[1.3, 7.8, 4.8, 9.6, 5.3]
        Interpolation::nonopt :
          Options expected (instead of 5.3`) beyond position 2 in Interpolation[1.3, 7.8, 4.8, 9.6, 5.3].
             An option must be a rule or a list of rules. ≫
Out[4]= Interpolation[1.3, 7.8, 4.8, 9.6, 5.3]
```

Wrapping the sequence of numbers in a list would work correctly.

```
In[5]:= Interpolation[{1.3, 7.8, 4.8, 9.6, 5.3}]
Out[5]= InterpolatingFunction[ Domain: {{1., 5.}}
                               Output: scalar ]
```

Section 6.2 introduces the framework for creating and issuing your own messages for the programs you develop in *Mathematica*.

Getting out of trouble

From time to time, you will evaluate an input which will cause *Mathematica* to misbehave in some way, perhaps by just going silent and not returning a result for a long time or by printing out screen after screen of not terribly useful information. In these cases, you can try to abort the calculation. How you do this depends on your computer's operating system (Table 1.3).

These attempts to stop the computation will sometimes fail. If after waiting a reasonable amount of time (say, a few minutes), *Mathematica* still seems to be stuck, you may have to "kill the kernel." Before attempting this, try to convince yourself that the computation is really in a loop from which it will not return and that it is not just an intensive computation requiring a lot of time. Killing the kernel is accomplished by selecting Quit Kernel from the Evaluation menu. The kernel can then be restarted without killing the front end (the user interface) by selecting Start Kernel ▸ Local under the Kernel menu, or you can simply evaluate a command in a notebook and a new kernel should start up automatically.

TABLE 1.3. *Interrupting and aborting calculations*

Operating system	Keyboard input	Description
Macintosh OS X	⌘[.]	the Command key and the period
Windows	ALT[.]	the Alt key and the period
Linux/Unix	CTRL[.]	then type a and then RET

Function information

Documentation on all built-in functions can be accessed in a variety of ways. If you know the name of a function but are unsure of its syntax or what it does or what types of arguments it takes, the easiest way to find out about it is to evaluate ? *function*. Here is the usage message for Map:

```
In[6]:= ? Map
```

Map[*f*, *expr*] or *f* /@ *expr* applies *f* to each element on the first level in *expr*.
Map[*f*, *expr*, *levelspec*] applies *f* to parts of *expr* specified by *levelspec*.
Map[*f*] represents an operator form of Map that can be applied to an expression. >>

If you are not sure of the name of a command, use wildcard characters to display all functions that contain certain characters. For example, this displays all functions that start with Random:

```
In[7]:= ? Random*
```

▼ System`

Random	RandomGraph	RandomReal
RandomChoice	RandomImage	RandomSample
RandomColor	RandomInteger	RandomSeed
RandomComplex	RandomPermutation	RandomVariate
RandomEntity	RandomPoint	RandomWalkProcess
RandomFunction	RandomPrime	

Clicking on one of these links will produce a short usage statement about that function. For example, clicking the RandomGraph link displays the following in your notebook.

RandomGraph[{*n*, *m*}] gives a pseudorandom graph with *n* vertices and *m* edges.
RandomGraph[{*n*, *m*}, *k*] gives a list of *k* pseudorandom graphs.
RandomGraph[*gdist*, …] samples from the random graph distribution *gdist*. >>

Clicking the >> hyperlink at the end of the usage message takes you directly to the Documentation Center where a much more detailed explanation of this function can be found.

You can also get help by highlighting any *Mathematica* function in a notebook and pressing the F1 key on the keyboard (or CMD+SHIFT+F on Macintosh OS X) to display documentation for that function.

You can create new documentation for your own functions and programs so that users of your programs can get help in exactly the same way as they would for *Mathematica*'s built-in functions. The framework for doing this is discussed in Section 6.2.

Documentation

Mathematica contains an extensive set of reference materials called the Documentation Center in which you can search for information and syntax of functions and browse examples, applications, and related items. Given that *Mathematica* (as of the writing of this book) contains 5000+ built-in functions, even experienced users make a regular habit of referring to the documentation when trying to find a function for a particular task or trying to learn about the intricacies of a function.

To open the documentation, select Wolfram Documentation under the Help menu. You should quickly see something like the following:

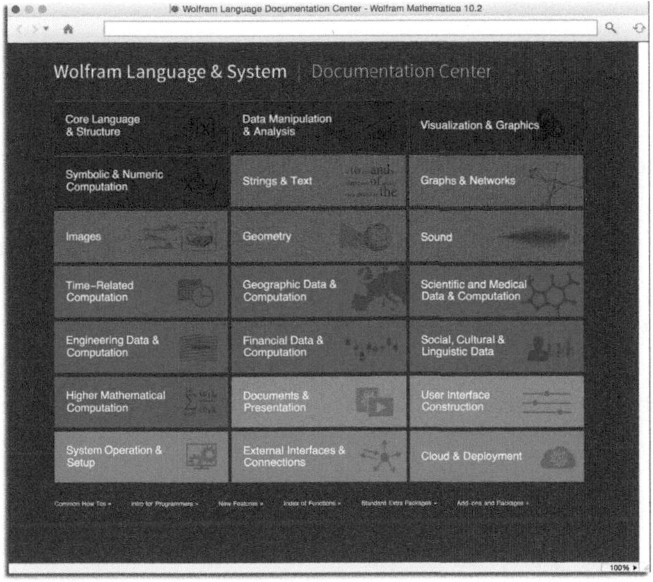

Clicking any of the twenty-one categories will open to an extended list of topics in that area. For example, suppose you were looking for information about visualizing geographical data. First click the Geographic Data & Computation category, then Maps & Cartography. The Documentation Center should look like this:

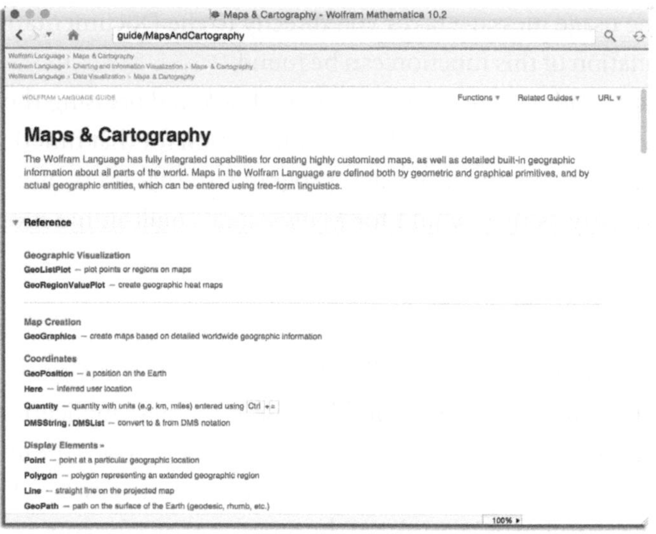

Clicking the `GeoGraphics` link takes you to the reference page for that function. Alternatively, you could evaluate `?GeoGraphics` in any notebook and then click the >> link at the end of the usage message.

1.4 Notes and further reading

For those interested in the history of modern programming, see the papers by Floyd (1979) and Knuth (2003). Also see language-specific references: on LISP (Graham 2002) and (McCarthy 1979); on C (Ritchie 1993); on PERL (Schwartz, foy, and Phoenix 2011); on JAVA (Sedgewick and Wayne 2007).

Palindromes are most easily understood in the context of integers and simple word play (Bergerson 1973), but they also are used in linguistics (Wier 2014), music (Hayden's *Symphony* 47, Hindemith's *Hin und Zurück*, and numerous pieces by J.S. Bach), and most recently in CRISPR techniques in microbiology (Bolotin et al. 2005).

2

The *Mathematica* language

__Expressions__ · Atoms · Normal expressions · Display of expressions · Evaluation of expressions · Compound expressions · Nesting expressions · __Numbers__ · Types of numbers · Digits and number bases · Random numbers · __Definitions__ · Defining variables and functions · Immediate vs. delayed assignments · Compound functions · Functions with multiple definitions · __Predicates and Boolean operations__ · Predicates · Relational and logical operators · __Attributes__ · Listable · Hold attributes · Protected · __Notes and further reading__

Throughout our history, humans have developed thousands of languages in order to communicate with each other. These *natural languages*, such as Mandarin, Bantu, or Finnish, evolved through ordinary usage over millennia, with rules for grammar developing organically and changing frequently. Then in 1879, Gottlieb Frege, in his *Begriffsschrift*, invented what is often referred to as the first *formal language*. Formal languages are designed for specific tasks; in Frege's case, he was attempting to formalize mathematical logic. Mathematics itself is a formal language, one used to express ideas about number, pattern, space, and other concepts. Although they too have evolved over many years, mathematics and logic differ from natural languages in that they have been formally constructed and have quite explicit and rigid rules regarding syntax.

Programming languages are, like mathematics, formal languages, but they are constructed to communicate with a machine and to command it to carry out certain instructions. Thought to have their origin in the 1940s and 1950s when the first digital computers came about, in fact programming languages go back much earlier to the creation of the Jacquard loom (1801), player pianos (mid-1800s), and mechanical organs (Anselmo Gavioli, 1892), all of which used physical punch cards or rolls to code and store instructions to weave fabric or play an instrument. The connection with computing probably begins with Herman Hollerith's innovation of using punch cards to store information for the US Census of 1890. Hollerith later founded a company to market his inventions and in 1924, that company became IBM.

Regardless of the mechanism used to store programs, all programming languages are described by specifying their syntax and semantics. *Syntax* refers to the form, indicating what symbols can be put together and in what order to make a meaningful construct in a given language. In other words, the syntax of a programming language is the set of rules that define what is a valid input or program. *Semantics*, however, refers to the meaning of expressions within a language.

Although we will not give a complete, rigorous description of the syntax of the *Mathematica* language here, it is important to understand some of the basic structures and their syntax, upon which everything is built. Fortunately, the *Mathematica* language can be understood quickly by learning about just a few elemental objects: atomic and normal expressions. After looking at these basic building blocks we discuss assignments and definitions, combining expressions using logical operators, and controlling properties of expressions through the use of attributes.

2.1 Expressions

When doing a simple arithmetic computation such as $3 + 4 \cdot 5$, usually you are not too concerned with the precise details of how a system such as *Mathematica* actually performs the additions or multiplications. Yet an understanding of the internals of such objects is key to being able to manipulate them in a consistent and powerful manner whenever they are encountered. These objects – numbers, strings, graphs, arrays, documents – have a similar underlying structure even though they may appear quite different at first sight. They are all *expressions*, and are divided into two kinds: atoms and normal expressions. These are the basic building blocks of all expressions you work with in *Mathematica* and, as such, they are essential to learning how to build larger and more complex programs and, ultimately, to mastering *Mathematica*. We start with atomic expressions.

Atoms

The primitive building blocks from which every expression is ultimately constructed are called *atoms*. The most basic atomic objects are symbols, numbers, and strings.

```
In[1]:= AtomQ[x31]
Out[1]= True
```

```
In[2]:= AtomQ[1.2345]
Out[2]= True
```

```
In[3]:= AtomQ["The rain in Spain"]
Out[3]= True
```

To identify types of objects, use the `Head` function. For numbers, it will report whether the number is an integer, a rational number, a real number, or a complex number.

```
In[4]:= Head[7]
Out[4]= Integer
```

```
In[5]:= Head[1 / 7]
Out[5]= Rational
```

```
In[6]:= Head[.522]
Out[6]= Real

In[7]:= Head[1 + 7 I]
Out[7]= Complex
```

In general, parts of an atom cannot be directly extracted; that is, atoms are not subdividable.

```
In[8]:= Part[1.2345, 1]
        Part::partd : Part specification 1.2345⟦1⟧ is longer than depth of object. >>
Out[8]= 1.2345⟦1⟧
```

Symbols consist of a sequence of letters and digits, starting with a letter. This applies to both user-defined symbols and to the built-in symbols. The built-in symbols are spelled out in full and are always capitalized.

```
In[9]:= Head[x31]
Out[9]= Symbol

In[10]:= Head[Integrate]
Out[10]= Symbol
```

In *Mathematica*, built-in constants are all symbols.

```
In[11]:= Head[π]
Out[11]= Symbol

In[12]:= Head[EulerGamma]
Out[12]= Symbol
```

Strings are also atomic objects; they are composed of characters and are enclosed in quotes.

```
In[13]:= Head["Mathematica"]
Out[13]= String
```

TABLE 2.1. *Basic atomic expressions*

Atom	Examples
Integer	-3, 0, 28,...
Rational	$-\frac{1}{2}, \frac{8}{9}, \ldots$
Real	0.2348,...
Complex	5-4i,...
String	"The cat in the hat."
Symbol	Plot, myFun,...

Atomic expressions do not necessarily need to be small and simple. In addition to the basic atomic objects listed in Table 2.1, graphs, images, and sparse arrays are also considered atomic.

Graphs are abstract objects consisting of vertices and edges.

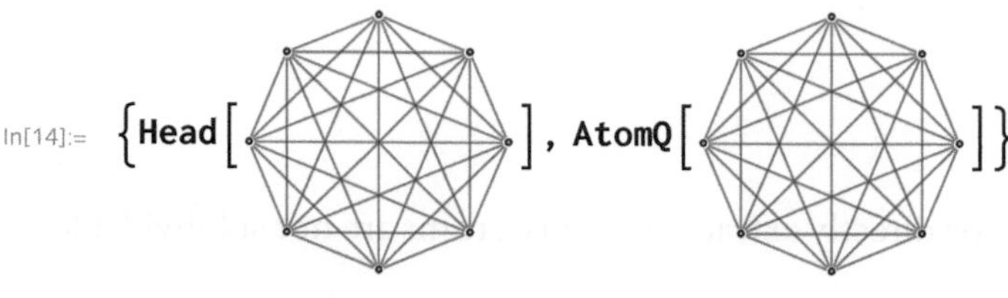

```
In[14]:= {Head[ ], AtomQ[ ]}
Out[14]= {Graph, True}
```

Images, which can be imported or created from arrays of numbers or from graphics, are atomic.

```
In[15]:= {Head[ ], AtomQ[ ]}
Out[15]= {Image, True}
```

Sparse arrays are a special kind of atomic expression. They give a compact and efficient means of representing large arrays of numbers, typically with many zero elements. Sparse arrays in *Mathematica* are represented by `SparseArray`, whose output form displays the number of nondefault elements and the dimensions of the array.

```
In[16]:= mat = SparseArray[{i_, i_} → 1, {5, 5}]
```

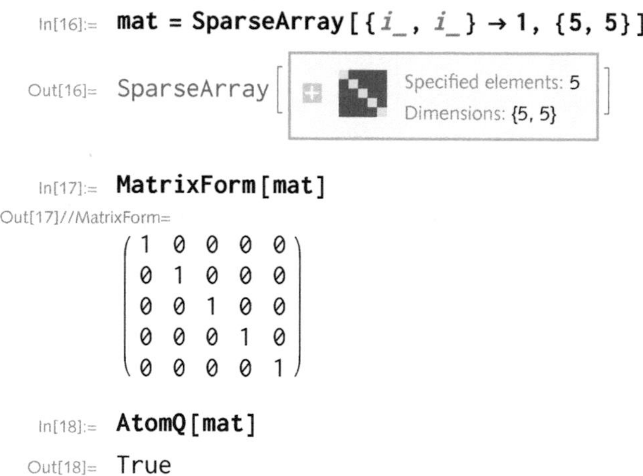

```
Out[16]= SparseArray[ Specified elements: 5
                      Dimensions: {5, 5} ]

In[17]:= MatrixForm[mat]
Out[17]//MatrixForm=
  1 0 0 0 0
  0 1 0 0 0
  0 0 1 0 0
  0 0 0 1 0
  0 0 0 0 1

In[18]:= AtomQ[mat]
Out[18]= True
```

Normal expressions

Everything in *Mathematica* is an expression – symbols, numbers, functions, formulas, programs, even the notebook object itself. Expressions are either atomic, as described in the previous section, or they are *normal expressions*, built up from atomic expressions, containing a head and zero or more elements. All normal expressions are of the following form, where h is the head of the expression and the e_i are the elements, which may be atomic or normal expressions:

$$h[e_1, e_2, \ldots, e_n]$$

For normal expressions, `Head` is used to find what type of an expression you are working with.

```
In[19]:= Head[a + b + c]
Out[19]= Plus
```

```
In[20]:= Head[{a, b, c}]
Out[20]= List
```

To see the full internal representation of an expression, use `FullForm`.

```
In[21]:= FullForm[a + b + c]
Out[21]//FullForm=
         Plus[a, b, c]
```

```
In[22]:= FullForm[{a, b, c}]
Out[22]//FullForm=
         List[a, b, c]
```

The important thing to notice is that both of these objects (the sum and the list) have very similar internal representations. Each is made up of a head (`Plus` and `List`, respectively), each encloses its arguments in square brackets, and each separates its arguments with commas. This is the form of every normal expression in *Mathematica*.

The number of elements in any expression is given by its length. The internal representation, as returned by `FullForm` above, displays this expression as a function with three arguments.

```
In[23]:= Length[a + b + c]
Out[23]= 3
```

Here is a more complicated expression:

```
In[24]:= expr = Sin[x] (a x^2 + b x + c)
Out[24]= (c + b x + a x^2) Sin[x]
```

Its head is `Times` because it is composed of the product of `Sin[x]` and the quadratic polynomial.

```
In[25]:= Head[expr]
Out[25]= Times
```

Its length is two since it only contains two factors.

```
In[26]:= Length[expr]
Out[26]= 2
```

Although the `FullForm` of this expression is a little harder to decipher, if you look carefully you should see that it is composed of the product of `Plus[...]` and `Sin[x]`. In other words, its head, `Times`, has two arguments.

```
In[27]:= FullForm[expr]
Out[27]//FullForm=
         Times[Plus[c, Times[b, x], Times[a, Power[x, 2]]], Sin[x]]
```

There are several important differences between atomic expressions and nonatomic, or, normal expressions. While the heads of all expressions are extracted in the same way – using the `Head` function – the head of an atom provides different information than the head of other expressions. The head of a symbol or string is the *kind* of atom that it is.

```
In[28]:= Head[Integrate]
Out[28]= Symbol
```

```
In[29]:= Head["hello"]
Out[29]= String
```

The head of a number is the specific kind of number that it is, its data type.

```
In[30]:= Head[2]
Out[30]= Integer
```

```
In[31]:= Head[5.21]
Out[31]= Real
```

The `FullForm` of an atom is the atom itself, indicating that it cannot be further subdivided.

```
In[32]:= FullForm[f]
Out[32]//FullForm=
         f
```

Although rational numbers have a compound internal representation, they cannot be subdivided.

In[33]:= FullForm$\left[\frac{5}{7}\right]$

Out[33]//FullForm=

```
Rational[5, 7]
```

In[34]:= Part$\left[\frac{5}{7}, 1\right]$

Part::partd : Part specification $\frac{5}{7}$⟦1⟧ is longer than depth of object. ≫

Out[34]= $\frac{5}{7}$⟦1⟧

In contrast to atomic expressions, normal expressions have parts. For example, the first part of the expression a + b is the symbol a.

```
In[35]:= Part[a + b, 1]
Out[35]= a
```

The second part is b.

```
In[36]:= Part[a + b, 2]
Out[36]= b
```

This should be clearer from looking at the internal representation of this expression:

```
In[37]:= FullForm[a + b]
Out[37]//FullForm=
         Plus[a, b]
```

So, `Part[a + b, 1]` is another way of extracting the first element of `Plus[a, b]`, which is simply the symbol a. In general, `Part[`*expr*`, `*n*`]` gives the *n*th element of *expr*. The zeroth part is the head of the expression.

```
In[38]:= Part[a + b, 0]
Out[38]= Plus
```

Trying to extract part of an atomic expression generates an error, because atomic expressions have no parts. (Technically, this statement is not quite correct as sparse arrays can be operated on with `Part` to extract rows, columns, and sub-arrays.)

```
In[39]:= Part["veni vidi vici", 1]

         Part::partd : Part specification veni vidi vici⟦1⟧ is longer than depth of object. >>

Out[39]= veni vidi vici⟦1⟧
```

Similarly, rational and complex numbers are atomic and hence have no parts. The expression *expr*`[[1]]` is shorthand for `Part[`*expr*`, 1]`.

```
In[40]:= 2 - 3 i[[1]]

         Part::partd : Part specification i⟦1⟧ is longer than depth of object. >>

Out[40]= 2 - 3 i⟦1⟧
```

Because all expressions in *Mathematica* have a common structure, most of the built-in functions that are used for list manipulation, such as `Part`, can also be used to manipulate the arguments of any other kind of normal expression.

```
In[41]:= Append[w + x y, z]
Out[41]= w + x y + z
```

This result can best be understood by looking at the `FullForm` of the following two expressions:

```
In[42]:= FullForm[w + x y]
Out[42]//FullForm=
         Plus[w, Times[x, y]]

In[43]:= FullForm[w + x y + z]
Out[43]//FullForm=
         Plus[w, Times[x, y], z]
```

Appending `z` to `w + x y` is equivalent to adding `z` as an argument to the `Plus` function. More generally:

```
In[44]:= Append[f[a, b], c]
Out[44]= f[a, b, c]
```

For more complicated expressions, you might find it useful to display the internal representation with `TreeForm`. In the following example, the root node of the tree is `Plus`, which then branches three times at c, bx, and at ax^2, the latter two branching further.

In[45]:= `TreeForm[a x^2 + b x + c]`

Out[45]//TreeForm=

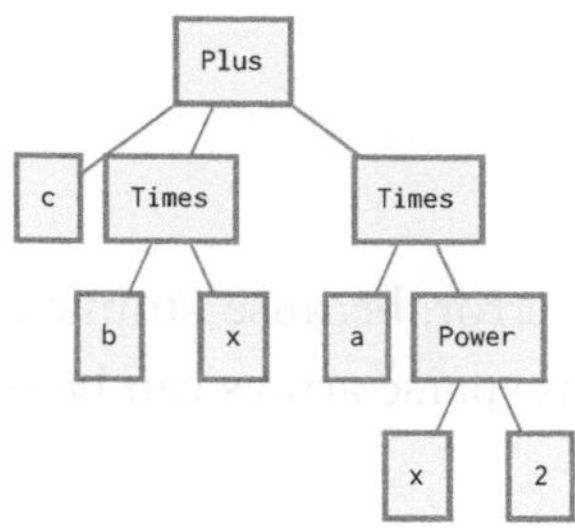

In[46]:= `Head[a x^2 + b x + c]`

Out[46]= `Plus`

The second element of this expression is the second term in the sum.

In[47]:= `Part[a x^2 + b x + c, 2]`

Out[47]= `b x`

The second element of that is the second factor in the product.

In[48]:= `FullForm[%]`

Out[48]//FullForm=

`Times[b, x]`

In[49]:= `Part[b x, 2]`

Out[49]= `x`

To extract the second part of the second element directly, use `Part` with the following syntax:

In[50]:= `Part[a x^2 + b x + c, 2, 2]`

Out[50]= `x`

Another useful function for looking at the structure of expressions is `Level`, which gives a list of the elements at a given level in the expression. For example, the elements at level one in `f[a, b, c]` are simply a, b, and c.

In[51]:= `Level[f[a, b, c], {1}]`

Out[51]= `{a, b, c}`

The elements at level two in the following matrix are the matrix elements themselves. The elements at level one are the rows of the matrix.

In[52]:= `Level[{{a, b}, {c, d}}, {2}]`

Out[52]= `{a, b, c, d}`

In[53]:= `Level[{{a, b}, {c, d}}, {1}]`

Out[53]= `{{a, b}, {c, d}}`

Display of expressions

Regardless of how an atomic or normal expression may appear in a notebook, its structure is uniquely determined by its head and parts, which can be seen with `FullForm` as described above. Some expressions, such as numbers and lists, display pretty much as you would type them as input.

```
In[54]:= {23, 3 + 4 ⅈ, x²}
Out[54]= {23, 3 + 4 ⅈ, x²}
```

But other expressions look a bit different in output than they do as input. For example, the standard output form for strings is to display without the quote characters surrounding the string.

```
In[55]:= "this is a string"
Out[55]= this is a string
```

`InputForm` shows what you would type as input to create the expression. `FullForm` shows the internal representation as a normal or atomic expression. Both use a purely linear syntax.

```
In[56]:= InputForm[{23, 3 + 4 ⅈ, x²}]
Out[56]//InputForm=
         {23, 3 + 4*I, x^2}

In[57]:= FullForm[{23, 3 + 4 ⅈ, x²}]
Out[57]//FullForm=
         List[23, Complex[3, 4], Power[x, 2]]
```

These functions are useful for discovering the internal form of any expression – graphical objects, numerical quantities, algebraic expressions, and so on.

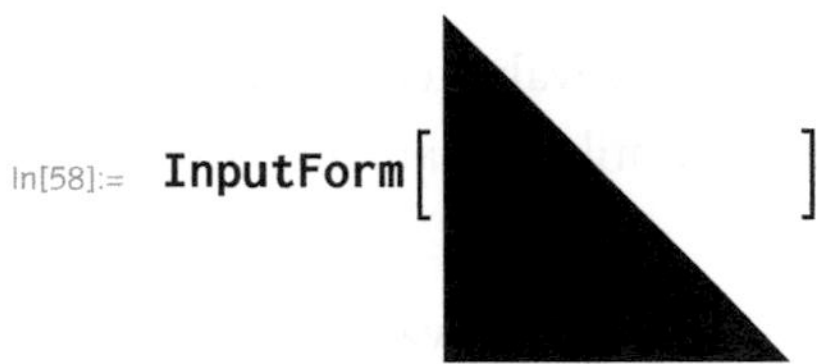

```
Out[58]//InputForm=
         Graphics[Triangle[{{0, 0}, {1, 0}, {0, 1}}]]
```

Another example of the difference between what you see in output and the internal form of expressions regards approximate numbers – by default, six digits are displayed.

```
In[59]:= N[π]
Out[59]= 3.14159
```

`InputForm` shows that these numbers are in fact carrying about sixteen digits of precision.

```
In[60]:= InputForm[%]
Out[60]//InputForm=
         3.141592653589793
```

To generate and display numbers with higher precision, use the two-argument form of `N`.

```
In[61]:= N[π, 70]
Out[61]= 3.141592653589793238462643383279502884197169399375105820974944592307816
```

Evaluation of expressions

The evaluator, the part of *Mathematica* that evaluates expressions, follows a well-prescribed set of rules to insure correctness and consistency in program evaluation. For example, in a logical expression such as $expr_1$ && $expr_2$ && $expr_3$, *Mathematica* evaluates the expressions $expr_i$ in order until it finds one to be false, at which point evaluation is terminated. Although there are many such rules built in, it is useful to identify a few that you will occasionally encounter.

Briefly, the evaluation sequence involves the following series of steps:

1. When you evaluate an expression (by pressing SHIFT+RET or SHIFT+ENTER), it is left unchanged if that expression is a number or string.
2. If the expression is a symbol, it is rewritten if there is an applicable rule, built-in or user-defined. If there is no such rule for the symbol, it is unchanged.

If the expression is not a number, string, or symbol, its parts are evaluated in a specific order:

3. The head of the expression is evaluated.
4. The elements of the expression are evaluated in order, except when the head is a symbol with a `Hold` attribute. In this case, some of its arguments are left unevaluated depending upon what is being held.
5. After the head and arguments of an expression are each completely evaluated, the expression is rewritten if there is an applicable rule (after making any necessary changes to the arguments based on the attributes of the head). User-defined rules are checked, then the built-in rule base.
6. After carrying out the previous steps, the resulting expression is evaluated in the same way and then the result of that evaluation is evaluated, and so on until there are no more applicable rules.

These steps give just an outline of what happens internally in the standard evaluation procedure. If you are interested in the details, including nonstandard evaluation, see the tutorials Evaluation and Evaluation of Expressions (WLDC).

As indicated in step 4 above, arguments of expressions are evaluated prior to being passed to the calling function (typically given by the head). This principle is common to many modern programming languages but it can cause some surprises occasionally. For example, asking for the internal representation of a simple sum like that below, you might expect something like `Plus[2, 2]`, but that is not what is returned after evaluation.

```
In[62]:= FullForm[2 + 2]
Out[62]//FullForm=
         4
```

This is a consequence of the fact that arguments to functions are evaluated before being passed up to the calling function, in this case, `Plus`. So, how can you see the internal form of an expression before the evaluator gets to it? The easiest way is to use `Defer`.

```
In[63]:= Defer[FullForm[2 + 2]]
Out[63]= Plus[2, 2]
```

Wrapping an expression in `Defer` causes that expression to be kept in an unevaluated form as it is passed up to `FullForm`.

Another approach is to use one of the many `Hold` functions.

```
In[64]:= FullForm[HoldForm[2 + 2]]
Out[64]//FullForm=
         HoldForm[Plus[2, 2]]
```

What is the difference between these two functions? With `Defer`, you can evaluate its output simply by putting your cursor in the corresponding output cell and evaluating. With `HoldForm`, you need to release the hold, typically by wrapping the output in `ReleaseHold`. We will have more to say about attributes such as `HoldForm` at the end of this chapter.

Compound expressions

Oftentimes your computations and programs consist of a series of steps that are performed in some order. There are several ways you can put the steps together, but perhaps the simplest is to put one after another, separating each complete expression by a semicolon. Such *compound expressions* look like the following:

$$expr_1;\ expr_2;\ \ldots;\ expr_m$$

The $expr_i$ can be any expression: a simple assignment or a user-defined function, for example. When a compound expression is evaluated, the $expr_i$ are evaluated in order and the result of the evaluation of the last expression is returned (by adding a semicolon after $expr_m$, the display of the final evaluation result can also be suppressed).

For example, the following compound expression first generates the list `{2, 4, 6, 8}`, then computes the square root of each element in the list, then sums up that list (remember, `%` refers to the value of the previous result).

```
In[65]:= Range[2, 8, 2];
         Sqrt[%];
         Total[%]
Out[67]= 2 + 3 √2 + √6
```

Removing the semicolons displays the output of each step. *Mathematica* interprets the (hidden) newline as the end of that line of input, that is, a complete expression.

```
In[68]:= Range[2, 8, 2]
Out[68]= {2, 4, 6, 8}

In[69]:= Sqrt[%]
Out[69]= {√2, 2, √6, 2 √2}

In[70]:= Total[%]
Out[70]= 2 + 3 √2 + √6
```

Nesting expressions

Using the output of one function as the input of another is key to becoming proficient with *Mathematica*. This nesting of functions is commonly referred to by mathematicians as the "composition of functions." In *Mathematica*, this sequential application of several functions is sometimes referred to as a *nested function call.*

For example, consider the computation from the previous section. Instead of the compound expression, we could give each input as the argument to the next function, returning the final result:

```
In[71]:= Total[Sqrt[Range[2, 8, 2]]]
Out[71]= 2 + 3 √2 + √6
```

This use of functions as arguments to other functions is an essential part of functional programming, but if you are new to it, it is instructive to step through the computation working from the inside out. In general, the *Mathematica* evaluator does the computation from the most deeply nested expression outward. The inner-most function is `Range` and it produces a list of numbers from two through eight in steps of two.

```
In[72]:= Range[2, 8, 2]
Out[72]= {2, 4, 6, 8}
```

Moving outwards, `Sqrt` is then applied to the result of the `Range` function to produce a list of the square roots.

```
In[73]:= Sqrt[%]
Out[73]= {√2, 2, √6, 2 √2}
```

Finally, `Total` adds up the elements in the list produced by `Sqrt`.

```
In[74]:= Total[%]
Out[74]= 2 + 3 √2 + √6
```

Wrapping `Trace` around the computation shows all the intermediate expressions that are used in this evaluation.

```
In[75]:= Trace[Total[Sqrt[Range[2, 8, 2]]]]
Out[75]= {{{Range[2, 8, 2], {2, 4, 6, 8}}, √{2, 4, 6, 8}, {√2, √4, √6, √8},
           {√2, √2}, {√4, 2}, {√6, √6}, {√8, 2 √2}, {√2, 2, √6, 2 √2}},
          Total[{√2, 2, √6, 2 √2}], 2 + 3 √2 + √6}
```

Nested functions are read in much the same way as they are created, starting with the innermost functions and working toward the outermost functions. The following two examples – computing a matrix norm and creating a random walk – provide more substantial numerical illustrations of this idea.

Spectral norm The spectral norm of a matrix is its largest singular value. It is found by taking the square root of the largest eigenvalue of the matrix product $\overline{A}^T A$, where $\overline{A}^T$ is the conjugate transpose of matrix A. There is a built-in function to compute singular values, but it is instructive to walk through a nested computation like this. For the 2 × 2 matrix 𝒜 given below, here is the computation:

```
In[76]:= 𝒜 = {{2, -1}, {5, 0}};
         N[Sqrt[Max[Eigenvalues[ConjugateTranspose[𝒜].𝒜]]]]
Out[77]= 5.39835
```

Let us step through the computation much the same as *Mathematica* does, from the inside out. Start by computing the matrix product of 𝒜 and its conjugate transpose.

```
In[78]:= ConjugateTranspose[𝒜].𝒜
Out[78]= {{29, -2}, {-2, 1}}
```

Next compute the eigenvalues of this matrix.

```
In[79]:= Eigenvalues[%]
```

Out[79]= $\left\{5\left(3+2\sqrt{2}\right), 5\left(3-2\sqrt{2}\right)\right\}$

Then find the maximum eigenvalue and take its square root.

```
In[80]:= Max[%]
```

Out[80]= $5\left(3+2\sqrt{2}\right)$

```
In[81]:= Sqrt[%]
```

Out[81]= $\sqrt{5\left(3+2\sqrt{2}\right)}$

And finally convert to a numerical approximation.

```
In[82]:= N[%]
Out[82]= 5.39835
```

Let's compare this computation with the built-in function `Norm`, which, in the following form, gives the spectral norm:

```
In[83]:= N[Norm[𝒜, 2]]
Out[83]= 5.39835
```

Random walks Imagine taking a walk in a one-dimensional world such as a number line: at each step you can go either right or left one step (ok, you also need to imagine *yourself* as a one-dimensional object!). Starting at the origin, if your choices to go left or right are equally likely, then this is a good model for a one-dimensional random walk. These random walks represent phenomena that are probabilistic in nature and have been used to model everything from particle movement in a gas or liquid, to predicting the movement of stock prices in the financial markets.

Let's create a short program to model and simulate this process. Starting from any location, adding 1 will represent a step to the right and adding −1 will represent a step to the left.

```
In[84]:= dirs = {-1, 1};
```

Starting at the origin, randomly choose one of these directions.

```
In[85]:= RandomChoice[dirs]
Out[85]= -1
```

To make multiple random choices, use a second argument with `RandomChoice`.

```
In[86]:= steps = RandomChoice[dirs, {5}]
Out[86]= {-1, 1, 1, 1, -1}
```

From these step directions how do we create the random walk? A moment's thought should convince you that we can add one step direction to the previous location to generate the "walk." `Accumulate` computes partial sums, which is clearer with an example using symbolic input.

```
In[87]:= Accumulate[{a, b, c, d, e}]
Out[87]= {a, a + b, a + b + c, a + b + c + d, a + b + c + d + e}
```

So if we accumulate the list `steps` above, this generates a list of the locations of a one-dimensional five-step walk starting at the origin (see Figure 2.1 for a graphical representation).

```
In[88]:= Accumulate[steps]
Out[88]= {-1, 0, 1, 2, 1}
```

FIGURE 2.1. *Five steps in a random walk on the number line with steps to the left pictured below the axis.*

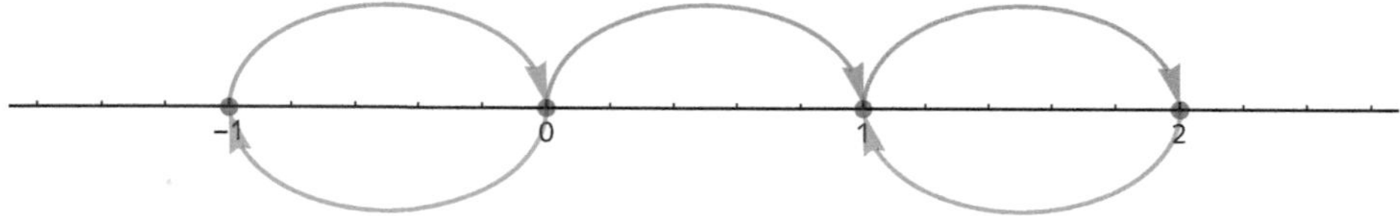

To visualize this random walk for 25 000 steps, we can use one of the built-in graphics functions. The visualization shows the number of steps on the horizontal axis and the displacement from the origin on the vertical axis. Alternatively, you could think of this walk as a time series with the horizontal axis representing time increments.

```
In[89]:= ListLinePlot[Accumulate[RandomChoice[dirs, 25000]]]
```

Out[89]=

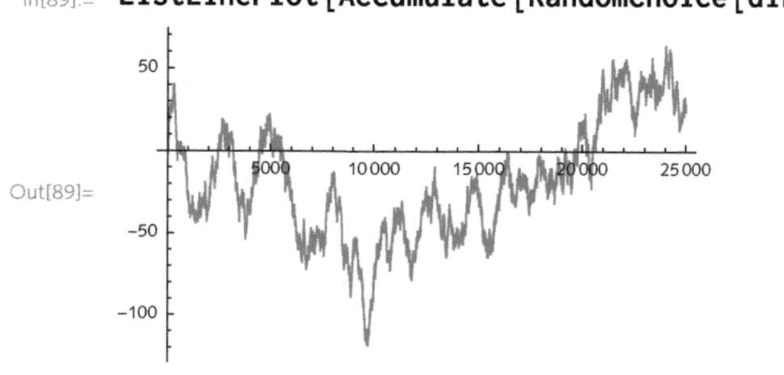

Notice the nested functions used in this example to create the random walk and visualize it. The code is compact, but quite readable, essentially describing the process itself.

Exercises

1. Determine if each of the following are atomic expressions. If the expression is not atomic, find its head.

   a. `8 / 5`

   b. `8 / 5 + x`

   c. `{{a, b}, {c, d}}`

   d. `"8/5 + x"`

2. Give the full (internal) form of the expression `a (b + c)`.

3. What is the traditional representation of `Times[a, Power[Plus[b, c], -1]]`.

4. What is the part specification of the symbol `b` in the expression $a\,x^2 + b\,x + c$?

5. What will be the result of evaluating each of the following? Use `FullForm` on the expressions to help you understand their structures.

   a. `((x^2 + y) z / w)[[2, 1, 2]]`

   b. `(a/b)[[2, 2]]`

6. Use `Level` to find all the factors in the following expression. Then find all the terms inside the parentheses of the output.

```
In[1]:= expr = LegendreP[5, x]
```

$$\text{Out[1]=}\quad \frac{1}{8}\left(15\,x - 70\,x^3 + 63\,x^5\right)$$

7. Explain why the following expression returns an integer instead of displaying the internal representation of the fraction.

```
In[2]:= FullForm[12/4]

Out[2]//FullForm=
    3
```

8. Modify the code for the one-dimensional random walk in this section to create two-dimensional random walks. In this case the step directions will be the vectors pointing in the compass directions, {0, 1}, {0, −1}, {1, 0}, and {−1, 0}.

2.2 Numbers

Numbers are probably the most common and familiar object that you will work with in *Mathematica*. They are used to quantify, to represent phenomena, and they are studied in their own right. In this section we take a more formal look at the various kinds of numbers that you will encounter, including the digits of integer and real numbers, different number bases, and random numbers and random number generators.

Types of numbers

There are four kinds of numbers represented in *Mathematica* – integer, rational, real, and complex. Additionally, mathematical constants like π and e are symbols but with numerical properties. Although numbers are atomic expressions and cannot be broken down into smaller parts, you can use the Head function to identify the type of number you are working with.

Integers Integers are considered to be exact and are represented without a decimal point.

```
In[1]:= {Head[3], FullForm[3]}
Out[1]= {Integer, 3}
```

Exact numbers can be thought of as having an infinite number of digits of precision (relative uncertainty in the value of that number) and accuracy (measuring the absolute uncertainty).

```
In[2]:= Precision[3]
Out[2]= ∞

In[3]:= Accuracy[3]
Out[3]= ∞
```

Rational numbers Rational numbers are quotients of integers and are also considered to be exact. *Mathematica* simplifies rational numbers to lowest terms and leaves them as exact numbers.

```
In[4]:= 36 / 16
        9
Out[4]= —
        4

In[5]:= {Head[9 / 4], FullForm[9 / 4], Precision[9 / 4]}
Out[5]= {Rational, Rational[9, 4], ∞}
```

The representation of rational numbers as a pair of integers has an important consequence. The pattern matcher in *Mathematica* works with the syntactical form of expressions as displayed by FullForm, not the output form that you see by default in your notebook. This is described in some detail in Section 4.1, where we discuss structured patterns.

Real numbers Any number containing a decimal point is categorized as a real number.

```
In[6]:= {Head[3.14], FullForm[3.14], Precision[3.14]}
Out[6]= {Real, 3.14`, MachinePrecision}
```

These numbers are not considered exact and hence are often referred to as *approximate* or *machine numbers*. This often leads to confusion for new users of *Mathematica*. You may know that the number 6.0 is identical to the number 6, *from a mathematical perspective*, but from the perspective of the floating-point unit (FPU) of your computer they are quite different, both in terms of their representation and in terms of the algorithms that are used to do arithmetic with them.

One way to see that these numbers are different is to compare them using the two functions `Equal` (==) and `SameQ` (===).

```
In[7]:=  6 == 6.0
Out[7]=  True
```

```
In[8]:=  6 === 6.0
Out[8]=  False
```

`Equal` effectively converts the integer 6 to an approximate number and then compares the last seven binary digits (roughly the last two decimal digits) of the two numbers. `SameQ`, however, checks to see if they are identical expressions. Since one is an exact integer and the other is an approximate real number, `SameQ` returns `False`.

Complex numbers Complex numbers are of the form $a + bi$, where a and b are any numbers – integer, rational, or real and i is equal to $\sqrt{-1}$, represented in *Mathematica* by the symbols `I` or $\mathbb{i}$.

```
In[9]:=  z = 3 + 4 ⅈ
Out[9]=  3 + 4 ⅈ
```

```
In[10]:= {Head[z], FullForm[z], Precision[z]}
Out[10]= {Complex, Complex[3, 4], ∞}
```

Although a complex number expression is atomic, you can get the real and imaginary parts using the selectors `Re` and `Im` (*selectors* are functions that return a component of a data object).

```
In[11]:= {Re[z], Im[z]}
Out[11]= {3, 4}
```

FIGURE 2.2. *Argand diagram showing complex numbers as points in the complex plane.*

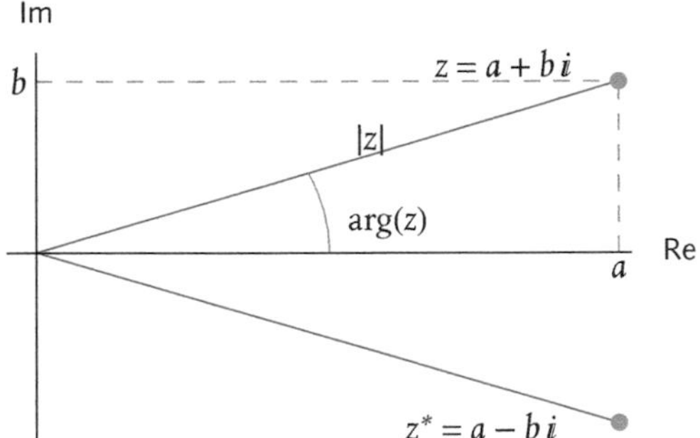

The absolute value of a number is its distance from the origin in the complex plane. The conjugate can be thought of as the reflection of the complex number in the real axis of the complex plane. The phase angle is given by the argument. Each of these properties of complex numbers can be visualized geometrically (Figure 2.2).

```
In[12]:=  {Abs[z], Conjugate[z], Arg[4 ⅈ]}
Out[12]=  {5, 3 - 4 ⅈ, π/2}
```

Mathematical constants Built-in constants such as π, e, i, and Degree are not treated as explicit numbers by *Mathematica*; internally, they are symbols.

```
In[13]:=  {Head[π], AtomQ[π], FullForm[π], Precision[π]}
Out[13]=  {Symbol, True, Pi, ∞}

In[14]:=  NumberQ[π]
Out[14]=  False
```

These mathematical constants have an attribute that essentially alerts *Mathematica* to the fact that they are numeric in nature. Functions with this attribute are assumed to have zero derivative with respect to any variables of that function. Here is a list of all those built-in symbols that have the Constant attribute. FunctionsWithAttribute is defined in Section 5.5. Any of the functions defined in the book packages can be loaded by evaluating the following input:

```
In[15]:=  << EPM`

In[16]:=  FunctionsWithAttribute[Constant]
Out[16]=  {Catalan, Degree, E, EulerGamma, Glaisher,
           GoldenAngle, GoldenRatio, Khinchin, MachinePrecision, Pi}
```

Mathematical constants and any expressions that are explicit numbers are considered numeric.

```
In[17]:=  {NumericQ[Catalan], NumericQ[E], NumericQ[Pi]}
Out[17]=  {True, True, True}
```

For purposes of comparison, *Mathematica* converts any symbol with this attribute to a real number, using what it perceives to be necessary precision.

```
In[18]:=  RandomReal[{ϕ, ⅇ}]
Out[18]=  1.72425

In[19]:=  ⅇ^π > π^ⅇ
Out[19]=  True

In[20]:=  NumericQ[π^ⅇ]
Out[20]=  True
```

Note, in particular, that the symbol ∞ is not numeric.

```
In[21]:=  NumericQ[∞]
Out[21]=  False
```

To distinguish between explicit numbers and symbols that represent numbers, use NumberQ.

```
In[22]:=  {NumberQ[3.14], NumberQ[π]}
Out[22]=  {True, False}
```

The important difference is that NumberQ returns a value of True for any argument that is explicitly a number (has head Integer, Rational, Real, Complex), whereas NumericQ returns a value of True for all explicit numbers as well as mathematical constants such as π, i, e, and so on.

```
In[23]:= NumericQ[ⅈ]
Out[23]= True
```

Digits and number bases

To extract a list of the digits of a number, use either IntegerDigits or RealDigits.

```
In[24]:= IntegerDigits[1293]
Out[24]= {1, 2, 9, 3}
```

RealDigits returns a list with two elements: the digits and an exponent that indicates the number of digits to the left of the decimal point.

```
In[25]:= RealDigits[N[EulerGamma]]
Out[25]= {{5, 7, 7, 2, 1, 5, 6, 6, 4, 9, 0, 1, 5, 3, 2, 9}, 0}
```

To reconstruct a number from a list of digits, use FromDigits.

```
In[26]:= FromDigits[{1, 2, 9, 3}]
Out[26]= 1293
```

Numbers in base 10 can be displayed in other bases by means of the BaseForm function. For example, the following displays 18 in base 2:

```
In[27]:= BaseForm[18, 2]
Out[27]//BaseForm=
         10010₂
```

The operator b ^^ n takes the number n in base b and converts it to base 10.

```
In[28]:= 2^^10010
Out[28]= 18
```

The letters of the alphabet are used for numbers in bases larger than 10. For example, here are the numbers 1 through 20 in base 16:

```
In[29]:= Table[BaseForm[j, 16], {j, 1, 20}]
Out[29]= {1₁₆, 2₁₆, 3₁₆, 4₁₆, 5₁₆, 6₁₆, 7₁₆, 8₁₆, 9₁₆,
          a₁₆, b₁₆, c₁₆, d₁₆, e₁₆, f₁₆, 10₁₆, 11₁₆, 12₁₆, 13₁₆, 14₁₆}
```

Numbers other than integers can be represented in bases different from 10. Here are the first few digits of π in base 2:

```
In[30]:= BaseForm[N[π], 2]
Out[30]//BaseForm=
         11.001001000011111111₂
```

You are not restricted to integral bases such as in the previous examples. The base can be any real number greater than one.

```
In[31]:= RealDigits[N[π], N[GoldenRatio]]
Out[31]= {{1, 0, 0, 0, 1, 0, 0, 1, 0, 1, 0, 1, 0, 0, 1, 0, 0, 0, 1, 0, 1, 0, 1, 0, 1, 0,
   0, 0, 0, 0, 1, 0, 1, 0, 0, 1, 0, 0, 0, 0, 1, 0, 0, 1, 0, 1, 0, 0, 1, 0,
   0, 0, 0, 0, 1, 0, 1, 0, 1, 0, 1, 0, 1, 0, 1, 0, 0, 0, 0, 0, 0, 1, 0}, 3}
```

Random numbers

Statistical work and numerical experimentation often require random numbers to test hypotheses or run simulations. We will use them frequently to create prototypical data as we develop programs throughout this book. Several different random number functions are used to generate random numbers in various ranges, domains, and distributions.

Using `RandomReal` without any arguments will generate a uniformly distributed random real number between zero and one.

```
In[32]:= RandomReal[]
Out[32]= 0.418897
```

`RandomReal` can be given a range of numbers. For example, this generates a random real in the range zero to one hundred:

```
In[33]:= RandomReal[{0, 100}]
Out[33]= 31.5761
```

Use a second argument to create vectors or arrays of random numbers.

```
In[34]:= RandomReal[{-10, 10}, {12}]
Out[34]= {4.77845, -7.65161, 5.61367, 7.25102, 0.0473111, 5.12344,
  -8.89018, 2.74638, 0.0286741, -1.38765, -6.81866, 4.71722}
```

```
In[35]:= RandomReal[1, {4, 4}] // MatrixForm
Out[35]//MatrixForm=
 ( 0.0965377  0.418897   0.315761  0.738922 )
 ( 0.117419   0.780683   0.862551  0.502366 )
 ( 0.756172   0.0554912  0.637319  0.501434 )
 ( 0.430617   0.159067   0.735861  0.983597 )
```

Similar functions are available for generating random integers and complex numbers; they have the same syntax as `RandomReal`.

```
In[36]:= RandomInteger[{-100, 100}, {8}]
Out[36]= {62, -5, -64, -34, 10, -63, 16, 51}
```

```
In[37]:= RandomComplex[]
Out[37]= 0.551023 + 0.916462 i
```

In addition to working with uniformly distributed random numbers (the default for `RandomReal`), you can also work with any of the built-in distributions or your own, user-defined distribution. `RandomVariate` is designed for generating numbers from any distribution, continuous or discrete, univariate or multivariate. For example, here are 2500 points in the plane, normally distributed about the origin with standard deviation one.

```
In[38]:= pts = RandomVariate[NormalDistribution[0, 1], {2500, 2}];

In[39]:= ListPlot[pts, AspectRatio → Automatic]
```

Out[39]=

This gives ten random numbers using the χ^2 distribution with four degrees of freedom.

```
In[40]:= RandomVariate[ChiSquareDistribution[4], 10]
Out[40]= {3.62443, 14.5423, 2.4547, 4.34218,
          0.586325, 1.08043, 2.99004, 1.91899, 3.4792, 2.34091}
```

Additional functions are available for generating random samples from lists, with or without replacement. For example, RandomChoice selects with equal probability elements from a list *with* replacement. That can be a list of numbers or any arbitrary expressions.

```
In[41]:= RandomChoice[{"red", "blue", "green"}, 20]
Out[41]= {green, blue, red, green, green, green, green, green, blue, blue,
          red, green, blue, green, red, green, green, green, red, green}
```

RandomSample, in contrast, selects *without* replacement and so its output is limited by the size of the list from which you are selecting. For example, this generates a random permutation on the first twenty integers:

```
In[42]:= RandomSample[Range[20], 20]
Out[42]= {4, 8, 14, 10, 17, 13, 20, 7, 19, 18, 5, 15, 1, 12, 11, 16, 3, 6, 9, 2}
```

Weights can be assigned with both RandomChoice and RandomSample. The following chooses ten zeros and ones, with a 25% chance of a zero being chosen and a 75% chance of a one:

```
In[43]:= RandomChoice[{0.25, 0.75} → {0, 1}, 10]
Out[43]= {0, 1, 1, 1, 0, 1, 0, 1, 1, 1}
```

Using a similar syntax to RandomReal and RandomInteger, you can create vectors, arrays, and tensors of random numbers.

```
In[44]:= RandomChoice[{0, 1}, {5, 5}] // MatrixForm
Out[44]//MatrixForm=
```

$$\begin{pmatrix} 1 & 1 & 1 & 0 & 1 \\ 1 & 1 & 1 & 1 & 0 \\ 1 & 0 & 1 & 1 & 0 \\ 1 & 1 & 0 & 1 & 0 \\ 0 & 0 & 0 & 0 & 0 \end{pmatrix}$$

Tip 2.1

Occasionally you will need repeatable results to test some code. SeedRandom is used to reseed the random number generator using a seed that is dependent upon the time of day and some aspects of the current *Mathematica* session.

```
In[45]:= SeedRandom[0]

In[46]:= RandomReal[1, {5}]

Out[46]= {0.652468, 0.63307, 0.682813, 0.566352, 0.935202}

In[47]:= SeedRandom[0]

In[48]:= RandomReal[1, {5}]

Out[48]= {0.652468, 0.63307, 0.682813, 0.566352, 0.935202}
```

Exercises

1. Is the expression $2 + \pi$ a number? Is it numeric? What is the difference?

2. Convert the base 10 integer 65 to base 2. Then convert back to base 10.

3. Define a function complexToPolar that converts complex numbers to their polar representations. Then, convert the numbers $3 + 3\,i$ and $e^{\pi i/3}$ to polar form.

4. Use NumberForm to display an approximate number with exactly four precise digits and three digits to the right of the decimal. Then use PaddedForm to display the numbers in the following vector with precisely two digits to the right of the decimal:

```
In[1]:= vec = RandomReal[{0, 1}, 8]

Out[1]= {0.897363, 0.629743, 0.657265, 0.959865, 0.681584, 0.706607, 0.995883, 0.111384}
```

5. Make a histogram of the frequencies of the first 100 000 digits of π. It is an open problem in number theory as to whether the digits are *normal*, meaning that each of the digits zero through nine occur with about the same frequency in the decimal expansion of π. See Bailey et al. (2012) for more information on normality and the digits of π.

6. Convert each of the characters in a string such as "Apple" to their eight-bit binary character code representation. For example, the character code for the letter A is 65:

```
In[2]:= ToCharacterCode["A"]

Out[2]= {65}
```

The eight-bit binary representation of 65 is 1000001, so your solution should return that base 2 number for the letter A. Binary representations of letters are used in certain ciphers such as the XOR cipher discussed in Exercise 5 of Section 7.1.

7. Graphs consist of a set of vertices and edges connecting some subset of those vertices. They are implemented in *Mathematica* with Graph, which takes two arguments: a list of vertices and a list of edges. Create a random graph on n vertices by choosing m edges from the $\binom{n}{2}$ possible edges. Such

random graphs are commonly specified as $G(n, m)$ and are essentially the model upon which the built-in `RandomGraph` is based.

8. Extract the first 5000 digits in the decimal expansion of 1/17 or any other rational number. Then play them using `ListPlay`, which emits sound whose amplitude is given by the sequence of digits. Compare with the first 5000 digits of π.

9. `RandomReal` by default outputs numbers uniformly distributed on the interval [0, 1].

```
In[3]:= data = RandomReal[{0, 1}, {10^4}];
        Histogram[data, 15]
```

Out[4]=

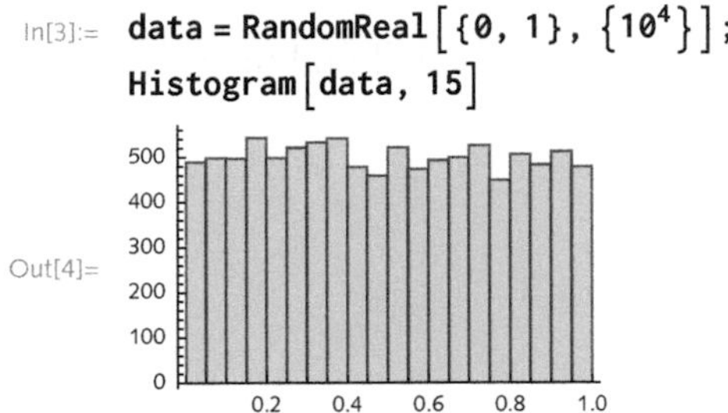

Bias the list of random numbers toward the lower end of this interval, giving a histogram similar to those in Figure 2.3.

FIGURE 2.3. *Distributions of random number data biased toward the lower end of the interval* [0, 1].

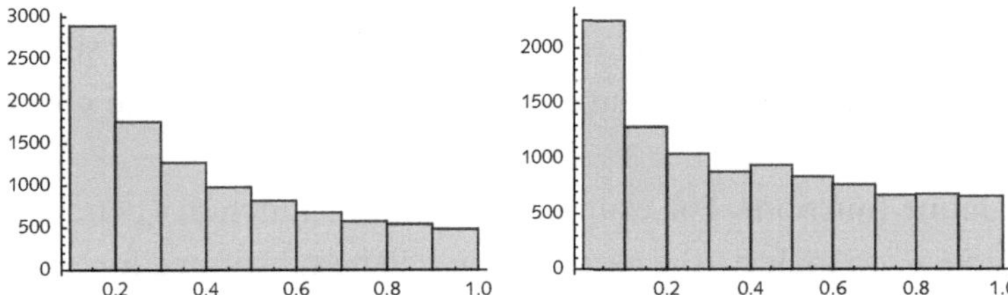

10. Information theory, as conceived by Claude Shannon in the 1940s and 1950s, was originally interested in maximizing the amount of data that can be stored and retrieved over some channel such as a telephone line. Shannon devised a measure, now called *entropy*, that gives the theoretical maxima for such a signal. Entropy can be thought of as the average uncertainty of a single random variable and is computed by the following, where $p(x)$ is the probability of event x over a domain X:

$$H(X) = -\sum_{x \in X} p(x) \log_2 p(x)$$

Generate a plot of the entropy (built into *Mathematica* as `Entropy`) as a function of success probability. You can simulate n trials of a coin toss with probability p using a Bernoulli distribution as follows:

```
RandomVariate[BernoulliDistribution[p], n]
```

2.3 Definitions

Defining variables and functions

One of the most common tasks in any programming environment is to define functions, constants, and procedures to perform various tasks. Sometimes a particular function that you need is not part of the built-in set of functions. Other times, you may need to use an expression over and over again and so it would be useful to define it once and have it available for future reference. By defining your own functions and constants you essentially expand the range of *Mathematica*'s capabilities in such a way that they work with all the built-in functions seamlessly.

For example, you might define a constant a to have a certain numeric value.

```
In[1]:= a = N[2 π]
Out[1]= 6.28319
```

Then, whenever a is used in a subsequent computation, *Mathematica* will find the rule associated with a and will substitute that value wherever a occurs.

```
In[2]:= Cos[a]
Out[2]= 1.
```

To check what definitions are associated with a, evaluate ? a.

```
In[3]:= ?a

Global`a

a = 6.28319
```

The expression a = N[2 π] is called an *assignment* – the value of the right-hand side is assigned to the symbol on the left-hand side. In this example, we have made an assignment of the constant 6.2831... to the symbol a.

Assignments are also used to define functions. For example, to define a function f, enclose its arguments in square brackets and use x_ to indicate the variable that will be substituted for x on the right-hand side.

```
In[4]:= f[x_] = 1/(1 + x)
Out[4]= 1/(1 + x)
```

The expression f[x_] on the left-hand side of this assignment is a pattern. It indicates the class of expressions for which this definition should be used. We will have much more to say about patterns and pattern matching in Chapter 4, but, for now, it is enough to say that the pattern f[x_] matches f[*any expression*].

Once you have defined the rule for f, you can evaluate it at different values by replacing x with any expression: numbers, symbolic expressions, images, anything!

```
In[5]:= f[.1]
Out[5]= 0.909091
```

```
In[6]:= f[1]
Out[6]= 1/2
```

```
In[7]:= f[α^2]
```

$$\text{Out[7]=} \quad \frac{1}{1 + \alpha^2}$$

```
In[8]:= f[ (graph) ]
```

$$\text{Out[8]=} \quad \frac{1}{1 + \text{(graph)}}$$

In this last example, the graph is a symbolic expression that is matched by the pattern `x_` in the definition for `f`. Although it might not make much mathematical sense to add and subtract integers from a graph, symbolically it is just an arbitrary expression matched by the pattern.

Clear the values of symbols that are no longer needed.

```
In[9]:= Clear[a, f]
```

Immediate vs. delayed assignments

When we set up the assignment for the symbol a above, the idea was to give the symbol a specific value so that we could use the symbol name to represent that value in subsequent computations. When you set up definitions for functions, those functions might depend upon the values of previously defined functions or other expressions. In such instances it is useful to delay the assignment until the function is actually used in a computation. This is the basic difference between *immediate* and *delayed assignments*.

An immediate assignment is written as follows:

lhs = *rhs*

Here *lhs* is an abbreviation for "left-hand side" and *rhs* abbreviates "right-hand side." Using `Defer`, you can see the internal form of this assignment before *Mathematica* has evaluated it (try it without `Defer`). The assignment is an expression with the head, `Set`, and two elements.

```
In[10]:= Defer[FullForm[x = 5]]
Out[10]= Set[x, 5]
```

As an example, consider defining a symbol `rand1` using an immediate assignment that generates a uniformly distributed random number between zero and one.

```
In[11]:= rand1 = RandomReal[]
Out[11]= 0.652468
```

Notice that the output of this assignment is the value of the right-hand side and that *Mathematica* evaluates the right-hand side immediately, that is, *when the assignment is made.*

Delayed assignments look similar to immediate assignments but use := instead of =.

lhs := *rhs*

Here is the internal representation of a delayed assignment:

```
In[12]:= Defer[FullForm[x := 5]]
Out[12]= SetDelayed[x, 5]
```

Consider the symbol `rand2` defined similarly to `rand1`, but instead uses a delayed assignment.

```
In[13]:= rand2 := RandomReal[]
```

Notice that the delayed assignment does not return a value when the assignment is made. In fact, the right-hand side will not be evaluated until the symbol `rand2` is used.

Let us call the function `rand1` three times.

```
In[14]:= Table[rand1, {3}]
Out[14]= {0.652468, 0.652468, 0.652468}
```

Because the right-hand side of `rand1` was evaluated when the definition was made, `rand1` was assigned the value `0.652468`. Each subsequent call to `rand1` returns that value.

```
In[15]:= ? rand1

Global`rand1

rand1 = 0.652468
```

In contrast, creating a table of values using `rand2` produces a very different result.

```
In[16]:= Table[rand2, {3}]
Out[16]= {0.63307, 0.682813, 0.566352}
```

Each of the three times that `rand2` is called inside `Table`, *Mathematica* looks up the definition of `rand2`, and sees that it should evaluate `RandomReal[]`. It does this each time it is called, generating a new random number each iteration inside `Table`.

```
In[17]:= ? rand2

Global`rand2

rand2 := RandomReal[]
```

So, when should you use immediate or delayed assignments? When you define a function, you usually do not want either the left-hand side or the right-hand side to be evaluated; you just want to make it available for use when the appropriate function call is made. This is precisely what occurs when `SetDelayed` is used, so the `SetDelayed` function is commonly used in writing function definitions. When you make a value declaration, you do not want the left-hand side to be evaluated; you just want to make it a nickname to serve as shorthand for a value. This is what happens when a

Set function is used and so the Set function is commonly used to make value declarations, such as assigning a numeric value to a constant or variable.

A new rule overwrites, or replaces, an older rule with the same left-hand side. However, keep in mind that two rules that only differ in the name of their pattern variables are considered the same by *Mathematica*.

Creating definitions with either immediate or delayed assignments creates a new rule (sometimes referred to as a rewrite rule) in *Mathematica*'s global rule base. Rules are used in *Mathematica* to rewrite expressions, that is, to transform an expression to another form. In *Mathematica*, you work with two kinds of rules: rules for built-in functions, which are part of every *Mathematica* session, and user-defined rules, which you enter during a particular session. User-defined rules essentially provide a mechanism for extending the rule base of *Mathematica*.

Information about both kinds of rules is obtained by evaluating ? *symbol_name*. In the case of a built-in function, the resulting usage message gives information about the syntax for using the function and a brief statement explaining what the function does.

```
In[18]:= ? Map
```

Map[*f*, *expr*] or *f* /@ *expr* applies *f* to each element on the first level in *expr*.
Map[*f*, *expr*, *levelspec*] applies *f* to parts of *expr* specified by *levelspec*.
Map[*f*] represents an operator form of Map that can be applied to an expression. >>

Clear[*name*] is used to remove user-defined rules from the global rule base. Built-in symbols like Map are protected and cannot be cleared.

```
In[19]:= Clear[x, rand1, rand2]
```

Compound functions

Let's return to the random walk example from Section 2.1 and turn it into a function, explicitly listing the separate steps. The idea is to create a compound expression on the right-hand side of a function definition. Recall that a compound expression has multiple expressions separated by semicolons.

```
In[20]:= walk[t_] := (
           dirs = {-1, 1};
           steps = RandomChoice[dirs, {t}];
           Accumulate[steps]
          )
```

Let's try out our function, first with a short five-step walk:

```
In[21]:= walk[5]
Out[21]= {1, 2, 3, 2, 3}
```

And then a visualization of a longer walk:

```
In[22]:= ListLinePlot[walk[1500]]
```

Out[22]=

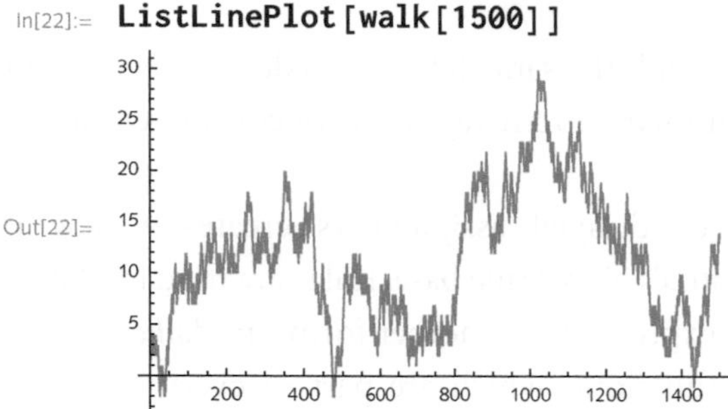

There are some important points to keep in mind regarding the right-hand side of a compound function definition:

- Since the expressions on the right-hand side are evaluated in order, assignments and function definitions should be given *before* they are used and the argument names used on the left-hand side of those function definitions *must* differ from the argument names used by the compound function itself.
- When you evaluate a compound function definition, you are creating not only the function but also the assignments and auxiliary function definitions. If you then remove the compound function definition using `Clear`, the auxiliary function definitions and assignments remain. This can cause a problem if you subsequently try to use the names of these auxiliary functions and values elsewhere. It is considered bad programming practice to leave auxiliary definitions in the global rule base if they are not explicitly needed by the user of your function.
- Note the use of parentheses wrapped around the compound expressions (those separated by semicolons). If you omit the parentheses, *Mathematica* will think the function definition ends at the first semicolon and will not know what value of *n* to use inside `RandomChoice`.

```
In[23]:= walkBad[n_] :=
           dirs = {-1, 1};
         steps = RandomChoice[dirs, {n}];
         Accumulate[steps]
         RandomChoice::array :
           The array dimensions {n} given in position 2 of RandomChoice[{-1, 1}, {n}] should be a list
              of non-negative machine-sized integers giving the dimensions for the result. >>

         Accumulate::tdlen : Objects of unequal length in RandomChoice[{-1, 1}, {n}] cannot be added. >>
Out[25]= Accumulate[RandomChoice[{-1, 1}, {n}]]
```

These issues are discussed in Section 6.1, where we introduce the scoping construct `Module`.

Functions with multiple definitions

When you create function definitions, usually the definition is associated with the head of the left-hand side of your definition. So, for example, the following assignment associates the rule $1 + x + x^2$ with the head f:

```
In[26]:= f[x_] := 1 + x + x^2
```

There can be many evaluation rules associated with one symbol. The following assignments associate additional rules with the symbol f:

```
In[27]:= f[x_, y_] := x + y
```

```
In[28]:= f[x_, y_, z_] := 1/(x + y - z)
```

To view all the rules associated with this symbol, use ? f.

```
In[29]:= ? f

Global`f

f[x_] := 1 + x + x^2

f[x_, y_] := x + y

f[x_, y_, z_] := 1/(x+y-z)
```

The advantage of this structure is that you can use one name for a function that behaves differently depending upon the number or form of arguments you give to that function. Using a different symbol for each of these tasks would require you and those who use your programs to remember multiple function names when one might be sufficient. For example, here are two definitions for a function, one for an arbitrary argument and the second for a list of two expressions:

```
In[30]:= fun[x_] := Abs[x]
```

```
In[31]:= fun[{x_, y_}] := Sqrt[x^2 + y^2]
```

Different rules will be called and evaluated depending upon the pattern match as determined by the argument structure.

```
In[32]:= fun[-12]
Out[32]= 12
```

```
In[33]:= fun[{2, 3}]
Out[33]= √13
```

```
In[34]:= fun[1 + 2 I]
Out[34]= √5
```

This is a very simplistic example, one that would need some modification if we wanted to consider it for, say, a norm computation and needed to be more careful about the arguments of the function.

```
In[35]:= fun["string"]
Out[35]= Abs[string]
```

```
In[36]:= fun[{{a, b}, {c, d}}]
```

Out[36]= $\{\sqrt{a^2 + c^2}, \sqrt{b^2 + d^2}\}$

Writing more explicit rules for such a computation is straightforward enough but requires a bit more discussion of patterns and predicates to do so properly. These topics will be discussed in Chapter 4 on patterns and rules.

Exercises

1. Create a function `reciprocal`$[\frac{a}{b}]$ that returns the reciprocal of the fraction a/b. Check your solution with numeric and symbolic fractions and with fractions containing zero in the numerator.
2. Using `Total`, create a function to sum the first n positive integers.
3. Create a function to compute the sum of the digits of any integer. Write an additional rule to give the sum of the base-b digits of an integer. Then use your function to compute the *Hamming weight* of any integer: the Hamming weight of an integer is given by the number of ones in the binary representation of that number. It has wide use in computer science (modular exponentiation and hash tables), cryptography, and coding theory (Knuth 2011).
4. Write a function `sumsOfCubes[`*n*`]` that takes a positive integer argument n and computes the sums of cubes of the digits of n (Hayes 1992).
5. What rules are created by each of the following functions? Check your predictions by evaluating them and then querying *Mathematica* with ?*function_name*.

   a. `randLis1[n_] := RandomReal[1, {n}]`

   b. `randLis2[n_] := (x = RandomReal[]; Table[x, {n}])`

   c. `randLis3[n_] := (x := RandomReal[]; Table[x, {n}])`

   d. `randLis4[n_] = Table[RandomReal[], {n}]`

6. Consider two functions `f` and `g`, which are identical except that one is written using an immediate assignment and the other using a delayed assignment.

   ```
   In[1]:= f[n_] = Sum[(1 + x)^j, {j, 1, n}];
   In[2]:= g[n_] := Sum[(1 + x)^j, {j, 1, n}]
   ```

   Explain why the outputs of these two functions *look* so different. Are they in fact different?

   ```
   In[3]:= f[2]
   ```

   Out[3]= $\frac{(1 + x)\ (-1 + (1 + x)^2)}{x}$

```
In[4]:= g[2]
Out[4]= 1 + x + (1 + x)^2
```

7. Write rules for a function `log` (note lowercase) that encapsulate the following identities:

$$\log(a\,b) = \log(a) + \log(b);$$
$$\log\left(\tfrac{a}{b}\right) = \log(a) - \log(b);$$
$$\log(a^n) = n\log(a).$$

8. Create a piecewise-defined function $g(x)$ based on the following; then plot the function from -2 to 0.

$$g(x) = \begin{cases} -\sqrt{1-(x+2)^2} & -2 \le x \le -1 \\ \sqrt{1-x^2} & x < 0 \end{cases}$$

9. The built-in function `RotateRight` rotates the elements in a list one place to the right, with the last element swinging around to the front.

```
In[5]:= RotateRight[{a, b, c, d, e}]
Out[5]= {e, a, b, c, d}
```

Create a function `IntegerRotateRight[n]` that takes an integer n and returns an integer with the original digits rotated one place to the right. Use this function to first verify that 142 857 is a divisor of its right rotation and then find all such numbers less than one million (Project Euler, Problem #168).

10. The Champernowne constant is a famous number that is created by concatenating successive integers and interpreting them as decimal digits. For example, here are the first 31 digits of the base-10 Champernowne number:

```
In[6]:= N[ChampernowneNumber[10], 31]
Out[6]= 0.1234567891011121314151617181920
```

Concatenation can be used to generate integers also. Create a function to generate the nth Smarandache–Wellin number, formed by concatenating the digits of successive primes. The first such number is 2, then 23, then 235, followed by 2357, 235711, and so on. Numerous open questions exist about these numbers: for example, it is not known if an infinite number of them are prime; see Crandall and Pomerance (2005) and Sloane (A019518).

2.4 Predicates and Boolean operations

Predicates

Suppose you are working with a data set consisting of temperatures collected by a sensor attached to a piece of equipment. As you collect and analyze the data, you need to know if the temperatures extend beyond some threshold value that the equipment needs to stay within. Or perhaps when the sensor fails, it inserts a nonnumeric value, say the string "NAN", in the set of data. One task of preprocessing the data is to find and adjust for nonnumeric values. Similarly, when you write programs, what to do next at any particular point in your program will often depend upon some test or condition being met. Every programming language has constructs for testing data or conditions, and some of the most useful are called predicates. A *predicate* is a function that returns a value of `True` or `False` depending upon whether its argument passes a test. For example, the predicate `PrimeQ` tests for the primality of its argument.

```
In[1]:= PrimeQ[2^31 - 1]
Out[1]= True
```

Predicates are available to test numbers to see whether they are even, odd, integral, and so on.

```
In[2]:= OddQ[21]
Out[2]= True

In[3]:= EvenQ[21]
Out[3]= False

In[4]:= IntegerQ[5/9]
Out[4]= False
```

Many other predicates are available for testing expressions such as atoms, lists, strings, various matrices, and much more.

```
In[5]:= AtomQ["string"]
Out[5]= True

In[6]:= ListQ[{a, b, c}]
Out[6]= True

In[7]:= StringQ["colorless green ideas sleep furiously"]
Out[7]= True

In[8]:= SymmetricMatrixQ[{{1, 2, 3}, {2, 4, 5}, {3, 5, 6}}]
Out[8]= True

In[9]:= ConnectedGraphQ[ ]
Out[9]= True
```

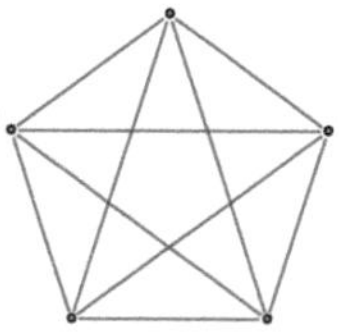

Some predicate functions take a second argument to test the form of the elements of an expression. For example, this tests whether the argument is a vector and if its elements are all prime:

```
In[10]:= VectorQ[{2^3 - 1, 2^7 - 1, 2^31 - 1}, PrimeQ]
Out[10]= True
```

Of course, you can define your own predicate functions as well. For example, the following function defines a test for perfect numbers, numbers that are equal to the sum of their proper divisors. `Divisors[n]` returns a list of divisors including the number n itself, hence the need for `2 n` on the right-hand side of the equality test.

```
In[11]:= PerfectQ[n_] := Total[Divisors[n]] == 2 n

In[12]:= PerfectQ[28]
Out[12]= True
```

Relational and logical operators

Another class of commonly used predicates are the relational operators. They are used to compare two or more expressions. The relational operators are `Equal` (==), `NotEqual` (≠), `Greater` (>), `Less` (<), `GreaterEqual` (≥), and `LessEqual` (≤). They can be used to compare numbers and arbitrary expressions and to set up equations and inequalities.

```
In[13]:= 7 < 5
Out[13]= False

In[14]:= 3 == 7 - 4 == 6/2
Out[14]= True

In[15]:= x^2 - 1 == (x^4 - 1)/(x^2 + 1) // Simplify
Out[15]= True
```

Note that the relational operators have lower precedence than the arithmetic operators. The second example above is interpreted as `3 == (7 - 4)` and not as `(3 == 7) - 4`. Table 2.2 lists the relational operators and their various input forms. A detailed listing of precedence for many operators is available in the built-in tutorial The Syntax of the Wolfram Language (WLDC).

TABLE 2.2. *Relational operators*

StandardForm	Long (functional) form	Meaning
$x == y$	`Equal[x, y]`	test for equality
$x \neq y$	`Unequal[x, y]`	unequal
$x > y$	`Greater[x, y]`	greater than
$x < y$	`Less[x, y]`	less than
$x \geq y$	`GreaterEqual[x, y]`	greater than or equal
$x \leq y$	`LessEqual[x, y]`	less than or equal

The logical operators (also called Boolean operators) determine the truth of an expression based on Boolean arithmetic. For example, the conjunction of two true statements is always true.

```
In[16]:= 4 < 5 && 8 > 1
Out[16]= True
```

The Boolean operation AND is represented in *Mathematica* by And, with shorthand notation && or ∧. Here is a table that gives all the possible values for the And operator. (The function TruthTable is developed in Exercise 12 of Section 5.6 and Exercise 3 of Section 6.3.)

```
In[17]:= << EPM`
```

```
In[18]:= TruthTable[A ∧ B, {A, B}]
```

Out[18]=

A	B	$A \wedge B$
T	T	T
T	F	F
F	T	F
F	F	F

The logical OR operator, represented by Or and with shorthand notation || (or ∨), is true when either of its arguments is true.

```
In[19]:= 4 == 3 || 3 == 6/2
```

```
Out[19]= True
```

```
In[20]:= 0 == 0.0001 ∨ π == 22/7
```

```
Out[20]= False
```

```
In[21]:= TruthTable[A ∨ B, {A, B}]
```

Out[21]=

A	B	$A \vee B$
T	T	T
T	F	T
F	T	T
F	F	F

Note the difference between this Boolean OR and the natural language notion of "or." A phrase such as "It is cold or it is hot" uses the word "or" in an *exclusive* sense, that is, it excludes the possibility that it is *both* cold and hot. The logical Or (∨) is inclusive in the sense that if A and B are both true, then $A \vee B$ is also true. Table 2.3 shows the logical operators and their input forms.

TABLE 2.3. *Logical operators*

StandardForm	TraditionalForm	Long form	Meaning
!x	$\neg x$	Not[x]	not
x && y	$x \wedge y$	And[x, y]	and
x || y	$x \vee y$	Or[x, y]	or
(x || y) && ! (x && y)	$x \veebar y$	Xor[x, y]	exclusive or
! (x || y)	$x \bar{\vee} y$	Nor[x, y]	negation of or
!x || y	$x \Rightarrow y$	Implies[x, y]	implication

The exclusive OR is represented by the operator `Xor`.

```
In[22]:= Xor[True, True]
Out[22]= False
```

```
In[23]:= Xor[True, False]
Out[23]= True
```

```
In[24]:= TruthTable[A ⊻ B, {A, B}]
```

Out[24]=

A	B	$A \veebar B$
T	T	F
T	F	T
F	T	T
F	F	F

Additionally, *bitwise logical operators* operate on integers as binary bits (see Table 2.4). For example, `BitOr[x, y]` gives the integer whose binary representation has ones wherever the binary representation of x or y has ones. Here is the bitwise OR of 21 and 19, given in binary form:

```
In[25]:= BaseForm[BitOr[2^^10101, 2^^10011], 2]
Out[25]//BaseForm=
         10111₂
```

```
In[26]:= BitOr[21, 19]
Out[26]= 23
```

```
In[27]:= BaseForm[23, 2]
Out[27]//BaseForm=
         10111₂
```

`BitXor[x, y]` gives the integer with ones at positions where either x or y have ones, but not both. Essentially, `BitXor` returns a 1 in positions where the two numbers' bits differ.

```
In[28]:= BaseForm[BitXor[2^^10101, 2^^10011], 2]
Out[28]//BaseForm=
         110₂
```

TABLE 2.4. *Bitwise operators*

Long (functional) form	Meaning
`BitAnd[x, y]`	bitwise AND of x and y
`BitOr[x, y]`	bitwise OR of x and y
`BitNot[x]`	bitwise NOT of x
`BitXor[x, y]`	bitwise XOR of x and y

In Section 5.6 we will look at an application of bitwise operators to an example involving error-correcting codes: the computation of Hamming distance.

Exercises

1. Create a predicate function that returns a value of `True` if its argument is between −1 and 1.
2. Define a predicate function `StringCharacterQ[str]` that returns `True` if its argument *str* is a single string character, and returns `False` otherwise.
3. Write a predicate function `NaturalQ[n]` that returns a value of `True` if *n* is a natural number and a value of `False` otherwise, that is, `NaturalQ[n]` gives `True` if *n* is among 0, 1, 2, 3, ...
4. Create a predicate function, `SquareNumberQ[n]` that returns `True` if *n* is a square number, such as 1, 4, 9, 16,....
5. Create a predicate function `TriangularNumberQ[t]` that returns `True` whenever its argument *t* is a triangular number. The *n*th triangular number T_n is given by the formula

$$T_n = \sum_{k=1}^{n} k = 1+2+3+\cdots+n = \frac{n(n+1)}{2} = \binom{n+1}{2}$$

6. Based on the solution to the two previous exercises, create a predicate function `SquareTriangularNumberQ[n]` that returns a value of `True` if *n* is *both* a square number and a triangular number. Then use this predicate to find all square triangular numbers less than one million.
7. Create a predicate function `RealPositiveQ[x]` that returns a value of `True` if *x* is a positive real number ("real" in the mathematical sense, i.e., $x \in \mathbb{R}$). Add a second rule that accepts vectors as arguments and returns `True` if every element of the vector argument is a positive real number.
8. The built-in function `CoprimeQ[a, b]` returns `True` if *a* and *b* are relatively prime (share no common factors other than 1) and returns `False` otherwise. Use `ArrayPlot` to visualize pairs of relatively prime numbers from 1 to 100. Use `Boole` to convert the table of `True/False` values returned by `CoPrimeQ` to zeros and ones.
9. An undirected graph *gr* is considered *dense* if the number of edges in *gr* is close to the maximum number of edges. The maximum for a graph with *n* edges occurs when *every* pair of vertices is connected by an edge and, assuming no self-loops and no multi-edges, is given by the number of two-element subsets of *n* objects, $\binom{n}{2}$. The density $\mathcal{D}$ of a graph can be defined as

$$\mathcal{D} = \frac{|E|}{|V|\,(|V|-1)}$$

where $|E|$ is the number of edges and $|V|$ is the number of vertices (given by `EdgeCount` and `VertexCount`, respectively). A graph with all possible edges has a density of 1 and a graph with no edges has density 0. Although there are differences of opinion as to where the cutoff is, assume that a graph is dense if its density is greater than or equal to 0.5.

Define a function `DenseGraphQ[gr]` that returns a value of `True` if *gr* is dense in the above sense and returns a value of `False` otherwise. As tests, `DenseGraphQ` should give `True` for `CompleteGraph[n]` for any *n* and it should return `False` for `RandomGraph[BernoulliGraphDistribution[n, pr]]` for small probabilities *pr*.

2.5 Attributes

All functions in *Mathematica* have certain properties that control various aspects of their behavior. These properties, called *attributes*, can make a function commutative or associative, or they may give the function the ability to be automatically threaded over a list. The attributes of any function are displayed with the `Attributes` function.

```
In[1]:= Attributes[Cos]
Out[1]= {Listable, NumericFunction, Protected}
```

You will often find it helpful to know the attributes of a built-in function in order to better understand how it behaves and in certain instances to help make your computations more efficient. Furthermore, functions that you create can inherit any of these attributes of the built-in functions. We will discuss a few of the more commonly used attributes below; other attributes of functions will be discussed in later chapters. For a complete list, see the tutorial Attributes (WLDC).

Listable

Functions with the `Listable` attribute are automatically applied to elements in lists.

In[2]:= $\text{Cos}\left[\left\{\frac{\pi}{6}, \frac{\pi}{4}, \frac{\pi}{3}\right\}\right]$

Out[2]= $\left\{\frac{\sqrt{3}}{2}, \frac{1}{\sqrt{2}}, \frac{1}{2}\right\}$

Functions that do not have the `Listable` attribute do not map over lists.

```
In[3]:= Area[{Disk[{0, 0}, r], Sphere[{0, 0, 0}, r]}]
        Area::reg : {Disk[{0, 0}, r], Sphere[{0, 0, 0}, r]} is not a correctly specified region. >>
Out[3]= Area[{Disk[{0, 0}, r], Sphere[{0, 0, 0}, r]}]
```

As we will see in Chapter 5, you will need to map such functions over lists manually.

```
In[4]:= Map[Area, {Disk[{0, 0}, r], Sphere[{0, 0, 0}, r]}]
```

Out[4]= $\{\pi r^2, 4 \pi r^2\}$

Hold attributes

Another important property that many built-in functions have is one of the many `Hold` attributes.

```
In[5]:= Attributes[Plot]
Out[5]= {HoldAll, Protected, ReadProtected}
```

Functions with one of the `Hold` attributes keep one or more of their arguments in an unevaluated form as they are passed into the body of the function. In some circumstances this can cause unintended results. For example, in the following, `Table` is not evaluated initially because the `Plot` function has the `HoldAll` attribute. As a result, the table is evaluated repeatedly for each value of `x` inside the body of `Plot`, causing the table of polynomials to be treated as a single vector-valued object and slowing down the computation.

```
In[6]:= Plot[Table[LegendreP[n, x], {n, 1, 15}], {x, 0, 1}] // Timing
```

```
Out[6]= {0.354403,
```

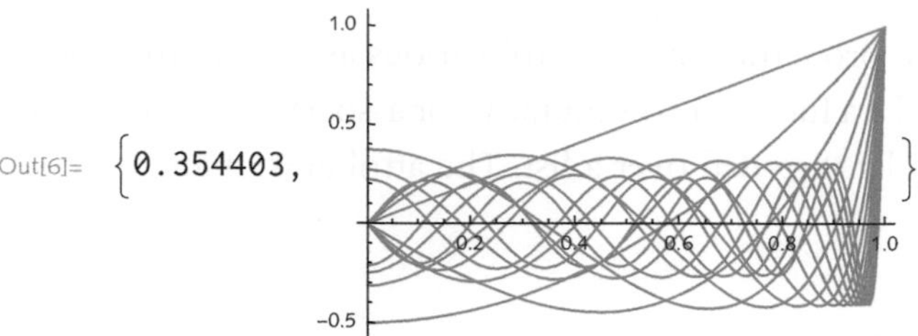


```
}
```

The table above is re-evaluated for each value of x. To override this hold behavior, use `Evaluate`.

```
In[7]:= Plot[Evaluate[Table[LegendreP[n, x], {n, 1, 15}]], {x, 0, 1}] // Timing
```

```
Out[7]= {0.106904,
```

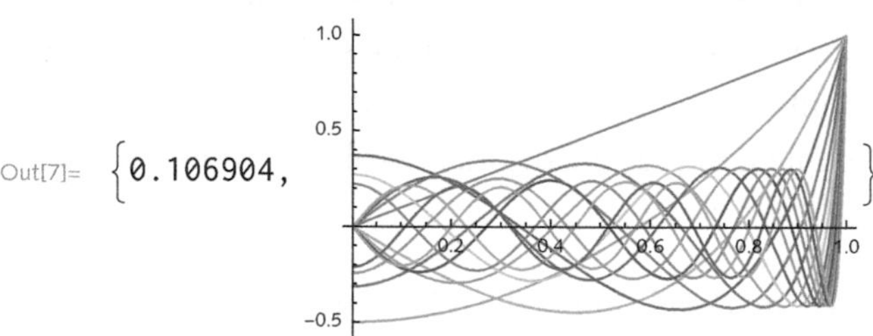


```
}
```

Protected

Although it is unusual to alter the attributes of a built-in function, it is fairly common to change the default attributes of a user-defined function. For example, suppose you had a function that you wanted to inherit the `Protected` attribute, an attribute possessed by all the built-in functions. Without explicitly setting that attribute, the function can be created and modified.

```
In[8]:= f[x_] := x^2 + 1
```

Once it is protected, no further modifications can be made to the function.

```
In[9]:= SetAttributes[f, Protected]
```

```
In[10]:= f[x_, y_] := x - y

         SetDelayed::write : Tag f in f[x_, y_] is Protected. >>

Out[10]= $Failed
```

A built-in function exists to reset functions to their default behavior regarding modification.

```
In[11]:= Unprotect[f]
Out[11]= {f}
```

We will see some applications of `SetAttributes` as well as ways to clear attributes in general in Sections 5.1 and 9.2.

Exercises

1. Ordinarily, when you define a function, it has no attributes. The arguments are evaluated before being passed up to the calling function. So, in the following case, 2 + 3 is evaluated before it is passed to g.

```
In[1]:= g[x_ + y_] := x^2 + y^2
In[2]:= g[2 + 3]
Out[2]= g[5]
```

Use one of the `Hold` attributes to give g the property that its argument is not evaluated first. The resulting output should look like this:

```
In[3]:= g[2 + 3]
Out[3]= 13
```

2. Define a function that takes each number, *x*, in a vector of numbers and returns *x* if it is within a certain interval, say $-0.5 < x < 0.5$, and returns $\sqrt{x}$ otherwise. Then make your function listable so that it can operate on vectors (lists) directly.

3. The definitions used in the solution to Exercise 1 of Section 2.3 for the `reciprocal` function failed to properly deal with the special case of zero in the numerator.

```
In[4]:= reciprocal[Rational[a_, b_]] := Rational[b, a]
In[5]:= reciprocal[0 / 5]
Out[5]= reciprocal[0]
```

Correct this problem by giving `reciprocal` the appropriate attribute.

2.6 Notes and further reading

The idea of using punched cards to store information and instruct machines to perform specific tasks predates Jacquard looms and player pianos. Charles Babbage, in the 1830s proposed his *Analytical Engine*, a mechanical computer that included looping and conditional branching structures as well as punch cards to store instructions and input. Although never fully realized in his day, it was, in many ways, the precursor of modern computers. See Ceruzzi (2012) for a discussion of the early history of computing.

The notion of formal languages began with Frege's *Begriffsschrift* (Frege 1879). Also see Enderton (1972) for an introduction to the language of mathematical logic, or Knuth (2003) for a discussion of the early development of programming languages.

The text by Manning and Schütze (1999) contains a discussion of entropy in the context of information theory generally and natural language processing in particular. Also, see Claude Shannon's very readable original paper on the mathematical theory of communication (Shannon 1948).

An excellent resource on computational problems surrounding prime numbers is Crandall and Pomerance (2005). For questions regarding any sequence of numbers, the indispensable resource is the On-Line Encyclopedia of Integer Sequences (Sloane A019518).

Although we could devote an entire book to numerical computation, this chapter only discusses different kinds of numbers and operations on them as they relate to the programming principles that are covered in this book. For a more thorough treatment of numbers and numerical issues in *Mathematica*, see Knapp (2001), Trott (2006), or Wellin (2013).

Random walks first appeared in print in 1905 in a letter to the journal *Nature* by the English mathematician Karl Pearson (1905). Since then they have been studied and applied to fields as wide-ranging as Brownian motion, genetic drift, population dynamics, modeling neuron activity in the brain, financial analysis, and much more. For introductions to random walks, see Weiss (1994), Barber and Ninham (1970), and Rudnick and Gaspari (2004). Several variations and improvements to the random walk problem will be added throughout the rest of the book, including walks in higher dimensions, off-lattice walks, and visualizations.

3

Lists and associations

Creating and displaying lists · *List structure and syntax* · *List construction* · *Displaying lists* · *Arrays* · ***Testing and measuring lists*** · *Testing a list* · *Measuring lists* · ***Operations on lists*** · *Extracting elements* · *Applying functions to lists* · *Rearranging lists* · *List component assignment* · *Multiple lists* · ***Associations*** · *Creating and displaying associations* · *Operations on associations* · *Creating a bibliography* · ***Differences from other languages*** · ***Notes and further reading***

Lists are the key data structure used in *Mathematica* to group objects together. They share some features with arrays in other languages such as C and JAVA, but they are more general and can be used to represent a wide range of objects: vectors, matrices, tensors, iterator and parameter specifications, and much more.

Because lists are so fundamental, an extensive set of built-in functions is available to manipulate them in a variety of ways. In this chapter, we start by looking at the structure and syntax of lists before moving on to constructing, measuring, and testing lists. We then introduce some of the built-in functionality used to manipulate lists such as sorting and partitioning. Finally, we will discuss associations, a feature first introduced in *Mathematica* 10. Associations provide a framework for efficient representation and lookup of large data structures such as associative arrays (for example, a large database of article and book references or a music library).

Many of the things you might wish to do with a list or association can be accomplished using built-in functions and the programming concepts in this book. And most of these operations extend to arbitrary expressions in a fairly natural way, as we will see in later chapters. As such, it is important to have a solid understanding of these functions before going further, since a key to efficient programming in *Mathematica* is to use the built-in functions whenever possible to manipulate lists and associations as well as general expressions.

3.1 Creating and displaying lists

List structure and syntax

The standard input form of a list is a sequence of elements separated by commas and enclosed in curly braces:

$\{e_1, e_2, \ldots, e_n\}$

Internally, lists are stored in the functional form using the `List` function with an arbitrary number of arguments.

`List[`$e_1, e_2, \ldots, e_n$`]`

`FullForm` gives the internal representation.

```
In[1]:= FullForm[{a, b, c}]
Out[1]//FullForm=
        List[a, b, c]
```

The arguments of the `List` function (the *list elements*) can be any type of expression, including numbers, symbols, functions, strings, images, and even other lists.

```
In[2]:= {2.4, Sin, "ossifrage", [image], {5, 3}, {}}
Out[2]= {2.4, Sin, ossifrage, [image], {5, 3}, {}}
```

List construction

Lists can be created from scratch using the `List` function or curly braces to collect various expressions as we did above. Lists can also be created programmatically using several different functions such as `Range` and `Table`.

`Range[`*imin*, *imax*, *di*`]` generates a list of ordered numbers starting from *imin* and going up to, but not exceeding, *imax* in increments of *di*.

```
In[3]:= Range[0, 30, 3]
Out[3]= {0, 3, 6, 9, 12, 15, 18, 21, 24, 27, 30}
```

If *di* is not specified, a value of one is used.

```
In[4]:= Range[4, 8]
Out[4]= {4, 5, 6, 7, 8}
```

If neither *imin* nor *di* is specified, then both are given the value of one.

```
In[5]:= Range[4]
Out[5]= {1, 2, 3, 4}
```

It is not necessary for *imin, imax,* or *di* to be integers.

```
In[6]:= Range[1.5, 6.3, .75]
Out[6]= {1.5, 2.25, 3., 3.75, 4.5, 5.25, 6.}
```

`Table[`*expr*`, {`*i*`, `*imin*`, `*imax*`, `*di*`}]` generates a list by evaluating *expr* a number of times as determined by the iterator list.

```
In[7]:= Table[2^i, {i, 1, 10, 2}]
Out[7]= {2, 8, 32, 128, 512}
```

The first argument, 2^i in the above example, is the expression that is evaluated to produce the elements in the list. The second argument to the `Table` function, the list `{`*i*`, `*imin*`, `*imax*`, `*di*`}`, is referred to as the *iterator list*. This list specifies the number of times the expression is evaluated and hence the number of elements in the list. The value *imin* is the value of *i* used in the expression to create the first list element. The value *di* is the incremental increase in the value of *i* used in the expression to create additional list elements. The value *imax* is the maximum value of *i* used in the expression to create the last list element. If incrementing *i* by *di* gives a valuc greater than *imax*, that value is not used.

```
In[8]:= Table[i, {i, 1, 10, 2}]
Out[8]= {1, 3, 5, 7, 9}
```

`Table[`*i*`, {`*i*`, `*imin*`, `*imax*`, `*di*`}]` is equivalent to `Range[`*imin*`, `*imax*`, `*di*`]`. As with the `Range` function, the arguments to `Table` can be simplified when the iterator increment is one.

```
In[9]:= Table[2^i, {i, 1, 10}]
Out[9]= {2, 4, 8, 16, 32, 64, 128, 256, 512, 1024}
```

Similarly, both *imin* and *di* can be omitted and are then assumed to be one.

```
In[10]:= Table[i^2, {i, 5}]
Out[10]= {1, 4, 9, 16, 25}
```

If the iterator variable does not appear in the expression being evaluated, the variable may be omitted as well. The expression will then simply be evaluated that many times.

```
In[11]:= Table[RandomReal[], {3}]
Out[11]= {0.63307, 0.682813, 0.566352}
```

The expression that the `Table` function evaluates can be completely arbitrary. In the following computation, it is used to create a list of plots.

```
In[12]:= Table[Plot[BesselJ[n, x], {x, 0, 10}], {n, 2, 4}]
```

Out[12]=

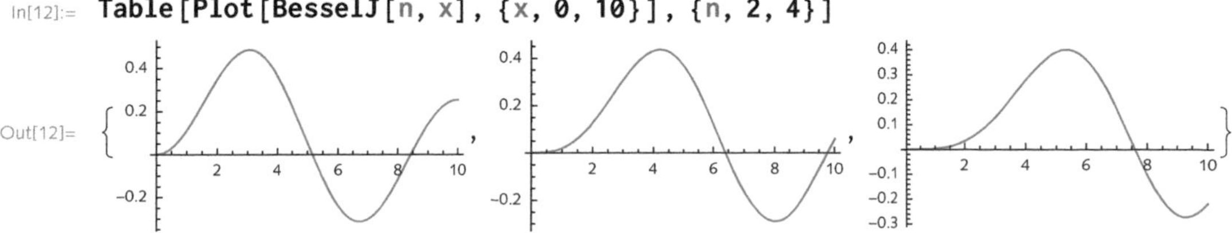

To create a *nested list* – a list containing other lists as elements – use additional iterators.

```
In[13]:= Table[i + j, {j, 1, 4}, {i, 1, 3}]
Out[13]= {{2, 3, 4}, {3, 4, 5}, {4, 5, 6}, {5, 6, 7}}
```

When there is more than one iterator, their order is important, because the value of the outer iterator is varied for each value of the inner iterator. In the above example, for each value of `j` (the inner iterator), `i` was varied from one to three, producing a three-element list for each of the four values of `j`. If you reverse the iterator order, you will get an entirely different list expression.

```
In[14]:= Table[i + j, {i, 1, 3}, {j, 1, 4}]
Out[14]= {{2, 3, 4, 5}, {3, 4, 5, 6}, {4, 5, 6, 7}}
```

The value of the outer iterator may depend on the value of the inner iterator; this can result in a nonrectangular list.

```
In[15]:= Table[i + j, {i, 1, 3}, {j, 1, i}]
Out[15]= {{2}, {3, 4}, {4, 5, 6}}
```

However, the inner iterator may not depend on the outer iterator because the inner iterator is fixed as the outer one varies.

```
In[16]:= Table[i + j, {i, 1, j}, {j, 1, 3}]
         Table::iterb : Iterator {i, 1, j} does not have appropriate bounds. >>
Out[16]= Table[i + j, {i, 1, j}, {j, 1, 3}]
```

Like the function being evaluated, the iterator structure can be quite arbitrary. In fact, it can be almost any expression, for example, a list of primes or a list of image effects.

```
In[17]:= Table[2^p - 1, {p, {2, 3, 5, 7, 13, 17}}]
Out[17]= {3, 7, 31, 127, 8191, 131 071}
```

```
In[18]:= Table[ImageEffect[ , effect],
           {effect, {"Charcoal", "Posterization", "Solarization"}}]
```

Out[18]= 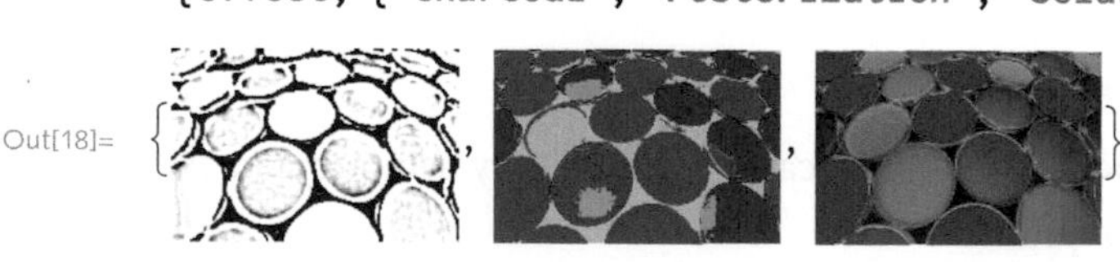

Rather than evaluating the iterator for a *range* of values, these arbitrary iterator specifications cause the function to be evaluated for *each* of the discrete values in the iterator list. So in the first example, the expression $2^p - 1$ is evaluated for each value of p equal to 2, 3, 5, 7, 13, 17; in the second example, `ImageEffect` is evaluated for each of the three different artistic image effects, `"Charcoal"`, `"Posterization"`, and `"Solarization"`.

Displaying lists

Regardless of whether `List` or the curly brace notation is used to enter a list expression, the default output form of a list uses the curly brace notation.

```
In[19]:= List[1, 2, 3]
Out[19]= {1, 2, 3}
```

Several formatting functions are available for displaying lists in different forms. For example, `MatrixForm` displays one-dimensional lists as column vectors.

```
In[20]:= MatrixForm[{a, b, c}]
Out[20]//MatrixForm=
```

$$\begin{pmatrix} a \\ b \\ c \end{pmatrix}$$

It displays rectangular arrays as traditional matrices.

```
In[21]:= MatrixForm[{{a, b, c}, {d, e, f}}]
Out[21]//MatrixForm=
```

$$\begin{pmatrix} a & b & c \\ d & e & f \end{pmatrix}$$

`TableForm` is useful for displaying nested lists such as multi-dimensional data in a basic rectangular array.

```
In[22]:= lis = Table[i + j, {i, 1, 3}, {j, 1, 2}]
Out[22]= {{2, 3}, {3, 4}, {4, 5}}

In[23]:= TableForm[lis]
Out[23]//TableForm=
         2    3
         3    4
         4    5
```

Another useful function for displaying nested lists is `Grid`. It contains numerous options specifically for formatting tabular data.

```
In[24]:= data = {{"Trial", "Value"}, {1, 0.264084}, {2, 0.185688},
            {3, 0.156994}, {4, 0.486455}, {5, 0.334819}, {6, 0.799379}};

In[25]:= Grid[data, Frame → All, Background → LightGray,
          ItemSize → {Automatic, 1.5}, FrameStyle → Thin]
```

Out[25]=

Trial	Value
1	0.264084
2	0.185688
3	0.156994
4	0.486455
5	0.334819
6	0.799379

Tip 3.1

Sometimes you need to display a list of expressions but do not want to display the curly braces and commas. This can be done using `Row`.

```
In[26]:= Row[{a, b, c, d, e}]
Out[26]= abcde
```

An optional second argument specifies a separator between each of the elements. In the following input the separator consists of a filled circle surrounded by a space on either side:

```
In[27]:= Row[{a, b, c, d, e}, " • "]
Out[27]= a • b • c • d • e
```

`Row` is particularly useful for constructing text cells of different kinds of expressions, something we will look at when building bibliographic expressions in Section 3.4.

Two plotting functions are commonly used to give a visual representation of data: `ListPlot` and `ListLinePlot`. For one-dimensional lists, both functions give the *y*-values as heights and the *x* data range showing the position, or index, of each data point in the list.

```
In[28]:= ListLinePlot[{5, 4, 3, 10, 8, 9, 0, 7}, Mesh → All]
```

Out[28]=

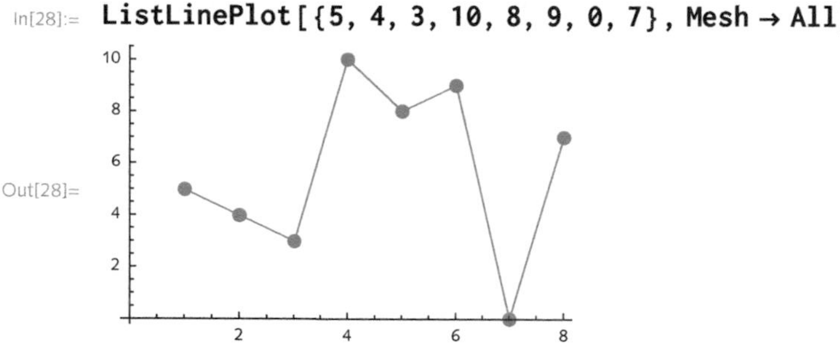

With two-dimensional data, the list-plotting functions essentially give scatter plots. Note that nonreal data is automatically ignored.

```
In[29]:= ListPlot[{{"Trial", "Value"}, {1.3, 6.7}, {2.7, 4.5},
           {-4.3, -2.}, {-6.6, -7.8}, {-6., 2.1}, {-1.1, 0.6}, {7.2, 7.7}}]
```

Out[29]=

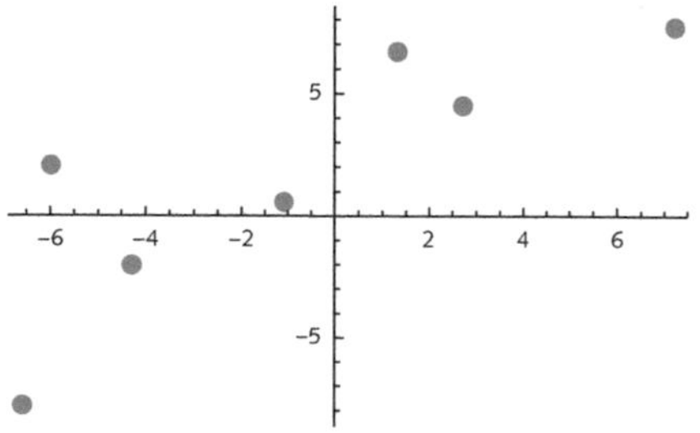

Large arrays of data present a special problem in terms of display. In general, you do not want to look at thousands of rows and columns of numbers from a large array. Functions like `ArrayPlot` and `MatrixPlot` are useful for visualizing the structure of such expressions. For small arrays, the correspondence between the array of numbers and the "cells" in the plot should be quite apparent.

```
In[30]:= mat = {{1, 0, 1}, {0, 2, 0}, {1, 0, 1}};
         MatrixForm[mat]
```

Out[31]//MatrixForm=

$$\begin{pmatrix} 1 & 0 & 1 \\ 0 & 2 & 0 \\ 1 & 0 & 1 \end{pmatrix}$$

```
In[32]:= ArrayPlot[mat, Mesh → All]
```

Out[32]=

These visualization functions are particularly useful for large arrays. For example, the following imported matrix is a representation of the topology of the US Western States power grid (Watts and Strogatz 1998):

```
In[33]:= grid =
          Import["http://www.cise.ufl.edu/research/sparse/MM/Newman/power.tar.gz",
           {"TAR", "power/power.mtx"}]
```

```
Out[33]= SparseArray[ Specified elements: 13 188
                      Dimensions: {4941, 4941} ]
```

`ArrayPlot` shows the structure of the array, in this case giving a visual sense that the underlying matrix is symmetric.

```
In[34]:= ArrayPlot[grid]
```

Out[34]=

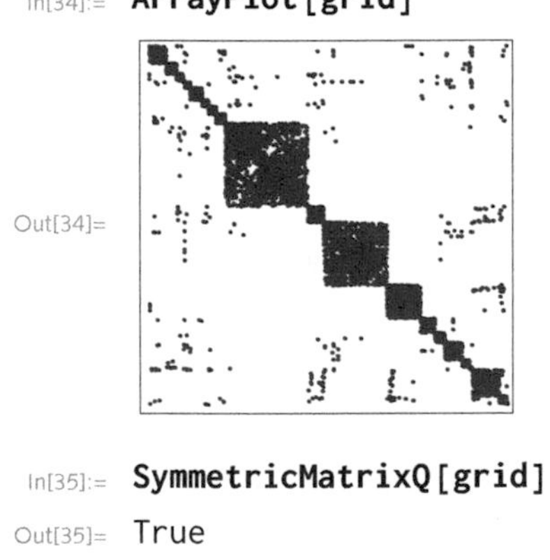

```
In[35]:= SymmetricMatrixQ[grid]
Out[35]= True
```

You could also visualize this sparse array as an adjacency graph where the edges represent the transmission lines between power stations (nodes). This representation only gives connectivity information; no geographic information is conveyed.

```
In[36]:= AdjacencyGraph[grid, GraphStyle → "BasicBlue"]
```

Out[36]=

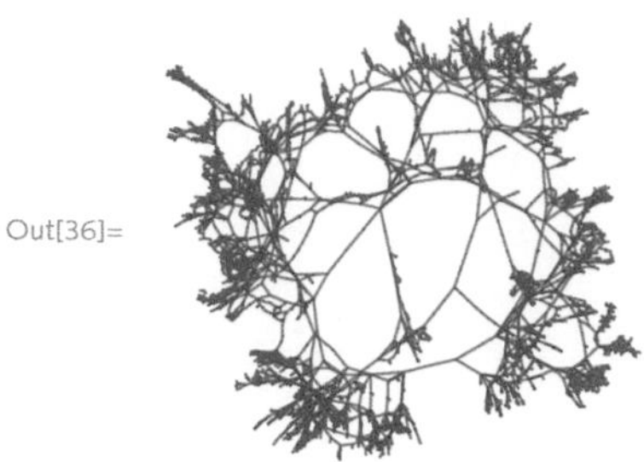

We will look at several other visualization approaches to working with data represented as lists, including time series, later in this book.

Arrays

In addition to `Table` and `Range`, several other functions can be used to construct lists from scratch, including `Array`, `ConstantArray`, and `SparseArray`. Each of these functions has a similar syntax to `Table` and `Range`.

`Array` is, in some sense, a generalization of `Table` in that you can create arrays of elements wrapped in arbitrary functions. For example, here is a 4×4 array where each element is wrapped in a symbolic function g:

```
In[37]:= Array[g, {4, 4}] // MatrixForm
Out[37]//MatrixForm=
 g[1, 1]  g[1, 2]  g[1, 3]  g[1, 4]
 g[2, 1]  g[2, 2]  g[2, 3]  g[2, 4]
 g[3, 1]  g[3, 2]  g[3, 3]  g[3, 4]
 g[4, 1]  g[4, 2]  g[4, 3]  g[4, 4]
```

If, instead of g, the function is `Greater`, we have the following:

```
In[38]:= Array[Greater, {4, 4}] // MatrixForm
Out[38]//MatrixForm=
 False  False  False  False
 True   False  False  False
 True   True   False  False
 True   True   True   False
```

Converting the `True`/`False` values to ones and zeros using `Boole` gives a lower-triangular matrix.

```
In[39]:= Boole[%] // MatrixForm
Out[39]//MatrixForm=
 0 0 0 0
 1 0 0 0
 1 1 0 0
 1 1 1 0
```

`ConstantArray` is useful for quickly creating constant vectors, arrays, and tensors.

```
In[40]:= ConstantArray[1, {12}]
Out[40]= {1, 1, 1, 1, 1, 1, 1, 1, 1, 1, 1, 1}
```

`SparseArray` is used to create arrays where most of the elements are some constant term, typically zero. The first argument to `SparseArray` is usually a list specifying the nondefault positions and their values. The optional second argument is used to specify the array dimensions. For example, this creates a 3×3 array with symbolic values α, β, and γ on the diagonal.

```
In[41]:= array = SparseArray[{{1, 1} → α, {2, 2} → β, {3, 3} → γ}, {3, 3}]

Out[41]= SparseArray[ Specified elements: 3
                      Dimensions: {3, 3} ]
```

The `SparseArray` object that is returned is a symbolic representation of the array, indicating that there are three nondefault elements and the dimensions are 3×3.

The array can be viewed in a traditional matrix form or converted to a regular list structure.

```
In[42]:= MatrixForm[array]
Out[42]//MatrixForm=
  ( α  0  0 )
  ( 0  β  0 )
  ( 0  0  γ )

In[43]:= Normal[array]
Out[43]= {{α, 0, 0}, {0, β, 0}, {0, 0, γ}}
```

You can plot sparse arrays just like normal lists (see the power grid example in the previous section); the list plotting functions are not only set up to work with them but are faster at representing these compact representations. We will have more to say about sparse arrays in Section 9.1.

Exercises

1. Create a list of the multiples of five less than or equal to one hundred.

2. Create a list of the reciprocals of the powers of two as the powers go from zero to sixteen.

3. Generate the list `{{0}, {0, 2}, {0, 2, 4}, {0, 2, 4, 6}, {0, 2, 4, 6, 8}}` in two different ways using the `Table` function.

4. Generate both of the following arrays using the `Table` function:

```
In[1]:= Array[f, 5]
Out[1]= {f[1], f[2], f[3], f[4], f[5]}

In[2]:= Array[f, {3, 4}]
Out[2]= {{f[1, 1], f[1, 2], f[1, 3], f[1, 4]},
   {f[2, 1], f[2, 2], f[2, 3], f[2, 4]}, {f[3, 1], f[3, 2], f[3, 3], f[3, 4]}}
```

5. Use `Table` to create an $n \times n$ matrix consisting of the positive integers one through n^2 arranged such that the first row is the list $\{1, 2, 3, \ldots, n\}$, the second row is the list $\{1 + n, 2 + n, 3 + n, \ldots, 2\,n\}$, and in general the kth row is the list $\{1 + (k-1)\,n, 2 + (k-1)\,n, 3 + (k-1)\,n, \ldots, n^2\}$. For example, for $n = 4$, you should have

```
{{1, 2, 3, 4}, {5, 6, 7, 8}, {9, 10, 11, 12}, {13, 14, 15, 16}}
```

In matrix form, this would be:

$$\begin{pmatrix} 1 & 2 & 3 & 4 \\ 5 & 6 & 7 & 8 \\ 9 & 10 & 11 & 12 \\ 13 & 14 & 15 & 16 \end{pmatrix}$$

6. Using `Table`, create a symmetric matrix of the binomial coefficients for any n similar to that in Table 3.1.

TABLE 3.1. *Pascal's matrix for $n = 5$*

$$\begin{pmatrix} 1 & 1 & 1 & 1 & 1 \\ 1 & 2 & 3 & 4 & 5 \\ 1 & 3 & 6 & 10 & 15 \\ 1 & 4 & 10 & 20 & 35 \\ 1 & 5 & 15 & 35 & 70 \end{pmatrix}$$

7. Given an $m \times m$ square lattice like the grid graph below, color all vertices on the bottom red, and on the top white. Your solution should be as general as possible, so that changing the size of the lattice (changing the value of m) will still work to color the lattice.

```
In[3]:= m = 5;
        GridGraph[{m, m}, VertexLabels → "Name"]
```

Out[4]=

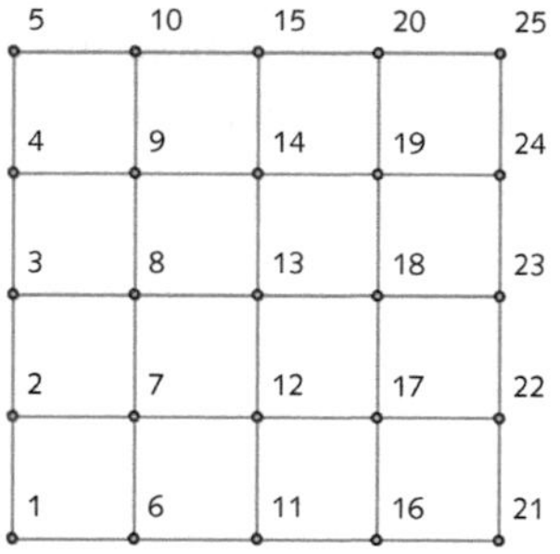

```
5    10   15   20   25
4    9    14   19   24
3    8    13   18   23
2    7    12   17   22
1    6    11   16   21
```

To change the property of select vertices in a graph, use `HighlightGraph`. For example, the following colors vertices 1, 13, and 25 red.

```
In[5]:= HighlightGraph[
          GridGraph[{m, m}, VertexLabels → "Name"],
          Style[{1, 13, 25}, Red], VertexSize → Medium]
```

Out[5]=

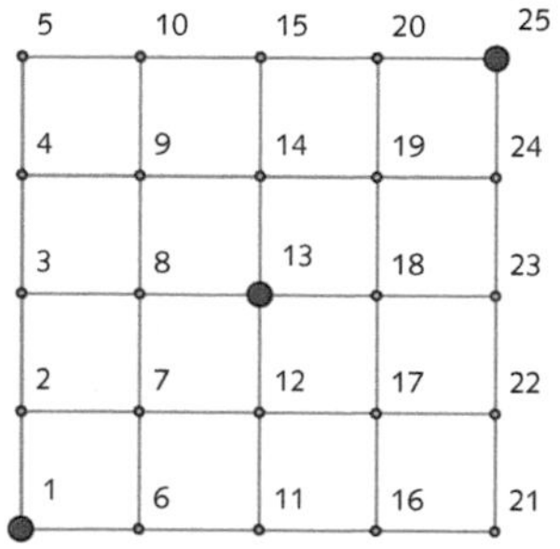

```
5    10   15   20   25
4    9    14   19   24
3    8    13   18   23
2    7    12   17   22
1    6    11   16   21
```

8. Import six images, resize them to the same dimensions, then display them inside a 3×2 grid using options for `Grid` to format the output.

9. Construct an integer lattice graphic like in Figure 3.1. Start by creating a list of the pairs of coordinate points. Then connect the appropriate pairs of coordinates with lines (use `Graphics[Line[...]]`). Add points with `Graphics[Point[...]]`. See Chapter 8 for details about creating plots from graphics primitives. Consider the function `CoordinateBoundsArray` to get the list of integer coordinates.

FIGURE 3.1. A 5×3 *rectangular lattice.*

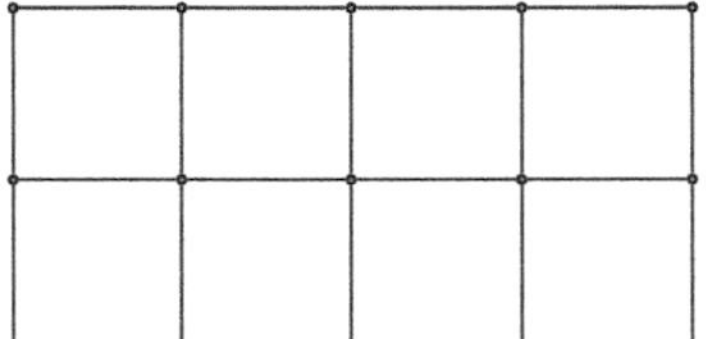

3.2 Testing and measuring lists

Testing a list

Imagine that you are given the task of analyzing ocean surface temperature data collected from several different sensors. Sensors occasionally fail and some insert the value -999 and others insert a string `"NA"` at those moments. To do your analysis on the data, you need numeric arrays and so you need to find and then replace or remove those anomalous values. When data is represented by lists, testing that list for different criteria is an important tool to have in your tool belt.

As an example, suppose you need to check if a list of data consists entirely of numbers. `AllTrue[`*lis*`,` *test*`]` checks if every element of *lis* passes the test, *test*. The test must be a predicate function, that is, a function that returns a value of `True` or `False`. Recall from Section 2.2 that the predicate `NumberQ` returns `True` if its argument is an explicit number.

```
In[1]:= AllTrue[{1.21, 17, "NA", -3.22}, NumberQ]
Out[1]= False
```

Alternatively, you could ask if the list contains any strings.

```
In[2]:= AnyTrue[{1.21, 17, "NA", -3.22}, StringQ]
Out[2]= True
```

To test if one particular expression is a member of a list, use `MemberQ`.

```
In[3]:= MemberQ[{5, 7, 5, 2, 1, 4}, 3]
Out[3]= False
```

Or you can test whether a list is free of a particular expression.

```
In[4]:= FreeQ[{5, 7, 5, 2, 1, 4}, 3]
Out[4]= True
```

To find the locations of specific elements in a list, use `Position`. For example, the following result indicates that the number 5 occurs in the first and third positions in the list.

```
In[5]:= Position[{5, 7, 5, 2, 1, 4}, 5]
Out[5]= {{1}, {3}}
```

The extra braces in the above output are used to avoid confusion with the case when elements are *nested* within a list. For example, in the following, the expression `f` occurs once, in the third position within the second inner list:

```
In[6]:= Position[{{a, b, c}, {d, e, f}}, f]
Out[6]= {{2, 3}}
```

Other functions select or count the number of elements in a list that match a certain pattern. For example, `Count` gives the frequency of an expression or pattern in a list.

```
In[7]:= Count[{5, 7, 5, 2, 1, 4}, 5]
Out[7]= 2
```

To test the equality of two lists, use `Equal` (==).

```
In[8]:= {a, 3.0, b, 4} == {a, 6 / 2, b, 12 / 3}
Out[8]= True
```

Notice above that each of the lists were evaluated first, simplifying the arithmetic expressions before testing element-wise for equality.

Tip 3.2

There are some subtleties in *Mathematica*'s notion of equality. For example, although the two lists above are equal, they are not identical. As mentioned in Section 2.2, a more rigorous equality is tested with `SameQ` (===) which tests if the two expressions are identical, both the elements and the structures.

```
In[9]:= {a, 3.0, b, 4} === {a, 6/2, b, 12/3}
Out[9]= False
```

Measuring lists

Recall from Chapter 2 that `Length[`*expr*`]` is used to give the number of elements in *expr*. For a simple unnested (linear) list, the `Length` function tells you how many elements are in the list.

```
In[10]:= Length[{a, b, c, d, e, f}]
Out[10]= 6
```

In a nested list, each inner list is an element of the outer list. Therefore, the `Length` of a nested list indicates the number of inner lists, not their sizes.

```
In[11]:= Length[{{{1, 2}, {3, 4}, {5, 6}}, {{a, b}, {c, d}, {e, f}}}]
Out[11]= 2
```

To find out more about the structure of nested lists, use the `Dimensions` function.

```
In[12]:= Dimensions[{{{1, 2}, {3, 4}, {5, 6}}, {{a, b}, {c, d}, {e, f}}}]
Out[12]= {2, 3, 2}
```

This indicates that there are two inner lists, that each inner list contains three lists, and that the innermost lists each have two elements.

The number of dimensions of a (possibly nested) list is given by `ArrayDepth`.

```
In[13]:= ArrayDepth[{{{1, 2}, {3, 4}, {5, 6}}, {{a, b}, {c, d}, {e, f}}}]
Out[13]= 3
```

This is identical to the number of levels in that expression as displayed by `TreeForm` (remember that the head of an expression is at level zero).

```
In[14]:= TreeForm[{{{1, 2}, {3, 4}, {5, 6}}, {{a, b}, {c, d}, {e, f}}}]
Out[14]//TreeForm=
```

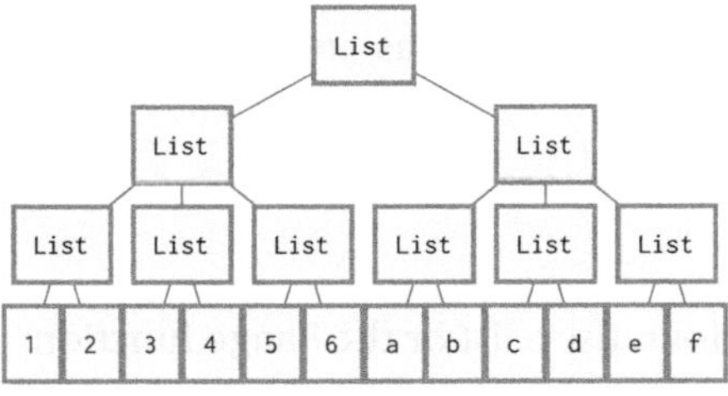

Exercises

1. What is the length of the following list? What are its dimensions? What is the position of g?

   `{{a, b}, {c, d}, {e, f}, {g, h}}`

2. The following input generates a list of 10 000 zeros and ones weighted heavily toward the ones. Determine if there are any zeros in this list and if there are, find how many.

   ```
   In[1]:= lis = RandomChoice[{.0001, .9999} → {0, 1}, {10000}];
   ```

3. Given a list of integers such as the following, count the number of zeros. Find a way to count all those elements of the list which are not ones.

   ```
   In[2]:= ints = RandomInteger[{-5, 5}, 30]
   Out[2]= {1, 4, -1, 2, -2, 4, 4, -5, 5, 3, 4, -3, -3, 1,
             0, 4, -1, -2, 2, 0, -5, 1, -5, -4, 3, -5, -2, -3, 3, 0}
   ```

4. Given the list `{{{1, a}, {2, b}, {3, c}}, {{4, d}, {5, e}, {6, f}}}`, determine its dimensions. Use the `Dimensions` function to check your answer.

5. Find the positions of the nines in the following list. Confirm using `Position`.

   `{{2, 1, 10}, {9, 5, 7}, {2, 10, 4}, {10, 1, 9}, {6, 1, 6}}`

6. Determine if there are any prime numbers in the interval [4 302 407 360, 4 302 407 713]. Once you have a list of the integers that you want to test for primality, use `Position` (see Section 4.1) and `Extract` to return the explicit primes.

3.3 Operations on lists

Extracting elements

The Part function is designed for extracting elements from expressions by identifying their position within that expression. For example, this extracts the third element in the list vec:

```
In[1]:= vec = {2, 3, 7, 8, 1, 4};

In[2]:= Part[vec, 3]
Out[2]= 7
```

The Part function is abbreviated using double brackets as shorthand notation.

```
In[3]:= vec[[3]]
Out[3]= 7
```

To get the elements from more than one location, use a list as an argument. For example, this picks out the second and fourth elements of vec:

```
In[4]:= vec[[{2, 4}]]
Out[4]= {3, 8}
```

To extract elements in positions two through four, use a list or the Range function; the argument to vec in the second input below will be evaluated first to produce the list {2, 3, 4}, before being passed up to the Part function.

```
In[5]:= vec[[{2, 3, 4}]]
Out[5]= {3, 7, 8}

In[6]:= vec[[Range[2, 4]]]
Out[6]= {3, 7, 8}
```

You can do this more compactly using a shorthand notation for the Span function.

```
In[7]:= vec[[2 ;; 4]]
Out[7]= {3, 7, 8}
```

For multi-dimensional lists, specify both the sublist and the position of the element in that sublist that you are interested in. Here is a sample 3×3 matrix to work with:

```
In[8]:= mat = Table[a_{i,j}, {i, 3}, {j, 3}];

In[9]:= MatrixForm[mat]
Out[9]//MatrixForm=
```

$$\begin{pmatrix} a_{1,1} & a_{1,2} & a_{1,3} \\ a_{2,1} & a_{2,2} & a_{2,3} \\ a_{3,1} & a_{3,2} & a_{3,3} \end{pmatrix}$$

This picks out the first part of the second sublist:

```
In[10]:= mat[[2, 1]]
Out[10]= a_{2,1}
```

To extract different parts of multi-dimensional lists, such as rows or columns from a matrix, several options are available. The following input extracts the entire second column of `mat`. Think of this as getting all rows, and the second column.

```
In[11]:= mat[[All, 2]] // MatrixForm
```

Out[11]//MatrixForm=

$$\begin{pmatrix} a_{1,2} \\ a_{2,2} \\ a_{3,2} \end{pmatrix}$$

And here is the third row of this matrix:

```
In[12]:= mat[[3, All]]
```

Out[12]= $\{a_{3,1}, a_{3,2}, a_{3,3}\}$

If you only specify one argument, the second argument is assumed to be `All`.

```
In[13]:= mat[[3]]
```

Out[13]= $\{a_{3,1}, a_{3,2}, a_{3,3}\}$

In addition to extracting elements from specific locations in a list, you can extract consecutively placed elements within the list using `Take`. Element positions are counted from either the front or the back of a list.

```
In[14]:= Take[{1, 9, 7, 17, 33, 57, 107, 197}, 2]
Out[14]= {1, 9}

In[15]:= Take[{1, 9, 7, 17, 33, 57, 107, 197}, -2]
Out[15]= {107, 197}
```

Keep in mind that the numbering of positions is different front-to-back and back-to-front.

```
In[16]:= Take[{1, 9, 7, 17, 33, 57, 107, 197}, {2, 4}]
Out[16]= {9, 7, 17}

In[17]:= Take[{1, 9, 7, 17, 33, 57, 107, 197}, {-5, -3}]
Out[17]= {17, 33, 57}
```

You can also take elements in steps. This takes the first through sixth element in increments of two, that is, it takes every other element:

```
In[18]:= Take[{1, 9, 7, 17, 33, 57, 107, 197}, {1, 6, 2}]
Out[18]= {1, 7, 33}
```

Another shorthand notation exists for ranges of this sort:

```
In[19]:= Take[{1, 9, 7, 17, 33, 57, 107, 197}, 1 ;; 6 ;; 2]
Out[19]= {1, 7, 33}
```

`Drop` is used to discard elements from a list, keeping the rest. Elements are removed from either end of the list or from consecutive locations.

```
In[20]:= Drop[{1, 9, 7, 17, 33, 57, 107, 197}, -1]
Out[20]= {1, 9, 7, 17, 33, 57, 107}
```

Use `Delete` to remove elements at specific locations.

```
In[21]:= Delete[{1, 9, 7, 17, 33, 57, 107, 197}, {{3}, {4}}]
Out[21]= {1, 9, 33, 57, 107, 197}
```

Certain extractions are used so often that a named function exists for the operation.

```
In[22]:= First[{1, 9, 7, 17, 33, 57, 107, 197}]
Out[22]= 1

In[23]:= Last[{1, 9, 7, 17, 33, 57, 107, 197}]
Out[23]= 197

In[24]:= Rest[{1, 9, 7, 17, 33, 57, 107, 197}]
Out[24]= {9, 7, 17, 33, 57, 107, 197}

In[25]:= Most[{1, 9, 7, 17, 33, 57, 107, 197}]
Out[25]= {1, 9, 7, 17, 33, 57, 107}
```

Applying functions to lists

One of the more surprising features of functional languages is the ability to operate on lists directly. In a procedural language, you typically create a temporary list for the result, extract each element one-by-one, operate on that element, and put it into the temporary list. In a functional style of programming, you operate on the list as a whole, dispensing with the need to maintain temporary lists and iterators.

For example, to take the square root of a list of numbers, simply wrap the `Sqrt` function around the list.

```
In[26]:= Sqrt[{2, 4, 6, 8}]
```

Out[26]= $\{\sqrt{2}, 2, \sqrt{6}, 2\sqrt{2}\}$

To take the cosine of a list, wrap `Cos` around the list.

In[27]:= $\text{Cos}\left[\left\{0, \frac{\pi}{6}, \frac{\pi}{4}, \frac{\pi}{3}, \frac{\pi}{2}\right\}\right]$

Out[27]= $\left\{1, \frac{\sqrt{3}}{2}, \frac{1}{\sqrt{2}}, \frac{1}{2}, 0\right\}$

What makes this possible is an attribute that many built-in functions have, listability.

```
In[28]:= Attributes[Sqrt]
Out[28]= {Listable, NumericFunction, Protected}
```

As introduced in Section 2.5, functions that have the `Listable` attribute automatically map or thread across lists of arguments. Not only is this a cleaner and more compact way to perform these operations, but it is also more efficient from the standpoint of memory and speed. Most of the arithmetic functions have this attribute, making them extremely efficient at operations on lists. This is discussed in more detail in Section 9.1.

Rearranging lists

Every list can be sorted into a canonical order. For lists of numbers or letters, this ordering is usually obvious.

```
In[29]:= Sort[{3, 223/71, 22/7, 355/113, 25/8}]
Out[29]= {3, 25/8, 223/71, 355/113, 22/7}

In[30]:= N[%]
Out[30]= {3., 3.125, 3.14085, 3.14159, 3.14286}

In[31]:= Sort[{"s", "p", "a", "m"}]
Out[31]= {a, m, p, s}
```

The following canonical orderings are used: numbers are ordered by numerical value with complex numbers first ordered by real part and then by absolute value of the imaginary part; symbols and strings are ordered alphabetically; powers and products are ordered in a manner corresponding to the terms in a polynomial; expressions are ordered depth-first with shorter expressions first.

```
In[32]:= Sort[{x^3, x^5, x}]
Out[32]= {x, x^3, x^5}

In[33]:= Sort[{Expand[(a + b)^2], a (b + c), a b}]
Out[33]= {a b, a^2 + 2 a b + b^2, a (b + c)}
```

You can also sort lists according to an ordering function specified as a second argument to `Sort`. For example, the following sorts the list in numerical order from greatest to smallest.

```
In[34]:= Sort[{3, 1.7, π, -4, 22/7}, Greater]
Out[34]= {22/7, π, 3, 1.7, -4}
```

When applied to a nested list, `Sort` uses the first element of each nested list to determine the order.

```
In[35]:= Sort[{{2, c}, {7, 9}, {e, f, g}, {1, 4.5}, {x, y, z}}]
Out[35]= {{1, 4.5}, {2, c}, {7, 9}, {e, f, g}, {x, y, z}}
```

For multi-dimensional lists, `SortBy` is also useful. Its second argument is a function that is applied to each element in the list; the result of that function gives the criterion used for the sort.

```
In[36]:= SortBy[{{b, 2}, {a, 3}, {c, 1}, {d, 0}}, Last]
Out[36]= {{d, 0}, {c, 1}, {b, 2}, {a, 3}}
```

In fact any list of expressions for which a canonical ordering exists can be sorted. For example, here is a list of random dates, sorted by absolute time.

```
In[37]:= dates = {"Thu 14 Apr 2016 02:45:33", "Wed 25 Sep 1996 21:26:13",
            "Fri 12 Apr 1946 12:34:35", "Wed 15 Nov 1933 19:36:24",
            "Mon 23 Nov 1981 01:01:18", "Sun 28 Aug 1977 00:56:01"};

In[38]:= SortBy[dates, AbsoluteTime]
Out[38]= {Wed 15 Nov 1933 19:36:24, Fri 12 Apr 1946 12:34:35,
          Sun 28 Aug 1977 00:56:01, Mon 23 Nov 1981 01:01:18,
          Wed 25 Sep 1996 21:26:13, Thu 14 Apr 2016 02:45:33}
```

In addition to sorting, various functions are available to rearrange lists. For example, this reverses the elements in a list:

```
In[39]:= Reverse[{1, 2, 3, 4, 5}]
Out[39]= {5, 4, 3, 2, 1}
```

This rotates the elements one position to the left:

```
In[40]:= RotateLeft[{1, 2, 3, 4, 5}]
Out[40]= {2, 3, 4, 5, 1}
```

To rotate the elements *two* positions to the right, give a second argument to `RotateRight`.

```
In[41]:= RotateRight[{1, 2, 3, 4, 5}, 2]
Out[41]= {4, 5, 1, 2, 3}
```

`Partition` divvies up lists by rearranging list elements to form nested lists. Several syntaxes are available. For example, the following partitions the list into nonoverlapping sublists of length two. The second argument to `Partition` specifies the length of the sublists.

```
In[42]:= Partition[{1, 4, 1, 5, 9, 2}, 2]
Out[42]= {{1, 4}, {1, 5}, {9, 2}}
```

You might be interested in only using some of the elements from a list. For example, this takes one-element sublists, with an offset of two; in other words, every other one-element sublist. The third argument specifies the length of the overlap.

```
In[43]:= Partition[{1, 4, 1, 5, 9, 2}, 1, 2]
Out[43]= {{1}, {1}, {9}}
```

You can also create overlapping inner lists, consisting of ordered pairs (two-element sublists) whose second element is the first element of the next ordered pair.

```
In[44]:= Partition[{1, 4, 1, 5, 9, 2}, 2, 1]
Out[44]= {{1, 4}, {4, 1}, {1, 5}, {5, 9}, {9, 2}}
```

The `Transpose` function pairs off the corresponding elements of the inner lists. Its argument is a single list consisting of two or more nested lists.

```
In[45]:= Transpose[{{x1, x2, x3, x4}, {y1, y2, y3, y4}}]
Out[45]= {{x1, y1}, {x2, y2}, {x3, y3}, {x4, y4}}
```

For rectangular lists, you might think of `Transpose` as exchanging the rows and columns of the corresponding matrix.

```
In[46]:= mat = {{x1, x2, x3, x4}, {y1, y2, y3, y4}, {z1, z2, z3, z4}};

In[47]:= MatrixForm[mat]
Out[47]//MatrixForm=
```

$$\begin{pmatrix} x_1 & x_2 & x_3 & x_4 \\ y_1 & y_2 & y_3 & y_4 \\ z_1 & z_2 & z_3 & z_4 \end{pmatrix}$$

```
In[48]:= MatrixForm[Transpose[mat]]
Out[48]//MatrixForm=
```

$$\begin{pmatrix} x_1 & y_1 & z_1 \\ x_2 & y_2 & z_2 \\ x_3 & y_3 & z_3 \\ x_4 & y_4 & z_4 \end{pmatrix}$$

Elements can be added to the front, the back, or to any specified position in a given list.

```
In[49]:= Append[{1, 2, 3, 4}, 5]
Out[49]= {1, 2, 3, 4, 5}

In[50]:= Prepend[{1, 2, 3, 4}, 0]
Out[50]= {0, 1, 2, 3, 4}

In[51]:= Insert[{1, 2, 3, 4}, 2.5, 3]
Out[51]= {1, 2, 2.5, 3, 4}
```

Elements at specific locations in a list can be replaced with other elements. Here, β replaces the element in the second position of the list:

```
In[52]:= ReplacePart[{a, b, c, d, e}, β, 2]
Out[52]= {a, β, c, d, e}
```

Some list operations result in deeply nested lists that you may need to flatten. The following removes all the inner braces, creating a linear list of elements:

```
In[53]:= Flatten[{{{3, 1}, {2, 4}}, {{5, 3}, {7, 4}}}]
Out[53]= {3, 1, 2, 4, 5, 3, 7, 4}
```

You can limit the degree of flattening, removing only some of the inner lists. For example, two inner lists, each having two ordered pairs, can be turned into a single list of four ordered pairs by only flattening down one level deep.

```
In[54]:= Flatten[{{{3, 1}, {2, 4}}, {{5, 3}, {7, 4}}}, 1]
Out[54]= {{3, 1}, {2, 4}, {5, 3}, {7, 4}}
```

List component assignment

Up until this point, most of the list-manipulation functions we have looked at are nondestructive. In other words, operating on a list by, say, reversing its elements does not change the original list.

```
In[55]:= lis = {0, 1, 2, 3, 4};

In[56]:= Reverse[lis]
Out[56]= {4, 3, 2, 1, 0}

In[57]:= lis
Out[57]= {0, 1, 2, 3, 4}
```

Sometimes, though, it is convenient to modify the list directly. This can be accomplished with *list component assignments*. The general syntax is

list_name [[*part_spec*]] = *expr*

The *part_spec* must evaluate to a valid position specification for the elements of the list. The assignment returns the value of *expr* (as assignments always do), but it resets the value of the list. In other words, this is a destructive operation, changing the value of the list on which you are operating.

For example, this replaces the first element of the above list, `lis`, with the value 10:

```
In[58]:= lis[[1]] = 10
Out[58]= 10
```

The value of `lis` itself has changed.

```
In[59]:= lis
Out[59]= {10, 1, 2, 3, 4}
```

Components of nested lists can be modified as well.

name [[$expr_1$, $expr_2$]] = *expr*

$expr_1$ and $expr_2$ are expressions that must evaluate to integers. $expr_1$ chooses the sublists of the list *name*, and $expr_2$ the element of that sublist.

Here is a 2×3 nested list:

```
In[60]:= A = {{1, 2, 3}, {4, 5, 6}};
```

This assigns the third element in the second sublist the value 20:

```
In[61]:= A[[2, 3]] = 20
Out[61]= 20

In[62]:= A
Out[62]= {{1, 2, 3}, {4, 5, 20}}
```

As a concrete example of list component assignment, let us create a matrix consisting of ones everywhere except for zeros on the border. Start by creating a matrix of ones:

```
In[63]:= mat = ConstantArray[1, {5, 5}];
```

```
In[64]:= MatrixForm[mat]
Out[64]//MatrixForm=
  1 1 1 1 1
  1 1 1 1 1
  1 1 1 1 1
  1 1 1 1 1
  1 1 1 1 1
```

Next, replace all elements on the borders with zeros. To specify the first and last rows of `mat`, use `mat[[{1, -1}, All]]`, and similarly for the columns.

```
In[65]:= mat[[{1, -1}, All]] = 0;
         mat[[All, {1, -1}]] = 0;
         MatrixForm[mat]
Out[67]//MatrixForm=
  0 0 0 0 0
  0 1 1 1 0
  0 1 1 1 0
  0 1 1 1 0
  0 0 0 0 0
```

Tip 3.3

Note that assigning one array name to another array makes a copy of the first; component assignments to either one will not affect the other.

```
In[68]:= B = A
Out[68]= {{1, 2, 3}, {4, 5, 20}}

In[69]:= B[[1, 2]] = 30
Out[69]= 30

In[70]:= B
Out[70]= {{1, 30, 3}, {4, 5, 20}}

In[71]:= A
Out[71]= {{1, 2, 3}, {4, 5, 20}}

In[72]:= A[[2, 1]] = 40
Out[72]= 40

In[73]:= B
Out[73]= {{1, 30, 3}, {4, 5, 20}}
```

This behavior differs from that of languages such as C, where aliasing can allow one list to *point* to another; with pointers, changing one array *will* have an effect on any array that points to it.

Because *Mathematica* is so efficient at list operations, many computations using list component assignment are often several orders of magnitude faster than other approaches. The reasons behind this are discussed in Chapter 9.

Multiple lists

A number of the functions described earlier in this chapter, such as `Transpose`, work with several lists if they are inside a nested list structure. The following functions, however, operate on multiple lists as arguments but without the need for the nesting. For example, `Join` concatenates two lists.

```
In[74]:= Join[{2, 5, 7, 3}, {d, a, e, j}]
Out[74]= {2, 5, 7, 3, d, a, e, j}
```

Here is the union of two lists:

```
In[75]:= {4, 1, 2} ⋃ {5, 1, 2}
Out[75]= {1, 2, 4, 5}
```

```
In[76]:= Union[{4, 1, 2}, {5, 1, 2}]
Out[76]= {1, 2, 4, 5}
```

When the `Union` function is used either on a single list or on a number of lists, a list is formed consisting of the original elements in canonical order with all duplicate elements removed. `Complement` gives all those elements in the first list that are not in the other list or lists. You can use `Intersection[`lis_1, lis_2, …`]` to find all those elements common to the lis_i.

```
In[77]:= Complement[{4, 1, 2}, {5, 1, 2}]
Out[77]= {4}
```

```
In[78]:= {4, 1, 2} ⋂ {5, 1, 2}
Out[78]= {1, 2}
```

These last three functions, `Union`, `Complement`, and `Intersection`, treat lists somewhat like sets in that there are no duplicates and the order of elements in the lists is not respected. To remove duplicates without sorting, use `DeleteDuplicates`.

```
In[79]:= DeleteDuplicates[{4, 1, 2, 5, 1, 2}]
Out[79]= {4, 1, 2, 5}
```

As a concrete example, consider the display of data in a tabular format. It is common to prepend a list of header information that will be displayed at the top of the columns in the table of data. This is straightforward with `Join` or `Prepend`, but some care must be taken to insure the elements being combined have a similar structure.

For example, here is a 5×2 array of data together with a list of header labels, one for each column:

```
In[80]:= data = RandomReal[1, {5, 2}]
Out[80]= {{0.691469, 0.928474}, {0.734368, 0.602864},
  {0.991845, 0.0567515}, {0.939638, 0.534616}, {0.588352, 0.5059}}
```

```
In[81]:= header = {"Column A", "Column B"};
```

When using Prepend[*expr*, *elem*], *elem* must have the same structure as the elements of *expr*.

```
In[82]:= Prepend[data, header]
Out[82]= {{Column A, Column B}, {0.691469, 0.928474}, {0.734368, 0.602864},
  {0.991845, 0.0567515}, {0.939638, 0.534616}, {0.588352, 0.5059}}
```

The following displays this list of headers and data, adding some formatting through the use of several options to Grid:

```
In[83]:= Grid[Prepend[data, header],
  Frame → All, FrameStyle → Thin, Alignment → Left, Spacings → {1, .75}]
```

Out[83]=

Column A	Column B
0.691469	0.928474
0.734368	0.602864
0.991845	0.0567515
0.939638	0.534616
0.588352	0.5059

You could try to use Join instead of Prepend, but the two lists have different structures – header is a list with two string elements; data is a list of lists.

```
In[84]:= Grid[Join[header, data]]
Out[84]= Grid[{Column A, Column B, {0.691469, 0.928474}, {0.734368, 0.602864},
  {0.991845, 0.0567515}, {0.939638, 0.534616}, {0.588352, 0.5059}}]

In[85]:= Dimensions[header]
Out[85]= {2}

In[86]:= Dimensions[data]
Out[86]= {5, 2}
```

To insure that the two lists have the same structure, header needs to be wrapped in {}.

```
In[87]:= Grid[Join[{header}, data]]
Out[87]=
Column A  Column B
0.691469  0.928474
0.734368  0.602864
0.991845 0.0567515
0.939638  0.534616
0.588352   0.5059
```

Exercises

1. Given a list of coordinate pairs such as the following:

   $\{\{x_1, y_1\}, \{x_2, y_2\}, \{x_3, y_3\}, \{x_4, y_4\}, \{x_5, y_5\}\}$

   separate the *x* and *y* components to get

   $\{\{x_1, x_2, x_3, x_4, x_5\}, \{y_1, y_2, y_3, y_4, y_5\}\}$

2. Use the `Part` function to extract the elements of a list that are in the even-indexed positions. So in the list below, the even-indexed elements are {3, 8, 3, 4, 2, 13}. Then extract all those elements in the odd-indexed positions.

```
In[1]:= lis = RandomInteger[{1, 20}, {12}]
Out[1]= {5, 3, 3, 8, 17, 3, 3, 4, 20, 2, 11, 13}
```

3. Given the following list of integers, find the five largest numbers in the list. Then find the five smallest numbers in the list.

```
In[2]:= nums = RandomInteger[{-100, 100}, {25}]
Out[2]= {38, 6, -15, -31, 44, 11, -100, 47, -14, 26, 50,
         48, -72, 24, 12, 66, 10, 31, 78, 85, 11, -67, 23, 63, -45}
```

4. Use `Table` to create the following matrix. Once created, use `Table` again to add all the elements on and above the diagonal.

$$\begin{pmatrix} 1 & 2 & 3 & 4 \\ 2 & 4 & 6 & 8 \\ 3 & 6 & 9 & 12 \\ 4 & 8 & 12 & 16 \end{pmatrix}$$

5. Rearrange the list of numbers one through ten so that any adjacent numbers (for example, 1 and 2, 2 and 3, and so on) are not adjacent in the output.

6. Create a list of all prime numbers less than 100. Repeat for a list of primes less than 1000. Consider using the functions `Prime` and `PrimePi`.

7. Take the partitioned list of integers from the solution to Exercise 5 in Section 3.1 and use `Grid` to display the partitioned list in a grid similar to that in Figure 3.2.

   FIGURE 3.2. *A 6 × 6 integer grid.*

1	2	3	4	5	6
7	8	9	10	11	12
13	14	15	16	17	18
19	20	21	22	23	24
25	26	27	28	29	30
31	32	33	34	35	36

8. Make a histogram of the frequencies of the leading digit in the first 10 000 Fibonacci numbers. The resulting distribution is an instance of Benford's law, which concerns the frequency of the leading digits in many kinds of data. The phenomenon, whereby a 1 occurs about 30% of the time, a 2 occurs

about 17.6% of the time, and so on, has been shown to occur in well-known numerical sequences, population counts, death rates, Fibonacci numbers, and has even been used to detect corporate and tax fraud.

9. Given a matrix, use list component assignment to swap any two rows.

10. In data mining and statistics, a matrix of data often needs to be centered on the matrix mean. This can be accomplished by subtracting the column mean from each point in a column. Create a function that takes a matrix and returns its centered matrix. Check that the mean of the centered matrix is a zero vector whose length is the same as the original matrix.

11. Create a function `AddColumn[mat, col, pos]` that inserts a column vector *col* into the matrix *mat* at the column position given by *pos*. For example:

```
In[3]:= mat = RandomInteger[9, {4, 4}];
        MatrixForm[mat]
Out[4]//MatrixForm=
 4 8 5 9
 9 4 1 9
 1 9 5 5
 9 5 6 7

In[5]:= AddColumn[mat, {a, b, c, d}, 3] // MatrixForm
Out[5]//MatrixForm=
 4 8 a 5 9
 9 4 b 1 9
 1 9 c 5 5
 9 5 d 6 7
```

12. How would you perform the same task as `Prepend[{x, y}, z]` using the `Join` function?

13. Starting with the lists `{1, 2, 3, 4}` and `{a, b, c, d}`, create the list `{2, 4, b, d}`. Then create the list `{1, a, 2, b, 3, c, 4, d}`.

14. Many lotteries include games that require you to pick several numbers and match them against the lottery's random number generator. The numbers are independent, so this is essentially random sampling with replacement. The built-in `RandomChoice` does this. For example, here are five random samples from the integers zero through nine:

```
In[6]:= RandomChoice[Range[0, 9], 5]
Out[6]= {5, 4, 1, 1, 3}
```

Write your own function `randomChoice[lis, n]` that performs a random sampling with replacement, where *n* is the number of elements being chosen from the list *lis*. Here is a typical result using a list of symbols:

```
In[7]:= randomChoice[{a, b, c, d, e, f, g, h}, 12]
Out[7]= {e, c, h, b, g, c, d, c, b, c, b, f}
```

15. Given two lists, find all those elements that are not common to the two lists. For example, starting with the lists `{a, b, c, d}` and `{a, b, e, f}`, your answer would return the list `{c, d, e, f}`.

16. One of the tasks in computational linguistics involves statistical analysis of text using what are called *n*-grams – sequences of *n* adjacent letters or words. Their frequency distribution in a body of text can be used to predict word usage based on the previous history or usage.

Import a file consisting of some text and find the twenty most frequently occurring word combinations. Pairs of words that are grouped like this are called *bigrams*, that is, *n*-grams for $n = 2$.

Use TextWords (new in *Mathematica* 10.1) to split long strings into a list of words that can then be operated on with the list manipulation functions.

```
In[8]:= TextWords["Use StringSplit to split long strings into words."]
Out[8]= {Use, StringSplit, to, split, long, strings, into, words}
```

17. Based on the previous exercise, create a function NGrams[*str*, *n*] that takes a string of text and returns a list of *n*-grams, that is, a list of the *n* adjacent words. For example:

```
In[9]:= NGrams["Use StringSplit to split long strings into words.", 3]
Out[9]= {{Use, StringSplit, to}, {StringSplit, to, split}, {to, split, long},
         {split, long, strings}, {long, strings, into}, {strings, into, words}}
```

18. Write your own user-defined functions using the Characters and StringJoin functions to perform the same operations as StringInsert and StringDrop.

19. Use ToCharacterCode and FromCharacterCode to perform the same operations as the built-in StringJoin and StringReverse functions.

20. Compute the first ten square-pyramidal numbers in three different ways. The first few square-pyramidal numbers are $1^2 = 1$, $1^2 + 2^2 = 5$, $1^2 + 2^2 + 3^2 = 14, \ldots$. The number of stacked spheres with a square base (Figure 3.3) are represented by these numbers. In addition, they give a solution to the problem of counting squares in an $n \times n$ grid.

FIGURE 3.3. *Graphical representation of square-pyramidal numbers.*

3.4 Associations

Although the expressions in a list can be quite arbitrary, there are situations where a more structured construct is useful. Imagine a bibliography consisting of books and articles, each of which has an author, title, date, journal, publisher, and other data that you need to manipulate, search, and perhaps generate reports from; or you might be working with a database of people consisting of names, contact information, and pictures. Traditionally, data structures such as associative arrays and indexed lists have been used to represent such objects. *Mathematica* provides a generalization of these ideas in what are called *associations*. Associations provide a mechanism for creating keys and values somewhat like a database, with quick lookup through built-in functions.

Associations are like lists in some ways. They share similar syntax for extracting values and their overall structures are also similar. But they are more general than lists and it is this generality that provides a framework for working with structured data as you would with a database say.

Creating and displaying associations

Associations are created from scratch by wrapping `Association` around a list of *key* → *value* expressions. You can think about `Association` as a wrapper for a list of rules.

```
In[1]:= assoc = Association[{key1 → val1, key2 → val2, key3 → val3}]
Out[1]= <|key1 → val1, key2 → val2, key3 → val3|>
```

To convert from an association to a list of rules, use `Normal`.

```
In[2]:= Normal[assoc]
Out[2]= {key1 → val1, key2 → val2, key3 → val3}
```

Use built-in functions to extract the list of keys and the list of values in an association.

```
In[3]:= Keys[assoc]
Out[3]= {key1, key2, key3}
```

```
In[4]:= Values[assoc]
Out[4]= {val1, val2, val3}
```

To look up the value associated with a particular key in the association, use `Lookup`.

```
In[5]:= Lookup[assoc, key1]
Out[5]= val1
```

Or you can use function notation to do the same thing.

```
In[6]:= assoc[key1]
Out[6]= val1
```

The syntax for extracting parts from a list can also be used. This gets the value associated with the first key.

```
In[7]:= assoc[[1]]
Out[7]= val1
```

If no key is found for the given association, `Missing` is returned.

```
In[8]:= assoc[key28]
Out[8]= Missing[KeyAbsent, key28]
```

Keys and values can be arbitrary expressions, thus making associations quite general objects to work with. For example, the following association creates a data structure containing publication information about an article, suitable for a bibliographic reference. Note that the keys in this example are all strings, something that will help avoid clashes with possible symbols (`Year` or `Address` could be symbols that are used elsewhere, for example).

```
In[9]:= art1 = Association@{
           "Authors" → "Hamming, Richard W.",
           "Title" → "Error detecting and error correcting codes",
           "Journal" → "The Bell System Technical Journal",
           "Year" → 1950,
           "Volume" → 29,
           "Issue" → 2,
           "Pages" → "147-160",
           "Url" → "https://archive.org/details/bstj29-2-147"
         }
Out[9]= <|Authors → Hamming, Richard W.,
         Title → Error detecting and error correcting codes,
         Journal → The Bell System Technical Journal,
         Year → 1950, Volume → 29, Issue → 2, Pages → 147-160,
         Url → https://archive.org/details/bstj29-2-147|>
```

In this example, there are eight keys: "Authors", "Title", "Journal", and so on.

```
In[10]:= Keys[art1]
Out[10]= {Authors, Title, Journal, Year, Volume, Issue, Pages, Url}
```

Values in associations can be any type of expression: some values are strings and others are integers. As noted above, values can be extracted in several different ways.

```
In[11]:= art1[[Key["Title"]]]
Out[11]= Error detecting and error correcting codes
```

If the key is a string, then you can extract its value directly.

```
In[12]:= art1["Title"]
Out[12]= Error detecting and error correcting codes
```

Or you can use the same syntax as Part to extract the value of a key, in this case, the third key, "Journal".

```
In[13]:= art1[[3]]
Out[13]= The Bell System Technical Journal
```

In fact, values can be quite arbitrary – they could be images or even other associations.

```
In[14]:= art2 = Association[{
            "Authors" → "Hathaway, David H.", "Title" → "The solar cycle",
            "Journal" → "Living Reviews in Solar Physics",
            "Year" → 2010, "Volume" → 7, "Issue" → "", "Pages" → "",
            "Url" → "http://dx.doi.org/10.12942/lrsp-2010-1", "Image" → LIVING REVIEWS in solar physics
          }];
```

This extracts the value of the "Image" key:

```
In[15]:= art2["Image"]
```

In[15]:= LIVING REVIEWS in solar physics

The following extracts the value of the "Url" key from art2. The value is a plain string. In the next section we will see how to turn this into a live, clickable hyperlink.

```
In[16]:= art2["Url"]
Out[16]= http://dx.doi.org/10.12942/lrsp-2010-1
```

Operations on associations

For database users, some common tasks include sorting, finding records with a certain value or within a certain threshold, merging records, and so on. All of these operations can be performed on associations. For example, to sort an association on the keys, use KeySort.

```
In[17]:= KeySort[<|"Title" → "Hop on Pop", "Author" → "Dr. Seuss", "Year" → 1963|>]
Out[17]= <|Author → Dr. Seuss, Title → Hop on Pop, Year → 1963|>
```

When you have multiple associations as part of a large data set, it is often useful to group them together in some way. This can be done by simply enclosing them in a list, as we have done below with two references.

```
In[18]:= articles = {
    <|"Title" → "The solar cycle", "Authors" → "Hathaway, David",
     "Year" → 2010, "Url" → "http://dx.doi.org/10.12942/lrsp-2010-1"|>,
    <|"Title" → "Error detecting and error correcting codes",
     "Authors" → "Hamming, Richard", "Year" → 1950,
     "Url" → "https://archive.org/details/bstj29-2-147"|>
   };
```

Alternatively, wrap them in Dataset to create a hierarchical list that can be operated on by a variety of functions. For example, this turns the above list into a data set:

```
In[19]:= bib = Dataset[articles]
```

Out[19]=

Title	Authors	Year	Url
The solar cycle	Hathaway, David	2010	http://dx.doi.org/10.12942/lrsp-2010-1
Error detecting and error correcting codes	Hamming, Richard	1950	https://archive.org/details/bstj29-2-147
2 levels | 2 rows			

Values from associations and data sets can be used like any other expression in *Mathematica* – they can be manipulated, formatted, and so on. For example, this sorts the data set bib first on the "Year" key and then on the "Authors" key:

```
In[20]:= bib[SortBy["Year"]]
```

Out[20]=

Title	Authors	Year	Url
Error detecting and error correcting codes	Hamming, Richard	1950	https://archive.org/details/bstj29-2-147
The solar cycle	Hathaway, David	2010	http://dx.doi.org/10.12942/lrsp-2010-1
2 levels | 2 rows			

```
In[21]:= bib[SortBy["Authors"]] // Normal
Out[21]= {<|Title → Error detecting and error correcting codes,
           Authors → Hamming, Richard, Year → 1950,
           Url → https://archive.org/details/bstj29-2-147|>,
          <|Title → The solar cycle, Authors → Hathaway, David,
           Year → 2010, Url → http://dx.doi.org/10.12942/lrsp-2010-1|>}
```

This extracts the first entry in the data set:

```
In[22]:= Hathaway2010 = bib[1]
```

Out[22]=

Title	The solar cycle
Authors	Hathaway, David
Year	2010
Url	http://dx.doi.org/10.12942/lrsp-2010-1
1 level	4 elements

To display the article author in a form suitable for a bibliography, use `Style` with some text-formatting options.

```
In[23]:= Style[Hathaway2010["Authors"], "TR"]
Out[23]= Hathaway, David
```

The following input extracts the value of the `"Url"` key and creates a hyperlink from it. `Hyperlink[`*label*`,` *url*`]` creates a live hyperlink with *label* as the displayed label and *url* as the underlying target uniform resource locator (URL). Clicking the link will open a web browser and display the web page specified by the URL.

```
In[24]:= Hyperlink[Style[Hathaway2010["Url"], "TR"], Hathaway2010["Url"]]
Out[24]= http://dx.doi.org/10.12942/lrsp-2010-1
```

Creating a bibliography

One of the most familiar structured data sets is a database. Databases are used for modeling customer accounts, inventories, personnel information, and much more. In this example we will create a sample bibliography using associations and then perform several typical operations on the data toward creating a nicely formatted report.

We will create functions to extract and format the author and title information and also create live links from the URLs of each reference.

First, here is a function to display the value of the `"Authors"` key in a Times-Roman font:

```
In[25]:= makeAuthor[ref_] := Style[ref["Authors"], "TR"]

In[26]:= makeAuthor[Hathaway2010]
Out[26]= Hathaway, David
```

Similarly, the following function extracts the value of the `"Title"` key and displays it in a Times-Italic font:

```
In[27]:= makeTitle[ref_] := Style[ref["Title"], "TI"]
```

```
In[28]:= makeTitle[Hathaway2010]
Out[28]= The solar cycle
```

And let's create a live hyperlink from the "Url" value using the example above. Clicking the resulting output will open that page in a web browser on your computer.

```
In[29]:= makeLink[ref_] := Hyperlink[Style[ref["Url"], "TR"], ref["Url"]]

In[30]:= makeLink[Hathaway2010]
Out[30]= http://dx.doi.org/10.12942/lrsp−2010−1
```

Next, let's put all these pieces together to create an item suitable for a simple bibliography listing. We will use Row, described earlier in Section 3.1, to display the output. The second argument to Row specifies the separator between elements; in this case, a newline character.

```
In[31]:= Row[{makeAuthor[Hathaway2010],
           makeTitle[Hathaway2010], makeLink[Hathaway2010]}, "\n"]
Out[31]= Hathaway, David
         The solar cycle
         http://dx.doi.org/10.12942/lrsp−2010−1
```

This could be turned into a function that can be applied to any other similarly constructed references. To do so, wrap the above code in TextCell to specify the style of cell to display ("Text" in this case) and then use CellPrint to display the text cell. The option ShowStringCharacters is set to False to suppress the display of quotes around strings.

```
In[32]:= MakeRef[ref_] := CellPrint[
           TextCell[Row[{makeAuthor[ref], makeTitle[ref], makeLink[ref]}, "\n"],
            "Text", ShowStringCharacters → False]]

In[33]:= MakeRef[Hathaway2010]
         Hathaway, David
         The solar cycle
         http://dx.doi.org/10.12942/lrsp−2010−1
```

Chapter 5 introduces the Map function, but if you are already familiar with it, you can use it to map MakeRef across the list of associations.

```
In[34]:= Hamming1950 = bib[2];

In[35]:= Map[MakeRef, {Hathaway2010, Hamming1950}];
         Hathaway, David
         The solar cycle
         http://dx.doi.org/10.12942/lrsp−2010−1

         Hamming, Richard
         Error detecting and error correcting codes
         https://archive.org/details/bstj29−2−147
```

There is much more that can be done with associations. For example, we saw in the previous section that by using `SortBy` you could sort on a key (`"Authors"`, say) to put the entries in alphabetical order. The bibliography could contain entries for books or online databases that contain different kinds of information and hence need to be formatted differently. And some conditional functions will need to be used to deal with multiple authors and missing values. We will postpone dealing with these issues until after we have discussed transformation rules, higher-order functions like `Map` and `SortBy`, and pure functions in Chapters 4 and 5.

Exercises

1. Create an association consisting of several songs in your music library. Include keys for song title, artist, release date, album cover. Once the association is defined, convert all the album covers to smaller images using `Thumbnail`.
2. Modify the `MakeRef` function to display the year of publication at the end of the line for authors. Adjust the style so that the year displays in a bold font.

```
In[1]:= MakeRef[hamming1950]
```

Hamming, Richard (**1950**)
Error detecting and error correcting codes
https://archive.org/details/bstj29–2–147

3.5 Differences from other languages

If you have some experience with other programming languages such as C or JAVA, you may find it helpful to understand the differences between *Mathematica* and these languages to better write programs that take advantage of *Mathematica*'s features. This can help you avoid trying to implement something that works in C say, but doesn't have a direct analog in *Mathematica*. Although there are many differences, we will mainly focus here on arrays and lists as these are fundamental data structures in almost every programming language.

Arrays are the structure with which you group objects together. The objects typically are numbers, characters, and possibly other arrays, representing vectors, strings, matrices, and many more structures. If you are already familiar with arrays in C or JAVA, then the closest thing to them in *Mathematica* is a list. Many of the operations on arrays have their analog in *Mathematica*, but lists are quite general objects and differ from arrays in some important ways. Table 3.2 contains a listing of array and list features in which the differences between traditional languages and *Mathematica* is pronounced.

TABLE 3.2. *Differences between arrays in C and Java and lists in Mathematica*

Feature	Traditional languages	*Mathematica*
Array type	must declare type ahead of time	lists can contain arbitrary types; no need to declare types
Array size	must declare ahead of time; in JAVA array size is fixed	no limit; no need to declare size; can change size by adding or deleting elements
Extract elements	a[i] to extract *i*th element of array named a	a[[i]] to extract *i*th element of list named a
Mixed types	not allowed in arrays	lists can contain mixed types
Pointers	used to hold and reference memory location	no pointers

In languages like C and JAVA, you declare the array size and type when you make the declaration. So, in C, the following would declare an array named numsC to consist of integers only and set aside space for five elements:

```
int numsC[5]={2,4,6,8,10}
```

In *Mathematica*, assignments are made without the need to declare the type of elements contained in the list or the size of the list itself.

```
In[1]:= numsM = {2, 4, 6, 8, 10};
```

To access the *i*th element of the array in C, you use the following notation:

```
numsC[i]
```

In *Mathematica* you use Part.

```
numsM[[i]]
```

Another important difference is that in C and JAVA, the index for arrays starts at zero. So to extract the first element of the array numsC, you use

```
numsC[0]
```

In *Mathematica*, the index starts at one, so this extracts the first element of numsM:

```
numsM[[1]]
```

Since *Mathematica* does not use pointers like in C or references as in JAVA, there is no aliasing. What this means is that if you make a copy of a list and modify an element of that copy, it will have no effect on the original list.

```
In[2]:= lisa = {2, 4, 6, 8, 10};

In[3]:= lisb = lisa
Out[3]= {2, 4, 6, 8, 10}
```

Make a change to `lisb` using list component assignment.

```
In[4]:= lisb[[3]] = 2^10;
```

`lisb` has changed, but since it does not point to `lisa`, the original list is unchanged.

```
In[5]:= lisb
Out[5]= {2, 4, 1024, 8, 10}
```

```
In[6]:= lisa
Out[6]= {2, 4, 6, 8, 10}
```

There is another very important difference between arrays in languages such as C and JAVA and lists in *Mathematica*. To operate on the elements of an array, you typically pull off one element, operate on it, put the transformed element in a different array of the same size as the original, then repeat this process looping through the array one-by-one. So, for example, the C code to reverse the elements in an array would look something like that in Program 3.1 (leaving out the parts to read in the array and print the result).

PROGRAM LISTING 3.1. *Partial C code to reverse the elements in an array.*

```
#include<stdio.h>

int main() {
   int array[100], i, j, num, temp;

   // code here to enter elements in array

   }

   j = i - 1;     // j points to the last element
   i = 0;         // i points to the first element

   while (i < j) {
      tmp = array[i];
      array[i] = array[j];
      array[j] = tmp;
      i++;               // increment i
      j--;               // decrement j
   }
```

In *Mathematica*, list-manipulation functions operate on the array directly and can automatically handle multiple data types. In the following case, a real number, rational, symbol, and an image:

```
In[7]:= Reverse[{3.0, 22 / 7, π, [image]}]
Out[7]= {[image], π, 22/7, 3.}
```

Another important distinction between C and *Mathematica* has to do with strings. C does not have built-in facilities to deal with strings. As a result, strings in C are essentially just arrays of characters. You declare them in one of two ways:

```
char mystring[] = "colourless green ideas";

char mystring[] = {'c', 'o', 'l', 'o', 'u', 'r', 'l','e', ... , '\0'};
```

In *Mathematica* you enter a string as any concatenation of characters enclosed in quotes; its type is automatically recognized.

```
In[8]:= str = "colourless green ideas";

In[9]:= Head[str]
Out[9]= String
```

Perhaps it is not fair to compare *Mathematica* with C and JAVA in terms of strings – JAVA and various extensions to C have sophisticated string-processing capabilities. And more robust and flexible languages have been designed with string processing specifically in mind (PERL and PYTHON, for example). But if you have a background in one of these other languages it is helpful to understand these differences so that you can make the most effective use of your programming experience with *Mathematica*. Throughout this book we will point out important distinctions as they arise.

3.6 Notes and further reading

Prime gaps (Exercise 6, Section 3.2) can get arbitrarily large and are an active area of research in number theory. The big news in this area is the recent result of Yitang Zhang on bounds of prime gaps. For a readable survey article see Cipra (2005).

The leading digits problem in Exercise 8, Section 3.3 is an example of Benford's law, a phenomenon known to exist in many different types of data sets, including population numbers, lengths of rivers, street addresses, and most famously, tax returns and corporate financial statements; see Nigrini (2012), Hill (1998), and especially the blog by Terence Tao (2009) on Benford's law, Zipf's law, and Pareto distributions.

Several sparse matrix collections are available to use in prototyping: matrices from both the University of Florida Sparse Matrix Collection (Davis and Hu 2011) and the Matrix Market collection curated at the National Institute of Standards and Technology (2014) are used in this book.

N-grams are used in linguistics to analyze and compare the computational complexity of text sources. They can be found in any natural language processing text. Two authoritative sources in natural language processing are Manning and Schütze (1999) and Jurafsky and Martin (2009). N-grams are also heavily used in bioinformatics in the statistical analysis of nucleotide and protein sequences (Cristianini and Hahn 2007).

For information on arrays in traditional languages, see the language-specific references: for C, Kernighan and Ritchie (1988); for JAVA, the textbook by Sedgewick and Wayne (2007); for PERL, Schwartz, foy, and Phoenix (2011); for PYTHON, Downey (2012).

4

Patterns and rules

Patterns · Blanks · Pattern matching by type · Explicit pattern matching · Structured patterns · Sequence pattern matching · Conditional pattern matching · Shorthand notation · Alternatives · Repeated patterns · Functions that use patterns · Transformation rules · Creating and using replacement rules · Applying transformation rules · Examples · Counting coins · Filtering and extracting data · Perimeter · Triangle area · Finding parts of expressions · Sorting a list · Sunspot activity · Notes and further reading

The idea of representing an idealized version of an object with something called a pattern is central to mathematics and computer science. For the purposes of search, patterns provide a template with which to compare expressions. They can be used to filter data by selecting only those parts that match the pattern. Because of the wide applicability of patterns, many modern programming languages have extensive pattern-matching capabilities that enable them to identify objects that meet some criteria in order to classify, select, or transform those objects through the use of rules.

Pattern matching in *Mathematica* is done through a powerful yet flexible pattern language. Used in rules to transform expressions from one form to another, they can be applied to broad classes of expressions or they can be limited to very narrowly-defined objects through the use of conditional and structured pattern matching. Pattern matching is the key to identifying which rules should be applied to expressions that you wish to transform.

If you have used regular expressions in languages such as PERL or RUBY, or via libraries in JAVA, PYTHON, or C++, then you are already familiar with pattern matching on strings (discussed further in Chapter 7). *Mathematica*'s pattern language generalizes this to arbitrary objects and expressions. Although the syntax may be new to you, with practice it becomes natural, providing a direct connection between the statement of a problem and its expression in a program. This chapter starts with an introduction to patterns and pattern matching and then proceeds to a discussion of transformation rules in which patterns are used to identify the parts of an expression that are to be transformed. The chapter concludes with several concrete examples that make use of pattern matching and transformation rules to show their application to some common programming tasks.

4.1 Patterns

Patterns are objects that represent classes of expressions. Pattern matching is the process by which an expression is determined to match a template pattern. Together with rules, you can transform any expression that matches a pattern representing something of interest. For example, using patterns, you can set up your own functions to only operate on certain kinds of expressions – for argument checking, say. We start by introducing basic pattern objects and then extend this to the many kinds of patterns that can be used to restrict the types of expressions you wish to operate on.

Blanks

When you make an assignment to a symbol, like x = 4, you are making a rule that should be applied to the literal expression x. Loosely speaking, the rule says replace x with the value 4 whenever x is encountered. As we have seen, you can also define functions of one or more arguments that allow you to substitute *arbitrary* expressions for those arguments.

```
In[1]:= f[x_] := x + 1
```

The left-hand side of the above assignment is a pattern. It contains a pattern object, the blank (underscore), that can stand for any expression, not just the literal expression x.

```
In[2]:= f[ξ]
Out[2]= 1 + ξ
```

```
In[3]:= f[Bob]
Out[3]= 1 + Bob
```

To start, we will define a *pattern* as an expression that may contain *blanks*; specifically, one of the following: a single blank (_), a double blank (__), or a triple blank (___). This is not quite accurate since arbitrary expressions can be used as patterns, but for now we will only discuss patterns involving blanks. We will focus on the single blank, saving discussion of the double and triple blank for the section on sequence pattern matching below.

It is often useful to identify a pattern so that it can be referred to by name elsewhere. For example, in the function f defined above, the argument is a pattern named x. The argument is referred to using the name x on the right-hand side of the definition. The right-hand side essentially describes what should be done with the argument to produce the desired output. So-called *labeled patterns* can be used with single, double, and triple blanks.

To see what expressions are matched by a given pattern, use MatchQ. For example, the following tests whether the symbol Bob is matched by any expression since the single underscore can stand for *any* expression:

```
In[4]:= MatchQ[Bob, _]
Out[4]= True
```

Often, we are interested in pattern matching classes of expressions (for example, an expression having Image as its head or a sequence of numbers within a certain range). This is accomplished through more restrictive patterns and pattern matching, the subject of the next few sections.

Pattern matching by type

Although the single blank matches every expression, oftentimes a more restrictive pattern is called for. For example, you might want to define a function that accepts only integers as arguments, or a function that only operates on strings or graphs. One way of restricting the class of expressions matched by a pattern is to match on the head of the expression. This is done with patterns of the form _*head*. For example, the following tests whether the number 3.14 is matched by any expression with head Real:

```
In[5]:= MatchQ[3.14, _Real]
Out[5]= True
```

Of course 3.14 does not match any expression with head Integer.

```
In[6]:= MatchQ[3.14, _Integer]
Out[6]= False
```

```
In[7]:= Head[3.14]
Out[7]= Real
```

Instead of working with a single expression, you can use Cases to take a list of expressions and extract those that are matched by a particular pattern. Cases[*expr*, *patt*] returns those elements of *expr* that are matched by the pattern *patt*. For example, the only two elements of the list below that have head Integer are 3 and 17. Notice the fourth element is a string.

```
In[8]:= Cases[{3, 3.14, 17, "24", 4 + 5 I}, _Integer]
Out[8]= {3, 17}
```

```
In[9]:= Cases[{3, 3.14, 17, "24", 4 + 5 I}, _String]
Out[9]= {24}
```

Tip 4.1

Remember that the OutputForm of strings is to display without the quote characters. If you want to check the structure of this last output, use InputForm or FullForm.

```
In[10]:= InputForm[%]
Out[10]//InputForm=
        {"24"}
```

This next example matches all those expressions with head g.

```
In[11]:= Cases[{g[x], f[x], g[h[x]], g[a, 0]}, _g]
Out[11]= {g[x], g[h[x]], g[a, 0]}
```

The only expression below that is matched by the pattern _Plus is a + b. The string has head String. But isn't 2 + 3 matched by the pattern _Plus?

```
In[12]:= Cases[{a + b, 2 + 3, "3+4"}, _Plus]
Out[12]= {a + b}
```

Recall from Section 2.1 that *Mathematica* evaluates the arguments to functions *before* passing them up to the calling function. So the expression 2 + 3 in this example is evaluated first and returns an expression that does not have head Plus.

```
In[13]:= FullForm[2 + 3]
Out[13]//FullForm=
         5
```

Pattern matching on heads is extremely useful for restricting the kinds of arguments on which a defined function can operate, essentially argument checking. For example, the following function sets up a rule for expressions of the form f[*integer*]. Only those expressions matched by this pattern will cause the rule to be invoked.

First, clear any previous definitions of f.

```
In[14]:= Clear[f]

In[15]:= f[x_Integer] := x + 1

In[16]:= f[5]
Out[16]= 6

In[17]:= f[1.25]
Out[17]= f[1.25]

In[18]:= Clear[f]
```

Explicit pattern matching

The patterns we have looked at up to this point match general classes of expressions such as all expressions with head Integer or all expressions with head String. Sometimes you need to match explicit expressions. For example, suppose you need to delete all zeros from a list of numbers.

```
In[19]:= vec = {0, 1, 1, 1, 0, 1, 1, 0, 1, 1, 0, 1};
```

DeleteCases has the same form as Cases, so using it with the explicit pattern 0 will do the job.

```
In[20]:= DeleteCases[vec, 0]
Out[20]= {1, 1, 1, 1, 1, 1, 1, 1}
```

Alternatively, you could use Cases to extract all those elements except 0.

```
In[21]:= Cases[vec, Except[0]]
Out[21]= {1, 1, 1, 1, 1, 1, 1, 1}
```

Structured patterns

Patterns can also be set up to match arbitrary expressions. In the following example, the pattern {p_, q_} matches any list with two elements:

```
In[22]:= Cases[{{a, b}, {}, {1, 0}, {c, d, 3}}, {p_, q_}]
Out[22]= {{a, b}, {1, 0}}
```

In fact, there is no need to name the patterns in this last example as they are not referred to elsewhere. Hence, the following is equivalent:

```
In[23]:= Cases[{{a, b}, {}, {1, 0}, {c, d, 3}}, {_, _}]
Out[23]= {{a, b}, {1, 0}}
```

The next result might be a bit surprising. The pattern used for matching is a symbolic expression involving a general pattern in both numerator and denominator.

In[24]:= $\text{Cases}\left[\left\{2, \frac{9}{3}, \frac{1}{3}, \frac{x}{y+z}\right\}, \frac{a\_}{b\_}\right]$

Out[24]= $\left\{\frac{x}{y+z}\right\}$

Why doesn't the pattern match 9/3? *Mathematica* evaluates the elements of expressions first and so when 9/3 is evaluated, it reduces to an integer.

In[25]:= $\frac{9}{3}$

Out[25]= 3

What is even more mysterious is the fact that the pattern a_ / b_ does not match 1/3. A look at the internal representation of this fraction gives a clue.

In[26]:= $\left\{\text{FullForm}\left[\frac{1}{3}\right], \text{FullForm}\left[\frac{a}{b}\right]\right\}$

```
Out[26]= {Rational[1, 3], Times[a, Power[b, -1]]}
```

The pattern matcher is a syntactic tool, not a semantic one. This means that patterns match expressions based on the explicit structure of the expression, not what that expression means or what it might reduce to. This is an important principle to keep in mind when you are creating and using patterns.

In[27]:= $\text{MatchQ}\left[\frac{1}{3}, \text{Rational}[a\_, b\_]\right]$

Out[27]= True

Structured arguments provide a clean mechanism for writing rules that only apply to the kinds of expressions for which you want them to apply. The following function definition is for an argument consisting of a list of two expressions:

In[28]:= $f[\{x\_, y\_\}] := \frac{x^2}{y^3}$

```
In[29]:= f[{a, b}]
```

Out[29]= $\frac{a^2}{b^3}$

The pattern does not match in the following case. The function f is expecting a list of two elements as an argument, but here it is getting a sequence of two elements, not a list.

```
In[30]:= f[a, b]
Out[30]= f[a, b]
```

The alternative to such a structured pattern on the left-hand side of this definition would be to use a more general pattern that matches the head of the expression. But this requires you to extract the various parts of the list in order to operate on them on the right-hand side of the definition. It's not wrong, just clumsier.

```
In[31]:= ff[list_List] := list[[1]]^2/list[[2]]^3

In[32]:= ff[{a, b}]
```

Out[32]= $\frac{a^2}{b^3}$

```
In[33]:= Clear[f, ff]
```

Sequence pattern matching

A *sequence* consists of a number of expressions separated by commas. For example, the elements of expressions are written as sequences, as can be seen in the full form representation for a list.

```
In[34]:= FullForm[{a, b, c, d, e}]
Out[34]//FullForm=
         List[a, b, c, d, e]
```

The double blank (BlankSequence) represents a sequence of one or more expressions. So, the pattern {p__} matches any list consisting of a sequence of one or more elements.

```
In[35]:= MatchQ[{a, b, c, d, e}, {p__}]
Out[35]= True
```

Using the name p is actually unnecessary here as it is never referred to elsewhere.

```
In[36]:= MatchQ[{a, b, c, d, e}, {__}]
Out[36]= True
```

Note how this differs from the pattern {_}, which is only matched by a list consisting of a single expression.

```
In[37]:= MatchQ[{a, b, c, d, e}, {_}]
Out[37]= False

In[38]:= MatchQ[{Bob}, {_}]
Out[38]= True
```

The triple blank (BlankNullSequence) represents a sequence of zero or more expressions, so the pattern {___} matches any list consisting of a sequence of zero or more elements.

```
In[39]:= Cases[{x, "ab", {}, {a}, {b, c}, {d, e, f}}, {___}]
Out[39]= {{}, {a}, {b, c}, {d, e, f}}
```

You can use double and triple blanks to match expressions by type as we did with the single blank above. For example, the pattern `{___Symbol}` matches any list consisting of a sequence of zero or more elements, all of which have head `Symbol`.

```
In[40]:= MatchQ[{a, b, c}, {___Symbol}]
Out[40]= True
```

```
In[41]:= MatchQ[{a, 2, c}, {___Symbol}]
Out[41]= False
```

The next example returns `True`, but not for the reason you might think.

```
In[42]:= MatchQ[{a, b, c}, __]
Out[42]= True
```

The pattern `__` is matched by a sequence of one or more expressions. In this case the entire list matches that pattern, regardless of the contents of that list.

```
In[43]:= MatchQ[{}, __]
Out[43]= True
```

The discussion about pattern matching on lists applies equally to any expression. For example, the following returns `True`, with `x` naming the sequence `a, b, c`:

```
In[44]:= MatchQ[f[a, b, c], f[x__]]
Out[44]= True
```

Tip 4.2

Sometimes expressions have more complicated or nested structures than the examples above. In such cases, you will often need to coax the pattern matcher to dig a little deeper in its search for a match. For example, using the structured pattern `(var_)^n_` to find expressions consisting of a variable raised to a power, the following fails initially:

```
In[45]:= Cases[a x^3 + b x^2 + c x + d, (var_)^n_]
Out[45]= {}
```

The reason `Cases` did not find any expressions matching the pattern is that the polynomial is deeply nested and `Cases`, by default, only looks at the first level of the expression.

```
In[46]:= FullForm[a x^3 + b x^2 + c x + d]
Out[46]//FullForm=
    Plus[d, Times[c, x], Times[b, Power[x, 2]], Times[a, Power[x, 3]]]
```

There certainly are some variables raised to powers in there. To get `Cases` to find them, give it a third argument that specifies the level to search down to. Rather than guessing or spending time trying to figure out that level, you can just use `Infinity` as the level specification and this means, go all the way down the expression tree in the search. Here we use the functional form of the pattern:

```
In[47]:= Cases[a x^3 + b x^2 + c x + d, Power[var_, n_], Infinity]
Out[47]= {x^2, x^3}
```

Conditional pattern matching

Suppose you are interested in finding the numbers in a list that meet a certain criterion. For example, say you wanted only numbers that were even, or square numbers. Conditions can be used to place a constraint on the labeled parts of a pattern that represent a criterion you are interested in. The general notation for conditional patterns is *expr_ /; test*. The pattern match is successful only if the predicate *test* returns `True`.

In this first example, the pattern named `n` must meet the condition that its square root passes the `IntegerQ` test; in other words, that `n` is a square number.

```
In[48]:= Cases[{1, 2, 3, 4, 5, 6, 7, 8, 9}, n_ /; IntegerQ[√n]]
Out[48]= {1, 4, 9}
```

In the following case, the expressions that are matched by the pattern are powers where the exponent passes the `EvenQ` test:

```
In[49]:= Cases[{x, x^2, x^3, x^4, x^5}, _^(n_) /; EvenQ[n]]
Out[49]= {x^2, x^4}
```

Let's try a more applied problem. Given an array, how can we test that it is a square matrix? One way is to check that the dimensions are identical.

```
In[50]:= mat = RandomReal[1, {4, 4}];
         MatrixForm[mat]
Out[51]//MatrixForm=
  0.336577 0.438783 0.56452  0.644591
  0.397034 0.103496 0.5157   0.947336
  0.985451 0.71404  0.258119 0.948957
  0.115993 0.015101 0.983933 0.186973

In[52]:= Dimensions[mat]
Out[52]= {4, 4}
```

In the definition below, the condition that the expression passes the matrix test is added to the left-hand side. This avoids having to check tensors where the first two dimensions might be identical but the tensor clearly should not be classified as a square matrix (without `MatrixQ` you would need to check that its array depth did not exceed two).

```
In[53]:= squareMatrixQ[mat_ /; MatrixQ[mat]] :=
          Dimensions[mat][[1]] == Dimensions[mat][[2]]

In[54]:= squareMatrixQ[mat]
Out[54]= True
```

```
In[55]:= mat = RandomReal[1, {3, 4}];
         MatrixForm[mat]
Out[56]//MatrixForm=
  0.400838 0.238144 0.681011 0.22226
  0.519637 0.791515 0.241791 0.492405
  0.677933 0.977262 0.396413 0.862713
```

```
In[57]:= squareMatrixQ[mat]
Out[57]= False
```

A 1×1 matrix is also square.

```
In[58]:= squareMatrixQ[{{1}}]
Out[58]= True
```

```
In[59]:= Dimensions[{{1}}]
Out[59]= {1, 1}
```

Shorthand notation

There is a convenient shorthand notation for conditional patterns that is commonly used. The condition *expr_ /; test* can be shortened to *expr_ ? test*.

```
In[60]:= Cases[{1, 2, 3, 4, 5, 6, 7, 8, 9}, _?PrimeQ]
Out[60]= {2, 3, 5, 7}
```

```
In[61]:= squareMatrixQ[mat_?MatrixQ] :=
          Dimensions[mat][[1]] == Dimensions[mat][[2]]
```

```
In[62]:= MatchQ[[image], _?ImageQ]
Out[62]= True
```

Note the difference in syntax between using a predicate and a head to pattern match: to match a class of expressions that have head *h*, you use _*h*. To match a class of expressions that evaluate to True when the predicate *test* is applied, use _ ? *test*.

```
In[63]:= MatchQ[{1, 2, 3}, _List]
Out[63]= True
```

```
In[64]:= MatchQ[{1, 2, 3}, _?NumberQ]
Out[64]= False
```

In the above example, even though the list {1, 2, 3} consists of numbers, it does not match ?NumberQ because its head (List) does not pass the NumberQ test. If you want to match the list consisting of a sequence of numbers, use the double blank as follows:

```
In[65]:= MatchQ[{1, 2, 3}, {__?NumberQ}]
Out[65]= True
```

To extract the elements of a list that meet a criterion, use Cases[*lis*, *patt*], which returns all elements of *lis* that match the pattern *patt*.

```
In[66]:= Cases[{1, 2, 3, a}, _?NumberQ]
Out[66]= {1, 2, 3}
```

The pattern _?Negative matches any expression that passes the Negative test, that is, those elements that return a value of True when Negative is applied to them.

```
In[67]:= Cases[{-2, 7, -1.2, 0, -5 - 2 I}, _?Negative]
Out[67]= {-2, -1.2}
```

Here is a basic application of attaching a predicate. This definition of the Fibonacci function for arbitrary *n* tests its argument to see if it is an integer (Fibonacci functions are introduced in Section 5.3). We start with the base cases defined as a double assignment, then the recursion.

```
In[68]:= f[1] = f[2] = 1;

In[69]:= f[n_?IntegerQ] := f[n - 1] + f[n - 2]
```

Because of the predicate, noninteger arguments do not match the pattern _?IntegerQ and the rules for f will not apply in those cases.

```
In[70]:= f[1.2]
Out[70]= f[1.2]

In[71]:= {f[5], f[10], f[20]}
Out[71]= {5, 55, 6765}
```

To test that the argument is both an integer *and* positive, use logical AND. This might require more verbose code, as in the following example:

```
In[72]:= Clear[f]
         f[1] = f[2] = 1;

In[74]:= f[n_ /; IntegerQ[n] && Positive[n]] := f[n - 1] + f[n - 2]

In[75]:= {f[5], f[10], f[20.0], f[-10]}
Out[75]= {5, 55, f[20.], f[-10]}
```

Tip 4.3

In general, try to use the condition operator /; on the smallest possible pattern expression to limit the amount of checking that is needed to find a match. The pattern matcher matches patterns sequentially so the sooner it finds a part of the condition that fails, the sooner it will terminate the entire pattern match.

Alternatives

Sometimes the criterion needed for pattern matching involves one of several alternatives. Alternatives are denoted $p_1 \mid p_2 \mid \ldots \mid p_n$, where the p_i are independent patterns. This pattern will match an expression whenever any one of the independent patterns match it.

In the following, the pattern matches any expression that has head Integer or Rational or Real:

```
In[76]:= Cases[{1, 3.1, x, 3 + 4 I, "Hello"}, _Integer | _Rational | _Real]
Out[76]= {1, 3.1}
```

You might also need to extract all expressions that do *not* match a pattern – in other words, an exception to the pattern. This can be done with the function Except. The following finds all numbers other than zero in a list:

```
In[77]:= Cases[{-4.7943, NAN, -8.0251, 7.2672, 4.8205, -4.2002, 0.0, "N/A"},
          Except[0, _?NumberQ]]
Out[77]= {-4.7943, -8.0251, 7.2672, 4.8205, -4.2002, 0.}
```

Why was 0. returned? Recall the pattern matcher is syntactic, not semantic, and so 0. does not match the pattern 0 even though they are numerically equivalent. An alternative, 0 | 0.0, will catch the two forms of zero, integer or real, that could be present.

```
In[78]:= Cases[{-4.7943, NAN, -8.0251, 7.2672, 4.8205, -4.2002, 0.0, "N/A"},
          Except[0 | 0.0, _?NumberQ]]
Out[78]= {-4.7943, -8.0251, 7.2672, 4.8205, -4.2002}
```

You should think of $p_1 \mid p_2 \mid \ldots \mid p_n$ as pattern p_1 or pattern p_2 or.... But note that this is different from the logical OR which requires predicates, not patterns, as its argument.

Repeated patterns

Double and triple blanks can be used to set up a function with a sequence of arguments whose length is not known ahead of time. For example, to match a list containing an arbitrary sequence of numbers, you could use the double blank with a test:

```
In[79]:= MatchQ[{1, 2, 3, 4, 5}, {__?NumberQ}]
Out[79]= True
```

Or, you could use Repeated[*pattern*] (shorthand notation *pattern* ..), which stands in for a sequence of one or more expressions all of which match *pattern*; in this case, repeated expressions all of which pass the NumberQ test.

```
In[80]:= MatchQ[{1, 2, 3, 4, 5}, {_?NumberQ ..}]
Out[80]= True
```

Similarly, there is RepeatedNull[*pattern*] (shorthand notation *pattern* ...), a pattern object that will match a sequence of zero or more expressions, all matching *pattern*.

```
In[81]:= MatchQ[{}, {_?NumberQ ...}]
Out[81]= True
```

Tip 4.4

If you use a named pattern with `Repeated` or `RepeatedNull`, note that each expression matching the named pattern part must be identical.

```
In[82]:= MatchQ[{{1, 2}, {1, 4}, {1, 5}}, {{_, _} ..}]
Out[82]= True
In[83]:= MatchQ[{{1, 2}, {1, 4}, {1, 5}}, {{_, q_} ..}]
Out[83]= False
In[84]:= MatchQ[{{1, 2}, {1, 4}, {1, 5}}, {{p_, _} ..}]
Out[84]= True
```

As an example of the use of these repeated pattern objects, let's create two rules for a function that we will use later to display random walks in two and three dimensions.

First, look at the form of the input this function should accept. Here are fifteen steps in a two- and three-dimensional random walk, respectively:

```
In[85]:= << EPM`RandomWalks`
In[86]:= RandomWalk[15, Dimension → 2]
Out[86]= {{1, 0}, {1, -1}, {1, 0}, {1, -1}, {1, -2}, {0, -2}, {0, -1}, {0, -2},
          {0, -3}, {-1, -3}, {-2, -3}, {-1, -3}, {0, -3}, {0, -4}, {0, -5}}
In[87]:= RandomWalk[15, Dimension → 3]
Out[87]= {{0, 1, 0}, {0, 1, -1}, {0, 1, 0}, {0, 1, 1}, {-1, 1, 1},
          {-1, 1, 2}, {-1, 0, 2}, {-1, 0, 1}, {-1, 1, 1}, {-2, 1, 1},
          {-2, 1, 0}, {-2, 2, 0}, {-2, 3, 0}, {-2, 3, 1}, {-2, 3, 2}}
```

For the first pattern we will use `{{_, _} ..}`, which matches any sequence of one or more two-dimensional coordinates. Similarly, `{{_, _, _} ..}` matches any sequence of one or more three-dimensional coordinates. We could be a bit more careful and insist that each element in the list pass the `NumberQ` test, but we will omit that here for purposes of clarity.

```
In[88]:= showWalk[coords : {{_, _} ..}] :=
           ListLinePlot[coords, AspectRatio → Automatic]
In[89]:= showWalk[coords : {{_, _, _} ..}] :=
           Graphics3D[Line[coords]]
```

This is defined as `ShowWalk` in Chapter 10. Loading the package from the materials that accompany this book, we generate a random walk and test one of the `showWalk` rules written here:

```
In[90]:= showWalk[RandomWalk[2500, Dimension → 3]]
```

Out[90]=
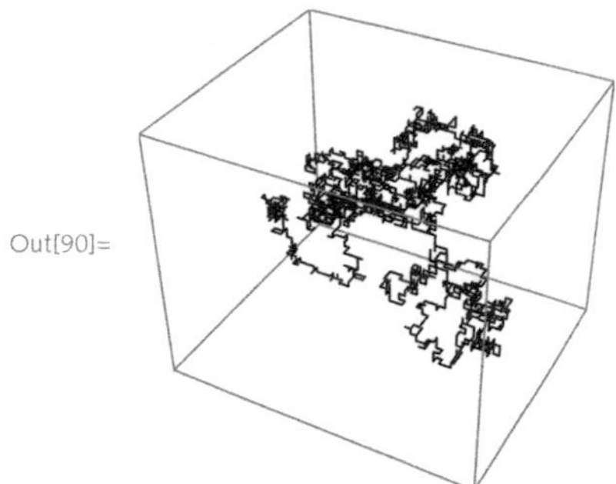

In the above example, upon seeing a list of triples generated by `RandomWalk[…, Dimension → 3]`, the pattern matcher checks each rule in turn until the match is made.

```
In[91]:= ? showWalk
```

```
Global`showWalk

showWalk[coords : {{_, _} ..}] :=
 ListLinePlot[coords, AspectRatio → Automatic]

showWalk[coords : {{_, _, _} ..}] := Graphics3D[Line[coords]]
```

Note that we have not yet written a rule for the one-dimensional case. Hence the following input returns unevaluated as there is no rule for `showWalk` when its argument is a one-dimensional vector. In Exercise 10 at the end of this section you are asked to write a rule for the one-dimensional case and to add another rule to handle the display of multiple walks.

```
In[92]:= showWalk[RandomWalk[5, Dimension → 1]]
Out[92]= showWalk[{-1, 0, -1, -2, -1}]
```

We have used one additional construct in these rules for `showWalk`, *named patterns*. The pattern `{{_, _} ..}` will be matched by any list of one or more lists of pairs. The pattern is named `coords` using the construction `coords : {{_, _} ..}`. We then refer to the entire argument by name inside the body of the function. This really is no different than an ordinary function definition like `f` below, where we name the argument `x` and refer to the argument by its name on the right-hand side of the function definition. The following two function definitions are equivalent. It is of course more convenient to use the more compact first definition.

```
In[93]:= f[x_] := x + 1

In[94]:= f[x : _] := x + 1
```

Functions that use patterns

We have already seen several functions that are used in working with patterns: `MatchQ` is used to check if an expression is matched by a pattern; `Cases` returns all those elements in an expression that are matched by a pattern. But there are several other functions that are quite useful and follow on the syntax of these two functions. For example, using Cases, this returns all those elements in a list of integers that are divisible by 3:

```
In[95]:= ints = RandomInteger[20, {12}]
Out[95]= {3, 20, 0, 13, 9, 2, 5, 14, 9, 17, 12, 11}

In[96]:= Cases[ints, x_ /; Mod[x, 3] == 0]
Out[96]= {3, 0, 9, 9, 12}
```

But what if you were interested in all those elements that are *not* divisible by 3? DeleteCases takes the same syntax as Cases but deletes those elements that are matched by the pattern.

```
In[97]:= DeleteCases[ints, x_ /; Mod[x, 3] == 0]
Out[97]= {20, 13, 2, 5, 14, 17, 11}
```

If you wanted the positions within the list at which the pattern is matched, Position is the function to use.

```
In[98]:= Position[ints, x_ /; Mod[x, 3] == 0]
Out[98]= {{1}, {3}, {5}, {9}, {11}}
```

To get the number of elements in the list that are matched by the pattern, use Count.

```
In[99]:= Count[ints, x_ /; Mod[x, 3] == 0]
Out[99]= 5
```

Notice how all four of these functions use the exact same syntax. They are all quite useful for the common task of finding information about the elements within an expression that meet some criterion in which you are interested.

As a nontrivial example, suppose you have a collector in the field that gives information about some phenomenon that you are studying, such as sea surface temperatures or UV levels. Normally, it returns a list of real numbers at specified intervals, but whenever it fails, it inserts a string such as "NAN". Using Count and Position, it would be straightforward to find the rate of failure and the positions (times) at which those failures occurred.

```
In[100]:= signal = Import["collectorData.dat", "List"];

In[101]:= Take[signal, 5062 ;; 5080]
Out[101]= {0.12694, 0.841523, NAN, 0.145962, -0.0842434, -0.62487,
  0.853251, -0.798156, -0.08864, -0.461193, -0.921515, 0.106368,
  0.0103998, 0.709147, 0.134594, 0.121745, 0.264044, NAN, -0.249447}

In[102]:= Dimensions[signal]
Out[102]= {8860}

In[103]:= badvals = Count[signal, _String]
Out[103]= 19
```

Or you could count all those elements of `signal` that are not numeric.

```
In[104]:= Count[signal, Except[_?NumericQ]]
Out[104]= 19
```

```
In[105]:= N[badvals / Length[signal]]
Out[105]= 0.00214447
```

```
In[106]:= Position[signal, _String]
Out[106]= {{299}, {700}, {1394}, {1488}, {1991}, {2195},
  {2360}, {2628}, {3413}, {3466}, {3553}, {3662}, {5064},
  {5079}, {5505}, {6861}, {6870}, {7118}, {7449}}
```

Exercises

1. Explain why the following pattern match fails. Then find two different patterns that correctly match a complex number such as 3 +4 *i*.

```
In[1]:= MatchQ[3 + 4 I, a_ + b_I]
Out[1]= False
```

2. Use conditional patterns to find all those numbers in a list of integers that are divisible by 2 or 3 or 5.
3. Write down four conditional patterns that match the expression `{4, {a, b}, "g"}`.
4. Explain why the expression `1 / y` is not matched by the pattern `a_/b_`.

```
In[2]:= MatchQ[1 / y, a_/b_]
Out[2]= False
```

   Determine the correct pattern that can be used to match the symbolic expression `x / y`.

```
In[3]:= MatchQ[x / y, Power[a_, -1]]
Out[3]= False
```

5. Write a function `Collatz` that takes an integer *n* as an argument and returns $3n + 1$ if *n* is an odd integer and returns $n/2$ if *n* is even.
6. Write the `Collatz` function from the above exercise, but this time you should also check that the argument to `Collatz` is positive.
7. Use alternatives to write a function `abs[x]` that returns *x* if $x \geq 0$, and $-x$ if $x < 0$, whenever *x* is an integer or a rational number. Whenever *x* is complex, `abs[x]` should return $\sqrt{\mathrm{re}(x)^2 + \mathrm{im}(x)^2}$.
8. Create a function `swapTwo[lis]` that returns *lis* with only its first two elements interchanged; for example, the input `swapTwo[{a, b, c, d, e}]` should return `{b, a, c, d, e}`. If *lis* has fewer than two elements, `swapTwo` just returns *lis*. Write `swapTwo` using three clauses: one for the empty list, one for one-element lists, and one for all other lists. Then write it using two clauses: one for lists of length zero or one and another for all longer lists.

9. Explain the different results from the following three pattern matches:

```
In[4]:= MatchQ[{4, 6, 8}, x_ /; Length[x] > 4]
Out[4]= False
In[5]:= MatchQ[{4, 6, 8}, {x___} /; Length[x] > 4]
        Length::argx : Length called with 3 arguments; 1 argument is expected. >>
Out[5]= False
In[6]:= MatchQ[{4, 6, 8}, {x___} /; Plus[x] > 10]
Out[6]= True
```

10. Write a rule for the one-dimensional case of `showWalk` described in this section. Then write an additional rule to handle multiple one-dimensional random walks.

```
In[7]:= Needs["EPM`RandomWalks`"]
In[8]:= walk = RandomWalk[1000, Dimension → 1];
        showWalk[walk]
Out[9]=
In[10]:= walks = Table[RandomWalk[1000, Dimension → 1], {25}];
         showWalk[walks]
Out[11]=
```

11. Given a set of data like that in Figure 4.1, remove all outliers, defined here by being greater than two standard deviations from the mean of the data.

```
In[12]:= rawData = RandomVariate[NormalDistribution[0, 2], {200}];
```

FIGURE 4.1. *Scatter plots of original data and data with outliers removed.*

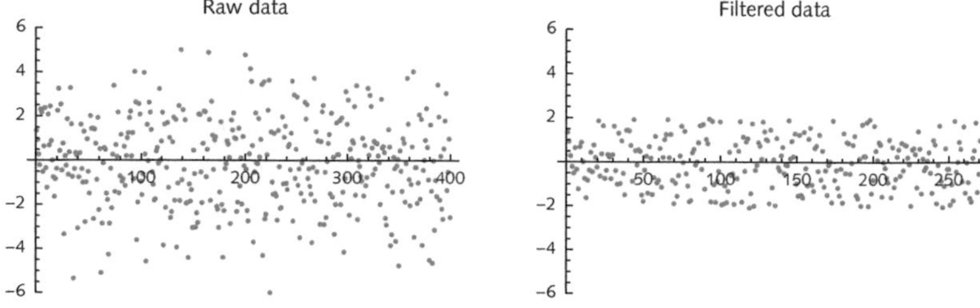

4.2 Transformation rules

Transformation rules are the mechanism by which *Mathematica* simplifies algebraic and mathematical expressions. In fact, much of its computation is really a process of pattern matching to find the appropriate rule to apply and then doing the transformation.

We have already seen how function assignments are created and used to transform an argument according to a rule specified as the right-hand side of the definition. These rules are applied automatically whenever possible. But sometimes it is preferable to apply a transformation to an expression manually. This is what replacement operators are for, and we will see how they can be used together with pattern matching to transform any kind of expression that you are working with.

Creating and using replacement rules

A replacement rule is of the form *pattern* → *replacement* or *pattern* :→ *replacement*. Just like traditional function definitions, the left-hand side of each of these rules matches an expression and the right-hand side describes the transformation of that expression.

expr /. *pattern* → *replacement*

The standard input form is

`ReplaceAll[`*expr*, *pattern* → *replacement*`]`

Any part of *expr* that is matched by the pattern will be rewritten according to the replacement. For example,

```
In[1]:= x + y /. y → α
Out[1]= x + α
```

Here is the standard input form of this rule:

```
In[2]:= ReplaceAll[x + y, y → α]
Out[2]= x + α
```

A rule that produces the same output but using assignments would look like this:

```
In[3]:= y = α;

In[4]:= x + y
Out[4]= x + α
```

The main difference between the replacement rule and the assignment is that the assignment will automatically be used whenever there is an appropriate pattern match during evaluation. When `x + y` was evaluated, a rule was found for `y` (specifically, `y = α`) and a substitution was automatically made. Another key difference is that no assignment was made in the first case (the replacement rule) but one was made in the latter case.

Whether you use the standard form with `ReplaceAll` or use the shorthand notation, there are some important things to note about the evaluation of transformation rules. To start, the expression itself is first evaluated. Then *both* the left-hand side and the right-hand side of the rule are evaluated, unless there are parts of the right-hand side that have the Hold attribute. Finally, everywhere that the evaluated left-hand side of the rule appears in the evaluated expression, it is replaced by the evaluated right-hand side of the rule.

```
In[5]:= {a, a} /. a → RandomReal[]
Out[5]= {0.509168, 0.509168}
```

Trace shows how the transformation rule works: the expression is evaluated first, then the right-hand side of the rule (RandomReal[]), and then the replacement occurs.

```
In[6]:= Trace[{a, a + a} /. a → RandomReal[]]
Out[6]= {{{a + a, 2 a}, {a, 2 a}},
  {{RandomReal[], 0.209463}, a → 0.209463, a → 0.209463},
  {a, 2 a} /. a → 0.209463, {0.209463, 2 × 0.209463},
  {2 × 0.209463, 0.418927}, {0.209463, 0.418927}}
```

Just as in the case of assignments, there are immediate and delayed transformation rules. In an immediate rule (*pattern* → *replacement*), the *replacement* will be evaluated immediately. For delayed rules (*pattern* :→ *replacement*), the *replacement* is only evaluated after the substitution is made.

```
In[7]:= {a, a} /. a :→ RandomReal[]
Out[7]= {0.303669, 0.371831}
```

```
In[8]:= Trace[{a, a} /. a :→ RandomReal[]]
Out[8]= {{a :→ RandomReal[], a :→ RandomReal[]}, {a, a} /. a :→ RandomReal[],
  {RandomReal[], RandomReal[]}, {RandomReal[], 0.859679},
  {RandomReal[], 0.940477}, {0.859679, 0.940477}}
```

In general, it is a good idea to use delayed rules whenever you have global symbols on the right-hand side of your rules, to avoid the possibility of global values for these symbols being used automatically during evaluation. If there are no global symbols on the right-hand side of your rules, it may be safe to use an immediate rule.

The kinds of patterns that you can use with transformation rules are limitless. For example, using the symbol List as the pattern, this changes the following list to a sum:

```
In[9]:= {a, b, c} /. List → Plus
Out[9]= a + b + c
```

Using labeled patterns can make it clearer what is being transformed. In the first example below, a pattern is used to identify and then swap the elements in the second and third column. In the second example, the pattern matches elements in the matrix with the same row and column index and replaces them with zero.

```
In[10]:= mat = {{a, b, c}, {d, e, f}};
         MatrixForm[mat]
Out[11]//MatrixForm=
```

$$\begin{pmatrix} a & b & c \\ d & e & f \end{pmatrix}$$

```
In[12]:= mat /. {col1_, col2_, col3_} :→ {col1, col3, col2} // MatrixForm
Out[12]//MatrixForm=
         ( a  c  b )
         ( d  f  e )

In[13]:= ReplacePart[mat, {i_, i_} → 0] // MatrixForm
Out[13]//MatrixForm=
         ( 0  b  c )
         ( d  0  f )
```

ReplacePart[*expr*, *i* → *val*] is used to replace the part of *expr* at position *i* with *val*. In the example above, we have used the pattern {i_, i_} to stand in for a two-dimensional position in which the row and column positions are the same, as indicated by the similarly named patterns i_.

To use multiple rules with an expression, enclose them in a list.

```
In[14]:= {a, b, c} /.{c :→ b, b :→ a}
Out[14]= {a, a, b}
```

A transformation rule is applied only once to each part of an expression (in contrast to a rewrite rule), and multiple transformation rules are used in parallel. Hence, in the above example, the symbol c is transformed into b but it is not further changed into a.

In some situations the transformation rules need to be applied again and again to an expression until it no longer changes. For example, the product of x and y below is replaced by the sum of x and y, but this is only done for the first such occurrence that matches.

```
In[15]:= a b c d /. x_ y_ :→ x + y
Out[15]= a + b c d
```

Using ReplaceRepeated, the rule is applied repeatedly until the expression no longer changes.

```
In[16]:= a b c d //. x_ y_ :→ x + y
Out[16]= a + b + c + d

In[17]:= Clear[y]
```

Applying transformation rules

The basic idea of transformation rules is that they can be applied on demand to transform one expression into another without the need to first create and then use a formal function definition. For example, this rule adds the elements in each ordered pair:

```
In[18]:= {{x1, y1}, {x2, y2}, {x3, y3}} /. {x_, y_} :→ x + y
Out[18]= {x1 + y1, x2 + y2, x3 + y3}
```

In the above example, we transformed a list. We could just as well transform a graphic. Here is a rule that interchanges the coordinate points that make up a plot, essentially reflecting in the line $y = x$:

```
In[19]:= gr = Plot[Sin[x], {x, 0, 2 π}];
```

```
In[20]:= Show[{gr, gr /. {x_?NumberQ, y_?NumberQ} :→ {y, x},
           Graphics[{Dashed, InfiniteLine[{{0, 0}, {1, 1}}]}]},
          PlotRange → All, AspectRatio → Automatic]
```

Out[20]=

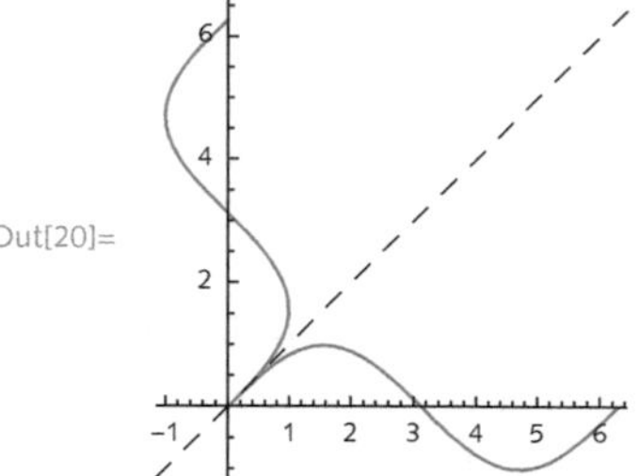

In fact, the expressions that you can transform are completely arbitrary. They could be strings or arrays or images. For example, here we give a list of replacement rules to be applied to the string.

```
In[21]:= StringReplace["acgttttccctgagcataaaaacccagcaatacg",
          {"ca" → "CA", "tt" → "TT"}]

Out[21]= acgTTTTccctgagCAtaaaaaccCAgCAatacg
```

In the following example, any strings in the array are replaced with `0.0`.

```
In[22]:= ( 0.4683  0.2699  "NAN"  )
         ( 0.8323  0.1458  0.683  ) /. (_String → 0.0) // MatrixForm
         ( "NAN"   0.4935  0.4033 )

Out[22]//MatrixForm=
         ( 0.4683  0.2699  0.     )
         ( 0.8323  0.1458  0.683  )
         ( 0.      0.4935  0.4033 )
```

To find expressions matching a certain pattern and then return a transformed version of them, `Cases` can be used with an alternate syntax. For example, to find all those elements in a list that are numbers and then return them squared, we could use a transformation rule.

```
In[23]:= lis = {f, 12, "64", 0.5, {a, b, c}, -0.2, π};

In[24]:= Cases[lis, n_?NumericQ :→ n^2]

Out[24]= {144, 0.25, 0.04, π^2}
```

Exercises

1. Here is a rule designed to switch the order of each pair of expressions in a list. It works fine on the first example, but fails on the second.

```
In[1]:= {{a, b}, {c, d}, {e, f}} /. {x_, y_} :→ {y, x}

Out[1]= {{b, a}, {d, c}, {f, e}}

In[2]:= {{a, b}, {c, d}} /. {x_, y_} :→ {y, x}

Out[2]= {{c, d}, {a, b}}
```

Explain what has gone wrong and rewrite this rule to correct the situation, that is, so that the second example returns `{{b, a}, {d, c}}`.

2. Given a 3×3 matrix, here is a rule intended to swap the elements in the second and third columns:

```
In[3]:= mat = {{a, b, c}, {d, e, f}, {g, h, i}};
In[4]:= mat /. {x_, y_, z_} :→ {x, z, y} // MatrixForm
Out[4]//MatrixForm=
 a b c
 g h i
 d e f
```

Explain what has gone wrong and rewrite the rule so that it correctly swaps columns two and three.

3. Use pattern matching to extract all negative solutions of the following polynomial:

$$x^9 + 3.4\,x^6 - 25\,x^5 - 213\,x^4 - 477\,x^3 + 1012\,x^2 + 111\,x - 123$$

Then extract all real solutions; that is, those which are not complex.

4. Create a rewrite rule that uses a repeated replacement to "unnest" the nested lists within a list.

```
In[5]:= unNest[{{α, α, α}, {α}, {{β, β, β}, {β, β}}, {α, α}}]
Out[5]= {α, α, α, α, β, β, β, β, β, α, α}
```

5. Define a function using pattern matching and repeated replacement to sum the elements of a list such as that produced by `Range[100]`.

6. Using the built-in function `ReplaceList`, write a function `cartesianProduct` that takes two lists as input and returns the Cartesian product of these lists.

```
In[6]:= cartesianProduct[{x1, x2, x3}, {y1, y2}]
Out[6]= {{x1, y1}, {x1, y2}, {x2, y1}, {x2, y2}, {x3, y1}, {x3, y2}}
```

7. Write a function to count the total number of multiplications in any polynomial expression. For example, given a power, your function should return one less than the exponent.

```
In[7]:= MultiplyCount[t^5]
Out[7]= 4
In[8]:= MultiplyCount[a x y t]
Out[8]= 3
In[9]:= MultiplyCount[a x y t^4 + w t]
Out[9]= 7
```

8. Create six graphical objects, one each to represent the faces of a standard six-sided die. `Dice[n]` should display the face of the appropriate die, as below. Then use the `Dice` function to create a function `RollDice[]` that "rolls" two dice and displays them side-by-side. Create an additional rule, `RollDice[n]`, that rolls a pair of dice *n* times and displays the result in a list or row.

```
In[10]:= Table[Dice[n], {n, 1, 6}]
Out[10]= {⚀, ⚁, ⚂, ⚃, ⚄, ⚅}
```

One way to approach this problem is to think of a die face as a grid of nine elements, some of which are turned on (white) and some turned off (blue above). Then create one set of rules for each of the six die faces. Once your rules are defined, you could use something like the following graphics code (a bit incomplete as written here) to create your images:

```
Dice[n_] := GraphicsGrid[
  Map[Graphics, Partition[Range[9], 3] /. rules[[n]], {2}]]
```

9. Make a scatter plot of the points used to construct the polygons in a torus, which is given parametrically as follows:

```
In[11]:= ParametricPlot3D[
  {(2 + Cos[v]) Sin[u], (2 + Cos[v]) Cos[u], Sin[v]}, {u, 0, 2π}, {v, 0, 2π}]
```

Out[11]=

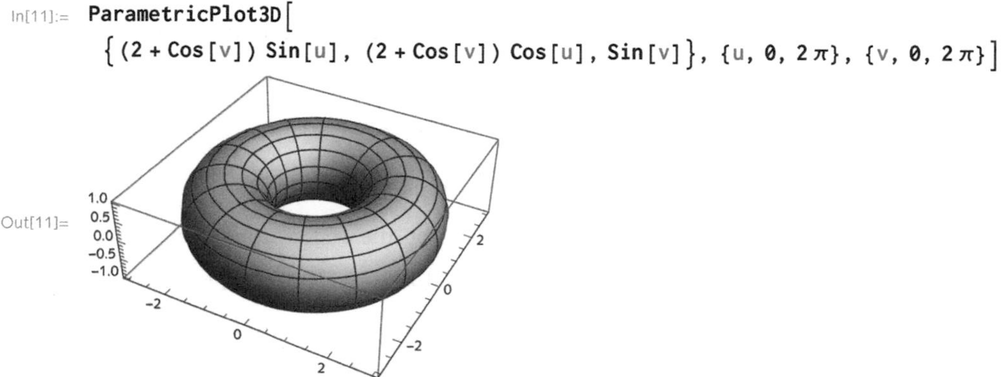

4.3 Examples

This section focuses on the application of transformation rules and pattern matching to solve several problems. First we will solve a simple problem in counting change, followed by two problems dealing with data – filtering and extracting elements based on first, removing outliers and second, finding records in water reservoir data that fall below some threshold. Next are two problems in geometry, computing the perimeter and the signed area of triangles. The fifth example wades through a graphical expression to extract coordinates that are used to construct the curve. We then use a rule-based approach to solve a classical problem in computer science, sorting. Finally, the last example is a substantial computation in astrophysics – determining the cycles in sunspot activity. It involves importing several hundred year's worth of time-series data, filtering, analyzing, and visualizing that data.

Counting coins

For our first example of the use of transformation rules, we will write a program to perform a common task: calculating the value of the change in your pocket.

Suppose you have the following collection of coins and assume *p*, *n*, *d*, and *q* represent pennies, nickels, dimes, and quarters, respectively (modify as appropriate for different currencies):

```
In[1]:= coins = {p, p, q, n, d, d, p, q, q, p};
```

Here are the values, given by a list of rules:

```
In[2]:= values = {p → .01, n → .05, d → .10, q → .25};
```

This replaces each coin by its value:

```
In[3]:= coins /. values
Out[3]= {0.01, 0.01, 0.25, 0.05, 0.1, 0.1, 0.01, 0.25, 0.25, 0.01}
```

And here is the value of the set of coins:

```
In[4]:= Total[coins /. values]
Out[4]= 1.04
```

Finally, here is a function that wraps up all these steps:

```
In[5]:= CountChange[coins_List] :=
          Total[coins /.{p → .01, n → .05, d → .10, q → .25}]

In[6]:= CountChange[{p, q, q, d, d, p, q, q, d, d}]
Out[6]= 1.42
```

Although we have used symbols to represent the coins, there is no reason you could not use other objects – in Exercise 6 at the end of this section you are asked to use images of coins as the patterns on the right-hand side of the rules.

Filtering and extracting data

One of the more important uses of pattern matching is to extract the elements of a set of data based on a criterion of interest. For example, to extract all those numbers from a list that are between two and five, a conditional pattern seems quite natural.

```
In[7]:= Cases[{1, 2, 3, 4, 5, 6, 7, 8}, x_ /; 2 < x < 5]
Out[7]= {3, 4}
```

This is essentially a filter, and we can use this technique to filter all sorts of data. For example, in the following, we first import a signal containing data clustered about the mean, plot it, and then remove outliers using a conditional pattern:

```
In[8]:= sig = Import["signal.dat", "List"];

In[9]:= ListPlot[sig, PlotRange → {-1, 1}]
```

Out[9]=

```
In[10]:= filtered = Cases[sig, p_ /; -0.3 < p < 0.3];
         ListPlot[filtered, PlotRange → {-1, 1}]
```

Out[11]=

1.0
0.5
200 400 600 800
-0.5
-1.0

Let's try a slightly more complicated example: finding those water reservoirs in a list of imported data that are less than 75% capacity of the historical average on the date of the imported report.

```
In[12]:= resData = Import["CAresevoir.csv", "CSV"]

Out[12]= {{Resevoir, Capacity 1000 AF, Hist Avg, 2014 AF, 2015 AF, % Avg},
          {UPPER KLAMATH, 515.6, 341.1, 195.7, 281.7, 83},
          {CLEAR LAKE, 526.8, 221, 33.2, 31.2, 14},
          {GERBER, 94.7, 48., 2., 1.9, 4},
          {SHASTA DWINNELL, 50, 21, 3., 7.1, 34},
          {TRINITY, 2447.7, 1953.8, 865.4, 825., 42},
          {LEWISTON, 14.7, 13.9, 13.9, 13.7, 99},
          {PILLSBURY, 80.5, 62.9, 50.1, 24.2, 38},
          {MENDOCINO (COYOTE), 122.4, 70., 38.8, 47.9, 68},
          {WARM SPRINGS, 381, 214, 163.2, 192.7, 90}}
```

The names of the reservoirs are in the first column and the percentages of average capacity are in the last column. The pattern `{res_, __, avg_ /; avg < 75}` is matched by those rows where the last element is less than 75. The rule causes only the reservoir name and the average to be returned for those rows that match the pattern.

```
In[13]:= Cases[resData, {res_, __, avg_ /; avg < 75} :→ {res, avg}]

Out[13]= {{CLEAR LAKE, 14}, {GERBER, 4}, {SHASTA DWINNELL, 34},
          {TRINITY, 42}, {PILLSBURY, 38}, {MENDOCINO (COYOTE), 68}}
```

Perimeter

When working with geometric regions you often need to find the length of a path across or through the region. For objects in plane geometry, the perimeter is a common measure of the extent of that object. Area, a two-dimensional notion, is another measure of the extent of an object. Although a function to compute the area of regions is built into *Mathematica*, perimeter is not. In this example we will create one.

To specify triangles *Mathematica* uses a graphics primitive, `Triangle`, which takes a list of three points as its argument. To display the triangle, wrap it with `Graphics`.

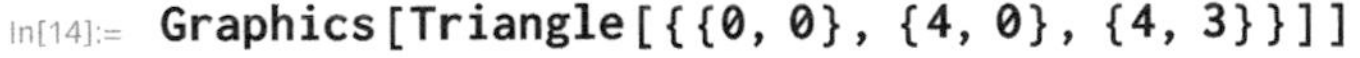

```
In[14]:= Graphics[Triangle[{{0, 0}, {4, 0}, {4, 3}}]]
```

Out[14]=

Since we will be using this triangle repeatedly in this section, let us assign a name to the points and also format the graphic a bit differently.

```
In[15]:= pts = {{0, 0}, {4, 0}, {4, 3}};
         Graphics[{EdgeForm[Gray], LightBlue, Triangle[pts]}]
```

Out[16]=

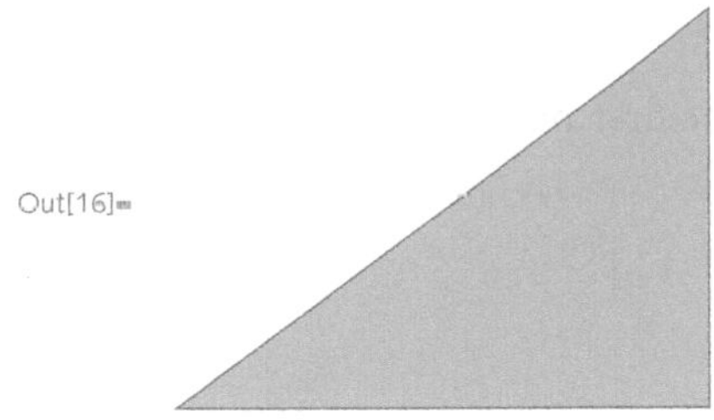

Our plan to solve this problem is to measure the arc length of the three lines on the boundary of the triangle; but simply passing the three points to `ArcLength` results in an error.

```
In[17]:= ArcLength[pts]

         ArcLength::reg : {{0, 0}, {4, 0}, {4, 3}} is not a correctly specified region. >>

Out[17]= ArcLength[{{0, 0}, {4, 0}, {4, 3}}]
```

`ArcLength` expects a region as its argument. `Triangle` is a two-dimensional region but if we use `Triangle[pts]` as the argument of `ArcLength`, it returns ∞ because arc length is a one-dimensional notion.

```
In[18]:= ArcLength[Triangle[pts]]

Out[18]= ∞
```

Since we are interested in a one-dimensional measure (length), we should pass `ArcLength` lines. We can do that by wrapping the list of points with `Line`.

```
In[19]:= ArcLength[Line[pts]]

Out[19]= 7
```

But this is wrong; the answer should be 12. The perimeter is the combined length of the three line segments on the boundary of the triangle. We have only given `ArcLength` two lines to work with.

```
In[20]:= Graphics[Line[pts]]
```

Out[20]=

So, from the three points, we need to create three lines; that is, we need to close up the region by connecting the third point to the first. There are several ways we could do that, but the most direct is with a transformation rule.

```
In[21]:= pts /. {p1_, pn__} :→ {p1, pn, p1}
Out[21]= {{0, 0}, {4, 0}, {4, 3}, {0, 0}}
```

Note the use of the double blank above. `p1_` represents the first point in the list `pts`, and `pn__` represents all the points that follow.

```
In[22]:= Graphics[Line[pts /. {p1_, pn__} :→ {p1, pn, p1}]]
```

Out[22]=

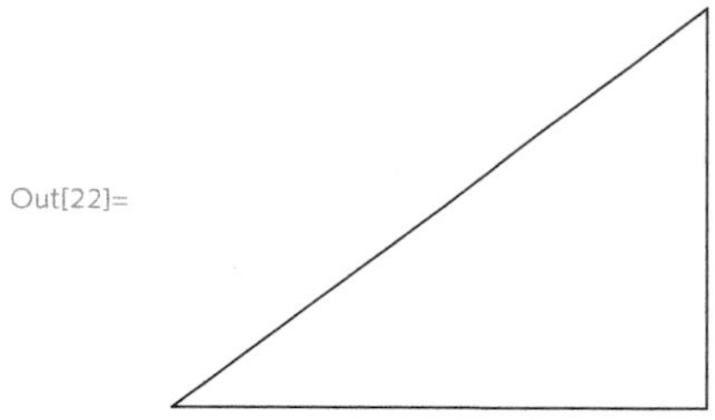

Now we get the correct value for the arc length of the triangle.

```
In[23]:= ArcLength[Line[pts] /. {p1_, pn__} :→ {p1, pn, p1}]
Out[23]= 12
```

Here then is our first perimeter definition for triangles. Note the left-hand side of this rule: `Perimeter` expects an argument that has head `Triangle`, which itself has an argument consisting of a list of three expressions, `p1`, `p2`, and `p3`. We have named that list `pts` for convenience in using it on the right-hand side of the definition.

```
In[24]:= Perimeter[Triangle[pts : {p1_, p2_, p3_}]] :=
          ArcLength[Line[pts] /. {pt1_, ptn__} :→ {pt1, ptn, pt1}]
```

Alternatively, we could have used `RegionMeasure`, of which `ArcLength` is a special case for one-dimensional regions. (Or use `RegionBoundary[Triangle[…]]`, which returns a line.)

```
In[25]:= Perimeter[Triangle[pts : {p1_, p2_, p3_}]] :=
          RegionMeasure[Line[pts /. {pt1_, pn__} :→ {pt1, pn, pt1}]]

In[26]:= Perimeter[Triangle[pts]]
Out[26]= 12
```

Triangle area

Although *Mathematica* has an `Area` function that will compute the area of `Triangle` objects, it has certain limitations that we will need to work around later in the book: it returns an error message for degenerate triangles and it only produces nonnegative areas. In the case where all three points of a triangle are collinear, we will need to have the area reported as zero (Exercise 10, Section 8.1); for problems in computational geometry such as point-in-polygon problems (Section 8.4), we need a signed area to help determine if a point is inside a polygon. In this section we will develop a function for computing the signed area of triangles.

The area of a triangle is commonly defined as one-half the length of the base times the length of the altitude. For arbitrary points, finding the altitude requires a bit of computation that does not generalize to higher dimensions. A different approach is to think about the cross product: the determinant of the cross product of two vectors having a common vertex gives the area of the parallelogram that they determine.

$$A_{\Delta} = \frac{1}{2} \left| v_1 \times v_2 \right|$$

But in fact, we can compute the signed area directly using the following determinant formula:

$$A_{\Delta} = \frac{1}{2} \begin{vmatrix} x_1 & y_1 & 1 \\ x_2 & y_2 & 1 \\ x_3 & y_3 & 1 \end{vmatrix}$$

Starting with a two-dimensional point $\{x_i, y_i\}$, a transformation rule will give us each row.

```
In[27]:= {xi, yi} /. {x_, y_} :→ {x, y, 1}
Out[27]= {xi, yi, 1}
```

Here then is the computation of the signed area:

```
In[28]:= pts = {{x1, y1}, {x2, y2}, {x3, y3}};
         Det[pts /. {x_, y_} :→ {x, y, 1}] / 2
```

Out[29]= $\frac{1}{2}(-x_2 y_1 + x_3 y_1 + x_1 y_2 - x_3 y_2 - x_1 y_3 + x_2 y_3)$

Let's mirror the argument structure we used for `Perimeter` and set up this function to accept `Triangle` objects as input:

```
In[30]:= SignedArea[Triangle[{v1_, v2_, v3_}]] :=
          1/2 Det[{v1, v2, v3} /. {x_, y_} :→ {x, y, 1}]
```

This function gives results that differ only by sign if the order of the triangle vertices are reversed.

```
In[31]:= pts = {{0, 0}, {4, 0}, {4, 3}};
         SignedArea[Triangle[pts]]
Out[32]= 6
```

```
In[33]:= SignedArea[Triangle[Reverse@pts]]
Out[33]= -6
```

Finding parts of expressions

As you work with more complicated expressions, you will occasionally need to deconstruct them in order to extract or operate on certain parts you are interested in. As an example, suppose you were interested in finding all the points used to construct the curve in a two-dimensional plot to better understand the adaptive sampling routine of the `Plot` function.

```
In[34]:= plot = Plot[Sin[x], {x, 0, 2 π}]
```

Out[34]=

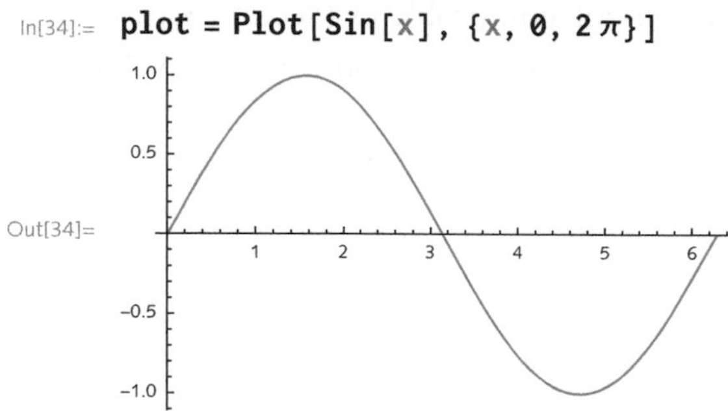

A look at the internal representation of this plot gives a clue as to how the curve is constructed.

```
In[35]:= Short[InputForm[plot], 8]
Out[35]//Short=
   Graphics[{{{}, {},
      {Directive[Opacity[1.], RGBColor[0.368417, 0.506779, 0.709798],
        AbsoluteThickness[0.7]], Line[{{1.28228 × 10^-7, 1.28228 × 10^-7},
         {0.0019271654532543384, 0.001927164260349845},
         {0.0038542026782371016, 0.003854193135958910 5},
         {0.0077082771282026286, << 1 >>}, {<< 2 >>},
         << 424 >>, {6.281028700305505, -0.002156605202368725},
         {6.283185178951315, -1.28228 × 10^-7}}]}}}, {<< 17 >>}]
```

The "curve" is actually a line connecting hundreds of points. The `Line` graphics primitive following `Directive[…]` is given the full list of coordinate points as its argument. To extract the coordinate pairs inside `Line[]`, we use `Cases` with the pattern `Line[{{_, _}..}]`. The structured pattern `{_, _}` represents a single coordinate pair and the repeated pattern `..` is needed to return all such two-element lists.

```
In[36]:= Short[Cases[plot, Line[{{_, _}..}], Infinity], 5]
Out[36]//Short=
   {Line[{{1.28228 × 10^-7, 1.28228 × 10^-7},
      {0.00192717, 0.00192716}, {0.0038542, 0.00385419}, <<426>>,
      {6.28103, -0.00215661}, {6.28319, -1.28228 × 10^-7}}]}
```

In fact, using an alternate form of `Cases`, we can return just the explicit coordinates named by the pattern named `pts`.

```
In[37]:= coords = Cases[plot, Line[pts : {{_, _} ..}] :> pts, Infinity];
         Short[coords, 5]
Out[37]//Short=
         {{{1.28228 × 10^-7, 1.28228 × 10^-7},
           {0.00192717, 0.00192716}, {0.0038542, 0.00385419}, <<426>>,
           {6.28103, -0.00215661}, {6.28319, -1.28228 × 10^-7}}}
```

Now we can work with these points directly. For example, here is a scatter plot of the coordinates showing that more points are sampled where the slope of the function is changing most rapidly, near $x = \pi/2$ and $x = 3\pi/2$:

```
In[38]:= ListPlot[coords]
```

Out[38]=

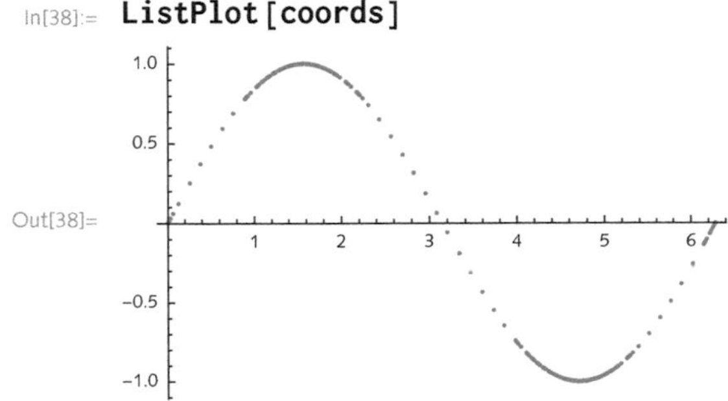

The exercises include a problem similar to the above but working with a three-dimensional plot instead, one in which the underlying structure is nested inside various graphics expressions.

Sorting a list

Sorting is one of the fundamental tasks in computer science going back to the dawn of modern programming. The idea is to take a sequence of objects and put them in some logical order. If the objects are letters, the order is typically alphabetic. If the objects are numbers, the order would likely be numeric. In this introductory example, we will incorporate several of the concepts discussed in this chapter – using a delayed rule, conditional patterns, and several types of sequence pattern matching – to sort lists of numbers.

We will create a rule named `listSort` that, upon repeated application, will put a list of numbers into numerical order. To account for the first and last elements in the list we use the triple blank (`___`), which matches a sequence of zero or more expressions.

```
In[39]:= listSort = {{x___, a_?NumericQ, b_?NumericQ, y___} :> {x, b, a, y} /; b < a};
```

The expression that has to match the pattern `{x___, a_, b_, y___}` is a list of at least two elements, since `x___` and `y___` will match zero or more elements. The condition on the right-hand side of the rule says that whenever `b` is less than `a`, switch the order of `a` and `b` in the original list to output `{x, b, a, y}`, where `x` and `y` represent sequences of zero or more elements.

Here is a list of ten real numbers between zero and one:

```
In[40]:= nums = RandomReal[1, {10}]
Out[40]= {0.311376, 0.566004, 0.627155, 0.129313, 0.791636,
  0.654409, 0.106783, 0.361809, 0.872012, 0.294215}
```

Applying the `listSort` rule to nums results in one transformation, in this case only the third and fourth numbers are sorted (the first two numbers in nums were already in numerical order).

```
In[41]:= nums /. listSort
Out[41]= {0.311376, 0.566004, 0.129313, 0.627155, 0.791636,
  0.654409, 0.106783, 0.361809, 0.872012, 0.294215}
```

To apply a transformation rule repeatedly until the expression being operated on no longer changes, use `ReplaceRepeated` (`//.`).

```
In[42]:= nums //. listSort
Out[42]= {0.106783, 0.129313, 0.294215, 0.311376, 0.361809,
  0.566004, 0.627155, 0.654409, 0.791636, 0.872012}
```

Because we used `?NumericQ` as part of the pattern match, `listSort` will work on expressions that may not be explicit numbers, but are numerical in nature; that is, expressions that return explicit numbers when `N` is applied to them.

```
In[43]:= {e, π, EulerGamma, GoldenRatio, 1} //. listSort
Out[43]= {EulerGamma, 1, GoldenRatio, e, π}
```

Tip 4.5

The built-in `Sort` function, because of its great generality, sorts symbols by their names and so does not return a numerically sorted list such as in the following example:

```
In[44]:= Sort[{e, π, EulerGamma, GoldenRatio, 1}]
Out[44]= {1, e, EulerGamma, GoldenRatio, π}
```

One way around this is to give `Sort` a second argument, causing it to sort by numerical value.

```
In[45]:= Sort[{e, π, EulerGamma, GoldenRatio, 1}, Less]
Out[45]= {EulerGamma, 1, GoldenRatio, e, π}
```

Although this implementation of `listSort` only works for numerical arguments, it can be overloaded to work on strings of characters (see Exercise 3, Section 7.3).

Our `listSort` algorithm is essentially an implementation of the classical bubble sort. It is far less efficient than many other, more commonly used, sorting algorithms, especially those that employ a divide-and-conquer strategy. This is because the pattern matcher generates all possible pairs of adjacent elements and then compares them. The computational complexity of the bubble sort algorithm is known to be $O(n^2)$, meaning that the running time is proportional to the square of the size of the input. This can be seen by timing the sort on lists of increasing size.

```
In[46]:= times =
  Table[First[Timing[(RandomReal[1, {n}] //. listSort);]], {n, 50, 150, 10}]
Out[46]= {0.03841, 0.05565, 0.114953, 0.14933, 0.205962,
  0.344053, 0.473374, 0.646739, 0.809276, 1.02434, 1.39299}

In[47]:= model = LinearModelFit[times, {x, x^2}, x]

Out[47]= FittedModel[ 0.0992068 - 0.050355 x + 0.0147969 x^2 ]

In[48]:= Show[{ListPlot[times], Plot[model[t], {t, 1, 11}]},
  PlotLabel → model["BestFit"]]
```

Out[48]=

The built-in `Sort` function uses a classical algorithm called *merge sort*, which starts by dividing the list into two parts of approximately equal size. It then sorts each part recursively and finally merges the two sorted sublists. For numerical input it has computational complexity $O(n \log(n))$.

Sunspot activity

Sunspots are dark spots on the sun where the surface temperature is reduced by the effects of strong magnetic activity. They were first observed and recorded by the Chinese over 2000 years ago. In the year 1610, soon after the invention of the telescope, Galileo (1564–1642) spotted them, thus dealing one of several blows to religious dogma of the time which insisted that the heavens and stars were perfect objects.

Extraordinary levels of ultraviolet and x-ray emissions from increased solar activity have pronounced effects on the Earth's upper atmosphere and so detecting patterns in the frequency of sunspot activity is an important aspect of current solar research. Fortunately, data is available going back to 1818. The time-series data that we will import in this example requires some extraction, cleaning, and filtering before we can analyze and visualize it, typical tasks when working with real data. Transformation rules provide a clean and efficient mechanism to perform these tasks.

Start by importing the data from the WDC-SILSO, Royal Observatory of Belgium.

```
In[49]:= data = Import["http://sidc.oma.be/silso/DATA/SN_d_tot_V2.0.txt", "Table"];
```

There are over 70 000 observations (or records).

```
In[50]:= Length[data]
Out[50]= 72165
```

Our task here is to filter all of the data and make a plot of the sunspot numbers over the time period covered by the data set. We start by converting the data to a form that can be used by `TimeSeries` and `DateListPlot`; that is, convert the data to a list of the form `{{`*date*`,` *value*`}, …}`. We will first prototype with a small number of data points and, when we are satisfied with the code, apply it to the entire data set.

Here are the first two and last two records or data points from the imported data.

```
In[51]:= test = Part[data, {1, 2, -2, -1}]
Out[51]= {{1818, 1, 1, 1818., -1, -1., 0}, {1818, 1, 2, 1818., -1, -1., 0},
  {2015, 7, 30, 2015.58, 74, 3.7, 17, *}, {2015, 7, 31, 2015.58, 114, 28.2, 3, *}}
```

Next we need to put the data into a form suitable for the time series functions. Each observation is of the form {*y*, *m*, *d*, *yf*, *sn*, *sd*, *obs*, *ind*}, where *y* is the year, *m* is the month, *d* is the day, *yf* is the date in fraction of a year, *sn* is the sunspot number, *sd* is the standard deviation of the sunspot numbers, *obs* is the raw number of observations used to compute *sn*, and *ind* is a value used to indicate if the sunspot number value is still provisional (see the SILSO website for details).

Notice that earlier data points have seven elements in each sublist while later data consists of eight-element lists. The following rule will remove the indicator element if present and leave seven-element lists unchanged.

```
In[52]:= test2 = test /. lis : {y_, m_, d_, _, _, _, _, _} :→ Most[lis]
Out[52]= {{1818, 1, 1, 1818., -1, -1., 0}, {1818, 1, 2, 1818., -1, -1., 0},
  {2015, 7, 30, 2015.58, 74, 3.7, 17}, {2015, 7, 31, 2015.58, 114, 28.2, 3}}
```

The next rule extracts just the date information and the sunspot number and then wraps the date in `DateList` to put it in a form suitable for the time series functions.

```
In[53]:= test3 = test2 /.
   {y_Integer, m_, d_, _Real, sn_Integer, __} :→ {DateList[{y, m, d}], sn}
Out[53]= {{{1818, 1, 1, 0, 0, 0.}, -1}, {{1818, 1, 2, 0, 0, 0.}, -1},
  {{2015, 7, 30, 0, 0, 0.}, 74}, {{2015, 7, 31, 0, 0, 0.}, 114}}
```

Some pruning of the data will help to better see the patterns in the sunspot activity. From the SILSO website, we find sunspot number values of –1 indicate a missing observation. We will replace those with `Missing[]` which the time series functions will ignore by default.

```
In[54]:= test4 = test3 /. {lis : {__}, sn_ /; sn == -1} :→ {lis, Missing[]}
Out[54]= {{{1818, 1, 1, 0, 0, 0.}, Missing[]}, {{1818, 1, 2, 0, 0, 0.}, Missing[]},
  {{2015, 7, 30, 0, 0, 0.}, 74}, {{2015, 7, 31, 0, 0, 0.}, 114}}
```

Finally, the data is converted to a `TimeSeries` object which will simplify visualization and analysis.

```
In[55]:= TimeSeries[test4]
Out[55]= TimeSeries[ Time: 01 Jan 1818 to 31 Jul 2015
                     Data points: 4 ]
```

Now we repeat the above steps for the entire data set.

```
In[56]:= data2 = data /. lis : {y_, m_, d_, _, _, _, _, _} :→ Most[lis];

In[57]:= data3 = data2 /.
           {y_Integer, m_, d_, _Real, sn_Integer, __} :→ {DateList[{y, m, d}], sn};

In[58]:= data4 = data3 /. {lis : {__}, sn_ /; sn == -1} :→ {lis, Missing[]};
```

This is the form we need for time series functions, so we are ready to convert the entire data set into a `TimeSeries` object.

```
In[59]:= tsData = TimeSeries[data4]

Out[59]= TimeSeries[ Time: 01 Jan 1818 to 31 Jul 2015
                     Data points: 72165 ]
```

The time series is ready to be passed to `DateListPlot` to get a quick visualization of the raw data.

```
In[60]:= DateListPlot[tsData, AspectRatio → 1 / 4, Filling → Bottom]
```

Out[60]=

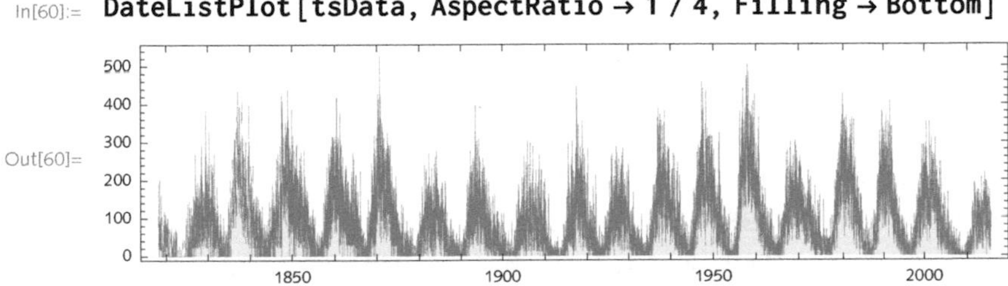

Although the periodic nature of the sunspot activity is already quite visible, some further work is needed: much of the sunspot data is known to be unreliable prior to 1849, so we will start the series at that point (using `TimeSeriesWindow`); and since the observations are relatively uncertain, the data is fairly noisy and so we smooth it using a 24-month Gaussian filter.

```
In[61]:= tsw = TimeSeriesWindow[tsData, {AbsoluteTime[{1849, 1, 1}], AbsoluteTime[]}]

Out[61]= TimeSeries[ Time: 01 Jan 1849 to 31 Jul 2015
                     Data points: 60842 ]

In[62]:= gfData = GaussianFilter[tsw, 24 × 30];
         DateListPlot[gfData, AspectRatio → 1 / 4]
```

Out[63]=

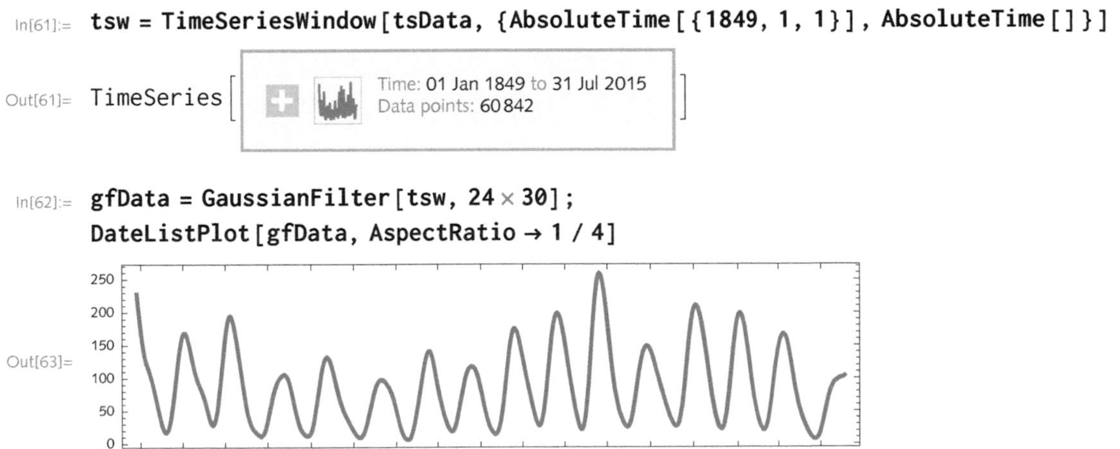

We could go a few steps further and compute the frequency of the peaks. Some experimentation is necessary to find the correct scale for `FindPeaks`.

```
In[64]:= peaks = FindPeaks[gfData, 365]

Out[64]= TimeSeries[ Time: 01 Jan 1849 to 31 Jul 2015
                     Data points: 16 ]

In[65]:= DateListPlot[{gfData, peaks}, AspectRatio → 1 / 4, Joined → {True, False},
           PlotStyle → {Automatic, {Red, PointSize[Medium]}}]

Out[65]=
```

To extract the dates from the time-series peaks and convert to date lists, we need to map `DateList` across these values (`Map` is discussed in the next chapter).

```
In[66]:= dates = Map[DateList, peaks["Times"]]

Out[66]= {{1849, 1, 1, 0, 0, 0.}, {1860, 3, 29, 0, 0, 0.},
          {1871, 1, 18, 0, 0, 0.}, {1883, 9, 19, 0, 0, 0.}, {1893, 11, 14, 0, 0, 0.},
          {1906, 5, 24, 0, 0, 0.}, {1917, 12, 16, 0, 0, 0.},
          {1927, 9, 8, 0, 0, 0.}, {1938, 1, 1, 0, 0, 0.}, {1948, 2, 11, 0, 0, 0.},
          {1958, 2, 5, 0, 0, 0.}, {1969, 2, 13, 0, 0, 0.}, {1980, 7, 2, 0, 0, 0.},
          {1990, 5, 24, 0, 0, 0.}, {2001, 4, 16, 0, 0, 0.}, {2015, 7, 31, 0, 0, 0.}}
```

To get the differences between each pair of peaks, we create successive pairs of the dates with `Partition` and then use a transformation rule to pass each pair of dates to `DateDifference`.

```
In[67]:= Partition[dates, 2, 1] /.
           {d1 : {__}, d2 : {__}} :→ DateDifference[d1, d2, "Year"]

Out[67]= {11.2404 yr , 10.8082 yr , 12.6685 yr , 10.1534 yr , 12.5233 yr ,
          11.5644 yr , 9.72877 yr , 10.3151 yr , 10.112 yr , 9.98356 yr ,
          11.0219 yr , 11.3825 yr , 9.89315 yr , 10.8959 yr , 14.2896 yr }
```

And here is the average time span between the cycles, sometimes known as the Schwabe cycle, due to Samuel Heinrich Schwabe who first discovered it in 1843:

```
In[68]:= Mean[%]

Out[68]= 11.1054 yr
```

Exercises

1. Create a predicate function `compositeQ` that tests whether a positive integer is composite. Check it against the built-in `CompositeQ`.

2. Plot the function `Sinc[x]` over the interval $[-2\pi, 2\pi]$ and then use a transformation rule to display a reflection in the *y*-axis. Use `Show[`*plot* `/.` *expr* `:→` *rule*`, PlotRange → All]` to display the transformed plot in such a way that a new plot range is computed.

3. Occasionally, when collecting data from an instrument, the collector fails or returns a bad value. In analyzing the data, the analyst has to make a decision about what to use to replace these bad values. One approach is to replace them with a column mean. Given an array of numbers such as the following, create a function to replace each "NAN" with the mean of the numbers that appear in that column:

```
In[1]:= data = ( 0.9034  "NAN"   0.7163  0.8588
                 0.3031  0.5827  0.2699  0.8063
                 0.0418  0.8426  "NAN"   0.8634
                 "NAN"   0.8913  0.0662  0.8432 );
```

4. Given a two-column array of data

```
In[2]:= data = RandomInteger[{0, 9}, {5, 2}];

In[3]:= MatrixForm[data, TableAlignments → "."]

Out[3]//MatrixForm=
  ( 7  0
    8  2
    1  5
    8  0
    6  7 )
```

create a new array that consists of three columns where the first two columns are identical to the original, but the third column consists of the mean of the two numbers from the first two columns.

$$\begin{pmatrix} 7 & 0 & \frac{7}{2} \\ 8 & 2 & 5 \\ 1 & 5 & 3 \\ 8 & 0 & 4 \\ 6 & 7 & \frac{13}{2} \end{pmatrix}$$

5. Given a graphic produced by `Plot`, use a transformation rule to halve the *y*-coordinate of each point used to construct the plot, then display the result.

6. Extend the counting coins example to take images of coins as the argument to the function.

```
Out[4]= 0.42
```

7. Create a function `FindSubsequence[digits, subseq]` to find the positions of a subsequence *subseq* within a sequence of numbers given by *digits*. Assume both *digits* and *subseq* are lists of numbers. Your function should return a list of the starting and ending positions where the subsequence occurs in the sequence, similar to what `Position` returns. For example, here are the first 50 digits of π:

```
In[5]:= pidigs = First[RealDigits[π, 10, 100]]

Out[5]= {3, 1, 4, 1, 5, 9, 2, 6, 5, 3, 5, 8, 9, 7, 9, 3, 2, 3, 8, 4, 6, 2, 6, 4, 3,
  3, 8, 3, 2, 7, 9, 5, 0, 2, 8, 8, 4, 1, 9, 7, 1, 6, 9, 3, 9, 9, 3, 7, 5, 1,
  0, 5, 8, 2, 0, 9, 7, 4, 9, 4, 4, 5, 9, 2, 3, 0, 7, 8, 1, 6, 4, 0, 6, 2, 8,
  6, 2, 0, 8, 9, 9, 8, 6, 2, 8, 0, 3, 4, 8, 2, 5, 3, 4, 2, 1, 1, 7, 0, 6, 7}
```

The subsequence 38 appears in two locations in `pidigs`.

```
In[6]:= FindSubsequence[pidigs, {3, 8}]

Out[6]= {{18, 19}, {26, 27}}
```

8. Write another definition of `FindSubsequence` that takes two integers as arguments. So, for example, the following should work:

```
In[7]:= SeedRandom[6];
        n = RandomInteger[10^200]

Out[8]= 38 962 167 906 640 602 500 170 931 211 955 779 575 023 497 774 170 227 858 878 429 522 794 \
  529 744 062 342 783 143 699 902 237 900 976 316 871 609 846 545 097 431 390 396 795 087 845 \
  924 977 005 230 435 025 177 652 637 766 538 981 421 277 296 525 589 205 107 229 653

In[9]:= FindSubsequence[n, 965]

Out[9]= {{181, 183}, {197, 199}}
```

9. Compute the area of a triangle using the following formula for three two-dimensional coordinates (x_i, y_i, z_i) embedded in three-dimensional space:

$$A_\Delta = \frac{1}{2}\sqrt{\left(\begin{vmatrix} x_1 & y_1 & 1 \\ x_2 & y_2 & 1 \\ x_3 & y_3 & 1 \end{vmatrix}^2 + \begin{vmatrix} y_1 & z_1 & 1 \\ y_2 & z_2 & 1 \\ y_3 & z_3 & 1 \end{vmatrix}^2 + \begin{vmatrix} z_1 & x_1 & 1 \\ z_2 & x_2 & 1 \\ z_3 & x_3 & 1 \end{vmatrix}^2\right)}$$

10. Using historical global surface temperatures, make a plot showing the difference in °C from the 1950–1980 average for each year. Data is available from numerous sources, including NASA's Goddard Institute for Space Studies (NASA 2015). After importing the data you will need to remove header and footer information before pouring the pairs `{year, yearly_temp}` into `TimeSeries`. Make the plot using `DateListPlot` and include a smoothed five-year moving average together with the plot of the raw data.

11. Sunspots are caused by magnetic fields which in turn are caused by the current generated by the motion of hot plasma inside the sun. In regions where the induced magnetic field is most intense, the increased pressure causes the region to rise to the surface causing darker regions – sunspots – where the temperature is lower. The mean magnetic field of the sun has been recorded since 1975 and is available from the Wilcox Solar Observatory at Stanford University:

```
In[10]:= data = Import["http://wso.stanford.edu/meanfld/MF_timeseries.txt", "Table"];
         Take[data, 10]
Out[11]= {{Date, Daily, MF, (uT)}, {1975:05:16_20h, 29},
          {1975:05:17_20h, 22}, {1975:05:18_20h, 24}, {1975:05:19_20h, 24},
          {1975:05:20_20h, 13}, {1975:05:21_20h, 4}, {1975:05:22_20h, 4},
          {1975:05:23_20h, XXXX}, {1975:05:24_20h, -3}}
```

Import the solar magnetic field data and create rules to convert the timestamps to a form that the time series functions can work with. You will need to convert the missing measurements (denoted `"XXXX"` in the data) of the magnetic field strength to `Missing[]` which the time series functions will handle more gracefully. Finally, make a plot of the data over the time period using `DateListPlot`.

To convert the date to a usable format, use `DateList` and specify the explicit delimiters.

```
In[12]:= DateList[{"1975:05:18_20h", {"Year", ":", "Month", ":", "Day", "_", "Hour", "h"}}]
Out[12]= {1975, 5, 18, 20, 0, 0.}
```

4.4 Notes and further reading

Several programming languages have included pattern matching as a mechanism to identify and operate on objects, the earliest widely used one being SNOBOL in which patterns were first class data types. Later languages include *Mathematica* and other functional languages such as HASKELL (HaskellWiki).

Collatz sequences, introduced in Exercise 5, Section 4.1 and used throughout this book, have been studied extensively, most notably in Lagarias (2010).

A large literature in computer science exists on sorting algorithms. See Knuth (1998), Sedgewick and Wayne (2011) for details on sorting algorithms and an analysis of their complexity, and also Press et al. (2007). See Maeder (1994) for animations of sorting in action.

The data on water reservoirs in Section 4.3 is from the California Department of Water Resources, which gives historical information on major reservoirs in northern California (CA Data Exchange Center 2015).

Sunspot activity has been observed for over 2000 years but the nature of the 11-year cycle was only first hypothesized at the end of the 18th century by Heinrich Schwabe. Other measures are used to measure solar activity including solar flux (radio emissions at 10.7cm wavelength), total radiant energy emitted at all wavelengths, magnetic fields, flares, coronal mass ejections, and geomagnetic activity. Sunspot numbers have the advantage of a long record of measurement, going back over two centuries. Data for the sunspot time series used in this chapter was imported from the Sunspot Index and Long-term Solar Observations database (Royal Observatory of Belgium 2015). The solar magnetic field data used in Exercise 11, Section 4.3 comes from the Wilcox Observatory at Stanford University (Wilcox 2015). An excellent and accessible survey on the current state of solar research can be found in Hathaway (2010). For a review of solar cycle prediction based on dynamo theory, see Petrovay (2010).

The global sea and land surface temperature data used in Exercise 10, Section 4.3 is from NASA's Goddard Institute for Space Studies (NASA 2015). For additional information about how the temperature data sets are collected, see the National Center for Atmospheric Research (2014).

5

Functions

Functions for manipulating expressions · *Map* · *Apply* · *Thread and MapThread* · *Listability* · *Inner and Outer* · *Select and Pick* · ***Iterating functions*** · *Nest* · *FixedPoint* · *NestWhile* · *Fold* · ***Recursive functions*** · *Fibonacci numbers* · *Thinking recursively* · *Dynamic programming* · ***Loops and flow control*** · *Conditional functions* · *Piecewise-defined functions* · *Which and Switch* · *Argument checking* · *Do and For loops* · *While loops* · ***Pure functions*** · *Syntax of pure functions* · *Multiple arguments* · *Pure predicate functions* · *Indexing with pure functions* · *Newton revisited* · *Example: searching for attributes* · ***Examples*** · *Hamming distance* · *The Josephus problem* · *Protein interaction networks* · *Operating on arrays* · *Enumerating binary matrices* · *Clustering data* · ***Notes and further reading***

Functional programming – the use and evaluation of functions as a programming paradigm – has a long and productive history in the world of programming languages. LISP came about in the 1950s in the search for a convenient language to represent mathematical concepts in programs, borrowing from the lambda calculus of the logician Alonzo Church. More recent languages have in turn embraced many aspects of LISP – in addition to LISP's offspring such as SCHEME and HASKELL, you will find elements of functional constructs in JAVA, PYTHON, RUBY, and PERL. *Mathematica* itself has clear bloodlines to LISP, including the ability to operate on data structures such as lists as single objects and in its representation of mathematical properties through rules.

Mathematica functions, unlike those in many other languages, are considered "first-class" objects, meaning that they can be used as arguments to other functions, they can be returned as values, and they can be part of many other kinds of data objects such as arrays. In addition, you can create and use functions at runtime, that is, when you evaluate an expression. This *functional* style of programming distinguishes *Mathematica* from traditional procedural languages like C and FORTRAN. Facility with functional programming is therefore essential for taking full advantage of the *Mathematica* language to solve your computational tasks.

We start with some of the most useful functional programming constructs – higher-order functions such as `Map`, `Apply`, `Thread`, `Select`, and `Outer`. We then introduce iteration, a mechanism by which the output of one computation is fed as input into the next. Recursive functions, a form of iteration in which earlier values of a discrete function are used for subsequent computation, are covered in Section 5.3.

Although looping and flow control are generally thought of as procedural constructs, they are implemented and used in *Mathematica* in a functional manner; that is, control structures such as `Do` and `For` are themselves functions. They are introduced in Section 5.4.

Section 5.5 introduces one of the unique features of a functional language such as *Mathematica* – the ability to create a function at runtime, meaning that you do not need to formally declare such a function before using it. This is implemented through the construct of pure functions.

The chapter closes with several applied examples: the detection of errors in signals; the Josephus problem, an ancient counting problem; the representation and visualization of protein–protein interaction networks; a problem in filtering and processing data arrays; enumeration problems on binary matrices with connections to graph theory; and the visualization of clustered data.

5.1 Functions for manipulating expressions

Three of the most commonly-used functions in *Mathematica* programs are `Map`, `Apply`, and `Thread`. They provide efficient and comprehensive means of operating on and transforming expressions. In this section we will discuss their syntax and look at some basic examples of their use. We will also briefly look at some additional functions (`Inner` and `Outer`), which will prove useful in manipulating lists in a variety of ways; finally, in this section we introduce `Select` and `Pick`, which are used to extract elements of an expression based on some criteria of interest. These higher-order functions are in the toolkit of every experienced *Mathematica* programmer and they will be used throughout the rest of this book.

Map

Performing the same operation on every element in a list is a common task; it is accomplished by mapping a function across that list. For example, this maps the `Head` function across a short list:

```
In[1]:= vec = {1.5, π, I};

In[2]:= Map[Head, vec]
Out[2]= {Real, Symbol, Complex}
```

More generally, mapping a function `h` over the expression `g[a, b, c]` essentially wraps the function `h` around each of the elements of `g`.

```
In[3]:= Map[h, g[a, b, c]]
Out[3]= g[h[a], h[b], h[c]]
```

This symbolic computation is structurally identical to `Map[h, {a, b, c}]`, except in that example `g` is replaced with `List` (remember that the internal form of `{a, b, c}` is `List[a, b, c]`).

The real power of Map is that you can map any function across any expression for which it makes sense. For example, to reverse the order of elements in each list of a nested list, map the Reverse function. Map operates on the elements of the outer list, that is, it operates on the sublists.

```
In[4]:= Map[Reverse, {{a, b}, {c, d}, {e, f}}]
Out[4]= {{b, a}, {d, c}, {f, e}}
```

Mapping Sort over a nested list sorts the inner lists, that is, it sorts the *elements* of the larger list, the expressions at level one.

```
In[5]:= Map[Sort, {{2, 6, 3, 5}, {7, 4, 1, 3}}]
Out[5]= {{2, 3, 5, 6}, {1, 3, 4, 7}}
```

Often, you will need to define your own function to perform a computation on each element of a list. For example, to square each element and add one, you could first define a function that performs this computation on its arguments.

```
In[6]:= f[x_] := x^2 + 1
```

Mapping this function over vec will wrap f around each element and evaluate f of those elements.

```
In[7]:= Map[f, vec]
Out[7]= {3.25, 1 + π^2, 0}
```

The Map function is such a commonly used function that a shorthand notation exists for it: *fun* /@ *expr* is equivalent to Map[*fun*, *expr*]. Hence, the above computation can also be written as

```
In[8]:= f /@ vec
Out[8]= {3.25, 1 + π^2, 0}
```

While it does make your code more compact, the use of such shorthand notation comes at the cost of readability. Experienced *Mathematica* programmers and those who prefer such an infix notation tend to use them liberally. We will use the longer form in general but encourage you to become comfortable with either syntax as it will make it easier for you to read programs created by others.

Apply

Whereas Map is used to perform the same operation on each element of an expression, Apply is used to change the structure of expressions. For example, applying the function h to the expression g[a, b, c] results in the head of g[a, b, c] being replaced with h.

```
In[9]:= Apply[h, g[a, b, c]]
Out[9]= h[a, b, c]
```

If the second argument is a list, applying h to that expression replaces its head (List) with h.

```
In[10]:= Apply[h, {a, b, c}]
Out[10]= h[a, b, c]
```

The following computation shows the same thing, except that we are using the internal representation of the list `{a, b, c}` here to better see how the structure is changed.

```
In[11]:= Apply[h, List[a, b, c]]
Out[11]= h[a, b, c]
```

The elements of `List` have become the arguments of `h`. You should think of `Apply[h, `*expr*`]` as replacing the head of *expr* with `h`.

In the following example, `List[1, 2, 3, 4]` has been changed to `Plus[1, 2, 3, 4]` or, in other words, the head `List` has been replaced by `Plus`:

```
In[12]:= Apply[Plus, {1, 2, 3, 4}]
Out[12]= 10
```

`Plus[1, 2, 3, 4]` is the internal representation of the sum of these four numbers that you would normally write 1 + 2 + 3 + 4.

```
In[13]:= Plus[1, 2, 3, 4]
Out[13]= 10
```

Tip 5.1

If you are a little unsure of what is happening in the above examples, consider the following and, instead of `plus`, think of `Plus`:

```
In[14]:= Apply[plus, {1, 2, 3, 4}]
Out[14]= plus[1, 2, 3, 4]
```

This is a useful general tip: use a symbol that has no built-in meaning like this to help you see the structure of the expressions after evaluation.

`Apply` has a shorthand notation: the expression *fun* @@ *expr* is equivalent to `Apply[`*fun*`, `*expr*`]`. So, the above computation could be written as follows:

```
In[15]:= Plus @@ {1, 2, 3, 4}
Out[15]= 10
```

One important distinction between `Map` and `Apply` has to do with the level in the expression at which each operates. By default, `Map` operates at level one. That is, in `Map[`*h*`, `*expr*`]`, *h* will be applied to each element at the top level of *expr*. So, for example, if *expr* consists of a nested list, *h* will be applied to each of the sublists, but not deeper, by default.

```
In[16]:= Map[h, {{a, b}, {c, d}}]
Out[16]= {h[{a, b}], h[{c, d}]}
```

To apply `h` at a deeper level, specify it explicitly with a third argument to `Map`.

```
In[17]:= Map[h, {{a, b}, {c, d}}, {2}]
Out[17]= {{h[a], h[b]}, {h[c], h[d]}}
```

Apply, in contrast, operates at level zero by default. That is, in Apply[*h*, *expr*], Apply looks at part zero of *expr* (its head) and replaces it with *h*.

```
In[18]:= Apply[h, {{a, b}, {c, d}}]
Out[18]= h[{a, b}, {c, d}]
```

To apply *h* at a different level, use a third argument to Apply.

```
In[19]:= Apply[h, {{a, b}, {c, d}}, {1}]
Out[19]= {h[a, b], h[c, d]}
```

For example, to apply Plus to each of the inner lists, you specify that Apply will operate at level one.

```
In[20]:= Apply[Plus, {{1, 2, 3}, {5, 6, 7}}, {1}]
Out[20]= {6, 18}
```

Applying at the default level zero is different. The outer List is replaced with Plus giving vector addition, adding element-wise.

```
In[21]:= Apply[Plus, {{1, 2, 3}, {5, 6, 7}}]
Out[21]= {6, 8, 10}
```

Applying functions at level one is also a common task and it too has a shorthand notation: *fun* @@@ *expr* is equivalent to Apply[*fun*, *expr*, {1}].

```
In[22]:= Plus @@@ {{1, 2, 3}, {5, 6, 7}}
Out[22]= {6, 18}
```

Thread and MapThread

The Thread function "threads" a function over several lists. Think of it as extracting the first element from each of the lists, wrapping a function around them, then extracting the next element in each list and wrapping the function around them, and so on.

```
In[23]:= Thread[g[{a, b, c}, {x, y, z}]]
Out[23]= {g[a, x], g[b, y], g[c, z]}
```

Using a slightly different syntax, you can accomplish the same thing with MapThread. It differs from Thread in that it takes two arguments – the function that you are mapping and a list of two (or more) lists as arguments of the function. It creates a new list in which the corresponding elements of the old lists are paired, or zipped, together.

```
In[24]:= MapThread[g, {{a, b, c}, {x, y, z}}]
Out[24]= {g[a, x], g[b, y], g[c, z]}
```

You could perform this computation manually by first zipping together the two lists using Transpose, and then applying g at level one.

```
In[25]:= Transpose[{{a, b, c}, {x, y, z}}]
Out[25]= {{a, x}, {b, y}, {c, z}}
```

```
In[26]:= Apply[g, %, {1}]
Out[26]= {g[a, x], g[b, y], g[c, z]}
```

With Thread, you can fundamentally change the structure of the expressions you are using. For example, threading Equal over the following two lists creates a list of equalities:

```
In[27]:= Thread[Equal[{x, y, z}, {a, b, c}]]
Out[27]= {x == a, y == b, z == c}
```

```
In[28]:= Map[FullForm, %]
Out[28]= {Equal[x, a], Equal[y, b], Equal[z, c]}
```

As another Thread example, we start off with a list of variables and a list of values.

```
In[29]:= vars = {x1, x2, x3, x4, x5};
```

```
In[30]:= values = {1.2, 2.5, 5.7, 8.21, 6.66};
```

From these two lists, we create a list of rules.

```
In[31]:= Thread[Rule[vars, values]]
Out[31]= {x1 → 1.2, x2 → 2.5, x3 → 5.7, x4 → 8.21, x5 → 6.66}
```

Notice how we started with a *rule of lists* and Thread produced a *list of rules*. In this way, you might think of Thread as a generalized transpose operation.

Thread and MapThread are designed for situations where you need to slot values into a function of two or more arguments and these values come from different lists. As an example, a circle, represented in *Mathematica* by the graphics primitive Circle, takes two arguments, the center coordinates and the radius. Wrapping Graphics around this primitive displays the object.

```
In[32]:= Graphics[Circle[{0, 0}, 1]]
```

Out[32]=

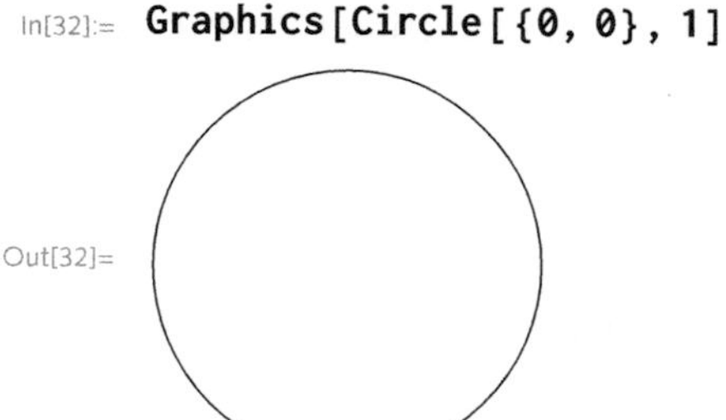

Suppose though that you want to display several circles with centers and radii coming from two different lists.

```
In[33]:= radii = {0.5, 1.0, 0.5};
         centers = {{-1, 0}, {0, 0}, {1, 0}};
```

Using Thread, you can slot these values into Circle as follows:

```
In[35]:= Thread[Circle[centers, radii]]
Out[35]= {Circle[{-1, 0}, 0.5], Circle[{0, 0}, 1.], Circle[{1, 0}, 0.5]}
```

```
In[36]:= Graphics[%]
```

Out[36]=

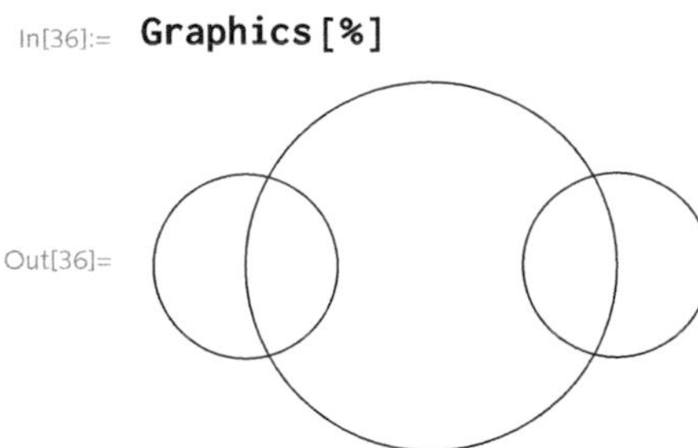

Using the same Graphics expression, any number of objects could be used.

```
In[37]:= radii = RandomReal[{.25, 1.25}, {40}];
         centers = RandomReal[{-1, 1}, {40, 2}];
         Graphics[Thread[Circle[centers, radii]]]
```

Out[39]=

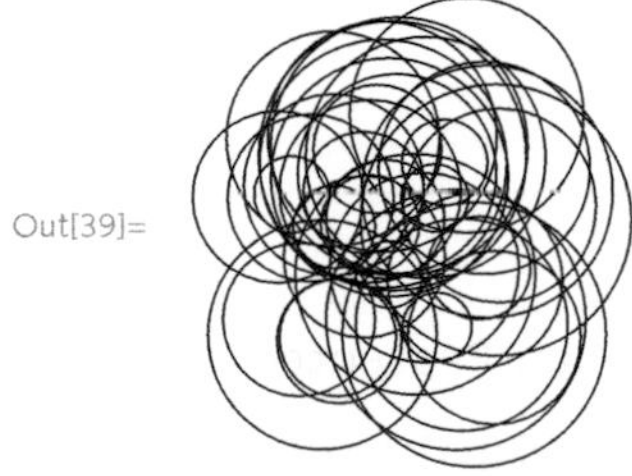

To use MapThread instead, give the second argument as a list of the centers and radii.

```
In[40]:= Graphics[MapThread[Circle, {centers, radii}]]
```

Out[40]=

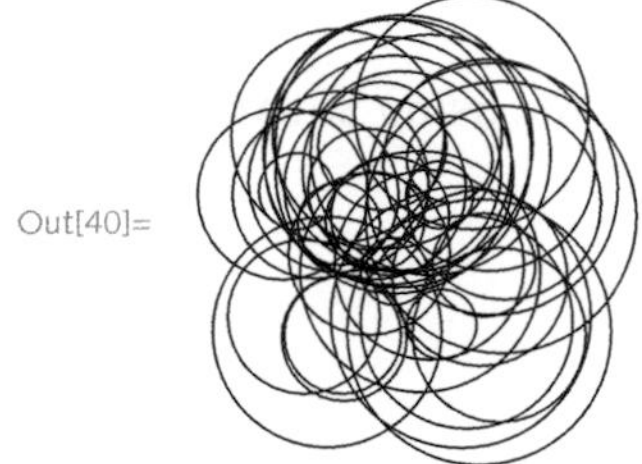

Listability

As we saw in Section 2.5, many of the built-in functions have the Listable attribute, making them automatically map across lists. For example, the Log function has this attribute:

```
In[41]:= Log[{a, E, 1}]
Out[41]= {Log[a], 1, 0}
```

You get the same result using Map, but it is a bit more to write and, as we will see in Chapter 9, the direct approach is much more efficient for large computations.

```
In[42]:= Map[Log, {a, E, 1}]
Out[42]= {Log[a], 1, 0}
```

Similarly, listable functions that take two or more arguments are automatically threaded onto the elements of the lists. For example, the following is essentially vector addition (`Plus` is listable):

```
In[43]:= Plus[{4, 6, 3}, {5, 1, 2}]
Out[43]= {9, 7, 5}
```

Of course, you can just use the more traditional notation.

```
In[44]:= {4, 6, 3} + {5, 1, 2}
Out[44]= {9, 7, 5}
```

This gives the same result as using the `Plus` function with `MapThread`.

```
In[45]:= MapThread[Plus, {{4, 6, 3}, {5, 1, 2}}]
Out[45]= {9, 7, 5}
```

Both `Log` and `Plus` have the `Listable` attribute.

```
In[46]:= Attributes[Log]
Out[46]= {Listable, NumericFunction, Protected}

In[47]:= Attributes[Plus]
Out[47]= {Flat, Listable, NumericFunction, OneIdentity, Orderless, Protected}
```

By default, user-defined functions do not have any attributes associated with them. So, for example, if you define a function g, it will not automatically thread over a list.

```
In[48]:= g[{a, b, c, d}]
Out[48]= g[{a, b, c, d}]
```

To make a function map and thread over lists, give it the `Listable` attribute using `SetAttributes`.

```
In[49]:= SetAttributes[g, Listable]

In[50]:= g[{a, b, c, d}]
Out[50]= {g[a], g[b], g[c], g[d]}
```

Tip 5.2

Clearing a symbol only clears values associated with that symbol. It does not clear any attributes associated with that symbol. So after clearing, g still has the attribute we gave it earlier.

```
In[51]:= Clear[g]

In[52]:= ?g

  Global`g

Attributes[g] = {Listable}
```

Use `ClearAttributes` to clear specific attributes associated with a symbol.

```
In[53]:= ClearAttributes[g, Listable]
```

To clear all values, definitions, attributes, and messages associated with a symbol, use `ClearAll`.

```
In[54]:= ClearAll[g]
```

```
In[55]:= ?g
```

```
Global`g
```

Inner and Outer

In linear algebra, the *outer product* of two vectors is the matrix obtained by multiplying each element of one vector by each element of the other vector. It generalizes to matrices and tensors as the tensor product. The `Outer` function applies a function to all the combinations of the elements in several lists and so is a generalization of the mathematical outer product.

```
In[56]:= Outer[f, {x, y}, {2, 3, 4}]
Out[56]= {{f[x, 2], f[x, 3], f[x, 4]}, {f[y, 2], f[y, 3], f[y, 4]}}
```

Using the `List` function as an argument, you can create lists of ordered pairs that combine the elements of several lists.

```
In[57]:= Outer[List, {x, y}, {2, 3, 4}]
Out[57]= {{{x, 2}, {x, 3}, {x, 4}}, {{y, 2}, {y, 3}, {y, 4}}}
```

The classical outer product of two vectors is obtained by wrapping `Times` around pairs of elements.

```
In[58]:= Outer[Times, {u1, u2, u3}, {v1, v2, v3, v4}] // MatrixForm
Out[58]//MatrixForm=
```

$$\begin{pmatrix} u_1 v_1 & u_1 v_2 & u_1 v_3 & u_1 v_4 \\ u_2 v_1 & u_2 v_2 & u_2 v_3 & u_2 v_4 \\ u_3 v_1 & u_3 v_2 & u_3 v_3 & u_3 v_4 \end{pmatrix}$$

With `Inner`, you can thread a function onto several lists and then use the result as the argument to another function.

```
In[59]:= Inner[f, {x, y, z}, {d, e, f}, g]
Out[59]= g[f[x, d], f[y, e], f[z, f]]
```

This function lets you carry out some interesting operations.

```
In[60]:= Inner[Equal, {x, y, z}, {a, b, c}, List]
Out[60]= {x == a, y == b, z == c}
```

```
In[61]:= Inner[Times, {x1, y1, z1}, {x2, y2, z2}, Plus]
```

Out[61]= $x_1 x_2 + y_1 y_2 + z_1 z_2$

This last example shows that `Inner` is really a generalization of the familiar matrix dot product.

```
In[62]:= Dot[{x1, y1, z1}, {x2, y2, z2}]
```

Out[62]= $x_1 x_2 + y_1 y_2 + z_1 z_2$

Select and Pick

Suppose you are interested in filtering out all numbers in an array that lie outside a certain range of threshold values. Or you might need to find all values in a file of recorded data that are not explicit numbers. Finding and extracting all those elements of a data set that meet some criteria of interest is a common computational task. We have already seen how you can use Cases with patterns to express the criteria of interest. In this section we will explore two additional functions that can be used for such problems.

Select[*expr*, *predicate*] returns all those elements in *expr* that pass the predicate *test*. For example, here we select those elements in this short list of integers that pass the EvenQ test:

```
In[63]:= Select[{1, 2, 3, 4, 5, 6, 7, 8, 9}, EvenQ]
Out[63]= {2, 4, 6, 8}
```

From a list of the first one hundred Mersenne numbers (numbers of the form $2^n - 1$), this selects those that are prime:

```
In[64]:= Select[Table[2^n - 1, {n, 1, 100}], PrimeQ]
Out[64]= {3, 7, 31, 127, 8191, 131071, 524287, 2147483647,
          2305843009213693951, 618970019642690137449562111}
```

You can also create your own predicates to specify the criteria in which you are interested. For example, given an array of numbers, we first create a function, inRange, that returns a value of True if its argument falls in a certain range, say between 20 and 30.

```
In[65]:= data = {24.39001, 29.669, 9.321, 10.8856, 23.4736, 22.1488, 14.7434,
             22.1619, 21.1039, 34.8177, 27.1331, 25.8705, 39.7676, 24.7762};

In[66]:= inRange[x_] := 20 ≤ x ≤ 30
```

Then, select those elements from data that pass the inRange test.

```
In[67]:= Select[data, inRange]
Out[67]= {24.39, 29.669, 23.4736, 22.1488, 22.1619, 21.1039, 27.1331, 25.8705, 24.7762}
```

Pick can also be used to extract elements based on predicates, but it is more general than just that. In its simplest form, Pick[*expr*, *selList*] returns those elements from *expr* whose corresponding value in *selList* is True.

```
In[68]:= Pick[{a, b, c, d, e}, {True, False, True, False, True}]
Out[68]= {a, c, e}
```

You can also use binary values in the second argument, but then you need to provide a third argument to Pick indicating what the selector value is. In this case, it is 1:

```
In[69]:= Pick[{a, b, c, d, e}, {1, 0, 1, 0, 1}, 1]
Out[69]= {a, c, e}
```

See Exercise 10, Section 5.6 for an applied example of the use of Pick to create random graphs.

Exercises

1. Use `Partition` and `Mean` to create a two-term moving average. Then repeat for a three-term moving average. Check your results against the built-in `MovingAverage` function.

```
In[1]:= MovingAverage[{a, b, c, d, e}, 2]
```

Out[1]= $\left\{\frac{a+b}{2}, \frac{b+c}{2}, \frac{c+d}{2}, \frac{d+e}{2}\right\}$

2. Use `Apply` to rewrite the definition of `squareMatrixQ` given in Section 4.1.

3. Use `Inner` to replicate the result in the text that used `Thread` to create a list of equations.

```
In[2]:= Thread[Equal[{x, y, z}, {a, b, c}]]
Out[2]= {x == a, y == b, z == c}
```

4. Heron's formula for the area of a triangle is given as follows:

$$A = \sqrt{s\,(s-a)\,(s-b)\,(s-c)}$$

where a, b, and c are the lengths of the three sides of the triangle and s is the semiperimeter of the triangle, defined by $s = (a+b+c)/2$. Compute the area of any triangle using Heron's formula. You can check your result against the built-in `Area` function.

```
In[3]:= pt1 = {0, 0}; pt2 = {5, 2}; pt3 = {3, 4};
        Graphics[Triangle[{pt1, pt2, pt3}], Axes → Automatic]
```

Out[4]=

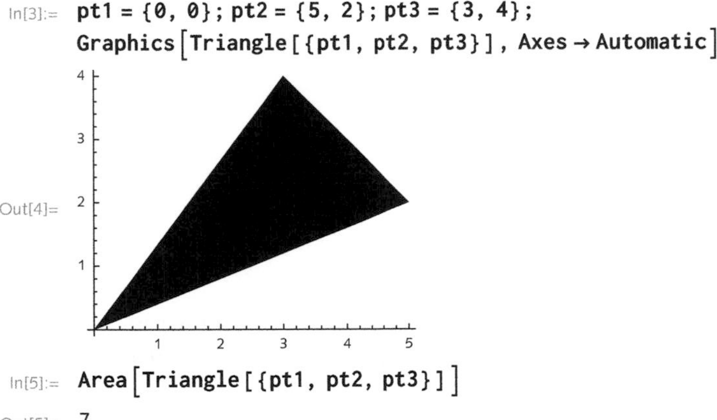


```
In[5]:= Area[Triangle[{pt1, pt2, pt3}]]
Out[5]= 7
```

5. Find all square numbers that contain the digits one through nine exactly once (see Madachy 1979). Use `SquareNumberQ` from Exercise 4 in Section 2.4.

6. In Section 2.4 we defined a predicate `PerfectQ[n]` that returns `True` if n is a perfect number (n is a perfect number if it is equal to the sum of its proper divisors). Create a function `PerfectSearch[n]` that finds all perfect numbers less than n. Then find all perfect numbers less than 10^6.

7. Turn the computation from Exercise 6 of Section 3.3 into a reusable function `PrimesLessThan[n]` that returns all prime numbers less than n.

8. One of the tasks in analyzing DNA sequences is determining the frequency with which the individual nucleotides G, C, A, and T occur. In addition, the frequency of longer "words" is often also of interest. For example, words of length two (or longer) such as AG, AT, CC are sometimes used to find locations in the sequence where an evolutionary change may have occurred.

Nucleotides are generally represented as strings, so starting with the list {"A", "T", "G", "C"}, create a list of all possible two-letter words from this alphabet. You can use StringJoin to return a string consisting of the concatenation of two strings.

```
In[6]:= StringJoin[{"A", "T"}] // InputForm
Out[6]//InputForm=
        "AT"
```

Finally, generalize this process to create words of length n for any such alphabet. For example, you could use a list of the amino acids as your alphabet.

```
In[7]:= aa = {"A", "R", "N", "D", "C", "E", "Q", "G", "H", "I",
          "L", "K", "M", "F", "P", "O", "U", "S", "T", "W", "Y", "V"};
```

9. Create a function LeadingDigit[*n*] that takes an integer *n* as an argument and returns the leading digit of *n* (see Exercise 7, Section 3.3). Set up your function so that it returns the leading digits of a list of numbers such as the first 10 000 Fibonacci numbers.

10. Given a set of points in the plane, find the bounding rectangle that fully encloses the points. For three-dimensional sets of points, find the bounding rectangular box. (See Figure 5.1.)

FIGURE 5.1. *Bounding boxes (dashed lines) for points in two and three dimensions.*

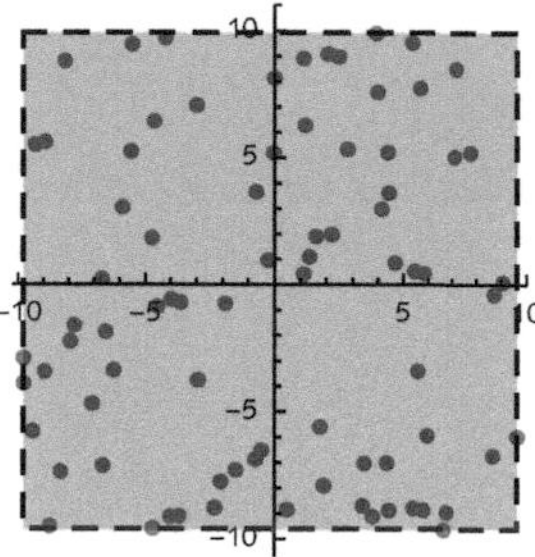

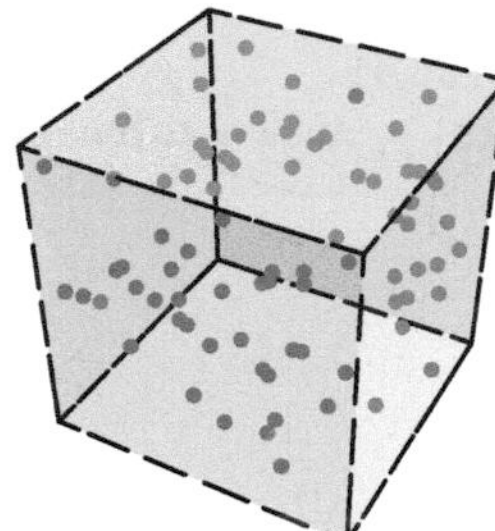

11. Given a set of points in the plane (or 3-space), find the maximum distance between any pair of these points. This is often called the *diameter* of the point set. If your definition is general enough it should be able to handle points in any dimension.

12. Create a graphic that consists of *n* randomly colored circles in the plane with random centers and random radii. Consider using Thread or MapThread to thread Circle[...] across the lists of centers and radii.

13. While matrices can easily be added using Plus, matrix multiplication is a bit more involved. The Dot function, written as a single period, is used.

```
In[8]:= {{1, 2}, {3, 4}}.{x, y}
Out[8]= {x + 2 y, 3 x + 4 y}
```

Perform matrix multiplication on {{1, 2}, {3, 4}} and {x, y} without using Dot.

14. An adjacency matrix can be thought of as representing a graph of vertices and edges where a value of one in position a_{ij} indicates an edge between vertex i and vertex j, whereas a value of zero indicates no such edge between vertices i and j.

```
In[9]:=  mat = RandomInteger[1, {5, 5}];
         MatrixForm[mat]

Out[10]//MatrixForm=
         ( 1 0 1 0 1 )
         ( 0 1 0 1 1 )
         ( 1 1 1 1 0 )
         ( 0 1 0 0 1 )
         ( 0 1 1 1 1 )

In[11]:= AdjacencyGraph[mat, VertexLabels → "Name"]

Out[11]=
```

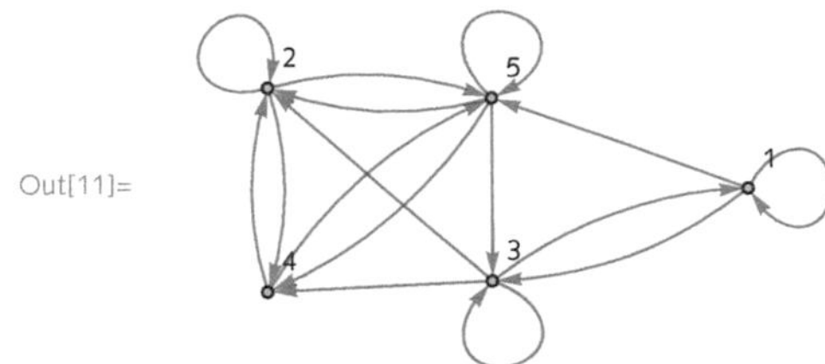

Compute the total number of edges for each vertex in both the adjacency matrix and graph representations. For example, you should get the following edge counts for the five vertices represented in the above graph. Note: self-loops count as two edges each.

```
{5, 7, 7, 5, 8}
```

15. Create a function `ToEdges[`*lis*`]` that takes a list of pairs of elements and transforms it into a list of directed edges suitable for a graph. For example:

```
In[12]:= lis = RandomInteger[9, {12, 2}]

Out[12]= {{1, 4}, {1, 5}, {1, 7}, {1, 9}, {8, 0},
          {3, 1}, {9, 2}, {6, 2}, {3, 4}, {4, 4}, {7, 6}, {2, 8}}

In[13]:= ToEdges[lis]

Out[13]= {1 → 4, 1 → 5, 1 → 7, 1 → 9, 8 → 0,
          3 → 1, 9 → 2, 6 → 2, 3 → 4, 4 → 4, 7 → 6, 2 → 8}
```

Make sure that your function also works in the case where its argument is a single list of a pair of elements.

```
In[14]:= ToEdges[{3, 6}]

Out[14]= 3 → 6
```

16. `FactorInteger[`*n*`]` returns a nested list of prime factors and their exponents for the number *n*.

```
In[15]:= FactorInteger[3628800]

Out[15]= {{2, 8}, {3, 4}, {5, 2}, {7, 1}}
```

Use `Apply` to reconstruct the original number from this nested list.

17. Repeat the above exercise but instead use `Inner` to reconstruct the original number *n* from the factorization given by `FactorInteger[`*n*`]`.

18. Create a function `PrimeFactorForm[`*n*`]` that formats its argument *n* in prime factorization form. You will need to use `Superscript` and `CenterDot` to format the factored integer.

```
In[16]:= PrimeFactorForm[12]
```

Out[16]= $2^2 \cdot 3^1$

19. The Vandermonde matrix arises in Lagrange interpolation and in reconstructing statistical distributions from their moments. Construct the Vandermonde matrix of order n:

$$\begin{pmatrix} 1 & x_1 & x_1^2 & \cdots & x_1^{n-1} \\ 1 & x_2 & x_2^2 & \cdots & x_2^{n-1} \\ \vdots & \vdots & \vdots & \ddots & \vdots \\ 1 & x_n & x_n^2 & \cdots & x_n^{n-1} \end{pmatrix}$$

20. Using `Inner`, write a function `div[`*vecs*`,` *vars*`]` that computes the divergence of an n-dimensional vector field, `vecs` = $\{e_1, e_2, \ldots, e_n\}$, dependent upon n variables, `vars` = $\{v_1, v_2, \ldots, v_n\}$. The divergence is given by the sum of the pairwise partial derivatives.

$$\frac{\partial e_1}{\partial v_1} + \frac{\partial e_2}{\partial v_2} + \cdots + \frac{\partial e_n}{\partial v_n}$$

21. Using `Outer`, create a function `JacobianMatrix[`*vec*`,` *vars*`]` that returns the Jacobian of the vector *vec* in the variables given by the list *vars*. Then use `JacobianMatrix` to compute the volume of the hypersphere in two (circle) and three (sphere) dimensions by integrating the absolute value of the determinant of the Jacobian.

22. The example in this section on `Select` and `Pick` found Mersenne numbers $2^n - 1$ that are prime for exponents n from 1 to 100. Modify that example to only use prime exponents – a basic theorem in number theory states that a Mersenne number with composite exponent must be composite (Crandall and Pomerance 2005).

5.2 Iterating functions

A common task in computer science, mathematics, and many sciences is the repeated application of a function to some expression. Iterating functions has a long tradition in the history of computing, with perhaps the most famous example being Newton's method for finding roots of functions.

In this section, we introduce several functions for iteration of functions and symbolic expressions. In later chapters we will apply these and other programming constructs to look at applications of iteration, including Newton's method, the visualization of Julia sets, and several iterative algorithms in numerical computation.

Nest

The `Nest` function is used to iterate functions. In this first example, g is iterated four times starting with initial value a:

```
In[1]:= Nest[g, a, 4]
Out[1]= g[g[g[g[a]]]]
```

`NestList` performs the same iteration but displays all the intermediate values.

```
In[2]:= NestList[g, a, 4]
Out[2]= {a, g[a], g[g[a]], g[g[g[a]]], g[g[g[g[a]]]]}
```

Using a starting value of 0.85, this generates a list of six iterates of the Cos function:

```
In[3]:= NestList[Cos, 0.85, 6]
Out[3]= {0.85, 0.659983, 0.790003, 0.703843, 0.76236, 0.723208, 0.749687}
```

The list elements above are the values of 0.85, Cos[0.85], Cos[Cos[0.85]], and so on.

```
In[4]:= {0.85, Cos[0.85], Cos[Cos[0.85]], Cos[Cos[Cos[0.85]]]}
Out[4]= {0.85, 0.659983, 0.790003, 0.703843}
```

Tip 5.3

As mentioned earlier, you can use a lowercase symbol cos to help you see the structure of the computations. But, be careful to keep the iteration count manageable; otherwise, you can easily generate many pages of symbolic output on your screen.

```
In[5]:= NestList[cos, 0.85, 8]
Out[5]= {0.85, cos[0.85], cos[cos[0.85]], cos[cos[cos[0.85]]],
  cos[cos[cos[cos[0.85]]]], cos[cos[cos[cos[cos[0.85]]]]],
  cos[cos[cos[cos[cos[cos[0.85]]]]]], cos[cos[cos[cos[cos[cos[cos[0.85]]]]]]],
  cos[cos[cos[cos[cos[cos[cos[cos[0.85]]]]]]]]}
```

The objects that you can iterate are entirely general – they could be formulas or graphics. For example, suppose you had a triangle in the plane that you wanted to rotate iteratively. Starting with a set of vertices, here is a display of the initial triangle, using some graphics directives to change its display attributes (see Section 8.1 for more on graphics directives):

```
In[6]:= vertices = {{0, 0}, {1, 0}, {1/2, √3/2}};

In[7]:= tri = Triangle[vertices];

In[8]:= Graphics[{LightBlue, EdgeForm[Gray], tri}]
```

Out[8]=

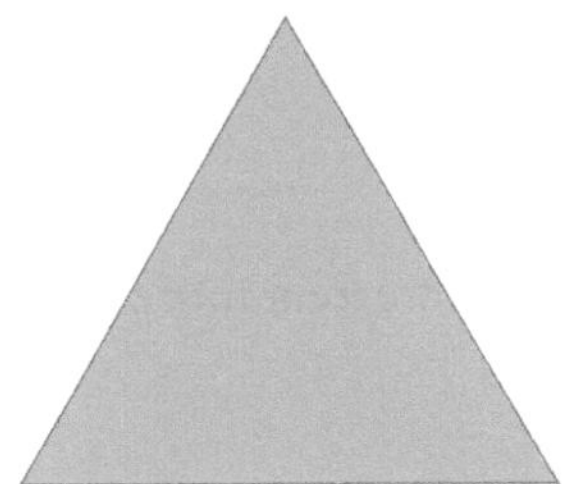

Next, we create the rotation function that will be iterated inside of NestList. The built-in function Rotate takes a graphics object (our triangle), an angle, and a point to rotate about; we will rotate about the center of mass of the triangle.

```
In[9]:= rotation[gr_] := Rotate[gr, π/13, RegionCentroid[tri]]
```

Here are ten steps of this iteration:

```
In[10]:= Graphics[{
           LightBlue, Opacity[.5], EdgeForm[Gray],
           NestList[rotation, tri, 10]
          }]
```

Out[10]=

Or you can iterate a translation. First, create some translation vectors.

```
In[11]:= vecs = 1 / 2 vertices
```

Out[11]= $\left\{\{0, 0\}, \left\{\frac{1}{2}, 0\right\}, \left\{\frac{1}{4}, \frac{\sqrt{3}}{4}\right\}\right\}$

The `translation` function creates three objects translated by the vectors `vecs`. `NestList` then iterates this translation function two times. The original triangle is displayed thick and red.

```
In[12]:= translation[gr_] := Translate[gr, vecs]
```

```
In[13]:= Graphics[{Opacity[0], EdgeForm[Gray],
           NestList[translation, tri, 2],
           EdgeForm[{Thick, Red}], tri
          }]
```

Out[13]=

The exercises at the end of this section build upon these examples to create a more interesting and well-known object, the Sierpiński triangle.

FixedPoint

The iterates of the cosine function in the previous section converge to a fixed point; that is, a point x such that $x = \cos(x)$. `Nest` requires you to specify how many iterations to perform, but how many are enough? To apply a function repeatedly to an expression until it no longer changes, use `FixedPoint`. For example, here is a function that, when iterated, converges to the Golden ratio:

In[14]:= `golden[ϕ_] := 1 +` $\frac{1}{\phi}$

```
In[15]:= FixedPoint[golden, 1.0]
Out[15]= 1.61803
```

`FixedPointList` displays all the intermediate results. `InputForm` shows all the digits computed, making it easier to see the convergence. Here we display every fourth element in the list:

```
In[16]:= phi = FixedPointList[golden, 1.0];

In[17]:= phi[[1 ;; -1 ;; 4]] // InputForm
Out[17]//InputForm=
         {1., 1.6, 1.6176470588235294, 1.6180257510729614,
          1.618033813400125, 1.618033985017358, 1.6180339886704433,
          1.6180339887482038, 1.618033988749859, 1.618033988749894}
```

It takes thirty-nine iterations to reach the fixed point (thirty-eight if you don't count the initial value).

```
In[18]:= Length[FixedPointList[golden, 1.0]]
Out[18]= 39
```

Sometimes, the iteration does not converge quickly and you need to relax the constraint on the closeness of successive iterates. Sometimes the iteration never settles down.

```
In[19]:= f[z_] := z^2 + -0.8 - 0.156 ⅈ
         julia[z_] := FixedPointList[f, z]

In[21]:= julia[-0.5 + 1.5 ⅈ] // Short

         General::ovfl : Overflow occurred in computation. ≫
Out[21]//Short=
         {-0.5 + 1.5 ⅈ, -2.8 - 1.656 ⅈ, <<51>>, Overflow[], Overflow[]}
```

In such cases, you can give an optional third argument to indicate the maximum number of iterations to perform, or you can specify a looser tolerance for the comparison of successive iterates, or, as in the following, you can specify a bound for the iterates:

```
In[22]:= julia[z_] := FixedPointList[f, z, SameTest → (Abs[#2] > 4.0 &)]
```

With this definition, the iteration stops when the distance to the origin of the complex values is greater than 4.0. (We discuss the odd notation involving # and & in Section 5.5, on pure functions.)

```
In[23]:= julia[-0.5 + 1.5 ⅈ]
Out[23]= {-0.5 + 1.5 ⅈ, -2.8 - 1.656 ⅈ, 4.29766 + 9.1176 ⅈ}
```

NestWhile

The `Nest` function iterates a fixed number of times, whereas `FixedPoint` iterates until a fixed point is reached. Sometimes you need to iterate until a condition is met. `NestWhile` (or `NestWhileList`) is perfect for this. For example, here we find the next prime after a given number by adding one and if the result passes the composite test, adding one and checking again. When the test fails – when the number fails to be composite – the iteration stops and returns the result of the last iteration.

```
In[24]:= addOne[n_] := n + 1

In[25]:= NestWhile[addOne, 2^100, CompositeQ]
Out[25]= 1 267 650 600 228 229 401 496 703 205 653

In[26]:= PrimeQ[%]
Out[26]= True
```

Verify with the built-in function that computes the next prime after a given number.

```
In[27]:= NextPrime[2^100]
Out[27]= 1 267 650 600 228 229 401 496 703 205 653
```

Fold

Whereas `Nest` and `NestList` operate on functions of one variable, `Fold` and `FoldList` generalize this notion by iterating a function of two arguments. In the following example, the function `f` is first applied to a starting value `x` and the first element from a list, then this result is used as the first argument of the next iteration, with the second argument coming from the second element in the list, and so on:

```
In[28]:= Fold[f, x, {a, b, c}]
Out[28]= f[f[f[x, a], b], c]
```

Use `FoldList` to see all the intermediate values.

```
In[29]:= FoldList[f, x, {a, b, c}]
Out[29]= {x, f[x, a], f[f[x, a], b], f[f[f[x, a], b], c]}
```

It may be easier to see what is going on with `FoldList` by working with an arithmetic operator. This generates “running sums”:

```
In[30]:= FoldList[Plus, 0, {a, b, c, d, e}]
Out[30]= {0, a, a + b, a + b + c, a + b + c + d, a + b + c + d + e}

In[31]:= FoldList[Plus, 0, {1, 2, 3, 4, 5}]
Out[31]= {0, 1, 3, 6, 10, 15}
```

The built-in `Accumulate` function also creates running sums but it does not return the initial value zero as in the `FoldList` examples above.

```
In[32]:= Accumulate[{1, 2, 3, 4, 5}]
Out[32]= {1, 3, 6, 10, 15}
```

Exercises

1. Use `NestWhileList` to iterate the `julia` function similarly to how it was iterated with `FixedPointList` in the text.
2. Use `NestList` to iterate the process of summing cubes of digits, that is, starting with an initial integer generate a list of the successive sums of cubes of its digits. For example, starting with 4, the list should look like `{4, 64, 280, 520, 133, …}`, since $4^3 = 64$, $6^3 + 4^3 = 280$, etc. Extend the list to at least fifteen values, experiment with other starting values, and look for patterns in the sequences.
3. Following on the example in this section iterating rotations of a triangle, use `Translate` to iterate the translation of a square or other polygon.
4. Using `Fold`, create a function `fac[n]` that takes an integer n as argument and returns the factorial of n, that is, $n(n-1)(n-2)\cdots 3\cdot 2\cdot 1$.
5. The naive way to multiply x^{22} would be to repeatedly multiply x by itself, performing 21 multiplications. But going as far back as about 200 BC in the Hindu classic *Chandah-sutra*, another method has been known that significantly reduces the total number of multiplications in performing such exponentiation. The idea is to first express the exponent in base 2.

```
In[1]:= IntegerDigits[22, 2]
Out[1]= {1, 0, 1, 1, 0}
```

   Then, starting with the second bit from the left, interpret a 1 to mean square the existing expression and multiply by x, and a 0 to mean multiply just by x. Implement this algorithm using `FoldList`.

6. The Sierpiński triangle is a classic iteration example. It can be constructed by starting with an equilateral triangle and removing the inner triangle formed by connecting the midpoints of each side of the original triangle.

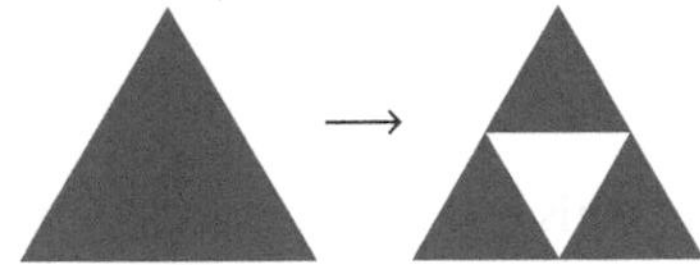

   The process is iterated by repeating the same computation on each of the resulting smaller triangles (other types of iteration can be used).

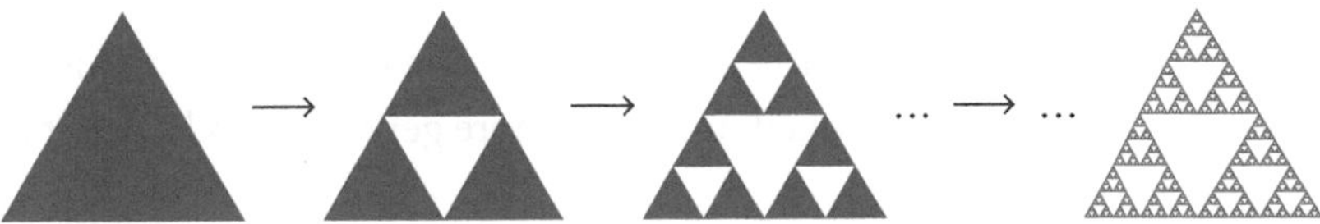

   One approach is to take the starting equilateral triangle and, at each iteration, perform the appropriate transformations using `Scale` and `Translate`, then iterate. Implement this algorithm, but be careful about nesting large symbolic graphics structures too deeply.

5.3 Recursive functions

Many important and classical problems in mathematics and computer science have solutions in terms of recursive definitions: the factorial function, the natural numbers, many divide-and-conquer algorithms, and parsers for programming languages all use recursion in fundamental ways.

A function is defined using recursion if, in its definition, it makes calls to itself. The great advantage of recursive definitions is their simplicity and directness. Their one major drawback, however, is the degree to which the depth and complexity of the operations can increase to the point of making your computations intractable. In this section we introduce recursive functions and look at ways of making them as efficient as possible.

Fibonacci numbers

Recursive definitions of mathematical quantities were used by mathematicians for centuries before computers even existed. One famous example arises from a special sequence of numbers first studied in the Middle Ages by the Italian mathematician Leonardo Fibonacci (*ca.* 1170 – *ca.* 1250).

The *Fibonacci numbers* are generated as follows: start with two 1s, then add them to generate the third number in the sequence; and generally, each new number in the sequence is created by adding the previous two numbers you have written down.

$$\begin{array}{ccccccccc} 1 & 1 & 2 & 3 & 5 & 8 & 13 & 21 & \dots \\ F_1 & F_2 & F_3 & F_4 & F_5 & F_6 & F_7 & F_8 & \dots \end{array}$$

The simplest way to define these numbers is with recursion.

$$F_1 = 1$$
$$F_2 = 1$$
$$F_n = F_{n-2} + F_{n-1}, \quad \text{for } n > 2$$

If we think of this sequence as a function, we would just change this to a functional definition.

$$F(1) = 1$$
$$F(2) = 1$$
$$F(n) = F(n-2) + F(n-1), \quad \text{for } n > 2$$

In this form, we can translate the definition directly into code. The condition $n > 2$ is unnecessary because specific rules such as `F[1] = 1` are looked up before more general rules like that for `F[n]`.

```
In[1]:= F[1] = 1;
        F[2] = 1;

In[3]:= F[n_] := F[n-2] + F[n-1]
```

Here is a list of the first twenty-six Fibonacci numbers:

```
In[4]:= Table[F[i], {i, 1, 26}]

Out[4]= {1, 1, 2, 3, 5, 8, 13, 21, 34, 55, 89, 144, 233, 377, 610, 987, 1597,
         2584, 4181, 6765, 10946, 17711, 28657, 46368, 75025, 121393}
```

It is somewhat amazing that this works, but note that whenever you want to compute F[*n*] for some $n > 2$, you only apply F to numbers smaller than *n*. Let us trace the evaluation of F[4] only looking at expressions that involve an F[*integer*] or a sum of two Fs.

```
In[5]:= TracePrint[F[4], F[_Integer] | F[_] + F[_]]
   F[4]
   F[4 - 2] + F[4 - 1]
      F[2]
      F[3]
      F[3 - 2] + F[3 - 1]
         F[1]
         F[2]
Out[5]= 3
```

The first two lines indicate that F[4] is rewritten to F[4 - 2] + F[4 - 1], and the lines that are indented show the calls of F[2] and F[3]. The lines showing calls to F[1] and F[2] do not have any indented lines under them, since those values are computed directly by a single rule, without making any recursive calls.

There are two key things to understand about recursion:

- You can always apply a function within its own definition, so long as you apply it only to *smaller* values.
- You can apply the function to smaller and smaller values, but you must eventually reach a value that can be computed *without* recursion. In the case of the Fibonacci numbers, the numbers that can be computed without recursion – the *base cases* – are F[1] and F[2].

Thinking recursively

Let us now look at recursive definitions for two basic functions: one that computes the length of a list, and another that performs pairwise addition on two vectors. Although these functions have more efficient implementations using other constructs, they provide a convenient vehicle for discussing and getting practice with the basic concepts of recursive programming.

As noted above, recursion works if the arguments of recursive calls are smaller than the original argument. The same principle applies to functions on lists. One common case is when the argument in the recursive call is the "tail" (think, Rest) of the original argument. An example is a recursively defined version of the built-in Length function. The idea is that the length of a list is always one greater than the length of its tail.

```
In[6]:= length[lis_] := length[Rest[lis]] + 1
```

Simply applying `length` to a list, however, leads to trouble.

```
In[7]:= length[{a, b, c}]

        Rest::norest : Cannot take Rest of expression {} with length zero. >>

        $RecursionLimit::reclim2 : Recursion depth of 1024 exceeded during evaluation of
            {Rest::norest, Rest::argx, Rest::norest, Rest::argx, Rest::norest, General::stop, Rest::argx,
             General::stop}. >>

Out[7]= Hold[length[Rest[Rest[Rest[]]]]]
```

Well, perhaps it is already obvious, but what we are experiencing is one of the most common errors in defining functions recursively – we forgot the base cases. For `length`, there is just one base case, the empty list.

```
In[8]:= length[{}] := 0
```

Now `length` works as intended.

```
In[9]:= length[{a, b, c}]
Out[9]= 3
```

Recursion is of course used for functions with multiple arguments as well. The following function `addPairs[`lis_1, lis_2`]` takes two lists of numbers of equal length and returns a list containing the pairwise sums; think vector addition.

The idea is to apply `addPairs` recursively to the tails of both lists. The base case consists of the two empty lists.

```
In[10]:= addPairs[{}, {}] := {}

In[11]:= addPairs[{x1_, r1___}, {x2_, r2___}] :=
          Join[{x1 + x2}, addPairs[{r1}, {r2}]]

In[12]:= addPairs[{1, 2, 3}, {4, 5, 6}]
Out[12]= {5, 7, 9}

In[13]:= addPairs[{x1, y1, z1}, {x2, y2, z2}]
Out[13]= {x1 + x2, y1 + y2, z1 + z2}
```

Dynamic programming

The function `F` defined in the previous section to compute Fibonacci numbers is simple, but quite "expensive" to execute: in the course of computing `F[`n`]`, there are numbers $m < n$ for which `F[`m`]` is computed many times. For instance, `F[`$n - 2$`]` is computed twice – it is called from `F[`n`]` and also from `F[`$n - 1$`]`; `F[`$n - 3$`]` is computed three times; and `F[`$n - 4$`]` five times. The number of calls to the Fibonacci function to compute `F[`n`]` is `F[`n`]` itself! This grows exponentially and is therefore quite impractical for large n. Even computing the first thirty Fibonacci numbers using this approach will be prohibitively slow.

This continual recalculation can be eliminated by memorizing these values as they are computed using a technique known as *dynamic programming*. The idea is to dynamically create rules *during* evaluation. Using dynamic programming, a delayed assignment whose right-hand side is an immediate assignment of the same name is defined.

`f[x_] := f[x] =` *right–hand side*

When an expression matches the pattern `f[x_]`, the immediate assignment is evaluated, creating a new rule. Since the global rule base is always consulted during evaluation, storing results as rules can cut down on computation time. It is like caching values, but in this case we are caching rules. In this way, dynamic programming can be described as a method in which rewrite rules are added to the global rule base *dynamically*, that is, during the running of a program. A well-known application of this is to speed up the computation of Fibonacci numbers.

The following definition of `fibD` (`D` for *dynamic*) is just like the definition of `F`, but it adds a rule `fibD[n] = fibD[n - 2] + fibD[n - 1]` to the global rule base the first time the value is computed. Since *Mathematica* always chooses the most specific rule to apply when rewriting, future requests for `fibD[n]` cause the new rule to be used instead of the more general rule. Thus, for every *n*, `fibD[n]` will be computed just once; after that, its value will be found in the rule base.

```
In[14]:= Clear[fibD]
         fibD[1] = 1; fibD[2] = 1;
         fibD[n_] := fibD[n] = fibD[n - 2] + fibD[n - 1]
```

Tracing the computation shows that there is only one evaluation of `fibD[3]` now, since the second evaluation of it is just a use of a global rule. Only those expressions in the following computation that match the pattern given by the second argument to `TracePrint` will be shown: either `fibD` with an integer argument or an assignment for `fibD`.

```
In[17]:= TracePrint[fibD[4], fibD[_Integer] | (fibD[_] = fibD[_] + fibD[_])]

          fibD[4]

          fibD[4] = fibD[4 - 2] + fibD[4 - 1]

           fibD[2]

           fibD[3]

           fibD[3] = fibD[3 - 2] + fibD[3 - 1]

            fibD[1]

            fibD[2]

           fibD[3]

          fibD[4]

Out[17]= 3
```

Another way to understand this is to look at the global rule base after evaluating `fibD[4]`.

```
In[18]:= ?fibD

Global`fibD

fibD[1] = 1

fibD[2] = 1

fibD[3] = 2

fibD[4] = 3

fibD[n_] := fibD[n] = fibD[n - 2] + fibD[n - 1]
```

The cost of executing `fibD` is dramatically lower (see Table 5.1). It is linear in n, rather than in `F[n]` which grows exponentially. Furthermore, these costs are only for the first time `fibD[n]` is computed; in the future, we can find `fibD[n]` for free, or rather, for the cost of looking it up in the global rule base.

```
In[19]:= Timing[fibD[100]]
Out[19]= {0.000546, 354 224 848 179 261 915 075}
```

TABLE 5.1. *Number of additions in Fibonacci algorithm – plain recursion vs. dynamic programming*

n	F[n] additions	fibD[n] additions
5	5	3
10	21	8
15	610	13
20	6765	18
25	75025	23

Dynamic programming can be a useful technique, but needs to be used with care. It will entail some increased cost in memory, as the global rule base is expanded to include the new rules. Furthermore, you could still bump up against the built-in limits with a large computation.

```
In[20]:= fibD[5000]
   $RecursionLimit::reclim2 :
     Recursion depth of 1024 exceeded during evaluation of fibD[2956 - 2] + fibD[2956 - 1]. >>
Out[20]= Hold[fibD[2956 - 2] + fibD[2956 - 1]]
```

In such cases, if you know that the algorithm is correct, you can temporarily increase the recursion limit. But you first need to clear out the values to `fibD` that were assigned during the previous, failed computation. (The localization construct `Block`, used below, is discussed in Section 6.1.)

```
In[21]:= Clear[fibD]
```

```
In[22]:= fibD[1] = 1;
         fibD[2] = 1;
         fibD[n_] := fibD[n] = fibD[n - 2] + fibD[n - 1]

In[25]:= Block[{$RecursionLimit = ∞},
          fibD[5000] // N
         ]
Out[25]= 3.878968454388326 × 10^1044
```

Exercises

1. Create a recursive function that computes the nth power of two.

2. Create a recursive function that returns the factorial of n, for n a nonnegative integer.

3. The Tower of Hanoi puzzle is a popular game invented by the French mathematician Édouard Lucas in 1883. Given three pegs, one of which contains n disks of increasing radii, the object is to move the stack of disks to another peg in the fewest number of moves without putting a larger disk on a smaller one (Figure 5.2).

   FIGURE 5.2. *Tower of Hanoi.*

   Create a recursive function `TowerOfHanoi[n]` that computes the minimal number of moves for a stack of n disks over three pegs. Results for $n = 1, 2, \ldots, 10$ are as follows:

   ```
   {1, 3, 7, 15, 31, 63, 127, 255, 511, 1023}
   ```

   Legend has it that the priests in the Indian temple Kashi Vishwanath have a room with a stack of 64 disks and three pegs and that when they complete moving the stack to a new peg, the world will end. If they move one disk per second, compute how long until the "end of the world."

4. For each of the following sequences of numbers, see if you can deduce the pattern and write a function to compute the general term:

   a.

2,	3,	6,	18,	108,	1944,	209 952,	…
A_1	A_2	A_3	A_4	A_5	A_6	A_7	…

   b.

0,	1,	−1,	2,	−3,	5,	−8,	13,	−21,	…
B_1	B_2	B_3	B_4	B_5	B_6	B_7	B_8	B_9	…

c.

0,	1,	2,	3,	6,	11,	20,	37,	68,	...
C_1	C_2	C_3	C_4	C_5	C_6	C_7	C_8	C_9	...

5. The Fibonacci sequence can also be defined for negative integers using the following formula (Graham, Knuth, and Patashnik 1994):

$$F_{-n} = (-1)^{n-1} F_n$$

The first few terms are

0	1	−1	2	−3	5	−8	13	−21	...
F_0	F_{-1}	F_{-2}	F_{-3}	F_{-4}	F_{-5}	F_{-6}	F_{-7}	F_{-8}	...

Write the definitions for Fibonacci numbers with negative integer arguments.

6. Create a recursive function to reverse the elements in a flat list.

7. Create a recursive function to transpose the elements of two lists. Write an additional rule to transpose the elements of three lists.

8. Using dynamic programming is one way to speed up the computation of Fibonacci numbers, but another is to use different algorithms. A more efficient algorithm is based on the following identities:

$$\begin{aligned} F_1 &= 1 \\ F_2 &= 1 \\ F_{2n} &= 2F_{n-1}F_n + F_n^2, \quad \text{for } n \geq 1 \\ F_{2n+1} &= F_{n+1}^2 + F_n^2, \quad \text{for } n \geq 1 \end{aligned}$$

Program a function to generate Fibonacci numbers using these identities.

9. You can still speed up the code for generating Fibonacci numbers in the previous exercise by using dynamic programming. Do so, and construct tables like those in this section, giving the number of additions performed by the two programs.

10. An Eulerian number, denoted $\left\langle {n \atop k} \right\rangle$, gives the number of permutations of n-element sets with k increasing runs of elements. For example, for $n = 3$ the permutations of {1, 2, 3} contain four increasing runs of length one, namely {1, 3, 2}, {2, 1, 3}, {2, 3, 1}, and {3, 1, 2}. Hence, $\left\langle {3 \atop 1} \right\rangle = 4$.

```
In[1]:= Permutations[{1, 2, 3}]
Out[1]= {{1, 2, 3}, {1, 3, 2}, {2, 1, 3}, {2, 3, 1}, {3, 1, 2}, {3, 2, 1}}
```

This can be programmed using the following recursive definition, where n and k are assumed to be integers:

$$\left\langle {n \atop k} \right\rangle = (k+1)\left\langle {n-1 \atop k} \right\rangle + (n-k)\left\langle {n-1 \atop k-1} \right\rangle, \quad \text{for } n > 0,$$

$$\left\langle {0 \atop k} \right\rangle = \begin{cases} 1 & k = 0 \\ 0 & k \neq 0. \end{cases}$$

Create a function `EulerianNumber[n, k]`. You can check your work against Table 5.2, which displays the first few Eulerian numbers.

TABLE 5.2. *Eulerian number triangle*

n	$\left\langle {n \atop 0} \right\rangle$	$\left\langle {n \atop 1} \right\rangle$	$\left\langle {n \atop 2} \right\rangle$	$\left\langle {n \atop 3} \right\rangle$	$\left\langle {n \atop 4} \right\rangle$	$\left\langle {n \atop 5} \right\rangle$	$\left\langle {n \atop 6} \right\rangle$	$\left\langle {n \atop 7} \right\rangle$	$\left\langle {n \atop 8} \right\rangle$
0	1								
1	1	0							
2	1	1	0						
3	1	4	1	0					
4	1	11	11	1	0				
5	1	26	66	26	1	0			
6	1	57	302	302	57	1	0		
7	1	120	1191	2416	1191	120	1	0	
8	1	247	4293	15 619	15 619	4293	247	1	0

Because of the triple recursion, you will find it necessary to use a dynamic programming implementation to compute any Eulerian numbers of even modest size.

Hint: Although the above formulas will compute it, you can add the following rule to simplify some of the computation (Graham, Knuth, and Patashnik 1994):

$$\left\langle {n \atop k} \right\rangle = 0, \quad \text{for } k \geq n$$

11. The Collatz sequence is generated as follows: starting with a number n, if it is even, then output $n/2$; if it is odd, then output $3\,n + 1$. Iterate this process while the value of the iterate is not equal to one. Using recursion and dynamic programming, create the function `collatz[n, i]`, which computes the ith iterate of the Collatz sequence starting with integer n. Compare its speed with that of the procedural approach in Exercise 10 of Section 5.4.

5.4 Loops and flow control

Conventional programming languages like C and FORTRAN embody a style of programming that has roots in the early days of computing, when resource constraints forced programmers to write their code in a step-by-step manner. These procedures, as they came to be known, typically involve certain basic elements: looping over an array, conditional statements that control the flow of execution, logical constructs to build up tests, and functions to jump from one place in a program to another. Although newer languages use many different programming paradigms, procedural programming continues to be used and remains appropriate for certain kinds of problems.

Conditional functions

Let us start with functions that control the flow of execution of an evaluation. Perhaps the most basic and easiest to understand is `If`. Here is a rather simplistic implementation of the absolute value function, using `If`:

```
In[1]:= abs[x_] := If[x ≥ 0, x, -x]
```

The `If` function takes three arguments: `If[`*test*, *then*, *else*`]`. If the first argument, *test*, evaluates to `True`, the second argument, *then*, is evaluated; if, however, *test* evaluates to `False`, the third argument, *else*, is evaluated.

Once defined, these functions can be used with any other computations. For example, they can be mapped over a list of numbers.

```
In[2]:= Map[abs, {-2, -1, 0, 1, 2}]
Out[2]= {2, 1, 0, 1, 2}
```

Tip 5.4

By default, functions you create, like `abs` above, will not *automatically* map across lists.

```
In[3]:= abs[{-2, -1, 0, 1, 2}]
Out[3]= If[{-2, -1, 0, 1, 2} ≥ 0, {-2, -1, 0, 1, 2}, -{-2, -1, 0, 1, 2}]
```

If you want `abs` to behave like many of the built-in functions and automatically map across lists, make the function `Listable` as described in Section 2.5.

```
In[4]:= SetAttributes[abs, Listable]
In[5]:= abs[{-2, -1, 0, 1, 2}]
Out[5]= {2, 1, 0, 1, 2}
```

Let us look at some additional examples using `If`. The following function checks if its argument is a number and returns it unchanged if it is; otherwise, it returns the string `"NAN"` to indicate that it is not a number:

```
In[6]:= f[x_] := If[NumericQ[x], x, "NAN"]
In[7]:= Map[f, {5, π, 0.27, I, x1, "a string"}]
Out[7]= {5, π, 0.27, ⅈ, NAN, NAN}
```

The following function resizes large images and leaves them alone if the width (the first dimension in `ImageDimensions`) is smaller than some threshold size:

```
In[8]:= img = [image];
In[9]:= ResizeImage[img_Image, target_ : 100] :=
          If[First@ImageDimensions[img] > target,
           ImageResize[img, target],
           img
          ]
```

```
In[10]:= ResizeImage[img, 75]
```

Out[10]=

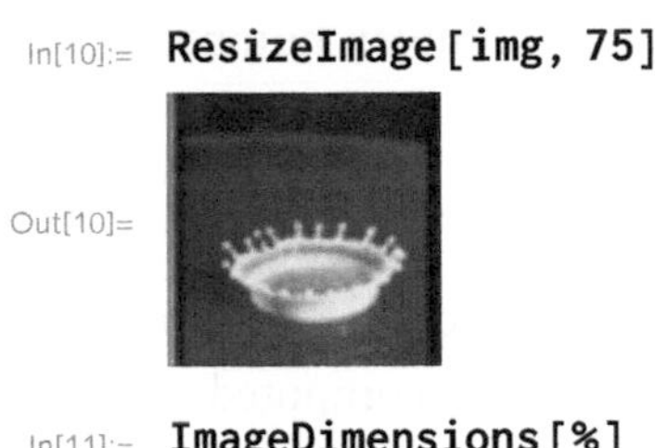

```
In[11]:= ImageDimensions[%]
Out[11]= {75, 75}
```

Conditional definitions can be written using another construct in *Mathematica*, the `Condition` operator `/;` that has already been introduced in the context of conditional patterns in Section 4.1. For example, the `abs` function can be entered, using two definitions, as follows:

```
In[12]:= Clear[abs]

In[13]:= abs[x_] := x /; x ≥ 0

In[14]:= abs[x_] := -x /; x < 0

In[15]:= Map[abs, {-2, 0, 5, z}]
Out[15]= {2, 0, 5, abs[z]}
```

The first definition should be interpreted as "`abs[x]` is equal to `x` whenever (or under the condition that) `x` is greater than or equal to zero" and the second definition as "`abs[x]` is equal to the opposite of `x` whenever `x` is less than zero."

The conditions can also be entered on the left-hand side of these definitions as follows:

```
In[16]:= Clear[abs]

In[17]:= abs[x_ /; x ≥ 0] := x

In[18]:= abs[x_ /; x < 0] := -x
```

This last notation has the advantage of preventing the right-hand side of the definitions from being evaluated whenever the pattern on the left does not match.

```
In[19]:= Map[abs, {-2, 0, 5, z}]
Out[19]= {2, 0, 5, abs[z]}
```

The `abs` function defined above is fine for integer and real number arguments, but, since the complex numbers cannot be ordered, comparisons with zero will fail.

```
In[20]:= abs[3 + 4 I]

         GreaterEqual::nord : Invalid comparison with 3 + 4 ⅈ attempted. ≫

         Less::nord : Invalid comparison with 3 + 4 ⅈ attempted. ≫

Out[20]= abs[3 + 4 ⅈ]
```

This can be resolved through the use of additional rules to deal with complex numbers as arguments (see Exercise 4 at the end of this section).

Piecewise-defined functions

The last absolute value function given in the previous section is defined piecewise. This means that for different intervals, or under different conditions, the values will be computed differently. `Piecewise` is designed specifically for such problems. The syntax is

```
Piecewise[{{e1, c1}, ..., {en, cn}}]
```

`Piecewise` outputs e_1 if the condition c_1 is true, e_2 if c_2 is true, … , e_n if c_n is true, and zero otherwise (the default). So, for example, here is the definition for the absolute value function given as a piecewise object:

```
In[21]:= abspw[x_] := Piecewise[{{x, x ≥ 0}, {-x, x < 0}}]
```

Piecewise objects display using traditional mathematical notation.

```
In[22]:= abspw[x]
```

$$\text{Out[22]=}\quad \begin{cases} x & x \geq 0 \\ -x & x < 0 \\ 0 & \text{True} \end{cases}$$

Compared with `Piecewise`, the conditional implementations in the previous approaches are not fully supported by many of the built-in functions.

```
In[23]:= Integrate[abs[x], {x, -1, 1}]
```

$$\text{Out[23]=}\quad \int_{-1}^{1} \text{abs}[x]\, dx$$

```
In[24]:= D[abs[x], x]

Out[24]= abs′[x]
```

`Piecewise`, in contrast, is fully integrated with the algebraic, symbolic, and graphical functions in *Mathematica* and in this sense it is preferable to other approaches.

```
In[25]:= Integrate[abspw[x], {x, -1, 1}]

Out[25]= 1

In[26]:= D[abspw[x], x]
```

$$\text{Out[26]=}\quad \begin{cases} -1 & x < 0 \\ 1 & x > 0 \\ \text{Indeterminate} & \text{True} \end{cases}$$

Which and Switch

Oftentimes you will find yourself using nested `If/Then/Else` chains to deal with multiple conditions that need to be checked. In the following example, we will create a dynamic interface of an interpolation of some data, displaying plot labels that are determined by the interpolation order chosen. To start, here is a single static plot:

```
In[27]:= data = Table[Sin[x y], {x, 0, 4, 0.5}, {y, 0, 4, 0.5}];
         ListPlot3D[data, InterpolationOrder → 0, PlotLabel → "Voronoi cells"]
```

Out[28]=

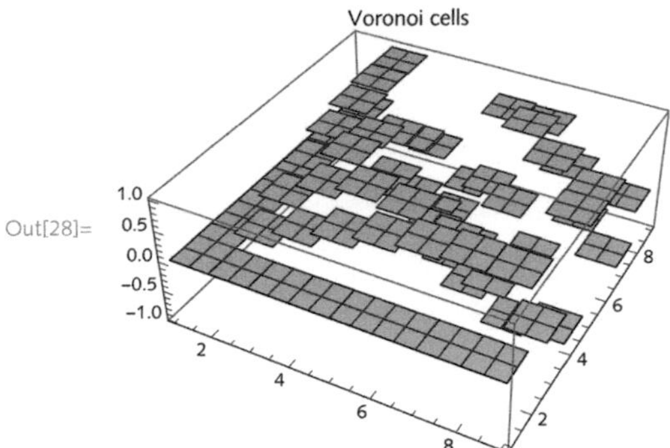

The plot labels in the following dynamic interface are set up so that they change depending upon the value of the parameter, `order`. Figure 5.3 displays the four panes from the dynamic interface.

```
In[29]:= Manipulate[
           ListPlot3D[data, InterpolationOrder → order,
            PlotLabel →
             If[order == "None", "Linear",
              If[order == 0, "Voronoi cells",
               If[order == 1, "Baricentric",
                If[order == 2, "Natural neighbor"
                ]
               ]
              ]
             ]
           ],
           {{order, "None", "InterpolationOrder"}, {"None", 0, 1, 2}}];
```

This code contains several nested `If`s, each occurring in the false clause of the previous one. The structure of the computation is a sequence of tests of predicates $cond_i$ until one is found to be true, at which point a result can be computed.

```
If[cond_1, result_1,
  If[cond_2, result_2,
    ⋮
      If[cond_n, result_n,
        …, result_n+1] …
  ]
]
```

FIGURE 5.3. *Manipulate showing different interpolation orders used to construct a surface.*

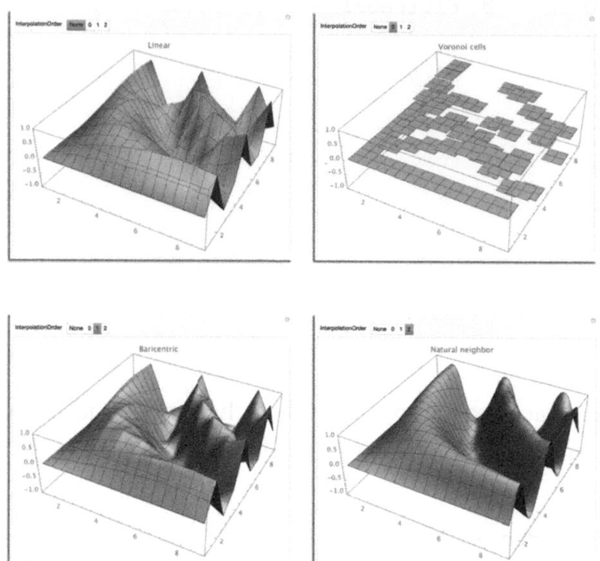

It can be a little difficult to read these nested `If` statements and figure out which clause goes with which `If`. Fortunately, cascaded `If`s are so common that there is a more direct and compact way of writing them using the function `Which`.

`Which[`
  $cond_1$, $result_1$,
  $cond_2$, $result_2$,
  $cond_n$, $result_n$,
  `True`, $result_{n+1}$
`]`

This has exactly the same effect as the cascaded `If` expression above: it tests each condition in turn, and, when it finds an i such that $cond_i$ is true, it returns $result_i$ as the result of the `Which` expression itself. If none of the conditions turns out to be true, then it will test the final condition, namely the expression `True`, which always evaluates to true, and it will then return $result_{n+1}$.

```
In[30]:= Manipulate[
           ListPlot3D[data, InterpolationOrder → order,
            PlotLabel →
             Which[
              order == "None", "Linear",
              order == 0, "Voronoi cells",
              order == 1, "Baricentric",
              order == 2, "Natural neighbor"]],
           {{order, "None", "Interpolation order"}, {"None", 0, 1, 2}}];
```

We have used `Which` to compare the `order` parameter with several different possible values. Since this is also a common form, *Mathematica* provides a special function for it, called `Switch`. Where `Which` compares values to determine which result to evaluate, `Switch` does pattern matching.

```
Switch[expr,
    pattern1, result1,
    pattern2, result2,
      ⋮
    patternn, resultn,
    _, resultn+1]
```

This evaluates *expr* and then checks each pattern sequentially to see whether *expr* matches; as soon as *expr* matches one, say $pattern_i$, it returns the value of $result_i$. Of course, if none of the patterns $pattern_1, \ldots, pattern_n$ matches, the general pattern _ certainly will and $result_{n+1}$ will be returned.

Here is a toy example showing how `Switch` works. If the expression `expr` matches the pattern `_Integer`, that is, if it has head `Integer`, then the string "I am an integer" will be returned. If not, but `expr` has head `Rational`, then "I am rational" is returned, and so on.

```
In[31]:= WhatAmI[expr_] := Switch[expr,
           _Integer, "I am an integer",
           _Rational, "I am rational",
           _Real, "I am real",
           _Complex, "I am complex",
           _, "I am not a number"]

In[32]:= WhatAmI[3 + 4 I]
Out[32]= I am complex

In[33]:= WhatAmI[fun]
Out[33]= I am not a number
```

Exercise 11 at the end of this section asks you to rewrite the `Manipulate` example with `ListPlot3D` that used `Which` to instead use `Switch`.

Argument checking

When creating functions, you often know ahead of time that their definitions are valid only for certain kinds of inputs. For example, the following recursive definition for the factorial function only makes sense for positive integers:

```
In[34]:= factorial[0] = 1;
         factorial[n_] := n factorial[n - 1]

In[36]:= factorial[5]
Out[36]= 120
```

If you were to give `factorial` an argument that was not a positive integer, the recursion could run away from you.

```
In[37]:= factorial[3.4] // Short
         $RecursionLimit::reclim2 :
           Recursion depth of 1024 exceeded during evaluation of factorial[-1018.6 - 1]. >>
Out[37]= Hold[factorial[-1018.6 - 1]]
```

Conditionals are a convenient way of checking that the arguments to a function are restricted in a certain way. For example, there are several ways that you could make the `factorial` function valid only under the condition that its argument is a positive integer. Here is how you might approach it using the `If` construct to test that n passes the appropriate criteria.

```
In[38]:= Clear[factorial]

In[39]:= factorial[0] = 1;

In[40]:= factorial[n_] := If[IntegerQ[n] && n > 0, n factorial[n - 1]]

In[41]:= {factorial[5], factorial[-3], factorial[2.4]}
Out[41]= {120, Null, Null}
```

The function works fine for positive integers, but since we did not give an alternative condition to the `If` function, nothing is returned (technically, `Null` is returned) when the test condition fails.

Do and For loops

One of the most famous of all iterative numerical algorithms is Newton's method for finding the roots of a function. Even though *Mathematica* includes a built-in function, `FindRoot`, that implements this method, this is a classical algorithm and so central to numerical analysis that it is well worth your time learning how to implement it.

Suppose you are given a function f and can compute its derivative f'. Then Newton's algorithm works as follows:

- give an initial estimate of the root, say x_0;
- keep generating better estimates $x_1, x_2, \ldots$ using the following rule until you are done (we will discuss the stopping conditions in a moment):

$$x_{i+1} = x_i - \frac{f(x_i)}{f'(x_i)}.$$

The method is illustrated in Figure 5.4. The basic idea, as learned in a first-year calculus course, is to choose an initial estimate x_0, draw the tangent to the function at $f(x_0)$, and set x_1 to the point where that tangent line intersects the x-axis. Then iterate. Under favorable circumstances, the estimates get closer and closer to the root. "Unfavorable conditions" include a poor choice for the initial estimate and the function not being continuously differentiable in a neighborhood of the root.

FIGURE 5.4. *Illustration of Newton's method.*

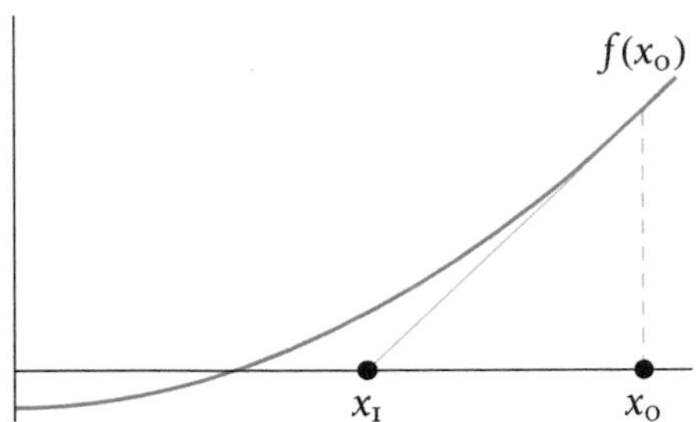

Before we discuss when to stop the iteration, first let us look at an example: computing the square root of two. The function $f(x) = x^2 - 2$ has a root at $\sqrt{2}$. Let us see what happens after five iterations of this procedure.

```
In[42]:= f[x_] := x^2 - 2

In[43]:= x0 = 1;

In[44]:= x1 = N[x0 - f[x0]/f'[x0], 16]

Out[44]= 1.500000000000000

In[45]:= x2 = N[x1 - f[x1]/f'[x1], 16]

Out[45]= 1.416666666666667

In[46]:= x3 = N[x2 - f[x2]/f'[x2], 16]

Out[46]= 1.414215686274510

In[47]:= x4 = N[x3 - f[x3]/f'[x3], 16]

Out[47]= 1.41421356237469

In[48]:= x5 = N[x4 - f[x4]/f'[x4], 16]

Out[48]= 1.41421356237310
```

As you can see, these values are getting closer and closer to the real square root of two, which is approximately 1.4142135. But how do we decide when the answer we have computed is accurate enough? For now, we will simply do ten iterations, repeating these steps using a Do loop and setting the initial value to 1.0.

```
In[49]:= xi = 1.0;
         Do[xi = N[xi - f[xi] / f'[xi]], {10}]
```

The Do loop itself yields no value (or rather, it yields the special value Null, which is a symbol that is used when there is no result from an evaluation; nothing is printed). But, more importantly, at the end of the iteration the value assigned to xi is very close to the square root of two.

```
In[50]:= {xi, √2 - xi}
Out[50]= {1.41421, 2.22045 × 10^-16}
```

The arguments of the Do function are the same as those of Table (see Section 3.1 and also Exercise 13 at the end of this section).

Do[*expr*, {*i*, i_{min}, i_{max}, *di*}]

This loop repeatedly evaluates *expr* with the variable *i* taking the values i_{min}, $i_{min} + di$, and so on, as long as the value of i_{max} is not exceeded. The loop is repeated a total of $\lfloor (i_{max} - i_{min})/di \rfloor$ times, where $\lfloor expr \rfloor$ gives the floor of *expr* (more precisely, the loop is actually repeated a total of $\max(0, \lfloor (i_{max} - i_{min})/di \rfloor + 1)$ times). Furthermore, if *di* is omitted, it is assumed to be one; if only *i* and i_{max} are given, both i_{min} and *di* are assumed to be one.

To print each approximation and label it with the current value of xi, use a compound expression – the Newton iteration and the Print statement – inside the body of the Do loop (\t prints as a tab space).

```
In[52]:= xi = 1;
         Do[xi = N[xi - f[xi] / f'[xi]];
          Print["iteration ", i, ":\t", xi], {i, 1, 5}]

         iteration 1:    1.5

         iteration 2:    1.41667

         iteration 3:    1.41422

         iteration 4:    1.41421

         iteration 5:    1.41421
```

Another commonly used control structure in procedural code is the For loop. It is similar to a Do loop, but instead of an iterator list, you explicitly specify a starting value and increment for the iterator. The For function has the following syntax:

For[*start*, *test*, *increment*, *body*]

Do loops and For loops are quite similar and you can often cast a problem using either construction. For example, here is a For implementation of the Do loop given above for the Newton iteration:

```
In[54]:= For[xi = 1; i = 0, i < 5, i++, xi = N[xi - f[xi]/f'[xi]]]

In[55]:= xi
Out[55]= 1.41421
```

The starting condition is the compound expression initializing `xi` and `i`; the test is `i < 5`; the increment is `i ++`, which is shorthand for increasing the value of `i` by one; the body of the function is the same as for the `Do` loop, namely, Newton's formula.

Several exercises later in this chapter as well as Section 9.1 explore efficiencies that can be gained from a careful look at the evaluations done within the iterations. But first, we turn to another looping construct, `While`.

While loops

Let us see how we can use a different control structure to improve the Newton root-finding computation by fine-tuning the number of iterations that are performed. In the previous section on `Do` and `For` loops, we explicitly stopped the iteration after five times through the loop. Five times might be okay for $f(x) = x^2 - 2$, but not always. Consider the function $x - \sin(x)$.

```
In[56]:= g[x_] := x - Sin[x]
```

It has a root at zero.

```
In[57]:= g[0]
Out[57]= 0
```

However, even after ten iterations of Newton's algorithm we are not getting very close to it.

```
In[58]:= xi = 1.0;
         Do[xi = N[xi - g[xi]/g'[xi]], {10}]

In[60]:= xi
Out[60]= 0.0168228
```

Twenty-five iterations does a bit better.

```
In[61]:= xi = 1.0;
         Do[xi = N[xi - g[xi]/g'[xi]], {25}]

In[63]:= xi
Out[63]= 0.0000384172
```

In practice, no fixed number of iterations is going to do the trick for all functions. We need to iterate repeatedly until our estimate is close enough to stop. When is that? When $f(x_i)$ is very close to zero. So, choose ϵ to be a very small number, and iterate until $|f(x_i)| < \epsilon$.

But how can we write a loop that will test some condition and stop when the condition is no longer met? The looping constructs `Do` and `For` iterate a fixed number of times. We need a new kind of iterative function. It is `While`, and it has the following form:

```
While[test, expr]
```

The first argument is the test or condition, the second is the body, *expr*. It works like this: evaluate the test; if it is true, evaluate the body and then the test again. If it is true, then again evaluate the body and the test. Continue this way until the test evaluates to `False`. Note that the body may not be evaluated at all (if the test is false the first time), or it may be evaluated once, or a thousand times.

This is just what we want – if the estimate is not yet close enough, compute a new estimate and try again. Newton's method insures, under suitable conditions, that the iteration will converge to the root. Those conditions are that the initial guess is near the root and not near a local minimum or maximum, and also that the function is continuously differentiable near the root. If the function is not differentiable, then a variation of Newton's method known as the secant method can be used to approximate the derivative using finite differences (see Exercise 15 at the end of this section).

```
In[64]:= f[x_] := x^2 - 2

In[65]:= ϵ = .0001;
         xi = 1.0;
         While[Abs[f[xi]] > ϵ,
           xi = N[xi - f[xi]/f'[xi]]]

In[68]:= xi
Out[68]= 1.41422
```

To finish, let us put all these pieces into a reusable function (jump ahead to Chapter 6 if you are not familiar with scoping constructs such as `Module`). And instead of simply returning the value of x_i, we will return a rule of the form $\{x \to value\}$ similar to the built-in functions such as `Solve`, `DSolve`, `FindRoot`, and others. In this version, we have also added a third argument, ϵ, so the user can set the tolerance of the approximations.

```
In[69]:= findRoot[fun_Symbol, {var_, init_}, ϵ_] := Module[{xi = init},
           While[Abs[fun[xi]] > ϵ,
             xi = N[xi - fun[xi]/fun'[xi]]];
           {var → xi}]

In[70]:= findRoot[f, {x, 2}, .0001]
Out[70]= {x → 1.41422}
```

Working with this example a little more, suppose that you would like to know how many iterations were needed to find the answer. Built-in numerics functions and many visualization functions use the option `EvaluationMonitor` to keep track of and display information derived from the numerical operations these functions are performing internally. For example, `EvaluationMonitor` is used here with the built-in function `FindRoot` to display intermediate values of `x`:

```
In[71]:= FindRoot[f[x], {x, 1}, EvaluationMonitor :→ Print[x]]
         1.
         1.5
         1.41667
         1.41422
         1.41421
         1.41421
Out[71]= {x → 1.41421}
```

We can mirror this functionality in our `findRoot` function in several different ways. One possibility is to insert a `Print` expression to show the value of `xi` each time through the loop.

```
In[72]:= findRoot[fun_Symbol, {var_, init_}, ϵ_] := Module[{xi = init},
           While[Abs[fun[xi]] > ϵ,
            Print["x = ", xi];
            xi = N[xi - fun[xi]/fun'[xi]]];
           {var → xi}]

In[73]:= findRoot[f, {x, 2.0}, 0.0001]
         x = 2.
         x = 1.5
         x = 1.41667
Out[73]= {x → 1.41422}
```

Counting the lines shows that the function converged after three iterations (we are seeing the value of `xi` at the *beginning* of each execution of the body). Alternatively, insert a counter that keeps track of the number of iterations and return that as part of the answer.

```
In[74]:= findRoot[fun_Symbol, {var_, init_}, ϵ_] := Module[{xi = init, count = 0},
           While[Abs[fun[xi]] > ϵ,
            count = count + 1;
            xi = N[xi - fun[xi]/fun'[xi]]];
           {{var → xi}, StringForm["Number of iterations → `1`", count]}]

In[75]:= findRoot[f, {x, 2}, 10^-12]
Out[75]= {{x → 1.41421}, Number of iterations → 5}
```

We will revisit this algorithm in Section 5.5 and improve the implementation there by using a more appropriate function (`NestWhile`) to do the iteration, and allow for general expressions and equalities in the first argument.

Exercises

1. Create a function `UpperTriangularMatrix[n]` that generates an $n \times n$ matrix with ones on and above the diagonal and zeros below the diagonal. Create an alternative rule that defaults to the value one for the upper values, but allows the user to specify a nondefault upper value.

```
In[1]:= UpperTriangularMatrix[3] // MatrixForm
Out[1]//MatrixForm=
 (0 1 1)
 (0 0 1)
 (0 0 0)

In[2]:= UpperTriangularMatrix[3, ξ] // MatrixForm
Out[2]//MatrixForm=
 (0 ξ ξ)
 (0 0 ξ)
 (0 0 0)
```

2. Write a function `sign[x]` which, when applied to an integer x, returns −1, 0, or 1 if x is less than, equal to, or greater than zero, respectively. Write it in four different ways: using three clauses, using a single clause with `If`, using a single clause with `Which`, and using `Piecewise`.

3. Use `If` to define a function that, given a list of numbers, doubles all the positive numbers but leaves the negative numbers unchanged.

4. The definition of the absolute value function in this section does not handle complex numbers well:

```
In[3]:= abs[3 + 4 I]

GreaterEqual::nord : Invalid comparison with 3 + 4 i attempted. >>

Less::nord : Invalid comparison with 3 + 4 i attempted. >>

Out[3]= abs[3 + 4 i]
```

Rewrite `abs` to include a specific rule for the case where its argument is complex.

5. One of the fastest methods for computing Fibonacci numbers (Section 5.3) involves iterating multiplication of the matrix {{0, 1}, {1, 1}} and pulling off the appropriate part. For example, the last element in the output of $\texttt{mat}^9$ is the tenth Fibonacci number.

```
In[4]:= mat = {{0, 1}, {1, 1}};
        MatrixPower[mat, 9]
Out[5]= {{21, 34}, {34, 55}}

In[6]:= Fibonacci[10]
Out[6]= 55
```

Without using `MatrixPower`, create a function `FibMat[n]` that iterates the matrix multiplication and then pulls off the correct element from the resulting matrix to give the nth Fibonacci number. Check the speed of your implementation against both `MatrixPower` and the built-in `Fibonacci`.

6. Using an `If` control structure, create a function `median[lis]` that computes the median (the middle value) of a one-dimensional list. You will need to consider the case when the length of the list is odd and the case when it is even. In the latter case, the median is given by the average of the middle two elements of the sorted list.

7. Given a set of data representing a sine wave, perform a clipping operation where values greater than 0.5 are clipped to 0.5, values less than −0.5 are clipped to −0.5, and all other values are left unchanged (Figure 5.5).

```
In[7]:= data = Table[{x, Sin[x]}, {x, 0, 2 π, 0.1}];
```

FIGURE 5.5. *Discrete data of sine wave together with data clipped at amplitude 0.5.*

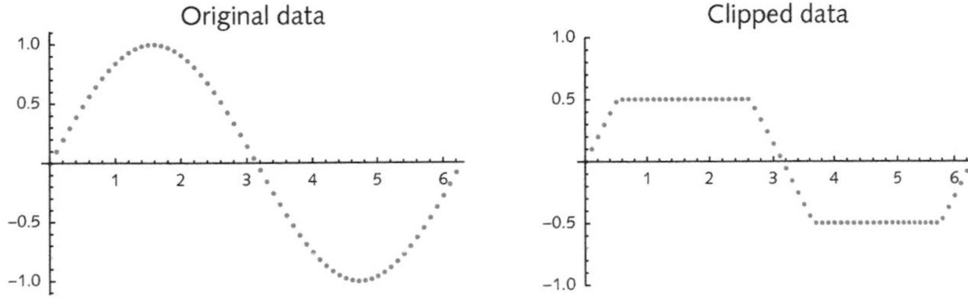

8. Rewrite the `WhatAmI` function from this section so that it properly deals with expressions such as π and *e* that are numerical but not explicit numbers.

9. The bibliography example in Section 3.4 is unable to properly handle a key that has a missing value. For example, the following association has no value for both the `"Issue"` key and the `"Pages"` key:

```
In[8]:= art2 = Association[{"Author" → "Hathaway, David H.",
          "Title" → "The solar cycle", "Journal" → "Living Reviews in Solar Physics",
          "Year" → 2010, "Volume" → 7, "Issue" → "", "Pages" → "",
          "Url" → "http://dx.doi.org/10.12942/lrsp-2010-1"}];

In[9]:= art2["Issue"]

Out[9]=
```

Suppose you were interested in creating a formatted bibliographic reference that displayed volume 7, issue 4 as 7(4). But if the issue value is missing, it should display the volume value only. Create a function that takes the volume and issue values and displays the correct information regardless of whether or not the issue number is present.

```
In[10]:= volIss[art2]

Out[10]= 7
```

10. In Exercise 11, Section 5.3 we introduced Collatz numbers using recursion. Write a procedural implementation, `CollatzSequence[n]`, that produces the Collatz sequence for any positive integer *n*. Consider using `NestWhileList`. Here is the Collatz sequence for initial value 22:

```
In[11]:= CollatzSequence[22]

Out[11]= {22, 11, 34, 17, 52, 26, 13, 40, 20, 10, 5, 16, 8, 4, 2, 1}
```

11. Write a version of the `Manipulate` example visualizing interpolation order that used `Which` to instead use `Switch`.

12. Compute the square root of two using `Nest` (see Section 5.2) and compare with the versions in this section using a `Do` loop.

13. `Do` is closely related to `Table`, the main difference being that `Do` does not return any value, whereas `Table` does. Use `Table` instead of `Do` to rewrite one of the `findRoot` functions given in this section. Compare the efficiency of the two approaches.

14. Compute Fibonacci numbers iteratively. The first few values in the Fibonacci sequence are 1, 1, 2, 3, 5, 8, 13, …, where, after the first two 1s, each number is the sum of the previous two numbers in the sequence. You will need two variables, say `this` and `prev`, giving the two most recent Fibonacci numbers, so that after the *i*th iteration, `this` and `prev` have the values F_i and F_{i-1}, respectively.

15. As mentioned in the discussion of Newton's method for root finding, one type of difficulty that can arise occurs when the derivative of the function in question is either difficult or impossible to compute. As a very simple example, consider the function $|x+3|$, which has a root at $x=-3$. Both the built-in function `FindRoot` and our user-defined `findRoot` will fail with this function, since a symbolic derivative cannot be computed.

```
In[12]:= D[Abs[x + 3], x]
Out[12]= Abs′[3 + x]
```

One way around such problems is to use a numerical derivative (as opposed to an analytic derivative). The *secant method* approximates $f'(x_k)$ using the difference quotient:

$$\frac{f(x_k)-f(x_{k-1})}{x_k-x_{k-1}}$$

Implement a version of `findRoot` using the secant method by creating a rule that takes two initial values: `findRoot[`*f*`, {`*var*`, `*a*`, `*b*`}]`.

16. Using a `While` loop, write a function `gcd[`*m*`, `*n*`]` that computes the greatest common divisor (gcd) of *m* and *n*. The Euclidean algorithm for computing the gcd of two positive integers *m* and *n*, sets $m=n$ and $n=m \bmod n$. It iterates this process until $n=0$, at which point the gcd of *m* and *n* is left in the value of *m*.

17. Write the function `gcd[`*m*`, `*n*`]` implementing the Euclidean algorithm using an `If` function.

18. A permutation of the elements of a list is a reordering of the elements such that the original list and the reordered list are in one-to-one correspondence. For example, the permutations of the list {*a*, *b*, *c*} are {{*a*, *b*, *c*}, {*a*, *c*, *b*}, {*b*, *a*, *c*}, {*b*, *c*, *a*}, {*c*, *a*, *b*}, {*c*, *b*, *a*}}.

One way to create a permutation of the elements of a list *lis* is to start by randomly selecting one element from *lis* and putting it in a temporary list, *lis2* say. Then select one element from the complement of *lis* and *lis2* and repeat the process. Using a `Do` loop, create a function `randomPermutation` that implements this procedure.

19. Create a program `InversePermutation[`*p*`]` that takes a list *p*, that is a permutation of the numbers one through *n*, and returns the inverse permutation *ip*. The inverse permutation *ip* is such that *p*⟦*ip*⟦*i*⟧⟧ = *ip*⟦*p*⟦*i*⟧⟧ = *i*. Check you answer against the built-in `Ordering` function. See Sedgewick and Wayne (2007) for a discussion of inverse permutations.

20. Create a procedural definition for each of the following functions. For each function, create a definition using a `Do` loop and another using `Table`.

For example, the following function first creates an array consisting of zeros of the same dimension as mat. Then inside the Do loop it assigns the element in position {j, k} in mat to position {k, j} in matA, effectively performing a transpose operation. Finally, it returns matA, since the Do loop itself does not return a value.

```
In[13]:= transposeDo[mat_] :=
          Module[{matA, rows = Length[mat], cols = Length[mat[[1]]], j, k},
           matA = ConstantArray[0, {rows, cols}];
           Do[matA〚j, k〛 = mat〚k, j〛,
            {j, 1, rows},
            {k, 1, cols}];
           matA]

In[14]:= mat1 = {{a, b, c}, {d, e, f}, {g, h, i}};
         MatrixForm[mat1]

Out[15]//MatrixForm=
         a b c
         d e f
         g h i

In[16]:= MatrixForm[transposeDo[mat1]]

Out[16]//MatrixForm=
         a d g
         b e h
         c f i
```

This same computation could be performed with a *structured iteration* using Table.

```
In[17]:= transposeTable[mat_?MatrixQ] := Module[{matA, rows, cols},
           {rows, cols} = Dimensions[mat];
           matA = ConstantArray[0, {rows, cols}];
           Table[matA[[j, k]] = mat[[k, j]], {j, rows}, {k, cols}]
          ]

In[18]:= transposeTable[mat1] // MatrixForm

Out[18]//MatrixForm=
         a d g
         b e h
         c f i
```

a. Create the function reverse[*vec*] that reverses the elements in the list *vec*.

b. Create a function rotateRight[*lis*, *n*] that rotates the elements in the list *lis* *n* places to the right.

21. The *digit sum* of a number is given by adding the digits of that number. For example, the digit sum of 7763 is $7 + 7 + 6 + 3 = 23$. If you iterate the digit sum until the resulting number has only one digit, this is called the *digit root* of the original number. So the digit root of 7763 is $7763 \to 7 + 7 + 6 + 3 = 23 \to 2 + 3 = 5$. Create a function to compute the digit root of any positive integer.

22. Quadrants in the Euclidean plane are traditionally numbered counterclockwise from quadrant I (x and y positive) to quadrant IV (x positive, y negative) with some convention adopted for points that lie on either of the axes. Use Piecewise to define a quadrant function that returns the quadrant value for any point in the plane.

23. Using a Do loop create a function to tally the elements in a list, returning a list of the form $\{\{elem_1, cnt_1\}, \ldots, \{elem_n, cnt_n\}\}$. Check your result against the built-in Tally function.

```
In[19]:= Tally[{a, c, a, a, c, b, a, a, b, c, a, b}]
Out[19]= {{a, 6}, {c, 3}, {b, 3}}
```

5.5 Pure functions

Many computations involve creating and using a function quickly to perform some transformation on an expression. Typically, you introduce a formal function definition and then use that function explicitly.

```
In[1]:= f[x_] := x^2

In[2]:= Map[f, {a, b, c, d, e}]
Out[2]= {a^2, b^2, c^2, d^2, e^2}
```

But what if you could use a function "on the fly" without creating an explicit definition? That is what you can do with pure functions. A pure function does not have a name and it can be used at the moment it is created. This is often convenient, especially if the function is only going to be used once or if it will be used as an argument to a higher-order function, such as Map, Fold, or Nest. The built-in function Function is used to create pure functions.

Syntax of pure functions

The basic form of a pure function is Function[*x*, *body*] for a pure function with a single variable *x* (any symbol can be used for the variable) and Function[{*x*, *y*, …}, *body*] for a pure function with more than one variable. The *body* looks like the right-hand side of a user-defined function definition, with the variables *x*, *y*, … where argument names would be. As an example, here is a pure function that squares its argument:

```
In[3]:= Function[z, z^2]
Out[3]= Function[z, z^2]
```

There is also a standard input form that can be used in creating a pure function which is easier to write than the Function notation but can be a bit cryptic to read. The right-hand side of the function definition is rewritten by replacing the variable with a number sign, or, hash symbol (#), and ending the expression with the ampersand symbol (&) to indicate that this is a pure function.

```
#^2 &
```

A pure function can be used exactly like more conventional-looking functions: by following the function with the argument values enclosed in square brackets. First we show the pure function using Function.

```
In[4]:= Function[z, z^2][6]
Out[4]= 36
```

Here is the same thing, but using the more cryptic shorthand notation; the parentheses in the following example are purely for readability and can be omitted if you wish:

```
In[5]:= (#^2 &) [6]
Out[5]= 36
```

In fact, you can do anything with a pure function that you can do with a formally defined function. You can evaluate it at a value, plot it, integrate it, and so on.

```
In[6]:= #^2 &[10]
Out[6]= 100
```

```
In[7]:= Plot[#^2 &[x], {x, -2, 2}]
```

Out[7]=


```
In[8]:= Integrate[#^2 &[x], x]
```

Out[8]= $\frac{x^3}{3}$

If you prefer, you can give a pure function a name and then use that name to call the function later. This has the same effect as defining the function in the more traditional manner (although, as we will see in Section 9.1, working with pure functions can give significant speed increases on many types of computations).

```
In[9]:= squared = #^2 &;
```

```
In[10]:= squared[6]
Out[10]= 36
```

Pure functions are commonly used with higher-order functions like `Map` and `Apply`, so, before going further, let us first look at a few basic examples of the use of pure functions.

Given a list of numbers, let us square each number and then add one to it. The pure function that does this is $\#^2 + 1$ &.

```
In[11]:= Map[#^2 + 1 &, {2, -5, 6.1}]
Out[11]= {5, 26, 38.21}
```

As another example, consider the visualization of complex numbers. The plotting functions can only work with real numbers to plot them in the plane, so we need to convert complex numbers to their real and imaginary parts to pass to the visualization functions. To convert a single complex number to a coordinate pair that can then be plotted, something like the following will work:

```
In[12]:= z = 3 - 4 I;
         {Re[z], Im[z]}
Out[13]= {3, -4}
```

But what should you do with a *list* of complex numbers?

```
In[14]:= lis = RandomComplex[1 + I, 3]
Out[14]= {0.63307 + 0.935202 i, 0.682813 + 0.976188 i, 0.566352 + 0.238452 i}
```

This is where a pure function can be used. If we had a function that extracts the real and imaginary parts of each complex number, we could map it across this list. But we just did that with the single complex number z. So instead of z, we use the pure function variable.

```
In[15]:= Map[{Re[#], Im[#]} &, lis]
Out[15]= {{0.63307, 0.935202}, {0.682813, 0.976188}, {0.566352, 0.238452}}
```

Let us look at one last example: recall the problem introduced in Section 3.4, where we used associations to create a bibliography. Typically, bibliographies are created by adding references one at a time as needed. At some point, the set of references have to be put in order and so the need to sort the association alphabetically by author, say, becomes apparent.

Here is a set of three references that were entered without consideration given to their order:

```
In[16]:= bib = {Association[{"Authors" → "Pearson, Karl",
             "Title" → "The problem of the random walk", "Journal" → "Nature",
             "Year" → 1905, "Volume" → 72, "Issue" → 1865, "Pages" → 294}],
           Association[{"Authors" → "Hathaway, David H.", "Title" →
              "The solar cycle", "Journal" → "Living Reviews in Solar Physics",
             "Year" → 2010, "Volume" → 7, "Issue" → "", "Pages" → ""}],
           Association[{"Authors" → "Hamming, Richard W.",
             "Title" → "Error detecting and error correcting codes",
             "Journal" → "The Bell System Technical Journal", "Year" → 1950,
             "Volume" → 29, "Issue" → 2, "Pages" → "147-160"}]};
```

To sort this association by the value of one of the keys, use `SortBy`. To sort on the `"Authors"` key, give a pure function `#["Authors"]&`. Each of the three associations in `bib` will be slotted into the pure function and the sort will be on the values of the `"Authors"` key.

```
In[17]:= SortBy[bib, #["Authors"] &]
Out[17]= {<|Authors → Hamming, Richard W.,
           Title → Error detecting and error correcting codes,
           Journal → The Bell System Technical Journal, Year → 1950, Volume → 29,
           Issue → 2, Pages → 147-160|>, <|Authors → Hathaway, David H.,
           Title → The solar cycle, Journal → Living Reviews in Solar Physics,
           Year → 2010, Volume → 7, Issue → , Pages → |>,
          <|Authors → Pearson, Karl, Title → The problem of the random walk,
           Journal → Nature, Year → 1905, Volume → 72, Issue → 1865, Pages → 294|>}
```

Multiple arguments

Multiple arguments to pure functions are identified using #1, #2, and so on. For example, here is a pure function that takes the cosine of the first argument and multiplies it by the sine of the second argument:

```
In[18]:= Cos[#1] Sin[#2] &[θ, ρ]
Out[18]= Cos[θ] Sin[ρ]
```

Let us try something a bit more ambitious and create a function that computes the median lines for any triangle (Figure 5.6). We will create a function `TriangleMedians` that takes a `Triangle` object as an argument and returns the lines which define each of the three medians: lines from a vertex to the midpoint of the opposite side. Pure functions are useful in this example in both the creation of a midpoint function and in threading coordinate points across lines.

FIGURE 5.6. *Triangle with medians (red) and centroid (blue).*

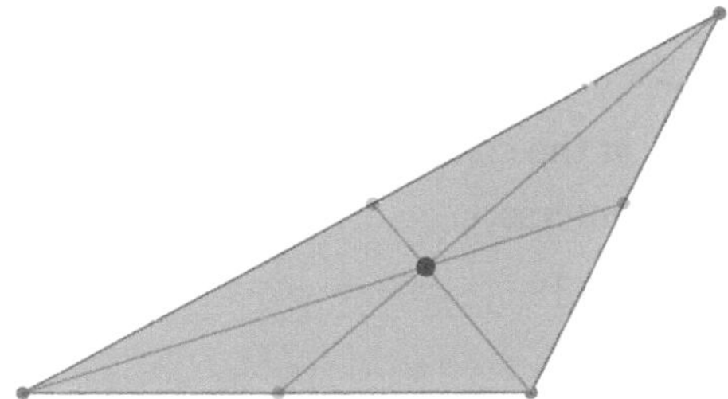

To start, we need the midpoints of the line connecting each pair of vertices. First, create the pairs of vertices that define each edge of the triangle.

```
In[19]:= {p1, p2, p3} = {{-1, 0}, {0, 2}, {1, 0}};
         pairs = Subsets[{p1, p2, p3}, {2}]
Out[20]= {{{-1, 0}, {0, 2}}, {{-1, 0}, {1, 0}}, {{0, 2}, {1, 0}}}
```

For two-dimensional points, here is a quick midpoint computation. Applying the pure function to `pairs` at level one causes the pure function to go inside the outer braces of `pairs` and operate on each of the three pairs of points in turn.

```
In[21]:= midpts = Apply[(#1 + #2) / 2 &, pairs, {1}]
```

Out[21]= $\left\{\left\{-\frac{1}{2}, 1\right\}, \{0, 0\}, \left\{\frac{1}{2}, 1\right\}\right\}$

The median lines are created by pairing up each vertex with the correct median on the opposite side. Using `MapThread`, we map `Line[{#1, #2}]`, slotting in the vertices in the first slot and the midpoints in the second. A bit of thought shows that the list of vertices needs to be reversed before pairing with the midpoints.

```
In[22]:= medians = MapThread[Line[{#1, #2}] &, {{p3, p2, p1}, midpts}]
```

$$Out[22]= \left\{Line\left[\left\{\{1, 0\}, \left\{-\frac{1}{2}, 1\right\}\right\}\right], Line[\{\{0, 2\}, \{0, 0\}\}], Line\left[\left\{\{-1, 0\}, \left\{\frac{1}{2}, 1\right\}\right\}\right]\right\}$$

Here then is the function that returns the medians as a list of lines. We are setting up the left-hand side so that `TriangleMedians` accepts a `Triangle` object as an argument. Rather than using a pure function as above, we set up the computation of the midpoints as a regular definition for readability purposes; the `MapThread` expression still uses pure functions. (You may want to look ahead to Chapter 6 to learn about the localization construct `Module` used here.)

```
In[23]:= TriangleMedians[Triangle[{p1_, p2_, p3_}]] := Module[{midpoint, midpts},
           midpoint[{pt1_, pt2_}] := (pt1 + pt2) / 2;
           midpts = Map[midpoint, Subsets[{p1, p2, p3}, {2}]];
           MapThread[Line[{#1, #2}] &, {{p3, p2, p1}, midpts}]
          ]
```

One of the properties of the medians is that they intersect at the centroid of the triangle. To see this, take the medians (`Line` objects) and find where these lines intersect.

```
In[24]:= medians = TriangleMedians[Triangle[{p1, p2, p3}]]
```

$$Out[24]= \left\{Line\left[\left\{\{1, 0\}, \left\{-\frac{1}{2}, 1\right\}\right\}\right], Line[\{\{0, 2\}, \{0, 0\}\}], Line\left[\left\{\{-1, 0\}, \left\{\frac{1}{2}, 1\right\}\right\}\right]\right\}$$

```
In[25]:= Solve[{x, y} ∈ medians[[1]] ∧
           {x, y} ∈ medians[[2]] ∧ {x, y} ∈ medians[[3]], {x, y}]
```

$$Out[25]= \left\{\left\{x \to 0, y \to \frac{2}{3}\right\}\right\}$$

```
In[26]:= RegionCentroid[Triangle[{p1, p2, p3}]]
```

$$Out[26]= \left\{0, \frac{2}{3}\right\}$$

Pure predicate functions

One of the primary tasks of signal processing is dealing with unwanted elements in a signal. Historical audio recordings often contain pops and clicks in addition to general hiss (noise). Electrical circuits are susceptible to spikes – short-duration transients – in voltage, current, and energy. Such spikes can be caused by lightning strikes, short circuits, electromagnetic impulses, and other sources. Much work goes into developing digital and analog filters to attenuate such spikes, as they can cause damage to any device whose circuitry is not designed to deal with voltages or currents above some specified threshold.

In this example we use `Select` to do a simple filtering of a signal containing a spike, first, importing the signal from a comma-separated file.

```
In[27]:= signal = Import["spikedata.csv", "List"];
         ListLinePlot[signal]
```

Out[28]=

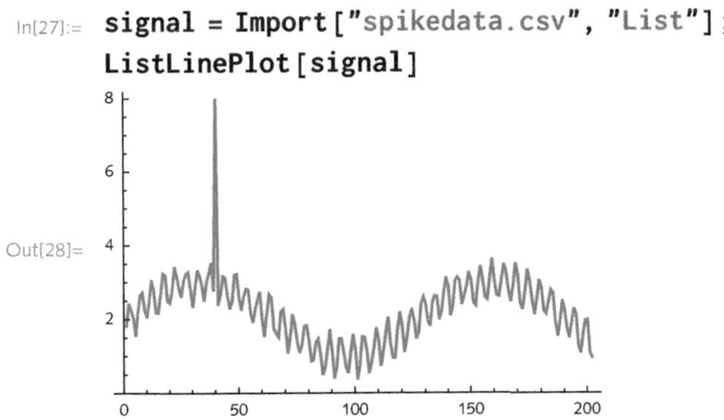

Most of the values fall within a narrow band.

```
In[29]:= RandomSample[signal, 12]

Out[29]= {3.07255, 3.32531, 2.17509, 2.52658, 2.25535, 0.69369,
          2.6599, 1.46555, 0.537821, 1.43433, 2.49226, 1.51776}
```

To remove the spike, we can select all those values that are below a certain threshold, essentially creating a lowpass filter. With a bit of experimentation, a threshold of 4 seems about right.

```
In[30]:= filtered = Select[signal, # < 4 &];
         ListLinePlot[filtered, PlotRange → {0, 5}]
```

Out[31]=

This was a simplistic filter. It works fine for a signal whose amplitudes are not widely varying or for signals whose spikes are fairly uniform. For most real-world signal processing, filters involving moving averages or convolutions are commonly used to reduce noise and spikes (Hamming 1989).

As another example of pure predicate functions, let us next create a function to sum the integers one through *n* using pure predicate functions for argument checking. The following works fine if *n* is a positive integer, but is not well-defined otherwise:

```
In[32]:= sumInts[n_] := Total[Range[n]]

In[33]:= sumInts[1.3]

Out[33]= 1

In[34]:= sumInts[-3]

Out[34]= 0
```

Argument checking using pure function predicates can rectify this.

```
In[35]:= Clear[sumInts]

In[36]:= sumInts[n_?(IntegerQ[#] && Positive[#] &)] := Total[Range[n]]

In[37]:= sumInts[-1.3]
Out[37]= sumInts[-1.3]

In[38]:= sumInts[100]
Out[38]= 5050
```

Because of the precedence *Mathematica* gives to different operators, it is necessary to enclose the entire function, including the &, in parentheses. For a complete list of operator precedence, see the tutorial Operator Input Forms (WLDC).

Indexing with pure functions

Occasionally it is necessary to index parts of an expression by the position of each element. MapIndexed is designed for this purpose and it is often used with pure functions.

Given an expression to index, the default behavior of MapIndexed is to create pairs (e_i, i), where e_i is the ith element in the expression, and then to pass them as arguments to a function given as the first argument to MapIndexed.

```
In[39]:= expr = {a, b, c, d, e};
         MapIndexed[f, expr]
Out[40]= {f[a, {1}], f[b, {2}], f[c, {3}], f[d, {4}], f[e, {5}]}
```

If, instead of a symbolic function f, we use List, we get pairs of the form $\{e_i, \{i\}\}$.

```
In[41]:= MapIndexed[List, expr]
Out[41]= {{a, {1}}, {b, {2}}, {c, {3}}, {d, {4}}, {e, {5}}}
```

Using pure functions you can modify this quite a bit by operating on either the index or the subexpression. With MapIndexed, #2 refers to the index and #1 to the element itself. For example, the following pure function is a list consisting of the first part of the index (strip away one set of braces) followed by the element in that position:

```
In[42]:= MapIndexed[{First[#2], #1} &, expr]
Out[42]= {{1, a}, {2, b}, {3, c}, {4, d}, {5, e}}
```

Let's use MapIndexed on a matrix to extract its diagonal. Here is a small matrix with random integer elements:

```
In[43]:= mat = RandomInteger[10, {4, 4}];
         MatrixForm[mat]
Out[44]//MatrixForm=
```

$$\begin{pmatrix} 7 & 2 & 5 & 4 \\ 1 & 4 & 6 & 3 \\ 7 & 2 & 2 & 4 \\ 2 & 0 & 0 & 8 \end{pmatrix}$$

Recall that Part[*lis*, *i*, *k*] gives the *i*th row, *k*th column of *lis*. In the following then, #1 refers to the row and #2, the index, gives the column number:

```
In[45]:= MapIndexed[Part[#1, #2] &, mat]
Out[45]= {{7}, {4}, {2}, {8}}
```

Flatten the list to reduce the nesting braces and then check against a built-in function that computes diagonals.

```
In[46]:= Flatten[%]
Out[46]= {7, 4, 2, 8}
```

```
In[47]:= Diagonal[mat]
Out[47]= {7, 4, 2, 8}
```

Newton revisited

In the last version of the findRoot function that we created in Section 5.4, a While loop was used to evaluate the body until the test failed. There is another function we could use to simplify this calculation – it is NestWhile.

```
NestWhile[f, init, test]
```

This function iterates *f* with initial value *init*, while *test* continues to be true.

To rewrite findRoot using this construct we have to identify the arguments to NestWhile: the first argument is the expression we are iterating; the second argument is the initial guess, the initial value for the iteration; the third argument is the test that will be performed each time through the loop until it returns False.

```
NestWhile[# - f[#]/f'[#] &, N[init], Abs[f[#]] > ϵ &]
```

We are going to add a new construct: a default value for ϵ. The syntax is ϵ_ : *val*; this is the syntax for an optional argument that, when omitted, takes the value *val*.

We also want to change the form of the first argument to allow a general expression such as $x^2 - 2$ or Cos[*x*], similar to what the built-in root-finding functions use. The key here is to create a pure function from the general expression and then use that in a similar manner to what we did previously. If our expression is *expr* in the variable *var*, then the pure function will be the following:

```
Function[var, expr]
```

Here then is a new findRoot using these constructs:

```
In[48]:= findRoot[expr_, {var_, init_}, ϵ_ : 0.0001] :=
  Module[{result, f = Function[Evaluate[var], expr]},
   result = NestWhile[# - f[#]/f'[#] &, N[init], Abs[f[#]] > ϵ &];
   {var → result}]
```

You will notice that we have wrapped `var` inside the pure function with `Evaluate`. Technically it is not necessary, as the `findRoot` function will still work, but without it *Mathematica* thinks there is a conflict between the `var` on the left-hand side of the rule and the `var` being initialized in the `Module`.

Here we compute the square root of two and a root of cosine near $x = 0.5$:

```
In[49]:= findRoot[x^2 - 2, {x, 2.0}]
Out[49]= {x → 1.41422}

In[50]:= findRoot[Cos[x], {x, .5}]
Out[50]= {x → 1.5708}
```

To compute the root of $x - \sin(x)$, we should try using a nondefault value for ϵ – a wider tolerance.

```
In[51]:= findRoot[x - Sin[x], {x, 1.0}, 10^-20]
Out[51]= {x → 2.95905 × 10^-7}
```

The exercises contain several variations and extensions of this root-finding function, including one that returns intermediate values and another that accepts equations – expressions of the form $x^2 - 2 == 0$ or `Cos[x] == 0` – as arguments.

Example: searching for attributes

With so many built-in functions available in *Mathematica*, the need often arises to find functions having a certain attribute in which you are interested. For example, listable functions are very efficient when operating on lists, and so it is useful to be able to identify and use them whenever possible. In this example we will create a function that searches the entire built-in symbol list for functions with a given attribute. We start by figuring out what to do with one function and then extend that to a list of functions.

It is easy to check one function: `MemberQ[`*list*`,` *form*`]` returns the value `True` if an element of *list* matches the pattern *form*.

```
In[52]:= MemberQ[Attributes[Sin], Listable]
Out[52]= True
```

Next, here is a list of all the built-in functions:

```
In[53]:= names = Names["System`*"];

In[54]:= RandomSample[names, 8]
Out[54]= {LoopFreeGraphQ, VertexShapeFunction, Gradient,
          FindProcessParameters, LocationTest, Blank, Parameter, FontVariations}
```

One minor point to note: the output of `Names` is a list of strings.

```
In[55]:= InputForm[%]
Out[55]//InputForm=
         {"LoopFreeGraphQ", "VertexShapeFunction", "Gradient",
          "FindProcessParameters", "LocationTest", "Blank", "Parameter",
          "FontVariations"}
```

Fortunately, `Attributes` can take either a symbol or a string as an argument, so we do not need to worry about the distinction here but we will need to worry about this when we do something similar for options in Exercise 17 at the end of this section.

```
In[56]:= Attributes["Sin"]
Out[56]= {Listable, NumericFunction, Protected}
```

Hopefully it is clear how we should proceed. We want to select all those `System`` symbols that have a given attribute. For example, this selects all `System`` symbols with the `Constant` attribute. Each symbol in the list `names` will be slotted in to the pure function and if its list of attributes include `Constant`, then it will be selected.

```
In[57]:= Select[names, MemberQ[Attributes[#], Constant] &]
Out[57]= {Catalan, Degree, E, EulerGamma, Glaisher,
          GoldenRatio, Khinchin, MachinePrecision, Pi}
```

Let us turn this into a function that takes the attribute as an argument. This function is self-contained – the user does not need to evaluate `Names["System`"]` prior to using it as we did above.

```
In[58]:= FunctionsWithAttribute[attrib_Symbol] :=
          Select[Names["System`*"], MemberQ[Attributes[#], attrib] &]

In[59]:= FunctionsWithAttribute[Constant]
Out[59]= {Catalan, Degree, E, EulerGamma, Glaisher,
          GoldenRatio, Khinchin, MachinePrecision, Pi}

In[60]:= FunctionsWithAttribute[Orderless]
Out[60]= {ArithmeticGeometricMean, BitAnd, BitOr, BitXor, CoprimeQ,
          DiracComb, DiracDelta, DiscreteDelta, Equivalent, GCD,
          HeavisideLambda, HeavisidePi, HeavisideTheta, KroneckerDelta,
          LCM, Majority, Max, Min, Multinomial, OrderlessPatternSequence,
          Plus, Times, UnitBox, UnitStep, UnitTriangle, Xnor, Xor}
```

Exercises

1. Using pure functions, compute $\sin(x)/x$ for each x in the list $\{0, \pi/6, \pi/4, \pi/3, \pi/2\}$. Check your answer against the built-in `Sinc` function.
2. Create a pure function to select all integers between one and one thousand that are square numbers; that is, numbers that are some integer squared.
3. In Exercise 11, Section 5.1 you were asked to create a function to compute the diameter of a set of points in n-dimensional space. Modify that solution by instead using the `Norm` function and pure functions to find the diameter.

4. Rewrite the code from Section 5.2 for finding the next prime after a given integer so that it uses pure functions instead of relying upon the auxiliary definition `addOne` and the built-in function `CompositeQ`.

5. Create a function `RepUnit[n]` that generates integers of length n consisting entirely of ones. For example, `RepUnit[7]` should produce 1111111.

6. Rewrite the example from Section 5.2 in which `NestList` was used to perform several rotations of a triangle to instead use pure functions and dispense with the auxiliary function `rotation` used to specify the rotation angles.

7. Given a set of numerical data, extract all those data points that are within one standard deviation of the mean of the data.

```
In[1]:= data = RandomVariate[NormalDistribution[0, 1], {2500}];
```

8. Using the built-in `Fold` function, write a function `fromDigits[lis, b]` that accepts a list of digits in any base b (less than 20) and converts it to a base 10 number. For example, 1101_2 is 13 in base 10, so your function should handle this as follows:

```
In[2]:= fromDigits[{1, 1, 0, 1}, 2]
Out[2]= 13
```

Check your solution against the built-in `FromDigits` function.

9. Write a pure function that moves a random walker from one location on a square lattice to one of the four adjoining locations with equal probability (a two-dimensional lattice walk). For example, starting at `{0, 0}`, the function should return `{0, 1}`, `{0, -1}`, `{1, 0}`, or `{-1, 0}` with equal likelihood. Use this pure function with `NestList` to generate the list of step locations for an n-step random walk starting at the origin.

10. Modify the `findRoot` function from this section to allow for equations of the form `x^2 == 2` or `Cos[x] == 0` as the first argument.

11. Create a function `findRootList` that is based on `findRoot` and returns all the intermediate values that are computed by the Newton iteration.

12. A naive approach to polynomial arithmetic would require three additions and six multiplications to carry out the arithmetic in the expression $a\,x^3 + b\,x^2 + c\,x + d$. Using Horner's method for fast polynomial multiplication, this expression can be represented as $d + x(c + x(b + a\,x))$, where there are now half as many multiplications. You can see this using the `MultiplyCount` function developed in Exercise 7 of Section 4.2.

```
In[3]:= MultiplyCount[a x^3 + b x^2 + c x + d]
Out[3]= 6

In[4]:= MultiplyCount[d + x (c + x (b + a x))]
Out[4]= 3
```

In general, the number of multiplications in an n-degree polynomial in traditional form is given by:

```
In[5]:= Binomial[n + 1, 2]
Out[5]= 1/2 n (1 + n)
```

This, of course, grows quadratically with n, whereas Horner's method grows linearly. Create a function `HornerPolynomial[lis, var]` that gives a representation of a polynomial in Horner form. Here is some sample output that your function should generate:

```
In[6]:= HornerPolynomial[{a, b, c, d}, x]
Out[6]= d + x (c + x (b + a x))

In[7]:= Expand[%]
Out[7]= d + c x + b x^2 + a x^3
```

13. Find all words in the dictionary that start with the letter q and are of length five. The following gets all the words in the dictionary that comes with *Mathematica* and displays a random sample:

```
In[8]:= words = DictionaryLookup[];
        RandomSample[words, 18]
Out[9]= {dare, condole, forums, attributive, impassible,
         minefields, skittish, thereabout, jugful, fishiest, canter,
         choral, Nanjing, toupee, solemner, Marlboro, Whigs, healthier}
```

14. Given a list of angles between zero and 2π, map them to points of the form $\{x, y\}$ on the unit circle.

```
In[10]:= angles = RandomReal[{0, 2 π}, {8}]
Out[10]= {5.8948, 2.50319, 1.93239, 5.65609, 0.571937, 5.32786, 4.96526, 5.49373}
```

Once created, display the points graphically using code similar to the following:

```
In[11]:= Graphics[{Circle[], Point[pts]}]
Out[11]=
```

Finally, create a set of lines from the origin to each of the points on the circle and display using code similar to the following:

```
In[12]:= Graphics[{Circle[], Point[pts], Line[lines]}]
Out[12]=
```

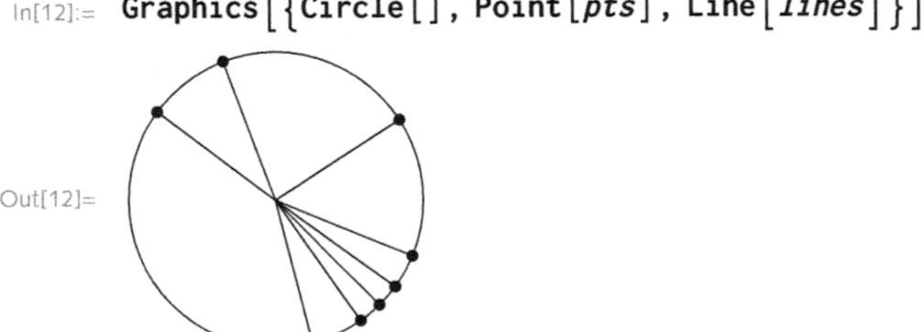

15. Use `FoldList` to compute an exponential moving average of a list $\{x_1, x_2, x_3\}$. You can check your result against the built-in `ExponentialMovingAverage`.

```
In[13]:= ExponentialMovingAverage[{x1, x2, x3}, α]
Out[13]= {x1, -(-1 + α) x1 + α x2, -(-1 + α) (-(-1 + α) x1 + α x2) + α x3}
```

16. A well-known programming exercise in many languages is to generate Hamming numbers, sometimes referred to as *regular numbers*. These are numbers that divide powers of 60 (the choice of that number goes back to the Babylonians, who used 60 as a number base). Generate a sorted sequence of all Hamming numbers less than 1000. The key observation is that these numbers have only 2, 3, and 5 as prime factors.

17. In the text, we developed `FunctionsWithAttributes` to find all built-in functions with a particular attribute. Create a new function to find all built-in functions with a given option. For example:

```
In[14]:= FunctionsWithOption[StepMonitor]

Out[14]= {FindArgMax, FindArgMin, FindFit, FindMaximum, FindMaxValue,
  FindMinimum, FindMinValue, FindRoot, NArgMax, NArgMin, NDSolve,
  NDSolveValue, NMaximize, NMaxValue, NMinimize, NMinValue,
  NonlinearModelFit, NRoots, ParametricNDSolve, ParametricNDSolveValue}
```

Several changes from `FunctionsWithAttributes` will be necessary: `Options` does not take a string as an argument; and options are often given as nested lists of rules, requiring mapping at the appropriate level. You might also want to delete all functions beginning with $, such as `$Context`, to help speed the computation.

18. Graphs that are not too dense are often represented using adjacency structures which consist of a list for each vertex v_i that includes those other vertices that v_i is connected to. Create an adjacency structure for any graph, directed or undirected. For example, consider the graph gr below.

```
In[15]:= gr = RandomGraph[{8, 12}, VertexLabels → "Name"]
```

Out[15]=

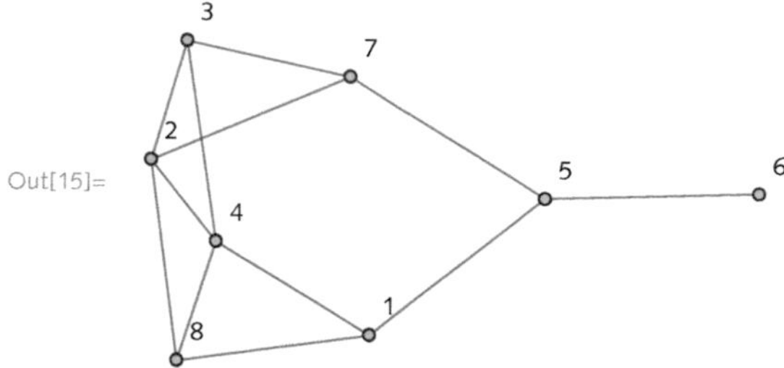

Start by creating an adjacency list for any given vertex; that is, a list of those vertices to which the given vertex is connected. The adjacency list for vertex 4 in the above graph would be `{1, 8, 2, 3}`.

The adjacency structure is then the list of adjacency lists for every vertex in that graph. It is common to prepend each adjacency list with its vertex; typically the adjacency structure takes the following form where this syntax indicates that vertex 1 is connected to vertices 4, 5, and 8; vertex 2 is connected to vertices 3, 4, 7, and 8; and so on.

```
{{1, {4, 5, 8}}, {2, {3, 4, 7, 8}}, {3, {2, 4, 7}}, {4, {1, 2, 3, 8}},
 {5, {1, 6, 7}}, {6, {5}}, {7, {2, 3, 5}}, {8, {1, 2, 4}}}
```

19. One common use of graphs is to analyze the relationships of the objects under study. For example, if you were interested in finding all objects a certain distance from a given object, you could use `NeighborhoodGraph`.

Here is a grid graph on which we can start prototyping:

```
In[16]:= gr = GridGraph[{7, 7}, VertexLabels → "Name"];
```

NeighborhoodGraph gives all those vertices up to distance two from vertex 25.

```
In[17]:= HighlightGraph[gr, NeighborhoodGraph[gr, 25, 2]]
```

Out[17]=

But suppose you were interested in all those vertices *precisely* distance two from vertex 25. Implement this using two different approaches: one in which you use NeighborhoodGraph and another using a two-argument form of VertexList in which the second argument is a pattern.

20. Create a "composition" using the digits of π to represent notes on the C scale, where a digit n is interpreted as a note n semitones from middle C. For example, the first few digits 1, 4, 1, 5 would give the notes one, four, one, and five semitones from middle C.

    You can generate tones using Sound and SoundNote. For example, this emits a tone five semitones above middle C of duration one second:

```
In[18]:= Sound[SoundNote[5, 1]] // EmitSound
```

    And this emits the same tone but using a midi instrument instead of the default:

```
In[19]:= Sound[SoundNote[5, 1, "Vibraphone"]] // EmitSound
```

21. A matrix is *nilpotent* if it is a square matrix all of whose eigenvalues are zero. Alternatively, a square matrix A is nilpotent if A^n is the zero matrix for some positive integer n. Create a predicate NilpotentMatrixQ[*mat*] that returns True if *mat* is nilpotent. Check your function by verifying that any directed acyclic graph (DAG) has a nilpotent adjacency matrix. A list of acyclic graphs is available via GraphData["Acyclic"]. See McKay et al. (2004) for information about acyclic graphs and the eigenvalues of their adjacency matrices.

```
In[20]:= gr = GraphData[{"CayleyTree", {5, 3}}]
```

Out[20]=

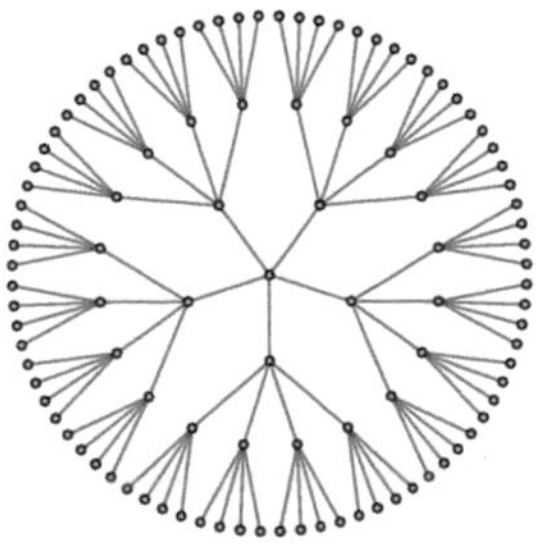

```
In[21]:= AcyclicGraphQ[gr]
Out[21]= True
```

5.6 Examples

In this section we will put many of the concepts we have explored to work in solving several concrete, real-world problems. Included is a problem from signal processing on computing Hamming distance; another from ancient history, the Josephus problem; a graphical problem from bioinformatics on the creation and display of protein–protein interaction networks; a data-processing problem on cleaning and filtering arrays of data in which nonnumerical elements arise; a large numerical problem in which we enumerate and count matrices whose eigenvalues have a certain form; and a numerical/graphical problem in clustering data.

Hamming distance

When a signal is transmitted over a channel in the presence of noise, errors often occur. A major concern in telecommunications is measuring (and of course, trying to minimize) that error. For two lists of binary symbols, their *Hamming distance* is defined as the number of nonmatching elements and so gives a measure of how well these two lists of binary digits match up. In this first example, we will create a function to compute the Hamming distance of binary signals.

How do we determine if two binary numbers are identical? Various tests of equality are available. `SameQ[x, y]` returns `True` if x and y are identical. It differs from `Equal` (==) in that, for numbers, `Equal` tests for numerical equality within a certain tolerance, but `SameQ` tests for identical structures.

```
In[1]:= SameQ[0, 0.0]
Out[1]= False
```

```
In[2]:= Equal[0, 0.0]
Out[2]= True
```

Here is what `SameQ` returns for the different pairings of binary numbers:

```
In[3]:= {SameQ[0, 0], SameQ[1, 0], SameQ[1, 1]}
Out[3]= {True, False, True}
```

So we need to thread `SameQ` over the two lists of binary numbers and then count up the occurrences of `False`.

```
In[4]:= MapThread[SameQ, {{1, 0, 0, 1, 1}, {0, 1, 0, 1, 0}}]
Out[4]= {False, False, True, True, False}
```

```
In[5]:= Count[%, False]
Out[5]= 3
```

Putting these last two pieces together, we have our first definition for Hamming distance.

```
In[6]:= HammingDistanceCnt[lis1_, lis2_] :=
          Count[MapThread[SameQ, {lis1, lis2}], False]
```

```
In[7]:= HammingDistanceCnt[{1, 0, 0, 1, 1}, {0, 1, 0, 1, 0}]
Out[7]= 3
```

Since we are dealing with binary information, we might try to solve this problem by a more direct approach using some of the logical binary operators built into *Mathematica*. `BitXor[x, y]` returns the bitwise XOR of x and y. So if x and y can only be among the binary integers zero or one, `BitXor` will return zero whenever they are the same and will return one whenever they are different. Note that `BitXor` is listable and so automatically threads over lists.

```
In[8]:= BitXor[{1, 0, 0, 1, 1}, {0, 1, 0, 1, 0}]
Out[8]= {1, 1, 0, 0, 1}
```

And here are the number of ones that occur in that list:

```
In[9]:= Total[%]
Out[9]= 3
```

Here then is our bit-operator version for the Hamming distance computation:

```
In[10]:= HammingDistanceBit[lis1_, lis2_] := Total[BitXor[lis1, lis2]]

In[11]:= HammingDistanceBit[{1, 0, 0, 1, 1}, {0, 1, 0, 1, 0}]
Out[11]= 3
```

Let us compare the running times of these implementations using a large data set, in this case two lists consisting of one million zeros and ones.

```
In[12]:= sig1 = RandomInteger[1, {10^6}];

In[13]:= sig2 = RandomInteger[1, {10^6}];

In[14]:= Timing[HammingDistanceCnt[sig1, sig2]]
Out[14]= {0.338938, 500169}

In[15]:= Timing[HammingDistanceBit[sig1, sig2]]
Out[15]= {0.016084, 500169}
```

That is quite a difference in the efficiency of these two approaches! Using bit operators gives a speedup of between one and two orders of magnitude. We will leave a discussion of the causes of this difference until Chapter 9. Until then, the exercises ask you to write additional implementations for computing Hamming distance that use pattern matching and modular arithmetic.

As an aside, the above computations are not a bad check on the built-in random number generator – we would expect that about half of the paired-up lists would contain different elements.

The Josephus problem

Flavius Josephus (37 – *ca.* 100 AD) was a Jewish historian who fought in the Roman–Jewish war of the first century AD. Through his writings comes the following story:

> *The Romans had chased a group of ten Jews into a cave and were about to attack. Rather than die at the hands of their enemy, the group chose to commit suicide one by one. Legend has it though, that they decided to go around their circle of ten individuals and eliminate every other person until only one was left.*

The Josephus problem is stated simply: who was the last to survive? Although a bit macabre, this problem has a definite mathematical interpretation that lends itself well to a functional style of programming. We will restate the problem to make it closer to the computational steps we will implement: *n* people are lined up; the first person is moved to the end of the line; the second person is removed from the line; the third person is moved to the end of the line; and so on until only one person remains in the line.

The statement of the problem indicates that there is a repetitive action, performed over and over. It can be encoded with the `RotateLeft` function (move the person at the front of the line to the back of the line) followed by the use of the `Rest` function (remove the next person from the line).

```
In[16]:= Rest[RotateLeft[{a, b, c, d}]]
Out[16]= {c, d, a}
```

At this point it should be fairly clear where this computation is headed. We want to take a list and, using the `Nest` function, iterate the pure function `Rest[RotateLeft[#]] &` until only one element remains. A list of *n* elements will need $n - 1$ iterations. We will create the list of *n* elements using `Range[n]`. Here then is the function `survivor`:

```
In[17]:= survivor[n_] := Nest[Rest[RotateLeft[#]] &, Range[n], n - 1]
```

Evaluating the `survivor` function on a list of ten, the survivor is in the fifth starting position.

```
In[18]:= survivor[10]
Out[18]= {5}
```

Tracing the applications of `RotateLeft` in this example gives a clearer picture of what is happening. Using `TracePrint` with a second argument shows only the results of the applications of `RotateLeft` that occur during evaluation of the expression `survivor[5]`.

```
In[19]:= TracePrint[survivor[5], RotateLeft]
           RotateLeft
           {2, 3, 4, 5, 1}
           RotateLeft
           {4, 5, 1, 3}
           RotateLeft
           {1, 3, 5}
           RotateLeft
           {5, 3}
Out[19]= {3}
```

Or, your could generate the list of survivors at each round by using `NestList` instead of `Nest`.

```
In[20]:= n = 5;
         NestList[Rest[RotateLeft[#]] &, Range[n], n - 1]
Out[21]= {{1, 2, 3, 4, 5}, {3, 4, 5, 1}, {5, 1, 3}, {3, 5}, {3}}
```

Protein interaction networks

Proteins interact with other proteins in biological processes as varied as DNA replication, signal transduction, movement of molecules into and between cells, and essentially all processes in living cells. In fact, signal transduction, a process in which proteins control the signaling into and out of the cell, is key to the study of diseases including many cancers. Their importance in all cellular activity has given rise to active work in the visualization of protein–protein interactions (PPIs). In this section, we will combine functional constructs, pattern matching, and graph tools to visualize networks of proteins that have a high level of interaction.

We will work with proteins from the worm *Caenorhabditis elegans*, a heavily studied organism. The data, courtesy the Center for Cancer Systems Biology at the Dana-Farber Cancer Institute, are in the form of a tab-separated text file.

```
In[22]:= data = Import[
           "http://interactome.dfci.harvard.edu/C_elegans/graphs/sequence_edges/
            wi2007.txt", "TSV"];
```

Tip 5.5

When importing data, one of the first things you need to figure out is the nature of what you are working with. Two very useful things to know after import are how big the data set is and what does a typical element look like? The first two computations below show that there are 1817 elements and that each element is a pair.

```
In[23]:= Length[data]
Out[23]= 1817

In[24]:= Dimensions[data]
Out[24]= {1817, 2}
```

Use `Take` to show a few representative elements. The data are of the form {*protein*$_1$, *protein*$_2$}, which indicates an interaction between these two named proteins.

```
In[25]:= Take[data, 8]
Out[25]= {{#IDA, IDB}, {AC3.3, F29G6.3}, {AC3.3, R05F9.10}, {AC3.3, Y69H2.3},
          {AC3.7, Y40B10A.2}, {B0001.4, F19B6.1}, {B0001.7, B0281.5}, {B0001.7, F37H8.1}}
```

Using the function `ToEdges`, developed in Exercise 15 of Section 5.1, we turn these lists into edges, where each edge represents an interaction between two proteins (vertices in the graph).

```
In[26]:= ToEdges[lis : {{_, _} ..}] := Apply[DirectedEdge, lis, {1}]
```

```
In[27]:= ToEdges[lis : {_, _}] := Apply[DirectedEdge, lis]

In[28]:= ToEdges[Take[data, 12]]

Out[28]= {#IDA → IDB, AC3.3 → F29G6.3, AC3.3 → R05F9.10,
          AC3.3 → Y69H2.3, AC3.7 → Y40B10A.2, B0001.4 → F19B6.1,
          B0001.7 → B0281.5, B0001.7 → F37H8.1, B0024.10 → C06A1.1,
          B0024.12 → C06E2.1, B0024.14 → B0228.1, B0024.14 → C05G6.1}
```

We need to delete the first entry ("#IDA" → "IDB"), which is meant as a comment. So we use ToEdges on Rest[data] and then visualize the result with Graph.

```
In[29]:= edges = ToEdges[Rest[data]];

In[30]:= gr = Graph[edges, GraphStyle → "BasicBlue"]

Out[30]=
```

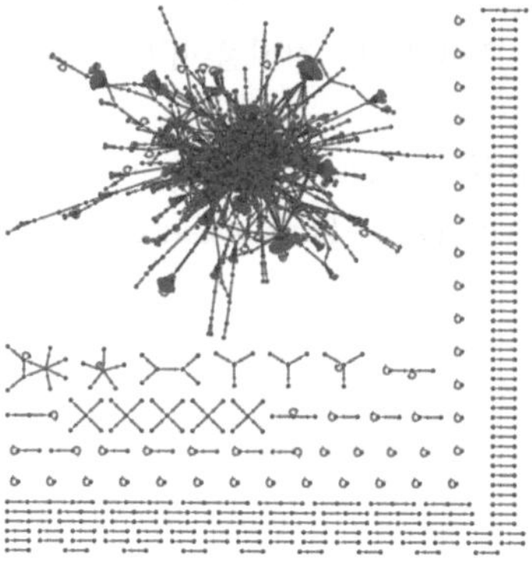

This is a fairly dense graph showing all the protein interactions, and, as a result, it is a bit difficult to discern detail. Many of the interactions involve only two proteins, as seen in the small components on the right and bottom of the above output. Our task in this example is to find the subgraph consisting of all those proteins with greater than n interactions with other proteins. We will take $n = 12$; that is, proteins that have more than 12 interactions with other proteins.

VertexDegree[*gr*, *vertex*] gives the number of edges incident to *vertex* in a graph *gr*. So in our protein network, the vertex degree for vertex v_i gives the number of interactions between that protein represented by v_i and all other proteins. The proteins are specified as strings.

```
In[31]:= VertexDegree[gr, "R05F9.10"]

Out[31]= 86
```

A slightly different syntax for VertexDegree gives the degree for every vertex in the graph. So, from the tally below, vertices with one edge occur 933 times in this network, vertices with two edges occur 246 times, and so on. There is only one vertex with 86 edges.

```
In[32]:= SortBy[Tally@VertexDegree[gr], First]

Out[32]= {{1, 933}, {2, 246}, {3, 107}, {4, 64}, {5, 40}, {6, 21}, {7, 19},
          {8, 6}, {9, 10}, {10, 6}, {11, 2}, {12, 11}, {13, 2}, {14, 1}, {15, 2},
          {16, 3}, {17, 2}, {18, 2}, {19, 3}, {21, 2}, {23, 1}, {24, 2}, {28, 1},
          {30, 1}, {31, 3}, {39, 1}, {44, 1}, {45, 1}, {47, 1}, {49, 1}, {86, 1}}
```

To extract all vertices with a vertex degree greater than 12, use `Select` with the appropriate predicate.

```
In[33]:= Select[VertexList[gr], (VertexDegree[gr, #] > 12 &)]
Out[33]= {R05F9.10, Y69H2.3, Y40B10A.2, DH11.4, K09B11.9, R02F2.5, ZK1053.5, W05H7.4,
  C18G1.2, T11B7.1, F52E1.7, F46A9.5, Y54E2A.3, ZK858.4, C50F4.1, K12C11.2,
  C06G1.5, Y65B4BR.4, F32B4.4, ZK849.2, C36C9.1, ZK1055.7, C06A5.9, W09C2.1,
  F44G3.9, ZK121.2, M04G12.1, T21G5.5, W10C8.2, F01G10.2, Y55F3C.6}
```

Or, thread the inequality over the list of vertex degrees and pick those vertices for which this inequality is true.

```
In[34]:= proteins = Pick[VertexList[gr], Thread[VertexDegree[gr] > 12]]
Out[34]= {R05F9.10, Y69H2.3, Y40B10A.2, DH11.4, K09B11.9, R02F2.5, ZK1053.5, W05H7.4,
  C18G1.2, T11B7.1, F52E1.7, F46A9.5, Y54E2A.3, ZK858.4, C50F4.1, K12C11.2,
  C06G1.5, Y65B4BR.4, F32B4.4, ZK849.2, C36C9.1, ZK1055.7, C06A5.9, W09C2.1,
  F44G3.9, ZK121.2, M04G12.1, T21G5.5, W10C8.2, F01G10.2, Y55F3C.6}
```

`Thread` is needed here because `Greater` (>) is not listable. Note that `Thread` can thread over two expressions that are not the same structurally, as in our example here:

```
In[35]:= {1, 2, 3, 4} > 3
Out[35]= {1, 2, 3, 4} > 3

In[36]:= Thread[{1, 2, 3, 4} > 3]
Out[36]= {False, False, False, True}
```

Now we get all those interactions that involve the list `proteins` as defined above. In other words, this is a list of all protein interactions involving proteins that have greater than 12 interactions:

```
In[37]:= edges = Cases[EdgeList[gr],
    (p1_ ↔ p2_) /; MemberQ[proteins, p1] && MemberQ[proteins, p2],
    Infinity];

In[38]:= {Length[edges], Take[edges, -1]}
Out[38]= {53, {ZK858.4 ↔ ZK858.4}}
```

We delete self-loops (although proteins certainly can interact with themselves).

```
In[39]:= gr1 = DeleteCases[edges, x_ ↔ x_];

In[40]:= {Length[gr1], Take[gr1, -1]}
Out[40]= {41, {W05H7.4 ↔ ZK121.2}}
```

Finally, we use Graph and several options to visualize this PPI network.

```
In[41]:= Graph[gr1, VertexStyle → Red, VertexSize → Large,
          GraphLayout → "SpringElectricalEmbedding", VertexLabels → "Name"]
```

Out[41]=

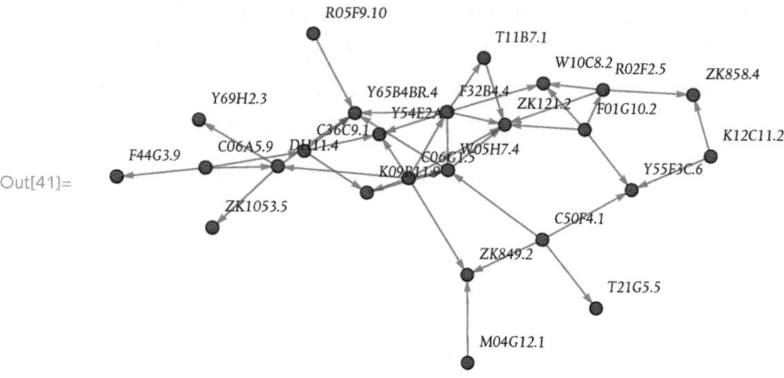

The exercises include an extension of this PPI visualization in which you are asked to color the vertices according to that protein's biological processes.

Operating on arrays

Up to this point, the solutions for many of the examples resulted in short programs, either what are often called "one-liners" or simply short, self-contained programs. One of the advantages of such an approach is that everything you might need to run the program is contained in the body of your function. Although it may seem convenient to put all auxiliary definitions into the body of a function, there are several good reasons not to do so. One large chunk of code with many definitions embedded is often difficult to debug. Running the program may fail, with several warning or error messages displayed and no clear indication of where in your program the problem lies. The same holds for a program that returns an incorrect result. From the standpoint of efficiency, if your program takes longer than you think it should to run, how do you locate the bottleneck?

Modern programming uses a modular design to break up computational or programmatic tasks into small separate chunks and then put the pieces together in one program in such a way that you can isolate each part and diagnose errors or inefficient code more readily. Although we have been trying to adhere to this approach implicitly up to this point, in this section we will explicitly look at how a modular approach is implemented in *Mathematica*, using a matrix-processing example: replacing "bad" entries in a matrix with the column mean.

In working with tabular data collected by an instrument or by some other means, you occasionally find nonnumeric values (strings, for example) in the matrix where either the instrument has failed to collect a datum point for some reason or the value is "out of range." If an analysis of the matrix depends upon numeric values, what should be used to replace the nonnumeric values? One solution is to replace them with the column mean; that is, take the column in which the nonnumeric value occurs, compute the column mean using only the numeric values, and then replace the nonnumeric value with this mean.

To prototype, we use a small matrix, making it easier to check our work along the way.

```
In[42]:= mat = ( 44     72  6      "NAN"
                 "NAN"  46  28     75
                 19     10  40     2
                 99     98  "NAN"  47 );
```

First, extract and work on the first column and then later extend this to all the other columns.

```
In[43]:= col1 = mat[[All, 1]];
         MatrixForm[col1]
Out[44]//MatrixForm=
  44
  NAN
  19
  99
```

We need to extract just the numeric values. `Cases`, with the appropriate pattern, will do that. Several approaches using different patterns could be used.

```
In[45]:= Cases[col1, _?NumberQ]
Out[45]= {44, 19, 99}
```

```
In[46]:= Cases[col1, Except[_String]]
Out[46]= {44, 19, 99}
```

Then compute the mean of these numeric values.

```
In[47]:= Mean[Cases[col1, _?NumberQ]]
Out[47]= 54
```

Replace the string "NAN" with the mean.

```
In[48]:= col1 /. "NAN" → Mean[Cases[col1, _?NumberQ]] // MatrixForm
Out[48]//MatrixForm=
  44
  54
  19
  99
```

This operation needs to be performed on each column, so we write a function that will be mapped across the columns of a matrix.

```
In[49]:= colMean[col_] := col /. "NAN" :→ Mean[Cases[col, _?NumberQ]]
```

```
In[50]:= Map[colMean, Transpose[mat]]
```

Out[50]= $\left\{\{44, 54, 19, 99\}, \{72, 46, 10, 98\}, \left\{6, 28, 40, \frac{74}{3}\right\}, \left\{\frac{124}{3}, 75, 2, 47\right\}\right\}$

Since we operated on the columns, the above array is a list of the column vectors. We need to transpose back.

```
In[51]:= MatrixForm[Transpose[%]]
Out[51]//MatrixForm=
```

$$\begin{pmatrix} 44 & 72 & 6 & \frac{124}{3} \\ 54 & 46 & 28 & 75 \\ 19 & 10 & 40 & 2 \\ 99 & 98 & \frac{74}{3} & 47 \end{pmatrix}$$

Finally, let us put these pieces together:

```
In[52]:= ReplaceElement[mat_] := Transpose[Map[colMean, Transpose[mat]]]
```

```
In[53]:= ReplaceElement[mat] // MatrixForm
Out[53]//MatrixForm=
```

$$\begin{pmatrix} 44 & 72 & 6 & \frac{124}{3} \\ 54 & 46 & 28 & 75 \\ 19 & 10 & 40 & 2 \\ 99 & 98 & \frac{74}{3} & 47 \end{pmatrix}$$

Perform a quick, manual check on the third column.

```
In[54]:= Mean[{6, 28, 40}]
```

$$\text{Out[54]=} \quad \frac{74}{3}$$

With just a few small adjustments, `ReplaceElement` can work with arbitrary strings, not just `"NAN"` as above. Instead of the "hard-coded" string `"NAN"` in `columnMean`, we introduce a new rule with a different argument structure that will work alongside the earlier rule. This one will take a second argument `str` and use that wherever `"NAN"` appeared in the previous rule.

```
In[55]:= colMean[col_, str_String] := col /. str :→ Mean[Cases[col, _?NumberQ]]
```

```
In[56]:= ReplaceElement[mat_, str_String] :=
          Transpose[Map[colMean[#, str] &, Transpose[mat]]]
```

Let's try out the new code.

```
In[57]:= mat2 = {{-0.4444, "N/A", 0.3319, 0.4242, 0.},
           {-0.5088, -0.6955, 0.8398, 0.4287, -0.9319},
           {"N/A", 0.8287, 0.5286, 0.2591, -0.6978}, {0.6499, 0.4035, -0.099,
            0.6052, 0.5332}, {0.2575, -0.0589, -0.4938, "N/A", -0.5924}};
```

```
In[58]:= ReplaceElement[mat2, "N/A"] // MatrixForm
Out[58]//MatrixForm=
```

$$\begin{pmatrix} -0.4444 & 0.11945 & 0.3319 & 0.4242 & 0. \\ -0.5088 & -0.6955 & 0.8398 & 0.4287 & -0.9319 \\ -0.01145 & 0.8287 & 0.5286 & 0.2591 & -0.6978 \\ 0.6499 & 0.4035 & -0.099 & 0.6052 & 0.5332 \\ 0.2575 & -0.0589 & -0.4938 & 0.4293 & -0.5924 \end{pmatrix}$$

Of course, we should check that this code is reasonably efficient. This creates a random matrix, then inserts strings here and there, and finally runs `ReplaceElement`.

```
In[59]:= size = 1000;
         mat = RandomReal[1, {size, size}];
         rmat = ReplacePart[mat, RandomInteger[{1, size}, {size, 2}] :→ "NAN"];

In[62]:= ReplaceElement[rmat, "NAN"]; // Timing

Out[62]= {0.53991, Null}
```

That is not too bad – processing a 1000×1000 matrix in under a second. That is on the same order of magnitude as some of the highly optimized built-in linear algebra functions.

In the exercises you are asked to go a bit further and rewrite `ReplaceElement` to accept an arbitrary list of strings as the nonnumeric values to be replaced with the column means.

Enumerating binary matrices

In this example we will perform an enumeration and search involving binary matrices, that is, matrices consisting only of zeros and ones. The problem is to count the number of $n \times n$ binary matrices all of whose eigenvalues are real and positive. It turns out that the number of such matrices has an interesting connection to graph theory: this number is in one-to-one correspondence with labeled directed acyclic graphs (DAGs) on n nodes, something conjectured by Eric Weisstein in 2003 and proved in McKay et al. (2004).

To start, here is one random 2×2 binary matrix:

```
In[63]:= SeedRandom[125];
         n = 2;
         mat = RandomInteger[{0, 1}, {n, n}];
         MatrixForm[mat]

Out[66]//MatrixForm=
         (1  1)
         (0  1)
```

In this case, both eigenvalues are real and positive.

```
In[67]:= Eigenvalues[mat]

Out[67]= {1, 1}
```

The task is to count all such matrices for $n = 2, 3, 4, \ldots$.

To solve this problem, for each n, we will first need a programmatic way of enumerating all $n \times n$ binary matrices. Once that is done, we will create a predicate function to check if the eigenvalues of these matrices consist of all real and positive values.

Starting with $n = 2$, there are $2^2 = 4$ elements in the 2×2 matrix and each element can take on one of two values, 0 or 1. That gives $2^{2^2} = 16$ possible matrices. The key observation is this: if we enumerate the numbers 0 through 15 in base two and then convert those representations to a matrix, we will cover all possible permutations of zero and one in a four-element list. Here are the base two representations of each of the integers 0 through 15:

```
In[68]:= n = 2;
         Table[IntegerDigits[i, 2], {i, 0, 2^(n^2) - 1}]
Out[69]= {{0}, {1}, {1, 0}, {1, 1}, {1, 0, 0}, {1, 0, 1},
          {1, 1, 0}, {1, 1, 1}, {1, 0, 0, 0}, {1, 0, 0, 1}, {1, 0, 1, 0},
          {1, 0, 1, 1}, {1, 1, 0, 0}, {1, 1, 0, 1}, {1, 1, 1, 0}, {1, 1, 1, 1}}
```

To turn these into lists of the same length, pad out to four places; a third argument to IntegerDigits gives the number of places to pad out to.

```
In[70]:= Table[IntegerDigits[i, 2, n^2], {i, 0, 2^(n^2) - 1}]
Out[70]= {{0, 0, 0, 0}, {0, 0, 0, 1}, {0, 0, 1, 0}, {0, 0, 1, 1},
          {0, 1, 0, 0}, {0, 1, 0, 1}, {0, 1, 1, 0}, {0, 1, 1, 1},
          {1, 0, 0, 0}, {1, 0, 0, 1}, {1, 0, 1, 0}, {1, 0, 1, 1},
          {1, 1, 0, 0}, {1, 1, 0, 1}, {1, 1, 1, 0}, {1, 1, 1, 1}}
```

Now, turn each sublist into a 2×2 matrix by partitioning.

```
In[71]:= Table[Partition[IntegerDigits[i, 2, n^2], n], {i, 0, 2^(n^2) - 1}]
Out[71]= {{{0, 0}, {0, 0}}, {{0, 0}, {0, 1}}, {{0, 0}, {1, 0}}, {{0, 0}, {1, 1}},
          {{0, 1}, {0, 0}}, {{0, 1}, {0, 1}}, {{0, 1}, {1, 0}}, {{0, 1}, {1, 1}},
          {{1, 0}, {0, 0}}, {{1, 0}, {0, 1}}, {{1, 0}, {1, 0}}, {{1, 0}, {1, 1}},
          {{1, 1}, {0, 0}}, {{1, 1}, {0, 1}}, {{1, 1}, {1, 0}}, {{1, 1}, {1, 1}}}
```

Since we will be repeating these computations for $n = 3$, $n = 4$, and so on, let's wrap up the above code into a reusable function.

```
In[72]:= Clear[n]

In[73]:= BinaryMatrix[n_Integer?Positive] :=
          Table[Partition[IntegerDigits[i, 2, n^2], n], {i, 0, 2^(n^2) - 1}]
```

Before we do the eigenvalue computation on these matrices, we first need to create a predicate function that checks to see if a vector (our lists of eigenvalues) consists of real and positive numbers only. The following is the solution to Exercise 7 from Section 2.4:

```
In[74]:= RealPositiveQ[n_?NumericQ] := Im[n] == 0 && Positive[n]

In[75]:= RealPositiveQ[vec_?VectorQ] := AllTrue[vec, RealPositiveQ]
```

Now we can find those binary matrices whose eigenvalues are all real and positive; for the 2×2 case, they happen to have identical sets of eigenvalues.

```
In[76]:= mats = BinaryMatrix[2];

In[77]:= Select[Map[Eigenvalues, mats], RealPositiveQ]
Out[77]= {{1, 1}, {1, 1}, {1, 1}}
```

There are three such.

```
In[78]:= Count[Map[Eigenvalues, mats], m_ /; RealPositiveQ[m]]
Out[78]= 3
```

We have all the pieces now to check for any n. Let us first try for all 3×3 matrices.

```
In[79]:= mats = BinaryMatrix[3];

In[80]:= Count[Map[Eigenvalues, mats], m_ /; RealPositiveQ[m]]
Out[80]= 25
```

And for $n = 4$:

```
In[81]:= mats = BinaryMatrix[4];

In[82]:= Count[Map[Eigenvalues, mats], m_ /; RealPositiveQ[m]] // AbsoluteTiming
Out[82]= {33.8273, 543}
```

These computations are starting to get more compute-intensive as the shear number of matrices we are working with is growing exponentially. For example, for $n = 4$, there are 2^{4^2} matrices whose eigenvalues need to be computed and checked.

```
In[83]:= Length[mats]
Out[83]= 65536
```

As it turns out, most of the time is spent in the eigenvalue computation, not the predicate check. We will wait until Chapter 9 to discuss profiling, where we can identify the bottlenecks and find ways to speed things up.

Clustering data

When working on large data sets you are faced with the task of trying to summarize the data in a comprehensible way. Descriptive statistics such as the mean or standard deviation give some information about the average value and the spread of values. Histograms give a visual picture of the distribution of the data from which you can compare with other distributions. But none of these processes give a good sense of the *closeness* or *similarity* of data. For example, given a large drug sample, it is often important to group samples together that evoke similar reactions in a certain population; or your data might consist of reports of crimes committed in a certain geographic region and it would be helpful to know if certain criteria are clustered in some way.

Clustering (or cluster analysis) is used to group sets of data so that all objects in the same group, or cluster, are more similar than those objects outside that cluster. A key aspect of clustering is determining what it means for two objects to be similar. This is done by using distance metrics that are defined for specific domains. When performing cluster analysis on genomic sequences to find functionally related proteins, the objects you are working with are strings of letters, and so edit distance or Hamming distance are used. For numeric data, you might use Euclidean distance as the metric to determine the similarity or closeness of two data points.

In this section we will explore a bit of cluster analysis on two-dimensional numeric data with the aim of using several programming constructs discussed in this and previous chapters to help visualize the data. We will visualize the clusters together with the centroid of each cluster, as well as a region around the centroid.

Let us start with a set of bivariate data imported from a spreadsheet.

```
In[84]:= data = Import["bivariatedata.xlsx", {"XLSX", "Data", 1}];
         RandomSample[data, 12]

Out[85]= {{-3.6, 3.9}, {-2., -1.2}, {-3.7, -3.5}, {5.2, 3.1},
          {-3.2, -0.8}, {-3.5, 3.}, {-3., 3.}, {-1.3, -0.7},
          {-2.5, 3.2}, {-1.3, 4.2}, {-3.3, -1.5}, {-0.5, -2.}}
```

Use `FindClusters` to partition the data into exactly three clusters (the default is four).

```
In[86]:= clusters = FindClusters[data, 3];
         ListPlot[clusters]
```

Out[87]=

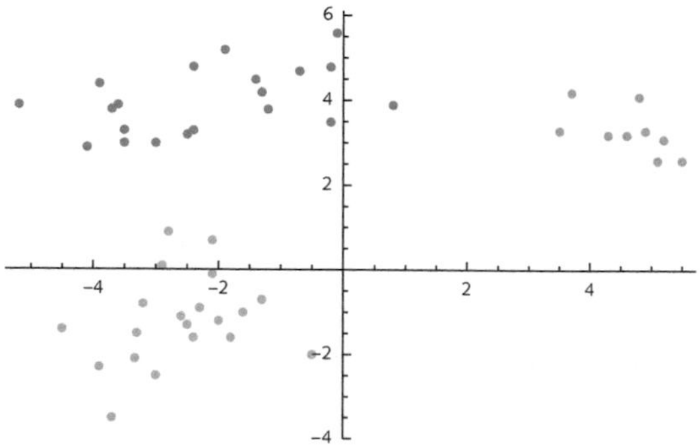

The centroids for each cluster can be found with `Mean` or with `RegionCentroid`.

```
In[88]:= Map[Mean, clusters]

Out[88]= {{-2.2, 3.985}, {4.62222, 3.28889}, {-2.5915, -1.195}}

In[89]:= centroids = Map[RegionCentroid[Point[#]] &, clusters]

Out[89]= {{-2.2, 3.985}, {4.62222, 3.28889}, {-2.5915, -1.195}}

In[90]:= ListPlot[clusters, Epilog → {
            Opacity[.4], PointSize[Large], Point[centroids]}]
```

Out[90]=

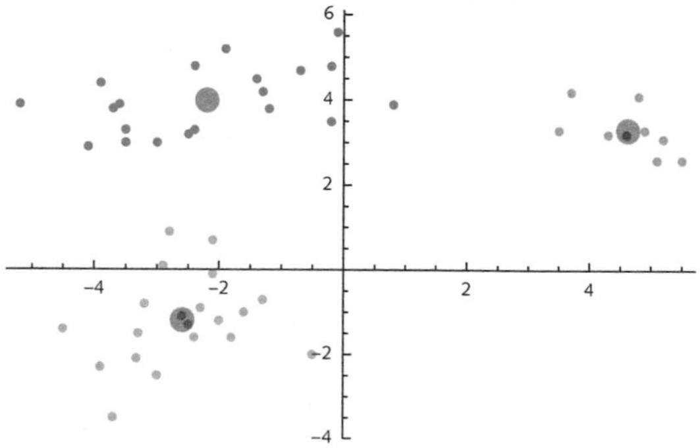

We will create disks centered on each centroid with radius equal to the mean of the distances of each point in the cluster to its centroid. Here is the computation for the first cluster only. What is returned are the distances from each point in the first cluster to the centroid for that cluster.

```
In[91]:= Map[EuclideanDistance[centroids[[1]], #] &, clusters[[1]]]
Out[91]= {3.0012, 1.46943, 3.0012, 1.51137, 2.64919, 2.18797,
  1.25149, 1.01697, 1.66169, 1.26895, 1.40258, 0.951433, 0.925324,
  0.839181, 1.63102, 2.15968, 0.7136, 1.74992, 2.05797, 0.840372}
```

Using Mean, this gives the average distances for each of the clusters.

```
In[92]:= distances = Table[
   Mean@Map[EuclideanDistance[centroids[[i]], #] &, clusters[[i]]],
   {i, 1, Length[clusters]}]
Out[92]= {1.61453, 0.723884, 1.20147}
```

The first visualization we will create will show the clusters as above together with a disk centered on each cluster with radius proportional to the average distance of the points in that cluster from their centroid. First, we create the disks. Disk takes two arguments: the center and the radius. MapThread is used here to slot these into Disk for each cluster.

```
In[93]:= disks = MapThread[Disk[#1, #2] &, {centroids, distances}]
Out[93]= {Disk[{-2.2, 3.985}, 1.61453],
  Disk[{4.62222, 3.28889}, 0.723884], Disk[{-2.5915, -1.195}, 1.20147]}
```

```
In[94]:= ListPlot[clusters, AspectRatio → Automatic, Epilog → {
    Opacity[0.4], PointSize[Large], Point[centroids],
    EdgeForm[Black], disks}]
```

Out[94]=

To color the disks the same color as the cluster they surround, we will grab the colors that the ListPlot function uses for multiple data sets.

```
In[95]:= colors = Take[ColorData[1, "ColorList"], Length[clusters]]
Out[95]= {■, ■, ■}
```

Lastly, we thread three lists: colors, centroids (disk center), and distances (disk radii).

```
In[96]:= disks = MapThread[{#1, Disk[#2, #3]} &, {colors, centroids, distances}]
Out[96]= {{■, Disk[{-2.2, 3.985}, 1.61453]},
  {■, Disk[{4.62222, 3.28889}, 0.723884]},
  {■, Disk[{-2.5915, -1.195}, 1.20147]}}
```

```
In[97]:= ListPlot[clusters, PlotStyle → colors,
          AspectRatio → Automatic, Epilog → {Opacity[.35],
            PointSize[Medium], Point[centroids], EdgeForm[Gray], disks}]
```

Out[97]=

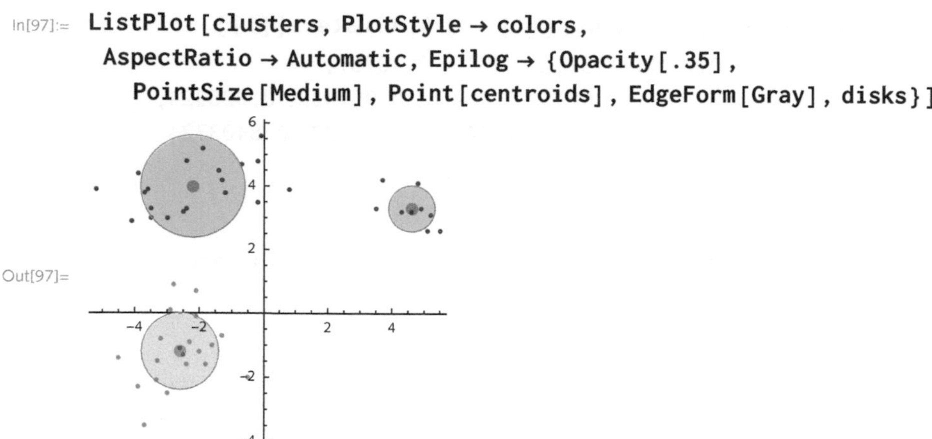

In the exercises you are asked to modify this code to have each disk enclose *all* points in its cluster.

Exercises

1. Write a version of the function that computes Hamming distance by using `Count` with an appropriate pattern to find the number of nonidentical pairs of corresponding numbers in two binary signals.
2. Write an implementation of Hamming distance using the `Total` function and modular arithmetic base 2 to compare two bits. Compare running times with the other versions discussed in this chapter.
3. Rewrite the `median` function from Exercise 6, Section 5.4 so that instead of using an `If` control structure, you create two separate rules: one rule for the case when the list has an odd number of elements and another rule for the case when the length of the list is even.
4. Extend the survivor function developed in this section to a function of two arguments, so that `survivor[`*n*`,` *m*`]` returns the survivor starting from a list of *n* people and executing every *m*th person.
5. In Section 4.3 we created a function `CountChange[`*lis*`]` that took a list of coins and, using transformation rules, returned the monetary value of that list of coins. Rewrite `CountChange` to use a purely functional approach. Consider using `Dot`, or `Inner`, or `Tally`.
6. Create a function `Regular2Graph[`*n*`]` that outputs an *n*-sided regular graph where every vertex has degree two.

```
In[1]:= Regular2Graph[5]
```

Out[1]=

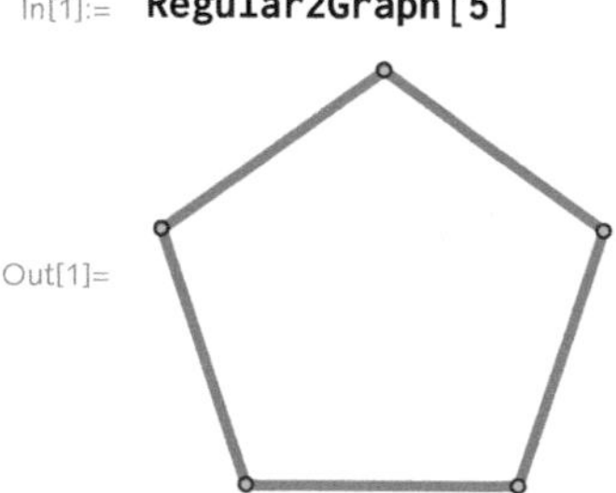

7. Extend the visualization of PPI networks from this section by coloring vertices according to the biological process in which they are involved. The built-in `ProteinData` contains this information, for example:

```
In[2]:= ProteinData["KLKB1", "BiologicalProcesses"]
Out[2]= {BloodCoagulation, Fibrinolysis, InflammatoryResponse, Proteolysis}
```

8. Extend the range of `ReplaceElement` developed in this section to accept a list of strings considered as nonnumeric matrix entries, each of which should be replaced by a column mean.

9. Imagine a random walk on a graph: starting at vertex v_i, the probability that you next move to vertex v_j is given by

$$P(v_i, v_j) = \begin{cases} \frac{1}{d_{v_i}}, & \text{if } v_i \leftrightarrow v_j \\ 0, & \text{otherwise} \end{cases}$$

where d_{v_i} is the degree of vertex v_i. This defines what is known as a *transition probability matrix* and can be used to create a Markov model to simulate random walks on graphs.

Given a graph, create its transition probability matrix where matrix element $a_{ij} = P(v_i, v_j)$ as defined above. You will need the built-in functions `VertexCount` and `VertexDegree` as well as `EdgeQ`. For more on random walks on graphs, see Lovász (1993) or Aldous and Fill (2014).

10. Random graphs have a rich and deep history in spite of the fact that they were only first defined in the mid-twentieth century in a paper by Erdős and Rényi (1959). They have since been used to study areas as diverse as percolation, telecommunications, social networks, and many more.

Perhaps the simplest random graph model is one in which both the number of vertices and the number of edges are fixed. In this model, $G(n, m)$, the m edges are placed at random among all $\binom{n}{2}$ possible edges. This is the model that the built-in function `RandomGraph` is based upon. In an alternate model, commonly referred to as $G(n, p)$, the probability of an edge between any two of the n vertices is fixed. As as result, the number of edges can vary from none, for example when $p = 0$, to $\binom{n}{2}$ when $p = 1$. In this exercise you are asked to create a simplified model of the $G(n, p)$ random graph.

Starting with a set of edges, assign a probability to each. The edges can be taken from a complete graph, a graph in which there is an edge between every pair of vertices.

```
In[3]:= n = 7;
        cg = CompleteGraph[n];
        EdgeRules[cg]
Out[5]= {1→2, 1→3, 1→4, 1→5, 1→6, 1→7, 2→3, 2→4, 2→5, 2→6,
         2→7, 3→4, 3→5, 3→6, 3→7, 4→5, 4→6, 4→7, 5→6, 5→7, 6→7}
```

Next choose an edge with probability p. An edge being chosen is a binary choice: either it is chosen or it isn't. This is essentially a coin toss distribution which, in *Mathematica*, is represented by `BernoulliDistribution`. We create a list of probabilities the same length as the number of edges in the complete graph.

```
In[6]:= p = 0.45;
        probs = RandomVariate[BernoulliDistribution[p], EdgeCount[cg]]
Out[7]= {1, 0, 0, 0, 1, 0, 0, 1, 0, 1, 0, 1, 1, 1, 1, 0, 1, 0, 0, 0, 1}
```

Finally, use Pick to include only edges whose corresponding probability is less than the threshold value p and display the resulting graph with Graph.

11. Extend the grid example from Exercise 5, Section 3.1 to color the prime grid elements (Figure 5.7).

FIGURE 5.7. *Grid of integers 1 through n^2 with prime elements highlighted.*

1	2	3	4	5	6	7
8	9	10	11	12	13	14
15	16	17	18	19	20	21
22	23	24	25	26	27	28
29	30	31	32	33	34	35
36	37	38	39	40	41	42
43	44	45	46	47	48	49

12. Using Grid, create a truth table for a logical expression such as $(A \vee B) \Rightarrow C$ (Figure 5.8).

FIGURE 5.8. *Truth table for $A \vee B \Rightarrow C$.*

A	B	C	$A \vee B \Rightarrow C$
T	T	T	T
T	T	F	F
T	F	T	T
T	F	F	F
F	T	T	T
F	T	F	F
F	F	T	T
F	F	F	T

13. Create a function RandomNote[*n*] that plays a random sequence of n notes taken from the twelve-tone scale. The twelve tones in C major can be generated using Sound and SoundNote to create the sound objects; use EmitSound to play them through the speakers of your computer.

```
In[8]:= Sound[Map[SoundNote, Range[0, 11]]] // EmitSound
```

A second argument to SoundNote can be used to alter the duration of each note, which, by default, is for one second. Set up RandomNote to have random durations as well as random notes. Finally, set up RandomNote to accept a second argument to set the MIDI instrument through which the sound will be played.

14. Because of the completely random nature of how the notes are chosen in the previous exercise, the resulting "tunes" will have no autocorrelation and the result is quite uninteresting. Create a new function to generate sequences of notes where the randomness is applied to the distance between notes, essentially performing a "random walk" through the C major scale. Music generated in such a way is called *Brownian* because it behaves much like the movement of particles suspended in liquid – Brownian motion.

15. If you read musical notation, take a musical composition such as one of Bach's *Brandenburg Concertos* and write down a list of the frequency intervals x between successive notes. Then find a function that interpolates the power spectrum of these frequency intervals and determine if this function is of the

form $f(x) = c/x$ for some constant c. (*Hint*: To get the power spectrum, you will need to square the magnitude of the Fourier transform: take `Abs[Fourier[...]]^2` of your data.) Compute the power spectra of different types of music using this procedure.

16. Modify the clustering example in this section so that the cluster disks enclose *every* point in their respective clusters (Figure 5.9).

FIGURE 5.9. *Clustering with each disk enclosing entire cluster.*

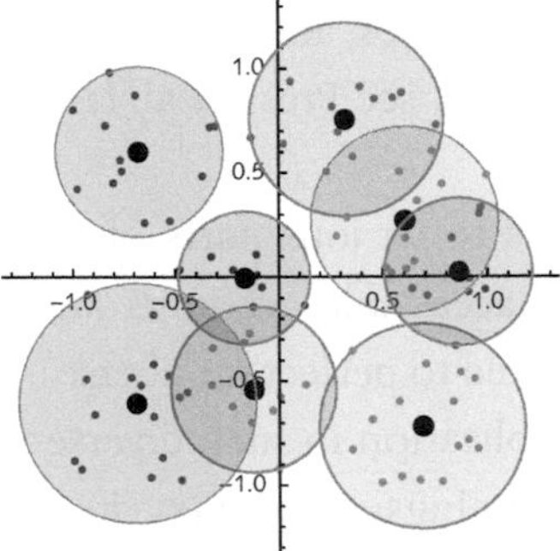

17. Given a set of n points in the plane, find a tour that visits each of them once, returning to the first point visited: choose a point v_1 from the set at random; then find the point that is closest to v_1, call it v_2; of the points not chosen so far, find the point that is closest to v_2; call it v_3. In this way create a running list $\{v_1, v_2, \ldots, v_n, v_1\}$ that gives the points to visit in order, returning to the first point visited. This is essentially a nearest-neighbor algorithm for solving the traveling salesman problem. It is known that this solution is sub-optimal but it will give you a good feeling for these kinds of problems. See Section 8.4 for some variations on traveling salesman-type problems.

18. Starting with a set of n random points in the unit square, find the proportion that are also in the square's inscribed disk (Figure 5.10). As n increases, this proportion (slowly!) approaches the value $\pi/4$.

FIGURE 5.10. *Monte Carlo simulation to approximate π.*

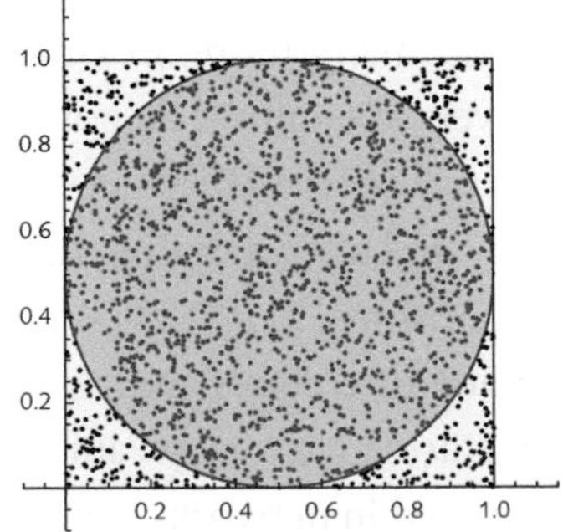

In Exercise 5, Section 9.2 this computation is run numerous times as a Monte Carlo simulation to get better and better approximations to the value of π.

5.7 Notes and further reading

For information on functional programming, see the article on the history of LISP by John McCarthy (1979) and also Paul Graham's blogs on the roots of LISP (Graham 2002).

The implementations of Newton's algorithm in this chapter are quite basic. Although they are fine for learning about procedural programming and iteration, they have some serious limitations regarding accuracy and precision; a more thorough treatment would require quite a bit more background in numerics and some more advanced programming techniques, and hence is outside the scope of this book. For more information on numerical root finding, see Press et al. (2007) or the tutorial Numerical Operations on Functions (WLDC).

Perfect numbers, although easy to define, have deep connections to various parts of number theory. See Gardner (1978) and Conway and Guy (1996) for very accessible accounts and also Shanks (1993) for a description of unsolved (and solved) problems related to perfect numbers.

The Fibonacci numbers have been studied extensively, finding application in such diverse areas as random number generation, compression algorithms, musical tunings, phyllotaxy in plants, population generation, and much more. See Knuth (1997) and Graham, Knuth, and Patashnik (1994) for a good general introduction to recursion and the Fibonacci numbers in particular.

The problem of exponentiation with large exponents (Exercise 5, Section 5.2) occurs in primality testing in cryptographic applications. For more information on this binary exponentiation method, see Knuth (1997). For the history of early Hindu mathematics where this problem was possibly first explored, see Datta and Singh (1938).

Additional information on the Sierpiński triangle, including alternative ways to generate it, can be found at Weisstein (Sierpinski Sieve) and Wagon (1999).

There is an extensive history of the Josephus survivor problem as a computational exercise. See Herstein and Kaplansky (1978) or Graham, Knuth, and Patashnik (1994).

Cluster analysis has extensive application in bioinformatics, image analysis, machine learning, and information retrieval. Numerous clustering algorithms are used such as hierarchical clustering, density-based clustering, subspace clustering for higher dimensions, and many more. In *k*-means clustering, common in data mining, means or centroids are used, iteratively assigning data points to the cluster that is nearest a median in such a way as to minimize the set of squared distances from the cluster. See MacKay (2003) for cluster analysis in information theory and also Manning, Raghavan, and Schütze (2008) regarding clustering in information retrieval algorithms.

Graphs and networks now model relationships and processes in many disciplines and, as such, they are used throughout this book. The paper on random graphs that started it all is by Paul Erdős and Alfred Rényi (1959). For a thorough treatment of graphs as they are used in networks generally, see the excellent book by Mark Newman (2010). For information on random walks on graphs with application to web search, see Chung and Zhao (2010) or Lovász (1993).

6

Programs

Scoping constructs · *Localizing names: Module* · *Localizing values: Block* · *Localizing constants: With* · *Matrix manipulation* · **Options and messages** · *Options* · *Messages* · **Examples** · *Sieve of Eratosthenes* · *Radius of gyration* · *Lag plots* · *Random walks* · **Notes and further reading**

Most of the programs we have created in the first five chapters are relatively short and compact, focused on solving problems that are quite manageable. These pieces of code are often sufficient when working on a problem and you are looking for a quick result. But before long, something more is needed: a series of computations that have to be repeated perhaps, with slight variations each time; or you need to share your code with colleagues or students; or perhaps you are developing an application for a client who knows little of the *Mathematica* environment or language and is looking for a solution that integrates with what they are already comfortable with.

Whether you are writing code for yourself or others, it is important to develop programs that are not dependent upon the current state of the user's *Mathematica* session: previously defined symbols should not interfere with code in any way; side-effects of an evaluation should not cause surprises; programs should respond gracefully when things go wrong. All modern programming languages have frameworks designed to deal with these things, and *Mathematica* is no exception. This chapter introduces these structures and incorporates them throughout the rest of the book.

The first construct we will look at is localization of variables. This is a mechanism to isolate symbols and definitions that are local to a function in order to keep them from interfering with, or being interfered by, global symbols.

Providing options to functions and issuing messages when things go wrong are common mechanisms for getting your programs to look and behave like built-in functions; they are introduced in Section 6.2.

The chapter concludes with several larger pieces of code that put many of these pieces together in one program. We will also start to include discussion of some meta-programming issues: testing for correctness, dealing with atypical input, and testing for efficiency (although most of the speed and efficiency issues will have to wait until Chapter 9). Not all of the examples in this chapter include every one of these pieces but as a whole, they should give you a good sense of what a complete program looks like and how to test it to insure that it does what you intended and does it efficiently.

6.1 Scoping constructs

Up until this point, each of the symbols for which we have set up definitions live in what is called the *global context*. Such global symbols have the advantage that, in general, you do not need to worry about certain details such as namespace management. You can start up a *Mathematica* session and just use such symbols right away. But this ease of use comes at a cost. Sometimes you will run into naming conflicts that have unintended consequences. In this section, we discuss ways of protecting the definitions of your symbols from clashing with each other. The mechanism for doing all this is to localize your variables, a mechanism common to all modern programming languages.

Localizing names: Module

When you define functions using assignments, the names of any values or functions defined on the right-hand side should be isolated from the outside world in order to avoid conflicts with the use of a name elsewhere in the session. This process of localizing variable names is done by wrapping the right-hand side of the function definition with the `Module` function.

```
name[arg1_, arg2_, …, argn_] := Module[{sym1, sym2 = value, …},
  body_of_function
 ]
```

The first argument of `Module` is a list of the symbols to be localized. If you wish, you can assign values to these symbols – initializing the variables – as is shown with sym_2 above; the assigned value is only an initial value and can be changed in the body of the function. The list of symbols to be localized is separated from the right-hand side by a comma and so the parentheses enclosing the right-hand side of a compound function (Section 2.3) are not needed.

So what does `Module` do exactly? Briefly, when `Module` is encountered, the symbols that are being localized are temporarily given new and unique names, and all occurrences of those symbols in the body of the `Module` are given those new names as well. In this way, these unique and temporary names, which are local to the function, will not interfere with any names of functions or values outside of the `Module`.

To see how `Module` works we'll trace a computation involving a simple function, showing some of the internals. The function `f` takes an argument *n*, creates and initializes a local variable `tmp`, and assigns it the value of the list of the integers one through *n*; the body of the function converts those integers to approximate numbers and takes the dot product of the list `tmp` with itself.

```
In[1]:= f[n_] := Module[{tmp = Range[n]},
          tmp = N[tmp];
          tmp.tmp]

In[2]:= f[4]
Out[2]= 30.

In[3]:= Trace[f[4]]
Out[3]= {f[4], Module[{tmp = Range[4]}, tmp = N[tmp];
          tmp.tmp], {Range[4], {1, 2, 3, 4}},
         {tmp$1523 = {1, 2, 3, 4}, {1, 2, 3, 4}}, {tmp$1523 = N[tmp$1523];
          tmp$1523.tmp$1523, {{{tmp$1523, {1, 2, 3, 4}}, N[{1, 2, 3, 4}],
            {1., 2., 3., 4.}}, tmp$1523 = {1., 2., 3., 4.}, {1., 2., 3., 4.}},
          {{tmp$1523, {1., 2., 3., 4.}}, {tmp$1523, {1., 2., 3., 4.}},
           {1., 2., 3., 4.}.{1., 2., 3., 4.}, 30.}, 30.}, 30.}
```

The trace shows the local variable `tmp` has been renamed `tmp$1523`, a unique and new name. In this way, the local variable will not interfere with any global variable whose name might also be `tmp`. Checking the global rule base for information about the global symbol `tmp` shows that it has been unaffected by the above computation – no values are associated with it.

```
In[4]:= ? tmp

        Global`tmp
```

Let's use `Module` to rewrite the `walk` function from Section 2.3. In this case we will localize the two symbols `dirs` and `steps`, initializing `dirs` with the directions {−1, 1}.

```
In[5]:= walk1D[t_] := Module[{dirs = {-1, 1}, steps},
          steps = RandomChoice[dirs, t]; Accumulate[steps]
         ]
```

Again, a quick test on a small walk and a visualization of a larger walk:

```
In[6]:= walk1D[5]
Out[6]= {1, 0, 1, 0, 1}

In[7]:= ListLinePlot[walk1D[1500]]
```

Out[7]=

A check shows that the global symbol `dirs` is unaffected by the local `dirs` (similarly for `steps`).

```
In[8]:= dirs
Out[8]= dirs
```

It is generally a good idea to wrap the right-hand side of all compound function definitions in the `Module` function. Another way to avoid conflicts between the names of auxiliary function definitions is to use a pure function, as these can be applied without being given a name (see Section 5.5).

Localizing values: Block

Occasionally, you will need to localize a *value* associated with a symbol without localizing the symbol *name* itself. For example, deeply recursive computations will often require you to temporarily reset the value of the system variable `$RecursionLimit`. You can do this with `Block`, thereby only localizing the *value* of `$RecursionLimit` during the evaluation inside `Block`. `Block` has the same syntax as `Module`.

```
In[9]:= Block[{$RecursionLimit = 20},
          x = g[x]]

        $RecursionLimit::reclim2 : Recursion depth of 20 exceeded during evaluation of g[x]. >>

Out[9]= Hold[g[x]]
```

Notice that the global value of `$RecursionLimit` is unchanged.

```
In[10]:= $RecursionLimit
Out[10]= 1024
```

`Module`, in contrast, would create an entirely new symbol, `$RecursionLimit$`*nn*, that has nothing to do with the global variable `$RecursionLimit`, and so `Module` would be inappropriate for this particular task. `Block` only affects the *values* of these symbols, not their names.

As another example, here is a computation that uses fixed ten-digit precision by locally setting the two system variables `$MaxPrecision` and `$MinPrecision` to 10. In general, you do not want to set these variables globally.

```
In[11]:= Block[{$MaxPrecision = 10, $MinPrecision = 10},
           Log[1000000`10]]
Out[11]= 13.81551056

In[12]:= Precision[%]
Out[12]= 10.
```

In fact, `Block` is used to localize the iterators in numerous built-in functions such as `Table`, `Do`, `Sum`, and `Product`.

Localizing constants: With

Another scoping construct is used when you simply need to localize constants. If, in the body of your function, you use a variable that is assigned a constant once and never changes, then `With` is the preferred means to localize that constant.

This sets the global variable y to have the value 5:

```
In[13]:= y = 5;
```

Here is a simple function that initializes y as a local constant:

```
In[14]:= f[x_] := With[{y = x + 1}, y]
```

The global symbol is unchanged and it does not interfere with the local symbol y inside of `With`.

```
In[15]:= f[2]
Out[15]= 3
```

```
In[16]:= y
Out[16]= 5
```

Tip 6.1

`With` is particularly handy when you want to perform a computation and experiment with some values of your parameters without setting them globally. For example, suppose you are prototyping code for a function that returns a lower-triangular matrix; that is, a matrix with zeros above the diagonal. In the following example, the matrix has ones on and below the diagonal. `With` is used here to temporarily set the value of n, the size of the matrix.

```
In[17]:= With[{n = 4},
           Table[If[j ≤ i, 1, 0], {i, n}, {j, n}]
          ] // MatrixForm
Out[17]//MatrixForm=
  1 0 0 0
  1 1 0 0
  1 1 1 0
  1 1 1 1
```

The advantage of this approach is that it is quite easy to turn this into a reusable function. Copying and pasting the line of code above, starting with `Table[…]`, essentially gives the right-hand side of the function definition without the need to modify any parameters.

```
In[18]:= LowerTriangularMatrix[n_] := Table[If[j ≤ i, 1, 0], {i, n}, {j, n}]

In[19]:= LowerTriangularMatrix[4] // MatrixForm
Out[19]//MatrixForm=
  1 0 0 0
  1 1 0 0
  1 1 1 0
  1 1 1 1
```

Finally, it should be noted that `With` is generally faster than `Module`, so if you are really working with local constants – that is, symbols whose values do not change in the body of your functions – you will see some speed improvements using `With`.

```
In[20]:= f1[n_] := Module[{tmp = N@Range[n]},
           tmp.tmp]
```

```
In[21]:= Timing[Do[f1[100], {5 × 10^5}]]
Out[21]= {2.02276, Null}

In[22]:= f2[n_] := With[{tmp = N@Range[n]},
           tmp.tmp]

In[23]:= Timing[Do[f2[100], {5 × 10^5}]]
Out[23]= {1.46233, Null}
```

Matrix manipulation

Let us look at an example in which the need for localization is critical: the creation of a function to swap the rows or columns of a matrix.

We prototype with a small 4×4 matrix.

```
In[24]:= SeedRandom[123];
         mat = RandomInteger[9, {4, 4}];

In[26]:= MatrixForm[mat]
Out[26]//MatrixForm=
```

$$\begin{pmatrix} 7 & 4 & 0 & 2 \\ 6 & 7 & 9 & 8 \\ 3 & 9 & 8 & 5 \\ 2 & 6 & 2 & 6 \end{pmatrix}$$

We could use a parallel assignment to switch two rows, say rows one and two.

```
In[27]:= {mat[[1]], mat[[2]]} = {mat[[2]], mat[[1]]}
Out[27]= {{6, 7, 9, 8}, {7, 4, 0, 2}}
```

The problem with this approach is that `mat` is changed by the assignment – list component assignment is direct and fast, but it is a destructive operation.

```
In[28]:= mat // MatrixForm
Out[28]//MatrixForm=
```

$$\begin{pmatrix} 6 & 7 & 9 & 8 \\ 7 & 4 & 0 & 2 \\ 3 & 9 & 8 & 5 \\ 2 & 6 & 2 & 6 \end{pmatrix}$$

We can avoid this problem by using a local variable, `lmat`, and only operating on that expression, not the original matrix. When the computation is done, we return the value of `lmat`.

```
In[29]:= switchRows[mat_, {r1_, r2_}] := Module[{lmat = mat},
           {lmat[[r1]], lmat[[r2]]} = {lmat[[r2]], lmat[[r1]]};
           lmat]
```

This can be written a bit more compactly using list component assignment on the correct parts.

```
In[30]:= switchRows[mat_, {r1_, r2_}] := Module[{lmat = mat},
           lmat[[{r1, r2}]] = lmat[[{r2, r1}]];
           lmat]
```

```
In[31]:= SeedRandom[123];
         mat = RandomInteger[9, {4, 4}];

In[33]:= switchRows[mat, {1, 2}] // MatrixForm
Out[33]//MatrixForm=
         6 7 9 8
         7 4 0 2
         3 9 8 5
         2 6 2 6
```

Using local variables in this situation is preferable, as the original matrix is left unchanged.

```
In[34]:= mat // MatrixForm
Out[34]//MatrixForm=
         7 4 0 2
         6 7 9 8
         3 9 8 5
         2 6 2 6
```

You can even use negative indices to count rows from the end. For example, this switches the first and the last row:

```
In[35]:= switchRows[mat, {1, -1}] // MatrixForm
Out[35]//MatrixForm=
         2 6 2 6
         6 7 9 8
         3 9 8 5
         7 4 0 2
```

These are fairly simplistic implementations and will fail if you are not careful with the row numbers.

```
In[36]:= switchRows[mat, {1, 6}]
         Part::partw : Part 6 of {{7, 4, 0, 2}, {6, 7, 9, 8}, {3, 9, 8, 5}, {2, 6, 2, 6}} does not exist. >>
         Set::partw : Part 6 of lmat$1004863[[{1, 6}]] does not exist. >>
Out[36]= {{7, 4, 0, 2}, {6, 7, 9, 8}, {3, 9, 8, 5}, {2, 6, 2, 6}}
```

Exercise 4 at the end of this section extends this example to column swapping. Exercise 2 of Section 6.2 asks you to do some argument checking and issue an appropriate message when bad arguments are passed to these functions.

Exercises

1. The condition number of a square matrix gives a measure of how close the matrix is to being singular. First proposed by Alan Turing, it is often defined as the ratio of the largest singular value of the matrix to the smallest singular value. The condition number can give a sense of how much the solution of the matrix equation $A.x = b$ can change for small perturbations of the vector b.

   Create a function `ConditionNumber[mat]` that takes a square matrix *mat* and returns its condition number. Then test it on several Hilbert matrices (`HilbertMatrix`), which are known to have very large condition numbers, thus rendering numerical computations with them problematic from a precision point of view.

2. Turn the random graph example in Exercise 10, Section 5.6 into a function `RandomGraphGnp[n, p]` that returns a random graph on *n* vertices with edges chosen randomly (`BernoulliDistribution`) using probability *p*.

3. Create a function `EquilateralTriangleQ` that takes a `Triangle` object as an argument and returns a value of `True` if that triangle is equilateral and returns a value of `False` if it is not. A triangle is equilateral if the lengths of its three sides are identical. Create two implementations, one using `EuclideanDistance` to measure the side lengths and another using `ArcLength` with `MeshRegion` and `MeshPrimitives`.

4. Based on the row-switching example in this section, create a function to swap matrix columns.

5. Rewrite the function `FindSubsequence` from Exercise 7, Section 4.3 using `Module` to localize the length of the subsequence `subseq`.

6. The `PerfectSearch` function defined in Exercise 6, Section 5.1 is impractical for checking large numbers because it has to check all numbers from 1 through *n*. It is inefficient to check all numbers from 1 to 1000 if you are only looking for perfect numbers in the range 500 to 1000. Modify `PerfectSearch` so that it is self-contained, defining the perfect predicate inside the body of the function. Also, set up the argument structure to accept two numbers as input and have the function output all perfect numbers between those inputs. For example, `PerfectSearch[a, b]` will return a list of all perfect numbers in the range from *a* to *b*.

7. A number *n* is *k*-perfect if the sum of its proper divisors equals *k n*. Redefine `PerfectSearch` from the previous exercise so that it accepts as input two numbers *a* and *b*, a positive integer *k*, and computes all *k*-perfect numbers in the range from *a* to *b*. Use your rule to find the only three 4-perfect numbers less than 2 200 000.

8. Often in processing files you are presented with expressions that need to be converted into a format that can be more easily manipulated. For example, a file may contain dates in the form 20160702 to represent July 2, 2016. *Mathematica* represents its dates as a list in the following form:

   {*year*, *month*, *day*, *hour*, *minutes*, *seconds*}

   Write a function `convertToDate[n]` to convert a number consisting of eight digits such as 20160702 into a list of the form `{2016, 7, 2}`.

```
In[1]:= convertToDate[20160702]

Out[1]= {2016, 7, 2}
```

9. Create a function `zeroColumns[mat, m ;; n]` that zeros out columns *m* through *n* in matrix *mat*. Include rules to handle the cases of zeroing out one column or a list of nonconsecutive columns.

10. Following on the code for the one-dimensional random walk, create a function `walk2D[n]` that generates *n* steps of a two-dimensional random walk on the integer lattice (see Exercise 8, Section 2.1). For such a walk, the directions can be thought of as the two-dimensional vectors {0, 1}, {0, −1}, {1, 0}, and {−1, 0} pointing in the direction of the compass directions north, south, east, and west. Then create a function `walk3D[n]` that returns an *n*-step random walk on the three-dimensional integer lattice.

6.2 Options and messages

When developing programs that will be used by your colleagues, students, or customers, it is important to give some thought to the user interface for your code. That is, how will the user figure out the correct syntax, how will they get information, and so on. The easier it is for a user (including yourself!) to actually use your code, the more likely it is to be used for its intended purpose. One of the hallmarks of modern languages is that they provide a framework to develop programs that look and behave in a consistent and predictable manner. One of the pieces of this framework is a mechanism for passing messages when a bad argument is given or a certain condition occurs. Another piece is using optional arguments to modify the default behavior of your functions. In this section we discuss how you can set up functions so that they inherit this framework, making them behave like the built-in functions in terms of argument structure and messaging.

Options

When creating programs it is of course important to think about the many uses they will be put to. You might write separate functions to handle special cases, but the problem with having a separate function for each special case is that the user can soon become overloaded with the variety of functions to learn. A cleaner approach, one used by the built-in functions in *Mathematica*, is to use optional arguments to specify some variant or special case rather than to have a separate function for each such case. In this section, we will describe how to write options for your functions so that they behave like the built-in options in *Mathematica*.

When you create a function, generally you design the argument structure in such a way that it covers the most common usage cases and produces output in a form as widely applicable as possible. For example, given the required arguments only, the `Plot` function returns a basic plot. In such a plot, many decisions have been made behind the scenes, so to speak, about whether to include axes, how thick and what color the curve should be, and so on. All of these decisions are set in the default argument structure of the `Plot` function.

```
In[1]:= Plot[Sin[x], {x, 0, 2 π}]
```

Out[1]=
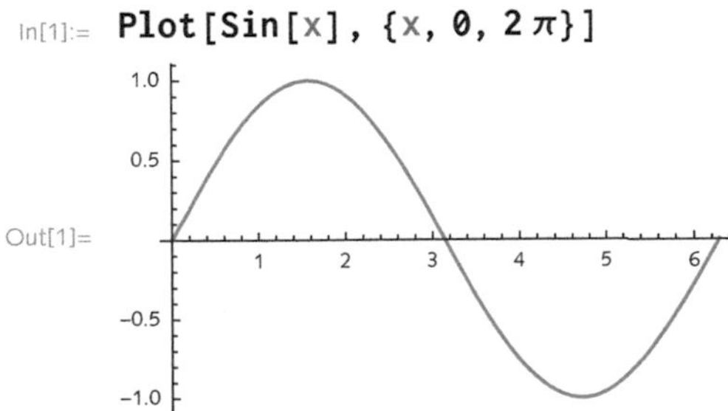

To override the default behavior, you specify different values for the optional arguments. These optional arguments, or *options*, can be included after the required arguments and are specified as a rule: *optionname* → *value*.

```
In[2]:= Plot[Sin[x], {x, 0, 2 π},
         GridLines → Automatic,
         Frame → True]
```

Out[2]=

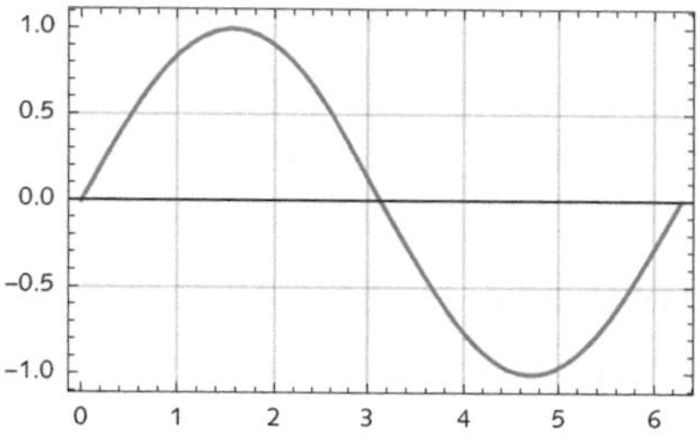

This provides a consistent framework for modifying the default behavior of the built-in functions. The first part of the framework is to declare that a function will have optional arguments and identify their names and default values. For example, the following indicates that a function named myFun will have two optional arguments, opt1 and opt2, with default values α and β, respectively:

```
In[3]:= Options[myFun] = {opt1 → α, opt2 → β}
Out[3]= {opt1 → α, opt2 → β}
```

The second piece of the options framework is to set up the argument structure on the left-hand side of your definition to allow for optional arguments. This is done by using OptionsPattern after any required arguments. In the example below, the required argument is x; some number (possibly zero) of optional arguments will follow the required argument.

```
myFun[x_, OptionsPattern[]] := …
```

The third piece of the framework is using OptionValue to extract the value of a given option on the right-hand side of your function definition.

```
In[4]:= myFun[x_, OptionsPattern[]] := 2 x + 3 OptionValue[opt1] + 4 OptionValue[opt2]
```

Let's try it out, first with default values for the options.

```
In[5]:= myFun[a]
Out[5]= 2 a + 3 α + 4 β
```

Now exercise the options.

```
In[6]:= myFun[a, opt1 → x, opt2 → y]
Out[6]= 2 a + 3 x + 4 y
```

So far, so good, but let's use the options framework to do something a bit more interesting. There are many times when it would be useful to inherit some or all of the options from a built-in function. This saves time and effort in that the structure already is in place, you just need to borrow it. Fortunately, this is quite straightforward using Options. To see how, we will create a function StemPlot that inherits options from ListPlot and displays discrete data as stems; that is, points at a height specified by the values of the data with lines drawn to the axis.

```
In[7]:= Options[StemPlot] = Options[ListPlot];
```

```
In[8]:= StemPlot[lis_List, opts:OptionsPattern[]] :=
          ListPlot[lis, opts, Filling → Axis]
```

We named the optional arguments `opts` so that we can slot whatever options are given into `ListPlot`. This is done by having `opts` precede any other options we wish to use. This way the user-passed options, appearing first, will override any similarly named options that come later.

```
In[9]:= StemPlot[RandomInteger[10, {12}]]
```

Out[9]=

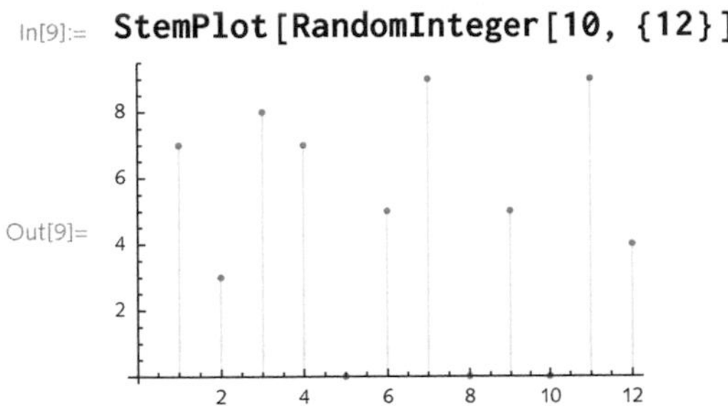

Let us exercise some of the options inherited from `ListPlot` but with a more substantial example. We will use some data from NASA Goddard Institute for Space Studies showing anomalous land temperatures in the northern and southern hemispheres measured from 1880 to 2014. The following shows the temperature difference from the mean using the period 1951 to 1980 as the base period mean (Ruedy, Sato, and Lo 2015):

```
In[10]:= data = Import["gistempland.csv"];

In[11]:= StemPlot[data, DataRange → {1880, 2014}, AspectRatio → 1 / 3,
           PlotLabel → "Hemispheric Land Temperature Anomalies (°C) 1880-2014",
           PlotLegends → SwatchLegend@{"N. hemisphere", "S. hemisphere"}]
```

Out[11]=

Hemispheric Land Temperature Anomalies (°C) 1880–2014

N. hemisphere
S. hemisphere

As an alternative to how we set up the options for `StemPlot`, you could also set up the inheritance of the options directly in the definition for the function, rather than setting the `Options[...] = ...` statement as we did above.

```
In[12]:= StemPlot[lis_List, opts:OptionsPattern[ListPlot]] :=
           ListPlot[lis, opts, Filling → Axis]
```

In Section 7.5, in the example on displaying DNA sequences and again in the visualization functions in Section 8.4, we will look at some variations of this options framework in which you can mix options from different functions.

Messages

Usage messages Every built-in function in *Mathematica* has a usage message that is accessed by evaluating ? *function*.

```
In[13]:= ? Map
```

Map[*f*, *expr*] or *f* /@ *expr* applies *f* to each element on the first level in *expr*.
Map[*f*, *expr*, *levelspec*] applies *f* to parts of *expr* specified by *levelspec*.
Map[*f*] represents an operator form of Map that can be applied to an expression. >>

User-defined functions can inherit the usage message framework as well. The syntax is as follows:

```
In[14]:= funName::usage = "funName[x,y] computes something using x and y.";
```

After evaluating the usage statement above, you get information about `funName` in the same way you do for built-in functions.

```
In[15]:= ? funName
```

funName[x,y] computes something using x and y.

The message starts with a template for the function. This template is used by *Mathematica* to provide a convenient user-interface feature: function templates. For any built-in function, you can get a template by entering the function name and then selecting Make Template from the Edit menu, or use a keyboard shortcut. When you do this, you should see something like the following:

```
Plot3D[f, {x, xmin, xmax}, {y, ymin, ymax}]
```

By starting your usage message with the template for your function – in the above example that is `funName[x, y]` – you automatically inherit this user-interface element:

```
funName[x, y]
```

Warning and error messages When you give an invalid argument to a *Mathematica* function, it returns a warning message.

```
In[16]:= Inverse[{1.2, 2.3, 4.5}]

Inverse::matsq : Argument {1.2, 2.3, 4.5} at position 1 is not a non–empty square matrix. >>

Out[16]= Inverse[{1.2, 2.3, 4.5}]
```

You can set up your own functions to do likewise. You do this by first defining the message and then using a rule to issue the message under the appropriate conditions.

Let's set up a message for `PalindromeQ` from Section 1.1. Here is the function definition:

```
In[17]:= PalindromeQ[num_Integer] := With[{digs = IntegerDigits[num]},
           digs == Reverse[digs]]
```

As written, this function returns unevaluated for any argument that does not match the pattern num_Integer. It is a good candidate for a warning message.

```
In[18]:= PalindromeQ[π]
Out[18]= PalindromeQ[π]
```

First, set up a message that will be issued whenever a bad argument is passed to PalindromeQ. Messages have names of the form *symbol*::*tag*, where *symbol* is the symbol with which you want to associate the message. The *tag* should be chosen to reflect the purpose of the message. For example: PalindromeQ::badarg.

```
In[19]:= PalindromeQ::badarg =
           "Bad argument to PalindromeQ. It should be a positive integer.";
```

To issue this message, we could create a general rule that covers all arguments other than integers, which is covered by the rule we wrote above.

```
In[20]:= PalindromeQ[n_] := Message[PalindromeQ::badarg]

In[21]:= PalindromeQ[π]
         PalindromeQ::badarg : Bad argument to PalindromeQ. It should be a positive integer.
```

So far, so good. We could go a bit further and pass the bad argument itself into the message. Built-in functions do this automatically.

```
In[22]:= FactorInteger[π]

         FactorInteger::exact : Argument π in FactorInteger[π] is not an exact number. >>

Out[22]= FactorInteger[π]
```

This is accomplished by using `1` to indicate the position in the string to slot in a value. Then use a two-argument form of Message to issue the warning with a value slotted into the string.

```
In[23]:= PalindromeQ::badarg =
           "Argument `1` in PalindromeQ[`1`] is not a positive integer.";

In[24]:= PalindromeQ[n_] := Message[PalindromeQ::badarg, n]

In[25]:= PalindromeQ[π]
         PalindromeQ::badarg : Argument π in PalindromeQ[π] is not a positive integer.
```

We can go one step further and create a more general rule, one that could cover multiple arguments or more complicated argument structures and, in addition to issuing the warning, also return the input unevaluated just like the built-in functions. The If statement below checks to see if the argument n is a positive integer. If it is, the If statement returns True, the conditional is satisfied, and the right-hand side of the definition will be invoked. If the argument is not a positive integer, then the message is issued and False is returned to the condition, making the pattern match fail (which causes the input to be returned), and so the right-hand side is not evaluated.

```
In[26]:= Clear[PalindromeQ]
```

```
In[27]:= PalindromeQ[n_] /; If[TrueQ[Head[n] == Integer && n > 1],
           True, Message[PalindromeQ::badarg, n];
           False] := IntegerDigits[n] == Reverse[IntegerDigits[n]]

In[28]:= PalindromeQ[123 454 321]

Out[28]= True

In[29]:= PalindromeQ[π]

         PalindromeQ::badarg : Argument π in PalindromeQ[π] is not a positive integer.

Out[29]= PalindromeQ[π]

In[30]:= PalindromeQ[{a, b, c}]

         PalindromeQ::badarg : Argument {a, b, c} in PalindromeQ[{a, b, c}] is not a positive integer.

Out[30]= PalindromeQ[{a, b, c}]
```

Of course, you could have multiple messages associated with any symbol by writing another *symbol*: :*tag* and modifying your code appropriately. This is what functions such as `Inverse` do for the various arguments that could be given.

```
In[31]:= Inverse[{a, b, c}]

         Inverse::matsq : Argument {a, b, c} at position 1 is not a non-empty square matrix. >>

Out[31]= Inverse[{a, b, c}]

In[32]:= Inverse[{{a, b}, {a, b}}]

         Inverse::sing : Matrix {{a, b}, {a, b}} is singular. >>

Out[32]= Inverse[{{a, b}, {a, b}}]
```

Exercises

1. Modify the random graph example in Exercise 2, Section 6.1 to inherit options from `Graph`.
2. In Section 6.1 we developed a function `switchRows` that interchanged two rows in a matrix. Create a message for this function that is issued whenever a row index greater than the size of the matrix is used as an argument. For example,

```
In[1]:= mat = RandomInteger[{0, 9}, {4, 4}];
        MatrixForm[mat]
Out[2]//MatrixForm=
        8 0 9 2
        7 2 1 9
        4 5 0 4
        2 8 6 4

In[3]:= switchRows[mat, {5, 2}]

        switchRows::badargs : The absolute value of the row indices 5
            and 2 in switchRows[mat,{5,2}] must be between 1 and 4, the size of the matrix.

Out[3]= {{8, 0, 9, 2}, {7, 2, 1, 9}, {4, 5, 0, 4}, {2, 8, 6, 4}}
```

You should also trap for a row index of zero.

```
In[4]:= switchRows[mat, {0, 2}]

switchRows::badargs : The absolute value of the row indices 0
    and 2 in switchRows[mat,{0,2}] must be between 1 and 4, the size of the matrix.

Out[4]= {{8, 0, 9, 2}, {7, 2, 1, 9}, {4, 5, 0, 4}, {2, 8, 6, 4}}
```

3. Create an error message for `StemPlot`, developed in this section, so that an appropriate message is issued if the argument is not a list of numbers.
4. Extend the definitions for `ToEdges` from Exercise 15, Section 5.1 to include an option to output directed or undirected edges.
5. The function `MultiplyCount` given in the solution to Exercise 7, Section 4.2 does not check that the expression passed to it is in fact a polynomial. Rewrite this function so that `MultiplyCount[`*poly*`,` *var*`]` checks that *poly* is a polynomial in the independent variable *var* and issues an appropriate message if the polynomial test fails.

6.3 Examples

Up until this point we have been mostly focused on learning different programming constructs that are available to solve problems. But as you progress in your understanding of programming in *Mathematica*, your focus will start to shift from simply figuring out how to get a program to run to thinking about correctness, robustness, usability, and a host of other meta-programming issues. In this section we start to implement these ideas, in particular, writing some nontrivial programs that include usage and warning messages as well as options to set and change the default behavior of your functions in some way.

Once your code is written, your job as a programmer is not done. You must test your code under both "regular" and "abnormal" conditions, that is, using what you think is typical input and also testing the code when given pathological or atypical input. You should include tests for correctness and efficiency. These notions will be discussed in what follows, although each example may not include every test and user-interface construct. Some of the examples on improving efficiency will have to wait for Chapter 9, where we introduce profiling, parallel programming, and compiling.

Sieve of Eratosthenes

One of the oldest algorithms in the history of computing is the Sieve of Eratosthenes. Named after the famous Greek astronomer Eratosthenes (*ca.* 276 – *ca.* 194 BC), this method is used to find all prime numbers below a given number *n*. It is one of a large class of sieving algorithms that continue to find use in number theory, cryptography, and lattice theory.

The great feature of the Sieve of Eratosthenes is that it finds prime numbers without doing any division, an operation that took considerable skill and concentration before the introduction of the Arabic numeral system. In fact, in our implementation the only operations are addition, multiplication, and component assignment.

The algorithm to find all the prime numbers less than an integer n can be summarized as follows:

1. create a list of the integers 1 through n;
2. starting with $p = 2$, cross out all multiples of p;
3. increment p (that is, add 1 to p) and cross out all multiples of p;
4. repeat the previous step until $p > \sqrt{n}$.

You should convince yourself that the numbers that are left after all the crossings out are in fact the primes less than n. This algorithm lends itself very well to a procedural approach, so let's walk through the steps.

We will start with the usage message. Stating it at this stage helps us to think about precisely what the algorithm is supposed to do and what the output should look like. We are of course free to modify it later as the need arises.

```
In[1]:= Sieve::usage =
          "Sieve[n] returns all prime numbers less than n using the classical
            Sieve of Eratosthenes algorithm.";
```

After reading the summary description above, a `For` loop seems to make sense for this problem. The syntax is `For[`*start*`,` *test*`,` *incr*`,` *body*`]`, where *start* will first be evaluated (initializing values), and then *incr* and *body* will be repeatedly evaluated until *test* fails.

1. Let `lis` be a list containing all the integers between 1 and n. We will prototype with $n = 20$.

```
In[2]:= n = 20;
        lis = Range[n]
Out[3]= {1, 2, 3, 4, 5, 6, 7, 8, 9, 10, 11, 12, 13, 14, 15, 16, 17, 18, 19, 20}
```

Set $p = 2$, then repeat the following two steps:

2. Starting at position $2p$, "cross out" every pth value in `lis`. By "cross out" we mean a value that is not prime and that we can safely delete when the loop has finished. Our approach is to assign 1 at positions $2p, 3p, \ldots$ in `lis`; the 1 will represent a crossed-out value.

```
In[4]:= p = 2;
        Do[lis[[i]] = 1, {i, 2 p, n, p}]

In[6]:= lis
Out[6]= {1, 2, 3, 1, 5, 1, 7, 1, 9, 1, 11, 1, 13, 1, 15, 1, 17, 1, 19, 1}
```

3. Increment p by 1, and while $p \leq \sqrt{n}$, repeat the iteration.

```
In[7]:= n = 20;
        lis = Range[n];
        For[p = 2,
         p ≤ Floor[Sqrt[n]],
         p++,
         Do[lis[[i]] = 1, {i, 2 p, n, p}]]
```

Deleting the 1s we are left with all the prime numbers less than or equal to *n*.

```
In[10]:= DeleteCases[lis, 1]
Out[10]= {2, 3, 5, 7, 11, 13, 17, 19}
```

Let's put these steps together in the function `Sieve`.

```
In[11]:= Clear[n, p, lis]

In[12]:= Sieve[n_Integer?Positive] := Module[{lis = Range[n], p},
           For[p = 2,
            p ≤ Floor[Sqrt[n]],
            p++,
            Do[lis[[i]] = 1, {i, 2 p, n, p}]];
           DeleteCases[lis, 1]
          ]
```

Finally, add a rule to catch arguments that are not positive integers.

```
In[13]:= Sieve::badarg = "Sieve was called with noninteger argument `1`.";

In[14]:= Sieve[n__] := Message[Sieve::badarg, n]
```

Here are a few simple tests to check the correctness of our function by comparing with the built-in functions that use a different algorithm (see below). First, for small *n*, we perform a basic check that `Sieve` returns the same list of primes as the built-in functions. The built-in function `PrimePi` gives the number of primes less than or equal to *x*.

```
In[15]:= Map[Prime, Range@PrimePi[100]]
Out[15]= {2, 3, 5, 7, 11, 13, 17, 19, 23, 29, 31, 37,
          41, 43, 47, 53, 59, 61, 67, 71, 73, 79, 83, 89, 97}

In[16]:= Sieve[100]
Out[16]= {2, 3, 5, 7, 11, 13, 17, 19, 23, 29, 31, 37,
          41, 43, 47, 53, 59, 61, 67, 71, 73, 79, 83, 89, 97}
```

Check that the list of primes less than 10 000 is the same as that produced by the built-in functions.

```
In[17]:= With[{n = 10^4},
          Sieve[n] == Map[Prime, Range@PrimePi[n]]
         ]
Out[17]= True
```

Next, we check that `Sieve` produces the correct *number* of primes less than a large integer.

```
In[18]:= Length[Sieve[10^5]]
Out[18]= 9592

In[19]:= PrimePi[10^5]
Out[19]= 9592
```

Next we exercise the usage and error messages.

```
In[20]:= ?Sieve
```

Sieve[*n*] returns all prime numbers less than *n* using the classical Sieve of Eratosthenes algorithm.

```
In[21]:= Sieve[π]
         Sieve::badarg : Sieve was called with noninteger argument π.

In[22]:= Sieve[{1, 2, 3}]
         Sieve::badarg : Sieve was called with noninteger argument {1, 2, 3}.
```

Finally, we do some simple timing tests to check the efficiency of this algorithm against the built-in functions that are optimized for this task.

```
In[23]:= Sieve[10^5]; // Timing
Out[23]= {0.538338, Null}

In[24]:= Map[Prime, Range@PrimePi[10^5]]; // Timing
Out[24]= {0.004371, Null}
```

For numbers in this range (less than about 10^5), sieving is fairly efficient. But beyond this range, it gets slower and slower. This implementation is quite basic and there are a number of things that we could do to optimize it. In Section 9.1 we will make several improvements to this sieving algorithm, reducing the overall number of computations performed by carefully structuring the `Do` loop.

Radius of gyration

In this next example we will work through the computation and visualization of a certain way of measuring the extent of a data set. Given some masses distributed about an axis, the radius of gyration gives the root-mean-square distance from the masses to their center of gravity or to the axis. It has application in structural engineering in determining where columns may buckle, polymer physics to describe certain properties of a polymer chain, and other physical systems.

Our focus will be on random walks. There are different ways of characterizing the shape of random walks. You could study their asphericity, a measure of how far the distribution of walk locations is from being spherically symmetric. As it turns out, this really is another way of measuring the anisotropic (not uniform in each dimension) nature of random walks. To get a sense of this, consider a two-dimensional off-lattice random walk. It is hard to tell much from one such walk – one might be severely elongated along the horizontal axis, another might be elongated along a different axis (Figure 6.1).

FIGURE 6.1. *Two 25 000-step, off-lattice walks.*

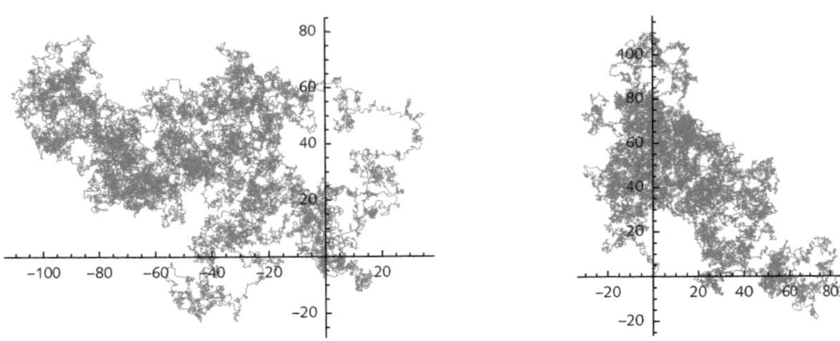

The measure we will use to characterize the shape of individual random walks is the *radius of gyration tensor*. It gives a good sense of the extent of these random walks in the sense of the length and direction of certain orthogonal vectors that span the walk (Figure 6.2).

FIGURE 6.2. A 20 000-step, *off-lattice walk. The two thick lines are in the direction of greatest and smallest extent of the walk. The center of mass is located at the intersection of these two lines.*

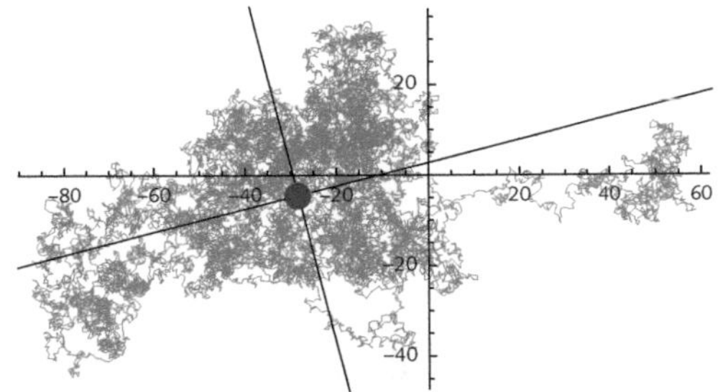

The radius of gyration tensor for a two-dimensional random walk is given by the following:

$$\mathcal{T} = \begin{pmatrix} \frac{1}{n}\sum_{i=1}^{n}(x_i - \langle x\rangle)^2 & \frac{1}{n}\sum_{i=1}^{n}(x_i - \langle x\rangle)(y_i - \langle y\rangle) \\ \frac{1}{n}\sum_{i=1}^{n}(x_i - \langle x\rangle)(y_i - \langle y\rangle) & \frac{1}{n}\sum_{i=1}^{n}(y_i - \langle y\rangle)^2 \end{pmatrix}$$

The quantities $\frac{1}{n}\sum_{i=1}^{n}(x_i - \langle x\rangle)^2$ and $\frac{1}{n}\sum_{i=1}^{n}(y_i - \langle y\rangle)^2$ are the sums of the squares of the distances of the step locations from the center of mass divided by the number of step locations, essentially the variance or second central moment. The *center of mass* is the sum of the step locations divided by the number of step locations and is denoted by $(\langle x\rangle, \langle y\rangle)$.

For example, for a 10 000-step, off-lattice walk, this computes the center of mass coordinates, labeled `mx` and `my` below. `RandomWalk` is defined in the package ``EPM`RandomWalks` `` that accompanies this book.

```
In[25]:= << EPM`RandomWalks`
```

```
In[26]:= SeedRandom[4];
         walk = RandomWalk[10^4, Dimension → 2, LatticeWalk → False];
```

```
In[28]:= {mx, my} = Mean[walk]
Out[28]= {72.7233, 32.084}
```

Here is a quick visual check, showing the center of mass as a large red point:

```
In[29]:= Show[{
           ShowWalk[walk, PlotStyle → Thin],
           Graphics[{PointSize[Medium], Red, Point[Mean[walk]]}]
          }, AspectRatio → Automatic]
```

Out[29]=

The radius of gyration tensor $\mathcal{T}$ defined above can be computed as follows. First, separate the x- and y-coordinates.

```
In[30]:= {x, y} = Transpose[walk];
```

Then compute the off-diagonal elements of the matrix $\mathcal{T}$.

```
In[31]:= xy = (x - mx).(y - my) / Length[walk]
Out[31]= -67.2011
```

The expression on the diagonal of $\mathcal{T}$, $\frac{1}{n}\sum_{i=1}^{n}(x_i - \langle x\rangle)^2$, is commonly called the second *central moment* of x (and similarly for y), so let's use a built-in function for that.

```
In[32]:= {μx, μy} = CentralMoment[walk, 2]
Out[32]= {1977.94, 761.669}

In[33]:= {{μx, xy}, {xy, μy}} // MatrixForm
Out[33]//MatrixForm=
  ( 1977.94   -67.2011 )
  ( -67.2011   761.669 )
```

These computations are bundled up in the function `RadiusOfGyrationTensor`.

```
In[34]:= RadiusOfGyrationTensor[lis_] := Module[{mx, my, x, y, xy, μx, μy},
           {mx, my} = Mean[lis];
           {x, y} = Transpose[lis];
           xy = (x - mx).(y - my) / Length[lis];
           {μx, μy} = CentralMoment[lis, 2];
           {{μx, xy}, {xy, μy}}]

In[35]:= RadiusOfGyrationTensor[walk]
Out[35]= {{1977.94, -67.2011}, {-67.2011, 761.669}}
```

This function is quite efficient, computing the radius of gyration tensor for a one-million-step random walk in under a second.

```
In[36]:= walk = RandomWalk[10^6, LatticeWalk → False];
         (𝒯 = RadiusOfGyrationTensor[walk]) // AbsoluteTiming
Out[37]= {0.219683, {{102109., 39176.1}, {39176.1, 28239.8}}}
```

Let's add a warning message to be issued if the argument to this function is not of the correct form. First, define the message.

```
In[38]:= RadiusOfGyrationTensor::badarg =
           "The argument to RadiusOfGyrationTensor should
             be a list of the form {{x1,y1},{x2,y2},...}.";
```

Now add a conditional on the left-hand side of the function definition to checks the form of the input. Also make the code more compact by applying the dot product to the correct expression.

```
In[39]:= Clear[RadiusOfGyrationTensor]

In[40]:= RadiusOfGyrationTensor[lis_] /; If[MatchQ[lis, {{_, _} ..}],
            True, Message[RadiusOfGyrationTensor::badarg];
            False] := Module[{xy, μx, μy},
          xy = Dot @@ (Transpose[lis] - Mean[lis]) / Length[lis];
          {μx, μy} = CentralMoment[lis, 2];
          {{μx, xy}, {xy, μy}}]

In[41]:= (𝒯 = RadiusOfGyrationTensor[walk]) // AbsoluteTiming
Out[41]= {0.277982, {{102109., 39176.1}, {39176.1, 28239.8}}}

In[42]:= RadiusOfGyrationTensor[{1, 2, 3}]
         RadiusOfGyrationTensor::badarg :
           The argument to RadiusOfGyrationTensor should be a list of the form {{x1,y1},{x2,y2},...}.
Out[42]= RadiusOfGyrationTensor[{1, 2, 3}]
```

The eigenvectors of $\mathcal{T}$ point in the directions of greatest and smallest spans of the walk and give a measure of how elongated the walk is in these directions. This can be seen by creating lines along each eigenvector of a length proportional to the corresponding eigenvalues (`EigenvectorPlot` is sketched out in Exercise 18 in Section 8.4 and is included in the packages accompanying this book).

```
In[43]:= << EPM`
         EigenvectorPlot[walk, 𝒯]
```

Out[44]=

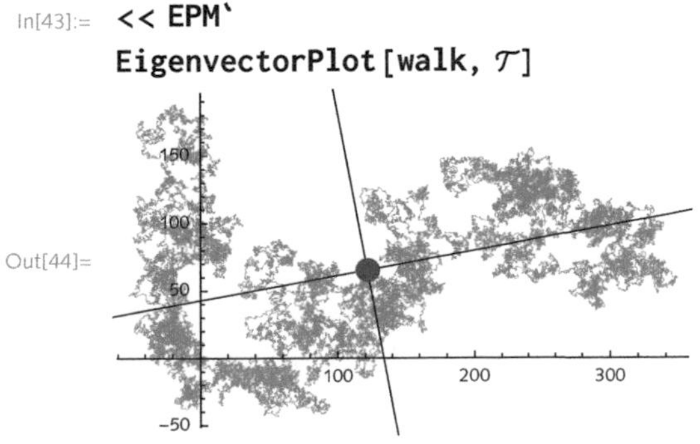

Lag plots

Time series data – data that is ordered in time – presents special problems when analyzing, modeling, and visualizing. Sometimes you look for *trends* in the data indicating a steady increase or decrease in the mean; *periodic fluctuations* such as are found in weather data are considered; and sometimes the data are not independent and observations appear to be related to each other over time in some way, showing a so-called *autocorrelation*. Such observations can be used to test the randomness of sequences of numbers or observed data.

In this example, we will create a function to visualize autocorrelation. For one-dimensional data, our function `LagPlot[`*data*`,` *lag*`]` will plot *data* against itself but lagged by a displacement. For example, if $lag = 1$, then the plot will display values $\{x_{i-1}, x_i\}$. If $lag = 2$, then the plot will display values $\{x_{i-2}, x_i\}$, and so on. Lag plots made from data that is autocorrelated tend to show patterns along the diagonal. With increasing levels of autocorrelation, the points in the lag plot cluster more around the diagonal.

Let's prototype with a small data set consisting of a random sequence of numbers.

```
In[45]:= data = RandomInteger[{1, 100}, {25}]

Out[45]= {59, 19, 57, 98, 17, 89, 87, 31, 66, 75, 23,
          62, 11, 76, 89, 74, 16, 59, 14, 65, 95, 36, 17, 49, 5}
```

The first task is to create pairs of numbers of the form $\{x_{i-1}, x_i\}$. If the data has length n, then we will end up with $n - 1$ pairs of this form. There are several different ways to form the pairs. We could pair up the original data with a shifted list of the data and then drop the last pair.

```
In[46]:= Most@Transpose[{RotateLeft[data], data}]

Out[46]= {{19, 59}, {57, 19}, {98, 57}, {17, 98}, {89, 17}, {87, 89},
          {31, 87}, {66, 31}, {75, 66}, {23, 75}, {62, 23}, {11, 62},
          {76, 11}, {89, 76}, {74, 89}, {16, 74}, {59, 16}, {14, 59},
          {65, 14}, {95, 65}, {36, 95}, {17, 36}, {49, 17}, {5, 49}}
```

Here is a different approach:

```
In[47]:= Transpose[{Drop[data, 1], Drop[data, -1]}]

Out[47]= {{19, 59}, {57, 19}, {98, 57}, {17, 98}, {89, 17}, {87, 89},
          {31, 87}, {66, 31}, {75, 66}, {23, 75}, {62, 23}, {11, 62},
          {76, 11}, {89, 76}, {74, 89}, {16, 74}, {59, 16}, {14, 59},
          {65, 14}, {95, 65}, {36, 95}, {17, 36}, {49, 17}, {5, 49}}
```

And this generalizes easily to different lag lengths:

```
In[48]:= With[{lag = 3},
          Transpose[{Drop[data, lag], Drop[data, -lag]}]
         ]

Out[48]= {{98, 59}, {17, 19}, {89, 57}, {87, 98}, {31, 17},
          {66, 89}, {75, 87}, {23, 31}, {62, 66}, {11, 75},
          {76, 23}, {89, 62}, {74, 11}, {16, 76}, {59, 89}, {14, 74},
          {65, 16}, {95, 59}, {36, 14}, {17, 65}, {49, 95}, {5, 36}}
```

So, here is a first attempt to create our function:

```
In[49]:= LagPlot[data_, lag_] :=
          ListPlot[Transpose[{Drop[data, lag], Drop[data, -lag]}]]
```

```
In[50]:= LagPlot[data, 1]
```

Out[50]=

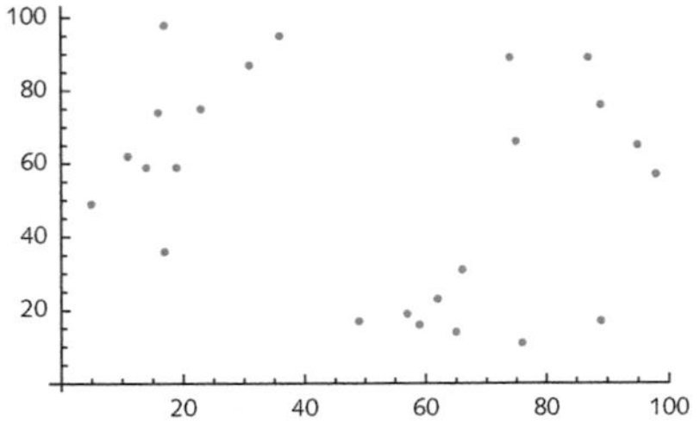

Actually, the options framework can be used to set up a default value for the lag option and to have our function inherit all the options from `ListPlot`.

```
In[51]:= Clear[LagPlot]

In[52]:= Options[LagPlot] = Join[Options[ListPlot], {Lag → 1}];

In[53]:= LagPlot[data_, opts : OptionsPattern[]] := Module[{lag = OptionValue[Lag]},
           ListPlot[Transpose[{Drop[data, lag], Drop[data, -lag]}],
            FilterRules[{opts}, Options[ListPlot]],
            PlotLabel → Style[StringForm["Lag = `1`", lag], 8]]
          ]

In[54]:= LagPlot[data, Lag → 3, PlotStyle → Directive[Blue, PointSize[Medium]]]
```

Out[54]=

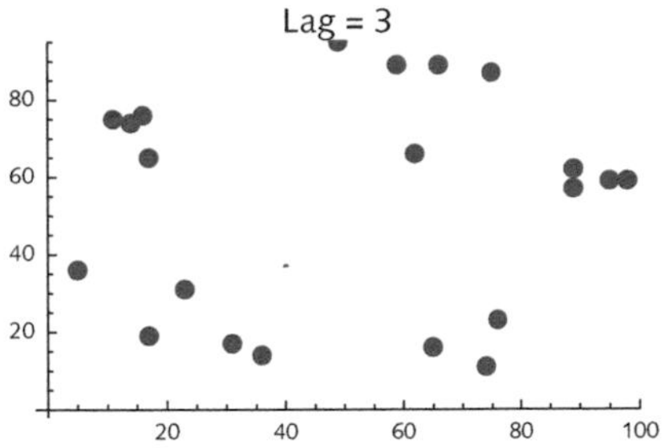

Lag = 3

If some autocorrelation was suspected, we would expect to see it in successive lag plots – random data should not show any structure in the lag plots. Our sequence of random numbers shows no signs of a lack of randomness.

```
In[55]:= Table[LagPlot[data, Lag → i], {i, 4}]
```

Out[55]= { Lag = 1, Lag = 2, Lag = 3, Lag = 4 }

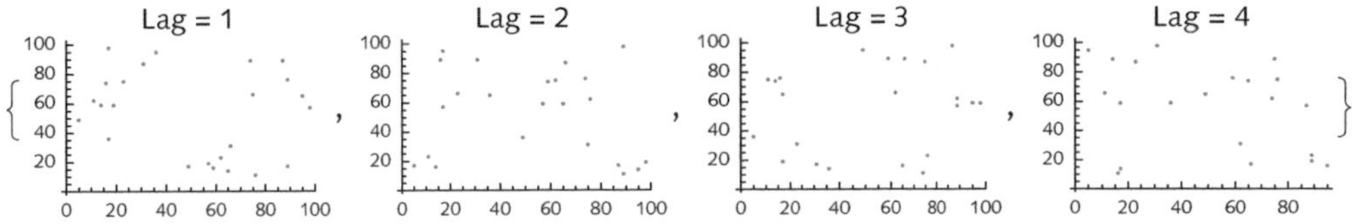

Let us now import a public data set whose lag plots indicate a known lack of randomness in the sequence of numbers: NIST's lew.dat, which consists of 200 deflections of a steel–concrete beam subjected to periodic pressure. A bit of post-processing is necessary to extract just the raw data from the file.

```
In[56]:= data = Import["http://itl.nist.gov/div898/education/eda/lew.dat", "Data"];
         Short[lewdata = Cases[data, {x_?NumberQ} :> x]]
Out[57]//Short=
         {-213, -564, -35, -15, <<192>>, 198, -218, -536, 96}
```

The analysis (NIST Lag plot 2015) asks if the data are drawn at random from a fixed distribution having fixed location and scale. The lag plot indicates that the data is not random and shows a few outliers as well.

```
In[58]:= LagPlot[lewdata, Lag → 1, ImageSize → Small]
```

Out[58]=

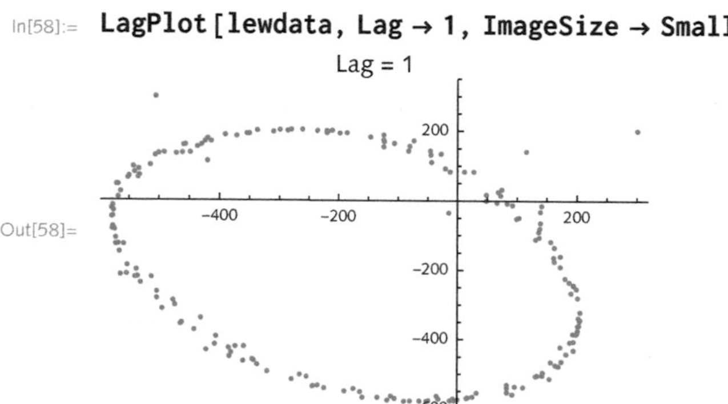

A scatter plot of the data with successive points connected by a line suggests that the data exhibits no shifting in location or scale over time.

```
In[59]:= ListLinePlot[lewdata, Mesh → All, PlotStyle → Thin]
```

Out[59]=

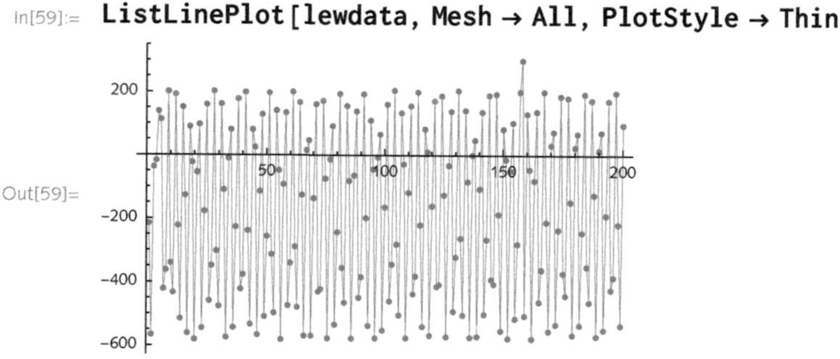

Finally, we look at some more interesting data consisting of sunspot activity, data which is known to be moderately autocorrelated. The data, curated by the Royal Observatory of Belgium, contains daily sunspot numbers going back to 1818. We will extract only the last year of data.

```
In[60]:= data = Import["http://sidc.oma.be/silso/DATA/SN_d_tot_V2.0.txt", "Table"];

In[61]:= data365 = Take[data, -365 ;; -1];
         Take[data365, -2]
Out[62]= {{2015, 7, 30, 2015.58, 74, 3.7, 17, *},
          {2015, 7, 31, 2015.58, 114, 28.2, 3, *}}
```

A bit of post-processing is necessary to put the data in a form that will work well with the time series functions, which expect a date and a value. The rule below uses a pattern that is matched by the list {y_, m_, d_, _, sn_, __} and from that returns a list with two elements: a date object and the sunspot activity value sn.

```
In[62]:= sunSpotNumbers = TimeSeries[
           data365 /. {y_Integer, m_, d_, _, sn_, __} :→ {DateObject[{y, m, d}], sn}]

Out[62]= TimeSeries[ Time: 01 Aug 2014 to 31 Jul 2015
                     Data points: 365 ]
```

```
In[63]:= DateListPlot[sunSpotNumbers, Mesh → All]
```

Out[63]=

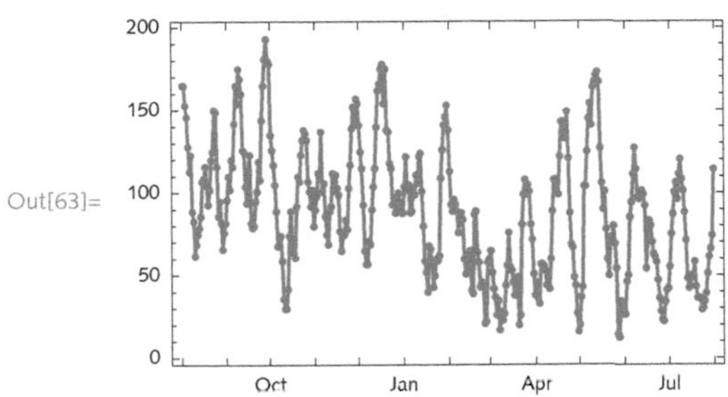

Extract the data values from the time series and make a lag plot.

```
In[64]:= LagPlot[sunSpotNumbers["Values"], Lag → 1]
```

Out[64]=

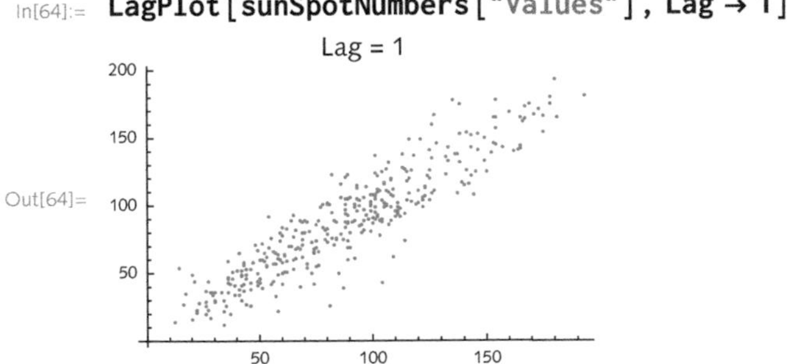

The points in the lag plot are clustering along the diagonal, which is a sign of moderate autocorrelation (NIST Lag plot 2015).

Random walks

Random walks are widely used to represent random processes in nature: they are used by physicists to model the transport of molecules, biologists work with them to model the locomotion of organisms, engineers use random walks to model heat conduction, and economists model the time behavior of financial markets with them. Random walks can be envisioned by thinking of a person taking a succession of steps that are randomly oriented with respect to one another. They provide a good application of programming to a diverse set of tasks: modeling, simulation, statistical analysis, visualization, and interface construction.

We will create an application for random walks in one, two, and three dimensions, and include an option for setting the dimension. We will add error and usage messages as well as functions for visualization and animation. We will wait until Chapter 10 to turn the programs into a package that can be distributed to others and used like any other *Mathematica* package.

Lattice walks From Section 6.1 we have the one-dimensional lattice walk already.

```
In[66]:= walk1D[t_] := Module[{dirs = {-1, 1}, steps},
           steps = RandomChoice[dirs, t];
           Accumulate[steps]]
```

To visualize such a random walk quickly, use `ListLinePlot`. The heights of the graph represent distances from the starting point and the number of steps is given along the horizontal axis.

```
In[67]:= ListLinePlot[walk1D[1000]]
```

Out[67]=

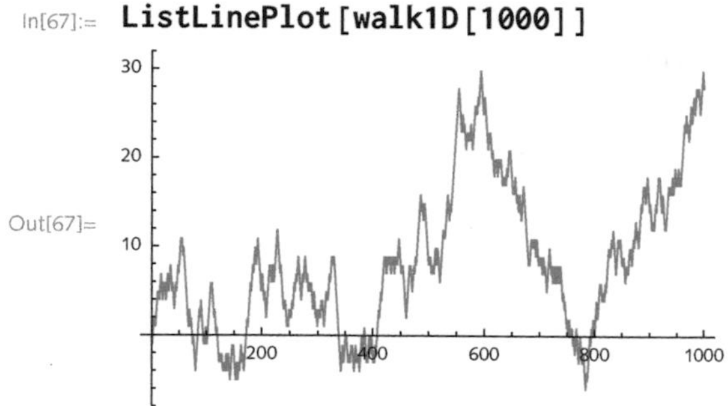

In one dimension, each step of the walk is either a forward step represented by 1 or a backward step represented by −1. In higher dimensions, a step can take a range of orientations with respect to previous steps. In two dimensions, on the rectangular lattice (Figure 6.3), each site has four nearest neighbors, points north, south, east, and west of the current site.

FIGURE 6.3. *A site (blue) with its four nearest neighbors (gray).*

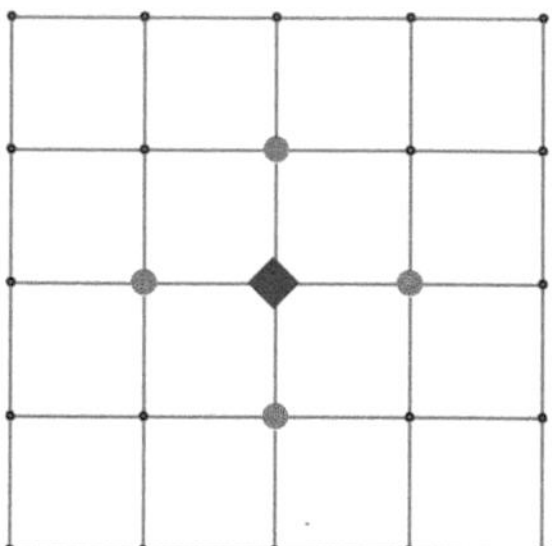

Just one change from the one-dimensional program is necessary – using two-dimensional directions. Otherwise the code is identical.

```
In[68]:= walk2D[t_] := Module[{dirs = {{1, 0}, {-1, 0}, {0, 1}, {0, -1}}, steps},
           steps = RandomChoice[dirs, t];
           Accumulate[steps]]
```

Try this out on a ten-step walk, that is, for $t = 10$.

```
In[69]:= walk2D[10]

Out[69]= {{1, 0}, {1, 1}, {2, 1}, {2, 2},
          {1, 2}, {1, 3}, {2, 3}, {3, 3}, {4, 3}, {4, 4}}
```

There is more than a little similarity between the two functions `walk1D` and `walk2D`. Both use `Accumulate`, randomly choosing t elements from some list. For one-dimensional walks, that list is simply {-1, 1}; for two-dimensional walks, it is the list {{1, 0}, {-1, 0}, {0, 1}, {0, -1}}. Although we could extend this idea to higher dimensions, the list of directions will start to get unwieldy. In three dimensions, there are six directions – each a triple of integers – that can be taken at any given step (Figure 6.4).

FIGURE 6.4. *A site (blue cube) with its six nearest neighbors in a three-dimensional rectangular lattice.*

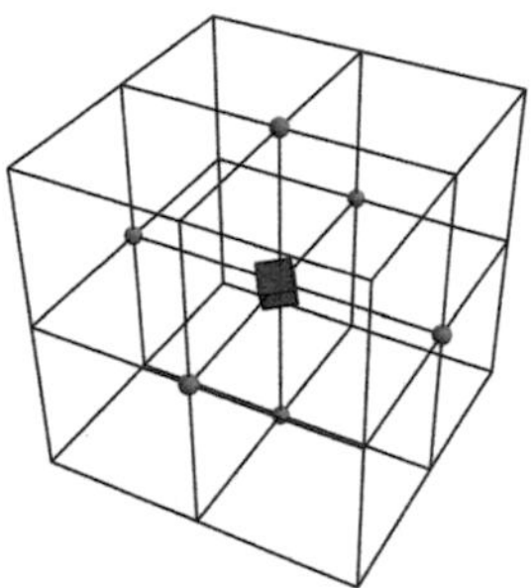

So let's try a slightly different approach, one that uses these similarities but simplifies and generalizes the lattice walk code. The key observation is to think about this as a vector problem. In two dimensions, the vectors chosen by RandomChoice are essentially the two orthogonal vectors {1, 0} and {0, 1}, together with the opposite of each of these. These vectors are given by the identity matrix of the appropriate dimension.

```
In[70]:= Join[IdentityMatrix[1], -IdentityMatrix[1]]
Out[70]= {{1}, {-1}}

In[71]:= Join[IdentityMatrix[2], -IdentityMatrix[2]]
Out[71]= {{1, 0}, {0, 1}, {-1, 0}, {0, -1}}

In[72]:= Join[IdentityMatrix[3], -IdentityMatrix[3]]
Out[72]= {{1, 0, 0}, {0, 1, 0}, {0, 0, 1}, {-1, 0, 0}, {0, -1, 0}, {0, 0, -1}}
```

This makes the code for the random walks consistent and generalizes to n-dimensional space easily. It is the approach we will take for the lattice walks.

Before writing the code for the n-dimensional lattice walk, we need to make one adjustment in the case of one-dimensional walks. IdentityMatrix[1] returns the list {{1}}, so we will need to flatten that list for this case only.

Here then is the code for an n-dimensional lattice walk:

```
In[73]:= latticeWalk[steps_, dim_] := Module[{mat, walk},
           mat = Join[IdentityMatrix[dim], -IdentityMatrix[dim]];
           walk = Accumulate[RandomChoice[mat, steps]];
           If[dim == 1, Flatten[walk], walk]]

In[74]:= latticeWalk[5, 2]
Out[74]= {{0, -1}, {1, -1}, {1, 0}, {1, 1}, {1, 2}}
```

To visualize the path these steps take in the plane, connect each successive point with a line. This displays a 2500-step random walk. We have set the AspectRatio so that our plot has a more natural ratio of height to width.

```
In[75]:= ListLinePlot[latticeWalk[2500, 2], AspectRatio → Automatic]
```

Out[75]=

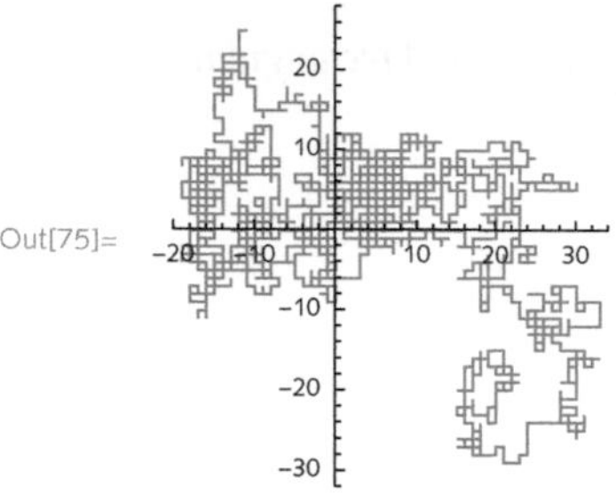

And here is a one-dimensional lattice walk:

```
In[76]:= ListLinePlot[latticeWalk[2500, 1]]
```

Out[76]=

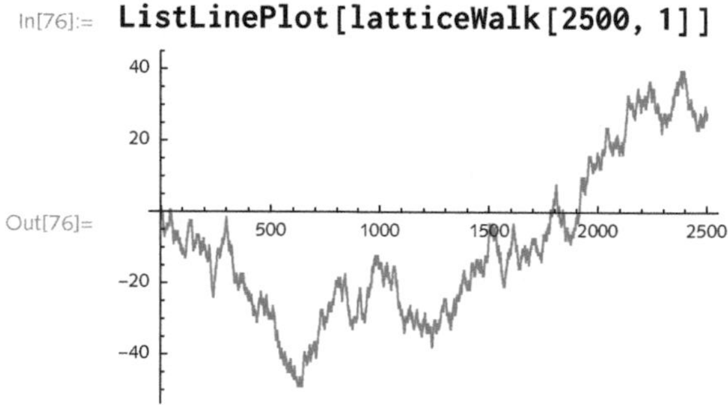

The visualization of these points in 3-space is straightforward – connect each point with a line (or tube, as below) and then convert to a graphical object to display.

```
In[77]:= Graphics3D[Tube[latticeWalk[2500, 3]]]
```

Out[77]=

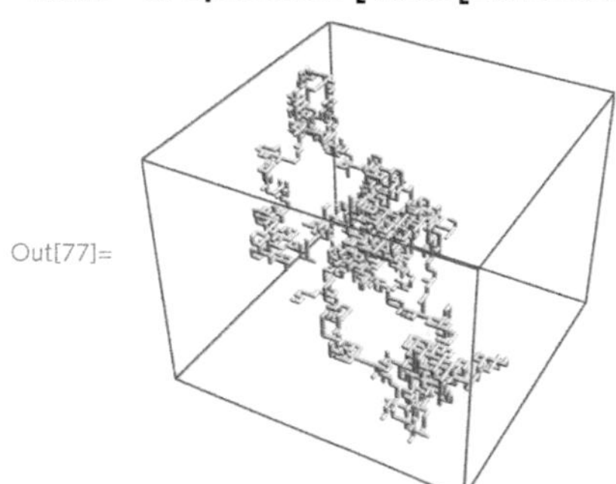

The latticeWalk function can be used to create n-dimensional walks for any positive integer $n > 0$. Although visualizing such objects is difficult, we can still ask questions about the nature of such walks. For example, here are five steps in a nine-dimensional random walk:

```
In[78]:= latticeWalk[5, 9]
Out[78]= {{0, 0, 0, 0, 0, 0, -1, 0, 0},
  {0, 0, 0, -1, 0, 0, -1, 0, 0}, {0, 1, 0, -1, 0, 0, -1, 0, 0},
  {0, 1, 0, -1, 0, -1, -1, 0, 0}, {0, 1, 0, -1, 1, -1, -1, 0, 0}}
```

This computes the distance from the last step to the origin in this nine-dimensional walk:

```
In[79]:= Norm[Last[%]]
Out[79]= √5
```

Although lattice walks are fairly easy to visualize and program, there are many physical phenomena, such as Brownian motion, for which walks off the lattice are more appropriate models. These off-lattice walks are similar to the lattice walk code, except that the step directions are real numbers in a certain range instead of integer lattice points. The exercises explore off-lattice walks in one, two, and three dimensions and they are given in full in the program listing in Section 10.3.

RandomWalk We have now developed the function `latticeWalk` for computing random walks in any dimension. We could add an off-lattice function and even a self-avoiding walk function. Our intention is that these would be auxiliary functions that the user should not have to remember but would be called by means of an option to the main function. It is preferable to have one function, `RandomWalk`, that has a simple, easy-to-remember interface that calls the appropriate function when needed. In computer languages, the `RandomWalk` function is often called the *public function*, the user's interface to the underlying code. The auxiliary function `latticeWalk` is referred to as a *private function* and is kept hidden from the user interface. The developer of such code is then free to change the underlying private constructs as the need arises and the user does not need to worry about them as the public interface remains unchanged.

We start by creating an optional argument to our `RandomWalk` function – `Dimension` – and give its default value. This is the value that will be used whenever explicit options to `RandomWalk` are not given. The idea is that if the `Dimension` option has been given a value of 3 say, that will be passed to the appropriate private function automatically.

```
In[80]:= Options[RandomWalk] = {Dimension → 2}
Out[80]= {Dimension → 2}
```

Here is the `RandomWalk` function with the option structure in place:

```
In[81]:= RandomWalk[t_, OptionsPattern[]] := Module[{dim, latticeQ},
           dim = OptionValue[Dimension];
           latticeWalk[t, dim]]
```

Some comments on this code are in order:

- To pass the options into the `RandomWalk` function, `OptionsPattern` is used on the left-hand side of the function definition.
- To extract the values from the options, we use `OptionValue[Dimension]`.
- We have assigned the value of the option to a local symbol `dim` inside the body of the `RandomWalk` function.

Let's add a message that will be issued if the value of `Dimension` is not a positive integer.

```
In[82]:= RandomWalk::baddim =
           "The value `1` of the option Dimension is not a positive integer.";
```

```
In[83]:= RandomWalk[t_, OptionsPattern[]] := Module[{dim, latticeQ},
           dim = OptionValue[Dimension];
           If[IntegerQ[dim] && Positive[dim],
            latticeWalk[t, dim], Message[RandomWalk::baddim, dim]]
          ]
```

This is the user interface to the random walk machinery we are building. The auxiliary function `latticeWalk` is private – the user does not need to know anything about it to use `RandomWalk`.

Next we exercise the options and check that each of the possible walks produces a sensible result.

```
In[84]:= RandomWalk[5, Dimension → 1]
Out[84]= {-1, 0, -1, 0, -1}

In[85]:= RandomWalk[5]
Out[85]= {{0, 1}, {0, 2}, {0, 1}, {1, 1}, {1, 0}}

In[86]:= RandomWalk[5, Dimension → 4]
Out[86]= {{0, 0, 0, 1}, {1, 0, 0, 1}, {2, 0, 0, 1}, {3, 0, 0, 1}, {3, 0, 0, 2}}
```

Check some bad values for the `Dimension` option.

```
In[87]:= RandomWalk[5, Dimension → -14]
         RandomWalk::baddim : The value -14 of the option Dimension is not a positive integer.
```

The `ShowWalk` function, discussed in Section 4.1 and developed in full in Chapter 10, can be used to display the random walks.

```
In[88]:= << EPM`RandomWalks`

In[89]:= ShowWalk[RandomWalk[2500, Dimension → 1]]
```

Out[89]=
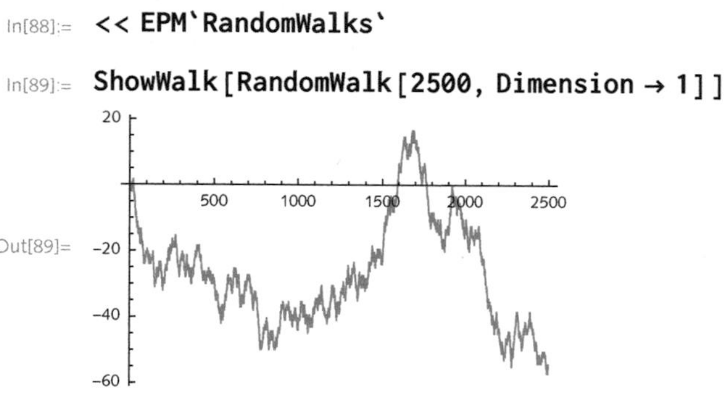


```
In[90]:= ShowWalk[RandomWalk[2500, Dimension → 2]]
```

Out[90]=
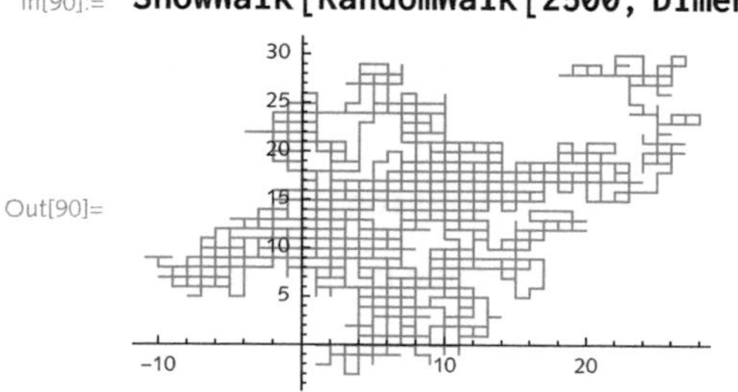

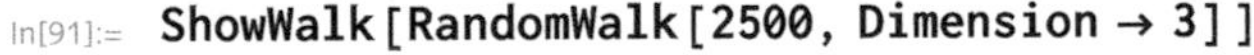

```
In[91]:= ShowWalk[RandomWalk[2500, Dimension → 3]]
```

Out[91]=

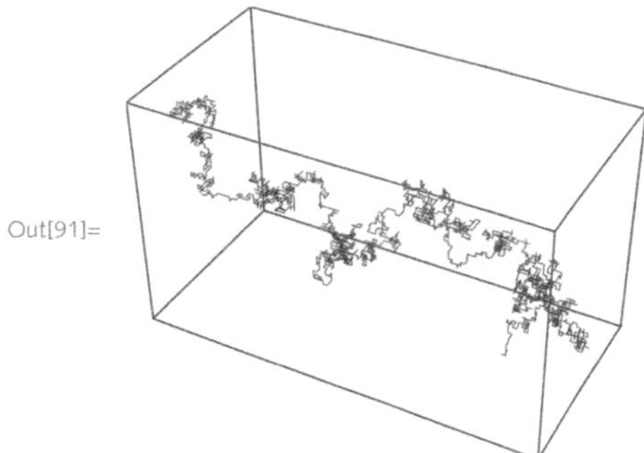

The fully developed random walk functions are contained in the package EPM`RandomWalks` that accompanies this book. The package itself is listed in Section 10.3.

Exercises

1. Add a message to the `RandomWalk` function developed in this chapter so that a warning is issued when a nonpositive integer is given as the first argument to `RandomWalk`.

2. Consider a sequence of numbers generated by the following iterative process: starting with the list of odd integers 1, 3, 5, 7, …, the first odd number greater than 1 is 3, so delete every third number from the list; from the list of remaining numbers, the next number is 7, so delete every seventh number; and so on. The numbers that remain are referred to as *lucky numbers*. Use a sieving method to find all lucky numbers less than 1000. See Weisstein (Lucky Number) for more information.

3. Create a function `TruthTable[`*expr*`, `*vars*`]` that takes a logical expression such as $A \wedge B$ and outputs a truth table similar to those in Section 2.4. You can create a list of truth values using `Tuples`:

```
In[1]:= Tuples[{True, False}, 2]
Out[1]= {{True, True}, {True, False}, {False, True}, {False, False}}
```

You will also find it helpful to consider threading rules over the tuples using `MapThread` or `Thread`. Alternatively, consider using the built-in function `BooleanTable`.

4. Given a list of expressions, *lis*, create a function `NearTo[`*lis*`, `*elem*`, {`*n*`}]` that returns all elements of *lis* that are exactly *n* positions away from *elem*, which is assumed to be a member of *lis*. For example:

```
In[2]:= chars = CharacterRange["a", "z"]
Out[2]= {a, b, c, d, e, f, g, h, i, j, k, l, m, n, o, p, q, r, s, t, u, v, w, x, y, z}

In[3]:= NearTo[chars, "q", {3}]
Out[3]= {{n}, {t}}
```

Write a second rule, `NearTo[lis, elem, n]`, that returns all elements in *lis* that are within *n* positions of *elem*.

```
In[4]:= NearTo[chars, "q", 4]
Out[4]= {{m, n, o, p, q, r, s, t, u}}
```

Finally, create your own distance function (`DistanceFunction`) and use it with the built-in `Nearest` to do the same computation. Two useful functions for these tasks are `Position` and `Extract`. `Extract[expr, pos]` returns elements from *expr* whose positions *pos* are given by `Position`.

5. A *Smith number* is a composite number such that the sum of its digits is equal to the sum of the digits of its prime factors. For example, the prime factorization of 852 is $2^2 \cdot 3^1 \cdot 71^1$, and so the sum of the digits of its prime factors is $2 + 2 + 3 + 7 + 1 = 15$, which is equal to the sum of its digits, $8 + 5 + 2 = 15$. Write a program to find all Smith numbers less than 10 000.

6. Develop auxiliary functions for one-, two-, and three-dimensional off-lattice random walks. Then create a function `offLatticeWalk[steps, dim]` that uses these auxiliary functions to return an off-lattice walk of length *steps*, in dimension *dim*. Finally, modify `RandomWalk` to include an option `LatticeWalk` that, when set to `True`, calls the `latticeWalk` auxiliary function and when set to `False`, calls this new `offLatticeWalk` auxiliary function.

7. Here is some code to run a bond percolation simulation on an $m \times n$ lattice grid. For each edge in the grid graph gg, it creates a probability from a Bernoulli distribution (think coin flip – only two possible outcomes) and then picks those edges that are below the threshold probability `prob`.

```
In[5]:= With[{m = 8, n = 13, prob = 0.47},
          gg = GridGraph[{m, n}];
          probs = RandomVariate[BernoulliDistribution[prob], EdgeCount[gg]];
          perc = Graph[Pick[EdgeList[gg], probs, 1]];
          HighlightGraph[gg, perc]]
```

Out[5]=

Turn the above code into a function `BondPercolation[{m, n}, prob, opts]` that outputs a graph like that above. Include a check on the arguments *m* and *n*, returning an appropriate message if they are not positive integers. Finally, have your function inherit options from `Graph` and pass them into the `GridGraph` function.

8. Create a function `ColorResidues[seq]` that takes an amino acid sequence *seq* and returns a visualization like that below where the amino acids are colored according to a scheme such as *Amino*, where more polar residues are brighter and more nonpolar residues are colored darker. In addition to a `ColorScheme` option, add options to control the frame around each residue.

```
In[6]:= Amino = {{"P", ■}, {"W", ■}, {"L", ■}, {"V", ■}, {"I", ■}, {"N", ■},
          {"Q", ■}, {"S", ■}, {"T", ■}, {"C", ■}, {"M", ■}, {"H", ■}, {"A", ■},
          {"G", ■}, {"F", ■}, {"Y", ■}, {"K", ■}, {"R", ■}, {"D", ■}, {"E", ■}};
```

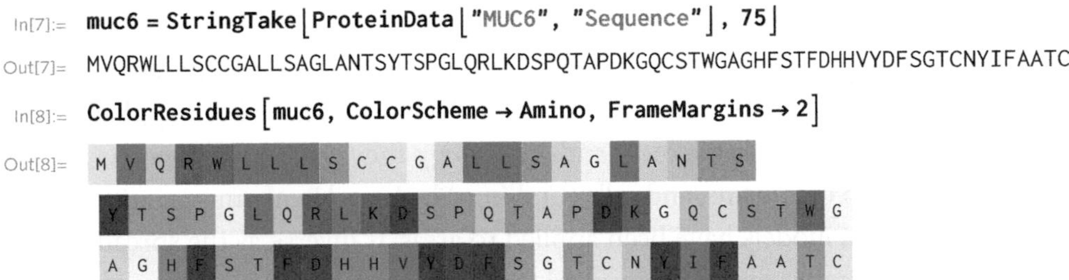

```
In[7]:= muc6 = StringTake[ProteinData["MUC6", "Sequence"], 75]
Out[7]= MVQRWLLLSCCGALLSAGLANTSYTSPGLQRLKDSPQTAPDKGQCSTWGAGHFSTFDHHVYDFSGTCNYIFAATC
In[8]:= ColorResidues[muc6, ColorScheme → Amino, FrameMargins → 2]
Out[8]= M V Q R W L L L S C C G A L L S A G L A N T S
        Y T S P G L Q R L K D S P Q T A P D K G Q C S T W G
        A G H F S T F D H H V Y D F S G T C N Y I F A A T C
```

6.4 Notes and further reading

The condition number of a matrix (Exercise 1, Section 6.1) gives a measure of the accuracy of solutions to matrix equations. Singular matrices have infinite condition numbers and a system is said to be ill-conditioned if the condition number is large. A "large" condition number c means roughly that the reciprocal of c approaches the machine's floating-point precision – typically about 10^{-15} for double floats. You can think of the logarithm of the condition number of a matrix $\mathcal{M}$ as giving a rough estimate of the number of digits that are lost when solving linear systems involving $\mathcal{M}$. See Blum (2012) for a discussion of the historical context of condition numbers including Alan Turing's original definition, or Press et al. (2007) for numerical implementations of the computation of condition numbers.

The NASA GISS Surface Temperature (GISTEMP) data used in Section 6.2 comes from the CO_2 Information Analysis Center at Oak Ridge National Laboratory. It covers global surface temperatures from 1880 to the present. The example in the text used land anomalous temperatures, that is, temperature deviations from the mean with anomalies relative to the 1951–1980 base period means (Ruedy, Sato, and Lo 2015).

The Sieve of Eratosthenes is one of the oldest algorithms known, but as noted in the text, it gets bogged down for large numbers. If you are interested in working with large numbers, it would be best to consider specialized algorithms that are asymptotically fast. For large integers, `PrimePi` uses an algorithm based on estimates of the density of primes by performing numerical integration of certain integral transforms of the Riemann ζ function (Lagarias and Odlyzko 1987).

Measuring the extent of data sets using eigenvectors has broad application not only to random-walk models (Rudnick and Gaspari 2004) but, somewhat surprisingly, also to PageRank, an algorithm used to rank web page importance in building search results (Chung and Zhao 2010).

Although much of the time series machinery is new to *Mathematica*, the subject has a long history and extends across many disciplines. Classic texts include Box, Jenkins, and Reinsel (2008) as well as Chatfield (2004). The sunspot time series data, curated by the Royal Observatory of Belgium, stretches back to 1818 and has been shown to be moderately autocorrelated (Hathaway 2010 and Petrovay 2010). Using lag plots to determine if data is autocorrelated is discussed in the *e-Handbook of Statistical Methods* (National Institute of Standards and Technology 2015).

Random walks, discussed throughout this book, have application to many branches of the sciences: in network science, they are used to estimate the size of the World Wide Web (Bar-Yossef and Gurevich 2006); walks on random graphs (Exercise 9, Section 5.6) have been applied to electrical network models (Chung and Zhao 2010); and in biology they have been used to model the movement of animals, micro-organisms, and cells (Codling, Plank, and Benhamou 2008).

Bond and site percolation models have been applied to areas as diverse as the spread of disease, propagation of computer viruses, electric power grids, and traffic flow. See Callaway et al. (2000) and Moore and Newman (2000) for more information.

Several schemes are commonly used to color amino acid sequences. The *Amino* scheme used in Exercise 8 of Section 6.3 colors according to the polarity of the residues. Other schemes might color for such attributes as hydrophobicity, size, position within the sequence, bond or angle energy, or protein secondary structure (Lesk 2010).

7

Strings

Structure and syntax · *Display of strings* · *Testing strings* · *Measuring strings* · *Character codes* · *Operations on strings* · *Basic string operations* · *Strings vs. lists* · *Encoding text* · *Anagrams* · *String patterns* · *Finding subsequences with strings* · *Alternatives* · *Regular expressions* · *Contractions* · *Examples* · *Abecedarian words* · *Random strings* · *Partitioning strings* · *DNA sequence analysis* · *Displaying DNA sequences* · *Blanagrams* · *Notes and further reading*

Strings are used across many disciplines to represent data, filenames, and other objects: they are used by linguists studying representation, classification, and patterns involved in audio and text usage; biologists working with genomic data as strings are interested in sequence structure and assembly and perform extensive statistical analysis on strings; programmers operate on string data for such tasks as text search, file manipulation, and text processing. Strings are so ubiquitous that almost every modern programming language has a string data type and dozens of functions for operating on strings.

In this chapter we will introduce the tools available for working with strings, starting with a look at their structure and syntax, then moving on to a discussion of the many high-level functions that are optimized for string manipulation. Many of the functions introduced in Chapter 3 for operating on lists have analogs with strings, and you would do well to first make sure you understand those before tackling the string functions.

String patterns follow on the discussion of more general patterns introduced in Chapter 4. We will introduce an alternative syntax – regular expressions – that provides a compact and efficient mechanism for working with strings. The chapter closes with several applied examples from bioinformatics (creating random strings, partitioning strings, analyzing GC content, displaying sequences in tables) and linguistics (text processing, corpus analysis, *n*-grams, collocation, word and sentence length frequency).

7.1 Structure and syntax

Strings are expressions consisting of a number of characters enclosed in quotes. The characters can be anything you can type from your keyboard, including uppercase and lowercase letters, numbers, punctuation marks, and spaces. Here is a list of the standard set of printable Ascii characters:

```
In[1]:= CharacterRange[" ", "~"]
Out[1]= { , !, ", #, $, %, &, ', (, ), *, +, ,, -, ., /, 0, 1, 2, 3, 4, 5, 6,
    7, 8, 9, :, ;, <, =, >, ?, @, A, B, C, D, E, F, G, H, I, J, K, L, M,
    N, O, P, Q, R, S, T, U, V, W, X, Y, Z, [, \, ], ^, _, `, a, b, c, d, e, f,
    g, h, i, j, k, l, m, n, o, p, q, r, s, t, u, v, w, x, y, z, {, |, }, ~}
```

Other character sets are available as well. For example, the lowercase Greek letters are typically entered from one of *Mathematica*'s built-in character palettes or by using a keyboard shortcut such as ESC-a-ESC for α.

```
In[2]:= CharacterRange["α", "ω"]
Out[2]= {α, β, γ, δ, ε, ζ, η, θ, ι, κ, λ, μ, ν, ξ, ο, π, ρ, ς, σ, τ, υ, φ, χ, ψ, ω}
```

Strings are atomic and so cannot be subdivided. Their data type is `String`.

```
In[3]:= Head["The magic words are squeamish ossifrage."]
Out[3]= String

In[4]:= Part["This is a string", 1]
        Part::partd : Part specification This is a string⟦1⟧ is longer than depth of object. >>
Out[4]= This is a string⟦1⟧
```

Display of strings

Strings displayed in output appear without quotes. This is the default behavior of the formatting rules for `OutputForm`:

```
In[5]:= "The magic words are squeamish ossifrage."
Out[5]= The magic words are squeamish ossifrage.
```

Use `InputForm` or `FullForm` to display these quotes in output:

```
In[6]:= FullForm["The magic words are squeamish ossifrage."]
Out[6]//FullForm=
        "The magic words are squeamish ossifrage."
```

Functions are available to convert expressions to strings and to convert strings to expressions.

```
In[7]:= ToString[word] // FullForm
Out[7]//FullForm=
        "word"

In[8]:= ToExpression["word"] // Head
Out[8]= Symbol
```

Testing strings

Various predicates test if a string consists entirely of letters, or uppercase and lowercase letters.

```
In[9]:= LetterQ["ossifrage"]
Out[9]= True
```

```
In[10]:= LetterQ["x1"]
Out[10]= False
```

```
In[11]:= LowerCaseQ["strings"]
Out[11]= True
```

`DigitQ` is used to test if all the characters in a string are digits.

```
In[12]:= DigitQ["12345"]
Out[12]= True
```

Use === (`SameQ`) to test for equality of strings.

```
In[13]:= "str" === "str "
Out[13]= False
```

Measuring strings

Counting the number of characters in a string is a common operation and a string function is devoted to that task.

```
In[14]:= StringLength["The magic words are squeamish ossifrage."]
Out[14]= 40
```

`StringLength` also works with lists of strings. In other words, it has the `Listable` attribute.

```
In[15]:= StringLength[{"How", "I", "wish", "I", "could", "calculate", "pi"}]
Out[15]= {3, 1, 4, 1, 5, 9, 2}
```

Character codes

Each character in a computer's character set is assigned a number, called its *character code*. By general agreement, almost all computers use the same character codes, together called the *Ascii code*. In this code, the uppercase letters *A*, *B*, …, *Z* are assigned the numbers 65, 66, …, 90 while the lowercase letters *a*, *b*, …, *z* have the numbers 97, 98, …, 122 (note that the number of an uppercase letter is 32 less than its lowercase version). The numbers 0, 1, …, 9 are coded as 48, 49, …, 57 while the punctuation marks period, comma, and exclamation point have the codes 46, 44, and 33, respectively. The space character is represented by the code 32. Table 7.1 shows the characters and their codes.

One way to work with strings is to convert them to a list of character codes and then operate on the codes using mathematical functions. To start, here are the printable Ascii characters:

```
In[16]:= FromCharacterCode[Range[32, 126]]
Out[16]=  !"#$%&'()*+,-./0123456789:;<=>?@ABCDEFGHIJKLMNOPQRSTUVWXYZ[\]^
         _`abcdefghijklmnopqrstuvwxyz{|}~
```

`ToCharacterCode[char]` converts any string character *char* to its Ascii code.

```
In[17]:= ToCharacterCode[%]
Out[17]= {32, 33, 34, 35, 36, 37, 38, 39, 40, 41, 42, 43, 44, 45, 46, 47, 48, 49, 50, 51, 52, 53,
  54, 55, 56, 57, 58, 59, 60, 61, 62, 63, 64, 65, 66, 67, 68, 69, 70, 71, 72, 73,
  74, 75, 76, 77, 78, 79, 80, 81, 82, 83, 84, 85, 86, 87, 88, 89, 90, 91, 92, 93,
  94, 95, 96, 97, 98, 99, 100, 101, 102, 103, 104, 105, 106, 107, 108, 109, 110,
  111, 112, 113, 114, 115, 116, 117, 118, 119, 120, 121, 122, 123, 124, 125, 126}
```

TABLE 7.1. *Ascii character codes*

Characters	Ascii codes
A, B, …, Z	65, 66, …, 90
a, b, …, z	97, 98, …, 122
0, 1, …, 9	48, 49, …, 57
. (period)	46
, (comma)	44
? (question mark)	63
␣ (space)	32

Characters from other languages can also be used, for example, Greek and Japanese.

```
In[18]:= FromCharacterCode[Range[913, 929]]
Out[18]= ΑΒΓΔΕΖΗΘΙΚΛΜΝΞΟΠΡ
```

```
In[19]:= FromCharacterCode[Range[30010, 30030]]
Out[19]= 町画甼甽甾甿畀畁畂畃畄畅畆畇畈畉畊畋界畍畎
```

Either Ascii decimal or hexadecimal values can be used to display characters. For example, the Kanji character 町 (cho or machi), which means "town," has hex value 753A and can be found using online Unicode charts (www.unicode.org/charts). This converts from base 16 and displays the character:

```
In[20]:= 16^^753A
Out[20]= 30010
```

```
In[21]:= FromCharacterCode[%]
Out[21]= 町
```

If you know the Unicode value, you can enter the character directly using `\:` before the hex value.

```
In[22]:= FullForm[%]
Out[22]//FullForm=
  "\:753a"
```

Exercises

1. Convert the first character in a string (which you may assume to be a lowercase letter) to uppercase.

2. Given a string of digits, for example, `"10495"`, convert it to its integer value.

3. Create a function `UniqueCharacters[str]` that takes a string as its argument and returns a list of the unique characters in that string. For example, `UniqueCharacters["Mississippi"]` should return `{M, i, s, p}`.

4. Using a first-name database, find all names consisting entirely of combinations of the first letters on the keys of a typical phone (Figure 7.1), that is, names that only contain the letters *a*, *d*, *g*, *j*, *m*, *p*, *t*, and *w*; for example, *PAT*. As a database source, the US Census Bureau curates lists of common names.

   FIGURE 7.1. *Telephone number pad.*

5. A somewhat simplistic cipher, known as the XOR cipher, uses binary eight-bit keys to encode strings. The idea is to first convert each letter in a plaintext string to their character code in eight-bit binary. So the letter A, whose character code is 65, is converted into 1000001. A key string, say the letter *K*, is similarly converted to an eight-bit binary representation. Then each letter in the plaintext is encoded by performing a bit XOR operation on the plaintext letter and the key, both using their eight-bit binary representation. The resulting ciphertext could remain in binary or it could be converted back from character codes to encoded text, the ciphertext.

   Create an XOR cipher and encode a plaintext string to produce a ciphertext. See Exercise 6, Section 2.2 for information on converting a string to its binary representation. As an aside, the XOR cipher is a terribly insecure cipher as simply reversing the encoding operations makes it easy to recover the key (Churchhouse 2001).

7.2 Operations on strings

Strings are expressions and, like other expressions such as numbers and lists, there are many built-in functions available to operate on them. In fact, many of these functions are quite similar to those for operating on lists. In this section we will first look at functions for working with strings and compare them to similar list manipulation operations, both from a structural point of view but also computationally. The section concludes with some applied examples: analyzing a large piece of text, encoding strings, and a word game for creating anagrams.

Basic string operations

StringTake is used to extract parts of a string; it has a similar syntax to Take. The second argument specifies the positions of the characters to extract. So, for example, this takes the first twelve characters in this string:

```
In[1]:= StringTake["Three quarks for Muster Mark!", 12]
Out[1]= Three quarks
```

And this takes the last twelve characters from the string:

```
In[2]:= StringTake["Three quarks for Muster Mark!", -12]
Out[2]= Muster Mark!
```

A list of the individual characters is returned by Characters.

```
In[3]:= Characters["Three quarks for Muster Mark!"]
Out[3]= {T, h, r, e, e,  , q, u, a, r, k, s,
          , f, o, r,  , M, u, s, t, e, r,  , M, a, r, k, !}
```

StringJoin concatenates strings and is, in some sense, the inverse of Characters.

```
In[4]:= StringJoin[%]
Out[4]= Three quarks for Muster Mark!
```

In addition to taking a list of characters, as above, StringJoin can take an arbitrary number of strings as arguments.

```
In[5]:= StringJoin["q", "u", "a", "r", "k", "s"]
Out[5]= quarks
```

The shorthand notation for StringJoin is str_1 <> str_2.

```
In[6]:= "x" <> "22"
Out[6]= x22
```

The following functions mirror those for list operations:

```
In[7]:= StringReverse["abcde"]
Out[7]= edcba

In[8]:= StringDrop["abcde", -1]
Out[8]= abcd

In[9]:= StringPosition["abcde", "bc"]
Out[9]= {{2, 3}}

In[10]:= StringCount["When you wish upon a star", "o"]
Out[10]= 2

In[11]:= StringInsert["abcde", "T", 3]
Out[11]= abTcde
```

```
In[12]:= StringReplace["abcde", "cd" → "CD"]
Out[12]= abCDe
```

Some functions are quite specific to strings and do not have analogs with lists, for example, conversion to uppercase and lowercase.

```
In[13]:= ToUpperCase["words"]
Out[13]= WORDS
```

This trims substrings from a string using alternative patterns (discussed further in Section 7.3). So, in the example below, if either " `http: //` " or " `/` " is found, they will be trimmed.

```
In[14]:= StringTrim["http://www.google.com/", "http://" | "/"]
Out[14]= www.google.com
```

Strings vs. lists

For some computations, you might be tempted to convert a string to a list of characters and operate on the list using list manipulation functions. Consider counting the number of characters in a string.

```
In[15]:= Characters["The magic words are squeamish ossifrage."]
Out[15]= {T, h, e,  , m, a, g, i, c,  , w, o, r, d, s,  , a, r, e,
           , s, q, u, e, a, m, i, s, h,  , o, s, s, i, f, r, a, g, e, .}

In[16]:= Length[%]
Out[16]= 40
```

But you can do it directly with `StringLength`.

```
In[17]:= StringLength["The magic words are squeamish ossifrage."]
Out[17]= 40
```

Using `StringLength` saves on a bit of typing and is one less evaluation, but this is a very small example. On a larger computation though, the differences begin to show.

For example, to count the occurrences of the letter B in a large text – Charles Darwin's *On the Origin of Species* – you could first construct a list of the individual characters and then use `Count`.

```
In[18]:= text = ExampleData[{"Text", "OriginOfSpecies"}];
         StringTake[text, 200]
Out[19]= INTRODUCTION. When on board H.M.S. 'Beagle,' as naturalist, I was much
           struck with certain facts in the distribution of the inhabitants
           of South America, and in the geological relations of the present

In[20]:= Count[Characters[text], "B"] // Timing
Out[20]= {0.142591, 427}
```

Since the string functions in *Mathematica* are optimized for working on strings directly, you will often find that they are much faster than the more general list manipulation functions.

```
In[21]:= StringCount[text, "B"] // Timing
Out[21]= {0.002565, 427}
```

This speedup results from the fact that string pattern matching algorithms are operating only on a well-defined finite alphabet and on the fact that string expressions are essentially flat structures, whereas the algorithms for more general expression matching are designed to operate on arbitrary expressions with potentially much more complicated structures.

In addition to efficiency issues, converting to lists and using list manipulation functions will often be more cumbersome than working with the string functions directly. For example, counting the occurrences of a word within a chunk of text by first converting to a list of characters would be quite indirect and computationally more taxing than simply using `StringCount` directly.

```
In[22]:= StringCount[text, "selection"] // Timing
Out[22]= {0.004854, 351}
```

In fact, sometimes you will find it more efficient to convert a numerical problem to one involving strings, do the work with string manipulation functions, and then convert back to numbers. See Section 7.3 for an example involving finding subsequences in the digits of π.

Encoding text

Encoding and decoding encrypted text goes back at least to the early Mesopotamian craftsmen (~1500 BC), who felt the need to encrypt formulas for their pottery glazes. Perhaps the most famous ancient use of encryption was the Roman general Julius Caesar who used a simple shift cipher to encode his military messages. Modern-day electronic communication would not be possible without encryption, which is used to protect the privacy of everything from email messages to bank transactions.

There are now many kinds of ciphers that one can implement: substitution, transposition, public-key, and many more. In this example we will look at one of the most basic of ciphers, a substitution cipher, essentially that used by Caesar. We will develop functions for coding and decoding strings of text. The particular coding we will use is quite simplistic compared with contemporary commercial-grade ciphers, but it will give us a chance to see how to combine string manipulation, the use of functional programming constructs, and rule-based programming, all in a practical example that should be easily accessible.

The problem in encryption is to develop an algorithm that can be used to encode a string of text and then a dual algorithm that can be used to decode the encrypted message. Typically, the input string is referred to as the *plaintext* and the encoded output as the *ciphertext*.

To start, we will limit ourselves to the 26 lowercase letters of the alphabet.

```
In[23]:= alphabet = CharacterRange["a", "z"]
Out[23]= {a, b, c, d, e, f, g, h, i, j, k, l, m, n, o, p, q, r, s, t, u, v, w, x, y, z}
```

The scheme used by Caesar is simply to shift each letter of the alphabet some fixed number of places to the left, and replace each character in the plaintext with the corresponding shifted letter. This is commonly referred to as a *substitution cipher*. Using `Thread`, we set up rules that implement this shift, here just shifting one place to the left:

```
In[24]:= CaesarCodeRules = Thread[alphabet → RotateLeft[alphabet]]
Out[24]= {a → b, b → c, c → d, d → e, e → f, f → g, g → h, h → i,
          i → j, j → k, k → l, l → m, m → n, n → o, o → p, p → q, q → r,
          r → s, s → t, t → u, u → v, v → w, w → x, x → y, y → z, z → a}
```

To encode a string, decompose it into individual characters, apply the code rules, and then join up the resulting characters into the ciphertext word.

```
In[25]:= Characters["hello"]
Out[25]= {h, e, l, l, o}

In[26]:= % /. CaesarCodeRules
Out[26]= {i, f, m, m, p}

In[27]:= StringJoin[%]
Out[27]= ifmmp
```

Here is the function to accomplish this:

```
In[28]:= encode[str_String, coderules_] := StringJoin[Characters[str] /. coderules]
```

The decoding rules are simply to reverse the encoding rules.

```
In[29]:= CaesarDecodeRules = Map[Reverse, CaesarCodeRules]
Out[29]= {b → a, c → b, d → c, e → d, f → e, g → f, h → g, i → h,
          j → i, k → j, l → k, m → l, n → m, o → n, p → o, q → p, r → q,
          s → r, t → s, u → t, v → u, w → v, x → w, y → x, z → y, a → z}
```

Similarly, here is the decoding function:

```
In[30]:= decode[str_String, decoderules_] :=
          StringJoin[Characters[str] /. decoderules]
```

Let's try it out on a phrase.

```
In[31]:= encode["squeamish ossifrage", CaesarCodeRules]
Out[31]= trvfbnjti pttjgsbhf

In[32]:= decode[%, CaesarDecodeRules]
Out[32]= squeamish ossifrage
```

We have shifted one position for each letter to encode (and decode). It is thought that Caesar (or his cryptographers) used a shift of length three to encode his military messages. In the exercises, you are asked to implement an arbitrary shift length in the encoding and decoding functions.

Even with longer shifts, the Caesar cipher is extremely insecure and highly prone to cracking, since there are only 26 possible shifts with this simple cipher. A slightly more secure cipher involves permuting the letters of the alphabet.

```
In[33]:= p = RandomSample[alphabet]
Out[33]= {h, p, z, s, t, c, d, o, q, x, n, f, y, e, w, l, k, m, i, r, a, g, b, v, j, u}
```

Using `Thread`, we create a rule for each letter paired up with the corresponding letter from the permutation p.

```
In[34]:= PermutationCodeRules = Thread[alphabet → p]
Out[34]= {a → h, b → p, c → z, d → s, e → t, f → c, g → d, h → o,
  i → q, j → x, k → n, l → f, m → y, n → e, o → w, p → l, q → k,
  r → m, s → i, t → r, u → a, v → g, w → b, x → v, y → j, z → u}
```

Again, the decoding rules are obtained by simply reversing the above rules.

```
In[35]:= PermutationDecodeRules = Thread[p → alphabet]
Out[35]= {h → a, p → b, z → c, s → d, t → e, c → f, d → g, o → h,
  q → i, x → j, n → k, f → l, y → m, e → n, w → o, l → p, k → q,
  m → r, i → s, r → t, a → u, g → v, b → w, v → x, j → y, u → z}
```

```
In[36]:= encode["squeamish ossifrage", PermutationCodeRules]
Out[36]= ikathyqio wiiqcmhdt
```

```
In[37]:= decode[%, PermutationDecodeRules]
Out[37]= squeamish ossifrage
```

Although these substitution ciphers are not too difficult to crack, they should give you some practice in working with strings, together with functional and rule-based programming constructs.

Anagrams

Anagrams are words that have the same set of letters but in a different order. Good Scrabble® players are adept at anagram creation. Anagrams can be programmed by taking a word, extracting and permuting its characters, and then finding which permutations are real words.

Start by getting the characters in a word and then permuting the characters.

```
In[38]:= chars = Characters["tame"]
Out[38]= {t, a, m, e}
```

```
In[39]:= p = Permutations[chars]
Out[39]= {{t, a, m, e}, {t, a, e, m}, {t, m, a, e}, {t, m, e, a},
  {t, e, a, m}, {t, e, m, a}, {a, t, m, e}, {a, t, e, m}, {a, m, t, e},
  {a, m, e, t}, {a, e, t, m}, {a, e, m, t}, {m, t, a, e}, {m, t, e, a},
  {m, a, t, e}, {m, a, e, t}, {m, e, t, a}, {m, e, a, t}, {e, t, a, m},
  {e, t, m, a}, {e, a, t, m}, {e, a, m, t}, {e, m, t, a}, {e, m, a, t}}
```

Concatenate the characters in each list to form possible words.

```
In[40]:= words = Map[StringJoin, p]
Out[40]= {tame, taem, tmae, tmea, team, tema, atme, atem, amte, amet, aetm, aemt,
  mtae, mtea, mate, maet, meta, meat, etam, etma, eatm, eamt, emta, emat}
```

Now, which of these "words" are really words? One way to check is to select those that are in the dictionary. Those elements in `words` that are not in the dictionary will return `{}` when run against `DictionaryLookup`, so we omit those using ≠.

```
In[41]:= Select[words, DictionaryLookup[#, IgnoreCase → True] ≠ {} &]
Out[41]= {tame, team, mate, meta, meat}
```

Putting all the pieces together, we have the function Anagrams:

```
In[42]:= Anagrams[word_String] := Module[{chars = Characters[word], words},
           words = Map[StringJoin, Permutations[chars]];
           Select[words, DictionaryLookup[#, IgnoreCase → True] ≠ {} &]]

In[43]:= Anagrams["parsley"] // Timing
Out[43]= {0.196837, {parsley, parleys, players, replays, sparely}}

In[44]:= Anagrams["elvis"]
Out[44]= {elvis, evils, levis, lives, veils}
```

Other than extracting the characters of a word and joining the permuted list of characters, the operations here are essentially those on lists (of strings) and pattern matching. Exercise 3 in Section 7.5 discusses a more direct approach to this problem, one that avoids the creation of permutations of the characters in the word.

Exercises

1. Create a function `PalindromeQ[str]` that returns a value of `True` if its argument *str* is a palindrome, that is, if the string *str* is the same forward and backward. For example, the word *refer* is a palindrome.

2. Several dozen words in an English dictionary contain two consecutive double letters: *balloon, coffee, succeed,* for example. Find all words in the dictionary that contain three consecutive double letters. This puzzle appeared on the *Car Talk* radio show (CarTalk 2007).

3. Given two strings of equal length, create a function `StringTranspose` that transposes the characters in the two strings and then joins them into a single string.

```
In[1]:= StringTranspose["abc", "def"]
Out[1]= adbecf
```

4. The built-in function `StringRotateLeft` rotates the characters in a string by a specified amount.

```
In[2]:= StringRotateLeft["a quark for Muster Mark ", 8]
Out[2]= for Muster Mark a quark
```

Perform the same operation without using `StringRotateLeft`.

5. Create a function `StringPermutations[str]` that returns all permutations of the string *str*. For example:

```
In[3]:= StringPermutations["ABC"] // InputForm
Out[3]//InputForm=
        {"ABC", "ACB", "BAC", "BCA", "CAB", "CBA"}
```

6. Rewrite the function `SmarandacheWellin` from Exercise 10 of Section 2.3 to instead use strings to construct these numbers. Test your implementation for speed against the function from Section 2.3 that uses numerical functions only.

7. When developing algorithms that operate on large structures (for example, large systems of equations), it is often helpful to be able to create a set of unique symbols with which to work. Create a function `MakeVarList` that creates unique symbols. For example:

```
In[4]:= MakeVarList[x, 8]
Out[4]= {x1, x2, x3, x4, x5, x6, x7, x8}

In[5]:= MakeVarList[var, {10, 15}]
Out[5]= {var10, var11, var12, var13, var14, var15}
```

8. Create a function `StringTally` that counts each unique character in a string and returns a list similar to that returned by the built-in `Tally` function. Include the option `IgnoreCase` with default value `False`. When set to `True`, your function should convert all characters to lowercase before doing the tally.

```
In[6]:= StringTally["One fish, two fish, red fish, blue fish"]
Out[6]= {{O, 1}, {n, 1}, {e, 3}, {  , 7}, {f, 4}, {i, 4}, {s, 4}, {h, 4},
         {,, 3}, {t, 1}, {w, 1}, {o, 1}, {r, 1}, {d, 1}, {b, 1}, {l, 1}, {u, 1}}

In[7]:= StringTally["One fish, two fish, red fish, blue fish", IgnoreCase → True]
Out[7]= {{o, 2}, {n, 1}, {e, 3}, {  , 7}, {f, 4}, {i, 4}, {s, 4}, {h, 4},
         {,, 3}, {t, 1}, {w, 1}, {r, 1}, {d, 1}, {b, 1}, {l, 1}, {u, 1}}
```

When done, import a sample text and do a frequency analysis on the letters in that text. Letter frequency analysis can be used to spot transposition ciphers in encoded messages as the frequency of the letters is unchanged in such simple encoding schemes.

Exercise 9 in Section 7.4 asks you to extend this function to include an option to specify if punctuation and digits should be included.

9. Generalize the Caesar cipher so that it encodes by shifting *n* places to the right. Include the space character in the alphabet.

10. A mixed-alphabet cipher is created by first writing a keyword followed by the remaining letters of the alphabet and then using this key to encode the text. For example, if the keyword is *django*, the encoding alphabet would be

    `djangobcefhiklmpqrstuvwxyz`

    So, *a* is replaced with *d*, *b* is replaced with *j*, *c* is replaced with *a*, and so on. As an example, the text

    the sheik of araby

    would be encoded as

    tcg scgeh mo drdjy

    Implement this cipher and go one step further to output the ciphertext in blocks of length five, omitting spaces and punctuation.

11. Modify the alphabet permutation cipher so that, instead of being based on single letters, it is based on adjacent pairs of letters. The single letter cipher has 26! permutations:

    $$26! = 403\,291\,461\,126\,605\,635\,584\,000\,000$$

    The adjacent pairs cipher will have $26^2! = 1.883707684133810 \times 10^{1621}$ permutations.

12. Create a function `StringPad[str, {n}]` that pads the end of a string with *n* whitespace characters. Then create a second rule `StringPad[str, n]` that pads the string out to length *n*. If the input string has length greater than *n*, issue a warning message. Finally, mirroring the argument structure for the built-in `PadLeft`, create a third rule `StringPad[str, n, m]` that pads with *n* whitespaces at the front and *m* whitespaces at the end of the string.

13. Fibonacci words are formed in a similar manner as Fibonacci numbers except, instead of adding the previous two elements, Fibonacci words *concatenate* the previous two elements (Knuth 1997). Starting with the two strings "0" and "01," create a function `FibonacciWord[n]` to generate the *n*th Fibonacci word. This can be generalized to start with any two strings, say "a" and "b." Fibonacci words are examples of a well-known object from combinatorics, Sturmian words.

14. In Exercise 8, Section 5.1 a function was created to generate *n*-grams from a given alphabet. For example, that function could be used to create all bigrams (words of length two) from the nucleotide alphabet `{"G", "C", "A", "T"}`.

    Import a nucleotide sequence such as the human mitochondrial genome `hsMito` below and then create a histogram (as in Figure 7.2) showing the frequency of each of the sixteen possible bigrams AA, AC, AT, etc.

```
In[8]:= hsMito = First@Import["ExampleData/mitochondrion.fa.gz"] // Short
Out[8]//Short= GATCACAGGTCTATCACCCT … CTTAAATAAGACATCACGATG
```

FIGURE 7.2. *Distribution of nucleotide words of length two in Homo sapiens mitochondria genome.*

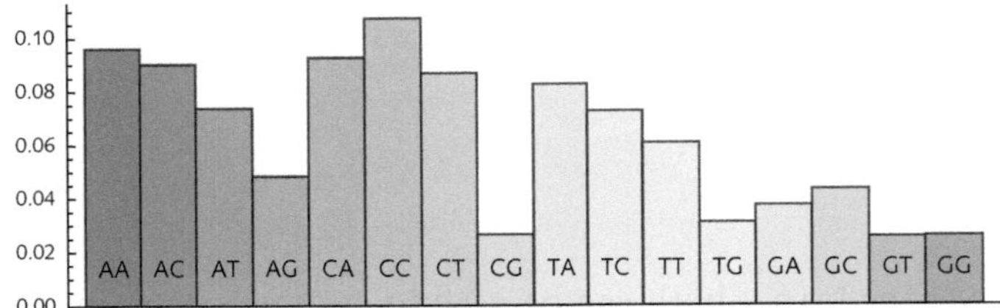

7.3 String patterns

Most of the string operations we have looked at up until this point have involved literal strings. For example, in string replacement, we have explicitly specified both the string that we are operating on as well as the replacement.

```
In[1]:= StringReplace["11/28/1986", "/" → "-"]
Out[1]= 11-28-1986
```

The real power of programming with strings comes with the use of patterns to represent different classes of strings. A string pattern is a string expression containing symbolic patterns. Much of the pattern matching discussed in the previous chapters extends to strings in a very natural manner. For example, the following uses patterns to change the first letter in a string to uppercase:

```
In[2]:= str = "colorless green ideas sleep furiously";
```

```
In[3]:= StringReplace[str, f_ ~~ rest__ :> ToUpperCase[f] <> rest]
Out[3]= Colorless green ideas sleep furiously
```

Or, use a conditional pattern to check if a word begins with an uppercase character.

```
In[4]:= StringMatchQ["Jekyll", f_?UpperCaseQ ~~ rest___]
Out[4]= True
```

To get started, you might find it helpful to think of strings as a sequence of characters and then use the same general principles on these expressions as you do with lists.

For example, the expression {a, b, c, c, d, e} matches the pattern {__, s_, s_, __} because it is a list that starts with a sequence of one or more elements, it contains an element repeated once, and then ends with a sequence of one or more elements.

```
In[5]:= MatchQ[{a, b, c, c, d, e}, {__, s_, s_, __}]
Out[5]= True
```

If we now use a string instead of a list and StringMatchQ instead of MatchQ, we get a similar result.

```
In[6]:= StringMatchQ["abccde", __ ~~ s_ ~~ s_ ~~ __]
Out[6]= True
```

*str*₁ ~~ *str*₂ is shorthand notation for StringExpression[*str*₁, *str*₂], which, for the purpose of pattern matching, represents a sequence of strings.

```
In[7]:= "a" ~~ "b"
Out[7]= ab

In[8]:= Defer[FullForm["a" ~~ "b"]]
Out[8]= StringExpression["a", "b"]
```

StringExpression is quite similar to StringJoin – both can be used to concatenate strings. But with StringExpression, you can also concatenate classes of characters and string patterns. StringJoin works only with explicit strings.

The next example also shows the similarity between the general expression pattern matching that we explored earlier in Chapter 4 and string patterns. Using Cases, the following returns all those expressions that match the pattern _Symbol, that is, it picks out all symbols from the list:

```
In[9]:= Cases[{1, f, g, 6, x, t, 2, 5}, _Symbol]
Out[9]= {f, g, x, t}
```

For strings, use StringCases whose second argument is a string pattern that represents a class of characters to match, returning those substrings that match the given pattern. Many named patterns are available for different purposes. For example, LetterCharacter matches a single letter.

```
In[10]:= StringCases["1fg6xt25", LetterCharacter]
Out[10]= {f, g, x, t}
```

Match single digits with `DigitCharacter` and one or more digits with `NumberString`.

```
In[11]:= StringCases["1fg6xt25", DigitCharacter]
Out[11]= {1, 6, 2, 5}
```

```
In[12]:= StringCases["1fg6xt25", NumberString]
Out[12]= {1, 6, 25}
```

To get a better idea of the generality of string patterns, suppose we were looking at a gene for a nucleotide sequence consisting of AA, followed by any character, followed by T. Using a gene from the human genome, the following string pattern neatly does the job:

```
In[13]:= gene = GenomeData["IGHV357"]
Out[13]= AAGTCCTGTGTGAAGTTTATTGATGGAGTCAGAGGCAGAAAATTGTACAGCCCAGTGGTTCACTGAGACTCTCCTGCAAAGCC⋱
         TCTGATTTCACCTTTACTGGCTACAGCATGAGCTTGGTCCAGCAGGCTTCATGACAGGGATTGGTGTGGGTGGAAACAG⋱
         TGAGTGATCAAGTGGGAGTTCTCAGAGTTACTCTCCATGAGTACAAATAAATTAACAGTCCCAAGCGACACCTTTTCAT⋱
         GTGCAGTCTACCTTACAATGACCAACCTGAAAGCCAAGGACAAGGCTGTGTATTACTGTGAGGGA
```

```
In[14]:= StringCases[gene, "AA" ~~ _ ~~ "T"]
Out[14]= {AAGT, AAGT, AAAT, AAGT, AAAT, AAAT}
```

Here are the starting and ending positions of these substrings. `StringPosition` takes the same syntax as `StringCases`, analogous to `Position` and `Cases`.

```
In[15]:= StringPosition[gene, "AA" ~~ _ ~~ "T"]
Out[15]= {{1, 4}, {13, 16}, {40, 43}, {41, 44},
          {172, 175}, {207, 210}, {211, 214}, {212, 215}}
```

And if you wanted to return those characters that follow all occurrences of the string `"GTC"`, you can name the pattern and use a rule to return it.

```
In[16]:= StringCases[gene, pat : "GTC" ~~ x_ :> pat <> x]
Out[16]= {GTCC, GTCA, GTCC, GTCC, GTCT}
```

The pattern named `pat` is the string `GTC` which is then followed by any character which is named `x` so that we can refer to it in the replacement expression on the right-hand side of the rule. The replacement expression is the pattern `pat` concatenated with the character named `x`.

As another example of the use of string patterns, suppose you were interested in scraping phone numbers from a web page; you need to construct a pattern that matches the form of the phone numbers. In this case use the form *n-nnn-nnn-nnnn,* which matches the form of North American phone numbers. `NumberString` comes in handy as it picks up strings of numbers of any length. Otherwise you would have to use `DigitCharacter ..` which matches repeating digits.

```
In[17]:= webpage = Import["http://www.wolfram.com/company/contact", "HTML"];
```

```
In[18]:= StringCases[webpage,
          NumberString ~~ "-" ~~ NumberString ~~
           "-" ~~ NumberString ~~ "-" ~~ NumberString]
Out[18]= {+1-217-398-0700, +1-217-398-0747}
```

Finding subsequences with strings

One of the big advantages of working with strings is that they are fast. In fact, for many algorithms that are naturally implemented using list manipulation functions, you can instead convert expressions to strings, operate on them using string manipulation functions, and then convert back to the original form of the expression and still gain in speed and efficiency. As an example, consider the problem of finding subsequences within a number sequence such as we developed in Exercises 7 and 8, Section 4.3. Here we will transform the problem from working with lists of digits to one in which we work with strings.

To start, we will prototype with a short sequence of digits of π, converted to a string.

```
In[19]:= num = ToString[N[π, 50]]
Out[19]= 3.1415926535897932384626433832795028841971693993751
```

Check that the output is in fact a string.

```
In[20]:= {Head[num], InputForm[num]}
Out[20]= {String, "3.1415926535897932384626433832795028841971693993751"}
```

For our purposes here, we are only interested in the digits following the decimal point. We can extract them by splitting the string of digits on the decimal point and then taking the second part of that expression. This will generalize for numbers with an arbitrary number of digits before the decimal point.

```
In[21]:= StringSplit[num, "."]
Out[21]= {3, 1415926535897932384626433832795028841971693993751}

In[22]:= Part[%, 2]
Out[22]= 1415926535897932384626433832795028841971693993751
```

The subsequence 3238 occurs starting fifteen positions to the right of the decimal point.

```
In[23]:= StringPosition[%, "3238"]
Out[23]= {{15, 18}}
```

Collecting the code fragments, we turn these steps into a function.

```
In[24]:= FindSubsequence[num_?NumberQ, subseq_?NumberQ] :=
          With[{n = ToString[num], s = ToString[subseq]},
           StringPosition[Part[StringSplit[n, "."], 2], s]]
```

Let's try it out on a more challenging example: finding occurrences of the sequence 314159 in the decimal expansion of π.

```
In[25]:= pi = N[π, 10^7];

In[26]:= FindSubsequence[pi, 314159] // Timing
Out[26]= {2.63908, {{176451, 176456},
            {1259351, 1259356}, {1761051, 1761056}, {6467324, 6467329},
            {6518294, 6518299}, {9753731, 9753736}, {9973760, 9973765}}}
```

Comparing with the function that takes lists of digits developed in the exercises in Section 4.3, our string implementation is about three to four times as fast.

```
In[27]:= pidigs = First[RealDigits[π, 10, 10^7, -1]];
         Timing[
          FindSubsequence[pidigs, {3, 1, 4, 1, 5, 9}]
         ]
Out[28]= {9.09755, {{176451, 176456}, {1259351, 1259356},
           {1761051, 1761056}, {6467324, 6467329}, {6518294, 6518299},
           {9753731, 9753736}, {9973760, 9973765}}}
```

Alternatives

We have already worked with alternatives in general patterns in Chapter 4, but they can also be used with string patterns. For example, a common task in genome analysis is determining the GC content or ratios of the bases guanine (G) and cytosine (C) to all four bases in a given fragment of genetic material.

```
In[29]:= gene = GenomeData["MRPS35P1"];
         StringTake[gene, 75]
Out[30]= AGAATGGAAACAAAATAAGACTGAAGCAGATGTGGGAGAATATATGTGGGAAAATAAATCCTTGGGATAAAAAAT
```

You could count the occurrences of G and the occurrences of C and add them together:

```
In[31]:= StringCount[gene, "G"] + StringCount[gene, "C"]
Out[31]= 41
```

But it is much easier to use alternatives to count all occurrences of either G or C. The syntax for using alternative string patterns is identical to that for general expressions, as introduced in Section 4.1.

```
In[32]:= StringCount[gene, "G" | "C"]
Out[32]= 41
```

The same idea can be used to find different forms of a word in a piece of text. For example, suppose you were interested in finding all occurrences of the character name *Cyclops* in Homer's *Odyssey*. This character also goes by the name *Polyphemus*.

```
In[33]:= odyssey = Import["http://www.gutenberg.org/ebooks/1727.txt.utf-8", "Text"];

In[34]:= StringCount[odyssey, "Cyclops" | "Polyphemus"]
Out[34]= 26
```

This approach is also useful for finding alternate spellings of words.

```
In[35]:= StringCount[odyssey, "Cyclops" | "Cyclopes" | "Polyphemus"]
Out[35]= 43
```

Exercises

1. Given a list of words, some of which start with uppercase characters, convert them all to words in which the first character is lowercase. You can use the words in the dictionary as a good sample set.

2. Create a function `Palindromes[n]` that finds all palindromic words of length *n* in the dictionary. For example, *kayak* is a five-letter palindrome.

3. Modify the `listSort` function from Section 4.3 by creating another rule that can be used to sort lists of string characters.

4. Find the number of unique words in a body of text such as *Alice in Wonderland*. This text can be imported from `ExampleData`:

   ```
   In[1]:= ExampleData[{"Text", "AliceInWonderland"}];
   ```

   After splitting the text into words, convert all uppercase characters to lowercase so that you count words such as *hare* and *Hare* as the same word.

5. Another important task in computational linguistics is comparing the complexity of text-based materials such as newspapers or school texts. There are many measures that you might use: the length of the text, average sentence length, levels of reasoning required, word frequency, and many more. One metric is word length. Use the built-in function `TextWords` (new in *Mathematica* 10.1) to generate a histogram like that in Figure 7.3 showing the word-length distribution for a text.

   FIGURE 7.3. *Word-length distribution for Alice in Wonderland.*

   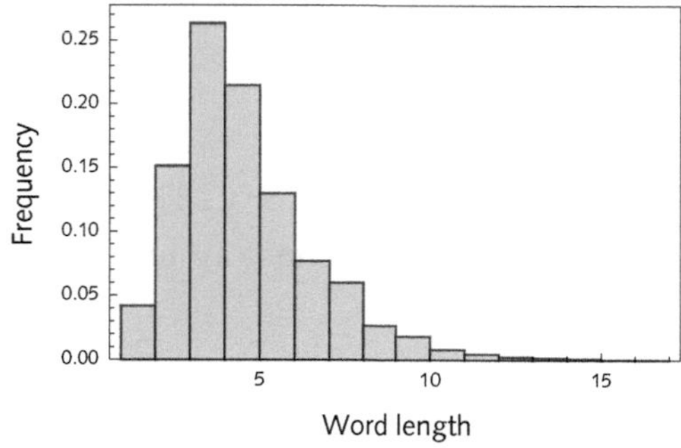

   Then compare the word-length distribution for several different text sources such as those available in `ExampleData["Text"]` or on gutenberg.org.

6. Repeat Exercise 5 but use sentence length instead of word length as the measure.

7. *Semordnilaps* ("palindromes" spelled backwards) are words that, when reversed, also spell a word. For example, *live* and *stressed* are semordnilaps because reversed, they still spell words: *evil* and *desserts*. Find all semordnilaps in the dictionary.

7.4 Regular expressions

Many modern programming languages use a construct called *regular expressions* (or *regex*) to define search patterns on strings. Regular expressions in *Mathematica* follow a syntax very close to that of the PERL programming language. This syntax is quite compact and powerful, but it comes at the cost of readability – regular expressions tend to be quite cryptic to humans. As a result, we will only cover a few examples of their use here and refer the interested reader to the set of tutorials Working with String Patterns (WLDC).

You should think of regular expressions as an alternative syntax for string patterns. To indicate that you are using a regular expression, wrap the expression in `RegularExpression`. For example, the regular expression `.` is a wildcard character. It matches any single character except a newline. To use it as a string pattern, write `RegularExpression["."]`.

```
In[1]:= StringMatchQ["a", RegularExpression["."]]
Out[1]= True
```

The string "abc" does not match the pattern because it does not consist of a single character.

```
In[2]:= StringMatchQ["abc", RegularExpression["."]]
Out[2]= False
```

You can also match a set or range of characters. For example, this matches any of the characters *a* through *z*:

```
In[3]:= StringMatchQ["a", RegularExpression["[a-z]"]]
Out[3]= True
```

Certain constructs give patterns with repeating elements. For example, "c*" is a pattern matched by a string with character c repeated zero or more times; "c+" stands in for the character c repeated one or more times.

```
In[4]:= StringMatchQ["aa", RegularExpression["a*"]]
Out[4]= True
```

```
In[5]:= StringMatchQ["aaab", RegularExpression["a+"]]
Out[5]= False
```

You can also match on concatenated characters using the syntax $c_1 c_2 \ldots$.

```
In[6]:= StringPosition["ACAACTGGAGATCATGACTG", RegularExpression["ACT"]]
Out[6]= {{4, 6}, {17, 19}}
```

The regular expression `a.*` matches any expression beginning with the character a followed by any sequence of characters.

```
In[7]:= StringMatchQ["all in good time", RegularExpression["a.*"]]
Out[7]= True
```

Several constructs are available for classes of characters. The named classes in the last two entries of Table 7.2 include *alpha, ascii, blank, digit, space, word,* and several more.

TABLE 7.2. *Regular expressions classes of characters*

Regular expression	Meaning
`\\d`	digit 0–9
`\\D`	nondigit
`\\s`	space, newline, tab, whitespace
`\\S`	non–whitespace character
`\\w`	word character, e.g. letter, digit
`\\W`	nonword character
`[[:`*class*`:]]`	characters in a named class
`[^[:`*class*`:]]`	characters not in a named class

The regular expression `\\d` represents any digit 0 through 9. Recall that `StringPosition` returns the starting and ending positions for each match.

```
In[8]:= StringPosition["a1b2c3d4", RegularExpression["\\d"]]
Out[8]= {{2, 2}, {4, 4}, {6, 6}, {8, 8}}
```

The regular expression `a.+\\d` matches any expression beginning with an a, followed by one or more instances of any character, followed by a digit.

```
In[9]:= StringCases["abc1, abd2, abc", RegularExpression["a.+\\d"]]
Out[9]= {abc1, abd2}
```

Let's try something more ambitious. This finds all words in a text that are of length 16 to 18:

```
In[10]:= text = ExampleData[{"Text", "OriginOfSpecies"}];
         StringCases[text, RegularExpression["\\b\\w{16,18}\\b"]] //
          DeleteDuplicates
Out[11]= {agriculturalists, disproportionably, malconformations,
          experimentalists, palaeontological, incomprehensibly, PALAEONTOLOGICAL,
          palaeontologists, intercommunication, incomprehensible}
```

The regular expression `\\b` matches any word boundary (typically whitespace, period, comma, etc.) and `\\w{16, 18}` matches any word of length 16 to 18.

Conveniently, you can mix regular expressions and other string patterns in various ways. This accomplishes the same thing as the previous computation, but using the built-in pattern symbol `WordBoundary` instead of the regular expression `\\b`. `WordBoundary` and various other shortcuts for some commonly used patterns are given in Table 7.3.

```
In[12]:= StringCases[text, WordBoundary ~~
            RegularExpression["\\w{16,18}"] ~~ WordBoundary] // DeleteDuplicates
Out[12]= {agriculturalists, disproportionably, malconformations,
          experimentalists, palaeontological, incomprehensibly, PALAEONTOLOGICAL,
          palaeontologists, intercommunication, incomprehensible}
```

TABLE 7.3. *Patterns for special locations within strings*

Pattern	Matches
`StartOfString`	beginning of entire string
`EndOfString`	end of entire string
`StartOfLine`	beginning of a line
`EndOfLine`	end of a line
`WordBoundary`	boundary between words

Sometimes you will need to refer to a pattern by name in order to perform some operation on it. This is similar to regular named patterns. For example, given a list of words, some of which are uppercase/lowercase, this uses string patterns to transform the list to all lowercase words, naming the pattern that is matched by the first character after a word boundary, a.

```
In[13]:= words = {"festively", "frolicking", "subcategories",
           "retreated", "recompiling", "Barbary", "Herefords", "geldings",
           "Norbert", "incalculably", "proselytizers", "topmast"};

In[14]:= StringReplace[words, WordBoundary ~~ a_ :→ ToLowerCase[a]]
Out[14]= {festively, frolicking, subcategories, retreated, recompiling, barbary,
          herefords, geldings, norbert, incalculably, proselytizers, topmast}
```

So how do you name a pattern with regular expressions in order to refer to it on the right-hand side of a rule? The syntax using regular expressions is to wrap the pattern in parentheses and then refer to it using `"$n"` where *n* is the *n*th occurrence of such named patterns. For example, `\\b(.)` is a pattern that is matched by an expression consisting of a word boundary followed by any character. The subexpression matching `(.)` is referenced by `"$1"` on the right-hand side of the rule.

```
In[15]:= StringReplace["the cat in the hat",
           RegularExpression["\\b(.)"] :→ ToUpperCase["$1"]]
Out[15]= The Cat In The Hat
```

To change the second character after the word boundary to uppercase, use `"$2"` to refer to the expression that matches the second named pattern.

```
In[16]:= StringReplace["the cat in the hat",
           RegularExpression["\\b([a-z])([a-z])"] :→ "$1" <> ToUpperCase["$2"]]
Out[16]= tHe cAt iN tHe hAt
```

A particularly useful tool in many situations is the lookahead/lookbehind construct. `(? = patt)` is used when the following text must match *patt* and `(? <= patt)` is used when the preceding text must match *patt*. For example, the following finds all those words in some example text that follow the string `"Raven, "`:

```
In[17]:= text = ExampleData[{"Text", "TheRaven"}];
```

```
In[18]:= StringCases[text,
          RegularExpression["(?<=Raven, )\\w+"]]
Out[18]= {sitting, never}
```

There are many more constructs available for operating on strings using regular expressions. We will explore some of these in the examples and exercises below, as well as in the applications in Section 7.5. For a more detailed discussion, see the tutorial Regular Expressions (WLDC) or the book on regular expressions by Friedl (2006).

Contractions

Prior to publishing a book every author goes through a tortuous process known as copy-edit. The undertaking involves a professional proofreader tearing apart your manuscript and making suggestions to correct grammar, improve readability, and generally make sure you haven't made some horrible and embarrassing mistakes. Recently, I went through this process with one of my books and the editor returned a long list of suggestions including one that was "house policy." Every publisher has certain styles that they want all of their books to adhere to and mine wanted all contractions converted to their full, uncontracted form. I could have said, "I ain't gonna' do it" but prudence got the better of me and I set about converting contractions such as *haven't* to *have not*.

As it turns out, replacing contractions with an uncontracted form is a good example of text processing and can be solved with some of the tools we have looked at up to this point. To start, let us find contractions in the dictionary that comes with *Mathematica*. We are using `Alternatives` to get words which match any of the patterns. This list is not complete but it will catch well over 90% of the contractions in the dictionary.

```
In[19]:= contractions =
          DictionaryLookup["*'t" | "*'ve" | "*'s" | "*'re" | "*'d" | "*'ll" | "o'*"]
Out[19]= {ain't, aren't, can't, couldn't, didn't, doesn't, don't, hadn't, hasn't, haven't, he'd,
          he'll, here's, he's, how's, I'd, I'll, isn't, it'd, it'll, it's, I've, let's,
          mayn't, mightn't, mustn't, needn't, o'clock, o'er, oughtn't, rec'd, shan't, she'd,
          she'll, she's, shouldn't, that's, there's, they'd, they'll, they're, they've,
          wasn't, we'd, we'll, we're, weren't, we've, what's, where's, who'd, who'll, who're,
          who's, who've, why'd, won't, wouldn't, would've, you'd, you'll, you're, you've}
```

Working with one contraction, **n't*, we need a rule that replaces it with * *not*. For example, the rule should replace *aren't* with *are not*. The regular expression `"\\b.+n't"` matches the start of a word followed by one or more characters and ending with the explicit three characters *n*, then the apostrophe, then *t*. We use the parentheses here to name the subpattern of the word which is referred to on the right-hand side of the transformation rule by `"$1"`. Here is the rule:

```
In[20]:= rules = {RegularExpression["\\b(.+)n't"] :> "$1" ~~ " not"};
```

This applies the rule to the list of contractions:

```
In[21]:= StringReplace[contractions, rules]
Out[21]= {ai not, are not, ca not, could not, did not, does not, do not, had not,
  has not, have not, he'd, he'll, here's, he's, how's, I'd, I'll, is not,
  it'd, it'll, it's, I've, let's, may not, might not, must not, need not,
  o'clock, o'er, ought not, rec'd, sha not, she'd, she'll, she's, should not,
  that's, there's, they'd, they'll, they're, they've, was not, we'd, we'll,
  we're, were not, we've, what's, where's, who'd, who'll, who're, who's,
  who've, why'd, wo not, would not, would've, you'd, you'll, you're, you've}
```

Ain't is a special case: it is contracted from *am not* or *is not*. Because it is a special case it needs a rule that will be checked before any others. Similarly for *can't* → *cannot*. Here are three rules, the two special cases listed first:

```
In[22]:= rules = {
    "ain't" → "am not",
    "can't" → "cannot",
    RegularExpression["\\b(.+)n't"] :→ "$1" ~~ " not"
   };
```

The order in which such rules are used is important. You do not want the last rule being used before any of the others – *ain't* would get replaced with *ai not* and then the other rules would not apply to that result. *Mathematica* will apply rules in the order in which they are given, assuming that they have roughly the same level of specificity.

```
In[23]:= StringReplace[contractions, rules]
Out[23]= {am not, are not, cannot, could not, did not, does not, do not, had not,
  has not, have not, he'd, he'll, here's, he's, how's, I'd, I'll, is not,
  it'd, it'll, it's, I've, let's, may not, might not, must not, need not,
  o'clock, o'er, ought not, rec'd, sha not, she'd, she'll, she's, should not,
  that's, there's, they'd, they'll, they're, they've, was not, we'd, we'll,
  we're, were not, we've, what's, where's, who'd, who'll, who're, who's,
  who've, why'd, wo not, would not, would've, you'd, you'll, you're, you've}
```

Here is a more complete list of exceptional and general rules:

```
In[24]:= rules = {
    "ain't" → "am not", "can't" → "cannot", "o'er" → "over",
    "rec'd" → "received", "shan't" → "shall not",
    RegularExpression["\\b(.+)n't"] :→ "$1" ~~ " not",
    RegularExpression["\\b(.+)'s"] :→ "$1" ~~ " is",
    RegularExpression["\\b(.+)'d"] :→ "$1" ~~ " would",
    RegularExpression["\\b(.+)'ll"] :→ "$1" ~~ " will",
    RegularExpression["\\b(.+)'ve"] :→ "$1" ~~ " have",
    RegularExpression["\\b(.+)'re"] :→ "$1" ~~ " are"
   };
```

```
In[25]:= StringReplace[contractions, rules]
Out[25]= {am not, are not, cannot, could not, did not, does not, do not, had not,
  has not, have not, he would, he will, here is, he is, how is, I would,
  I will, is not, it would, it will, it is, I have, let is, may not, might not,
  must not, need not, o'clock, over, ought not, received, shall not, she would,
  she will, she is, should not, that is, there is, they would, they will,
  they are, they have, was not, we would, we will, we are, were not, we have,
  what is, where is, who would, who will, who are, who is, who have, why would,
  wo not, would not, would have, you would, you will, you are, you have}
```

Exercises

1. Use regular expressions to count the occurrences of the vowels (*a, e, i, o, u*) in the following text:

```
In[1]:= text = "How many vowels do I have?";
```

2. Using regular expressions, find all words in the text *Alice in Wonderland* that contain the letter *q*. Then find all words that contain either *q* or Q. The text can be imported with the following:

```
In[2]:= words = TextWords[ExampleData[{"Text", "AliceInWonderland"}]];
        Take[words, 11]
Out[3]= {I, DOWN, THE, RABBIT-HOLE, Alice, was, beginning, to, get, very, tired}
```

3. Rewrite the genomic example in Section 7.3 to use regular expressions instead of string patterns to find all occurrences of the sequence AA*anything*T. Here is the example using general string patterns:

```
In[4]:= gene = GenomeData["IGHV357"];
        StringCases[gene, "AA" ~~ _ ~~ "T"]
Out[5]= {AAGT, AAGT, AAAT, AAGT, AAAT, AAAT}
```

4. Rewrite the web page example in Section 7.3 to use regular expressions to find all phone numbers on the page, that is, expressions of the form *nnn-nnn-nnnn*. Modify accordingly for other web pages and phone numbers formatted for other regions.

5. Use a regular expression to find all words given by `DictionaryLookup` that consist only of the letters *a, e, i, o, u,* and *y* in any order with any number of repetitions of the letters.

6. Use regular expressions to rewrite the solution to Exercise 2 in Section 7.2 to find all words containing three double letter repeats in a row.

7. The basic rules for pluralizing words in the English language are roughly, as follows: if a noun ends in *ch, s, sh, j, x,* or *z*, it is made plural by adding *es* to the end. If the noun ends in *y* and is preceded by a consonant, replace the *y* with *ies*. If the word ends in *ium*, replace with *ia* (*Chicago Manual of Style*, 2010). Of course, there are many more rules and even more exceptions, but you can implement a basic set of rules to convert singular words to plural based on these rules and then try them out on the following list of words:

```
In[6]:= words = {"building", "finch", "fix",
          "ratio", "envy", "boy", "baby", "faculty", "honorarium"};
```

8. A common task in transcribing audio is cleaning up text, removing certain phrases such as um, er, and so on, and other tags that are used to make a note of some sort. For example, the following transcription of a lecture from the University of Warwick, Centre for Applied Linguistics (Base

Corpus) contains quite a few fragments that should be removed, including newline characters, parenthetical remarks, and nonwords. Use `StringReplace` with the appropriate rules to clean this text and then apply your code to a larger corpus.

```
In[7]:= text =
   "okay well er today we're er going to be carrying on with the er French \nRevolution
     you may have noticed i was sort of getting rather er enthusiastic \nand
     carried away at the end of the last one i was sort of almost er like i sort
     \nof started at the beginning about someone standing on a coffee table and
     s-, \nshouting to arms citizens as if i was going to sort of leap up on the
     desk and \nsay to arms let's storm the Rootes Social Building [laughter] or er
     let's go \nout arm in arm singing the Marseillaise or something er like that";
```

9. Modify the solution to Exercise 8 in Section 7.2 so that `StringTally` includes an option `IncludeCharacters` that, by default, has value `LetterCharacters`, which should mean that `StringTally` only tallies letters; that is, excludes non-letter characters from the tally. Other values for `IncludeCharacters` could be `All` (include all characters in the tally), `WordCharacters` (include only word characters), `PunctuationOnly` (include only punctuation).

10. In web searches and certain problems in natural language processing, it is often useful to filter out certain words prior to performing a search or processing of text to help with the performance of the algorithms. Words such as *and*, *the*, and *is* are commonly referred to as *stop words* for this purpose. Lists of stop words are almost always created manually based on the constraints of a particular application. Sample lists of stop words are also commonly available across the Internet. For our purposes here, we will use one such list included with the materials for this book.

```
In[8]:= stopwords = Rest@Import["StopWords.dat", "List"];
        RandomSample[stopwords, 12]

Out[9]= {who'll, recently, ninety, be, no,
          taking, isn't, unless, what, soon, name, beside}
```

Using the above list of stop words, or any other that you are interested in, first filter some sample "search phrases" and then remove all stop words from a larger piece of text. If your function was called `FilterText`, it might work like this:

```
In[10]:= searchPhrases = {"Find my favorite phone",
            "How deep is the ocean?", "What is the meaning of life?"};

In[11]:= Map[FilterText[#, stopwords] &, searchPhrases]

Out[11]= {{Find, favorite, phone}, {deep, ocean}, {meaning, life}}
```

11. Modify the previous exercise so that the user can supply a list of punctuation in addition to the list of stop words to be used to filter the text.

7.5 Examples

This section puts together many of the concepts and techniques developed earlier in the chapter to solve a number nontrivial applied problems. We include several functions that are quite useful for work in genomic research, including creating random strings, partitioning strings, and analyzing and visualizing amino acid and nucleotide sequences. Also included are several word puzzles that should be accessible to anyone.

Abecedarian words

A common task in studying word or language structure is to find all words within a corpus that meet some criterion. In this brief example, we will operate on lists of characters to find *abecedarian* words, that is, words whose letters are "in order" when read from the first letter to the last. For example, the word "best" is abecedarian but "brag" is not. We will create a predicate `AbecedarianQ` that returns `True` or `False` depending upon whether its argument is in alphabetic order. Then we will use this predicate to find all words in a dictionary that are ordered in this sense.

We might start by ordering strings according to the individual character codes.

```
In[1]:= ToCharacterCode["best"]
Out[1]= {98, 101, 115, 116}
```

Then we only need to know if this list of codes is in order.

```
In[2]:= OrderedQ[%]
Out[2]= True
```

```
In[3]:= OrderedQ[ToCharacterCode["brag"]]
Out[3]= False
```

But before we get too carried away, note that this approach fails on words that are capitalized.

```
In[4]:= OrderedQ[ToCharacterCode["Jack"]]
Out[4]= True
```

This is due to the fact that the uppercase letters all appear earlier in the character codes than the lowercase letters.

```
In[5]:= {ToCharacterCode["J"], ToCharacterCode["a"]}
Out[5]= {{74}, {97}}
```

Although we could first convert all uppercase letters to lowercase, we will take a different approach. The sort algorithm used by `OrderedQ` is the same as that used by `Sort`, whose canonical order is that which is used in a dictionary. So we can simply use `OrderedQ` on the list of characters.

```
In[6]:= Characters["Jack"]
Out[6]= {J, a, c, k}
```

```
In[7]:= OrderedQ[%]
Out[7]= False
```

Here is a predicate that returns `True` if its argument is ordered in this alphabetic sense:

```
In[8]:= AbecedarianQ[word_String] := OrderedQ[Characters[word]]
```

Now we will find all the words in a dictionary file that are ordered in this way. Start by getting a list of all words in the dictionary that comes with *Mathematica*.

```
In[8]:= words = DictionaryLookup[];
```

```
In[9]:=  RandomSample[words, 12]
Out[10]= {terrapins, stubbier, shipped, cursoriness, projection, trickiest,
          toolkit, newsgirls, caps, segmentation, multiprogramming, shantung}
```

Next select those words that pass the test, randomly sampling 40 of them.

```
In[11]:= orderedwords = Select[words, AbecedarianQ];

In[12]:= RandomSample[orderedwords, 40]
Out[12]= {CD, deist, hilt, or, Finn, hip, kW, gloss, bet, no, ells, DDT, hoops, bee,
          chino, Eggo, Deimos, chintz, gory, beery, chills, adept, Dix, dill, dens,
          Hill, fops, hot, ms, DJ, knot, chivy, ans, ah, psst, CPU, ill, GI, ems, begin}
```

Random strings

A blasphemous sect suggested ... that all men should juggle letters and symbols until they constructed, by an improbable gift of chance, these canonical books.

— Jorge L. Borges, *The Library of Babel*

Those who work with genomic data often need to test their algorithms on prototypical strings. While it may be sensible to test against real data – genes on the human genome – random data might be more appropriate to quickly test and measure the efficiency of an algorithm. Although *Mathematica* has a variety of functions for creating random numbers, random variates, and so on, it does not have a function to create random sequences of strings. In this section we will create one.

To start, we will choose the characters A, C, T, and G – representing the nucleotide, or DNA, bases – as our alphabet.

```
In[13]:= chars = {"A", "C", "T", "G"};
```

We want to choose characters at random from this list. Since we need to repeat this *n* times, we need to choose with replacement. That is the function of RandomChoice.

```
In[14]:= RandomChoice[chars, 10]
Out[14]= {G, T, G, A, G, A, T, G, A, G}
```

This expression is a list of strings:

```
In[15]:= InputForm[%]
Out[15]//InputForm=
         {"G", "T", "G", "A", "G", "A", "T", "G", "A", "G"}
```

Finally, we concatenate the strings.

```
In[16]:= StringJoin[%] // FullForm
Out[16]//FullForm=
         "GTGAGATGAG"
```

As a first attempt at putting these pieces together, we set a default value of one for the second argument n, so if that argument is omitted, a string of length one will be returned.

```
In[17]:= RandomString[chars_List, n_Integer:1] := StringJoin[RandomChoice[chars, n]]
```

```
In[18]:= RandomString[{"A", "C", "T", "G"}, 400]

Out[18]= GCACTATATGTGCCAAACTTCGATTTCTTGAGTTATGTATCGTACTTGCGAGTTGTACAGCCCTATCTAACGCGGTACACGGCG⋱
           CACCAAACCTTAAGTCTTCACTGGCCTTCCATGGGGATTGCCGACGGGACGCAGAGCGGGAATCATACGTGCCTACATCG⋱
           GGACGCTTCATTAACCGGGGTCCCAATGCCTGACGGAATGCTGGAACGTGCCGGTGATTATCAGTCCTTATGTTAATGTC⋱
           CCAAGGGAAGGTGTTTTCGGCAGCAGCGCCAACTTCGGTCACACATCCTCGACTACCTGACGTTGTTCTAGTGAGAGGCA⋱
           CATGCAGGACAATAGCCGGAAAAATGATAGAAGACTTACGAGGCGGAAGACTAACGTCAGCAGTGTTAGGATGAAA

In[19]:= RandomString[{"A", "C", "T", "G"}]

Out[19]= C
```

Using structured patterns, we get a little tighter argument checking. The first argument in this next version must be a list consisting of a sequence of one or more strings.

```
In[20]:= Clear[RandomString]

In[21]:= RandomString[{ch__String}, n_: 1] := StringJoin[RandomChoice[{ch}, n]]

In[22]:= RandomString[{"a", "b", "d"}, 12]

Out[22]= ddbbbbadaadd
```

Using a different alphabet, here is a ten-character password generator:

```
In[23]:= RandomString[CharacterRange[",", "~"], 10]

Out[23]= W5pJr7V:YI
```

It is not hard to extend RandomString to create *n* random strings of a given length. We essentially pass that argument structure to RandomChoice.

```
In[24]:= RandomString[{ch__String}, {n_Integer, len_Integer}] :=
          Map[StringJoin, RandomChoice[{ch}, {n, len}]]

In[25]:= RandomString[{"A", "C", "T", "G"}, {4, 12}]

Out[25]= {TCATTTATTGGT, TTGATTACGAGT, CCCGGTTCTCTT, TTAAGAGCACTA}

In[26]:= RandomString[{"A", "C", "T", "G"}, {50, 1}]

Out[26]= {A, G, A, A, A, G, A, C, A, T, T, A, C, C, C, A, T, A, C, T, A, C, G, T, A,
          C, T, T, G, A, G, G, A, C, T, G, G, C, G, A, C, C, A, A, C, G, G, A, C, A}
```

For prototyping problems in genomics and linguistics it would be helpful to be able to create random strings in which certain characters are more likely to be chosen than others. The exercises at the end of this section include a problem that asks you to add an option that provides a mechanism to weight the individual characters in the random string.

Partitioning strings

Some types of string analysis require strings to be broken up into blocks of a certain size before performing computations on those blocks. Although there is a built-in function for partitioning strings, it has some limitations that are relevant for our work here with nucleotide sequences. For example, suppose we have a short string of length 15 and we need to create blocks of substrings of length four.

```
In[27]:= str = RandomString[{"A", "C", "T", "G"}, 15]
Out[27]= GGCAAGTAAGACTAT
```

The built-in `StringPartition` has no way to deal with uneven partitions and so simply omits the characters after the last block of length four.

```
In[28]:= StringPartition[str, 4]
Out[28]= {GGCA, AGTA, AGAC}
```

Dropping the last few characters will give incorrect results, for example, in genomic analysis. For our purposes, it would be preferable to append the short blocks at the end. In this example, we will create a function that behaves like the built-in function but extends its capabilities by using the more flexible argument structure of `Partition`.

The `Partition` function requires a list as its first argument. To start, we will give it a list of the characters in a prototype string, a small pseudogene on the human genome.

```
In[29]:= GenomeData["IGHVII671", "Name"]
Out[29]= immunoglobulin heavy variable (II)-67-1

In[30]:= str = GenomeData["IGHVII671"]
Out[30]= ATGTCCTATTCAGGAGCAGCTACAGCAGTCATGCCTAGGTGTGAAGATCACACACTGACCTCACCCATGCTGTCTCTGGCCACTT
          CATCACAACCAATGCTTAATATTGGACGTGGATCTGCCAGTCCCCGGGGAATGGGTTGAATGGAT

In[31]:= StringLength[str]
Out[31]= 150

In[32]:= Characters[str]
Out[32]= {A, T, G, T, C, C, T, A, T, T, C, A, G, G, A, G, C, A, G, C, T, A, C, A, G, C, A, G, T, C, A,
          T, G, C, C, T, A, G, G, T, G, T, G, A, A, G, A, T, C, A, C, A, C, A, C, T, G, A, C, C, T,
          C, A, C, C, C, A, T, G, C, T, G, T, C, T, C, T, G, G, C, C, A, C, T, T, C, A, T, C, A, C,
          A, A, C, C, A, A, T, G, C, T, T, A, A, T, A, T, T, G, G, A, C, G, T, G, G, A, T, C, T, G,
          C, C, A, G, T, C, C, C, C, G, G, G, G, A, A, T, G, G, G, T, T, G, A, A, T, G, G, A, T}
```

Now, partition this list of characters into lists of length four with offset one.

```
In[33]:= Partition[Characters[str], 4, 4, 1]
Out[33]= {{A, T, G, T}, {C, C, T, A}, {T, T, C, A}, {G, G, A, G}, {C, A, G, C},
          {T, A, C, A}, {G, C, A, G}, {T, C, A, T}, {G, C, C, T}, {A, G, G, T},
          {G, T, G, A}, {A, G, A, T}, {C, A, C, A}, {C, A, C, T}, {G, A, C, C},
          {T, C, A, C}, {C, C, A, T}, {G, C, T, G}, {T, C, T, C}, {T, G, G, C}, {C, A, C, T},
          {T, C, A, T}, {C, A, C, A}, {A, C, C, A}, {A, T, G, C}, {T, T, A, A}, {T, A, T, T},
          {G, G, A, C}, {G, T, G, G}, {A, T, C, T}, {G, C, C, A}, {G, T, C, C}, {C, C, G, G},
          {G, G, A, A}, {T, G, G, G}, {T, T, G, A}, {A, T, G, G}, {A, T, A, T}}
```

Because the number of characters in `str` is not a multiple of four, this use of `Partition` has padded the last sublist with the first two characters from the original string; in other words, this has treated the list cyclically – not quite what we want here.

```
In[34]:= Mod[StringLength[str], 4] == 0
Out[34]= False
```

A slightly different syntax for `Partition` gives an uneven subset at the end. We need to use this form so as not to lose or introduce any information.

```
In[35]:= parts = Partition[Characters[str], 4, 4, 1, {}]
Out[35]= {{A, T, G, T}, {C, C, T, A}, {T, T, C, A}, {G, G, A, G}, {C, A, G, C}, {T, A, C, A},
  {G, C, A, G}, {T, C, A, T}, {G, C, C, T}, {A, G, G, T}, {G, T, G, A}, {A, G, A, T},
  {C, A, C, A}, {C, A, C, T}, {G, A, C, C}, {T, C, A, C}, {C, C, A, T},
  {G, C, T, G}, {T, C, T, C}, {T, G, G, C}, {C, A, C, T}, {T, C, A, T},
  {C, A, C, A}, {A, C, C, A}, {A, T, G, C}, {T, T, A, A}, {T, A, T, T},
  {G, G, A, C}, {G, T, G, G}, {A, T, C, T}, {G, C, C, A}, {G, T, C, C},
  {C, C, G, G}, {G, G, A, A}, {T, G, G, G}, {T, T, G, A}, {A, T, G, G}, {A, T}}
```

Finally, convert each sublist into a contiguous string.

```
In[36]:= Map[StringJoin, parts]
Out[36]= {ATGT, CCTA, TTCA, GGAG, CAGC, TACA, GCAG, TCAT, GCCT, AGGT, GTGA, AGAT,
  CACA, CACT, GACC, TCAC, CCAT, GCTG, TCTC, TGGC, CACT, TCAT, CACA, ACCA, ATGC,
  TTAA, TATT, GGAC, GTGG, ATCT, GCCA, GTCC, CCGG, GGAA, TGGG, TTGA, ATGG, AT}
```

This puts everything together in a function:

```
In[37]:= stringPartition[str_String, blocksize_] :=
  Map[StringJoin, Partition[Characters[str], blocksize, blocksize, 1, {}]]
```

This partitions the string into nonoverlapping blocks of length 12:

```
In[38]:= stringPartition[str, 12]
Out[38]= {ATGTCCTATTCA, GGAGCAGCTACA, GCAGTCATGCCT, AGGTGTGAAGAT,
  CACACACTGACC, TCACCCATGCTG, TCTCTGGCCACT, TCATCACAACCA,
  ATGCTTAATATT, GGACGTGGATCT, GCCAGTCCCCGG, GGAATGGGTTGA, ATGGAT}
```

This function operates on large strings fairly fast. Here we partition a random string of length ten million into nonoverlapping blocks of length 16.

```
In[39]:= data = RandomString[{"A", "T", "C", "G"}, 10^7];

In[40]:= Timing[stringPartition[data, 16];]
Out[40]= {2.31799, Null}
```

Exercise 6 at the end of this section includes variations to this function that use the full argument structure of `Partition`.

DNA sequence analysis

DNA molecules are composed of sequences of the nitrogenous bases guanine (G), cytosine (C), thymine (T), and adenine (A). Guanine and cytosine bond with three hydrogen bonds and thymine and adenine bond with two. Research has indicated that high GC content DNA is more stable than that with lower GC. In addition, the importance of GC content in the hierarchical classification of bacteria and other organisms has made it a central tool in biomolecular research.

GC content is defined as a percentage of the guanine and cytosine nucleotides compared with the entire nucleotide content. In this section we will create a function to compute the ratio of GC in any given DNA sequence or fragment. We will start by importing a FASTA file consisting of human mitochondrial DNA.

```
In[41]:= hsMito = Import["ExampleData/mitochondrion.fa.gz"];

In[42]:= Import["ExampleData/mitochondrion.fa.gz", {"FASTA", "Header"}]
Out[42]= {gi|17981852|ref|NC_001807.4| Homo sapiens mitochondrion, complete genome}

In[43]:= StringLength[hsMito]
Out[43]= {16571}

In[44]:= StringTake[hsMito, 300]
Out[44]= {GATCACAGGTCTATCACCCTATTAACCACTCACGGGAGCTCTCCATGCATTTGGTATTTTCGTCTGGGGGGTGTGCACGCG⋱
          ATAGCATTGCGAGACGCTGGAGCCGGAGCACCCTATGTCGCAGTATCTGTCTTTGATTCCTGCCTCATTCTATTATT⋱
          TATCGCACCTACGTTCAATATTACAGGCGAACATACCTACTAAAGTGTGTTAATTAATTAATGCTTGTAGGACATAA⋱
          TAATAACAATTGAATGTCTGCACAGCCGCTTTCCACACAGACATCATAACAAAAAATTTCCACCA}
```

To count the number of occurrences of G or C in this sequence, use StringCount with the pattern expressed using alternatives (|).

```
In[45]:= gc = StringCount[hsMito, "G" | "C"]
Out[45]= {7372}
```

And here is the number of occurrences of A or T:

```
In[46]:= at = StringCount[hsMito, "A" | "T"]
Out[46]= {9199}
```

The GC percentage is given by the following ratio:

```
In[47]:= N[gc/(gc + at)]
Out[47]= {0.444874}
```

Here then is an auxiliary function we will use in what follows:

```
In[48]:= gcRatio[seq_String] := Module[{gc, at},
           gc = StringCount[seq, "G" | "C"];
           at = StringCount[seq, "A" | "T"];
           N[gc / (gc + at)]
          ]
```

Note that gcRatio expects a string as an argument, but this fails with hsMito, imported from an external source.

```
In[49]:= Short[gcRatio[hsMito], 3]
Out[49]//Short=
         gcRatio[{GATCACAGGTCTATCACCCTATTAACCACTCACGGGAGCTCTCCATGCATTTGGTATTTTCGTCTGG ...
            TGGTTCCTACTTCAGGGCCATAAAGCCTAAATAGCCCACACGTTCCCCTTAAATAAGACATCACGATG}]
```

It fails because Import returns a *list* consisting of a string, not a raw string. We can remedy this by writing a rule to deal with this argument structure and then call the first rule.

```
In[50]:= gcRatio[{str_String}] := gcRatio[str]
```

```
In[51]:= gcRatio[hsMito]
Out[51]= 0.444874
```

Typically, one studies the GC ratio on particular fragments of DNA. It might be important to locate high or low GC ratios on a specific genome or compare it with similar fragments from a different, but possibly related, organism. One common way of doing this is to compute the GC ratio for blocks of nucleotides of some given length. We will use the function `stringPartition` (developed in the previous section) to partition the sequence into blocks of a given size, using a small random sequence to prototype.

```
In[52]:= blocksize = 10;
         str = RandomString[{"A", "C", "T", "G"}, 125];
         lis = stringPartition[str, blocksize]
Out[54]= {CGATGACGCT, CTCGGGCTAA, CACCCCTAGT, GCTGAGATGG, CCGTACGAAG, GGCACTTCAA,
          TACTGGTCGT, TCGAGGGTAA, CCAGACTCAG, AGAATGGGCG, GAGAATGTGA, GGGAAGGCAC, ATGTA}
```

Here are the GC ratios for each of the blocks given by `lis`:

```
In[55]:= Map[gcRatio, lis]
Out[55]= {0.6, 0.6, 0.6, 0.6, 0.6, 0.5, 0.5, 0.5, 0.6, 0.6, 0.4, 0.7, 0.2}
```

Finally, it is helpful to be able to identify each block by its starting position. So we first create a list of the starting positions for each block and then transpose that with the ratios.

```
In[56]:= Table[i, {i, 1, StringLength[str], blocksize}]
Out[56]= {1, 11, 21, 31, 41, 51, 61, 71, 81, 91, 101, 111, 121}
```

```
In[57]:= Transpose[
          {Table[i, {i, 1, StringLength[str], blocksize}], Map[gcRatio, lis]}]
Out[57]= {{1, 0.6}, {11, 0.6}, {21, 0.6}, {31, 0.6}, {41, 0.6}, {51, 0.5}, {61, 0.5},
          {71, 0.5}, {81, 0.6}, {91, 0.6}, {101, 0.4}, {111, 0.7}, {121, 0.2}}
```

Here then are all the pieces in one function, `GCRatio`:

```
In[58]:= GCRatio[str_String, blocksize_Integer] := Module[{lis, blocks},
           lis = stringPartition[str, blocksize];
           blocks = Table[i, {i, 1, StringLength[str], blocksize}];
           Transpose[{blocks, Map[gcRatio, lis]}]
          ]
```

And again, a second rule in case the string is wrapped in a list.

```
In[59]:= GCRatio[{str_String}, blocksize_Integer] := GCRatio[str, blocksize]
```

Let's try it out first on our short prototype sequence.

```
In[60]:= GCRatio[str, 10]
Out[60]= {{1, 0.6}, {11, 0.6}, {21, 0.6}, {31, 0.6}, {41, 0.6}, {51, 0.5}, {61, 0.5},
          {71, 0.5}, {81, 0.6}, {91, 0.6}, {101, 0.4}, {111, 0.7}, {121, 0.2}}
```

And then on the human mitochondrial DNA with block size 1000.

```
In[61]:= gcdata = GCRatio[hsMito, 1000]
Out[61]= {{1, 0.46}, {1001, 0.441}, {2001, 0.43}, {3001, 0.478}, {4001, 0.427},
  {5001, 0.439}, {6001, 0.474}, {7001, 0.438}, {8001, 0.434},
  {9001, 0.461}, {10001, 0.396}, {11001, 0.448}, {12001, 0.429},
  {13001, 0.471}, {14001, 0.435}, {15001, 0.446}, {16001, 0.464098}}
```

Various types of analysis can then be performed on these blocks. For example, using `Select`, this quickly finds a region of low GC content:

```
In[62]:= Select[gcdata, Last[#] ≤ 0.40 &]
Out[62]= {{10001, 0.396}}
```

Here is a quick visualization of the GC content across the blocks:

```
In[63]:= ListLinePlot[gcdata, Mesh → All]
```

Out[63]=

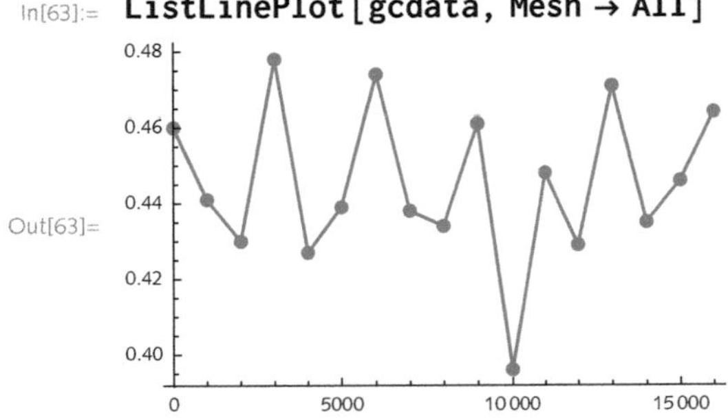

With a smaller block size, the low-GC region is more pronounced.

```
In[64]:= ListLinePlot[GCRatio[hsMito, 500], Mesh → All]
```

Out[64]=

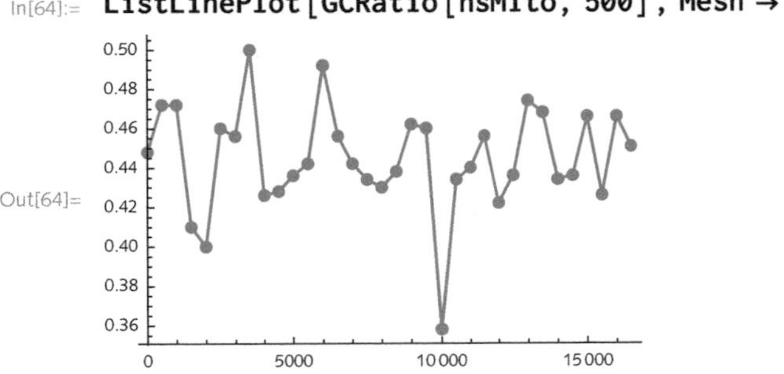

Displaying DNA sequences

DNA sequences are represented as long strings of nucleotides. Because they are difficult to visualize simply by looking at the string of characters, various visualization tools have been used to work with them. In this section we will look at a common way of viewing them in a formatted table.

We will prototype with a short random string consisting of nucleotide characters G, C, A, and T.

```
In[65]:= str = RandomString[{"G", "C", "A", "T"}, 125]
Out[65]= TTATTTTGTAATCTACTGACTGTTCATACAGTCCATTACGCAAAATCTAAAATACACGTCGGCTGTACGGCCAA
  CGGGCTAAGTGGCATCACGCACGCAAGCCCCCCCTGTTACCAAACGGCGCG
```

Using `stringPartition` developed earlier, we split the string into blocks of a desired size.

```
In[66]:= str1 = With[{blockLength = 10},
           stringPartition[str, blockLength]]
Out[66]= {TTATTTTGTA, ATCTACTGAC, TGTTCATACA, GTCCATTACG,
          CAAAATCTAA, AATACACGTC, GGCTGTACGG, CCAACGGGCT,
          AAGTGGCATC, ACGCACGCAA, GCCCCCCCTG, TTACCAAACG, GCGCG}
```

We have 13 blocks here, but for readability purposes, we will put five blocks on each line of output. We use the blank string " " to pad out any string shorter than the block size, in this case 10.

```
In[67]:= str2 = With[{rowLength = 5},
           Partition[str1, rowLength, rowLength, 1, " "]]
Out[67]= {{TTATTTTGTA, ATCTACTGAC, TGTTCATACA, GTCCATTACG, CAAAATCTAA},
          {AATACACGTC, GGCTGTACGG, CCAACGGGCT, AAGTGGCATC, ACGCACGCAA},
          {GCCCCCCCTG, TTACCAAACG, GCGCG,  ,  }}
```

The following code gives the starting positions for each line once we have set the block length and row length:

```
In[68]:= With[{blockSize = 10, rowLength = 5},
          ind =
           Select[Range[StringLength[str]], Mod[#, rowLength * blockSize] == 1 &]]
Out[68]= {1, 51, 101}
```

Prepend the starting position of each row at the head of the row. Recall that the second argument to Prepend is the expression you wish to put in front (the indices) of the target expression (the rows).

```
In[69]:= MapThread[Prepend[#1, #2] &, {str2, ind}]
Out[69]= {{1, TTATTTTGTA, ATCTACTGAC, TGTTCATACA, GTCCATTACG, CAAAATCTAA},
          {51, AATACACGTC, GGCTGTACGG, CCAACGGGCT, AAGTGGCATC, ACGCACGCAA},
          {101, GCCCCCCCTG, TTACCAAACG, GCGCG,  ,  }}
```

This is what the formatted output should look like:

```
In[70]:= Grid[%, Alignment → {{Right, {Left}}, Automatic}]
           1 TTATTTTGTA ATCTACTGAC TGTTCATACA GTCCATTACG CAAAATCTAA
Out[70]=  51 AATACACGTC GGCTGTACGG CCAACGGGCT AAGTGGCATC ACGCACGCAA
         101 GCCCCCCCTG TTACCAAACG GCGCG
```

Finally we put this all together, setting up options BlockSize and RowLength that are combined with the inherited options from Grid.

```
In[71]:= Options[SequenceTable] =
          Join[{BlockSize → 12, RowLength → 5}, Options[Grid]]
Out[71]= {BlockSize → 12, RowLength → 5, Alignment → {Center, Baseline},
          AllowedDimensions → Automatic, AllowScriptLevelChange → True,
          AutoDelete → False, Background → None, BaselinePosition → Automatic,
          BaseStyle → {}, DefaultBaseStyle → Grid, DefaultElement → □,
          DeleteWithContents → True, Dividers → {}, Editable → Automatic,
          Frame → None, FrameStyle → Automatic, ItemSize → Automatic,
          ItemStyle → None, Selectable → Automatic, Spacings → Automatic}
```

```
In[72]:= SequenceTable[lis_String, opts : OptionsPattern[]] :=
  Module[{n = OptionValue[BlockSize], len = StringLength[lis],
    rl = OptionValue[RowLength], str, blocks, ind},
   str = stringPartition[lis, n];
   blocks = Partition[str, rl, rl, 1, " "];
   ind = Select[Range[len], Mod[#, rl * n] == 1 &];
   Grid[MapThread[Prepend[#1, #2] &, {blocks, ind}],
    FilterRules[{opts}, Options[Grid]],
    ItemStyle → {8}, Alignment → {{Right, {Left}}, Automatic},
    Frame → True, Dividers → {{True, False}, All}]
  ]
```

```
In[73]:= str = RandomString[{"C", "A", "T", "G"}, 178]
Out[73]= GCCTTACACCATTGTGCAAATCCCAGAAATTTGGAGTAATGTCCGAATCATACTTCGTTGTGCGTGCACCCCGGGTACAC
   TAACCTCCGCCCTCCTCGGGGTGTTGTGTGTCTATCAACCAACTAAGACCTCAGTGAGCGGGGACCGAGCGGTTGCA
   CCATTACCCCCTGCCTTTAAT
```

```
In[74]:= SequenceTable[str]
```

Out[74]=

1	ACCTTGGTCTGC	GTTGTGAATTAT	CAGCCAGGATGC	CAGTGCACGCCT	GTCTATCGGGAT
61	GAATGTGAGGAT	CCTATACCTTGA	AGAGAGCATTAA	ATCCAAAGAGCG	CAAACAAAACGT
121	CACCTCCGTTTG	TGTCCACTCCTA	GCACGTGACTTA	GAGCTTTAGCTG	ATGTCACTTC

Display the sequence using the same block and row size as the GenBank format, adding some display options for the underlying `Grid` function.

```
In[75]:= SequenceTable[str, BlockSize → 12,
  FrameStyle → Directive[Thin, Gray], Background → LightYellow]
```

Out[75]=

1	GCCTTACACCAT	TGTGCAAATCCC	AGAAATTTGGAG	TAATGTCCGAAT	CATACTTCGTTG
61	TGCGTGCACCCC	GGGTACACTAAC	CTCCGCCCTCCT	CGGGGTGTTGTG	TGTCTATCAACC
121	AACTAAGACCTC	AGTGAGCGGGGA	CCGAGCGGTTGC	ACCATTACCCCC	TGCCTTTAAT

Blanagrams

A blanagram is an anagram for another word except for the substitution of one letter. Think of Scrabble with a blank square (blank + anagram = blanagram). For example, *phyla* is a blanagram of *glyph*: replace the *g* with an *a* and find anagrams. In this section we will create a function that finds all blanagrams of a given word.

We will prototype with a simple word, *glyph*.

```
In[76]:= Characters["glyph"]
Out[76]= {g, l, y, p, h}
```

Start by replacing the first letter in *glyph* with an *a* and then find all anagrams (using `Anagrams` from Section 7.2). The third argument to `StringReplacePart` is a list of beginning and ending positions for the replacement.

```
In[77]:= StringReplacePart["glyph", "a", {1, 1}]
Out[77]= alyph
```

```
In[78]:= Anagrams[%]
Out[78]= {haply, phyla}
```

Now do the same for each character position in the word.

```
In[79]:= Map[StringReplacePart["glyph", "a", {#, #}] &,
          Range[StringLength["glyph"]]]
Out[79]= {alyph, gayph, glaph, glyah, glypa}
```

Running Anagrams on each of these strings, only two appear as words in the dictionary.

```
In[80]:= Flatten[Map[Anagrams, %]]
Out[80]= {haply, phyla}
```

Having done this for the letter *a*, we now repeat for all other single characters.

```
In[81]:= CharacterRange["a", "z"]
Out[81]= {a, b, c, d, e, f, g, h, i, j, k, l, m, n, o, p, q, r, s, t, u, v, w, x, y, z}

In[82]:= blana = Table[
           Map[StringReplacePart["glyph", ch, {#, #}] &,
            Range[StringLength["glyph"]]],
           {ch, CharacterRange["a", "z"]}]
Out[82]= {{alyph, gayph, glaph, glyah, glypa}, {blyph, gbyph, glbph, glybh, glypb},
          {clyph, gcyph, glcph, glych, glypc}, {dlyph, gdyph, gldph, glydh, glypd},
          {elyph, geyph, gleph, glyeh, glype}, {flyph, gfyph, glfph, glyfh, glypf},
          {glyph, ggyph, glgph, glygh, glypg}, {hlyph, ghyph, glhph, glyhh, glyph},
          {ilyph, giyph, gliph, glyih, glypi}, {jlyph, gjyph, gljph, glyjh, glypj},
          {klyph, gkyph, glkph, glykh, glypk}, {llyph, glyph, gllph, glylh, glypl},
          {mlyph, gmyph, glmph, glymh, glypm}, {nlyph, gnyph, glnph, glynh, glypn},
          {olyph, goyph, gloph, glyoh, glypo}, {plyph, gpyph, glpph, glyph, glypp},
          {qlyph, gqyph, glqph, glyqh, glypq}, {rlyph, gryph, glrph, glyrh, glypr},
          {slyph, gsyph, glsph, glysh, glyps}, {tlyph, gtyph, gltph, glyth, glypt},
          {ulyph, guyph, gluph, glyuh, glypu}, {vlyph, gvyph, glvph, glyvh, glypv},
          {wlyph, gwyph, glwph, glywh, glypw}, {xlyph, gxyph, glxph, glyxh, glypx},
          {ylyph, gyyph, glyph, glyyh, glypy}, {zlyph, gzyph, glzph, glyzh, glypz}}
```

Because of the extra nesting (Table[Map[...]]), we need to flatten the output at a deeper level and delete duplicates.

```
In[83]:= Flatten[Map[Anagrams, blana, {2}]] // DeleteDuplicates
Out[83]= {haply, phyla, glyph, lymph, sylph}
```

Finally, put all the pieces together to create the function `Blanagrams`.

```
In[84]:= Blanagrams[word_String] := Module[{blana},
           blana = Table[
             Map[StringReplacePart[word, ch, {#, #}] &, Range[StringLength[word]]],
             {ch, CharacterRange["a", "z"]}];
           DeleteDuplicates[Flatten[Map[Anagrams, blana, {2}]]]
         ]
```

This turns out to be fairly quick for small words, but it starts to bog down as the words get longer.

```
In[85]:= Blanagrams["corn"] // Timing
Out[85]= {2.89661, {roan, narc, born, corn, cord, cone, once, core,
           horn, iron, coin, icon, coir, conk, cork, rock, lorn, morn,
           norm, corm, coon, porn, crop, cons, torn, worn, crow, cony}}
```

```
In[86]:= Blanagrams["glyph"] // Timing
Out[86]= {5.19078, {haply, phyla, glyph, lymph, sylph}}
```

```
In[87]:= Blanagrams["zydeco"] // Timing
Out[87]= {8.16601, {zydeco, cloyed, comedy, decoys}}
```

We will wait until Section 9.2 to optimize this code by identifying slow computational chunks (by profiling) and using parallel processing to speed them up.

Exercises

1. Rewrite the small auxiliary function `gcRatio` introduced in this section to eliminate the step in counting the AT content and instead use the length of the entire string in the denominator of the ratio. For large strings (length over 10^5), this could speed up the computation by a factor of two.
2. Generalize the `RandomString` function to allow for a `Weights` option so that you can provide a weight for each character in the generated string. Include a rule to generate a message if the number of weights does not match the number of characters or if the sum of the weights does not equal one. For example:

```
In[1]:= RandomString[{"A", "T", "C", "G"}, 30, Weights → {.1, .2, .3, .4}]
Out[1]= GTCCTGTGATTCGGTTCCAGTAGCCCGCTT
In[2]:= RandomString[{"A", "T", "C", "G"}, {5, 10}, Weights → {.1, .4, .4, .1}]
Out[2]= {CCTATCCTAG, CACCTCACCC, CCTCACTTCG, CCCTCCCCAC, TCCCTCTGTT}
In[3]:= RandomString[{"A", "T", "C", "G"}, {5, 10}, Weights → {.1, .4}]
        RandomString::badwt :
          The length of the list of weights must be the same as the length of the list of characters.
```

3. Rewrite the function Anagrams developed in Section 7.2 without resorting to the use of Permutations. Consider using the Sort function to sort the characters. Note the difference in speed of the two approaches: one involving string functions and the other list functions that operate on lists of characters. Increase the efficiency of your search by only searching for words of the same length as your source word.

4. Create a function that searches the built-in dictionary for words containing a specified substring. Set up an option to your function whose value specifies where in the string the substring occurs: start, middle, end, anywhere. For example:

```
In[4]:= FindWordsContaining["cite", WordPosition → "End"]
Out[4]= {anthracite, calcite, cite, excite,
         incite, Lucite, overexcite, plebiscite, recite}
```

5. Using texts from several different sources, compute and then compare the number of punctuation characters per 1000 characters of text. ExampleData["Text"] gives a listing of many different texts that you can use.

6. The function stringPartition was developed specifically to deal with genomic data where one often needs uniformly sized blocks to work with. Generalize stringPartition to fully accept the same argument structure as the built-in Partition.

7. Rewrite the text-encoding example from Section 7.2 using StringReplace and regular expressions. First create an auxiliary function to encode a single character based on a key list of the form {{pt_1, ct_1}, …}, where pt_i is a plaintext character and ct_i is its ciphertext encoding. For example, the pair {z, a} would indicate the character z in the plaintext will be encoded as an a in the ciphertext. Then create an encoding function encode[*str*, *key*] using regular expressions to encode any string *str* using the *key* made up of the plaintext/ciphertext character pairs.

8. Word collocation refers to expressions of two or more words that create a familiar phrase, such as *black coffee* or *sharp as a tack*. They are important in many linguistic applications: natural language translation and corpus research involving social phenomena, for example. In this exercise you will create functions for extracting pairs of words of a predetermined form involving parts of speech such as {*adjective, noun*}.

   Start by creating some functions to preprocess your text: split the text into pairs of words and, for simplicity, convert all words to lowercase. Next, filter out words that are not contained in the dictionary. Then, find all remaining pairs that are of a certain form involving the parts of speech. This information is contained in WordData:

```
In[5]:= WordData["split", "PartsOfSpeech"]
Out[5]= {Noun, Adjective, Verb}
```

   Finally, create a function Collocation[*expr*, {PoS_1, PoS_2}] that returns all pairs in *expr* that consist of the part of speech PoS_1 followed by the part of speech PoS_2. For example:

```
In[6]:= sentence =
          "Alice was beginning to get very tired of sitting by her sister on the
            bank, and of having nothing to do. Once or twice she
            had peeped into the book her sister was reading, but ";
```

```
In[7]:= PreProcessString[sentence]

Out[7]= {{was, beginning}, {beginning, to}, {to, get}, {get, very},
  {very, tired}, {tired, of}, {of, sitting}, {sitting, by}, {by, her},
  {her, sister}, {sister, on}, {on, the}, {the, bank}, {bank, and},
  {and, of}, {of, having}, {having, nothing}, {nothing, to}, {to, do},
  {do, once}, {once, or}, {or, twice}, {twice, she}, {she, had},
  {had, peeped}, {peeped, into}, {into, the}, {the, book}, {book, her},
  {her, sister}, {sister, was}, {was, reading}, {reading, but}}

In[8]:= Collocation[%, {"Verb", "Noun"}]

Out[8]= {{was, beginning}, {having, nothing}, {was, reading}}
```

Both `PreProcessString` and `Collocation` are included in the packages that accompany this book, but you may need to create your own versions for your applications.

9. Generating a list of all built-in symbols and then searching for those that have a certain property is a not uncommon task. Examples include finding all built-in functions with the attribute `Listable`, or all functions that have the `StepMonitor` option (see Section 5.5). The full list of built-in functions includes symbols that should be omitted from such searches. Here we display the first and last four symbols in the ``System` `` context, that is, the built-in symbols.

```
In[9]:= Drop[Names["System`*"], 5 ;; -5]

Out[9]= {à, ḃ, ċ, ḋ, $VersionNumber, $WolframID, $WolframUUID, ƛ}
```

Use regular expressions to create a list of only those built-in functions that begin with a capital letter. Then use that code to rewrite `FunctionsWithOption` (Exercise 17 in Section 5.5) so it only checks this smaller list of functions for options.

7.6 Notes and further reading

The rich string pattern language in *Mathematica*, including regular expressions, can be found in other languages such as PERL (Wall, Christiansen, and Orwant 2000) and PYTHON (Downey 2012). A fairly comprehensive treatment of regular expressions can be found in the book by Friedl (2006).

Natural language processing and computational linguistics are extremely active fields of research, given their wide applicability to web search, language and speech recognition and translation, and text analysis. The two texts consulted in this chapter are Manning and Schütze (1999) and Jurafsky and Martin (2009). In addition, the book on information retrieval by Manning, Raghavan and Schütze (2008) discusses problems in term–document incidence matrices used to compare the occurrence of certain terms across a set of documents.

For a very readable introduction to computational genomics, from which many examples and exercises in this book were derived, see the wonderful little book by Cristianini and Hahn (2007). The problem of splitting blocks of DNA sequences into rows and columns is one instance of a general partitioning problem in which you try to keep the column and row lengths as close to equal as possible. See Chapter 3, Integer functions, of Graham, Knuth, and Patashnik (1994).

Numerous online databases provide an endless source of genomic data and problems from which to choose. These include the DNA Databank of Japan (International Nucleotide Sequence Database Collaboration 2015), the Nucleotide Database (National Center for Biotechnology Information 2015), and the Genome Composition Database (National Institute of Genetics 2015).

The history of ciphers is a long one, going back thousands of years. For accessible historical surveys, see Churchhouse (2001) or Sinkov (2009). Modern commercial-grade ciphers such as public-key ciphers are often based on the difficulty of factoring large integers (Paar and Pelzl 2010).

8

Graphics and visualization

The graphics language *· Primitives · Directives · Options · Three-dimensional graphics · Structure of built-in graphics functions ·* ***Dynamic graphics*** *· Manipulate and locators · Dynamic building blocks ·* ***Efficient structures*** *· Multi-objects · GraphicsComplex · Numeric vs. symbolic expressions ·* ***Examples*** *· Root plots · Venn diagrams · Dot plots · Hypocycloids · Space-filling plots · Simple closed paths · Points in a polygon · Triangle centers ·* ***Notes and further reading***

Visualization is a means to organize, model, and ultimately make sense of information. Functions, numerical and abstract data, text, and many other objects are commonly analyzed and studied using visual representations. Sometimes the representation is fixed spatially, as with mathematical functions or geometric objects; other times, as with information visualization, a spatial representation is not given and must be created; and sometimes the information is ordered temporally and so time itself becomes a visualization parameter. In any of these domains, the idea is to find a representation that best conveys the information and relationships under study.

Although built-in graphics functions are often sufficient for your visualizations, you will periodically need to create your own customized code to visualize the objects under study. Sometimes it is more efficient to build upon existing functions, modifying them as needed. Other times you will find it best to create such visualizations from scratch, using the graphics building blocks that make up *Mathematica*'s symbolic graphics language.

This chapter covers how to construct functions for visualizing different kinds of data and objects using the basic building blocks of graphical expressions in *Mathematica* – primitives, directives, and options. We also look at ways to make dynamic graphics, including constructs for changing graphics dynamically using a pointing device such as a mouse. We then address ways to make your graphics more efficient by looking at the internal representation of graphics objects, as well as the use of multi-objects and an alternative representation that results in a compressed graphics object, `GraphicsComplex`. Finally, the chapter closes with several problems in bioinformatics, chemistry, geometry, and computer science, in which we use built-in graphics functionality together with the graphics language to create visualizations for some nontrivial problems.

8.1 The graphics language

A line is a dot that went for a walk.
— PAUL KLEE

Cultivate your curves… they may be dangerous but they won't be avoided.
— MAE WEST

All *Mathematica* graphics are built up from three graphical elements: primitives, directives, and options. These building blocks, together with rules for combining them, are used by the built-in functions such as `Plot` to create graphics. You can create your own graphics scenes using these components to visualize functions, data, and information in many forms. This section introduces these elements and discusses how to put them together to make graphical objects and scenes.

Briefly, the three elements can be summarized as follows:

- *Primitives.* The two-dimensional graphics primitives include objects to create points, lines, polygons, disks, circles, rectangles, Bézier curves, arrows, text, and so on (see Table 8.1 for a brief list or consult the documentation for a complete listing).
- *Directives.* Primitives are modified by directives which change the style, shape, or size of the graphics primitive they are modifying. Such properties as hue, point size, thickness, opacity, and so on are all directives that can be modified.
- *Options.* The complete graphics scene is modified by options that give control over the style of the entire plot, adding and modifying grid lines, plot frames, the aspect ratio of the graphic, the size of the overall image, and so on. A list of options is displayed by evaluating `Options[…]` for any function whose options you need to modify.

An outline of the structure of a graphical object built up from these elements looks like this:

```
Graphics[{
    {directive, primitive},
    {directive, primitive},
    …
  },
  options]
```

Primitives

`Triangle` is a graphics primitive that takes a list of three points as an argument. Evaluating this input simply returns the primitive triangle object:

```
In[1]:= {p1, p2, p3} = {{-2, 0}, {0, 2}, {1, 0}};
        Triangle[{p1, p2, p3}]
Out[2]= Triangle[{{-2, 0}, {0, 2}, {1, 0}}]
```

To display two-dimensional graphics primitives, wrap them in `Graphics`.

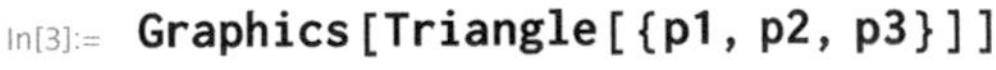

```
In[3]:= Graphics[Triangle[{p1, p2, p3}]]
```

Out[3]=

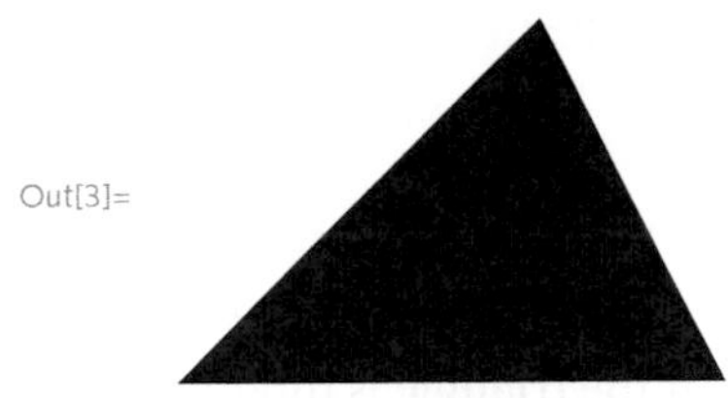

To display more than one graphics primitive, put them in a list. `Circle` is a graphics primitive that takes two arguments: its center and its radius. `Point` is a primitive that automatically maps across lists; that is, it is listable.

```
In[4]:= Graphics[{
          Triangle[{p1, p2, p3}],
          Circle[{-1 / 2, 1 / 2}, √(5 / 2)],
          Point[{p1, p2, p3}]
        }]
```

Out[4]=

Table 8.1 lists some of the two-dimensional graphics primitives. For a complete list, see the guide page Graphics Objects (WLDC).

TABLE 8.1. *Basic two-dimensional graphics primitives*

Graphics primitive	Usage
`Point[{`x, y`}]`	point at position $\{x, y\}$
`Line[{{`x_1, y_1`}, {`x_2, y_2`}, …}]`	line through the points $\{x_i, y_i\}$
`Arrow[{`pt_1, pt_2`}]`	arrow from pt_1 to pt_2
`Polygon[{{`x_1, y_1`}, {`x_2, y_2`}, …}]`	filled polygon
`Triangle[{`pt_1, pt_2, pt_3`}]`	triangle with vertices pt_1, pt_2, pt_3
`Circle[{`x, y`}, `r`, {`θ_1, θ_2`}]`	circular arc of radius r
`Disk[{`x, y`}, `r`]`	filled disk of radius r
`Raster[{{`x_{11}, x_{12}`, …}, {`x_{21}, x_{22}`, …}, …}]`	rectangular array of gray levels
`Text[`$expr$`, {`x, y`}]`	text centered at $\{x, y\}$

Directives

The display of graphics primitives is modified by using *graphics directives*. Graphics directives work by changing only those objects within their scope. The directive *dir* will affect each of the primitives $prim_i$ occurring within its scope, delineated by the curly braces:

$$\{dir, prim_1, prim_2, \ldots, prim_n\}$$

Typically, graphics directives are used to change the color, size, thickness, or other display properties of a primitive object. For example, in the following input the triangle is modified with the `LightBlue` and `EdgeForm` directives; the circle with the `Gray` and `Thick` directives; and the points with `Blue` and `PointSize` directives. Each of the primitives `Triangle`, `Circle`, and `Point` are scoped by means of the curly braces.

```
In[5]:= Graphics[{
          {LightBlue, EdgeForm[Gray], Triangle[{p1, p2, p3}]},
          {Gray, Thick, Circle[{-1/2, 1/2}, √(5/2)]},
          {Blue, PointSize[Medium], Point[{p1, p2, p3}]}
        }]
```

Out[5]=

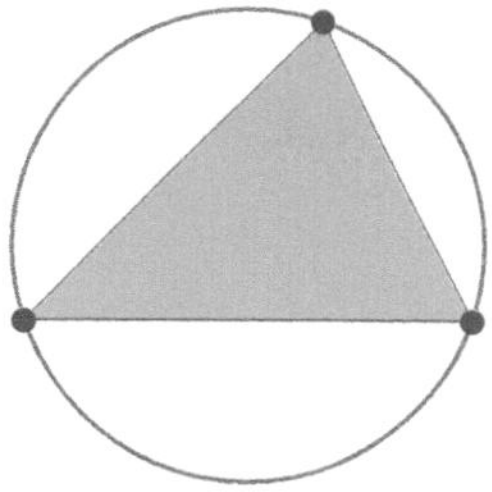

Using this graphics framework, let us create a visualization of a triangle, its centroid, and the triangle medians. The *centroid* is also referred to as the center of mass or center of gravity of the triangle. The *median* is the line segment from a vertex to the midpoint of the side opposite that vertex (`TriangleMedians` was developed in Section 5.5).

```
In[6]:= Needs["EPM`"]

In[7]:= medians = TriangleMedians[Triangle[{p1, p2, p3}]]
Out[7]= {Line[{{1, 0}, {-1, 1}}],
         Line[{{0, 2}, {-1/2, 0}}], Line[{{-2, 0}, {1/2, 1}}]}
```

The midpoints are the second list in each `Line` in `medians`.

```
In[8]:= midpts = Cases[medians, Line[{a_, b_}] :> b]
Out[8]= {{-1, 1}, {-1/2, 0}, {1/2, 1}}
```

To find the centroid of the triangle, use the built-in function `RegionCentroid`.

```
In[9]:= centroid = RegionCentroid[Triangle[{p1, p2, p3}]]
```

Out[9]= $\left\{-\frac{1}{3}, \frac{2}{3}\right\}$

Here then are all the pieces. Note that the medians intersect at the centroid.

```
In[10]:= Graphics[{
           {LightBlue, EdgeForm[Gray], Triangle[{p1, p2, p3}]},
           {Blue, PointSize[Medium], Point[{p1, p2, p3}]},
           {Gray, medians, Point@midpts},
           {Red, PointSize[Large], Point@centroid}
          }]
```

Out[10]=

Options

Whereas directives are used to modify the primitives that are within their scope, options are used to modify the entire graphic. Options to functions are placed after any required arguments, separated by commas. All of *Mathematica*'s graphics functions have options that allow you to modify some attribute of the entire graphic. For example, the following adds axes and a frame around the graphic. `Axes` and `Frame` are options to the `Graphics` function. Their default values turn these features off.

```
In[11]:= Options[Graphics, {Axes, Frame}]
Out[11]= {Axes → False, Frame → False}
```

```
In[12]:= Graphics[{
           {LightBlue, EdgeForm[Gray], Triangle[{p1, p2, p3}]},
           {Blue, PointSize[Medium], Point[{p1, p2, p3}]},
           {Gray, medians, Point@midpts},
           {Red, PointSize[Large], Point@centroid}
          }, Axes → False, Frame → True]
```

Out[12]=

2.0
1.5
1.0
0.5
0.0
−1.0 −0.5 0.0 0.5 1.0 1.5 2.0

Three-dimensional graphics

To display three-dimensional graphics primitives, a different wrapper is used: `Graphics3D`. It has some different options to those of `Graphics` but otherwise, the syntax is the same. In the following, the two sphere primitives are within the scope of the `Red` directive, the cylinder is within the scope of the `Blue` directive, and the plane is within the scope of the `Opacity` directive. The option `FaceGrids` adds a grid to each of the box faces in the image.

```
In[13]:= Graphics3D[{
           {Red, Sphere[{0, 0, 0}], Sphere[{4, 4, 4}]},
           {Blue, Cylinder[{{0, 0, 0}, {4, 4, 4}}, .2]},
           {Opacity[.5],
            InfinitePlane[{0, 0, 0}, {{1, 0, 0}, {1, Cos[π / 4], Sin[π / 4]}}]}
          }, FaceGrids → All]
```

Out[13]=

Three-dimensional versions of `Point`, `Line`, `Polygon`, and `Text` are available for building three-dimensional graphics. A full listing of `Graphics3D` primitives and directives is in the tutorials Three-Dimensional Graphics Primitives and Three-Dimensional Graphics Directives (WLDC).

Structure of built-in graphics functions

Graphics created with functions such as `Plot` and `ListPlot` are constructed using the same syntax as described above for creating graphics from primitive elements: primitives such as lines connecting points and options governing the overall display. Although you generally do not need to be aware of this syntax to use such functions, insight into the structure of the built-in functions is useful when you need to transform or modify a graphic created with `Plot` or `ListPlot` say.

Let's start by looking at the internal representation of a plot of the sine function.

```
In[14]:= sinplot = Plot[Sin[x], {x, 0, 2 π}]
```

Out[14]=

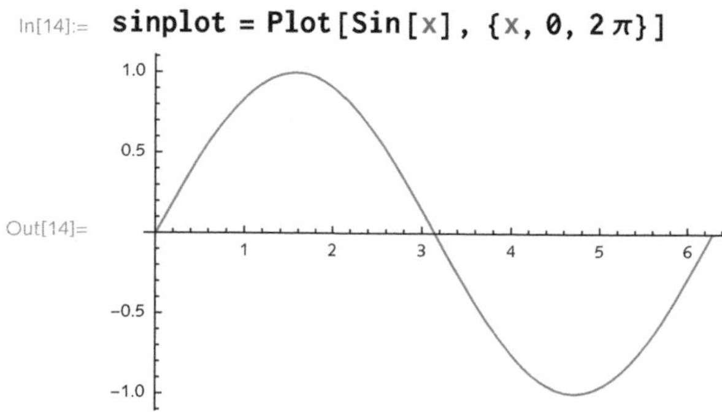

`InputForm` displays the expression that could have been entered manually to get the same plot. `Short` is used here to display an abbreviated listing of that expression. (*Note*: The formatted output from `Short` will vary slightly depending upon the width of your notebook.)

```
In[15]:= Short[InputForm[sinplot], 7]
Out[15]//Short=
     Graphics[
      {{{}, {}, {Directive[Opacity[1.], RGBColor[0.368417, 0.506779, 0.709798],
          AbsoluteThickness[0.7]], Line[{{1.28228×10^-7, 1.28228×10^-7},
           {0.0019271654532543384, 0.001927164260349845},
           {0.0038542026782371016, 0.0038541931359589105}, << 426 >>,
           {<< 2 >>}, {6.283185178951315, -1.28228×10^-7}}]}}}, {<< 17 >>}]
```

This graphic consists of a series of coordinates, or points, in the plane connected by lines of a certain hue. There are several hundred points that are sampled to make this plot, some of which are explicitly displayed above and the rest implicitly indicated by the notation <<*n*>>. The following shows that there are precisely 431 points in this plot (we have previously seen `Cases` used for this sort of thing in Section 4.3).

```
In[16]:= pts = First@Cases[sinplot, Line[coords_List] :→ coords, Infinity];

In[17]:= Dimensions[pts]
Out[17]= {431, 2}
```

Plotting these points shows the adaptive sampling that the `Plot` function uses to construct plots of functions: more points sampled where the derivative of the function is changing more rapidly and fewer points sampled where the function is locally linear.

```
In[18]:= Graphics[Point[pts]]
```

Out[18]=

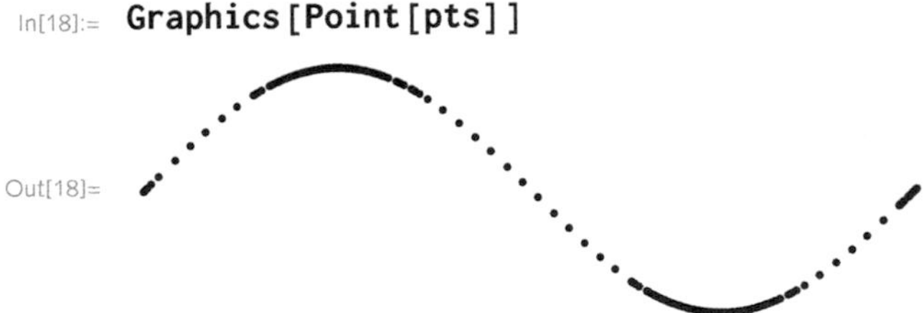

Connecting each coordinate point with a line gives the sine curve.

```
In[19]:= Graphics[Line[pts]]
```

Out[19]=

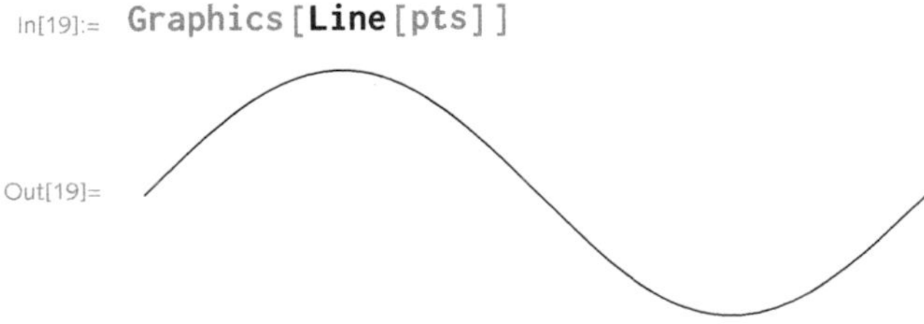

Add a directive to change the color of the curve.

```
In[20]:= Graphics[{
           Hue[0.67, .6, .6], Line[pts]
         }]
```

Out[20]=

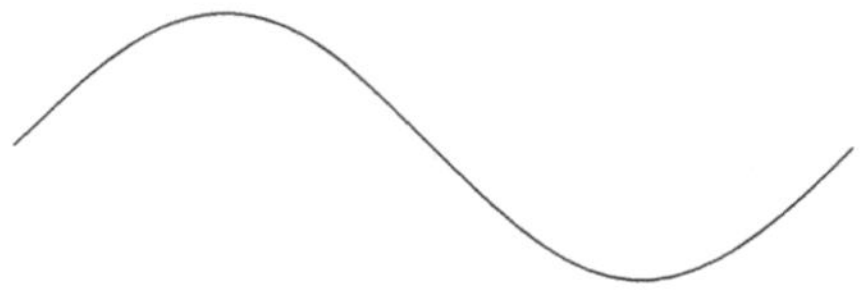

And finally, add several options to modify the overall appearance of the graphic.

```
In[21]:= Graphics[{
           Hue[0.67, 0.6, 0.6], Line[pts]
         }, Axes → Automatic, AspectRatio → 1 / GoldenRatio]
```

Out[21]=

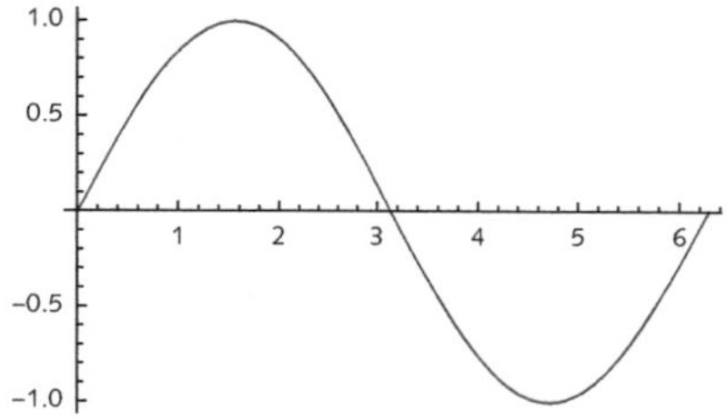

With an understanding of this internal structure you can transform graphical objects in a variety of ways. For example, the following uses a geometric transformation on the lines to essentially perform a reflection in the line $y = x$. Show is used to display multiple graphics objects.

```
In[22]:= Show[{
           sinplot,
           Graphics[{Dashed, InfiniteLine[{{0, 0}, {1, 1}}]}],
           sinplot /.
            line_Line :→ GeometricTransformation[line, ReflectionTransform[{1, -1}]]
         }, PlotRange → All, AspectRatio → 1]
```

Out[22]=

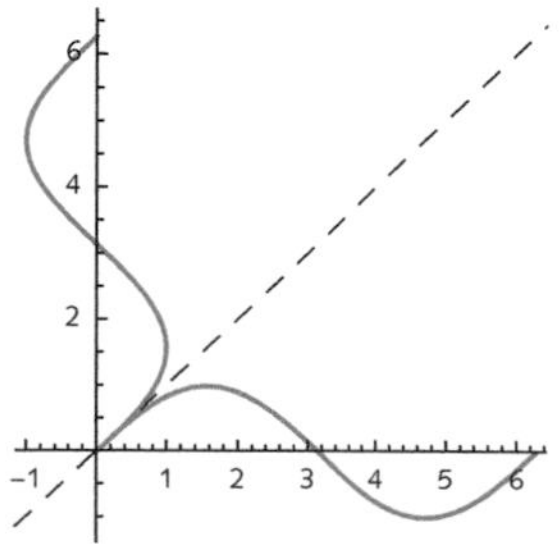

The three graphical elements in this plot are: the original `sinplot`, a dashed line on $y = x$, and the transformed `sinplot`. In the transformation rule, the pattern `line_Line` matches any expression in `sinplot` with head `Line`. It will be transformed into a line that is reflected according to `ReflectionTransform`. The reflection is in a line normal to the vector through the origin and {1, −1}.

Exercises

1. Create a color wheel by coloring successive sectors of a disk according to the `Hue` directive.

2. Construct a graphic containing a circle, a triangle, and a rectangle. Your graphic should include an identifying label for each object.

3. Create a three-dimensional graphic that includes six `Cuboid` graphics primitives, randomly placed in the unit cube. Add an opacity directive to make them transparent.

4. Create a graphic consisting of a cube together with a rotation of 45° about the vertical axis through the center of that cube. Then create a dynamically rotating cube using `Manipulate` or `Animate`.

5. Create a three-dimensional graphic consisting of twenty-four random points in the unit cube with every pair of points connected by a line. Add directives to make the points red and large and the lines gray and transparent.

6. Construct a graphic that consists of 500 points randomly distributed about the origin with standard deviation 1. Then, set the points to have random radii between 0.01 and 0.1 and colored randomly according to a `Hue` function.

7. Create a random walk on the binary digits of π. For a one-dimensional walk, use `RealDigits[`*num*`, 2]` to get the base 2 digits and then convert each 0 to −1 so that you have a vector of ±1s for the step directions; then use `Accumulate`.

   For the two-dimensional walk, use `Partition` to pair up digits and then use an appropriate transformation to have the four pairs, `{0, 0}`, `{0, 1}`, `{1, 0}`, and `{1, 1}` map to the compass directions; then use `Accumulate`. See Bailey et al. (2012) for more on visualizing digits of π.

8. Create a graphic that represents the solution to the following algebraic problem that appeared in the *Calculus&Mathematica* courseware (Porta, Davis, and Uhl, 1994). Find the positive numbers r such that the following system has exactly one solution in x and y:

$$(x-1)^2 + (y-1)^2 = 2$$
$$(x+3)^2 + (y-4)^2 = r^2$$

   Once you have found the right number r, plot the resulting circles on the same axes, plotting the first circle with solid lines and the two solutions with dashed lines.

9. Create a graphic of the sine function over the interval $(0, 2\pi)$ that displays vertical lines at each point calculated by the `Plot` function to produce the curve.

10. Bundle up the code fragments for the visualization of the triangle centroid into a function `CentroidPlot` that takes a `Triangle` graphics primitive as its argument and returns a graphic similar to that in this section. Set up your function to inherit options from `Graphics`.

    Add a check to `CentroidPlot` to return a message if the three vertices of the triangle are collinear.

```
In[1]:= pts = {{0, 0}, {1, 1}, {2, 2}};
        CentroidPlot[Triangle[pts]]
        CentroidPlot::collinpts : The points {{0, 0}, {1, 1}, {2, 2}} are collinear, giving a degenerate triangle.
```

11. The centroid of a triangle is only one kind of triangle center. The *circumcenter* is located at the intersection of the perpendicular bisectors of the sides of the triangle and is also the center of the circle passing through the vertices of the triangle, the circumcircle. The *incenter* is located at the intersection of the angle bisectors and is the center of the largest circle inside the triangle. The *orthocenter* is located at the intersection of the altitudes of the triangle (Kimberling 1994).

FIGURE 8.1. *Triangle centers.*

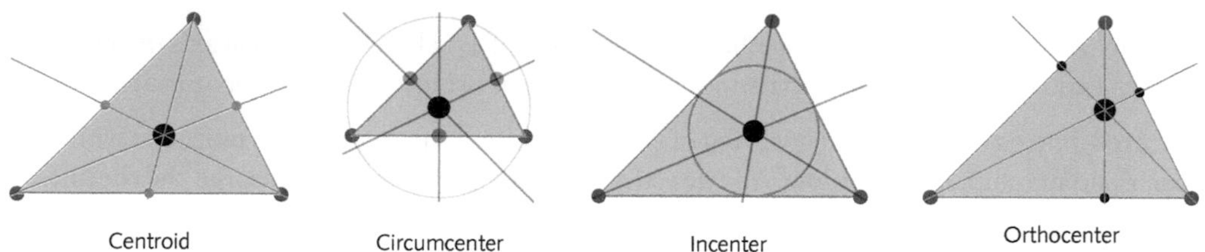

Create a graphic for each of these centers similar to that created for the centroid and the medians.

12. Using options to the `Plot` function, create a plot showing the probability density function (PDF) of a normal distribution together with vertical lines at the first and second standard deviations. Your plot should look something like that in Figure 8.2 for a normal distribution with $\mu = 0$ and $\sigma = 1$.

FIGURE 8.2. *PDF of normal distribution with standard deviation lines.*

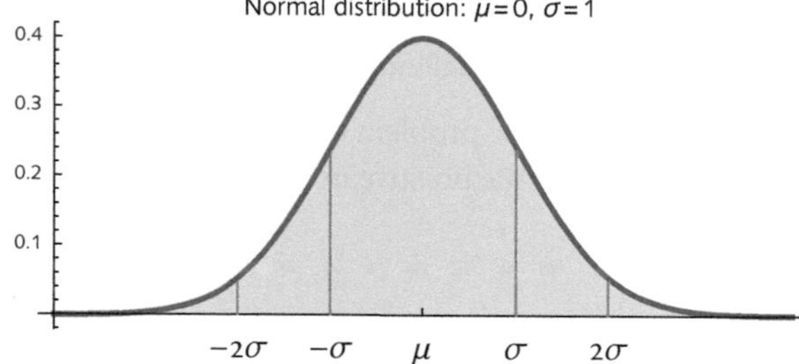

8.2 Dynamic graphics

Up to this point, all the examples we have discussed have involved the creation of graphics expressions that produce static output. Changing the value of a symbol does not change the value of a previously computed expression. But you can set things up so that *Mathematica* automatically updates symbols and expressions throughout your notebooks. This is done through a symbolic dynamic language. At its heart is the `Dynamic` construct that is used to update an arbitrary expression essentially in real time. This primitive dynamic building block, together with numerous control objects, provides a dynamic language with which you can construct arbitrary dynamic expressions including dynamic graphics. And, like the graphics language, high-level functions are available that provide a clean and simple interface to many of these dynamic features.

We will start this section with a look at some of the higher-level functions that can be used to create dynamic expressions. We then turn to the primitive elements `Dynamic` and `DynamicModule` that are used to construct those higher-level functions such as `Manipulate`.

Before going further we should note that discussing dynamic objects in a static book is a bit problematic. Dynamic objects, as their name suggests, change dynamically when their values change. This is quite different from the situation with static symbols. For this reason, this section is best read by evaluating the examples in order in your own *Mathematica* notebooks and observing changes to previous computations as subsequent expressions are evaluated.

Manipulate and locators

When you create a graphic, either from a built-in function or from graphics primitives, the output is a static expression. To change the output, you have to change the input and re-evaluate. For example, here is a plot of the sinc function:

```
In[1]:= Plot[Sinc[x], {x, -4π, 4π}]
```

Out[1]=

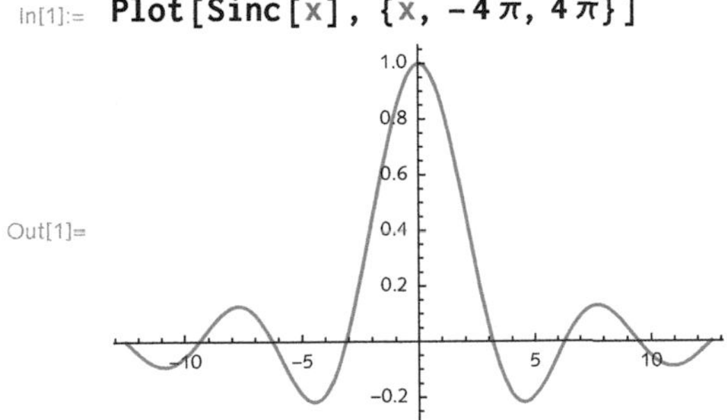

Using `Manipulate`, you can create an interface to display the plot together with controls to change any parameter. In the following example, we have inserted a parameter `b` into the sinc function. The iterator list `{b, 1, 5}` sets the minimum and maximum values for the parameter `b`.

```
In[2]:= Manipulate[
          Plot[Sinc[b x], {x, -4π, 4π}, PlotRange → 1],
          {b, 1, 5}]
```

Out[2]=

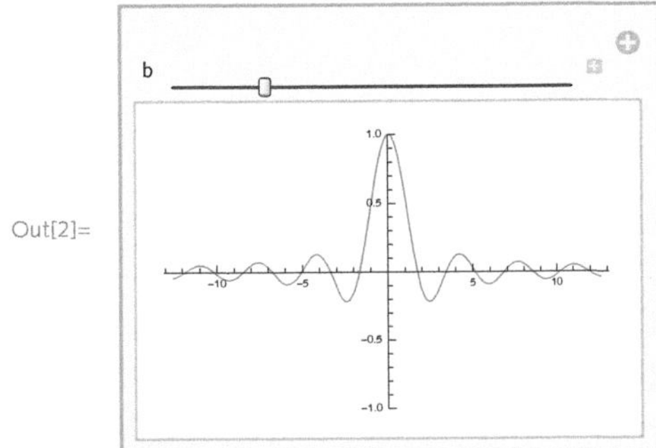

The expressions you can manipulate are quite arbitrary – they can be graphics primitives. Here, the dynamic parameter is θ, the angle of rotation:

```
In[3]:= Manipulate[
  Graphics[{Opacity[.5], Rotate[Rectangle[{-1, -1}, {1, 1}], θ]},
   PlotRange → √2 , Axes → True],
  {θ, 0, 2 π}]
```

Out[3]=

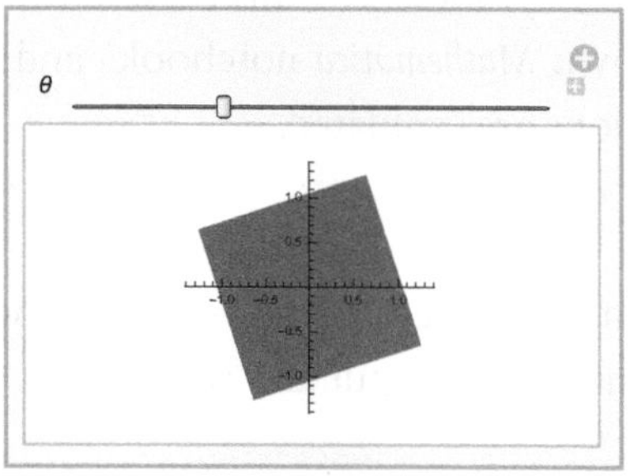

In addition to the general interface created by `Manipulate` in which parameters are controlled by sliders, other control objects can be used: checkboxes to toggle values on and off, two-dimensional sliders to manipulate two parameters at once, input fields to enter expressions from the keyboard, and much more. We will show just a few control objects here. A complete listing and links to documentation can be found in the guide page Control Objects (WLDC).

In the following expression, the parameter `pt` is controlled by a two-dimensional slider because the parameter list is of the form that generates a `Slider2D` control object. The value of the `pt` parameter is a list of two numbers that are passed dynamically to both `BezierCurve` and `Point`. As you move the slider, the control points change as does the location of the curve itself.

```
In[4]:= Manipulate[
  Graphics[{
    BezierCurve[{{1, 0}, pt, {3, -1}, {4, 0}}],
    Red, PointSize[Medium], Point[{{1, 0}, pt, {3, -1}, {4, 0}}]}],
  {pt, {2, 1}, {3, 3}}, ControlPlacement → Left]
```

Out[4]=

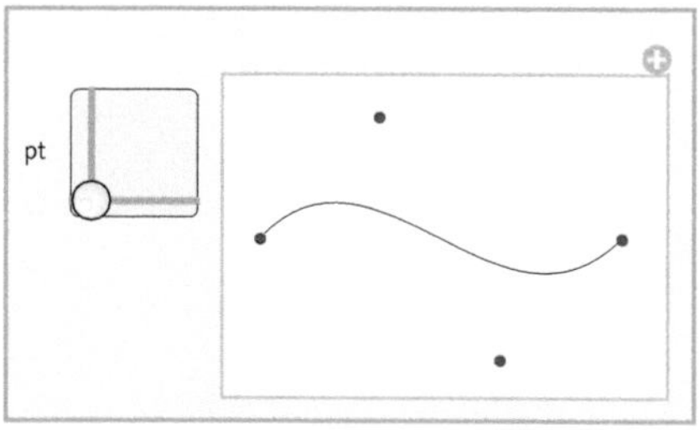

It would be much more convenient to be able to grab and manipulate objects in the graphic directly rather than using an intermediary like the `Slider2D` control object. This is what locators are for – they give you direct control over some object in the dynamic output. We will return to the Bézier curve example shortly, but first we introduce locators with a simple graphical object: three points wrapped in `Triangle`.

```
In[5]:= Graphics[{EdgeForm[Gray], LightBlue, Triangle[{{0, 0}, {2, 0}, {1, 1}}]}]
```

Out[5]=

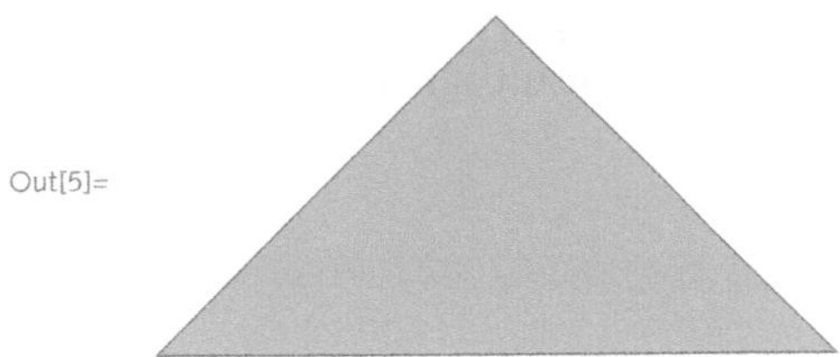

In the Bézier example, a two-dimensional slider was used to control one point, but here we will use the `Locator` control object to manipulate the point. In fact, one of the advantages of locators is that you can have as many of them as you wish. So let us turn all the vertices of this triangle into locators.

```
In[6]:= Manipulate[
         Graphics[{EdgeForm[Gray], LightBlue, Triangle[pts]}],
         {{pts, {{0, 0}, {2, 0}, {1, 1}}}, Locator}]
```

Out[6]=

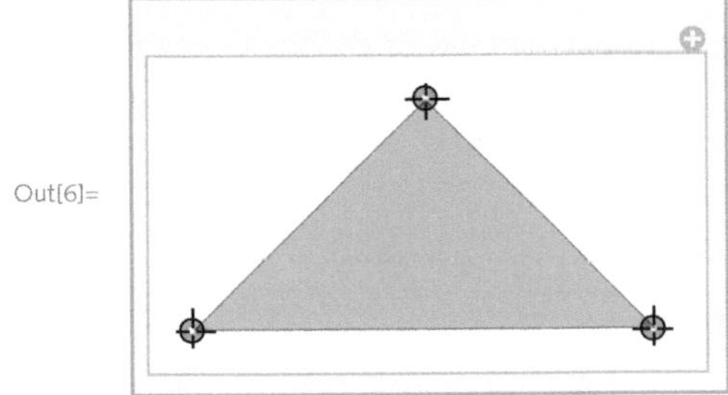

After moving some of the vertices with your mouse, here is how the graphic might look.

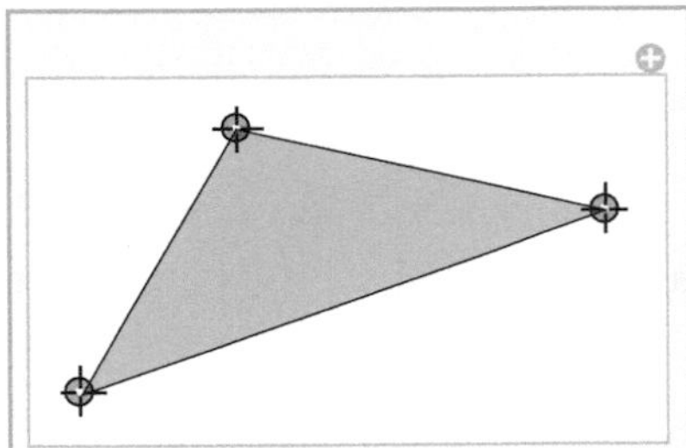

New locators can be added by Alt-clicking your mouse (holding ALT while clicking); this requires setting the option `LocatorAutoCreate`. New locator objects will be created at whatever position you click the mouse and they will be added to the list of existing locators. So, instead of `Triangle`, let's use `Polygon` so that we are not limited to the number of points in the object.

```
In[7]:= Manipulate[
          Graphics[{EdgeForm[Gray], LightBlue, Polygon[pts]}],
          {{pts, {{0, 0}, {2, 0}, {1, 1}}}, Locator, LocatorAutoCreate → True}]
```

Out[7]=

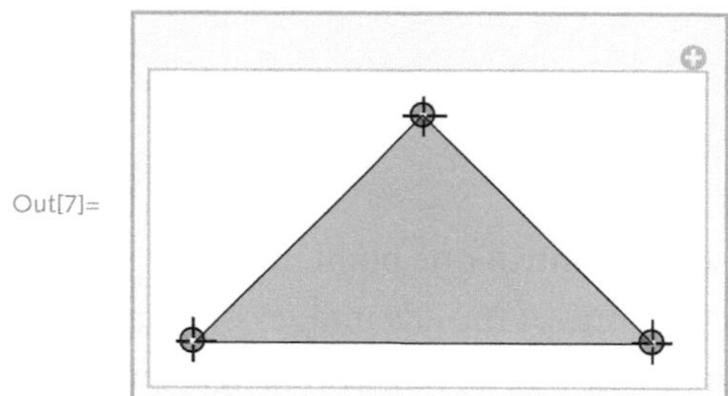

And here is how the graphic might look after clicking several times:

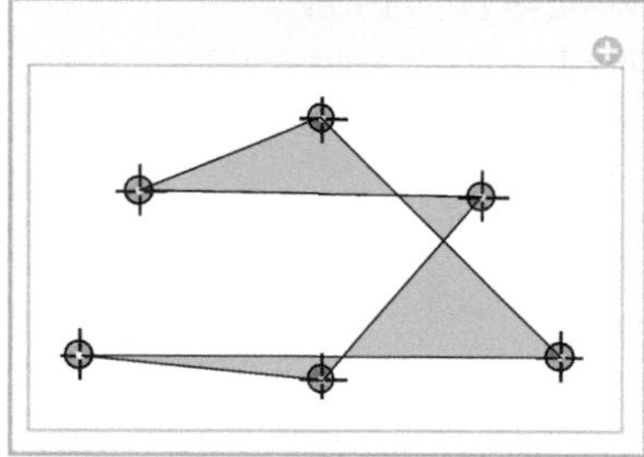

Dynamic building blocks

Whenever you make an assignment, the value of a symbol is fixed at the time the definition is made. For example, the symbol t is given the value 10 here:

```
In[8]:= t = 10
Out[8]= 10
```

Whenever you use t, its (static) value will be automatically substituted.

```
In[9]:= 4 t - 1
Out[9]= 39
```

Change the value associated with t and all *subsequent* evaluations will use the new value.

```
In[10]:= t = 5;
         4 t - 1
Out[11]= 19
```

The outputs of previous computations involving t all retain the history, essentially showing you the value *when the assignment was evaluated*. The rule, t = 10, is stored in memory by the kernel. Close the kernel and that rule is no longer known; you will need to re-evaluate the rule in a new session to give the symbol t that value again.

Another kind of output is possible: a dynamic output which is automatically updated to reflect the current value of the symbol.

```
In[12]:= t + 1
Out[12]= 6
```

```
In[13]:= Dynamic[t + 1]
Out[13]= 1 + Bobby
```

Change the value of t and any dynamic outputs will change immediately.

```
In[14]:= t = Bobby
Out[14]= Bobby
```

The value of the expression t + 1 in In[12] is 6, reflecting that the symbol t in that expression is static: it gets its value from the last assigned value for t, which in this case was 5. But note that the expression Dynamic[t + 1] has a different value. The dynamic expression has automatically updated to reflect the current value of its argument. Even though we evaluated t = Bobby later in the session, it is that, most current, value that is used inside of Dynamic.

It is important to note that Dynamic[*expr*] displays as *expr* but internally it is represented as a dynamic object.

```
In[15]:= Dynamic[3 + w]
Out[15]= 3 + w
```

```
In[16]:= InputForm[%]
Out[16]//InputForm=
         Dynamic[3 + w]
```

Any expression can be dynamic. For example, running ImageConvolve with an appropriate kernel on this image returns a static object. When it was evaluated immediately following the evaluation of img, it used that current value to perform the operation.

In[17]:= img =  ;

```
In[18]:= ImageConvolve[img, {{-1, 0, 1}, {-4, 0, 4}, {-1, 0, 1}}]
```

Out[18]= 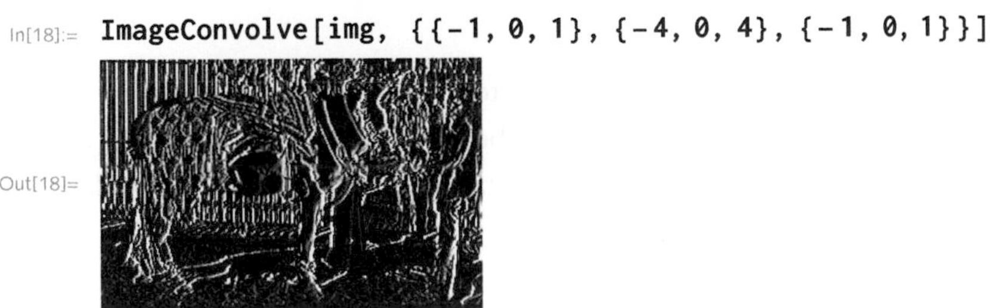

Change the value of img in a subsequent computation and the above expression does not change, but any dynamic version does.

```
In[19]:= img = ;
```

```
In[20]:= Dynamic[ImageConvolve[img, {{-1, 0, 1}, {-12, 0, 12}, {-1, 0, 1}}]]
```

Out[20]=

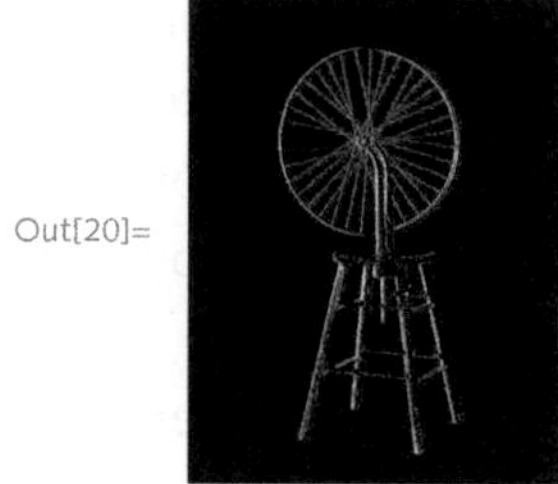

Let's start to build up interactive expressions using the dynamic building blocks. First, here is a slider object; by default it moves between values 0 and 1. You can move the slider with your mouse, but without an argument, it is not connected to anything.

```
In[21]:= Slider[]
```

Out[21]=

Let's give it a dynamic variable z, and display the value of z to the right of the slider.

```
In[22]:= Clear[z]

In[23]:= {Slider[Dynamic[z]], z}
```

```
Out[23]= { , z}
```

If you move the above slider, you will see that the value of z displayed to the right of the slider is not updating. The symbol z is not dynamic so it does not update. To make it dynamic, wrap it in `Dynamic`. We can also set a range of values that the dynamic value can take on, here from .01 to 1.

```
In[24]:= {Slider[Dynamic[z], {.01, 1}], Dynamic[z]}
```

```
Out[24]= { , 0.}
```

Now, moving this latest slider causes the value of z to update dynamically. As you move the slider you will notice that the previous slider also moves! This is because it too has a dynamic z as argument. The plot below will also automatically update as you change the value of z in the slider above.

```
In[25]:= Dynamic[Plot[Sin[x + 4 z], {x, 0, 2 π}]]
```

Out[25]=

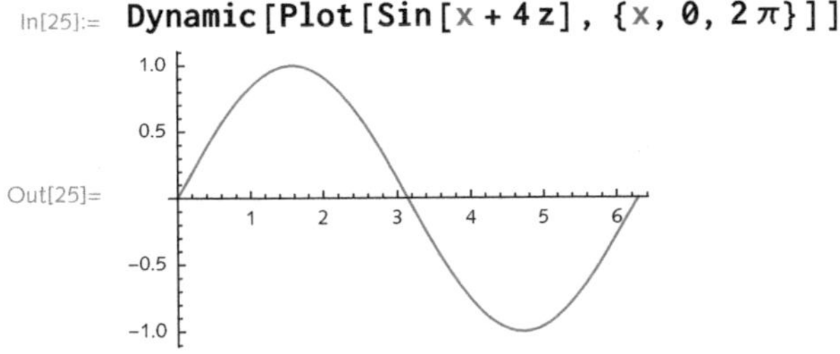

Tip 8.1

When creating dynamic plots, be careful to not simply wrap the variable `z` in `Dynamic` as this will not create a dynamic plot.

```
In[26]:= Plot[Sin[x + 4 Dynamic[z]], {x, 0, 2 π}]
```

Out[26]=

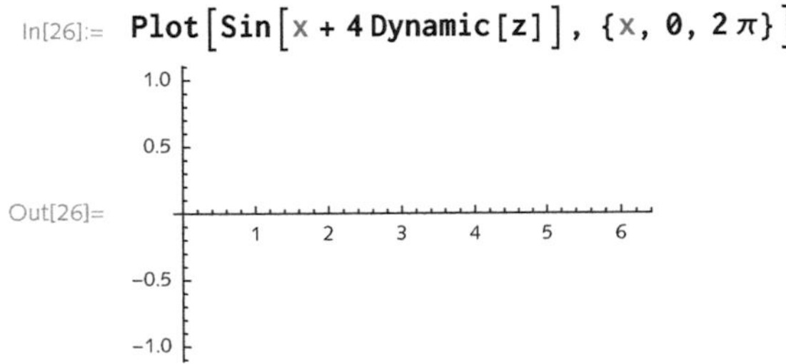

In fact, no curve is generated because `Plot` needs specific values to create the curve. It is the plot itself that we want to update dynamically, so `Plot` should be wrapped in `Dynamic`.

Putting the slider together with the dynamic plot, you can essentially build up a scene much like `Manipulate` which uses these very objects to construct its interfaces.

```
In[27]:= Panel[Column[{
            Slider[Dynamic[z]],
            Dynamic[Plot[Sin[x + 4 z], {x, 0, 2 π}]]}]]
```

Out[27]=

There is an important potential issue with the above example. If you were to assign a value to a global symbol `z`, it would conflict with the `z` in the dynamic expression. Fortunately, there is a way to localize (and initialize) variables in dynamic expressions using a dynamic analog of the `Module` function: `DynamicModule`.

```
In[28]:= DynamicModule[{z = 0.5}, {
           Panel[Column[{
              Slider[Dynamic[z]],
              Dynamic[Plot[Sin[x + 4 z], {x, 0, 2 π}]]
             }]
          ]}]
```

Out[28]=

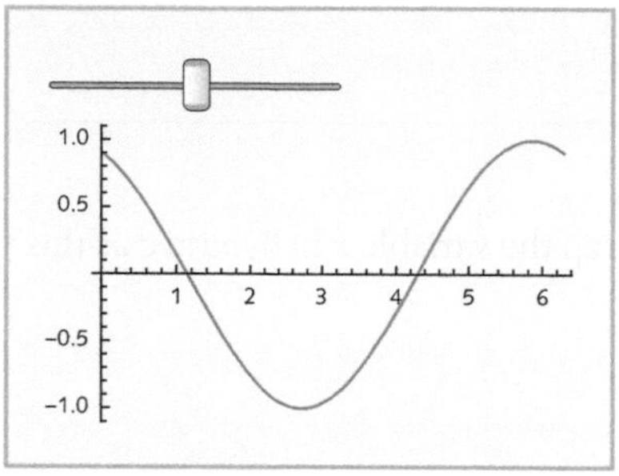

One of the advantages of `DynamicModule` is that it saves state. What this means is that you can end your *Mathematica* session, close the notebook, restart *Mathematica*, reopen the notebook and any output created with a `DynamicModule` will be in the same state as when you closed the notebook. This is because the output of a `DynamicModule` includes an expression embedded in the output that is initialized when it is displayed again. That expression includes values of local variables created with `DynamicModule`. Another way of thinking about this is that global variables are known to (and in a sense, owned by) the kernel; variables that are created by `DynamicModule`, however, live in the front end.

Let's recreate some of the objects from earlier in this chapter that used `Manipulate`, but instead, we will put them together using the dynamic building blocks. We will start with the dynamic triangle from the previous section. The variable `pts` is localized inside `DynamicModule` and initialized with three points. `LocatorPane[`*pos*`, `*expr*`]` is a low-level object that creates a pane with locators given at the positions specified by *pos* and a background given by the expression *expr*. So, in this example, `Dynamic[`*pts*`]` gives the dynamic locator positions and `Graphics[…]` displays in the background.

```
In[29]:= DynamicModule[{pts = {{-1, 0}, {1, 0}, {0, 1}}},
          LocatorPane[Dynamic[pts], Graphics[{
             LightBlue, EdgeForm[Gray], Dynamic[Polygon[pts]]}]]]
```

Out[29]=

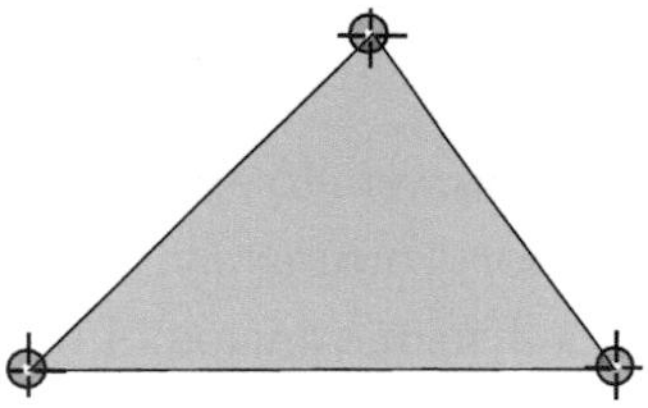

As another example of the use of `LocatorPane`, here is a dynamic Bézier curve as defined by several control points:

```
In[30]:= DynamicModule[{pts = {{0, 0}, {1, 1}, {2, 1}}},
          LocatorPane[Dynamic[pts], Graphics[Dynamic@BezierCurve[pts]]]]
```

Out[30]=

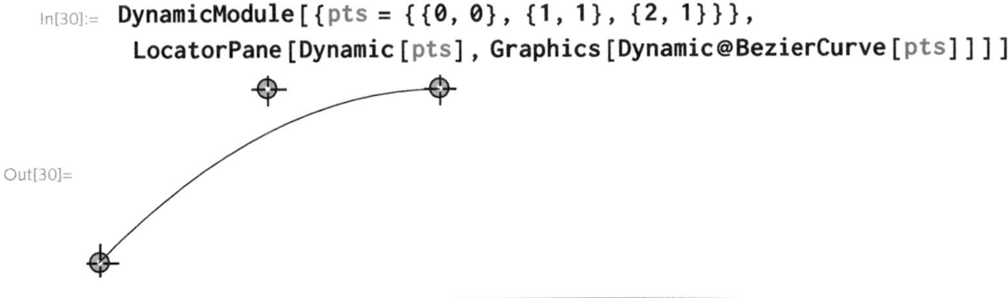

Exercises

1. In the `Manipulate` examples in this section, the parameters were controlled by sliders. Moving the slider changes the value of the parameter and any expression dependent upon that parameter inside the `Manipulate` expression. Sometimes you want to choose values for a parameter from a list of discrete values. A setter bar is a convenient control object for this. One way to set it is to use a different syntax for the parameter list: $\{param, \{val_1, val_2, \ldots, val_n\}\}$ will cause `Manipulate` to automatically use a setter bar instead of a slider. Create a `Manipulate` object showing plots of sin, cos, or tan, each selectable from a setter bar.

2. Modify the above exercise to use a popup menu to choose the function to plot. You can explicitly set the control by using `ControlType→ "PopupMenu"`.

3. Here is a graphic showing an ellipsoid together with its two foci:

```
In[1]:= With[{a = 5, b = 3},
         f = √(a² - b²);
         Graphics[{
           Circle[{0, 0}, {a, b}],
           Point[{f, 0}], Point[{-f, 0}]
          }, Axes → Automatic]]
```

Out[1]=

Turn this into a dynamic graphic by making the semi-major and semi-minor axes lengths a and b dynamic which, upon updating, will cause the ellipse to change shape. Some thought will be needed to properly deal with the situation $b > a$.

4. Create a dynamic interface that displays various structure diagrams and space-filling plots of the amino acids. A list of the amino acids is given by

```
In[2]:= ChemicalData["AminoAcids"]

Out[2]= {glycine, L-alanine, L-serine, L-proline, L-valine, L-threonine, L-cysteine, L-isoleucine,
  L-leucine, L-asparagine, L-aspartic acid, L-glutamine, L-lysine, L-glutamic acid,
  L-methionine, L-histidine, L-phenylalanine, L-arginine, L-tyrosine, L-tryptophan}
```

The diagrams and plots that should be included are built into `ChemicalData`:

```
In[3]:= StringCases[ChemicalData["Properties"], __ ~~ "Diagram" | (__ ~~ "Plot")] // Flatten

Out[3]= {BlackStructureDiagram, CHBlackStructureDiagram, CHColorStructureDiagram,
  ColorStructureDiagram, MoleculePlot, SpaceFillingMoleculePlot}
```

5. Using the code developed in Section 8.1 for plotting the centroid of a triangle, create a dynamic interface that displays the triangle, the medians (lines from each vertex to the midpoint of the opposite side), and the triangle vertices as locators.

6. In the 1920s and 1930s the artist Marcel Duchamp created what he termed *rotoreliefs*, spinning concentric circles giving a three-dimensional illusion of depth (Duchamp 1926). Create your own rotoreliefs: start with several concentric circles of different radii, then vary their centers around a path given by another circle, and animate.

7. Create a plot of $\sin(\theta)$ side-by-side with a circle and a dynamic point that moves along the curve and the circle as θ varies from 0 to 2π (Figure 8.3).

FIGURE 8.3. *Dynamic visualization of sin function.*

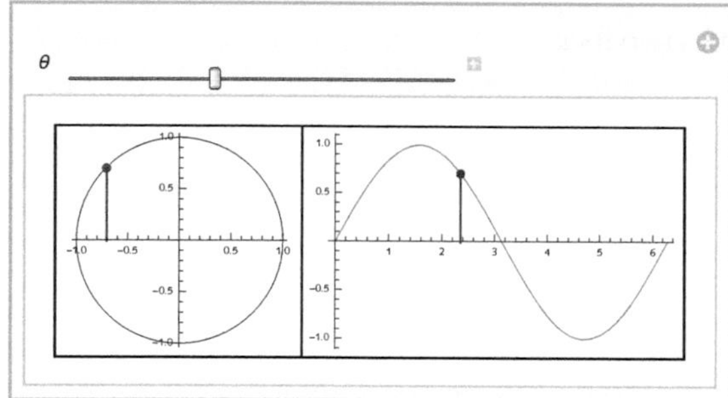

8. Take one of the two-dimensional random walk programs developed elsewhere in this book (Sections 6.3 and 10.3) and create an animation displaying successive steps of the random walk.

9. Looking forward to Chapter 10, where we develop a full application for computing and visualizing random walks, create a dynamic interface that displays random walks, adding controls to select the number of steps from a pulldown menu, the dimension from a setter bar, and a checkbox to turn on and off lattice walks.

10. Create a visualization of two-dimensional vector addition (Figure 8.4). The interface should include either a 2D slider for two vectors in the plane or locators to change the position of each vector; the display should show the two vectors as well as their vector sum. Extend the solution to three dimensions. (The solution of this vector interface is due to Harry Calkins of Wolfram Research.)

FIGURE 8.4. *Dynamic visualization of vector arithmetic.*

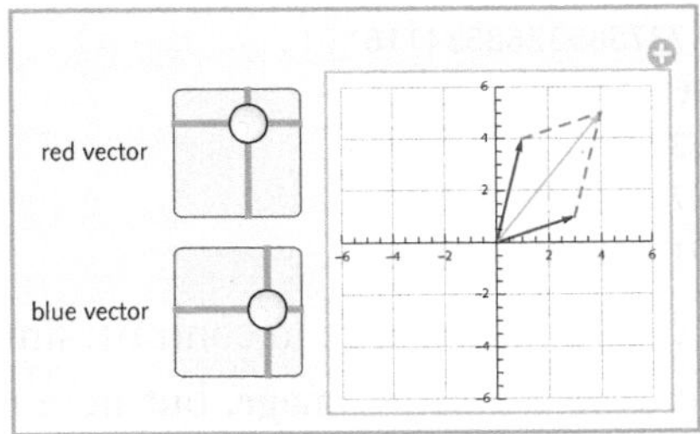

11. Create a dynamic interface consisting of a locator constrained to the unit circle. Check the documentation on `Locator` for information on constraining the movement of locators.

12. Create a dynamic interface that displays twenty random points in the unit square whose locations are randomized each time you click your mouse on the graphic. Add a checkbox to toggle the display of the shortest path (`FindShortestTour`) through the points (look up `EventHandler` and `MouseClicked` in the documentation).

    A suggested addition would be to add a control to change the number of points that are used but take care to keep the total number of points manageable (see the note on Traveling Salesman problems at the end of the chapter).

8.3 Efficient structures

In general, the built-in graphics functions are designed to operate on a broad set of possible arguments and they do so while constructing and displaying their graphics scenes quickly and efficiently, keeping the size of the resulting expression manageable. But when creating visualizations of sizable data sets you can find yourself with very large graphical objects that are not optimal in terms of memory usage, storage on disk, and interactivity. In this section we will look at several approaches to optimizing graphical expressions, introducing multi-objects and `GraphicsComplex` as two efficient structures for working with larger objects. Lastly, we will look at the use of numeric vs. symbolic expressions in the internal representation of graphical expressions.

Multi-objects

Visualizations involving a lot of graphics primitives often contain large data structures with numerous instances of a single primitive object like points and lines. For example, mapping `Point` across a set of pairs of coordinates is one way to create a graphic.

```
In[1]:= data = RandomReal[NormalDistribution[0, 1], {5, 2}];
        gr1 = Graphics[Map[Point, data]];
```

```
In[3]:= FullForm[gr1]
Out[3]//FullForm=
        Graphics[List[Point[List[0.7285501648713001`, 0.7375853268534116`]],
          Point[List[1.0917945215285878`, 1.9811188983886165`]],
          Point[List[-0.9200713876779407`, 1.5538709383530065`]],
          Point[List[-0.52477030742108`, 0.5016926303037705`]],
          Point[List[0.07590381445857085`, -0.12371375591301512`]]]]
```

Point occurs five times in the above expression, once for each point created. In contrast, simply wrapping Point around the entire list of coordinate pairs creates the same image, but note that Point is only used once in the underlying expression.

```
In[4]:= gr2 = Graphics[Point[data]];
        FullForm[gr2]
Out[5]//FullForm=
        Graphics[Point[List[List[0.7285501648713001`, 0.7375853268534116`],
           List[1.0917945215285878`, 1.9811188983886165`],
           List[-0.9200713876779407`, 1.5538709383530065`],
           List[-0.52477030742108`, 0.5016926303037705`],
           List[0.07590381445857085`, -0.12371375591301512`]]]]
```

The form in this latter case is referred to as a *multi-point expression*, and is treated differently than expressions with numerous primitives. The internal representation of multi-element objects is more compact and the *Mathematica* front end is able to render these objects much more quickly. For example, here are the kernel times to create a three-dimensional graphic consisting of 7500 points.

```
In[6]:= data = RandomVariate[NormalDistribution[0, 1], {7500, 3}];

In[7]:= Timing[Graphics3D[{PointSize[Tiny], Map[Point, data]}]]
```

Out[7]= {0.0032, 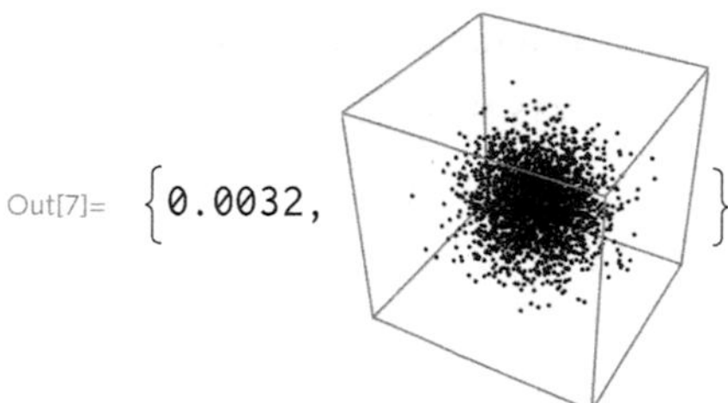 }

```
In[8]:= Timing[Graphics3D[{PointSize[Tiny], Point[data]}]]
```

Out[8]= {7. × 10^{-6}, 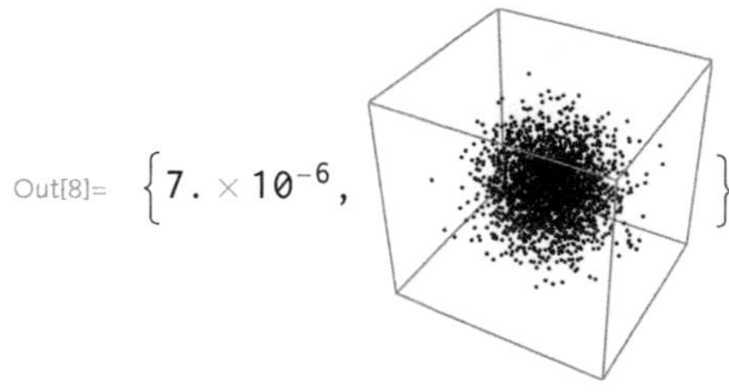 }

These timings are quite small, so small in fact that they might be misleading. The built-in granularity of the timing functions is given by the following:

```
In[9]:=  $TimeUnit

          1
Out[9]=  ───
         100
```

So, to get more trustworthy timing comparisons, either increase the size (number of points) of the computation or repeat it many times inside a loop. We choose the latter approach here as the increasingly larger graphical objects can make the size of your notebooks unwieldy.

```
In[10]:= Timing[Do[Graphics3D[{PointSize[Tiny], Map[Point, data]}], {500}]]
Out[10]= {1.61307, Null}
```

```
In[11]:= Timing[Do[Graphics3D[{PointSize[Tiny], Point[data]}], {500}]]
Out[11]= {0.000346, Null}
```

The differences in kernel timings are impressive – three to four orders of magnitude in this example. But the difference in the time it takes the front end to render these two objects is also significant, with the first expression taking much much longer.

Since `Timing` and `AbsoluteTiming` measure kernel times, you will have to use a different function, `SessionTime`, to measure total wall clock time for a computation, including the time it takes the front end to format and render the resulting expression.

```
In[12]:= t1 = SessionTime[];
         gr1 = Graphics3D[{PointSize[Tiny], Map[Point, data]}]
         t2 = SessionTime[];
         (t2 - t1) Seconds
```

Out[13]=

```
Out[15]= 0.265984 Seconds
```

```
In[16]:= t1 = SessionTime[];
         gr2 = Graphics3D[{PointSize[Tiny], Point[data]}]
         t2 = SessionTime[];
         (t2 - t1) Seconds
```

Out[17]= 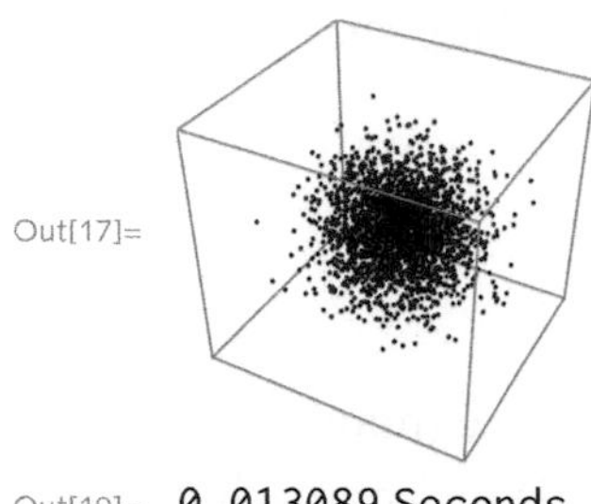

Out[19]= 0.013089 Seconds

Moreover, the memory needed to represent these objects is also vastly different, with that for the multi-point expression being some seven to ten times smaller.

```
In[20]:= {ByteCount[gr1], ByteCount[gr2], N[ByteCount[gr1] / ByteCount[gr2]]}
Out[20]= {1 381 600, 180 352, 7.66057}
```

Point, Line, Polygon, Arrow are the only graphics primitives that have multi-element forms. To make your graphics as efficient as possible, try to use them whenever possible.

GraphicsComplex

Graphical expressions often contain repetitions of the coordinate points used in the graphic. For example, a coordinate triple $\{x, y, z\}$ might have several polygons that share that vertex and it would be repeated for each of those polygons (Figure 8.5).

A GraphicsComplex is an expression that you can use to compress the representation of such objects. It works by specifying each coordinate once, and then only referring to the coordinate by an index, given by its position in the coordinate list.

FIGURE 8.5. *Three-dimensional graphics object with multiple polygons sharing vertices.*

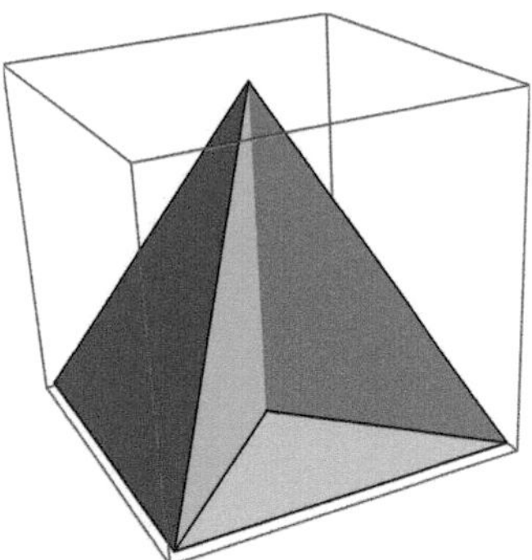

Another reason to think about using GraphicsComplex concerns limitations of some of the built-in functions when working with large data sets. For example, ListPlot and ListLinePlot will become bogged down as the size of your data increases. For example, for 500 000 pairs of numbers, these functions are quite slow. Here we use RandomWalk, defined in the packages that accompany this book, to generate a long list of pairs of numbers suitable for ListLinePlot:

```
In[21]:= Needs["EPM`RandomWalks`"]

In[22]:= walk = RandomWalk[5 × 10^5];
         ListLinePlot[walk] // Timing

Out[23]= {8.07687, [graphic]}
```

Although ListLinePlot doesn't use GraphicsComplex, many of the three-dimensional and region-plotting functions do in order to represent the graphical expression that would otherwise be quite a bit larger.

```
In[24]:= plt = Plot3D[Sqrt[1 - x^2 - y^2], {x, -1, 1}, {y, -1, 1}]
```

Out[24]=

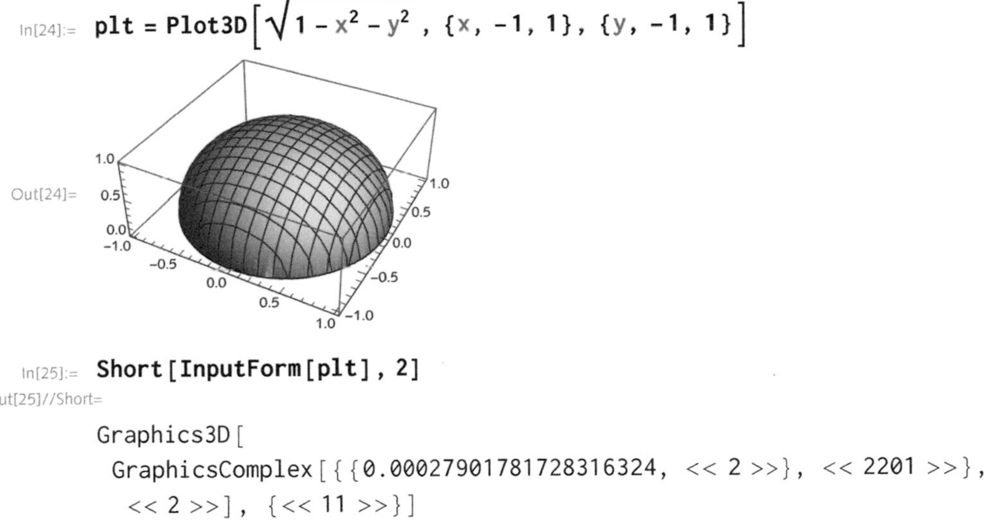

```
In[25]:= Short[InputForm[plt], 2]
Out[25]//Short=
         Graphics3D[
          GraphicsComplex[{{0.00027901781728316324, << 2 >>}, << 2201 >>},
           << 2 >>], {<< 11 >>}]
```

So, how do you create graphics using this machinery? GraphicsComplex takes two arguments: a list of coordinate points in 2- or 3-space, followed by a list of graphics primitives where each point is referenced by its position within the coordinate point list.

GraphicsComplex[{pt_1, pt_2, …}, *primitives*]

For example, here is a simple expression consisting of five points on the unit circle:

```
In[26]:= coords = N@CirclePoints[5]
Out[26]= {{0.587785, -0.809017}, {0.951057, 0.309017},
          {0., 1.}, {-0.951057, 0.309017}, {-0.587785, -0.809017}}
```

The following creates a line connecting the points in order. The explicit coordinates are given as the first argument. The second argument contains the primitives, in this case, a single Line object. In the Line primitive, the points are referred to by their position in the list coords.

```
In[27]:= GraphicsComplex[coords, Line[{1, 2, 3, 4, 5, 1}]]
Out[27]= GraphicsComplex[{{0.587785, -0.809017}, {0.951057, 0.309017}, {0., 1.},
           {-0.951057, 0.309017}, {-0.587785, -0.809017}}, Line[{1, 2, 3, 4, 5, 1}]]
```

Wrapping Graphics (or Graphics3D) around a GraphicsComplex displays the expression.

```
In[28]:= Graphics[GraphicsComplex[coords, Line[{1, 2, 3, 4, 5, 1}]]]
```

Out[28]=

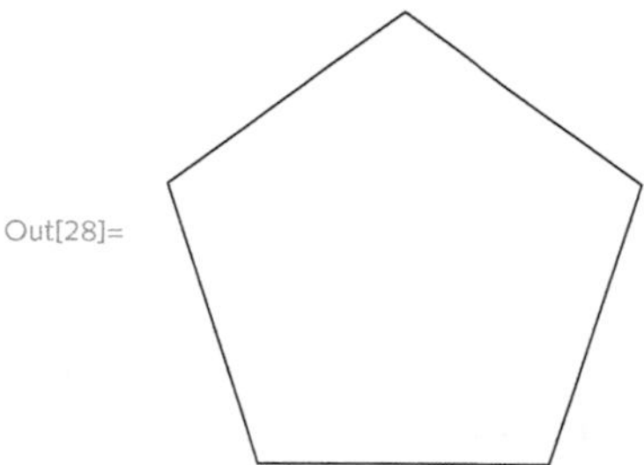

Changing the indices used in the second argument results in lines connecting the same coordinates but in a different order. Here we have added Text graphics primitives to label the points:

```
In[29]:= Graphics[GraphicsComplex[coords, {
            Line[{1, 3, 5, 2, 4, 1}],
            Map[Text[#, #] &, Range[5]]
          }]]
```

Out[29]=

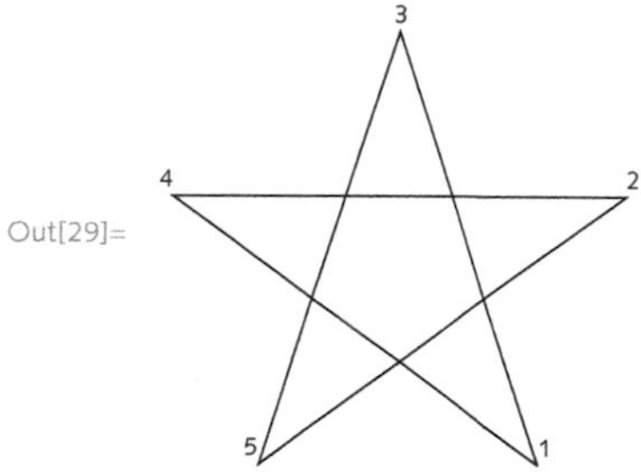

To include points at each coordinate, add them in the second argument to GraphicsComplex.

```
In[30]:= Graphics[GraphicsComplex[coords, {
            Line[{1, 3, 5, 2, 4, 1}],
            Blue, PointSize[Medium], Point[{1, 2, 3, 4, 5}]
          }]]
```

Out[30]=

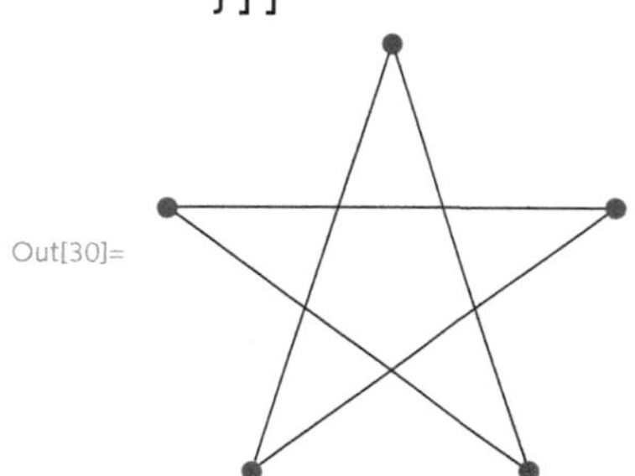

Once the list of coordinate points is specified as the first argument of GraphicsComplex, the points can be referenced as many times as needed. In the following example, the same set of points is referred to in the first line object as well as in the second and third rotated line objects.

```
In[31]:= Graphics[{
           GraphicsComplex[coords, {
             {Line[{1, 2, 3, 4, 5, 1}]},
             {Dashed, Rotate[Line[{1, 2, 3, 4, 5, 1}], 45 Degree]},
             {Thick, Rotate[Line[{1, 2, 3, 4, 5, 1}], 90 Degree]}
           }]
         }]
```

Out[31]=

Numeric vs. symbolic expressions

One of the great strengths of *Mathematica* is that you generally do not need to focus on the type of numbers you are working with when performing most operations. This is true of graphical as well as other kinds of computation. You can work with approximate numbers or symbolic/exact expressions and your graphics will just work. But for large graphical expressions, you may want to think about the types of numbers used.

For example, here is a graphics primitive, a polygon, generated from a list of exact coordinates:

```
In[32]:= tri = Graphics[{■, Polygon[{{0, 0}, {1, 0}, {1/2, √3/2}}]}]
```

Out[32]=

The front end, which renders the graphic, converts this list of exact coordinates into a numeric representation and maintains this in a cached form for purposes of efficiency. You can see this by converting to the internal box structure.

```
In[33]:= ToBoxes[tri]
Out[33]= GraphicsBox[{■, PolygonBox[NCache[
           {{0, 0}, {1, 0}, {1/2, √3/2}}, {{0, 0}, {1, 0}, {0.5, 0.866025}}]]}]
```

The exact coordinates, as well as the numeric approximations, are both part of this internal representation. Although this allows the front end to render the graphic quickly, it comes at a cost. Here is the size of this little graphic expression:

```
In[34]:= ByteCount[tri]
Out[34]= 856
```

Turning off this cache results in a simpler internal representation, one in which the symbolic expression is not stored.

```
In[35]:= tri2 = Graphics[Polygon[{{0, 0}, {1, 0}, {1/2, √3/2}}],
            Method → {"CacheSymbolicGraphics" → False}];

In[36]:= ToBoxes[tri2]
Out[36]= GraphicsBox[PolygonBox[{{0, 0}, {1, 0}, {0.5, 0.866025}}],
          Method → {CacheSymbolicGraphics → False}]
```

Fortunately, there is an easier way to get around this issue and that is simply to give the coordinates as numeric values rather than symbolic expressions.

```
In[37]:= ntri = Graphics[{■, Polygon[{{0, 0}, {1, 0}, {0.5, 0.866}}]}]
Out[37]=
```

```
In[38]:= ToBoxes[ntri]
Out[38]= GraphicsBox[{■, PolygonBox[{{0, 0}, {1, 0}, {0.5, 0.866}}]}]
```

The size of the resulting expression is reduced by about one-third over that of the cached version.

```
In[39]:= ByteCount[ntri]
Out[39]= 592
```

This becomes more important as the size and complexity of your graphics increase. Here is a random collection of cylinders in 3-space, first using symbolic coordinates:

```
In[40]:= pts =
           RandomChoice[Join[Range[8], {1/2, √2/2, √3/2, 1/2 (1 - √5)}], {100, 3}];
         pairs = Partition[pts, 2];
```

```
In[41]:= cylinders = Graphics3D[{Opacity[.5], EdgeForm[Blue],
             FaceForm[LightBlue], Map[Cylinder[#, .2] &, pairs]}] // Timing
```

Out[42]= {0.000102, 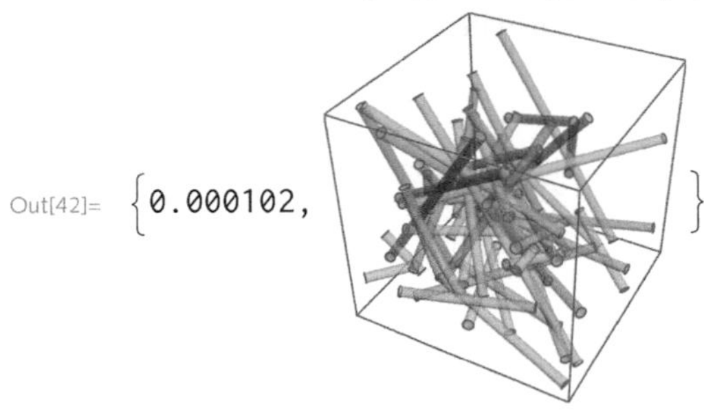 }

```
In[43]:= ByteCount[cylinders]
Out[43]= 37600
```

Here is the same graphic but using numerical coordinates only:

```
In[44]:= npairs = N@pairs;
         cylindersN = Graphics3D[{Opacity[.5], EdgeForm[Blue],
             FaceForm[LightBlue], Map[Cylinder[#, .2] &, npairs]}] // Timing
```

Out[45]= {0.000039, 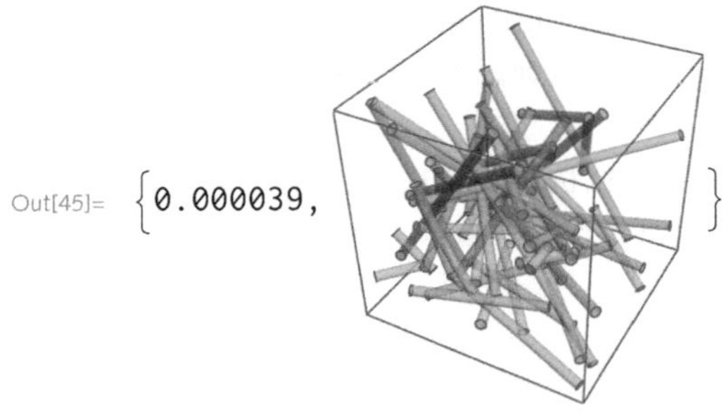 }

```
In[46]:= ByteCount[cylindersN]
Out[46]= 18808
```

The version using numerical approximations for the coordinates is half the size of the exact version. Also, the time to render the graphic is about two to three times as fast from the kernel's perspective, and about twice as fast for the front end (you could use a similar approach to that in the previous section, where we used `SessionTime`). This is mostly a result of not having to carry around all that extra information with the exact coordinates. Of course, if your graphical expression is highly dependent upon exact/symbolic expressions, then these suggestions might be moot. In that case, using either `GraphicsComplex` and/or multi-objects should make the representation more efficient.

Exercises

1. Create a hexagonal grid of polygons like that in Figure 8.6. First create the grid by performing appropriate translations using `Translate` or the geometric transformation `TranslationTransform`. Compare this approach with a multi-polygon approach.

FIGURE 8.6. *Two-dimensional hexagonal lattice.*

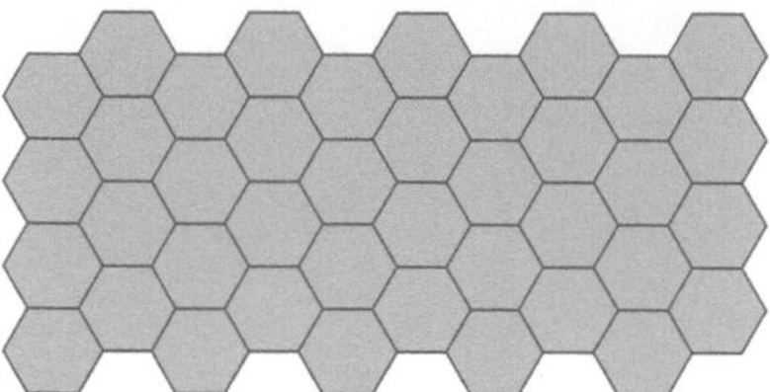

2. Take the example visualizing a 500 000-step random walk at the beginning of this section and replicate the output using `GraphicsComplex` instead of `ListLinePlot`. Compare the running times for each as the number of steps increases.

3. The `ShowWalk` function discussed in Section 4.1 for displaying random walks uses `ListLinePlot` to display the data. As mentioned in this section, `ListLinePlot` will get bogged down for large numbers of points. Using the solution to the previous exercise, create a new version for both the two- and three-dimensional cases of `ShowWalk` that uses `GraphicsComplex` instead; then test the new implementation against the one developed in Chapter 4.

4. Create a graphic consisting of a three-dimensional lattice, that is, lines passing through the integer coordinates in 3-space (Figure 8.7). Compare approaches that use multi-lines as opposed to those that do not.

FIGURE 8.7. *Three-dimensional integer lattice.*

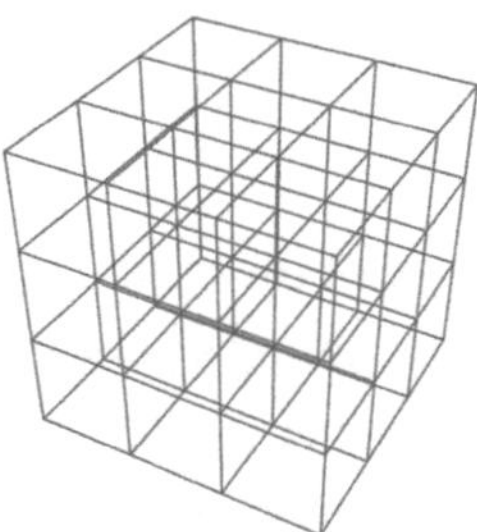

5. A common problem in computational geometry is finding the boundary of a given set of points in the plane. One way to think about the boundary is to imagine the points as nails in a board and then to stretch a rubber band around all the nails. The stretched rubber band lies on a convex polygon commonly called the *convex hull* of the point set.

   Create a function `ConvexHullPlot` for visualizing the convex hull together with the points on the interior of the convex hull. Your function should inherit options for `Graphics`. The built-in function `ConvexHullMesh` can be used to generate the hull polygon:

```
In[1]:= pts = RandomReal[1, {28, 2}];
        ℛ = ConvexHullMesh[pts]
```

Out[2]=

The zero-dimensional objects in the mesh are points and the one-dimensional objects are lines (two-dimensional objects would be polygons). These are the points and lines on the convex hull.

```
In[3]:= MeshPrimitives[ℛ, 0];
        Take[%, 2]

Out[4]= {Point[{0.992746, 0.379391}], Point[{0.0394433, 0.0418121}]}

In[5]:= MeshPrimitives[ℛ, 1];
        Take[%, 2]

Out[6]= {Line[{{0.0383976, 0.960283}, {0.0394433, 0.0418121}}],
         Line[{{0.0394433, 0.0418121}, {0.225102, 0.00814885}}]}
```

Your function should generate output similar to the following:

```
In[7]:= ConvexHullPlot[pts, Axes → Automatic]
```

Out[7]=

0.8
0.6
0.4
0.2
0.2 0.4 0.6 0.8 1.0

6. Modify `ConvexHullPlot` from Exercise 5 to accept an option `Dimension`. With default value of two, `ConvexHullPlot` should produce output like that in Exercise 5. For `Dimension → 3`, it should generate the convex hull together with large red points at each vertex of the hull (Figure 8.8).

FIGURE 8.8. *Three-dimensional convex hull with hull points highlighted.*

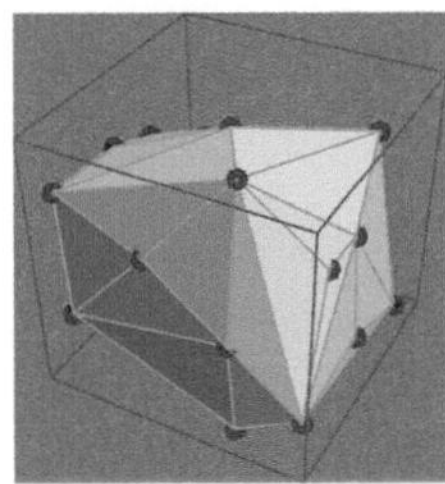

7. Extend Exercise 7 from Section 8.1 to random walks on the base-n digits of π. For example, in base 3, a 1 corresponds to an angle of 120° from the current position, 2 corresponds to 240°, and 0 to 360°. In base 4 the step angles will be multiples of 90° and in general, for base n, the step angles will be multiples of $360\,°/n$. Use `GraphicsComplex` to visualize the walks. Include a color function that depends on the length of the walk.

8.4 Examples

Up until this point, we have constructed relatively simple graphical objects in *Mathematica* using the graphics building blocks – primitives, directives, and options. We now turn to problems that are more involved or whose solution requires geometric insight as we construct our programs. We will not restrict our programs to those only constructed from graphics primitives, but will also build upon and modify some of the built-in functions for our purposes here.

We begin with four problems that use built-in functions in order to take advantage of established algorithms for computation and options for formatting and styling: root plotting, constructing Venn diagrams of logical expressions, protein dot plots for comparing protein and nucleotide sequences, and a visualization of hypocycloids. The last four examples involve building functions from primitive graphics elements: creating space-filling plots for proteins and other chemicals, finding simple closed paths through a set of data, determining if a point lies inside or outside of a polygon, and visualizing triangle centers.

Root plots

Whenever you write programs, one of the decisions that you need to make is whether to build your solution from scratch or to use some built-in constructs to solve your problem. This decision can only be made on a case-by-case basis. In this example we will make modifications to existing visualization functions as they provide a quick and sufficient solution.

In this problem we will plot a function together with all its roots in a given interval. Finding all the roots of a real-valued function on an interval is made straightforward by using the meshing algorithms built into `Plot` to extract and plot those roots on the horizontal axis. The advantage is that these options do a lot of the computational work that can be harnessed for our purposes here.

We will prototype with the sinc function as it has numerous roots in the interval below.

```
In[1]:= Plot[Sinc[x], {x, -10, 10}]
```

Out[1]=

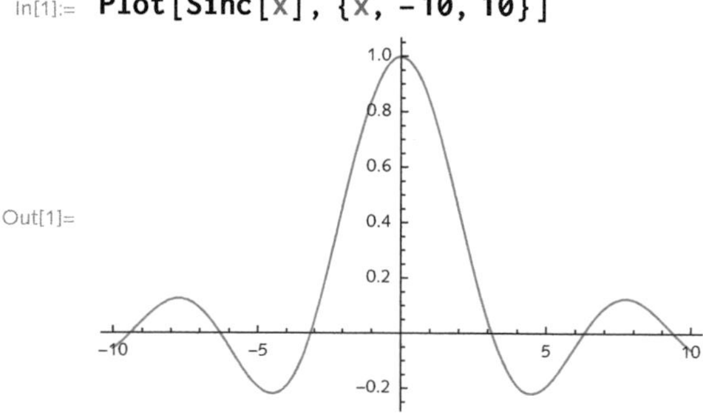

The key observation is this: two-dimensional plotting functions like `Plot` mesh their curves using points as the mesh objects; if you set the option `Mesh → All` in the above plot, you will see all the points used to construct the curve. Setting `Mesh` to `{{0.0}}` creates only mesh points at height 0.0, that is, on the horizontal axis. `MeshFunctions` should be given a value that places the mesh points on the curve itself.

```
In[2]:= Plot[Sinc[z], {z, -10, 10}, Mesh → {{0.0}},
         MeshFunctions → {Sinc[x] /. x → # &},
         MeshStyle → {Red, PointSize[Medium]}]
```

Out[2]=

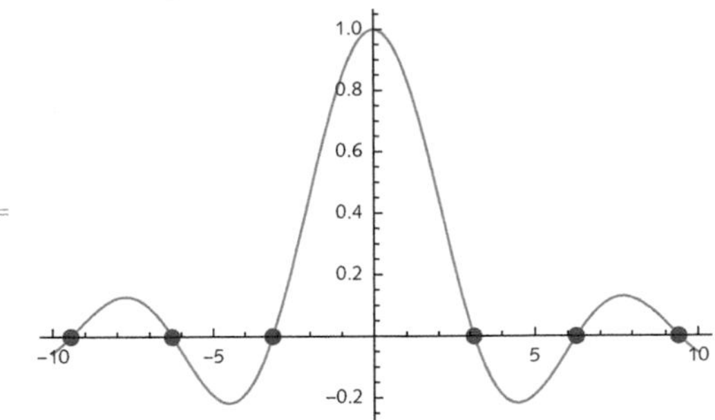

As a first step in creating the function RootPlot, set its options to inherit all those from Plot.

```
In[3]:= Options[RootPlot] = Options[Plot];
```

Using OptionsPattern after the required arguments indicates that the argument structure of RootPlot may include options following the required arguments. The set of options is given a name, opts, and used inside of Plot, where we want any optional arguments to be. As noted previously, it is important to put opts before any explicitly given options as *Mathematica* will only honor the first occurrence of an option if it occurs more than once.

```
In[4]:= RootPlot[fun_, {var_, varmin_, varmax_}, opts : OptionsPattern[]] :=
         Module[{f = fun},
          Plot[f, {var, varmin, varmax},
           opts,
           Mesh → {{0}}, MeshFunctions → {f /. var → # &},
           MeshStyle → {Red, PointSize[Medium]}]]
```

Let us now exercise some of the options on a more computationally complex function.

```
In[5]:= RootPlot[RiemannSiegelZ[z], {z, 1050, 1100},
          PlotStyle → Gray,
          MeshStyle → {Red, PointSize[Small]}] // Timing
```

Out[5]= {0.342027, }

Exercise 3 at the end of this section asks you to use Mesh in a similar manner to find and display curves of intersection for two surfaces in 3-space.

Tip 8.2

An alternative syntax for using directives in graphics is to enclose them in the `Directive` wrapper. This makes it a bit cleaner to use composite directives and to specify them for multiple expressions that you might be plotting. So, the above plot could also be written as follows:

```
In[6]:= RootPlot[RiemannSiegelZ[z], {z, 1050, 1100}, PlotStyle → Gray,
          MeshStyle → Directive[Red, PointSize[Small]]];
```

Venn diagrams

Venn diagrams are used to describe all possible logical relations between different sets. Many people first encounter them in elementary set theory or when learning about basic relationships in probability theory and computer science. In this example, we will create a visualization of the basic logical operators using a Venn diagram on two sets. We will combine the functionality from a built-in function (`RegionPlot`) with some graphics primitives.

An outline of the plan is as follows: create two circles aligned vertically; place text identifying the sets *A* and *B*; use `RegionPlot` to display inequalities as regions inside these circles; use options to label the plot with the logical expression.

To start, create two circles *A* and *B* with the given centers `c1` and `c2` (the default radius for `Circle` is one).

```
In[7]:= c1 = {-.5, 0}; c2 = {.5, 0};
        Graphics[{Circle[c1], Circle[c2],
          Text["A", {-.5, .75}], Text["B", {.5, .75}]}]
```

Out[8]=

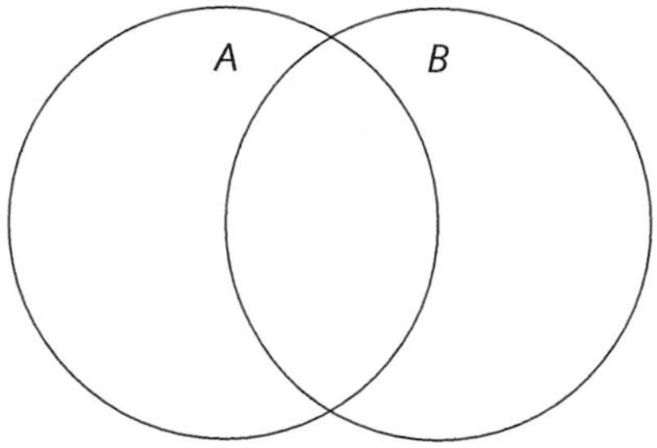

A B

We will prototype with the logical AND operator. The region representing $A \wedge B$ (that is, "*A* and *B*") consists of all those points common to *A* and *B*. By describing the regions as inequalities, `RegionPlot` can be used to display those regions.

```
In[9]:= regions = Apply[(x - #1)^2 + (y - #2)^2 < 1 &, {c1, c2}, {1}]
Out[9]= {(0.5 + x)^2 + y^2 < 1, (-0.5 + x)^2 + y^2 < 1}
```

```
In[10]:= RegionPlot[Apply[And, regions], {x, -1, 1}, {y, -1, 1}]
```

Out[10]=
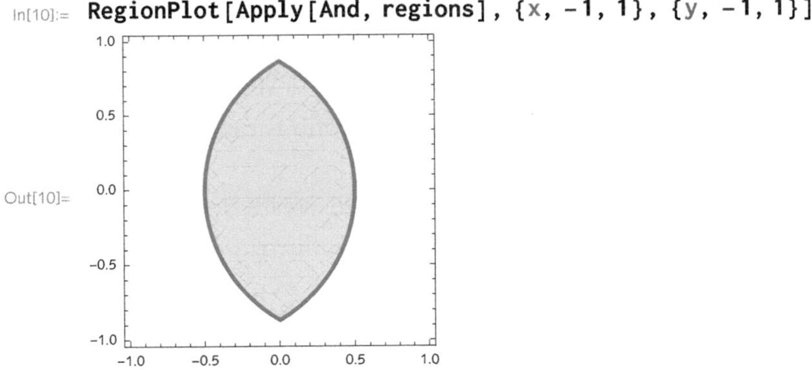

Putting the two graphics together, using an arbitrary logical function `f`, adjusting for plot ranges, and adding some labels, we have the following:

```
In[11]:= VennDiagram[f_, vars : {A_, B_}] :=
          Module[{regions, x, y, c1 = {-.5, 0}, c2 = {.5, 0}},
           regions = Apply[(x - #1)^2 + (y - #2)^2 < 1 &, {c1, c2}, {1}];
           Show[
            RegionPlot[Apply[f, regions], {x, -2, 2}, {y, -2, 2},
             Frame → True, FrameTicks → None, PlotLabel → f @@ vars,
             AspectRatio → Automatic, PlotRange → {{-2, 2}, {-1.2, 1.2}}],
            Graphics[{Circle[c1], Circle[c2],
              Text[First[vars], {-.5, .75}], Text[Last[vars], {.5, .75}]}]
           ]]

In[12]:= VennDiagram[Xor, {A, B}]
```

Out[12]=
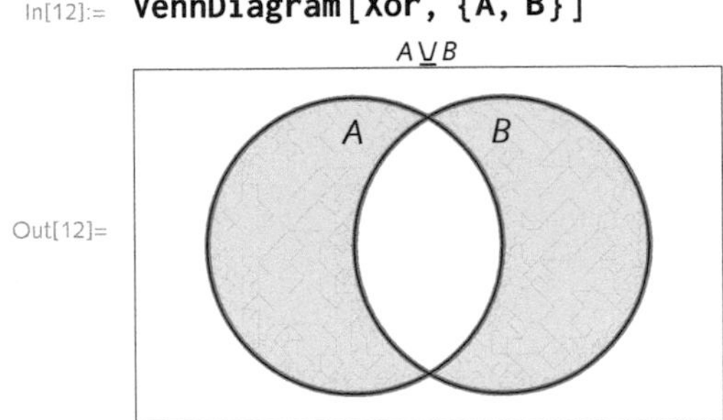

This is a very basic implementation. In the exercises you are asked to generalize `VennDiagram` to accept logical expressions of the form $A \Rightarrow B$, to create a version that does not need `Graphics` at all, and also to create a Venn diagram on three sets. Exercise 7 at the end of this section extends this to a dynamic visualization in which you can choose the operator to visualize by clicking a tab.

Dot plots

When studying the evolutionary changes of a protein or nucleic acid sequence within and across species, it is important to determine how similar two such sequences are. This is typically done using a similarity matrix called a dot plot. The idea is to compare two sequences, one along the vertical and the other along the horizontal axis of an array, coloring a cell black if the two amino acids (in the case of a protein) or nucleotides (in the case of a DNA or RNA molecule) are the same and white otherwise. If the sequences are identical, you would see a dark black line along the diagonal. With some analysis, insertions, deletions, and other alterations can be detected with the help of dot plots (Gibbs and Mcintyre 1970).

In this example we will use a built-in function, `ArrayPlot`, to create dot plots. We start by reading in two messenger RNA (mRNA) sequences of the Avian Influenza A virus, one infecting chickens, the other infecting ducks. These two fast-mutating strains were heavily studied during influenza outbreaks in the late 1990s to determine if a cross-species link could be established. The sequences are available from the National Center for Biotechnology Information (NCBI) website and also from the data files accompanying this book.

```
In[13]:= seq1 = First@Import["H5N1ChickenDQ023146.1.fasta"];
         seq2 = First@Import["H5N1DuckDQ232610.1.fasta"];
```

Here are the first six nucleotides in each sequence.

```
In[15]:= s1 = Characters@StringTake[seq1, 1 ;; 6]
         s2 = Characters@StringTake[seq2, 1 ;; 6]
Out[15]= {A, C, A, T, C, A}

Out[16]= {G, T, A, G, A, T}
```

In this alignment the third positions are identical. But in sequence alignments we are interested in all such matchings as a shift of one of the sequences may align better with the other. So we need all possible pairings and for this, `Outer` should be used. For example, the following similarity matrix shows that the first element in `s1` is the same as the third element is `s2`. Similarly, the fourth element in `s1` and the second element in `s2` are identical.

```
In[17]:= Outer[Equal, s1, s2] // MatrixForm
Out[17]//MatrixForm=
  False False True  False True  False
  False False False False False False
  False False True  False True  False
  False True  False False False True
  False False False False False False
  False False True  False True  False
```

To turn these `True`/`False` values into something `ArrayPlot` can use, we use `Boole` to convert to zeros and ones.

```
In[18]:= Boole[%]
Out[18]= {{0, 0, 1, 0, 1, 0}, {0, 0, 0, 0, 0, 0}, {0, 0, 1, 0, 1, 0},
          {0, 1, 0, 0, 0, 1}, {0, 0, 0, 0, 0, 0}, {0, 0, 1, 0, 1, 0}}
```

```
In[19]:= ArrayPlot[%]
```

Out[19]=

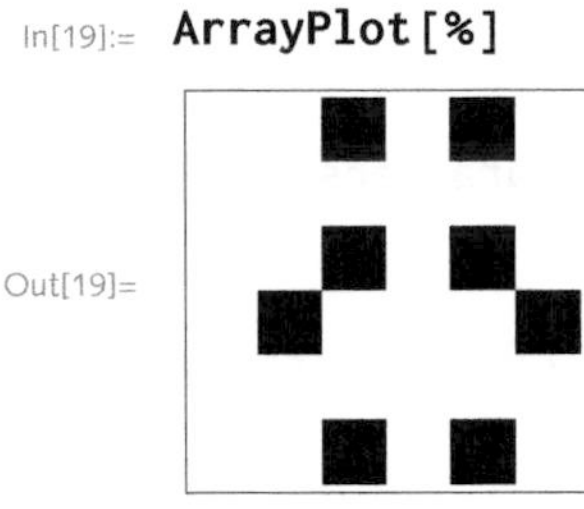

We are ready to put the parts together to make a reusable function, trying it out on the full sequences. Here we are taking `Outer` of `Boole[...]` whereas above we had `Boole[Outer[...]]`. Both work in this case.

```
In[20]:= ArrayPlot[Outer[Boole[#1 == #2] &, Characters[seq1], Characters[seq2]]]
```

Out[20]=

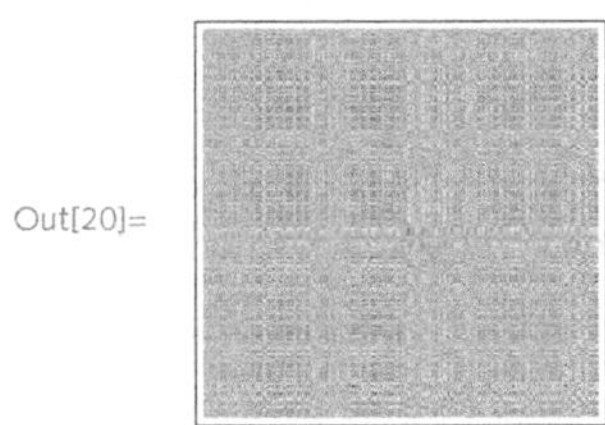

Let's add labels along the vertical and horizontal axes identifying the two sequences. `FrameLabel` requires the `Frame` option to be turned on. Here then is our dot plot function:

```
In[21]:= DotPlot[s1_, s2_, {name1_String, name2_String}] :=
          ArrayPlot[Outer[Boole[#1 == #2] &, Characters[s1], Characters[s2]],
           Frame → True, FrameLabel → {name1, name2}]
```

We will use the FASTA accession numbers to label these sequences.

```
In[22]:= label1 = First@Import["H5N1DuckDQ232610.1.fasta", {"FASTA", "Accession"}]
Out[22]= DQ232610.1

In[23]:= label2 = First@Import["H5N1ChickenDQ023146.1.fasta", {"FASTA", "Accession"}]
Out[23]= DQ023146.1

In[24]:= DotPlot[seq1, seq2, {label1, label2}]
```

Out[24]=

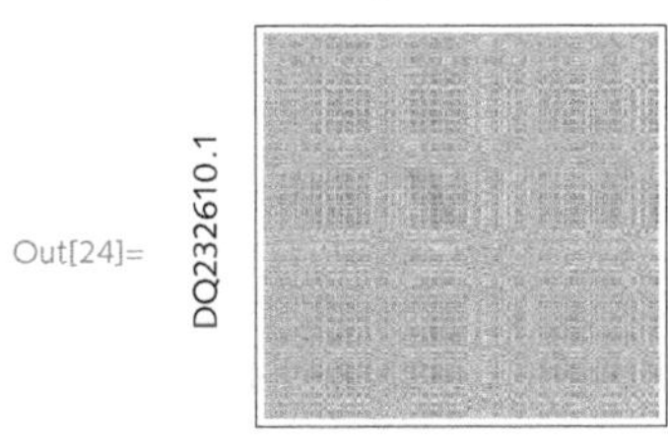

Finally, let's add a few options to `ArrayPlot` to set the frame and labels.

```
In[25]:= DotPlot[p1_, p2_, {name1_String, name2_String},
           opts : OptionsPattern[ArrayPlot]] :=
          ArrayPlot[Outer[Boole[#1 == #2] &, Characters[p1], Characters[p2]],
           opts, Frame → True, FrameLabel → {name1, name2}]
```

```
In[26]:= DotPlot[seq1, seq2, {label1, label2}, ColorRules → {1 → Red, 0 → White}]
```

Out[26]=

DQ232610.1

DQ023146.1

Sequences that are nearly identical will show a line down the diagonal. In the above dot plot, there appear to be many matches off the diagonal, but this is to be expected for a small alphabet (A, T, G, C) and relatively short sequences. This "noise" can be reduced by changing the *window size* – consider a match only if sequences of length two or three (or any number greater than one) match.

Another limitation of `DotPlot` as coded above is the hard-wiring of the `Frame` and `FrameLabel` options. Exercise 8 at the end of this section asks you to modify the options framework for this function to include an option for window size together with inheriting options from `ArrayPlot`.

Hypocycloids

Hypocycloids are curves generated by following a fixed point on a smaller circle rolling around the inside of a larger circle (Figure 8.9). In what follows, we will combine graphics primitives and directives together with a built-in graphics function to create a visualization of hypocycloids.

FIGURE 8.9. *Hypocycloid generated by rolling a smaller circle inside a larger circle.*

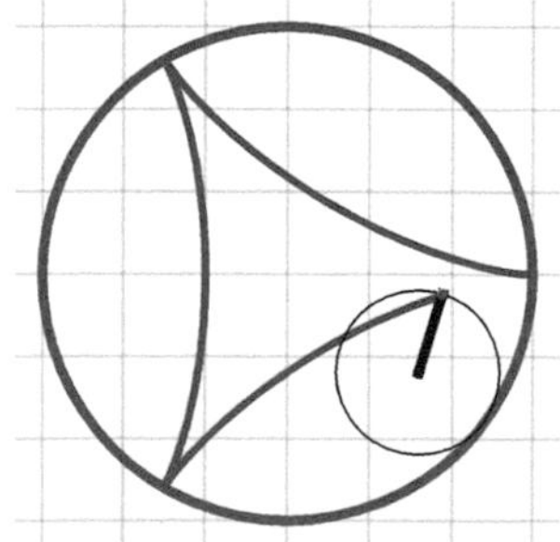

The formula for a hypocycloid is given parametrically by the following, where r is the radius of the smaller circle and R is the radius of the larger circle:

```
In[27]:= Hypocycloid[{a_, b_}, θ_] :=
          {(a - b) Cos[θ] + b Cos[θ (a - b)/b], (a - b) Sin[θ] - b Sin[θ (a - b)/b]}
```

$$\left\{(a-b)\,\mathrm{Cos}[\theta] + b\,\mathrm{Cos}\left[\theta\,\frac{a-b}{b}\right],\ (a-b)\,\mathrm{Sin}[\theta] - b\,\mathrm{Sin}\left[\theta\,\frac{a-b}{b}\right]\right\}$$

```
In[28]:= Hypocycloid[{R, r}, θ] // TraditionalForm
```

Out[28]//TraditionalForm=

$$\left\{\cos(\theta)\,(R-r)+r\cos\left(\frac{\theta\,(R-r)}{r}\right),\ \sin(\theta)\,(R-r)-r\sin\left(\frac{\theta\,(R-r)}{r}\right)\right\}$$

Here is a plot of the curve for various values of the two radii, where the ratio R/r is an integer:

```
In[29]:= Table[
          ParametricPlot[Hypocycloid[{R, 1}, θ], {θ, 0, 2π}, Axes → None],
          {R, 3, 7, 1}]
```

Out[29]= { , , , , }

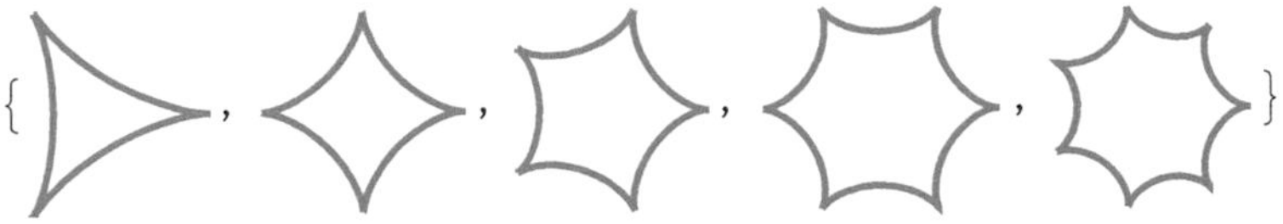

And here are some curves for rational, noninteger values of R/r:

```
In[30]:= Table[ParametricPlot[Hypocycloid[{R, 1}, θ],
           {θ, 0, 2 Denominator[R] π}, Axes → None], {R, {3/2, 5/3, 7/2, 13/5, 21/13}}]
```

Out[30]= { , , , , }

In fact, the curve only closes up when the ratio R/r is an integer or a rational number (see Maor 1998 or visit the *MathWorld* page on hypocycloids – Weisstein, Hypocycloid).

To create the graphic shown in Figure 8.9, we need to include the following pieces: inner and outer circles, radius of inner circle, point on inner circle used to sketch curve, the hypocycloid curve itself. We will fix the two radii for the purposes of developing the code and then make them parameters that can be set by the user when the code is ready. Here is the outer circle, thick and blue:

```
In[31]:= With[{R = 3, r = 1},
          Graphics[{Thick, Blue, Circle[{0, 0}, R]}]
         ]
```

Out[31]=

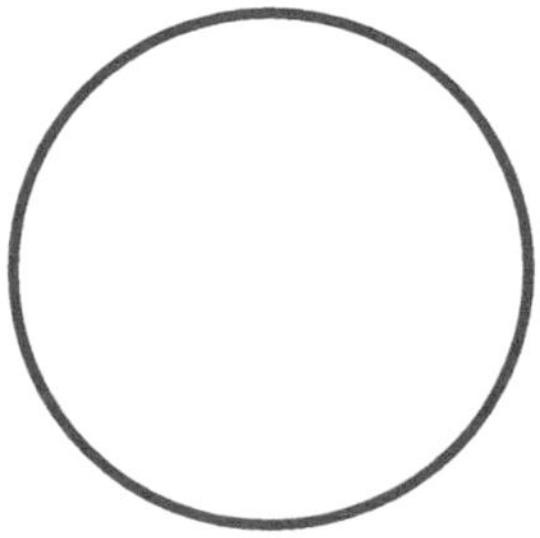

To draw the smaller inner circle, we first need to know its center. This will change as the smaller circle rotates around. In fact, it is dependent upon the parameter θ and is given by the following:

```
In[32]:= center[θ_, R_, r_] := (R - r) {Cos[θ], Sin[θ]}
```

Here then are the two circles together, with the smaller circle given with a fixed (for now) center set by the angle θ:

```
In[33]:= With[{θ = π / 6, R = 3, r = 1},
          Graphics[{
            {Thick, Blue, Circle[{0, 0}, R]},
            {Circle[center[θ, R, r], r]}
          }]]
```

Out[33]=

We know where the center of the smaller circle is, so let's draw a point there together with a thick line from the center to the hypocycloid. Also we include a red point that shows the fixed point on the smaller circle that will trace out the hypocycloid as the angle θ changes.

```
In[34]:= With[{θ = π/6, R = 3, r = 1}, Graphics[{
            {Thick, Blue, Circle[{0, 0}, R]},
            {Circle[center[θ, R, r], r]},
            {PointSize[.015], Point[center[θ, R, r]]},
            {Thick, Line[{center[θ, R, r], Hypocycloid[{R, r}, θ]}]},
            {Red, PointSize[.02], Point[Hypocycloid[{R, r}, θ]]}
          }]]
```

Out[34]=

Of course we want to include the hypocycloid itself, from zero to θ. We will combine a parametric plot of the curve with the graphics primitives we have developed so far. Because the plot ranges are quite different for the `ParametricPlot[...]` and the `Graphics[...]` pieces of the code, we need to add `PlotRange → All` as an option to the entire graphic, that is, as part of `Show`.

```
In[35]:= With[{θ = π / 6, R = 3, r = 1},
           Show[{
             ParametricPlot[Hypocycloid[{R, r}, t],
              {t, 0, θ}, PlotStyle → Red, Axes → None],
             Graphics[{
               {Thick, Blue, Circle[{0, 0}, R]},
               {Circle[center[θ, R, r], r]},
               {PointSize[.015], Point[center[θ, R, r]]},
               {Thick, Line[{center[θ, R, r], Hypocycloid[{R, r}, θ]}]},
               {Red, PointSize[.015], Point[Hypocycloid[{R, r}, θ]]}
             }]
           }, PlotRange → All, GridLines → Automatic]];
```

Finally, using `Hypocycloid` as defined above, we put all the pieces together in the function `HypocycloidPlot` and then sketch out the entire curve by having θ range from 0 to 2π.

```
In[36]:= HypocycloidPlot[R_, r_, θ_] := Module[{center},
          center[th_, R1_, r2_] := (R1 - r2) {Cos[th], Sin[th]};

          Show[{
            ParametricPlot[Hypocycloid[{R, r}, t],
             {t, 0, θ}, PlotStyle → Red, Axes → None],

            Graphics[
             {{Blue, Thick, Circle[{0, 0}, R]}, {Circle[center[θ, R, r], r]},
              {PointSize[.02], Point[center[θ, R, r]]},
              {Thick, Line[{center[θ, R, r], Hypocycloid[{R, r}, θ]}]},
              {Red, PointSize[.02], Point[Hypocycloid[{R, r}, θ]]}}]

          }, PlotRange → All, GridLines → Automatic]]

In[37]:= HypocycloidPlot[3, 1, 2 π]

Out[37]=
```

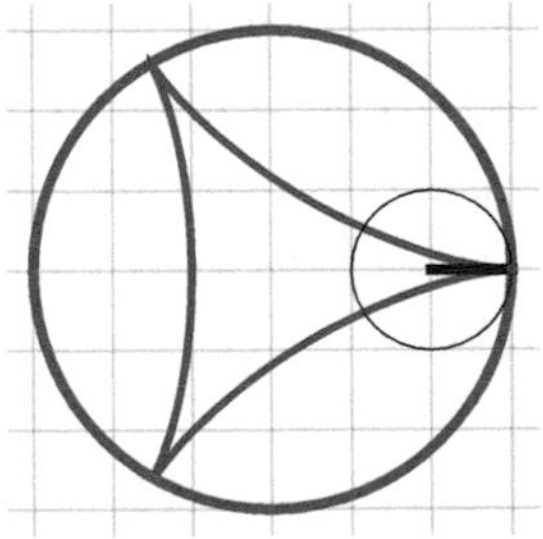

This hypocycloid example is a good candidate for a dynamic interface: the phenomenon it describes involves varying a parameter (the angle θ) that causes more and more of the curve to be sketched out.

Inside the `Manipulate` interface, we would like a control for each of the two radii. The syntax of the parameter list `{R, {3, 4, 5, 6, 7, 8}, Setter}` specifies `R` as the parameter that can take on the values {3, 4, 5, 6, 7, 8} with a control consisting of a setter button to select the different radii. Also, with a little mathematics, you should find that the number of rotations until the curve closes up is given by `2 π Denominator[(R - r) / r]`, although you may need to be careful if `R / r` is irrational as the curve will never close up in that case!

```
In[38]:= Manipulate[
           HypocycloidPlot[R, r, θ],
           {{θ, 1}, 0, 2 π Denominator[(R - r) / r]},
           {R, {3, 4, 5, 6, 7, 8}, Setter},
           {r, {1, 2, 3, 4, 5}, Setter}, SaveDefinitions → True]
```

Out[38]=

θ
R 3 4 5 6 7 8
r 1 2 3 4 5

It might not be obvious, but there is a small problem: at $\theta = 0$ the `ParametricPlot` starts off ranging from zero to zero, which returns an error. It might be easiest to have the animation start just a little past zero, say at 0.01.

```
In[39]:= Manipulate[
            HypocycloidPlot[R, r, θ],
            {θ, 0 + 0.01, 2 π Denominator[(R - r) / r]},
            {R, {3, 4, 5, 6, 7, 8}, Setter},
            {r, {1, 2, 3, 4, 5}, Setter}];
```

There is one additional issue that may arise: when the radius *r* of the inner circle is larger than the radius *R* of the outer circle. In this case, the graphic will bounce around a bit as different plot ranges are computed for these radii values. In Exercise 10 at the end of this section you are asked to deal with this problem. Exercise 11 asks you to create a dynamic interface for epicycloids, curves that are generated by rolling a smaller circle around the *outside* of a larger circle.

Space-filling plots

Our next graphics example uses three-dimensional graphics primitives to construct a visualization of molecular structures. The built-in data collection `ChemicalData` contains a property for generating these plots – `"SpaceFillingMoleculePlot"` – but you cannot use this with other objects such as a protein or any object not in `ChemicalData`.

```
In[40]:= ChemicalData["AceticAcid", "SpaceFillingMoleculePlot"]
```

Out[40]=

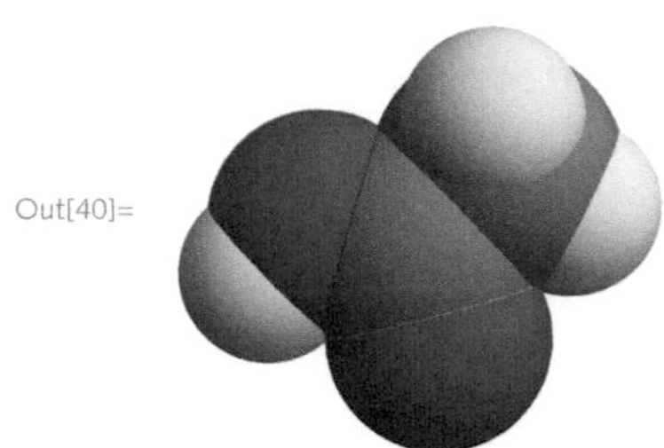

We will create a function that takes any file that includes the appropriate molecular information and output a space-filling plot like that above. The information needed to construct such a plot for any given molecule is:

- the positions in space of each atom;
- the radius of each atom;
- the color for each atom.

These data can come from a variety of places. For our purposes, we will combine several different sources: information imported from a structure data file (SDF) together with `ElementData` and `ColorData`, data collections built into *Mathematica*.

Let's start by importing an SDF file for the neurotransmitter serotonin that we have downloaded from the Open Chemistry Database (National Center for Biotechnology Information 2015).

```
In[41]:= Import["5hydroxytryptamine.sdf", "Elements"]
Out[41]= {EdgeRules, EdgeTypes, FormalCharges, Graphics3D, Header, MassNumbers,
          Metadata, StructureDiagram, VertexCoordinates, VertexTypes}
```

The list of atoms is given by the `"VertexTypes"` property for the SDF format.

```
In[42]:= atoms = First@Import["5hydroxytryptamine.sdf", "VertexTypes"]
Out[42]= {O, N, N, C, C, C, C, C, C, C, C, C, C, H, H, H, H, H, H, H, H, H, H, H, H}
```

Their positions in space are given by `"VertexCoordinates"`.

```
In[43]:= positions = First@Import["5hydroxytryptamine.sdf", "VertexCoordinates"]
Out[43]= {{273.52, 246.2, 9.75}, {11.21, -234.78, -11.23}, {-424.02, 156.78, -28.8},
          {-118.57, -60.4, 33.72}, {14.87, -13.61, 17.81}, {-237.44, 21.67, 64.4},
          {94.28, -124.99, -10.3}, {-117.61, -196.73, 15.23}, {-308.73, 73.69, -61.78},
          {75.91, 113.2, 24.66}, {232.23, -115.86, -31.98}, {213.79, 123.86, 3.2},
          {290.57, 10.96, -24.68}, {-308.28, -37.36, 124.06}, {-208.42, 106.54, 127.69},
          {-196.88, -270.18, 18.46}, {41.09, -329.68, -28.95},
          {-342.25, -10.74, -123.12}, {-238.88, 132.12, -122.84},
          {16.35, 201.49, 46.25}, {292.07, -203.71, -53.68}, {397.62, 20.86, -41.11},
          {-464.55, 193.95, -114.61}, {-393.63, 237.34, 25.74}, {206.01, 313.24, 29.95}}
```

The van der Waals radius of any atom is the radius of an imaginary sphere circumscribed about the atom. It has been computed for many atoms (not all) and is built into *Mathematica* via `ElementData`.

The units are picometers, where 1 pm = 10^{-12} m = 10^{-2} Å (ångströms). Atoms typically have radii in the range 60–520 pm, or 0.6–5.2 Å.

```
In[44]:= radii = Map[ElementData[#, "VanDerWaalsRadius"] &, atoms]

Out[44]= {152. pm , 155. pm , 155. pm , 170. pm , 170. pm , 170. pm ,
  170. pm , 170. pm , 170. pm , 170. pm , 170. pm , 170. pm ,
  170. pm , 120. pm , 120. pm , 120. pm , 120. pm , 120. pm , 120. pm ,
  120. pm , 120. pm , 120. pm , 120. pm , 120. pm , 120. pm }
```

We will need the raw values, stripped of their units. These will be the radii passed to Sphere.

```
In[45]:= rad = QuantityMagnitude@radii

Out[45]= {152., 155., 155., 170., 170., 170., 170., 170., 170., 170., 170., 170., 170.,
  120., 120., 120., 120., 120., 120., 120., 120., 120., 120., 120., 120.}
```

A commonly used color scheme for atoms was developed in the 1950s and 1960s by Corey, Pauling, and later Koltun, known as the CPK model. It is built into *Mathematica* via ColorData.

```
In[46]:= colors = Map[ColorData["Atoms", #] &, atoms]

Out[46]= {■, ■, ■, ■, ■, ■, ■, ■, ■, ■, ■,
  ■, ■, □, □, □, □, □, □, □, □, □, □, □, □}
```

We now have three lists: colors, positions, and radii that we will slot into a list of the form {*color*, Sphere[*pos*, *radius*]} for each atom. We use MapThread, where #1 pulls an element from the first list, colors; #2 pulls an element from the second list, positions; and #3 pulls an element from the third list, rad.

Here is an image using the information we have so far:

```
In[47]:= Graphics3D[{
   MapThread[{#1, Sphere[#2, #3]} &, {colors, positions, rad}]
  }]

Out[47]=
```

This is the basic structure we need. Next we add some directives and options to modify the overall plot. The Specularity directive gives control over the reflection of the lights. Setting the Lighting option to "Neutral" sets the light sources used to illuminate the object to be white in color.

```
In[48]:= Graphics3D[{Specularity[White, 40],
           MapThread[{#1, Sphere[#2, #3]} &, {colors, positions, rad}]
          }, Lighting → "Neutral"]
```

Out[48]=

Putting all these pieces together, here is the function `ChemicalSpaceFillingPlot`. It is dependent upon `ElementData` for the atomic data and `ColorData` for the atom colors. If you have other sources that you are drawing from, you will have to modify it accordingly.

```
In[49]:= ChemicalSpaceFillingPlot[file_String] :=
          Module[{pos, elements, radii, colors},
           {pos, elements} =
            Map[First, Import[file, {{"VertexCoordinates", "VertexTypes"}}]];
           radii = QuantityMagnitude[
             Map[ElementData[#, "VanDerWaalsRadius"] &, elements]];
           colors = Map[ColorData["Atoms", #] &, elements];
           Graphics3D[{Specularity[White, 50],
             MapThread[{#1, Sphere[#2, #3]} &, {colors, pos, radii}]
            }, Lighting → "Neutral"]]
```

Try it out on an amino acid, l-tryptophan (downloaded from the National Institute of Health).

```
In[50]:= ChemicalSpaceFillingPlot["ltryptophan.sdf"]
```

Out[50]=

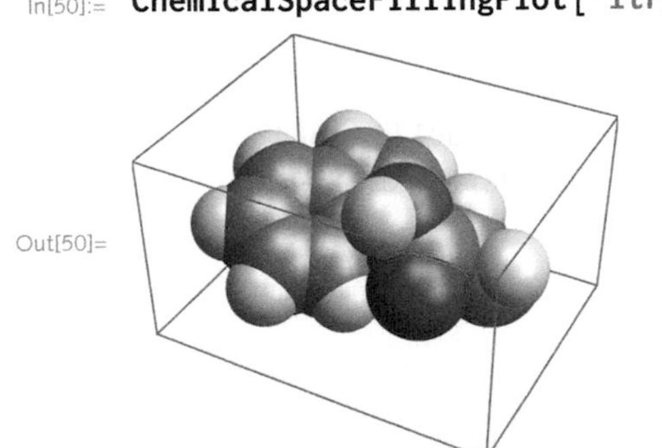

We could go further with this function and add legends giving identifying information for each atomic element, add a plot label, and do some argument checking to make sure the file to be imported is available and of the right type. These are left to the reader in Exercise 15 at the end of this section.

Simple closed paths

Our next example solves a very basic variation of what are known as *traveling salesman problems*. The traveling salesman problem asks for the *shortest* closed path that connects an arbitrary set of points. The traveling salesman problem is one of great theoretical, as well as practical, importance. Airline routing and power transmission line placement over large regions are examples of problems that could benefit from a solution to the traveling salesman problem.

Our focus will be on a variation that is a substantial simplification of the traveling salesman problem. We will find a *simple closed path* through a set of n points. For a given set of points, a *closed path* is one that travels to every point and returns to the starting point; the path is *simple* if it does not intersect itself. Our path will visit every point but in general it will not be the shortest such path. Figure 8.10 displays a simple closed path through fifteen points chosen at random in the plane.

FIGURE 8.10. *A simple closed path for fifteen points.*

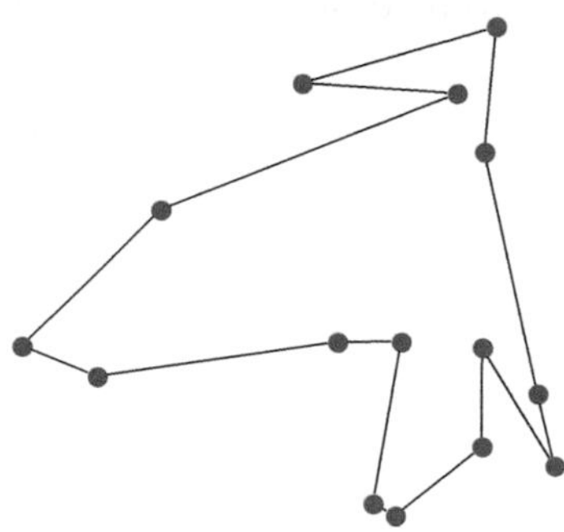

To solve the problem we will prototype with a small set of points and then generalize to point sets of arbitrary size. Let us first create a set of ten pairs of points in the unit square.

```
In[51]:= SeedRandom[1234];
         coords = RandomReal[1, {10, 2}]
Out[52]= {{0.876608, 0.521964}, {0.0862234, 0.377913},
          {0.0116446, 0.927266}, {0.543757, 0.479332},
          {0.245349, 0.759896}, {0.984993, 0.217045}, {0.459017, 0.884729},
          {0.583854, 0.263973}, {0.91956, 0.423835}, {0.98729, 0.587943}}
```

Here is a first attempt to visualize a path through the points:

```
In[53]:= Graphics[Line[coords]]
Out[53]=
```

There are two problems: first, the "path" is not simple in that it crosses itself; second, the path is not closed. We can solve the second problem using a transformation rule, in a manner similar to that with the Perimeter function developed in Section 4.3. Here is a function that takes a list of coordinates, colors them red, and passes a line through them, appending the first point to the end of the list to close up the path.

```
In[54]:= PathPlot[coords_List] := Graphics[{
           Line[coords /. {a_, b__} :→ {a, b, a}],
           PointSize[Medium], Red, Point[coords]
          }]
```

```
In[55]:= PathPlot[coords]
```

Out[55]=

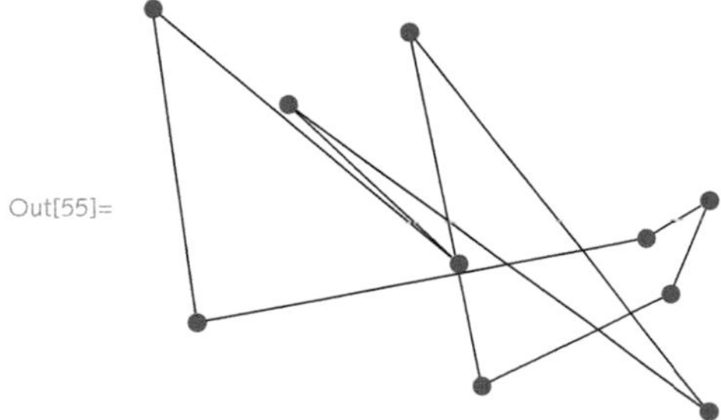

A simple path is one that does not cross itself. Merely taking the coordinates in the order in which they are given is not going to work here. Finding an ordering of the points such that a simple closed path results is geometric in nature. To develop an algorithm that insures our path does not cross itself for *any* set of points in the plane, we will implement the following plan: first, we will pick a base point and then compute the counterclockwise (polar) angle between a horizontal line and each of the other points, using the base point as the vertex of the angle (Figure 8.11). Then, sorting the points according to this angle and connecting the points in this order should give a path that does not cross itself and is closed.

To start, pick a point from our set at random and call this the *base* point.

```
In[56]:= base = RandomChoice[coords]
Out[56]= {0.0862234, 0.377913}
```

Next, we need to compute the polar angle between two points a and b (you should verify the trigonometry necessary to find this angle in the various cases).

```
In[57]:= angle[a_List, b_List] := Apply[ArcTan, (b - a)]
```

We will use this function to compute the polar angle between our base point and each of the points in the list coords. But we need to make sure that we do not compute the angle between the base point and itself as this will evaluate to ArcTan[0, 0], which is undefined. To avoid this case, we remove the base point from the list of coordinates when computing the angles.

```
In[58]:= remain = Complement[coords, {base}]
Out[58]= {{0.0116446, 0.927266}, {0.245349, 0.759896}, {0.459017, 0.884729},
  {0.543757, 0.479332}, {0.583854, 0.263973}, {0.876608, 0.521964},
  {0.91956, 0.423835}, {0.984993, 0.217045}, {0.98729, 0.587943}}
```

```
In[59]:= Map[angle[base, #] &, remain]
Out[59]= {1.70573, 1.17608, 0.936601, 0.218137,
  -0.225085, 0.180276, 0.0550508, -0.177111, 0.229001}
```

FIGURE 8.11. *Sorting points by polar angle.*

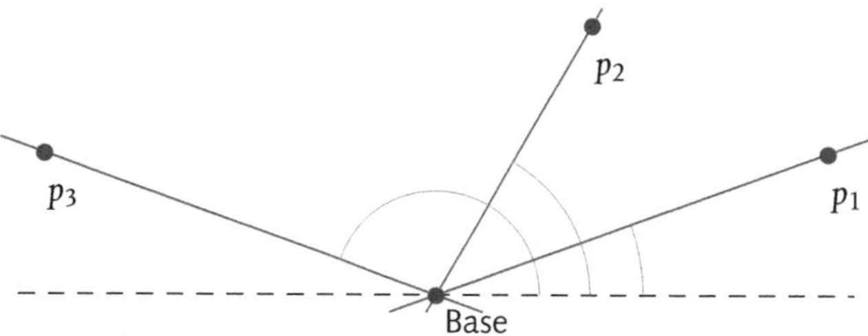

Now we need to sort the points according to their polar angles. `Sort[`*list*`,` *orderFun*`]` sorts *list* according to the ordering function *orderFun*, which, in the example below, is a two-argument predicate. We use the `angle` function to give an ordering on the list of coordinates by sorting on the angles between each point and the base point.

```
In[60]:= s = Sort[remain, angle[base, #1] ≤ angle[base, #2] &]
Out[60]= {{0.583854, 0.263973}, {0.984993, 0.217045}, {0.91956, 0.423835},
  {0.876608, 0.521964}, {0.543757, 0.479332}, {0.98729, 0.587943},
  {0.459017, 0.884729}, {0.245349, 0.759896}, {0.0116446, 0.927266}}
```

Finally, prepend the sorted list, `s`, with the base point.

```
In[61]:= path = Join[{base}, s]
Out[61]= {{0.0862234, 0.377913}, {0.583854, 0.263973},
  {0.984993, 0.217045}, {0.91956, 0.423835}, {0.876608, 0.521964},
  {0.543757, 0.479332}, {0.98729, 0.587943}, {0.459017, 0.884729},
  {0.245349, 0.759896}, {0.0116446, 0.927266}}
```

`PathPlot` defined above will close up the path by appending the first coordinate pair to the end of the list and then connecting every pair in the resulting list with a line.

```
In[62]:= PathPlot[path]
```

Out[62]=

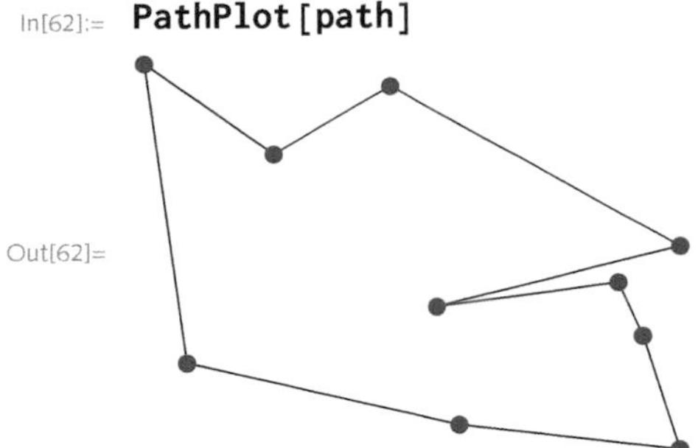

As an aside, this is not the *shortest* tour through the points, although it is close. In Figure 8.12, the shortest tour is on the right (obtained with `FindShortestTour`). Also note that solutions to the Traveling Salesman problem as given by `FindShortestTour` are not, in general, simple even though the one below right happens to be.

FIGURE 8.12. *Tours obtained with SimplePath (left) and with FindShortestTour (right).*

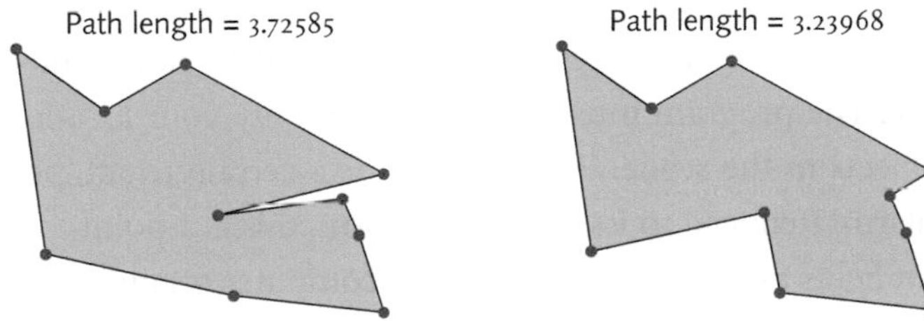

Collecting the above commands into a program, we have the following function, `SimplePath`:

```
In[63]:= SimplePath[lis_] := Module[{base, angle, sorted},
           base = RandomChoice[lis];
           angle[a_, b_] := Apply[ArcTan, b - a];
           sorted =
            Sort[Complement[lis, {base}], angle[base, #1] ≤ angle[base, #2] &];
           Join[{base}, sorted]]
```

Now we can create larger sets of points and find the corresponding simple closed paths.

```
In[64]:= data = RandomReal[1, {25, 2}];

In[65]:= PathPlot[SimplePath[data]]
```

Out[65]=

```
In[66]:= data = RandomReal[1, {100, 2}];

In[67]:= PathPlot[SimplePath[data]]

Out[67]=
```

Although this algorithm seems to work fairly well, there are certain conditions under which it will still fail. The exercises at the end of this section investigate some of those conditions and walk you through how best to improve the algorithm.

Points in a polygon

Imagine yourself a character in a video game in which the set of actions that befall you depend upon your location within the graphics scene. The program must determine not only your location but also where you are relative to other objects in the scene. If you are inside a certain room, perhaps the lighting model changes to reflect alarm. Reduced to its most basic form, this is a point-location problem and it has broad application in fields as varied as robot vision, computer graphics, motion sensing, and geographic information systems. We will look at a basic version of this problem: determining whether a point in the plane is inside a polygon. It is the basis of many algorithms in computational geometry and we will solve it first, by working with an idealized situation – convex polygons. The second implementation will be more general (and more involved), solving the problem for nonconvex polygons.

Convex polygons We start with a simplification of this problem, one in which the polygons are convex. A polygon is *convex* if any line segment connecting a pair of vertices is completely contained in the polygon; otherwise it is *concave* (Figure 8.13).

FIGURE 8.13. *Convex (left) and concave polygons.*

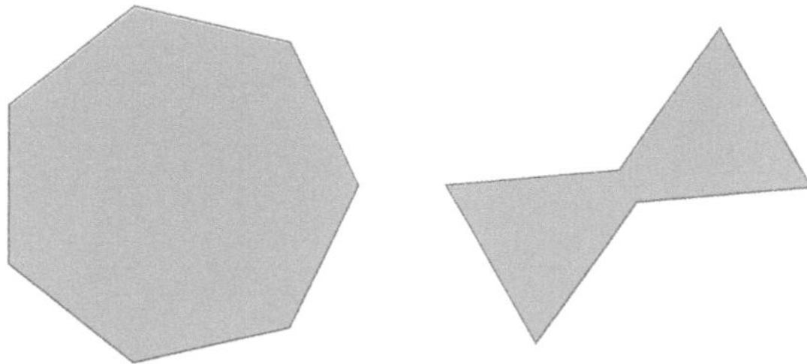

To solve the problem, we need one important fact: given a line determined by two points, (x_1, y_1), (x_2, y_2), a third point (x_3, y_3) is to the left of the other two if the triangle formed by these three points has positive area, where the signed area of a triangle is given by one-half of the determinant of the following 3×3 matrix:

$$\text{Area}_\triangle = \frac{1}{2}\begin{vmatrix} x_1 & y_1 & 1 \\ x_2 & y_2 & 1 \\ x_3 & y_3 & 1 \end{vmatrix}$$

We can check this with a simple example.

```
In[68]:= pt1 = {0, 0}; pt2 = {1, 1};
         ptL = {2 / 5, 4 / 5}; ptR = {4 / 5, 2 / 5};
```

```
In[70]:= Graphics[{
           Point[{pt1, pt2}], Line[{pt1, pt2}],
           Text["ptL", ptL, {0, -2}], Text["ptR", ptR, {0, -2}],
           Red, Point[{ptL, ptR}]
          }, Axes → Automatic]
```

Out[70]=

Fortunately, we have already programmed a function `SignedArea` in Section 4.3. It is included with the packages that accompany this book.

```
In[71]:= Needs["EPM`"]
```

```
In[72]:= SignedArea[Triangle[{pt1, pt2, ptL}]]
```

Out[72]= $\frac{1}{5}$

Now use `ptR` instead of `ptL`.

```
In[73]:= SignedArea[Triangle[{pt1, pt2, ptR}]]
```

Out[73]= $-\frac{1}{5}$

This negative quantity indicates that `ptR` is not to the left of the line formed by `pt1` and `pt2`. The following predicate returns a value of `True` if the given point is to the left of the other two:

```
In[74]:= leftOfQ[line : {a : {_, _}, b : {_, _}}, pt : {_, _}] :=
          SignedArea[Triangle[{a, b, pt}]] ≥ 0
```

```
In[75]:= Map[leftOfQ[{pt1, pt2}, #] &, {ptL, ptR}]
Out[75]= {True, False}
```

Now we are ready to answer the question posed at the beginning of this section: given a convex polygon and a point, how do you determine if that point is inside or outside the polygon (Figure 8.14)? The basic idea is to take each line segment making up the polygon (its edges) and determine if the given point is to the left of *each* segment. If the point is to the left of every edge as you travel from one edge to the next, then the point is inside the polygon.

FIGURE 8.14. *One point inside and one point outside a polygon.*

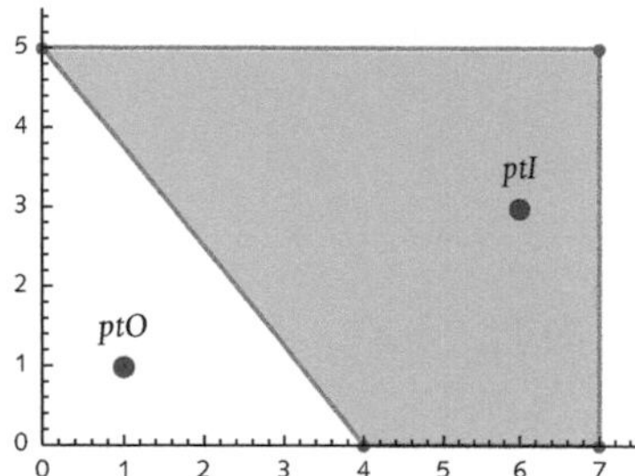

Partitioning that list of vertices of the polygon into pairs will give us the line segments we need. Note the need to use an overlap in the partition so that the last line consists of the last point paired with the first.

```
In[76]:= poly = {{4, 0}, {7, 0}, {7, 5}, {0, 5}};
         ptI = {6, 3};
         ptO = {1, 1};

In[78]:= lines = Partition[poly, 2, 1, 1]
Out[78]= {{{4, 0}, {7, 0}}, {{7, 0}, {7, 5}}, {{7, 5}, {0, 5}}, {{0, 5}, {4, 0}}}
```

Now map `leftOfQ` with `ptO` across these lines.

```
In[79]:= Map[leftOfQ[#, ptO] &, lines]
Out[79]= {True, True, True, False}
```

The given point is not to the left of all the lines. In fact, this test fails for the last line, the diagonal from the upper left to lower right. But the other point, `ptI`, is to the left of all lines of the polygon. This point is inside:

```
In[80]:= Map[leftOfQ[#, ptI] &, lines]
Out[80]= {True, True, True, True}
```

To check that `leftOfQ` returns `True` for all lines, we take the conjunction of the list of Boolean values. If one or more are `False`, `AllTrue` will return `False`.

```
In[81]:= pointInPolygonQ[poly_, pt_] :=
          AllTrue[Partition[poly, 2, 1, 1], leftOfQ[#, pt] &]

In[82]:= pointInPolygonQ[poly, ptI]
Out[82]= True
```

```
In[83]:= pointInPolygonQ[poly, pt0]
Out[83]= False
```

Nonconvex polygons The case of nonconvex polygons is a bit more complicated. A moment's thought should convince you that the algorithm we used for convex polygons will fail for nonconvex polygons. The point inside the polygon in Figure 8.15 will give `False` for the `leftOfQ` function for at least one of the edges of the polygon.

FIGURE 8.15. *Point-in-polygon problem, nonconvex case.*

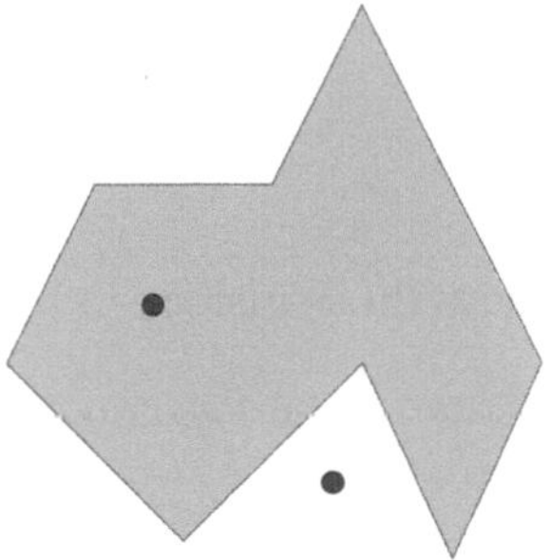

We can solve the problem of finding points in general polygons using some built-in computational geometry functions that work with regions and meshes. The key is to operate on the regions themselves using this machinery. One of the advantages to using this framework is that it generalizes well to arbitrary dimensions and generally scales well also.

To start, create a set of points in the plane and a polygonal region.

```
In[84]:= pts = RandomReal[{-2, 3}, {2500, 2}];
         ℛ = Polygon[{
              {-0.5, 0}, {0.5, -1}, {1.5, 0},
              {2., -1.1}, {2.5, 0}, {1.5, 2}, {1., 1}, {0., 1}
            }];
```

Here is a picture of the points and the polygon. At this point we have not yet identified or colored those points that lie inside the polygon.

```
In[86]:= Graphics[{{LightGray, PointSize[Small], Point[pts]},
           {Opacity[.5], EdgeForm[Black], Blue, ℛ}}, Axes → Automatic]
```

Out[86]=

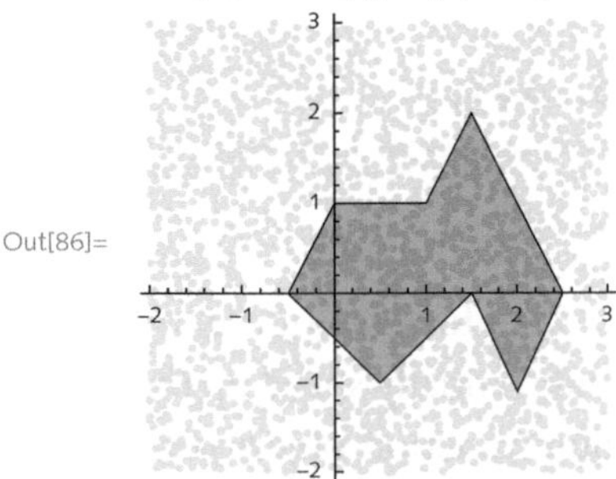

From the graphic we can see that the point {0, 0} lies inside the polygon and the point {−1, 2} lies outside. `RegionMember[ℛ, pt]` returns a value of `True` if the point *pt* is a member of region ℛ.

```
In[87]:= RegionMember[ℛ, {0, 0}]
Out[87]= True

In[88]:= RegionMember[ℛ, {-1, 2}]
Out[88]= False
```

So we need to select all those points that return a value of `True` when `RegionMember[ℛ, #] &` is applied to them.

```
In[89]:= in = Select[pts, RegionMember[ℛ, #] &];
         Length[in]
Out[90]= 493
```

The points on the outside should be the complement of all the points with those inside.

```
In[91]:= out = Complement[pts, in];
         Length[out]
Out[92]= 2007
```

All the heavy lifting is done. We now piece together these parts in our graphics scene.

```
In[93]:= Graphics[{{PointSize[Tiny], Gray, Point@out},
           {PointSize[Tiny], Red, Point@in},
           {Opacity[.5], EdgeForm[{Black, Thickness[Medium]}], Blue, ℛ}}]
```

Out[93]=

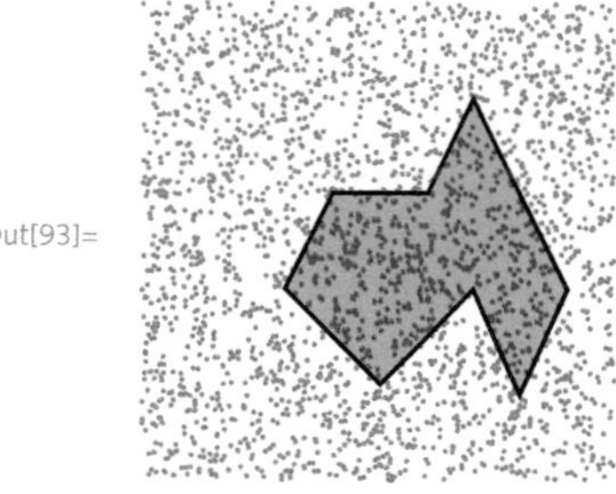

The only wrinkle here is that `RegionMember` can be a bit slow for large sets of points – the following computation on 10 000 points takes about half a minute:

```
In[94]:= pts = RandomReal[{-2, 4}, {10000, 2}];
         ℛ = Polygon@{{-0.5, 0}, {0.5, -1}, {1.5, 0},
              {2., -1.1}, {2.5, 0}, {1.5, 2}, {1., 1}, {0., 1}};

In[96]:= Select[pts, RegionMember[ℛ, #] &]; // Timing
Out[96]= {26.3612, Null}
```

What is slowing things down? A `RegionMember` function is created for each of the 10 000 points for which the comparison is done. Fortunately, there is a way to substantially speed up this computation using a one-argument form of `RegionMember` to build a pure function object once and then apply it to the entire set of points (see the discussion of built-in pure functions in Section 9.1).

Triangle centers

In earlier parts of this book we created visualizations of various triangle centers. In this last example, we will create a dynamic visualization of the triangle circumcenter – the point that is the center of the circle circumscribing the triangle. The circumcenter lies at the intersection of the perpendicular bisectors of the three sides, so we will add those elements to the graphic as well.

We will start with a static graphic containing a triangle, its circumcircle, and a point at the center of the circle.

```
In[97]:= pts = {{-2, 0}, {1, 4}, {2, 0}};
         Graphics[{
           {EdgeForm[Gray], LightBlue, Triangle[pts]},
           {Gray, Circumsphere[pts]},
           {PointSize[Medium], Point[First@Circumsphere[pts]]}}]
```

Out[98]=

To turn just this much into a dynamic object, we use `DynamicModule` and initialize the variable `pts` with the three points of the triangle. We have wrapped `Graphics` in `Dynamic` as every element of the triangle – the vertices, the center, the triangle itself – will all change as we manipulate the locations of the vertices. We have also added an element to change the appearance of the locators.

```
In[99]:= DynamicModule[{pts = {{-2, 0}, {1, 4}, {2, 0}}},
          LocatorPane[Dynamic[pts],
           Dynamic@Graphics[{
              {EdgeForm[Gray], LightBlue, Triangle[pts]},
              {Gray, Circumsphere[pts]},
              {PointSize[Medium], Point[First@Circumsphere[pts]]}
             }], Appearance → Style[⊕, 12]]]
```

Out[99]=

To compute the perpendicular bisectors of each side, we need to do a little geometry. The perpendicular bisector of each side is the point on that side closest to the center of the circumscribing circle. To find that point, we will create line objects on each side and then find the point on that line closest to the center.

To start, here are the vertices of our triangle and the center of the circumcircle of that triangle:

```
In[100]:= {p1, p2, p3} = {{-2, 0}, {1, 4}, {2, 0}};
          Circumsphere[{p1, p2, p3}]
```

Out[101]= $\text{Sphere}\left[\left\{0, \frac{13}{8}\right\}, \frac{5\sqrt{17}}{8}\right]$

```
In[102]:= center = First[%]
```

Out[102]= $\left\{0, \frac{13}{8}\right\}$

Next, Subsets is used to pair up the vertices and then InfiniteLine is mapped across that list to create the three lines that are incident with the sides of the triangle.

```
In[103]:= lines = Map[InfiniteLine, Subsets[{p1, p2, p3}, {2}]]

Out[103]= {InfiniteLine[{{-2, 0}, {1, 4}}],
           InfiniteLine[{{-2, 0}, {2, 0}}], InfiniteLine[{{1, 4}, {2, 0}}]}
```

This gives the point on each line closest to the center.

```
In[104]:= pbs = Map[RegionNearest[#, center] &, lines]
```

Out[104]= $\left\{\left\{-\frac{1}{2}, 2\right\}, \{0, 0\}, \left\{\frac{3}{2}, 2\right\}\right\}$

Finally, we want a line from each of these points to the center.

```
In[105]:= perpbis = Map[InfiniteLine[{center, #}] &, pbs]
```

Out[105]= $\left\{\text{InfiniteLine}\left[\left\{\left\{0, \frac{13}{8}\right\}, \left\{-\frac{1}{2}, 2\right\}\right\}\right], \text{InfiniteLine}\left[\left\{\left\{0, \frac{13}{8}\right\}, \{0, 0\}\right\}\right], \text{InfiniteLine}\left[\left\{\left\{0, \frac{13}{8}\right\}, \left\{\frac{3}{2}, 2\right\}\right\}\right]\right\}$

Let us add these three lines and points first to the static graphic.

```
In[106]:= Graphics[{
            {EdgeForm[Gray], LightBlue, Triangle[pts]},
            {LightGray, Circumsphere[pts]},
            {PointSize[Medium], Point[First@Circumsphere[pts]]},
            {Gray, perpbis}, Point@pbs
          }]
```

Out[106]=

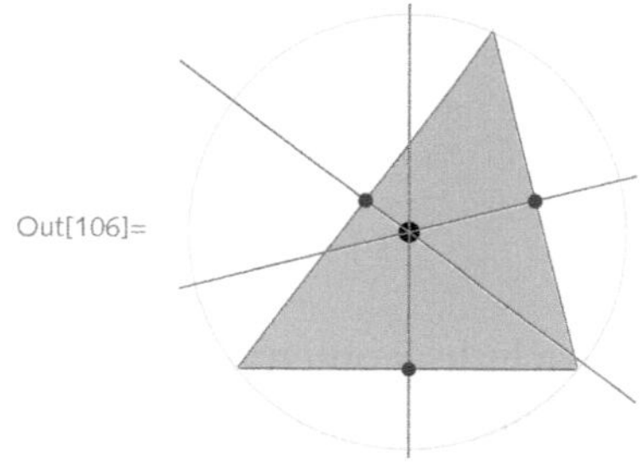

Now we implement these elements in the dynamic expression. Note that the code below is more verbose as we have made it self-contained by including the computations of pbs and perpbis above.

```
In[107]:= DynamicModule[{pts = {{-2, 0}, {1, 4}, {2, 0}}},
  LocatorPane[Dynamic[pts],
   Dynamic@Graphics[{
      {EdgeForm[Gray], LightBlue, Triangle[pts]},
      {LightGray, Circumsphere[pts]},
      {PointSize[Large], Point[First@Circumsphere[pts]]},
      {Gray, Map[InfiniteLine[{First@Circumsphere[pts], #}] &,
        Map[RegionNearest[#, First@Circumsphere[pts]] &,
         InfiniteLine /@ Subsets[pts, {2}]]], PointSize[Medium],
       Point[Map[RegionNearest[#, First@Circumsphere[pts]] &,
         InfiniteLine /@ Subsets[pts, {2}]]]}
     }], Appearance → Style[⊕, 12]]]
```

Out[107]=

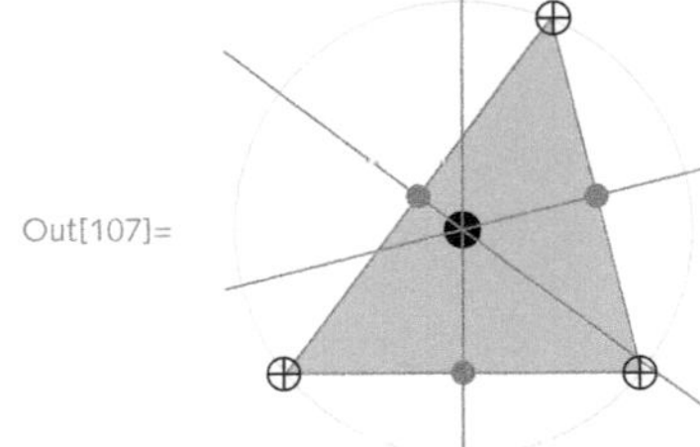

Exercises

1. Create a function `ComplexListPlot` that plots a list of complex numbers in the complex plane using `ListPlot`. Set initial options so that the `PlotStyle` is red, the `PointSize` is a little larger than the default, and the horizontal and vertical axes are labeled "Re" and "Im," respectively. Set up options to `ComplexListPlot` that are inherited from `ListPlot`.
2. Create a function `ComplexRootPlot` that plots the complex zeros of a polynomial in the plane. Use your implementation of `ComplexListPlot` that you developed in the previous exercise.
3. Use `Mesh` in a manner similar to its use in the `RootPlot` function to highlight the intersection of two surfaces, say $\sin(2x - \cos(y))$ and $\sin(x - \cos(2y))$. You may need to increase the value of `MaxRecursion` to get the sampling just right.
4. The version of `VennDiagram` developed in this section used `Graphics` to create the circles and then combined them with `RegionPlot` using `Show`. Modify `VennDiagram` so that the circles are created entirely inside `RegionPlot`.
5. Create a new rule for `VennDiagram` that takes a logical expression as its first argument instead of a logical function. For example, your function should be able to handle input such as the following:

```
In[1]:= VennDiagram[A ⊻ B, {A, B}]
```

Out[1]=

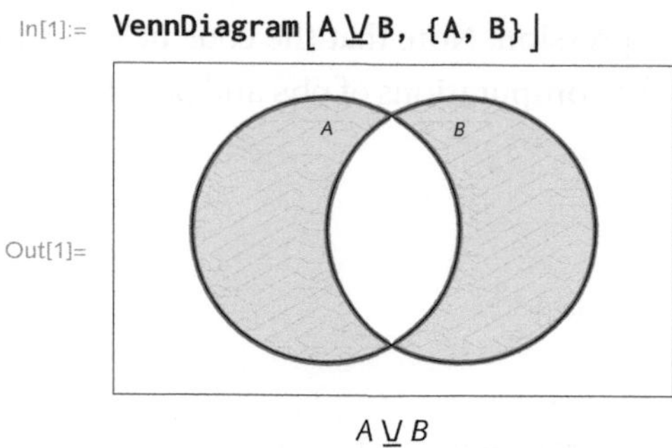

A ⊻ B

6. Extend the previous exercise to a Venn diagram on three sets, using logical expressions as the first argument.

```
In[2]:= VennDiagram[(A ∨ B ∨ C) && ¬ (A ∧ B ∧ C), {A, B, C}]
```

Out[2]=

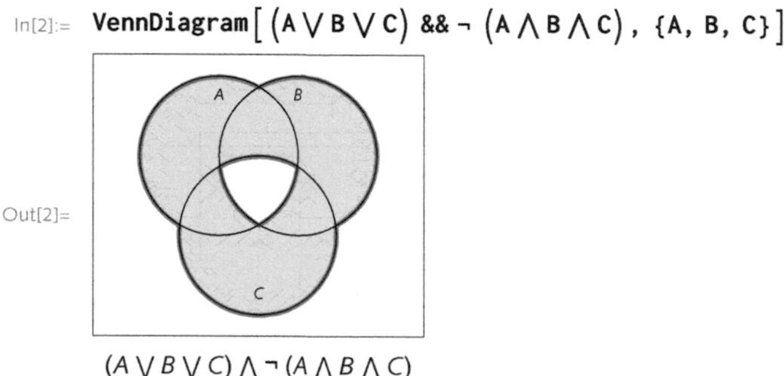

(A ∨ B ∨ C) ∧ ¬ (A ∧ B ∧ C)

7. Modify the dynamic Venn diagram created in this section to also display a truth table like that in Figure 8.16. Include the truth table side-by-side with the Venn diagram. `TruthTable` was developed in Exercise 3 in Section 6.3.

FIGURE 8.16. *Dynamic visualization of logical expressions.*

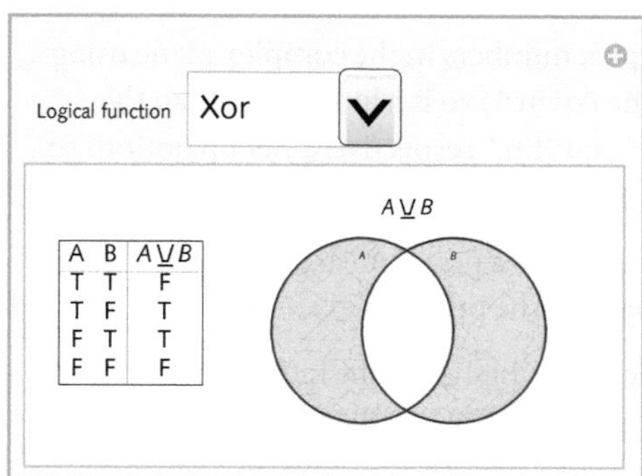

8. The `DotPlot` function developed in this section uses a fixed window size, meaning that it only colors a dot black if a string of length one matches a string of length one in the two sequences under comparison. Add a `WindowSize` option to `DotPlot` that allows you to set the length of the sequences to match – you will likely need `stringPartition` developed in Section 7.5. Finally, set up `DotPlot` to inherit the options from `ArrayPlot`.

```
In[3]:= DotPlot[seq2, seq1, WindowSize → 3, FrameLabel → {"DQ023146.1", "DQ232610.1"}]
```

Out[3]=

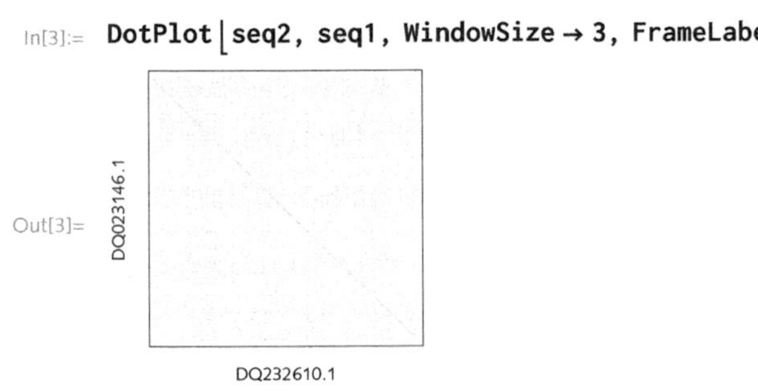

9. When making dot plots like in the previous exercise, if you knew you were *always* working with FASTA files, you could automate both the extraction of the frame labels from the FASTA accession ids and their insertion in the `FrameLabel` option of `ArrayPlot`.

```
In[4]:= Import["H5N1ChickenDQ023146.1.fasta", {"FASTA", "Accession"}]
Out[4]= {DQ023146.1}
```

Create a version of `DotPlot` that accepts two FASTA files as input and has the same options structure as in the previous exercise.

```
In[8]:= DotPlot["H5N1ChickenDQ023146.1.fasta", "H5N1DuckDQ232610.1.fasta", WindowSize → 3]
```

Out[8]=

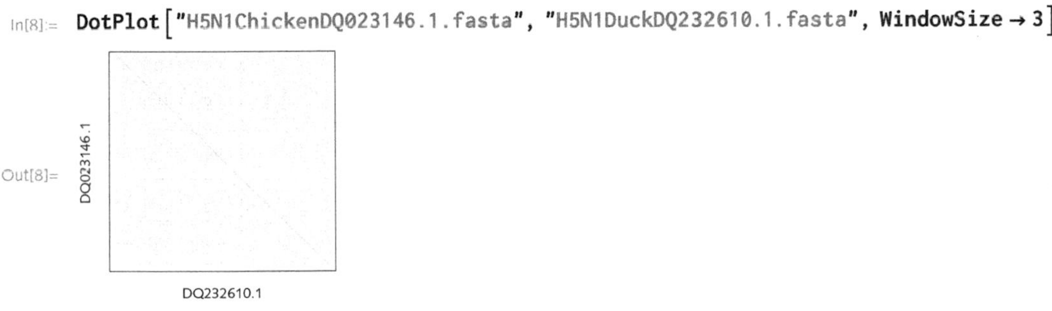

10. Modify the `Manipulate` expression animating the hypocycloid so that the plot range deals with the case where the radius of the inner circle is larger than the radius of the outer circle.

11. An *epicycloid* is a curve generated by tracing out a fixed point on a circle rolling around the outside of a second circle. The parametric formula for an epicycloid is similar to that for the hypocycloid:

$$x = (a + b)\cos(\theta) - b\cos\left(\frac{a+b}{b}\,\theta\right),$$
$$y = (a + b)\sin(\theta) - b\sin\left(\frac{a+b}{b}\,\theta\right).$$

Create a dynamic animation of the epicycloid similar to that for the hypocycloid in this section.

12. Modify `PathPlot` so that it inherits options from `Graphics` as well as having its own option, `PathClosed`, that can take on values of `True` or `False` and closes the path accordingly by appending the first point to the end of the list of coordinate points.

13. Modify `SimplePath` so that the point with the smallest x-coordinate of the list of data is chosen as the base point; repeat but with the largest y-coordinate; then try ordering the points about the polar angle each makes with the centroid of the set of points.

14. There are conditions under which the program `SimplePath` will occasionally fail (think collinear points). Experiment by repeatedly computing `SimplePath` for a set of ten integer-valued points until you see the failure. Determine the conditions that must be imposed for the program to work consistently.

15. Modify the `ChemicalSpaceFillingPlot` function to add legends that give identifying information for each atomic element in the plot (Figure 8.17). Consider using `Legended` and `SwatchLegend`.

FIGURE 8.17. *Space-filling plot of serotonin (with legends).*

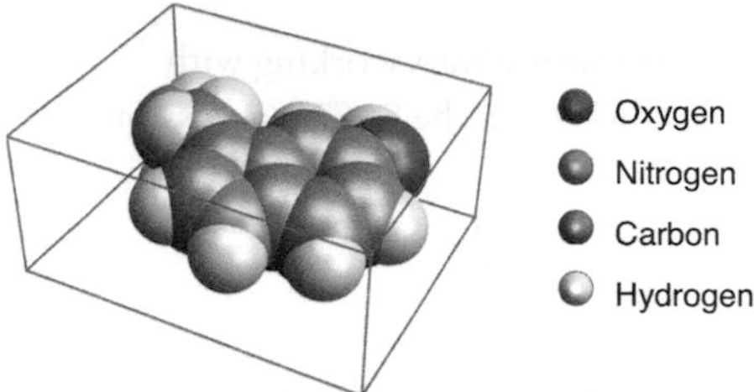

16. Create a dynamic interface similar to the triangle circumcenter example in this section but instead compute the *orthocenter*, which is located at the intersection of the three altitudes of the triangle (Figure 8.18). The *altitude* of a triangle is a line through a vertex perpendicular to the opposite side.

FIGURE 8.18. *Triangle orthocenter at the intersection of the altitudes.*

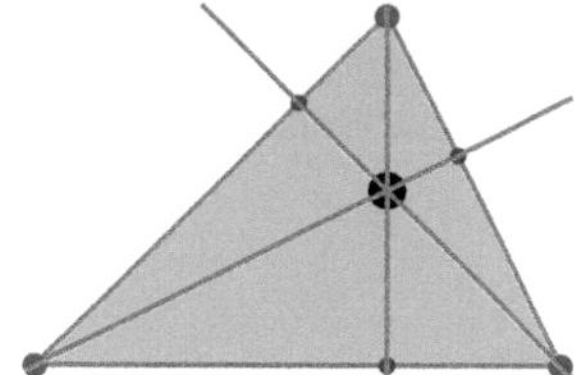

17. Leonhard Euler in 1765 showed that for any triangle, the centroid, circumcenter, and orthocenter are collinear. In fact, the line that passes through these triangle centers also passes through several other notable points such as the incenter, the nine-point center, the de Longchamps point, and others. And, remarkably, when you change the shape of the triangle, the relative distances between the centers is unchanged.

    Construct an interface to display a triangle with dynamic vertices together with the triangle's centroid, circumcenter, orthocenter, and the Euler line. Give distinct colors to each of the four sets: incenter and angle bisectors, medians and centroid, perpendicular bisectors and circumcenter and circumcircle, altitudes and orthocenter. Add a legend that identifies the objects by color.

18. One way to get a sense of the extent of data, such as a two-dimensional random walk, is to superimpose the eigenvectors of a certain tensor over a line plot of the walk. This tensor, called the radius of gyration tensor $\mathcal{T}$, is discussed in Section 6.3. For a given walk, the eigenvectors of $\mathcal{T}$ point in the direction of the greatest and smallest spans of the walk, while the eigenvalues of $\mathcal{T}$ give a measure of how elongated the walk is in the directions pointed by the corresponding eigenvectors.

    Create a function `EigenvectorPlot[`*walk*, $\mathcal{T}$, *opts*`]` that takes a two-dimensional list *walk*, the radius of gyration tensor $\mathcal{T}$ of that walk, and generates a visualization of the walk using `ListLinePlot` together with the eigenvector/value lines as described above.

8.5 Notes and further reading

Visualization of functions, data, information, and relationships between objects is a vast field with an enormous amount of resources to choose from. For a collection of examples on the display of visual information, see Lima (2011). Also the book by Heckbert (1994) is filled with interesting graphical problems.

Venn diagrams are used to show logical relations between sets and are used in elementary set theory as well as in probability and statistics and computer science. A survey, including historical information and extensions to large numbers of sets, is included in Ruskey and Weston (2005). Also, the brief article by Branko Grunbaum (1984) includes a discussion of Venn diagrams with regions other than circles.

Dot plots (Section 8.4) are used to make comparisons of nucleotide and protein sequences between organisms as well as to compare a sequence to itself to discover anomalies. A good introduction to dot plots is available in Schulz (2008). Numerous online databases are available containing information about chemical and molecular structures. We have used the PubChem Compound Database (National Center for Biotechnology Information 2015).

From a theoretical point of view, the traveling salesman problem is part of a large class of problems that are known as *NP-complete* problems. These are problems that can be solved in polynomial time using nondeterministic algorithms. A *nondeterministic algorithm* has the ability to "choose" among many options when faced with numerous choices, and then to verify that the solution is correct. The outstanding problem in computer science at present is known as the $\mathcal{P} = \mathcal{NP}$ problem. This equation says that any problem that can be solved by a nondeterministic algorithm in polynomial time ($\mathcal{NP}$) can be solved by a deterministic algorithm in polynomial time ($\mathcal{P}$). It is widely believed that $\mathcal{P} \neq \mathcal{NP}$ and considerable effort has gone into solving this problem. See Cook (2000), Lawler et al. (1985), or Pemmaraju and Skiena (2003).

The point-in-polygon problems discussed in this chapter have simple solutions for simple polygons (convex), but the real action is for nonconvex polygons. Although we have chosen to use the built-in computational geometry machinery to do most of the heavy lifting, it is still instructive to try and implement many of the classical algorithms using the programming ideas developed here. The point in polygon for nonconvex polygons is classically solved using a ray-crossing algorithm. The idea is to draw a horizontal ray starting at the point in question, extending out to infinity (the restriction of the ray being horizontal can be relaxed with suitable adjustments to the algorithm). Then the point is in or out of the polygon if the number of crossings of edges is odd or even, respectively (try it with the two points and polygon in Figure 8.15). Another commonly used algorithm for point-in-polygon problems involves winding numbers. This method computes the subtended angle from the point in question to each edge of the polygon and determines the number of turns the boundary of the polygon makes about the point. These algorithms are fairly involved, but they can be implemented with the tools discussed in this book. The interested reader is directed to O'Rourke (1998) or Heckbert (1994).

The problem of determining the convex hull of a set of points has application in computer vision, pattern recognition, image processing, and many other areas. Convex hull algorithms are discussed in Graham (1972) and the book on computational geometry by O'Rourke (1998).

9

Program optimization

Efficient programs · Low-level vs. high-level functions · Pattern matching · Reducing size of computation · Symbolic vs. numeric computation · Listability · Packed arrays · Pure functions · Built-in pure functions · Parallel processing · Basic examples · Profiling · Compiling · Compile · Compiling to C · Notes and further reading

We should forget about small efficiencies, say about 97% of the time: premature optimization is the root of all evil.

— Donald E. Knuth

When you first start to program your emphasis is usually on correctness, that is, getting your programs to run and return accurate and error-free results – and rightly so. There is little point in trying to speed up a program that returns incorrect answers! You develop your programs, prototyping with simple inputs so that you can see at a glance how things are progressing. At some point in the development process you start to increase the size or complexity of the inputs to your program and, if all goes well, the program scales well. But commonly, there are bottlenecks at various stages of the computation that slow things down; or there may be a large increase in the amount of memory needed to represent or store an expression or result. Some of these situations may be unavoidable, but often you can find optimizations that improve the efficiency and running time of your programs. This chapter introduces some of the optimization principles to think about both during the development process and after your programs are complete and you are satisfied that they produce the desired output.

How, you might ask, does one quantify efficiency? There are two measures we will focus on – timing and memory footprint. The importance of these two measures is highly subjective. Squeezing another tenth of a second out of a computation that is only going to be run once or twice does not make a lot of sense. However, if that computation is part of a loop that is going to be evaluated thousands of times, little things really start to add up. You will be the best judge of where to focus your efforts.

This chapter provides several case studies and tips to guide you in your efforts to improve your *Mathematica* programs: so-called high-level functions compared with more basic constructs; the efficiency of pattern matching; how to reduce the sheer bulk of your computations; symbolic versus numeric; listability; packed arrays; and the efficiency of pure functions. The chapter also includes an introduction to parallel processing and compilation in *Mathematica*, two tools that can be used to significantly increase the speed of your programs.

9.1 Efficient programs

Low-level vs. high-level functions

Many computational tasks are programmed as procedures that loop through an expression, extracting and operating on various pieces, putting the transformed pieces into a temporary list or array as they proceed. Typical examples include adding lists of numbers, operating on rows or columns from a matrix, and so on. This low-level approach to a common task is typical of procedural languages. But using tools that are optimized for these tasks can save time and effort, not just in coding and debugging but in the running of your programs.

As an example, consider the task of reversing pairs of elements in an $n \times 2$ array. The standard procedural approach starts by setting up a temporary list of the same size as the input, initialized here as a vector of zeros. Then, inside a `Do` loop, parts are extracted and put in a list in the order we want and assigned to the appropriate element in the temporary list.

```
In[1]:= mat = {{a, b}, {c, d}, {d, e}};

In[2]:= temp = ConstantArray[0, {Length[mat]}];

In[3]:= Do[temp[[i]] = {mat[[i, 2]], mat[[i, 1]]},
          {i, 1, Length[mat]}
         ];
        temp

Out[4]= {{b, a}, {d, c}, {e, d}}
```

Reversing the elements in a list is a fairly common task and a functional construct is available for just this.

```
In[5]:= Map[Reverse, mat]

Out[5]= {{b, a}, {d, c}, {e, d}}
```

Not only is the code compact and quite readable, but this functional approach is much faster in practice. For example, here is a matrix consisting of one million pairs of numbers:

```
In[6]:= mat = RandomReal[1, {10^6, 2}];
```

Reversing each pair with a procedural approach takes several seconds, whereas the functional approach speeds this up by over an order of magnitude.

```
In[7]:=  Timing[
          temp = ConstantArray[0, {Length[mat]}];
          Do[temp[[i]] = {mat[[i, 2]], mat[[i, 1]]},
           {i, 1, Length[mat]}]]
Out[7]=  {2.71782, Null}

In[8]:=  AbsoluteTiming[Map[Reverse, mat];]
Out[8]=  {0.150963, Null}
```

The point is that although you *can* program in a procedural manner in *Mathematica*, there often are some good reasons not to, the main ones being ease of coding and the efficiency of running your programs. The built-in *Mathematica* functions are optimized to be as fast as possible for the types of input and computations for which they are designed. So the first bit of advice is to use built-in functions wherever possible.

As a second example, consider summing the numbers one through one million. Several different implementations are possible.

```
In[9]:=  sumDo[n_] := Module[{i = 0, result = 0},
           Do[result = result + i, {i, 1.0, n}];
           result]

In[10]:= Timing[sumDo[10^6]]
Out[10]= {0.643772, 5.00001 × 10^11}

In[11]:= sumTable[n_] := Module[{result = 0.0},
           Table[result = result + i, {i, 1.0, n}];
           result]

In[12]:= Timing[sumTable[10^6]]
Out[12]= {0.532427, 5.00001 × 10^11}

In[13]:= Timing[Sum[i, {i, 1.0, 10^6}]]
Out[13]= {0.147193, 5.00001 × 10^11}

In[14]:= sumApply[n_] := Apply[Plus, N@Range[n]]

In[15]:= Timing[sumApply[10^6]]
Out[15]= {0.197198, 5.00001 × 10^11}
```

Of all these approaches (and there are many more!), using `Total` is optimal. It is designed expressly for the task of adding lists of numbers.

```
In[16]:= sumTotal[n_] := Total[N@Range[n]]

In[17]:= Timing[sumTotal[10^6]]
Out[17]= {0.007163, 5.00001 × 10^11}
```

You might wonder why `Sum`, which is also designed for adding expressions, is slower than both the functional approach with `Apply` and the approach with `Total`. The `Sum` function contains hundreds of rules for the various expressions it can handle and also has to keep track of an iterator `i`. Although these constructs are necessary for complicated summations, this extra overhead comes at a cost that is reflected in the timings here.

As an aside, some mathematical knowledge goes a long way in this particular case. The sum of the integers one through n is given by the binomial expression $\binom{n+1}{2}$.

```
In[18]:= Binomial[10^6 + 1, 2] // Timing
Out[18]= {0.000152, 500 000 500 000}

In[19]:= Binomial[10^6 + 1, 2] == Total[Range[10^6]]
Out[19]= True
```

Pattern matching

As we have seen throughout this book, pattern matching is one of the key features of *Mathematica*, distinguishing it from most other programming languages. It provides a natural mechanism to identify classes of expressions on which to operate or transform, based on some criteria of interest. But for computations where speed is at a premium, the convenience of pattern matching can be overshadowed by slower overall evaluation. In this section we will look at some larger examples that highlight this issue and discuss other approaches that you might want to consider.

A fairly common task is counting the number of elements in an expression that are of a certain form. For example, suppose you want to count the positive numbers in a vector. You could use `Count` with the appropriate pattern.

```
In[20]:= vec = RandomReal[{-1, 1}, {15}]
Out[20]= {-0.926813, 0.491359, -0.412521, -0.981969, 0.263568,
          -0.170956, 0.604117, -0.187172, -0.646797, -0.684245,
          0.970202, 0.0654069, 0.406671, -0.220314, 0.936063}

In[21]:= Count[vec, _?Positive]
Out[21]= 7
```

For a more arithmetic approach, you could use `Sign`, which returns –1 for negative numbers and 1 for positive numbers; then add 1 to each element, turning the –1s into 0s and the 1s into 2s.

```
In[22]:= Sign[vec]
Out[22]= {-1, 1, -1, -1, 1, -1, 1, -1, -1, -1, 1, 1, 1, -1, 1}

In[23]:= Sign[vec] + 1
Out[23]= {0, 2, 0, 0, 2, 0, 2, 0, 0, 0, 2, 2, 2, 0, 2}
```

Lastly, add up the numbers and divide by 2.

```
In[24]:= Total[Sign[vec] + 1] / 2
Out[24]= 7
```

The first approach using Count seems much more natural and easier to code and read, while the second approach involves a lot of steps to get the same result. You might think that the more natural, compact approach using Count would be faster. But, for large vectors, this is not the case.

```
In[25]:= vec = RandomReal[{-1, 1}, {10^6}];

In[26]:= Count[vec, _?Positive] // Timing
Out[26]= {0.438462, 499870}

In[27]:= Total[Sign[vec] + 1] / 2 // Timing
Out[27]= {0.028337, 499870}
```

Why is this? The pattern matcher can work with many different kinds of expressions – numbers, strings, functions, images, and so on. One of the things it must do in order to maintain this generality is to work with arbitrary arrays of numbers, so that it can identify different types that may be present in that array. Total and Sign, in contrast, are purely arithmetic functions and they can and do operate on packed arrays of numbers whenever possible. Packed arrays are internal array objects that take advantage of compiled code and are thus quite fast to work with. We will return to a more detailed discussion of packed arrays later in this chapter.

As another pattern-matching example, we consider two approaches for generating upper-triangular matrices – matrices with zeros below the diagonal and, in this case, ones everywhere else. We will start by using SparseArray. The pattern matcher is invoked to determine the value of the nonzero elements.

```
In[28]:= With[{n = 5},
           SparseArray[{i_, j_} /; i ≤ j → 1, {n, n}]
          ] // MatrixForm
Out[28]//MatrixForm=
         1 1 1 1 1
         0 1 1 1 1
         0 0 1 1 1
         0 0 0 1 1
         0 0 0 0 1

In[29]:= With[{n = 500},
           matSA = SparseArray[{i_, j_} /; i ≤ j → 1, {n, n}]
          ] // Timing
Out[29]= {0.289827, SparseArray[ Specified elements: 125250
                                  Dimensions: {500, 500} ]}
```

Using a procedural approach similar to that in Section 6.1 is significantly faster.

```
In[30]:= With[{n = 5},
           Table[If[j ≥ i, 1, 0], {i, n}, {j, n}]
         ] // MatrixForm
Out[30]//MatrixForm=
         1  1  1  1  1
         0  1  1  1  1
         0  0  1  1  1
         0  0  0  1  1
         0  0  0  0  1
```

```
In[31]:= With[{n = 500},
           matT = Table[If[j ≥ i, 1, 0], {i, n}, {j, n}];
         ] // Timing
Out[31]= {0.010814, Null}
```

That is about thirty times faster using `If`. The comparison is a bit unfair since we are not accounting for the internals of `Table` compared with `SparseArray`. But you could check that, in general, creating sparse array objects is quite fast compared with using `Table` for similarly sized expressions.

```
In[32]:= matT = Table[0, {i, 10^4}, {j, 10^4}]; // Timing
Out[32]= {2.48243, Null}
```

```
In[33]:= matSA = SparseArray[{_, _} → 0, {10^4, 10^4}]; // Timing
Out[33]= {0.000034, Null}
```

Only one rule was necessary to create this sparse array of zeros.

```
In[34]:= ArrayRules[matSA]
Out[34]= {{_, _} → 0}
```

So why is the procedural approach faster? When using patterns in `SparseArray`, the position index for every element had to be compared with the pattern to determine its value. The approach using `Table` had just as many comparisons to make but it did not invoke the pattern matcher to do so.

Tip 9.1

We should check to make sure that the matrices produced by these two approaches are the same. `Equal` (==) is the basic test for equality.

```
In[35]:= matSA == matT
Out[35]= True
```

The two matrices are not identical though, as one has the structure of a sparse array and the other is a list. `SameQ` (===) tests if they have identical structures and elements.

```
In[36]:= matSA === matT
Out[36]= False
```

Reducing size of computation

Although it may seem obvious, you should look to reduce the raw number of computations performed when trying to optimize your programs. Such inefficiencies are often difficult to spot. As an example, consider the following two loops used to add up the first one million integers:

```
In[37]:= (
           For[i = 0; result = 0, i ≤ 10^6, i++, result = result + i];
           result
         ) // Timing

Out[37]= {1.40554, 500 000 500 000}
```

```
In[38]:= (
           result = 0;
           Do[result = result + i, {i, 1, 10^6}];
           result
         ) // Timing

Out[38]= {0.511211, 500 000 500 000}
```

Why is the Do loop faster? Think about how many computations are done in each loop: in the For loop, compare i with 10^6, increment i, sum result + i, make an assignment to result. That is essentially four computations each time through the loop. The Do loop has the sum result + i, the assignment, and the increment of the iterator i. There are fewer raw computations with the Do loop.

As a more applied example, consider the Sieve of Eratosthenes we implemented in Section 6.3. For each value of p inside the For loop, the Do loop runs for i = 2 p to i = n in increments of p. In the code below, we have made a slight modification to Sieve to add a counter that gives the number of iterations of the inner Do loop.

```
In[39]:= SieveCnt[n_Integer] := Module[{ints = Range[n], p, cnt = 0},
           For[p = 2,
            p ≠ 1 && p ≤ Floor[Sqrt[n]],
            p++,
            Do[ints[[i]] = 1; cnt++, {i, 2 p, n, p}]];
           DeleteCases[ints, 1];
           cnt]
```

For this computation, 532 988 iterations of the inner Do loop were performed.

```
In[40]:= SieveCnt[10^5] // Timing

Out[40]= {0.716083, 532 988}
```

So how could we reduce the overall number of computations? We will use list component assignment but try to be a bit clever about picking out the parts. Inside the Do loop we will cross out values (assign a value of 1) to multiples of p in the list ints. But instead of using the For loop to get those values of p, we use the Part function with the Span shorthand 2 p ;; -1 ;; p indicating that we extract parts 2 p through the end in steps of p, that is, the multiples of p.

```
In[41]:= Sieve2[n_Integer] := Module[{ints = Range[n]},
           Do[ints[[2 p ;; -1 ;; p]] = 1,
            {p, 2, √n}];
           DeleteCases[ints, 1]]
```

First let's do a few basic checks for correctness.

```
In[42]:= Sieve2[100]
Out[42]= {2, 3, 5, 7, 11, 13, 17, 19, 23, 29, 31, 37,
          41, 43, 47, 53, 59, 61, 67, 71, 73, 79, 83, 89, 97}

In[43]:= Length[Sieve2[1000]]
Out[43]= 168

In[44]:= PrimePi[1000]
Out[44]= 168
```

Next we check the speed of this function.

```
In[45]:= Sieve2[10^5]; // Timing
Out[45]= {0.024918, Null}
```

That is between one and two orders of magnitude faster! Now count the number of iterations inside the `Do` loop in `Sieve2`.

```
In[46]:= Sieve2Cnt[n_Integer] := Module[{ints = Range[n], cnt = 0},
           Do[ints[[2 p ;; -1 ;; p]] = 1;
            cnt++,
            {p, 2, √n}];
           DeleteCases[ints, 1];
           cnt]

In[47]:= Sieve2Cnt[10^5] // Timing
Out[47]= {0.025125, 315}
```

Although it appears as if we have reduced the sheer number of computations from over 500 000 to about 300, that is not quite accurate – it is a bit subtle as to why things have in fact been sped up. For `Sieve2`, there is an implicit iteration given by `ints⟦2 p ;; -1 ;; p⟧ = 1` that is, in fact, handled in compiled C code. So what we are seeing is the difference between explicit iteration in *Mathematica* and implicit iteration being done at the level of compiled C code. The list component assignment, in effect, transfers that iteration to compiled code and this is what has caused the significant speedup.

Symbolic vs. numeric computation

Another issue to think about in trying to improve the speed and efficiency of your programs is the contrast between numeric and symbolic computation. In general, numeric-based computation can be quite fast, especially if it is done on the hardware of your machine rather than in software where symbolic computation often is performed.

For example, consider a simple operation: taking the sin of a vector of one million numbers. The computation with real numbers is quite fast but that with integers is several orders of magnitude slower.

```
In[48]:= With[{n = 10^6},
          vec = RandomReal[{-10, 10}, {n}];
          AbsoluteTiming[Sin[vec];]]

Out[48]= {0.000808, Null}

In[49]:= With[{n = 10^6},
          vec = RandomInteger[{-10, 10}, {n}];
          AbsoluteTiming[Sin[vec];]]

Out[49]= {0.874928, Null}
```

As another example, let us revisit the radius of gyration tensor computation from Section 6.3. Here is the code developed in that section. We have removed the argument-checking part of the code here for readability purposes.

```
In[50]:= RadiusOfGyrationTensor[lis_] := Module[{xy, vx, vy},
           xy = Apply[Dot, Transpose[lis] - Mean[lis]] / Length[lis];
           {vx, vy} = CentralMoment[lis, 2];
           {{vx, xy}, {xy, vy}}]
```

First, let us compute the tensor for an exact matrix (a lattice walk) and also for a matrix consisting of approximate numbers (the off-lattice walk is defined in the EPM`RandomWalks package and is accessed by means of an option to the RandomWalk function).

```
In[51]:= << EPM`RandomWalks`

In[52]:= walkLat = RandomWalk[10^6, LatticeWalk → True];

In[53]:= RadiusOfGyrationTensor[walkLat] // Timing
```

$$\text{Out[53]}= \left\{9.31648, \left\{\left\{\frac{30\,426\,873\,733\,494\,351}{1\,000\,000\,000\,000}, -\frac{641\,554\,050\,977\,181}{200\,000\,000\,000}\right\}, \left\{-\frac{641\,554\,050\,977\,181}{200\,000\,000\,000}, \frac{986\,449\,334\,503\,911}{40\,000\,000\,000}\right\}\right\}\right\}$$

```
In[54]:= walkOffLat = RandomWalk[10^6, LatticeWalk → False];

In[55]:= RadiusOfGyrationTensor[walkOffLat] // Timing

Out[55]= {0.261631, {{30892.9, -15004.6}, {-15004.6, 64895.7}}}
```

The off-lattice (approximate) computation is about one order of magnitude faster compared with the exact computation. So what is causing this difference? We will focus on the three computations at the heart of this function: computing column means, the dot product, and the central moment computation. This process of *profiling* code to isolate the parts in which the most time is spent is something that can be done using integrated development environments (IDEs), such as Wolfram *Workbench*. We will adopt a very basic approach here since our function is fairly simple to deconstruct. Section 9.2 discusses profiling in more detail.

First, here is the column mean computation for the two walks:

```
In[56]:= lisLat = Transpose[walkLat] - Mean[walkLat]; // Timing
Out[56]= {0.948657, Null}
```

```
In[57]:= lisOffLat = Transpose[walkOffLat] - Mean[walkOffLat]; // Timing
Out[57]= {0.029993, Null}
```

Second, this is the dot product computation:

```
In[58]:= (Dot @@ lisLat) / Length[walkLat]; // Timing
Out[58]= {0.968617, Null}
```

```
In[59]:= (Dot @@ lisOffLat) / Length[walkOffLat]; // Timing
Out[59]= {0.009218, Null}
```

And finally, this is the central moment computation:

```
In[60]:= CentralMoment[walkLat, 2]; // Timing
Out[60]= {7.23865, Null}
```

```
In[61]:= CentralMoment[walkOffLat, 2]; // Timing
Out[61]= {0.236898, Null}
```

Well, all of these computations are significantly slower for the exact input. A bit more digging into this example shows the real culprit causing the slowdown in the exact computations: large exact rational expressions.

```
In[62]:= Part[lisLat, 1, {1, -1}]
```

Out[62]= $\left\{-\frac{315\,658\,343}{1\,000\,000}, \frac{66\,341\,657}{1\,000\,000}\right\}$

If we were only working with exact integers, the times for these computations would be comparable to those with the approximate numbers. But at each stage, arithmetic is performed on large fractions and this is quite time- and resource-intensive.

So what can you take away from this discussion? To speed up your programs, profiling is a sensible way to find those computations to optimize. Once you find the bottlenecks, try to see if you can replace an exact computation with one using approximate numbers. Of course, if you need an exact result for some reason, then simply switching to approximate arithmetic is not an option and you will have to consider one of the other approaches discussed in this chapter.

Tip 9.2

There is often more going on with linear algebra computations than meets the eye. First, the linear algebra libraries that are optimized for your computer (such as BLAS) may contain slightly slower or faster implementations for integer or floating-point computation than those for another machine. In addition, multi-threading occurs automatically. You can get a hint of this by comparing the two functions `Timing` and `AbsoluteTiming` for these operations.

```
In[63]:= matRe = RandomReal[1, {1500, 1500}];

In[64]:= AbsoluteTiming[matRe.matRe;]
Out[64]= {0.05329, Null}

In[65]:= Timing[matRe.matRe;]
Out[65]= {0.185829, Null}
```

On the machine on which these computations were run, `Timing` is adding the total time spent on all threads that were launched to do this computation. In other words, the dot product (and many other linear algebra functions) automatically threads across your computer's processor. This is distinct from multiprocessing as is done in parallel computation. Because *Mathematica* automatically threads such linear algebra computations over any multiple cores that are available, some of these operations will see significant speedups on machines with larger numbers of cores.

Listability

Many *Mathematica* functions have the `Listable` attribute. Functions with this attribute automatically thread across lists element-wise. We have seen examples of this in many places in this book, for example, with vector and matrix operations:

```
In[66]:= {1, 2, 3, 4} + {10, 20, 30, 40}
Out[66]= {11, 22, 33, 44}

In[67]:= 10 {1, 2, 3, 4, 5}
Out[67]= {10, 20, 30, 40, 50}
```

But there is much more to listable functions. Large inputs can automatically take advantage of multi-threading on vector operations for machines whose hardware supports this. Most of the elementary functions call specialized code that performs this multi-threading behind the scenes. The way to best take advantage of this behavior is to use these functions directly on the vectors or matrices with which you are working.

Mapping elementary functions like `Sin` across a vector is fast, but it does not take direct advantage of the listability attribute.

```
In[68]:= vec = RandomReal[{-100, 100}, 10^6];

In[69]:= AbsoluteTiming[Map[Sin, vec];]
Out[69]= {0.063995, Null}
```

Simply wrapping Sin around vec causes a vectorized version of Sin to be called and this is the fastest way to perform the computation, essentially working at the speeds of compiled code.

```
In[70]:= AbsoluteTiming[Sin[vec];]
Out[70]= {0.0019, Null}
```

User-defined functions can inherit the Listable attribute and this can give modest improvements in speed. But you can squeeze even more speed out of functions by defining them as pure functions that are listable. This is done by giving Function a third argument, Listable.

```
In[71]:= f[x_] := If[-1 < x < 1, Exp[x], x^2]

In[72]:= pureF = Function[{x}, If[-1 < x < 1, Exp[x], x^2], Listable];

In[73]:= {AbsoluteTiming[Map[f, vec];], AbsoluteTiming[pureF[vec];]}
Out[73]= {{1.82835, Null}, {0.157504, Null}}
```

To generate a list of all built-in functions that have the listable attribute, you can use the function FunctionsWithAttributes defined in Section 5.5.

```
In[74]:= lis = FunctionsWithAttribute[Listable];
         Length[lis]
Out[75]= 279

In[76]:= RandomSample[lis, 12]
Out[76]= {Log2, PrimeQ, MathieuC, ExtendedGCD,
          AlgebraicNumberDenominator, IntegerPart, BitClear, Plus,
          SphericalBesselY, EllipticE, PolynomialLCM, StruveH}
```

Packed arrays

When you perform computations with floating-point numbers, *Mathematica* determines the type of numbers you are working with and then either it performs the computation on your machine's floating-point processor (if working with numbers that fit there) or it does the computation using extended-precision software routines. Similarly, computations involving integers will be done in hardware or using special software routines depending upon the size of the integers relative to your machine's hardware constraints.

However, all this comes at a cost, and the cost involves the administrative overhead necessary to determine the appropriate routine and whether to perform the computation in hardware or software. For small computations, this overhead is not noticeable, but for large computations involving tens of thousands of rows and columns of a matrix, say, this overhead could cause your computations to slow down considerably.

Fortunately, there is a way to bypass some of this overhead and get significant speed improvements together with a smaller memory footprint. The technology that does this is referred to as *packed arrays*. Whenever possible, *Mathematica* will automatically represent a list of a single type of machine numbers (integer, real, or complex) as an array, in fact, a packed array object. So a matrix consisting of all machine real numbers will be represented internally as a packed array. This internal representation is transparent to the user.

Here is a 1000 × 1000 array consisting of random real numbers:

```
In[77]:= mat = RandomReal[1, {1000, 1000}];
```

Mathematica recognizes that this array consists entirely of machine numbers and so it *packs* the array automatically.

```
In[78]:= Developer`PackedArrayQ[mat]
Out[78]= True
```

Let's also create an array that is not packed. We can do this by replacing one of the elements in `mat` with a number that is not a machine floating-point number, in this case, replacing the element in the first row, second column of `mat` with the integer `1`.

```
In[79]:= matUnp = ReplacePart[mat, 1, {1, 2}];

In[80]:= Developer`PackedArrayQ[mat2]
Out[80]= False
```

The first thing to notice is the memory saving obtained by using packed arrays.

```
In[81]:= Map[ByteCount, {mat, matUnp}]
Out[81]= {8 000 152, 24 208 200}
```

It takes three times as much memory to store the unpacked array over the packed array.

What about the speed of computations? Linear algebra and other arithmetic operations on such objects is significantly sped up with packed arrays.

```
In[82]:= Timing[Do[mat + Transpose[mat], {100}];]
Out[82]= {0.530168, Null}

In[83]:= Timing[Do[matUnp + Transpose[matUnp], {100}];]
Out[83]= {9.16468, Null}
```

Now we can return to the pattern-matching example earlier in this chapter and see where packed arrays are involved.

```
In[84]:= vec = RandomReal[{-1, 1}, {10^6}];

In[85]:= Count[vec, _?Positive] // Timing
Out[85]= {0.417061, 500 100}

In[86]:= Total[Sign[vec] + 1] / 2 // Timing
Out[86]= {0.027393, 500 100}
```

To see that `Count` is not taking advantage of packed arrays, turn on the display of a message that is issued whenever an array is unpacked internally.

```
In[87]:= SetSystemOptions["PackedArrayOptions" → "UnpackMessage" → True]
Out[87]= PackedArrayOptions → {ListableAutoPackLength → 250,
           PackedArrayMathLinkRead → True, UnpackMessage → True}
```

```
In[88]:= Count[vec, _?Positive]

         Developer`FromPackedArray::unpack : Unpacking array in call to Count. >>

Out[88]= 500100
```

```
In[89]:= Total[Sign[vec] + 1] / 2
Out[89]= 500100
```

The call to `Count` caused the packed vector to be unpacked, essentially for the purposes of pattern matching. This was not the case with the example using `Total` and `Sign`.

Reset the packed array message option to its default value.

```
In[90]:= SetSystemOptions["PackedArrayOptions" → "UnpackMessage" → False]
Out[90]= PackedArrayOptions → {ListableAutoPackLength → 250,
           PackedArrayMathLinkRead → True, UnpackMessage → False}
```

Tip 9.3

A simpler and faster way to turn the packing messages on and off is to use `On` and `Off`.

```
In[91]:= On["Packing"]
```

```
In[92]:= Count[vec, _?Positive]

         Developer`FromPackedArray::unpack : Unpacking array in call to Count. >>

Out[92]= 500100
```

```
In[93]:= Off["Packing"]
```

```
In[94]:= Count[vec, _?Positive]
Out[94]= 500100
```

When packed arrays are used in *Mathematica*, the compiler is invoked, thus generally improving the time it takes for the computation to take place. Many of the built-in functions are designed to take advantage of the packed-array technology. But they do *not* invoke the compiler whenever the time it takes to compile is close to the running time of the computation itself. There are length limits on many common *Mathematica* functions that determine whether the compiler will be used or not. For example, the length limit for `Table` is 250.

```
In[95]:= m1 = Table[i^2, {i, 1.0, 249}];
         Developer`PackedArrayQ[m1]
Out[96]= False
```

```
In[97]:= m2 = Table[i^2, {i, 1.0, 250}];
         Developer`PackedArrayQ[m2]
Out[98]= True
```

For NestList, it is 100 (remember that NestList[*f*, *init*, *n*] produces a list of $n+1$ elements because it prepends the initial value to the list of iterates).

```
In[99]:= n1 = NestList[Sin, .5, 98];
         Developer`PackedArrayQ[n1]
Out[100]= False
```

```
In[101]:= n2 = NestList[Sin, .5, 99];
          Developer`PackedArrayQ[n2]
Out[102]= True
```

These length limits are system parameters that can be displayed and set with SystemOptions.

```
In[103]:= SystemOptions["CompileOptions"]
Out[103]= {CompileOptions → {ApplyCompileLength → ∞, ArrayCompileLength → 250,
    AutoCompileAllowCoercion → False, AutoCompileProtectValues → False,
    AutomaticCompile → False, BinaryTensorArithmetic → False,
    CompileAllowCoercion → True, CompileConfirmInitializedVariables → True,
    CompiledFunctionArgumentCoercionTolerance → 2.10721,
    CompiledFunctionMaxFailures → 3, CompileDynamicScoping → False,
    CompileEvaluateConstants → True, CompileOptimizeRegisters → False,
    CompileParallelizationThreshold → 10, CompileReportCoercion → False,
    CompileReportExternal → False, CompileReportFailure → False,
    CompileValuesLast → True, FoldCompileLength → 100, InternalCompileMessages → False,
    ListableFunctionCompileLength → 250, MapCompileLength → 100,
    NestCompileLength → 100, NumericalAllowExternal → False,
    ProductCompileLength → 250, ReuseTensorRegisters → True, SumCompileLength → 250,
    SystemCompileOptimizations → All, TableCompileLength → 250}}
```

So how do you best take advantage of packed arrays when you write your code? First, whenever possible, it is important that you insure that your lists and arrays consist of machine numbers *all of the same type* – integer, real, or complex. In addition, whenever possible, try to operate on lists and arrays all at once instead of looping through your arrays. Listable operations with packed-array input will use the compiler and will produce packed-array output. Fortunately, many of the commonly used functions have this attribute.

One more suggestion is to coerce unpacked arrays that are operated on a lot to be packed. As an example, consider the two-dimensional random walk model we have touched upon throughout this book. It involves repeatedly operating on an array of compass directions.

```
In[104]:= NSEW = {{0, 1}, {0, -1}, {1, 0}, {-1, 0}};
```

By default, this array is not packed.

```
In[105]:= Developer`PackedArrayQ[NSEW]
Out[105]= False
```

Many functions, such as RandomChoice, will return a nonpacked array when given a nonpacked array as input.

```
In[106]:= Developer`PackedArrayQ[RandomChoice[NSEW, {1000}]]
Out[106]= False
```

To get around this, convert NSEW into a packed array and then pass that to RandomChoice. Notice that the output form of this packed array is the familiar list notation. But internally it is a different, packed, object.

```
In[107]:= nsewPacked = Developer`ToPackedArray[NSEW]
Out[107]= {{0, 1}, {0, -1}, {1, 0}, {-1, 0}}

In[108]:= Developer`PackedArrayQ[nsewPacked]
Out[108]= True
```

Now RandomChoice, upon receiving a packed array as input, returns a packed-array result.

```
In[109]:= Developer`PackedArrayQ[RandomChoice[nsewPacked, {100}]]
Out[109]= True
```

What is the point of this? Speed and memory! Here are two versions of the two-dimensional lattice walk that have been discussed in this book, one using the unpacked array NSEW and the other using nsewPacked:

```
In[110]:= walk2D[n_] := Accumulate[RandomChoice[NSEW, {n}]]

In[111]:= walk2DPacked[n_] := Accumulate[RandomChoice[nsewPacked, {n}]]
```

They both produce the same output.

```
In[112]:= With[{steps = 1000},
            {SeedRandom[0]; ListLinePlot[walk2D[steps]],
             SeedRandom[0]; ListLinePlot[walk2DPacked[steps]]}
          ]
```

Out[112]= { [plot] , [plot] }

But the speed and memory differences are substantial.

```
In[113]:= AbsoluteTiming[w = walk2D[10^7];]
Out[113]= {2.05906, Null}

In[114]:= AbsoluteTiming[wP = walk2DPacked[10^7];]
Out[114]= {0.621493, Null}
```

```
In[115]:= {ByteCount[w], ByteCount[wP]}
Out[115]= {960000080, 160000152}
```

That is better than a four-times improvement in speed and a six-times improvement in the size of the resulting expressions.

Pure functions

Several examples in this chapter have alluded to efficiency issues surrounding the use of pure functions vs. formally defined functions. As a simple example, consider two functions, one defined using pure functions and a second defined using a formal function assignment.

```
In[116]:= funP = Function[{x}, x^2 + 1];

In[117]:= fun[x_] := x^2 + 1

In[118]:= vec = RandomReal[{-100, 100}, 10^6];

In[119]:= AbsoluteTiming[Map[funP, vec];]
Out[119]= {0.073392, Null}

In[120]:= AbsoluteTiming[Map[fun, vec];]
Out[120]= {1.32606, Null}
```

What accounts for this substantial difference in timing? For expressions above a certain size, Map will automatically try to compile that expression. Below is a list of the system options that are involved with internal compilation.

```
In[121]:= Take["CompileOptions" /. SystemOptions["CompileOptions"], -10]
Out[121]= {InternalCompileMessages → False, ListableFunctionCompileLength → 250,
  MapCompileLength → 100, NestCompileLength → 100,
  NumericalAllowExternal → False, ProductCompileLength → 250,
  ReuseTensorRegisters → True, SumCompileLength → 250,
  SystemCompileOptimizations → All, TableCompileLength → 250}
```

For expressions whose size is below the threshold of MapCompileLength, there is little absolute difference in timing results.

```
In[122]:= vecSmall = RandomReal[{-100, 100}, {99}];

In[123]:= AbsoluteTiming[Map[funP, vecSmall];]
Out[123]= {0.000128, Null}

In[124]:= AbsoluteTiming[Map[fun, vecSmall];]
Out[124]= {0.000123, Null}
```

Turning off the autocompile feature by setting the threshold to ∞ shows nearly identical timings for the computations on the large arrays.

```
In[125]:= SetSystemOptions["CompileOptions" → "MapCompileLength" → ∞];

In[126]:= AbsoluteTiming[Map[funP, vec];]
Out[126]= {1.51693, Null}

In[127]:= AbsoluteTiming[Map[fun, vec];]
Out[127]= {1.24301, Null}
```

For programs that call functions within loops in particular, you will see speed improvements by using pure functions on larger arrays whenever possible.

Reset the system option to its default value.

```
In[128]:= SetSystemOptions["CompileOptions" → "MapCompileLength" → 100];
```

Built-in pure functions

Mathematica has several functions built in that behave like pure functions. They are returned as the output of certain computations. For example, when you do an interpolation of some data, an `InterpolatingFunction` object is returned.

```
In[129]:= data = Table[{x, Sin[x]}, {x, 0, 2π, .5}];

In[130]:= f = Interpolation[data]

Out[130]= InterpolatingFunction[ Domain: {{0., 6.}} Output: scalar ]
```

This object behaves much like a pure function. You can evaluate values with it, plot it, differentiate it, and so on.

```
In[131]:= Plot[{f[x], f'[x]}, {x, 0, 2π}]
```

Out[131]=

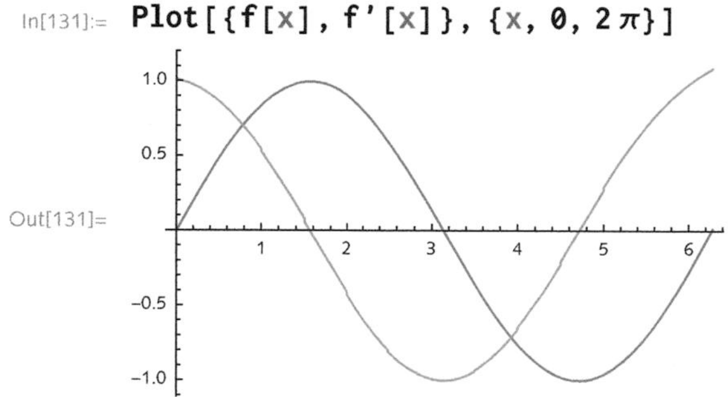

One of the advantages of using such functions is that they are very compact representations of fairly complicated expressions. But for our purposes here, another reason to consider them is that they are generally very fast to compute with. They work by building internal data structures such as trees and heaps, which allow for very fast queries.

As a concrete example, consider the program developed in Section 8.4 for determining if a point is inside or outside a polygon. We saw there that using `RegionMember` on a large set of points was computationally expensive.

```
In[132]:= pts = RandomReal[{-2, 4}, {10000, 2}];
          ℛ = Polygon[{{-0.5, 0}, {0.5, -1}, {1.5, 0},
               {2., -1.1}, {2.5, 0}, {1.5, 2}, {1., 1}, {0., 1}}];

In[134]:= in = Select[pts, RegionMember[ℛ, #] &]; // AbsoluteTiming
Out[134]= {26.0911, Null}
```

Instead of calling `RegionMember` on each of the 10 000 points under consideration, create a `RegionMemberFunction` using the one-argument form of `RegionMember`.

```
In[135]:= rmFun = RegionMember[ℛ]
Out[135]= RegionMemberFunction[ Embedding dimension: 2
                                Region dimension: 2 ]

In[136]:= inRMF = Select[pts, rmFun[#] &]; // AbsoluteTiming
Out[136]= {0.014485, Null}
```

That is over two orders of magnitude faster!

```
In[137]:= in == inRMF
Out[137]= True
```

Other built-in pure functions that can be used similarly include `BezierFunction`, `BooleanFunction`, `CompiledFunction`, `LinearSolveFuntion`, `NearestFunction`, and several others.

Exercises

1. One of the problems with measuring the time it takes to complete a computation is that computers are often busy doing many things simultaneously: checking mail, running system scripts in the background, and so on. To give a more accurate measure of the time spent on a computational task, create a function `AverageTiming` that runs several trials and then averages the results. Set up the function to return both the result and the timing, similar to `Timing` and `AbsoluteTiming`. Be careful that your function does not evaluate its input before it is passed into the body of the function.

2. The nth triangular number is defined as the sum of the integers 1 through n. They are so named because they can be represented visually by arranging rows of dots in a triangular manner (Figure 9.1). Program several different approaches to computing triangular numbers and compare their efficiency.

FIGURE 9.1. *Pictorial representation of the first five triangular numbers.*

3. Recall the Anagrams function in Section 7.2 that used Select to find words in the dictionary consisting of a permutation of the letters of a given word. Here is another implementation, converting the word to a list of characters, getting all permutations of that list of characters, joining the characters in each sublist, and then checking against actual words in the dictionary.

```
In[1]:= Anagrams1[word_String] := Module[{words},
          words = Map[StringJoin, Permutations[Characters[word]]];
          DictionaryLookup[x__ /; MemberQ[words, x]]]

In[2]:= Timing[Anagrams1["alerts"]]

Out[2]= {16.3502, {alerts, alters, salter, staler}}
```

And here is an implementation that uses Alternatives instead of the conditional pattern above:

```
In[3]:= Anagrams2[word_String] := Module[{chars = Characters[word], words},
          words = Map[StringJoin, Permutations[chars]];
          DictionaryLookup[Alternatives @@ words]
         ]

In[4]:= Timing[Anagrams2["alerts"]]

Out[4]= {0.940914, {alerts, alters, salter, staler}}
```

The following implementation from Chapter 7 uses regular expressions and Select but only checks words in the dictionary of the same length as the test word:

```
In[5]:= Anagrams3[word_String] := Module[{len = StringLength[word], words},
          words = DictionaryLookup[RegularExpression["\\w{" <> ToString[len] <> "}"]];
          Select[words, Sort[Characters[#]] == Sort[Characters[word]] &]
         ]

In[6]:= Timing[Anagrams3["alerts"]]

Out[6]= {0.052693, {alerts, alters, salter, staler}}
```

Determine what is causing the sharp differences in timing between these three implementations.

4. Several different implementations of the Hamming distance computation were given in Section 5.6; some run much faster than others. For example, the version with bit operators runs about one-and-a-half orders of magnitude faster than the version using Count and MapThread. Determine what is causing these differences.

```
In[7]:= HammingDistance1[lis1_, lis2_] :=
         Count[MapThread[SameQ, {lis1, lis2}], False]

In[8]:= HammingDistance2[lis1_, lis2_] := Total[BitXor[lis1, lis2]]

In[9]:= sig1 = RandomInteger[1, {10^6}];
        sig2 = RandomInteger[1, {10^6}];

In[11]:= Timing[HammingDistance1[sig1, sig2]]

Out[11]= {0.325111, 499258}

In[12]:= Timing[HammingDistance2[sig1, sig2]]

Out[12]= {0.012189, 499258}
```

5. Consider the computation of the diameter of a set of points in d-dimensional space, $\mathbb{R}^d$, as was done in Exercise 11, Section 5.1.

```
In[13]:= PointsetDiameter[pts_List] :=
          Max[Apply[EuclideanDistance, Subsets[pts, {2}], {1}]]
```

This function suffers from the fact that computing subsets is computationally expensive. Computing pairs of subsets typically is $O(n^2)$ and so the time to do this computation will grow quadratically with the size of the point set. Beyond about 10 000 points, the time is substantial.

```
In[14]:= pts = RandomReal[1, {5000, 2}];
         PointsetDiameter[pts] // Timing

Out[15]= {21.2414, 1.39259}
```

Try to speed up the computation of the diameter by using some computational geometry. In particular, note that the two points contained in the diameter must lie on the convex hull of the point set. Use this observation to substantially reduce the number of subsets that are computed (see O'Rourke 1998).

6. Searching for numbers which are both square and palindromic can be done by using the two predicate functions developed earlier, `SquareNumberQ` (Exercise 4, Section 2.4) and `PalindromeQ` (Section 1.1). For example, using these functions, the following finds all square palindromic numbers below 10^6:

```
In[16]:= With[{n = 10^6},
           Select[Select[Range[n], SquareNumberQ], PalindromeQ]] // Timing

Out[16]= {10.1161, {1, 4, 9, 121, 484, 676, 10201,
           12321, 14641, 40804, 44944, 69696, 94249, 698896}}
```

Somewhat surprisingly, checking for palindromes first and then finding square numbers amongst those, is about three to four times faster.

```
In[17]:= With[{n = 10^6},
           Select[Select[Range[n], PalindromeQ], SquareNumberQ]] // Timing

Out[17]= {3.79878, {1, 4, 9, 121, 484, 676, 10201,
           12321, 14641, 40804, 44944, 69696, 94249, 698896}}
```

Determine why this is so.

7. Consider the Monte Carlo approach to approximating π discussed in several places in this book. One way to perform the simulation is to create a large vector of random points in the square and count the number of such points that lie within the circle $x^2 + y^2 \leq 1$. Here are two approaches, the first using `Apply` at level one, the second using `Map`:

```
In[18]:= pts = RandomReal[{-1, 1}, {10^6, 2}];
         4. Total[Apply[Boole[#1^2 + #2^2 ≤ 1] &, pts, {1}]]/Length[pts] // Timing

Out[19]= {3.31052, 3.1408}

In[20]:= 4. Total[Map[Boole[First[#]^2 + Last[#]^2 ≤ 1] &, pts]]/Length[pts] // Timing

Out[20]= {0.27429, 3.1408}
```

Determine why the approach with `Apply` at level one is over an order of magnitude slower.

9.2 Parallel processing

Most modern computers now come with multiple core processors enabling numerous tasks to be performed in parallel. Many system operations are automatically distributed across multiple processors and *Mathematica* also does some automatic parallelization, particularly for many linear algebra operations. But there are plenty of computations that can be done in parallel that are not otherwise automatically threaded or parallelized. In this section we will see how you can use *Mathematica*'s parallel-processing framework to speed up many kinds of computation.

Depending upon your licensing, *Mathematica* can be launched and run on each available core on your computer. In general, it will handle the communication between the master kernel and the subkernels automatically and when the computation is done, it will also gather the results from the subprocesses. Although there are tools for getting fine control over many of these aspects of parallel computation, in this section we will introduce the basic functionality only and point you at other resources for further study.

Basic examples

Let's start with a straightforward example – factoring a list of large integers. (These integers were created by multiplying several large prime numbers together, giving numbers that are generally more difficult to factor than a random integer of the same size.)

```
In[1]:= ints = {6 816 621 442 891 306 800 904 744 383 119 905 653 635 103 851,
          73 388 383 728 563 244 425 930 590 337 481 080 121 879 717 077,
          52 013 328 811 529 395 666 589 446 962 910 372 930 994 642 737,
          505 513 202 541 467 917 512 749 204 086 148 326 575 935 117 323};
```

Doing the computation on one processor takes about five seconds.

```
In[2]:= AbsoluteTiming[Map[FactorInteger, ints]]
Out[2]= {5.32529, {{{322 901 609 390 167, 1}, {3 515 118 683 942 573, 1}, {6 005 635 550 849 761, 1}},
          {{2 294 373 045 611 351, 1}, {3 323 461 128 609 971, 1}, {9 624 378 352 212 737, 1}},
          {{1 570 432 314 085 519, 1}, {5 086 852 194 050 141, 1}, {6 510 979 192 425 803, 1}},
          {{7 415 796 267 244 853, 1}, {7 673 045 464 769 561, 1}, {8 883 967 089 924 631, 1}}}}
```

The machine on which this computation was performed has four processors on which *Mathematica* can run kernels.

```
In[3]:= $ProcessorCount
Out[3]= 4
```

This launches *Mathematica* on each of the available processors. (In fact, for many of the parallel functions, you do not need to manually launch the kernels like this as most of the parallel functions automatically launch kernels.)

```
In[4]:= LaunchKernels[]
Out[4]= {KernelObject[1, local], KernelObject[2, local],
          KernelObject[3, local], KernelObject[4, local]}
```

To do the factorization in parallel, use `ParallelMap` instead of `Map`. *Mathematica* will automatically distribute the computations across the subkernels and return the result of each.

```
In[5]:= AbsoluteTiming[ParallelMap[FactorInteger, ints]]
Out[5]= {1.46719, {{{322 901 609 390 167, 1}, {3 515 118 683 942 573, 1}, {6 005 635 550 849 761, 1}},
    {{2 294 373 045 611 351, 1}, {3 323 461 128 609 971, 1}, {9 624 378 352 212 737, 1}},
    {{1 570 432 314 085 519, 1}, {5 086 852 194 050 141, 1}, {6 510 979 192 425 803, 1}},
    {{7 415 796 267 244 853, 1}, {7 673 045 464 769 561, 1}, {8 883 967 089 924 631, 1}}}}
```

The results are the same but the computations were distributed across the available kernels, which gives a roughly four-times speedup.

When finished, terminate the *Mathematica* subkernel processes by evaluating `CloseKernels`.

```
In[6]:= CloseKernels[]
Out[6]= {KernelObject[1, local, <defunct>], KernelObject[2, local, <defunct>],
    KernelObject[3, local, <defunct>], KernelObject[4, local, <defunct>]}
```

If you prefer, launching and closing kernels can be managed using a graphical user interface by selecting Parallel Kernel Status from the Evaluation menu. From this interface (Figure 9.2) you can set properties that you want to monitor as well as set various configuration parameters for your kernels.

FIGURE 9.2. *Parallel kernel user interface.*

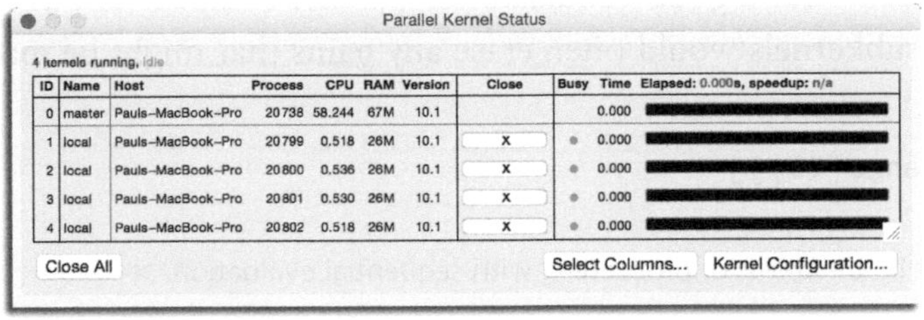

Parallel Kernel Status

4 kernels running, idle

ID	Name	Host	Process	CPU	RAM	Version	Close	Busy	Time	Elapsed: 0.000s, speedup: n/a
0	master	Pauls-MacBook-Pro	20738	58.244	67M	10.1			0.000	
1	local	Pauls-MacBook-Pro	20799	0.518	26M	10.1	X	•	0.000	
2	local	Pauls-MacBook-Pro	20800	0.536	26M	10.1	X	•	0.000	
3	local	Pauls-MacBook-Pro	20801	0.530	26M	10.1	X	•	0.000	
4	local	Pauls-MacBook-Pro	20802	0.518	26M	10.1	X	•	0.000	

Close All | Select Columns... | Kernel Configuration...

Let's look at a larger computation, drawn from Section 5.6, where we computed eigenvalues of binary matrices. First, here is the time to compute the eigenvalues of all the 4×4 binary matrices on a single kernel:

```
In[7]:= Needs["EPM`"]

In[8]:= mats = BinaryMatrix[4];
        AbsoluteTiming[Map[Eigenvalues, mats];]
Out[9]= {31.3737, Null}
```

This is a good problem to parallelize as we are doing the same computation (eigenvalues) on over 65 000 different matrices.

```
In[10]:= Length[mats]
Out[10]= 65 536
```

To start, launch kernels if they are not already running.

```
In[11]:= LaunchKernels[];
```

Let's try the parallel version of Map.

```
In[12]:= ParallelMap[Eigenvalues, mats]; // AbsoluteTiming
Out[12]= {17.5221, Null}
```

Another function, Parallelize, automatically handles much of the parallelization.

```
In[13]:= Parallelize[Map[Eigenvalues, mats]]; // AbsoluteTiming
Out[13]= {18.216, Null}
```

A Method option is available to the parallel functions with which you can set the size of the pieces that are sent to the kernels to give you some additional control of overhead and load balancing amongst the kernels. Setting the method to "FinestGrained" breaks up the computation into the smallest possible chunks. "CoarsestGrained" in contrast, breaks up the computation into as many pieces as there are kernels and is more appropriate when all the computational chunks take about the same amount of time.

```
In[14]:= Parallelize[Map[Eigenvalues, mats],
           Method → "CoarsestGrained"]; // AbsoluteTiming
Out[14]= {18.2943, Null}
```

Of course, some computations do not parallelize neatly. For example, any computation that depends upon previous values is generally not a good candidate for parallel computation as the overhead of communicating between subkernels would often erase any gains that might be made by splitting the computation.

```
In[15]:= Parallelize[Accumulate[Range[25]]]
         Parallelize::nopar1 :
           Accumulate[Range[25]] cannot be parallelized; proceeding with sequential evaluation. >>
Out[15]= {1, 3, 6, 10, 15, 21, 28, 36, 45, 55, 66, 78, 91,
          105, 120, 136, 153, 171, 190, 210, 231, 253, 276, 300, 325}
```

It is important also to note that many of the built-in functions automatically multi-thread, thus gaining a significant degree of parallelism. What this means is that trying to run some of these functions using the parallel framework will not give any further speedup as they already are running in parallel, but behind the scenes so to speak.

```
In[16]:= vec = RandomReal[1, 10^7];

In[17]:= Do[Total[vec], {100}] // AbsoluteTiming
Out[17]= {0.262111, Null}

In[18]:= ParallelDo[Total[vec], {100}] // AbsoluteTiming
Out[18]= {0.710878, Null}
```

Profiling

When you are developing programs it is not always obvious where speed bottlenecks may live. Especially with longer programs, there are numerous steps where the evaluation can bog down. If you are trying to determine which steps will benefit from running in parallel, you need to get some sense of where most of the time is being spent. One way to help locate the computational bottlenecks is to profile the code. Integrated development environments such as Wolfram *Workbench* have built-in profilers, but here we will create a simple set of profiling steps to determine where we should focus our efforts in improving the running time of our code.

Recall the `Blanagrams` function from Section 7.5.

```
Blanagrams[word_String] := Module[{blana},
  blana = Table[
    Map[StringReplacePart[word, ch, {#, #}] &, Range[StringLength[word]]],
    {ch, CharacterRange["a", "z"]}];
  DeleteDuplicates[Flatten[Map[Anagrams, blana, {2}]]]
 ]
```

The nested functions obscure the numerous computations being done here, but if you look carefully, you will see that there are essentially three computations:

- using `Table` to create a list of alternate "words" by sequentially replacing each letter in `word` with one of the twenty-six letters *a* through *z*;
- mapping `Anagrams` across the list produced by `Table`;
- flattening and deleting duplicates.

To profile the steps in this code, we first create a small auxiliary function that wraps `AbsoluteTiming` around an expression and adds a tag to make it easy to identify the various steps of the computation. To prevent `AbsoluteTiming` from evaluating before its argument is passed to it, the `HoldAll` attribute is given to the `timing` function.

```
In[19]:= timing[expr_, tag_] :=
          Print[{NumberForm[First@AbsoluteTiming[expr], 10], tag}]

In[20]:= SetAttributes[timing, HoldAll];
```

For the test word, `"string"`, here are the three steps pulled out of the `Blanagrams` function. First, load the package containing the definition of `Anagrams`.

```
In[21]:= Needs["EPM`"]

In[22]:= word = "string";

In[23]:= timing[tmp = Table[
             Map[StringReplacePart[word, ch, {#, #}] &, Range[StringLength[word]]],
             {ch, CharacterRange["a", "z"]}];, "table of letter combinations"];

         timing[Flatten[tmp2 = Map[Anagrams, tmp, {2}]];, "map Anagrams"];

         timing[DeleteDuplicates[Flatten[tmp2]];, "flatten and delete duplicates"]
```

```
{0.000372, table of letter combinations}

{9.601291, map Anagrams}

{0.000025, flatten and delete duplicates}
```

Creating the many letter combinations is very quick. Similarly, flattening and deleting duplicates at the end is not too expensive. The greatest part of this computation is spent mapping `Anagrams` across the many word combinations. So we can simply try to parallelize that using `ParallelMap`.

```
In[26]:= BlanagramsParallel[word_String] := Module[{blana},
           blana = Table[
             Map[StringReplacePart[word, ch, {#, #}] &, Range[StringLength[word]]],
             {ch, CharacterRange["a", "z"]}];
           DeleteDuplicates@Flatten[ParallelMap[Anagrams, blana, {2}]]]
```

There is no need to distribute `BlanagramsParallel` across the subkernels as the only parallel piece in it is `ParallelMap`. But `ParallelMap` is mapping `Anagrams`, which is not a built-in function, so we need to distribute that definition across the subkernels.

```
In[27]:= LaunchKernels[];
         DistributeDefinitions[Anagrams]

Out[28]= {Anagrams}

In[29]:= BlanagramsParallel["strands"] // AbsoluteTiming
Out[29]= {3.95019, {strands, stander, sanders, strains, tundras}}
```

For comparison, here is the computation done serially on one kernel:

```
In[30]:= Blanagrams["strands"] // AbsoluteTiming
Out[30]= {13.9307, {strands, stander, sanders, strains, tundras}}
```

On the machine on which this computation was run, we are getting about a four-times speedup. Recall that each evaluation of `Anagrams` makes a call to `DictionaryLookup` to check that the string is in fact a word appearing in the dictionary. This bit of extra overhead is a further bottleneck in this particular code. We could next look to `Anagrams` as another source of code to optimize and speed up, but we will leave that as an exercise for the interested reader (see Exercise 3, Section 9.1).

Tip 9.4

There is a cleaner mechanism for sharing package definitions across subkernels: use `ParallelNeeds`.

```
In[31]:= ParallelNeeds["EPM`"]
```

You can then see that the package has been added to the context path of each subkernel.

```
In[32]:= ParallelEvaluate[$ContextPath, Kernels[]]
Out[32]= {{EPM`, PacletManager`, System`, Global`}, {EPM`, PacletManager`, System`, Global`},
          {EPM`, PacletManager`, System`, Global`}, {EPM`, PacletManager`, System`, Global`}}
```

`ParallelNeeds["package`"]` effectively evaluates `Needs["package`"]` on each subkernel. Note though that `ParallelNeeds` does *not* load the package on the master kernel.

```
In[33]:= CloseKernels[];
```

Exercises

1. Many different methods can be used to smooth a noisy signal. Depending upon the nature of the data (periodic, for example) and the nature of the noise, some smoothing methods are more appropriate than others. Given a noisy signal, compare a variety of smoothing methods in parallel by displaying the original signal together with each smoothed version. For example, this displays the original signal together with an eight-term weighted moving average:

```
In[1]:= signal = Table[Sin[t] + RandomReal[0.2], {t, -2 π, 2 π, 0.05}];
In[2]:= ma = MovingAverage[signal, {1, 2, 6, 8, 6, 2, 1} / 8];
        ListPlot[{signal, ma}, Joined → {False, True}, PlotStyle → {Automatic, Red}]
Out[3]=
```

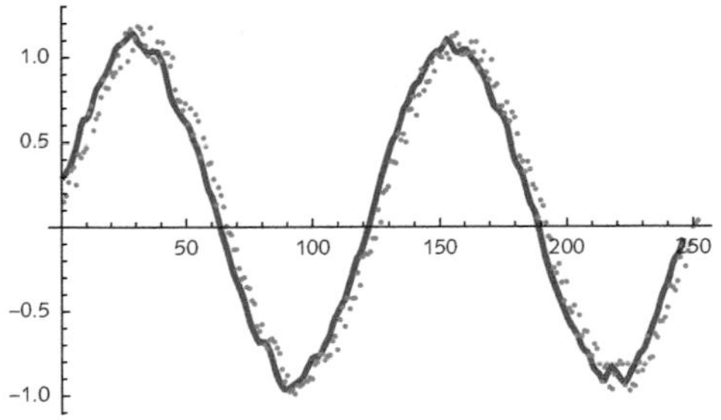

Example smoothers to consider include moving averages with different numbers of terms and weights, a convolution with a Gaussian kernel, a lowpass filter, and any others you might be familiar with (wavelets, for example).

2. The search for perfect numbers programmed in Exercise 6 in Section 5.1 gets bogged down for searches of more than one million numbers. Try to speed it up by considering the range of numbers searched, the built-in functions used, and the possibility of doing the computation in parallel.

3. In the eighteenth century, Leonhard Euler proved that all even perfect numbers must be of the form $2^{p-1}(2^p - 1)$ for $2^p - 1$ prime and p a prime number. (No one has yet proved that any odd perfect numbers exist.) Use this fact to find all even perfect numbers for $p < 10^4$.

4. A common task in many areas of computational linguistics is comparing certain features of a text across a broad corpus. One such comparison is counting the occurrence of a certain word across numerous texts. This is a good problem for parallel computation. Use the parallel tools to import and count the occurrence of a word, say *history*, across four different texts. Gutenberg.org is a good source for importing entire texts, but any available source could be used as well.

5. Monte Carlo simulations are computations that use random sampling to approximate a numerical result. One of the classical examples is the approximation to π. The idea is to generate a large number of random numbers in a square and compute the proportion that lie within the inscribed circle (Figure 9.3). The approximation to π is four times this proportion. This method converges quite slowly, so a large number of points and averaging many trials is needed to get better approximations.

FIGURE 9.3. *Monte Carlo simulation for approximating π.*

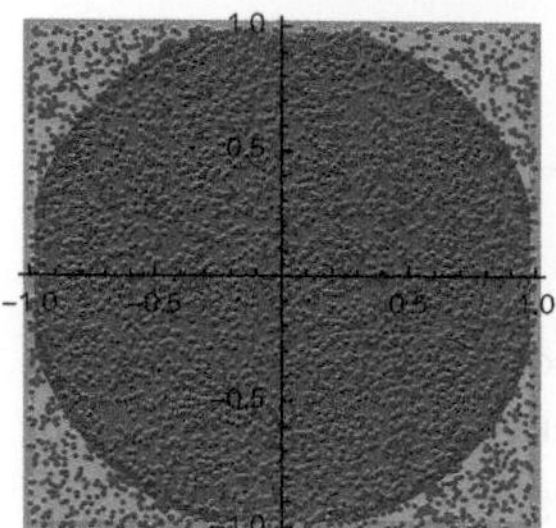

Use `RandomReal` to create points in a square, then count points inside the inscribed disk using two different implementations – one with a `Do` loop and another using the computational geometry machinery (`RegionMember` in particular). Compare the efficiency of these two implementations.

6. The following code can be used to create a plot of the Mandelbrot set. It uses `Table` to compute the value for each point in the complex plane on a small grid. We have deliberately chosen a relatively coarse grid ($n = 100$) as this is an intensive and time-consuming computation. The last argument to `NestWhileList`, 250 here, sets a limit on the number of iterations that can be performed for each input. Increase the resolution of the graphic by running the computation of the table of points in parallel.

```
In[4]:= Mandelbrot[c_] := Length[NestWhileList[#^2 + c &, 0, Abs[#] < 2 &, 1, 250]]

In[5]:= data = With[{n = 100},
           Table[Mandelbrot[x + I y], {y, -1.3, 1.3, 1/n}, {x, -2, 0.6, 1/n}]];

In[6]:= ArrayPlot[data, ColorFunction → "GreenPinkTones"]
```

Out[6]=

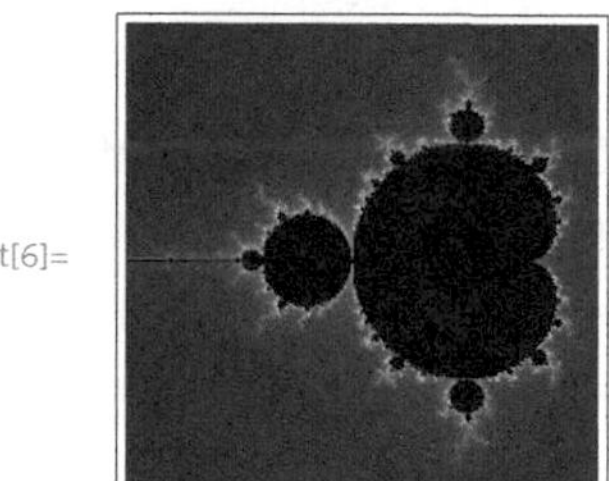

9.3 Compiling

Compiled functions are objects that can be executed quickly by being close to the machine code of your computer. The great advantage of working with compiled functions is that they are very fast. Part of the reason they are fast is that they do not need to worry about all the possible kinds of expressions upon which they might be called to operate.

For example, the built-in `Plus` function has to handle any kind of argument it might be given – integer, complex, real, rational, symbolic.

```
In[1]:= {1 / 3 + 2, 2 - 4 I + 5.1, 2 + 7, x + x}
Out[1]= {7/3, 7.1 - 4. i, 9, 2 x}
```

This kind of generality comes at a cost: *Mathematica* needs to keep track of the kinds of numbers you are passing to arithmetic functions so that the correct internal rule is applied, precision and accuracy are tracked and maintained, and so on. A compiled function, however, has its argument type explicitly specified so that it only operates on arguments of that type.

Many of the built-in functions make use of automatic compilation to speed things up behind the scenes. You don't need to do anything special to take advantage of this for many of the numeric and optimization functions. For your critical computations – those that are repeated many times or are bottlenecks in larger computations – you can improve the running times by compiling parts of your code. In this section we will see how.

Compile

Let's start with a basic example: creating a compiled function called `cfun` that does some simple arithmetic on its argument. It is expecting an argument `x` that must match the pattern `_Real`, that is, the argument must have head `Real`.

```
In[2]:= cfun = Compile[{{x, _Real}}, x^2 + 1]
Out[2]= CompiledFunction[ WVM Argument count: 1
                              Argument types: {_Real} ]
```

A `CompiledFunction` object is created using something called the *Mathematica* virtual machine. Essentially, *Mathematica* contains a compiler that can be used for this purpose. The advantage is that it is easy to use and does not require you to have a C compiler installed on your computer.

You use a compiled function like any other; for example, you can evaluate it at an argument or plot it, or map it across an array.

```
In[3]:= cfun[2.0]
Out[3]= 5.
```

```
In[4]:= Plot[cfun[x], {x, -1, 1}]
```

Out[4]=


```
In[5]:= Map[cfun, {{-10., -9.}, {7., -10.}}, {2}]
Out[5]= {{101., 82.}, {50., 101.}}
```

The point of creating and working with compiled functions is that they can speed up computations. This is most pronounced with expressions that have to be evaluated many times. For example, let's return to one of the functions created in Section 9.1.

```
In[6]:= fun[x_] := If[-1 < x < 1, Exp[x], x^2]

In[7]:= vec = RandomReal[{-100, 100}, 10^6];

In[8]:= AbsoluteTiming[Map[fun, vec];]
Out[8]= {1.57955, Null}
```

Here is the compiled version:

```
In[9]:= compfun = Compile[{{x, _Real}}, If[-1 < x < 1, Exp[x], x^2]]

Out[9]= CompiledFunction[ Argument count: 1
                          Argument types: {_Real} ]

In[10]:= AbsoluteTiming[Map[compfun, vec];]
Out[10]= {0.216692, Null}
```

Not bad, but we can go a bit further and add a runtime attribute to the compiled function that makes it listable.

```
In[11]:= compfunListable = Compile[{{x, _Real}},
           If[-1 < x < 1, Exp[x], x^2], RuntimeAttributes → {Listable}]

Out[11]= CompiledFunction[ Argument count: 1
                           Argument types: {_Real} ]

In[12]:= AbsoluteTiming[compfunListable[vec];]
Out[12]= {0.057439, Null}
```

Another option, `Parallelization → True`, sets the function to run in parallel if run on a multicore machine.

```
In[13]:= compfunParallel = Compile[{{x, _Real}}, If[-1 < x < 1, Exp[x], x^2],
           RuntimeAttributes → {Listable}, Parallelization → True]

Out[13]= CompiledFunction[ Argument count: 1
                           Argument types: {_Real} ]

In[14]:= AbsoluteTiming[compfunParallel[vec];]
Out[14]= {0.050209, Null}
```

An additional option can be specified to optimize for speed: `RuntimeOptions` with the value `"Speed"`. The caveat here is that this turns off checks and warning messages that might be issued if underflow or overflow errors were caught. Use it with caution.

```
In[15]:= compfunSpeed = Compile[{{x, _Real}},
           If[-1 < x < 1, Exp[x], x^2], RuntimeAttributes → {Listable},
           Parallelization → True, RuntimeOptions → "Speed"
         ]
Out[15]= CompiledFunction[ Argument count: 1
                           Argument types: {_Real} ]
```

```
In[16]:= AbsoluteTiming[compfunSpeed[vec];]
Out[16]= {0.051625, Null}
```

If you want to see some of the internals of what `Compile` produces, use `CompilePrint`, which is defined in the ``CompiledFunctionTools` `` package (we only show a short fragment of the code).

```
In[17]:= << CompiledFunctionTools`

In[18]:= CompilePrint[compfunSpeed] // Short
Out[18]//Short=
                1 argument
                1 Boolean reg … uare[ R0]
         9    R4 = R2
         10    Return
```

In general, compiling using *Mathematica*'s virtual machine is not going to compete in optimized code with a commercial C compiler. We look at compiling to C next.

Compiling to C

If you have a third-party C compiler installed on your computer, you can compile your functions to C, thus taking advantage of any optimizations inherent in your C compiler. If you are not sure if your system has a C compiler installed, evaluate `SystemInformation[]` and look under the section External Compilers ▸ Available C Compilers. Alternatively, you can list any C compilers that are installed on your computer as follows:

```
In[19]:= Needs["CCompilerDriver`"]

In[20]:= CCompilers[]
Out[20]= {{Name → Clang, Compiler → CCompilerDriver`ClangCompiler`ClangCompiler,
           CompilerInstallation → /usr/bin, CompilerName → Automatic},
          {Name → GCC, Compiler → CCompilerDriver`GCCCompiler`GCCCompiler,
           CompilerInstallation → /usr/bin, CompilerName → Automatic}}
```

The syntax to compile to C code is `Compile[…, CompilationTarget → "C"]`. For example, the following code compiles the function from the last section to C:

```
In[21]:= compfunC =
          Compile[{{x, _Real}}, If[-1 < x < 1, Exp[x], x^2], CompilationTarget → "C"]

Out[21]= CompiledFunction[ Argument count: 1
                           Argument types: {_Real} ]
```

For this example, the C compiler provides a speedup over using *Mathematica*'s virtual machine in the example done without runtime attributes or options.

```
In[22]:= AbsoluteTiming[Map[compfunC, vec];]
Out[22]= {0.073619, Null}
```

You could also compile to an executable file (using `CreateExecutable`) and run that either inside or outside *Mathematica*. We will not cover that here.

Finally, let's combine several of the optimization suggestions in this chapter in one nontrivial computation. We will create a compiled function that computes the points in the Julia set, defined as the set of points in the complex plane that remain bounded under iteration of a function such as $z^2 + c$. The basic idea is to fix a value of c in the complex plane and then iterate the function for points z on a fine grid in the complex plane. For most values of $c \in \mathbb{C}$ (the set of complex numbers), this iteration generates fractals when coloring points according to their iteration length. Since there are many points and many iterations for each point, this is very computationally intensive and so it is a good candidate for some of the techniques we have been discussing in this chapter.

First, here is the compiled version of the Julia set function. `Length` returns the length of the list of iterates. We will iterate each point until the iterate is a certain distance from the origin.

```
In[23]:= cJulia = Compile[{{z, _Complex}, {c, _Complex}},
           Length@FixedPointList[(#^2 + c &), z, 100, SameTest → (Abs[#2] > 2.0 &)],
           CompilationTarget → "C", RuntimeAttributes → {Listable},
           RuntimeOptions → "Speed"]

Out[23]= CompiledFunction[ Argument count: 2
                           Argument types: {_Complex, _Complex} ]
```

The grid of values that the function will evaluate is given by `ParallelTable` below. The result is passed to `ArrayPlot`, which colors each point in the grid according to its iteration length as given by the output of `cJulia`.

```
In[24]:= LaunchKernels[];

In[25]:= DistributeDefinitions[cJulia]
Out[25]= {cJulia}
```

Different Julia sets are generated for different complex numbers c. Here is the Julia set for the complex number $c = -0.8 - 0.156\,i$:

```
In[26]:= With[{res = 500}, ArrayPlot[
           ParallelTable[-cJulia[x + y ⅈ, -0.8 - 0.156 ⅈ], {y, -.85, .85, 1/res},
            {x, -1.5, 1.5, 1/res}], ColorFunction → "Pastel"]] // AbsoluteTiming
```

Out[26]= {4.04318, }

Changing c means changing both its real and imaginary parts, so this is a good candidate for a dynamic interface. We could use a 2D slider, but as we saw in Section 8.2, it is a bit more convenient to use a locator instead to manipulate the point c directly. Below, we include a different implementation of the Julia function as part of the initialization, as well as a dynamic plot label to display the value of the parameter c as the locator is moved.

```
In[27]:= Manipulate[Graphics[{
            PointSize[Tiny], Point[Transpose[{Re[#], Im[#]}] &@
              Nest[julia[Apply[Complex, loc], #] &, {0.0}, 12]]
           }, PlotLabel → StringForm["c = `1`", Apply[Complex, loc]]],
          {{loc, {-0.4, 0.6}}, {-2, -2}, {2, 2}, Locator},
          Initialization :→ {julia = Compile[{{c, _Complex}, {z, _Complex, 1}},
              Flatten[{√(z - c), -√(z - c)}], CompilationTarget → "C"]
          }]
```

Out[27]= 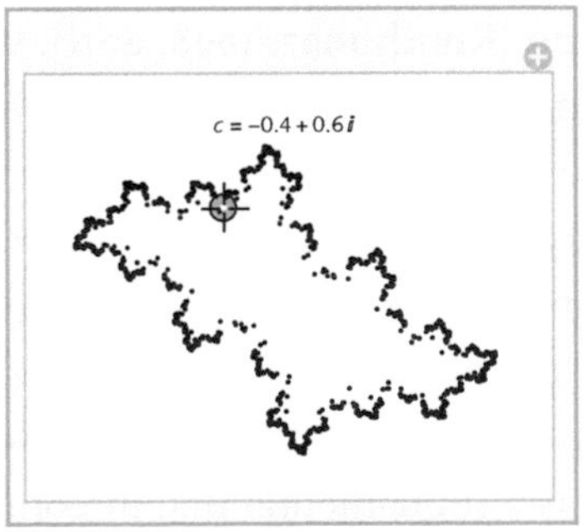


```
In[28]:= CloseKernels[];
```

Exercises

1. Create a compiled function that computes the distance to the origin of a two-dimensional point. Then compare it to some of the built-in functions such as `Norm` and `EuclideanDistance` to compute the distances for a large set of points. If you have a C compiler installed on your computer, use the `Compile` option `CompilationTarget→ "C"` and compare the results.

2. Modify the previous exercise under the assumption that complex numbers are given as input to your compiled function.

3. Padé approximants are rational functions that are often used to approximate functions whose Taylor series does not converge. For example, the Taylor series for $\ln(1 + x)$ has poor convergence on $0 \leq x \leq 1$. Here is its third-order Padé approximant:

```
In[1]:= PadeApproximant[Log[1 + x], {x, 0, 3}]
```

Out[1]=
$$\frac{x + x^2 + \frac{11 x^3}{60}}{1 + \frac{3 x}{2} + \frac{3 x^2}{5} + \frac{x^3}{20}}$$

   Create a compiled function that computes the above expression for x a real number and then evaluate a range of values from zero to two and make a discrete plot of the differences between the approximated values and `Log[1 + x]`.

4. Many other iteration functions can be used for the Julia set computation. Experiment with some other functions such as $c \sin(z)$, $c\, e^z$, or Gaston Julia's original function:

$$z^4 + z^3/(z - 1) + z^2/(z^3 + 4 z^2 + 5) + c.$$

   For these functions, you will have to adjust the test to determine if a point is unbounded upon iteration. Try `(Abs[Im[#]] > 50 &)`.

9.4 Notes and further reading

For a look at the algorithmic side of program optimization, see Skiena (2008) but of course also Donald Knuth's books on the art of computer programming (Knuth 1997, 1998, 2011), which contain a seemingly endless trove of useful and practical information on algorithms and the problems that inspire them.

Monte Carlo simulation is widely used to get numerical approximations to quantities using random sampling. For an interesting look at the early history of Monte Carlo techniques on the ENIAC computer, see Metropolis (1987). For more recent treatments, see Press et al. (2007) and Wagon (1999). For an application to computational geometry, see Clarkson and Shor (1989).

The problem of computing the diameter of a point set is a fundamental one in computational geometry and has application to robotic vision, pattern recognition, and image processing. Information can be found in Har-Peled (2001), Malandain and Boissonnat (2002), and O'Rourke (1998).

In addition to the built-in tutorials Numerical Operations on Functions and also Numbers (WLDC), a comprehensive tome on numerical computation in *Mathematica* is Trott (2006), which includes many useful insights into the intricacies of numerical computation in *Mathematica*.

10

Packages

Working with packages · *Loading and using packages* · *Package location* · ***Creating packages*** · *Contexts* · *Package framework* · *Creation and deployment* · ***RandomWalks package*** · *Package source code* · *Running the package* · ***Notes and further reading***

After you have developed several programs for some related tasks, you will find it convenient to group them together and make them available as a cohesive whole. Packages are designed to make it easy to distribute your programs to others, but they also provide a framework for you to write programs that integrate with *Mathematica* seamlessly.

A package is simply a text file containing *Mathematica* code. Typically you put related functions in a package. So there might be a computational geometry package or a random walks package that includes functions in support of those tasks. The package framework includes a *name-localizing* construct, analogous to `Module`, but for entire files of definitions. The idea is to allow you, the programmer, to define a collection of functions for *export*. These exported functions are what the users of your package will work with and are often referred to as *public* functions. Other functions, those that are *not for export*, are auxiliary, or *private* functions, and are not intended to be accessible to users. The package framework, and contexts specifically, provide a convenient way to declare some functions public and others private. In this chapter we will describe this framework and show how to write, install, and use the packages developed with it.

10.1 Working with packages

Loading and using packages

Upon starting a *Mathematica* session, the built-in functions are immediately available for you to use. There are, however, many more functions that you can access that reside in files supplied with *Mathematica*. The definitions in those files are placed in special structures called *packages*. Indeed, these files themselves are often called "packages" instead of "files."

Mathematica packages have been written for many different domains. They are provided with each version of *Mathematica* and are referred to as the Standard Extra Packages. Their documentation is available in the Documentation Center (under the Help menu) and they provide a good set of examples for learning about package creation and usage.

For example, one of the packages listed under the Standard Extra Packages is the Statistical Plots package. It provides functionality for visualizing such things as Pareto plots, stem–leaf plots, and pairwise scatter plots.

To load a package that you want to use, use Get. For example, the following uses the shorthand notation for Get to read the package; that is, << *package*` is shorthand for Get["*package*`"]. Actually, the argument of << is a string, but the quotation marks can be omitted.

```
In[1]:= << StatisticalPlots`
```

Alternatively, you can use Needs["StatisticalPlots`"] to read the package. This is just like Get, but will only load the package if it has not previously been loaded.

```
In[2]:= Needs["StatisticalPlots`"]
```

Once a package has been loaded into the *Mathematica* kernel, you can access and use the functions defined in that package just like any built-in function. For example, you can use ? to get the usage message for any of those functions.

```
In[3]:= ?ParetoPlot
```

ParetoPlot[*list*] creates a Pareto plot from the frequencies of the elements in *list*.
ParetoPlot[{{cat_1, $freq_1$}, {cat_2, $freq_2$}, ...}]
creates a Pareto plot from categories cat_i with frequencies $freq_i$. >>

Using a function from a package is just like using a built-in function. For example, this computes a Pareto plot which shows a bar chart of frequency for each category in a data set together with a line showing cumulative percentages for each category:

```
In[4]:= data = {v, u, y, w, w, u, u, z, v, u, v, u, u};
        ParetoPlot[data]
```

Out[5]=

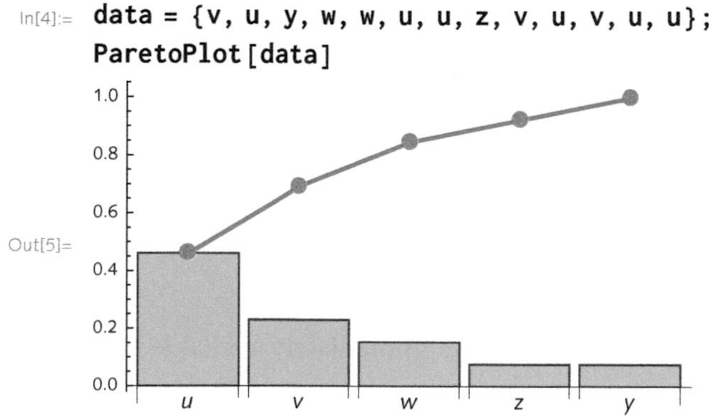

To display a list of the names defined in the package use Names.

```
In[6]:= Names["StatisticalPlots`*"]

Out[6]= {BoxExtraSpacing, BoxFillingStyle, BoxLabels, BoxLineStyle, BoxMedianStyle,
  BoxOrientation, BoxOutlierMarkers, BoxOutliers, BoxQuantile,
  BoxWhiskerPlot, ColumnLabels, DataLabels, DataRanges, DataSpacing,
  DataTicks, IncludeEmptyStems, IncludeStemCounts, IncludeStemUnits, Leaves,
  PairwiseScatterPlot, ParetoPlot, PlotDirection, StemExponent, StemLeafPlot}
```

If you forget the name of the package, you can browse through the Documentation Center which lists all packages, names, and usage messages of the functions defined in these packages. Alternatively, you can locate where the directory of packages is stored on your system and browse through it using your operating system's file browsing interface.

Package location

All the built-in *Mathematica* packages are located in one of several directories on *Mathematica*'s search path. If you put your package in one of these special directories, it will be found quickly when you try to load it with Get or Needs. This search path is given by $Path. Here we display only some of these locations.

```
In[7]:= Take[$Path, 8] // TableForm

Out[7]//TableForm=
  /Applications/Mathematica.app/Contents/SystemFiles/Links
  /Users/paulwellin/Library/Mathematica/Kernel
  /Users/paulwellin/Library/Mathematica/Autoload
  /Users/paulwellin/Library/Mathematica/Applications
  /Library/Mathematica/Kernel
  /Library/Mathematica/Autoload
  /Library/Mathematica/Applications
  .
```

Typically, packages are put in one of the following Applications directories on the path:

```
In[8]:= Select[$Path, MatchQ[FileNameTake[#], "Applications"] &] // TableForm

Out[8]//TableForm=
  /Users/paulwellin/Library/Mathematica/Applications
  /Library/Mathematica/Applications
  /Applications/Mathematica.app/Contents/AddOns/Applications
```

Certain special directories are identified on your system by means of a built-in symbol.

```
In[9]:= $UserBaseDirectory

Out[9]= /Users/paulwellin/Library/Mathematica

In[10]:= $BaseDirectory

Out[10]= /Library/Mathematica
```

These directories will be different on different operating systems, but putting a package in one of the Applications directories will work across systems consistently. For example, the instructions to install the packages that accompany this book specify that you should put them in one of the directories given by evaluating the following inputs on your computer:

```
In[11]:= FileNameJoin[{$BaseDirectory, "Applications"}]
Out[11]= /Library/Mathematica/Applications

In[12]:= FileNameJoin[{$UserBaseDirectory, "Applications"}]
Out[12]= /Users/paulwellin/Library/Mathematica/Applications
```

Alternatively, you could use the Install item in the File menu to be guided through the process somewhat automatically. This is described in the section below on creating and installing packages.

If you know the name of your package, you can use `FindFile` to see precisely where the package is located. Specifically, using the package name as an argument returns the location of the Kernel/init.m file. This works whether your package has been loaded or not.

```
In[13]:= FindFile["EPM`"]
Out[13]= /Users/paulwellin/Library/Mathematica/Applications/EPM/Kernel/init.m
```

Typically, the Kernel/init.m file contains initialization code that needs to be evaluated whenever your package is loaded. For example, the init.m file that is part of the packages that accompany this book includes commands such as `Get["EPM`RandomWalks`"]` to load particular packages.

10.2 Creating packages

Packages provide a framework to organize a collection of related functions that extend the functionality of *Mathematica* in some way. With them, you can identify private functions and constants that the user, or client, of the package will not ordinarily see. Usage and warning messages for the public functions, those that the user of your package will interact with, are also defined in the package. When set up properly using contexts, packages help to avoid naming collisions, or shadowing, with other definitions of those names.

Contexts

Your packages will usually contain several new rules that define the functionality of your package. Of course you want the symbols associated with these rules – typically the head of your functions – to behave much like the built-in function names. And, importantly, those symbols which might have similar names to other symbols should not conflict with any existing symbols. The way to organize the symbols in your packages and keep their names isolated from any others is to put them into a *context*, which is a mechanism for organizing the namespace in *Mathematica*.

Every symbol you use in a computation in *Mathematica* has a *full name* consisting of the symbol preceded by the *context* in which the name was first mentioned. The context is a means for organizing symbols. You can think of the context like a namespace – different symbols are in different contexts just like different files on your computer live in different directories.

When you first start your session, the current context is `Global`` (note the back quote), and any symbol you mention will have full name given by `Global``*symbol*.

For example, here is a function created, by default, in the `Global`` context:

```
In[1]:= f[x_] := x + 1
```

`Context[sym]` gives the context of the symbol *sym*.

```
In[2]:= Context[f]
Out[2]= Global`
```

You can use the function by specifying its full name.

```
In[3]:= Global`f[3]
Out[3]= 4
```

But, of course, it is much more convenient to use the regular, short form.

```
In[4]:= f[3]
Out[4]= 4
```

Mathematica first searches the current context for definitions associated with any symbols; by default, this is the `Global`` context. `$Context` gives the current context.

```
In[5]:= $Context
Out[5]= Global`
```

To see a list of the contexts that *Mathematica* uses to search for symbols, use `$ContextPath`. Note that the `StatisticalPlots`` context is included as we loaded that package in the previous section.

```
In[6]:= $ContextPath
Out[6]= {StatisticalPlots`, PacletManager`, System`, Global`}
```

Built-in functions have context `System``. Symbols defined in packages have their context set by the package (discussed below).

```
In[7]:= Map[Context, {Integrate, f, ParetoPlot}]
Out[7]= {System`, Global`, StatisticalPlots`}
```

To use a different context for any new symbols you mention, use the function `Begin`.

```
In[8]:= Begin["ContextA`"]
Out[8]= ContextA`

In[9]:= g[x_] := x + 2
```

This uses g by specifying its full name.

```
In[10]:= ContextA`g[3]
Out[10]= 5
```

Or, since we are currently in the `ContextA`` context, use the short name. In this new context, the name g is an abbreviation for `ContextA`g`.

```
In[11]:= g[3]
Out[11]= 5
```

Here is the current context:

```
In[12]:= $Context
Out[12]= ContextA`
```

Note that we can still refer to f, even though it was not defined in this context. This is because f lives in the Global` context, which is searched as part of $ContextPath.

```
In[13]:= Map[Global`f, {5, 7, 9}]
Out[13]= {6, 8, 10}

In[14]:= Map[f, {5, 7, 9}]
Out[14]= {6, 8, 10}
```

After exiting the context using End, you could define a different g, having context Global`.

```
In[15]:= End[]
Out[15]= ContextA`

In[16]:= g[x_] := x + 3

In[17]:= g[3]
Out[17]= 6

In[18]:= Context[g]
Out[18]= Global`
```

There are now two definitions of g: one definition of Global`g and one of ContextA`g. Since the current context is Global`, when we just say g we get Global`g; but we can still refer to ContextA`g by its full name.

```
In[19]:= g[3]
Out[19]= 6

In[20]:= ContextA`g[3]
Out[20]= 5
```

The question arises: when you enter a symbol *sym*, how does *Mathematica* decide which version of *sym* to use? And how can you tell which one it has chosen? As we saw above, the function Context gives the context of a symbol.

```
In[21]:= Context[Map]
Out[21]= System`

In[22]:= Context[ContextA`g]
Out[22]= ContextA`
```

You can also use ?.

```
In[23]:= ?g
```

```
Global`g

g[x_] := x + 3
```

How does *Mathematica* decide which definition to use? It maintains two variables, `$Context` and `$ContextPath`. `$Context` contains the current context; `$ContextPath` contains a list of contexts. *Mathematica* looks in `$Context` first, then in the contexts in `$ContextPath` in the order in which they appear there; if it does not find the symbol, it creates it in context `$Context`. None of this applies if you give the symbol's full name.

```
In[24]:= $Context
Out[24]= Global`

In[25]:= Begin["ContextA`"]
Out[25]= ContextA`

In[26]:= $Context
Out[26]= ContextA`

In[27]:= $ContextPath
Out[27]= {StatisticalPlots`, PacletManager`, System`, Global`}

In[28]:= End[]
Out[28]= ContextA`

In[29]:= $Context
Out[29]= Global`
```

The effect of entering a new context using `Begin` is simply to change the value of `$Context`; evaluating `End[]` changes it back. In either case, `$ContextPath` is not changed.

```
In[30]:= $ContextPath
Out[30]= {StatisticalPlots`, PacletManager`, System`, Global`}
```

Contexts can be nested, that is, you can have context names like `` A`B`C` ``.

```
In[31]:= Begin["A`"]        (* enter context A` *)
Out[31]= A`

In[32]:= Begin["`B`"]       (* enter context A`B` *)
Out[32]= A`B`

In[33]:= End[]              (* back in context A` *)
Out[33]= A`B`

In[34]:= End[]              (* back in context Global` *)
Out[34]= A`
```

Note the back quote *before* the context name in the second and third `Begin`. This is used to indicate that the new context should be a subcontext of the current context. We could have also indicated this as follows:

```
In[35]:= Begin["A`"]
Out[35]= A`

In[36]:= Begin["A`B`"]
Out[36]= A`B`
```

Nested contexts are a way of managing the multiplicity of contexts. In fact, package names are contexts. When you load a package using `Needs` or <<, *Mathematica* translates the package name directly into a path name in the hierarchical file system on your computer.

For example, you can load the package `RandomWalks.m` that lives in a directory EPM according to the commands given in Table 10.1.

TABLE 10.1. *Commands to load packages on different systems*

Operating system	Input
Windows	`<< EPM\RandomWalks.m`
Unix X/Linux	`<< EPM/RandomWalks.m`

Since *Mathematica* provides a system-independent means of loading packages, the preferred way to load the package is to simply use `Get` with the following system-independent syntax and *Mathematica* will automatically translate this into a path name appropriate for your computer:

```
<< EPM`RandomWalks`
```

Package framework

In this section, we will lay out the package framework that you can use as a template for developing your packages. This framework contains several elements that you need to include in your package (Program Listing 10.1). You can create these in a new *Mathematica* notebook or use the PackageTemplate.nb notebook that accompanies this book's support materials (see Preface).

PROGRAM LISTING 10.1. *Package template*

```
BeginPackage["packName`"]

(* usage messages *)
package::usage = "usage message here...";

(* options *)
Options[package] = {opt1 → value1, opt2 → value2, ...}

(* private context *)
Begin["`Private`"]
```

```
(* function definitions *)
fun[x_] := ...
fun2[x_, y_] := ...

(* end private context *)
End[]

EndPackage[]
```

BeginPackage and EndPackage Packages start with a `BeginPackage` statement and end with an `EndPackage`. Evaluating `BeginPackage["`*packName*`` ` ``"]` sets `$Context` to *packName*`` ` ``, and also sets `$ContextPath` to `{`*packName*`` ` ``, ``System` ``}`. `EndPackage[]` resets both variables to their values prior to the evaluation of `BeginPackage[]`, and then prepends *packName*`` ` `` to `$ContextPath`.

It is important to realize, too, that *Mathematica* determines the full name of any symbol when it reads it in. Thus, if `g` calls `f`, then the occurrence of `f` in the body of `g` becomes *packName*`` `f `` when *packName* is loaded. `g` will always call this `f`, even if there is a different `f` defined in the context in which the call to `g` is made.

The `BeginPackage` function can be given multiple arguments. The second and subsequent arguments are the names of other packages that this one uses. They are treated as if they were arguments to the `Needs` function, that is, they are loaded if they are not already loaded. Furthermore, they are included in `$ContextPath` *during the loading* of this package, so its functions can be referred to by their short names.

Usage and warning messages Put usage messages for all public functions immediately after the `BeginPackage`. Defining usage messages for the functions in your packages creates symbols for the functions in the current context. Each of the functions for which you define a usage message will be exported for public use, that is, those functions are visible and usable immediately after loading the package. This is in contrast to any functions that are defined in your package for which you do not have usage messages (or, more precisely, for those functions that you have not explicitly exported by mentioning that symbol before the `Begin` statement). Those functions will be private, unavailable for the user of your package to access.

Options Options for each public function should follow next. Options for private functions should follow the `Begin` statement, that is, options for private functions should themselves be private.

`Options[`*functionName*`] = {`$opt_1 \to value_1$`, `$opt_2 \to value_2$`}`

Begin private context The `Begin` command changes the current context without affecting the context path. Starting the argument ``` `Private` ``` with a context mark `` ` `` changes to a subcontext of the current context.

Function definitions Definitions for both public and private functions follow next. Only those functions that have been declared public (typically via usage messages before the `Begin` statement) will be available to the user of your package.

End private context The `End[]` command closes the `Begin[]` and returns you to the package context *packName*`` ` ``. Symbols defined in the subcontext *packName*`` `Private` `` can no longer be accessed.

EndPackage The `EndPackage[]` command puts you back in the context you were in prior to the `BeginPackage[]` command, typically `` Global` ``.

Creation and deployment

Since a package is simply a text file, you could create and develop it in a text editor if you preferred. But there are much more convenient environments in which you can do package development. One such application is the integrated development environment (IDE), Wolfram *Workbench*. With IDEs, you can develop your code, debug it, profile (look for bottlenecks), and create and deploy documentation. Working with IDEs is beyond the scope of this book (several resources are available on the Wolfram website). Instead, we will focus on package development using an environment you should already be familiar with: the *Mathematica* notebook interface.

Using a *Mathematica* notebook as your programming environment provides several useful tools for package development that we will outline here. In particular, converting your notebook into a package and installing it are both straightforward using the front end. Probably the most useful aspect of using *Mathematica* notebooks as your programming environment is the fact that you can experiment and try out code snippets or large-scale programs all in the same environment that you are already familiar with.

Tip 10.1

As you are creating your package, keep each function definition, each option statement, and so on in separate cells. This is generally a good practice whether you are developing packages or not. If a problem arises, an error or warning message will be issued immediately after the cell that triggers that message. If you had dozens of definitions in one cell, warning messages would still be issued after that input cell, but you would have a difficult time trying to determine which part of your code was causing the problem.

Once you have completed the code development in your notebook, select all Input cells (Option-click on Mac OS X or Alt-click on Windows) and then convert them to initialization cells by selecting Cell Properties ▶ Initialization Cell from the Cell menu. This marks those cells that will be included in the package. Saving your notebook at this point should trigger a dialog to create an autogenerated package from this notebook. Answering yes will cause a package (a text file with the .m extension) to be saved in the same location as your notebook (if not, you may have to set the notebook file option AutoGeneratedPackage to Automatic in the Option Inspector available under the Format menu). Furthermore, that package will be automatically updated whenever you save any changes to the corresponding notebook.

Finally, to install the package, select Install from the File menu. This will bring up a dialog (Figure 10.1) in which you can identify the type of item to install (Package), the source (point to your newly created and saved .m package), the install name (typically the name of your package), and whether the package should be made available to all users of your computer or just you.

FIGURE 10.1. *Deploying packages through the* File ▸ Install *menu item.*

10.3 RandomWalks package

Package source code

Let's now create a small package that contains all the pieces in the package framework as described in the first two sections of this chapter. We will use the random walk examples as described throughout this book as our application.

```
BeginPackage["EPM`RandomWalks`"]

RandomWalk::usage =
  "RandomWalk[t] generates a t-step random walk. The default behavior gives
    a two-dimensional lattice walk with steps in one of the four
    compass directions. The option LatticeWalk takes values True or
    False. The value of the option Dimension can be any of 1, 2, or 3.";

Dimension::usage =
  "Dimension is an option to RandomWalk that determines whether
    the random walk will be a one-, two-, or
    three-dimensional walk. Possible values are 1, 2, or 3.";

LatticeWalk::usage =
  "LatticeWalk is an option to RandomWalk that determines
    whether the random walk will be a lattice walk or an
    off-lattice walk. Possible values are True and False.";
```

```
ShowWalk::usage =
  "ShowWalk[walk] displays a one, two, or three-dimensional random
    walk connecting each site with a line. Graphics
    options can be passed to ShowWalk. E.g., ShowWalk[walk,
    Background→GrayLevel[0]] to produce a black background.";

RandomWalk::rwn = "Argument `1` is not a positive integer.";

RandomWalk::baddim =
  "The value `1` of the option Dimension is not a positive integer.";

RandomWalk::baddimlat = "The value `1` of the option
    Dimension is not a positive integer between 1 and 3.";

Options[RandomWalk] = {LatticeWalk → True, Dimension → 2};

Begin["`Private`"]

latticeWalk[steps_, dim_] := Module[{w, mat},
  mat = Join[IdentityMatrix[dim], -IdentityMatrix[dim]];
  w = Accumulate[RandomChoice[mat, steps]];
  If[dim == 1, Flatten[w], w]
 ]

offLatticeWalk[t_, dim_] := Module[{f1, f2, f3},
  f1 := RandomReal[{-1, 1}, t];
  f2 := Map[{Cos[#], Sin[#]} &, RandomReal[{0, 2 π}, t]];
  f3 := MapThread[{Cos[#1] Sqrt[1 - #2^2], Sin[#1] Sqrt[1 - #2^2], #2} &,
    {RandomReal[{0, 2 Pi}, t], RandomReal[{-1, 1}, t]}];
  Which[
   dim == 1, Accumulate[f1],
   dim == 2, Accumulate[f2],
   dim == 3, Accumulate[f3]
  ]]

RandomWalk[t_, OptionsPattern[]] := Module[{dim, latticeQ},
  {latticeQ, dim} = OptionValue[{LatticeWalk, Dimension}];
  Which[
   ! (IntegerQ[t] && t > 0), Message[RandomWalk::"rwn", t],
   (latticeQ && (! IntegerQ[dim] || NonPositive[dim])),
   Message[RandomWalk::baddim, dim],
   (! latticeQ && FreeQ[{1, 2, 3}, dim]),
   Message[RandomWalk::baddimlat, dim],
   latticeQ, latticeWalk[t, dim],
   True, offLatticeWalk[t, dim]]]

RandomWalk[x__] /; Message[RandomWalk::rwn, x] := Null
RandomWalk[] /; Message[General::argx, RandomWalk, 0] := Null;
```

```
ShowWalk[coords_?VectorQ, opts : OptionsPattern[]] :=
 ListLinePlot[coords, FilterRules[{opts}, Options[ListLinePlot]]]

ShowWalk[coords : {{_, _} ..}, opts : OptionsPattern[]] :=
 ListLinePlot[coords, Append[
   FilterRules[{opts}, Options[ListLinePlot]], AspectRatio → Automatic]]

ShowWalk[coords : {{_, _, _} ..}, opts : OptionsPattern[]] :=
 Graphics3D[Line[coords], FilterRules[{opts}, Options[Graphics3D]]]

End[]

EndPackage[]
```

Running the package

It is a good idea, when doing package development, to start with a new session before testing out your package. This way you can avoid some issues with contexts that might arise if you evaluated some context-changing commands in one context and then loaded a package in another.

```
In[9]:= Quit[]
```

Assuming that the `RandomWalks` package has been installed in a directory/folder where *Mathematica* can find it (as described in Section 10.2), this loads the package:

```
In[1]:= << EPM`RandomWalks`
```

Let's start by checking the usage message for the `RandomWalk` function.

```
In[2]:= ? RandomWalk
```

RandomWalk[*t*] generates a *t*-step random walk. The default behavior gives a two-dimensional lattice walk with steps in one of the four compass directions. The option LatticeWalk takes values True or False. The value of the option Dimension can be any of 1, 2, or 3.

This gives a random walk of length ten in two dimensions:

```
In[3]:= RandomWalk[10, Dimension → 2]
Out[3]= {{0, 1}, {-1, 1}, {0, 1}, {0, 0},
  {1, 0}, {0, 0}, {0, 1}, {0, 2}, {-1, 2}, {-2, 2}}
```

Check that `RandomWalk` does the right thing when passed a bad argument or given a value for the `Dimension` option that the function is not set up to handle.

```
In[4]:= RandomWalk[-5]
  RandomWalk::rwn : "Argument -5 is not a positive integer.

In[5]:= RandomWalk[100, Dimension → -6.5]
  RandomWalk::baddim : The value - 6.5 of the option Dimension is not a positive integer.
```

This shows a 10 000-step lattice random walk using the default of two dimensions:

```
In[6]:= ShowWalk[RandomWalk[10000]]
```

Out[6]=

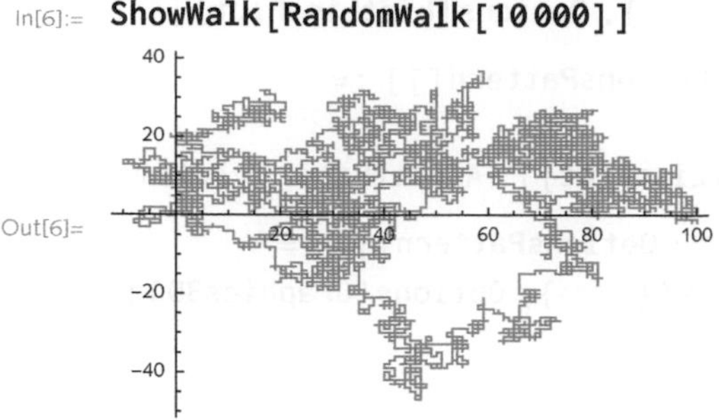

Here is a 20 000-step three-dimensional off-lattice random walk with some graphics options added:

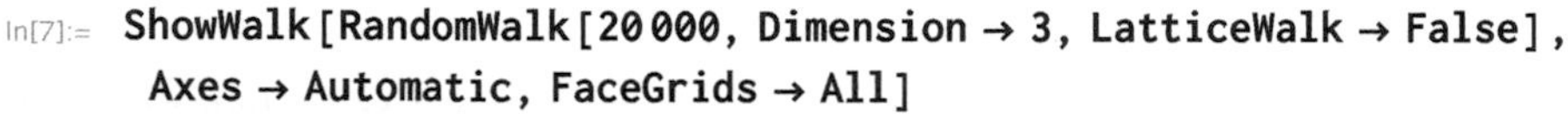

```
In[7]:= ShowWalk[RandomWalk[20000, Dimension → 3, LatticeWalk → False],
          Axes → Automatic, FaceGrids → All]
```

Out[7]=

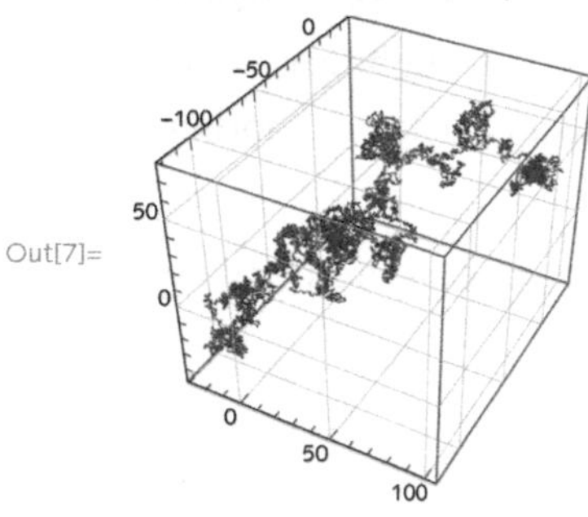

Exercises

1. The following set of exercises will walk you through the creation of a package `Collatz`, a package of functions for performing various operations related to the Collatz problem that we investigated earlier (Exercises 5 and 6 of Section 4.1, Exercise 11 of Section 5.3, and Exercise 10 of Section 5.4). Recall that the Collatz function, for any integer n, returns $3n + 1$ for odd n, and $n/2$ for even n. The (as yet unproven) Collatz conjecture is the statement that, for any initial positive integer n, the iterates of the Collatz function always reach the cycle 4, 2, 1,…. Start by creating an auxiliary function `collatz[n]` that returns $3n + 1$ for n odd and $n/2$ for n even.

   a. Create the function `CollatzSequence[n]` that lists the iterates of the auxiliary function `collatz[n]`. Here is some sample output of the `CollatzSequence` function:

```
In[1]:= CollatzSequence[7]

Out[1]= {7, 22, 11, 34, 17, 52, 26, 13, 40, 20, 10, 5, 16, 8, 4, 2, 1}
```

   b. Create a usage message for `CollatzSequence` and warning messages for each of the following situations:

      `noint`: the argument to `CollatzSequence` is not a positive integer

      `argx`: `CollatzSequence` was called with the wrong number of arguments.

c. Modify the definition of `CollatzSequence` that you created in part a. above so that it does some error trapping and issues the appropriate warning message that you created in part b.

d. Finally, put all the pieces together and write a package `Collatz`` that includes the appropriate `BeginPackage` and `Begin` statements, usage messages, warning messages, and function definitions. Make `CollatzSequence` a public function and `collatz` a private function. Put your package in a directory where *Mathematica* can find it on its search path and then test it to see that it returns correct output such as in the examples below.

```
In[2]:= Quit[];

In[1]:= << EPM`Collatz`

In[2]:= ?CollatzSequence
```

CollatzSequence[*n*] computes the sequence of Collatz iterates starting with initial value *n*. The sequence terminates as soon as it reaches the value 1.

Here are various cases in which `CollatzSequence` is given bad input:

```
In[3]:= CollatzSequence[-5]
```

CollatzSequence::notint : The argument, −5, to CollatzSequence must be a positive integer.

```
In[4]:= CollatzSequence[{a, b}]
```

CollatzSequence::notint : The argument, {a, b}, to CollatzSequence must be a positive integer.

And this computes the sequence for starting value 27:

```
In[5]:= CollatzSequence[27]

Out[5]= {27, 82, 41, 124, 62, 31, 94, 47, 142, 71, 214, 107, 322, 161, 484, 242, 121, 364,
  182, 91, 274, 137, 412, 206, 103, 310, 155, 466, 233, 700, 350, 175, 526, 263,
  790, 395, 1186, 593, 1780, 890, 445, 1336, 668, 334, 167, 502, 251, 754, 377,
  1132, 566, 283, 850, 425, 1276, 638, 319, 958, 479, 1438, 719, 2158, 1079, 3238,
  1619, 4858, 2429, 7288, 3644, 1822, 911, 2734, 1367, 4102, 2051, 6154, 3077,
  9232, 4616, 2308, 1154, 577, 1732, 866, 433, 1300, 650, 325, 976, 488, 244, 122,
  61, 184, 92, 46, 23, 70, 35, 106, 53, 160, 80, 40, 20, 10, 5, 16, 8, 4, 2, 1}
```

2. Take the `StemPlot` function developed in Section 6.2 and create a package around it. Include a usage message and appropriate warning messages that are issued when bad input is supplied.

10.4 Notes and further reading

The random walk model has been studied extensively in mathematics and physics but has also found wide application in fields from chemistry and biology to economics and finance. The original letter to *Nature* magazine that started it all can be found in Pearson (1905). Formal treatments can be found in Barber and Ninham (1970) and the two books by Weiss (1983, 1994). A graduate-level introduction to random walks can be found in Rudnick and Gaspari (2004). For self-avoiding walks – walks that do not return to a previously visited site – see Madras and Slade (2012).

A survey of random walks on graphs is contained in Lovász (1993); using Markov chains with random walks on graphs is discussed in Aldous and Fill (2014). For a look at how random walk models can be used to understand biological processes, see Codling, Plank, and Benhamou (2008).

Bibliography

In addition to those reference items listed here, tutorials and guide pages can be accessed in *Mathematica* under the Help menu or online at reference.wolfram.com. They are referred to throughout the book using the label WLDC for Wolfram Language Documentation Center. PDF and CDF versions of this bibliography, with live links for references, can be downloaded from www.cambridge.org/wellin_essentials.

ABBOTT, PAUL. 1998. Finding roots in an interval. *The Mathematica Journal*, 7(2), 108–112. www.mathematica-journal.com/issue/v7i2/tricks/contents/html/Links/tricks_lnk_5.html.

ALDOUS, DAVID and JAMES ALLEN FILL. 2002. Reversible Markov Chains and Random Walks on Graphs. *unfinished monograph, recompiled* 2014. www.stat.berkeley.edu/~aldous/RWG/book.pdf (accessed 27 June 2015).

BAILEY, DAVID H., JONATHAN M. BORWEIN, CRISTIAN S. CALUDE, MICHAEL J. DINNEEN, MONICA DUMITRESCU, and ALEX YEE. 2012. Normality and the digits of π, in *Exploratory Experimentation in Mathematics: Selected Works*. Perfectly Scientific Press.

BARBER, MICHAEL N. and BARRY W. NINHAM. 1970. *Random and Restricted Walks: Theory and Applications*. Gordon and Breach.

BAR-YOSSEF, ZIV and MAXIM GUREVICH. 2006. Random sampling from a search engine's index, in *Proceedings of the 15th International Conference on World Wide Web, WWW '06*. ACM. dx.doi.org/10.1145/1135777.1135833.

BERGERSON, HOWARD W. 1973. *Palindromes and Anagrams*. Dover.

BIRD, STEVEN, EWAN KLEIN, and EDWARD LOPER. 2009. *Natural Language Processing with Python: Analyzing Text with the Natural Language Toolkit*. O'Reilly Media.

BLUM, LENORE. 2012. Alan Turing and the other theory of computation, in *Proceedings of the 17th Annual Conference on Innovation and Technology in Computer Science Education, ITiCSE '12*. ACM. dx.doi.org/10.1145/2325296.2325299.

BOLLOBÁS, BÉLA. 2001. *Random Graphs*, second edition. Cambridge University Press.

BOLOTIN, ALEXANDER, BENOIT QUINQUIS, ALEXEI SOROKIN, and S. DUSKO EHRLICH. 2005. Clustered regularly interspaced short palindrome repeats (CRISPRs) have spacers of extrachromosomal origin. *Microbiology*, 151(8), 2551–2561. dx.doi.org/10.1099/mic.0.28048-0.

BORGES, JORGE LUIS. 2007. The Library of Babel, in *Labyrinths: Selected Short Stories & Other Writings*. New Directions.

BOURKE, PAUL. 2001. *Julia Set Fractal*(2D). www.paulbourke.net/fractals/juliaset.

BOWERMAN, BRUCE L., RICHARD T. O'CONNELL, and ANNE B. KOEHLER. 2005. *Forecasting, Time Series, and Regression: An Applied Approach*, fourth edition. Thomson Brooks/Cole.

BOX, GEORGE E.P., GWILYM M. JENKINS, and GREGORY C. REINSEL. 2008. *Time Series Analysis: Forecasting and Control*, fourth edition. John Wiley & Sons.

BOYER, CARL B. 1991. *A History of Mathematics*, second edition. Princeton University Press.

BRENT, RICHARD P. 1980. An improved Monte Carlo factorization algorithm. *BIT*, 20(2), 176–184. maths-people.anu.edu.au/~brent/pd/rpb051i.pdf.

CALIFORNIA DEPARTMENT OF WATER RESOURCES. Storage in major reservoirs, *Data Exchange Center*. cdec.water.ca.gov/cgi-progs/reservoirs/STORAGE (accessed 15 Aug 2015).

CALLAWAY, DUNCAN S., MARK E.J. NEWMAN, STEVEN H. STROGATZ, and DUNCAN J. WATTS. 2000. Network robustness and fragility: percolation on random graphs. *Physical Review Letters*, **85**(25), 5468–5471. arxiv.org/pdf/cond-mat/0007300.pdf.

CAR TALK. 2007. *This week's puzzler*, June 25. www.cartalk.com/content/puzzlers.

CENTER FOR CANCER SYSTEMS BIOLOGY. *Caenorhabditis elegans, Worm interactome database*. interactome.dfci.harvard.edu/C_elegans (accessed 24 Mar 2015).

CENTRE FOR APPLIED LINGUISTICS, UNIVERSITY OF WARWICK. Text transcripts and tagged texts, *British Academic Spoken English (Base)*. www2.warwick.ac.uk/fac/soc/al/research/collect/base/lecturetranscripts (accessed 13 June 2014).

CERUZZI, PAUL E. 2012. *Computing: A Concise History*. MIT Press.

CHATFIELD, CHRISTOPHER. 2004. *The Analysis of Time Series: An Introduction*, sixth edition. Chapman & Hall/CRC Press.

CHOMSKY, NOAM. 2002. *Syntactic Structures*, second edition. Mouton de Gruyter.

CHUNG, FAN and WENBO ZHAO. 2010. PageRank and random walks on graphs, in *Fete of Combinatorics and Computer Science: Bolyai Society Mathematical Studies*, Volume 20. Springer. dx.doi.org/10.1007/978-3-642-13580-4_3.

CHURCHHOUSE, ROBERT F. 2001. *Codes and Ciphers: Julius Caesar, the Enigma, and the Internet*. Cambridge University Press.

CIPRA, BARRY. 2005. Third time proves charm for Prime-Gap Theorem. *Science*, **308**(5726), 1238. dx.doi.org/10.1126/science.308.5726.1238.

CLARKSON, KENNETH L. and PETER W. SHOR. 1989. Applications of random sampling in computational geometry, II. *Discrete & Computational Geometry*, 4(1), 387–421. dx.doi.org/10.1007/BF02187740.

CODLING, EDWARD A., MICHAEL J. PLANK, and SIMON BENHAMOU. 2008. Random walk models in biology. *Journal of The Royal Society Interface*, 5(25), 813–834. dx.doi.org/10.1098/rsif.2008.0014.

CONWAY, JOHN H. and RICHARD K. GUY. 1996. Perfect numbers, in *The Book of Numbers*. Springer-Verlag.

COOK, STEPHEN. 2000. The *P* versus *NP* Problem. *The Clay Mathematics Institute for Millennium Prize Problems*. www.claymath.org/sites/default/files/pvsnp.pdf.

COSTA, LUCIANO DA FONTOURA and ROBERTO MARCONDES CESAR. 2001. *Shape Analysis and Classification: Theory and Practice*. CRC Press.

COVER, THOMAS M. and JOY A. THOMAS. 2006. *Elements of Information Theory*, second edition. Wiley Interscience.

CRANDALL, RICHARD E. 1994. *Projects in Scientific Computation.* TELOS/Springer-Verlag.

CRANDALL, RICHARD E. 1996. *Topics in Advanced Scientific Computation.* TELOS/Springer-Verlag.

CRANDALL, RICHARD E. and CARL POMERANCE. 2005. *Prime Numbers: A Computational Perspective,* second edition. Springer.

CRISTIANINI, NELLO and MATTHEW W. HAHN. 2007. *Introduction to Computational Genomics: A Case Studies Approach.* Cambridge University Press.

DATTA, BIBHUTIBHUSAN and AVADHESH N. SINGH. 1938. *History of Hindu Mathematics: A Source Book.* Asia Publishing House.

DAVIS, TIMOTHY A. and YIFAN HU. 2011. The University of Florida sparse matrix collection. *ACM Transactions on Mathematical Software,* 38(1), 1–25. dx.doi.org/10.1145/2049662.2049663.

DICEWARE. Time to add a word, *The Diceware Security Blog.* diceware.blogspot.com (accessed 14 Jul 2015).

DIJKSTRA, EDSGER. 1981. Hamming's exercise in SASL, Report EWD792. www.cs.utexas.edu/users/EWD/ewd07xx/EWD792.PDF.

DOWNEY, ALLEN B. 2012. *Think Python: How to Think Like a Computer Scientist.* O'Reilly Media.

DUCHAMP, MARCEL. 1926. Anémic Cinéma. *UbuWeb.* www.ubu.com/film/duchamp_anemic.html.

DUFF, IAIN S., ROGER G. GRIMES, and JOHN G. LEWIS. 1989. Sparse matrix test problems. *ACM Transactions on Mathematical Software,* 15(1), 1–14. dx.doi.org/10.1145/62038.62043.

EDELMAN, ALAN and GILBERT STRANG. 2004. Pascal matrices. *American Mathematical Monthly,* 111(3), 361–385. dx.doi.org/10.2307/4145127.

ENCYCLOPEDIA OF TRIANGLE CENTERS. Introduction and centers, faculty.evansville.edu/ck6/encyclopedia/ETC.html (accessed 25 Mar 2015).

ENDERTON, HERBERT B. 1972. *A Mathematical Introduction to Logic.* Academic Press.

ERDŐS, PAUL and ALFRED RÉNYI. 1959. On random graphs I. *Publicationes Mathematicae Debrecen,* 6, 290–297. www.renyi.hu/~p_erdos/1959-11.pdf.

FLOYD, ROBERT W. 1962. Algorithm 97: shortest path. *Communications of the ACM,* 5(6), 345. dx.doi.org/10.1145/367766.368168.

FLOYD, ROBERT W. 1979. The paradigms of programming. *Communications of the ACM,* 22(8), 455–460. dx.doi.org/10.1145/359138.359140.

FREGE, GOTTLOB. 1879. *Begriffsschrift,* a formal language, modeled upon that of arithmetic, for pure thought, in *From Frege to Gődel: A Source Book in Mathematical Logic,* 1879–1932, ed. Jean van Heijenoort. Harvard University Press.

FRIEDL, JEFFREY E.F. 2006. *Mastering Regular Expressions,* third edition. O'Reilly Media.

GARDNER, MARTIN. 1978. Perfect, amicable, sociable, in *Mathematical Magic Show: More Puzzles, Games, Diversions, Illusions and Other Mathematical Sleight-of-Mind from Scientific American.* Random House.

GARDNER, MARTIN. 1992. *Fractal Music, Hypercards, and More ... Mathematical Recreations from Scientific American Magazine.* W.H. Freeman.

GAYLORD, RICHARD J. and PAUL R. WELLIN. 1995. *Computer Simulations with Mathematica: Explorations in Complex Physical and Biological Systems.* TELOS/Springer-Verlag.

GIBBS, ADRIAN J. and GEORGE A. MCINTYRE. 1970. The Diagram, a method for comparing sequences; its use with amino acid and nucleotide sequences. *European Journal of Biochemistry,* 16(1), 1–11. dx.doi.org/10.1111/j.1432-1033.1970.tb01046.x.

GOLDREICH, ODED. 2010. *P, NP, and NP-Completeness: The Basics of Computational Complexity.* Cambridge University Press.

GOLIN, MORDECAI and ROBERT SEDGEWICK. 1988. Analysis of a simple yet efficient convex hull algorithm, in *Proceedings of the Fourth Annual Symposium on Computational Geometry.* dx.doi.org/10.1145/73393.73409.

GRAHAM, PAUL. 2002. The roots of Lisp. www.paulgraham.com/lisp.html.

GRAHAM, RONALD. 1972. An efficient algorithm for determining the convex hull of a finite planar set. *Information Processing Letters,* 1(4), 132–133. dx.doi.org/10.1016/0020-0190(72)90045-2.

GRAHAM, RONALD, DONALD E. KNUTH, and OREN PATASHNIK. 1994. *Concrete Mathematics: A Foundation for Computer Science,* second edition. Addison-Wesley.

GRIMMETT, GEOFFREY. 1999. *Percolation,* second edition. Springer.

GRÜNBAUM, BRANKO. 1984. On Venn diagrams and the counting of regions. *The College Mathematics Journal,* 15(5), 433–435. www.jstor.org/stable/2686559.

HAMMING, RICHARD W. 1950. Error detecting and error correcting codes. *The Bell System Technical Journal,* 29(2), 147–160. archive.org/details/bstj29-2-147.

HAMMING, RICHARD W. 1989. *Digital Filters,* third edition. Prentice-Hall.

HAR-PELED, SARIEL. 2001. A practical approach for computing the diameter of a point set, in *Proceedings of the Seventeenth Annual Symposium on Computational Geometry, SCG'01.* Association of Computing Machinery. doi.acm.org/10.1145/378583.378662.

HASKELLWIKI. The Fibonacci sequence, *The Haskell Programming Language.* www.haskell.org/haskellwiki/The_Fibonacci_sequence (accessed 13 Jan 2015).

HATHAWAY, DAVID H. 2010. The solar cycle. *Living Reviews in Solar Physics,* 7, dx.doi.org/10.12942/lrsp-2010-1.

HAYES, ALLAN. 1992. Sums of cubes of digits, driven to abstraction. *Mathematica in Education,* 1(4), 3–11.

HECKBERT, PAUL S. 1994. *Graphics Gems IV.* AP Professional.

HERSTEIN, ISRAEL N. and IRVING KAPLANSKY. 1978. *Matters Mathematical,* second edition. AMS Chelsea Publishing.

HILL, TED P. 1998. The first digit phenomenon. *American Scientist,* 86(4), 358–362. dx.doi.org/10.1511/1998.4.358.

HOFFMAN, PAUL. 1998. *The Man Who Loved Only Numbers: The Story of Paul Erdős and the Search for Mathematical Truth.* Hyperion.

HONSBERGER, ROSS. 1995. *Episodes of Nineteenth and Twentieth Century Euclidean Geometry.* The Mathematical Association of America.

INTERNATIONAL NUCLEOTIDE SEQUENCE DATABASE COLLABORATION. *DNA Databank of Japan.* www.ddbj.nig.ac.jp/searches (accessed 24 Mar 2015).

JARVIS, RAY A. 1973. On the identification of the convex hull of a finite set of points in the plane. *Information Processing Letters*, 2(1), 18–21. dx.doi.org/10.1016/0020-0190(73)90020-3.

JOYCE, JAMES. 1939. *Finnegan's Wake*. Viking Penguin.

JURAFSKY, DANIEL and JAMES H. MARTIN. 2009. *Speech and Language Processing: An Introduction to Natural Language Processing, Computational Linguistics, and Speech Recognition*, second edition. Pearson Prentice Hall.

KERNIGHAN, BRIAN W. and DENNIS M. RITCHIE. 1988. *The C Programming Language*, second edition. Prentice Hall.

KIMBERLING, CLARK. 1994. Central points and central lines in the plane of a triangle. *Mathematics Magazine*, 67(3), 163–187. dx.doi.org/10.2307/2690608.

KIMBERLING, CLARK. 1998. *Triangle Centers and Central Triangles*, Congressus Numerantium, 129. Utilitas Mathematica Publishing.

KNAPP, ROB. 2001. Numerical *Mathematica*, in 2001 *International Mathematica Symposium*.

KNUTH, DONALD E. 1992. *Literate Programming*. Center for the Study of Language and Information, Lecture Notes, no. 27.

KNUTH, DONALD E. 1993. *The Stanford GraphBase: A Platform for Combinatorial Computing*. ACM Press.

KNUTH, DONALD E. 1997. *The Art of Computer Programming, Volume 1: Fundamental Algorithms*, third edition. Addison-Wesley.

KNUTH, DONALD E. 1998. *The Art of Computer Programming, Volume 3: Sorting and Searching*, second edition. Addison-Wesley.

KNUTH, DONALD E. 2000. Textbook examples of recursion, in *Selected Papers on Analysis of Algorithms*. Center for the Study of Language and Information, Lecture Notes, no. 102. arxiv.org/abs/cs/9301113.

KNUTH, DONALD E. 2003. The early development of programming languages, in *Selected Papers on Computer Languages*. Center for the Study of Language and Information, Lecture Notes, no. 139.

KNUTH, DONALD E. 2011. *The Art of Computer Programming, Volume 4A: Combinatorial Algorithms, Part 1*. Addison-Wesley.

LAGARIAS, JEFFREY C., VICTOR S. MILLER, and ANDREW M. ODLYZKO. 1985. Computing $\pi(x)$: the Meissel–Lehmer method. *Mathematics of Computation*, 44(170), 537–560. dx.doi.org/10.1090/S0025-5718-1985-0777285-5.

LAGARIAS, JEFFREY C. and ANDREW M. ODLYZKO. 1987. Computing $\pi(x)$: an analytic method. *Journal of Algorithms*, 8(2), 173–191. dx.doi.org/10.1016/0196-6774(87)90037-X.

LAGARIAS, JEFFREY C. and K. SOUNDARARAJAN. 2006. Benford's law for the $3x + 1$ function. *Journal of the London Mathematical Society*, 74(2), 289–303. dx.doi.org/10.1112/S0024610706023131.

LAGARIAS, JEFFREY C. 2010. The $3x + 1$ problem and its generalizations, in *The Ultimate Challenge: The $3x + 1$ Problem*. American Mathematical Society.

LAWLER, EUGENE L., JAN KAREL LENSTRA, A.H.G. RINNOOY KAN, and D.B. SHMOYS. 1985. *The Traveling Salesman Problem: A Guided Tour of Combinatorial Optimization*. John Wiley & Sons.

LESK, ARTHUR M. 2010. *Introduction to Protein Science: Architecture, Function, and Genomics*, second edition. Oxford University Press.

LIMA, MANUEL. 2011. *Visual Complexity: Mapping Patterns of Information.* Princeton Architectural Press.

LIN, SHEN. 1965. Computer solutions of the traveling salesman problem. *Bell System Technical Journal,* **44**, 2245–2269. ieeexplore.ieee.org/stamp/stamp.jsp?arnumber=6767727.

LOVÁSZ, L. 1993. Random walks on graphs: a survey. *Combinatorics, Paul Erdős is Eighty,* 2, 1–46. www.cs.elte.hu/~lovasz/erdos.pdf.

MACKAY, DAVID J.C. 2003. *Information Theory, Inference and Learning Algorithms.* Cambridge University Press.

MADACHY, JOSEPH S. 1979. *Madachy's Mathematical Recreations.* Dover Publications.

MADRAS, NEAL and GORDON SLADE. 2012. *The Self-Avoiding Walk.* Birkhäuser.

MAEDER, ROMAN E. 1994. Animated algorithms. *The Mathematica Journal,* 4(4), 37–43. www.mathematica-journal.com/issue/v4i4/columns/maeder.

MAEDER, ROMAN E. 1997. *Programming in Mathematica,* third edition. Addison-Wesley.

MAEDER, ROMAN E. 2000. *Computer Science with Mathematica: Theory and Practice for Science, Mathematics, and Engineering.* Cambridge University Press.

MALANDAIN, GRÉGOIRE and JEAN-DANIEL BOISSONNAT. 2002. Computing the diameter of a point set, in *Discrete Geometry for Computer Imagery.* Lecture Notes in Computer Science, Vol. 2301. dx.doi.org/10.1007/3-540-45986-3_18.

MANDELBROT, BENOÎT. 1982. *The Fractal Geometry of Nature.* W.H. Freeman.

MANGANO, SALVATORE. 2010. *Mathematica Cookbook.* O'Reilly Media.

MANNING, CHRISTOPHER D. and HINRICH SCHÜTZE. 1999. *Foundations of Statistical Natural Language Processing.* MIT Press.

MANNING, CHRISTOPHER D., PRABHAKAR RAGHAVAN, and HINRICH SCHÜTZE. 2008. *Introduction to Information Retrieval.* Cambridge University Press.

MAOR, ELI. 1998. *Trigonometric Delights.* Princeton University Press.

MARSAGLIA, GEORGE. 1972. Choosing a point from the surface of a sphere. *The Annals of Mathematical Statistics,* 43(2), 645–646. dx.doi.org/10.1214/aoms/1177692644.

MATHEWS, MAX V., JOAN E. MILLER, F. RICHARD MOORE, JOHN R. PIERCE, and J.C. RISSET. 1969. *The Technology of Computer Music.* The MIT Press.

MCCARTHY, JOHN. 1979. History of Lisp. *Artificial Intelligence Laboratory,* Stanford University. www-formal.stanford.edu/jmc/history/lisp/lisp.html.

MCKAY, BRENDAN D., FRÉDÉRIQUE E. OGGIER, GORDON F. ROYLE, N.J.A. SLOANE, IAN M. WANLESS, and HERBERT S. WILF. 2004. Acyclic digraphs and eigenvalues of (0,1)-matrices. *Journal of Integer Sequences,* 7(3), arxiv.org/abs/math/0310423.

MERINGER, MARKUS and ERIC W. WEISSTEIN. Regular graph. *MathWorld.* mathworld.wolfram.com/RegularGraph.html.

MERSENNE RESEARCH, INC. List of known Mersenne primes, *Great Internet Mersenne Prime Search.* www.mersenne.org/prime.htm (accessed 24 Mar 2015).

METROPOLIS, NICHOLAS. 1987. The beginning of the Monte Carlo method, in *Los Alamos Science, 1987 Special Issue dedicated to Stanislaw Ulam.* library.lanl.gov/la-pubs/00326866.pdf.

MONNEROT-DUMAINE, ALEXIS. 2009. The Fibonacci word fractal. *HAL Archives-Ouvertes.* hal.archives-ouvertes.fr/hal-00367972.

MOORE, CRISTOPHER and MARK E.J. NEWMAN. 2000. Exact solution of site and bond percolation on small-world networks. *Physical Review E,* 62(5), 7059–7064. dx.doi.org/10.1103/PhysRevE.62.7059.

NASA. Global temperature, *Global Climate Change.* climate.nasa.gov/vital-signs/global-temperature (accessed 24 Mar 2015).

NATIONAL CENTER FOR ATMOSPHERIC RESEARCH. Global temperature data sets: overview & comparison table, *The Climate Data Guide.* climatedataguide.ucar.edu/collections/overview-comparison-page (accessed 12 Dec 2014).

NATIONAL CENTER FOR BIOTECHNOLOGY INFORMATION. *Nucleotide Database.* www.ncbi.nlm.nih.gov/nuccore (accessed 25 Mar 2015).

NATIONAL CENTER FOR BIOTECHNOLOGY INFORMATION. Serotonin, CID=5202, *PubChem Compound Database.* pubchem.ncbi.nlm.nih.gov/compound/5202 (accessed 25 Mar 2015).

NATIONAL INSTITUTE OF GENETICS. List of species, *Genome Composition Database.* esper.lab.nig.ac.jp/genome/?page=genome_composition_database_species_list (accessed 25 Mar 2015).

NATIONAL INSTITUTE OF STANDARDS AND TECHNOLOGY. Lag plot, *e-Handbook of Statistical Methods.* www.itl.nist.gov/div898/handbook/eda/section3/eda33f.htm (accessed 21 Apr 2015).

NATIONAL INSTITUTE OF STANDARDS AND TECHNOLOGY. Matrix Market, *Sparse Matrix Collection.* math.nist.gov/MatrixMarket/index.html (accessed 9 Oct 2014).

NEWMAN, MARK E.J. 2010. *Networks: An Introduction.* Oxford University Press.

NIGRINI, MARK J. 2012. *Benford's Law: Applications for Forensic Accounting, Auditing, and Fraud Detection.* John Wiley & Sons.

OAK RIDGE NATIONAL LABORATORY. NASA GISS surface temperature (GISTEMP) analysis, *Carbon Dioxide Information Analysis Center.* dx.doi.org/10.3334/CDIAC/cli.001 (accessed 20 Apr 2015).

O'ROURKE, JOSEPH. 1998. *Computational Geometry in C,* second edition. Cambridge University Press.

PAAR, CHRISTOF and JAN PELZL. 2010. *Understanding Cryptography: A Textbook for Students and Practitioners.* Springer.

PEARSON, KARL. 1905. The problem of the random walk. *Nature,* 72(1865), 294.

PEITGEN, HEINZ-OTTO, HARTMUT JÜRGENS, and DIETMAR SAUPE. 2004. *Chaos and Fractals: New Frontiers in Science,* second edition. Springer-Verlag.

PEMMARAJU, SRIRAM V. and STEVEN S. SKIENA. 2003. *Computational Discrete Mathematics: Combinatorics and Graph Theory with Mathematica.* Cambridge University Press.

PETROVAY, KRISTÓF. 2010. Solar cycle prediction. *Living Reviews in Solar Physics,* 7(6), dx.doi.org/10.12942/lrsp-2010-6.

PLATZMAN, LOREN K. and JOHN J. BARTHOLDI III. 1989. Spacefilling curves and the planar traveling salesman problem. *Journal of the ACM,* 36(4), 719–737. dx.doi.org/10.1145/76359.76361.

PORTA, HORACIO, WILLIAM DAVIS, and JERRY UHL. 1994. *Calculus&Mathematica.* Addison-Wesley.

PREPARATA, FRANCO P. and MICHAEL IAN SHAMOS. 1985. *Computational Geometry: An Introduction.* Springer-Verlag.

PRESS, WILLIAM H., SAUL A. TEUKOLSKY, WILLIAM T. VETTERLING, and BRIAN P. FLANNERY. 2007. *Numerical Recipes: The Art of Scientific Computing,* third edition. Cambridge University Press.

PROJECT EULER. Problem #168: Number rotations, *Problems Archives.* projecteuler.net/problem=168 (accessed 17 Feb 2015).

PROJECT GUTENBERG. *Portrait of the Artist as a Young Man,* www.gutenberg.org/ebooks/4217 (accessed 24 Mar 2015).

RAMÍREZ, JOSÉ L. and GUSTAVO N. RUBIANO. 2014. Properties and generalizations of the Fibonacci word fractal: exploring fractal curves. *The Mathematica Journal,* 16(2), www.mathematica-journal.com/2014/02/.

RAMÍREZ, JOSÉ L., GUSTAVO N. RUBIANO, and RODRIGO DE CASTRO. 2014. A generalization of the Fibonacci word fractal and the Fibonacci snowflake. *arXiv.org.* arxiv.org/abs/1212.1368.

RITCHIE, DENNIS M. 1993. The development of the C language, in *The Second ACM SIGPLAN Conference on History of Programming Languages, HOPL-II.* Association of Computing Machinery. dx.doi.org/10.1145/154766.155580.

DE LAS RIVAS, JAVIER and CELIA FONTANILLO. 2010. Protein–protein interactions essentials: key concepts to building and analyzing interactome networks. *PLoS Computational Biology,* 6(6), dx.doi.org/10.1371/journal.pcbi.1000807.

ROEDERER, JUAN G. 2008. *The Physics and Psychophysics of Music: An Introduction,* fourth edition. Springer.

ROSENKRANTZ, DANIEL J., RICHARD E. STEARNS, and PHILIP M. LEWIS II. 1977. An analysis of several heuristics for the traveling salesman problem. *SIAM Journal of Computing,* 6(3), 563–581. dx.doi.org/10.1137/0206041.

ROYAL OBSERVATORY OF BELGIUM. The international sunspot number, *Silso World Data Center.* www.sidc.be/silso (accessed 17 Feb 2015).

RUDNICK, JOSEPH and GEORGE GASPARI. 2004. *Elements of the Random Walk: An Introduction for Advanced Students and Researchers.* Cambridge University Press.

RUEDY, R., M. SATO, and K. LO. 2015. NASA GISS surface temperature (GISTEMP) analysis, in *Trends: A Compendium of Data on Global Change.* Carbon Dioxide Information Analysis Center, Oak Ridge National Laboratory, U.S. Department of Energy. dx.doi.org/10.3334/CDIAC/cli.001.

RUMP, S.M. 1991. A class of arbitrarily ill-conditioned floating-point matrices. *SIAM Journal of Matrix Analysis and Applications,* 12(4), 645–653. dx.doi.org/10.1137/0612049.

RUSKEY, FRANK and MARK WESTON. 2005. A survey of Venn diagrams. *The Electronic Journal of Combinatorics,* DS5, www.combinatorics.org/files/Surveys/ds5/VennEJC.html.

SCHULZ, JAN. 2008. Introduction to dot plots. *Code 10.* www.code10.info/index.php?option=com_content&view=article&id=64:inroduction-to-dot-plots&catid=52:cat_coding_algorithms_dot-plots&Itemid=76.

SCHWARTZ, RANDAL L., BRIAN D FOY, and TOM PHOENIX. 2011. *Learning Perl,* sixth edition. O'Reilly & Associates.

SEDGEWICK, ROBERT and KEVIN WAYNE. 2007. *Introduction to Programming in Java: An Interdisciplinary Approach.* Addison-Wesley.

SEDGEWICK, ROBERT and KEVIN WAYNE. 2011. *Algorithms,* fourth edition. Addison-Wesley.

SHAMOS, MICHAEL I. and DAN HOEY. 1975. Closest-point problems, in *16th Annual Symposium on Foundations of Computer Science.* IEEE. dx.doi.org/10.1109/SFCS.1975.8.

SHANKS, DANIEL. 1993. *Solved and Unsolved Problems in Number Theory,* fourth edition. Chelsea.

SHANNON, CLAUDE E. 1948. A mathematical theory of computation. *The Bell System Technical Journal,* 27(3,4), 379–423, 623–656. dx.doi.org/10.1002/j.1538-7305.1948.tb01338.x.

SHEPARD, ROGER N. 1962. The analysis of proximities: multidimensional scaling with an unknown distance function, I. *Psychometrika,* 27(2), 125–140. dx.doi.org/10.1007/BF02289630.

SINKOV, ABRAHAM. 2009. *Elementary Cryptanalysis: A Mathematical Approach,* second edition. The Mathematical Association of America.

SKIENA, STEVEN S. 2008. *The Algorithm Design Manual,* second edition. Springer Science+Business Media.

SLOANE, N.J.A. A019518, Smarandache–Wellin numbers. *The On-Line Encyclopedia of Integer Sequences.* oeis.org/A019518.

STAUFFER, DIETRICH and AMMON AHARONY. 1994. *Introduction to Percolation Theory,* second edition. Taylor & Francis.

TAO, TERENCE. 2009. Benford's law, Zipf's law, and the Pareto distribution. terrytao.wordpress.com/2009/07/03/benfords-law-zipfs-law-and-the-pareto-distribution.

TEETOR, PAUL. 2011. *R Cookbook.* O'Reilly Media.

THOMSON, DIETRICH E. 1982. Making music–fractally. *Journal of the Acoustical Society of America,* 72(6), 2036. dx.doi.org/10.1121/1.388637.

TROTT, MICHAEL. 2004. *The Mathematica Guidebook for Graphics.* Springer-Verlag.

TROTT, MICHAEL. 2004. *The Mathematica Guidebook for Programming.* Springer-Verlag.

TROTT, MICHAEL. 2006. *The Mathematica Guidebook for Numerics.* Springer Science+Business Media.

THE UNICODE CONSORTIUM. Unicode 8.0 Character Code Charts, *Unicode Standard.* www.unicode.org/charts (accessed 25 Mar 2015).

UNIVERSITY OF CHICAGO PRESS. 2010. *The Chicago Manual of Style,* sixteenth edition. University of Chicago Press.

VOSS, RICHARD F. and JOHN CLARKE. 1978. 1/*f* noise in music: music from 1/*f* noise. *Journal of the Acoustical Society of America,* 63(1), 258–263. dx.doi.org/10.1121/1.381721.

WAGON, STAN. 1999. *Mathematica in Action,* second edition. TELOS/Springer-Verlag.

WALL, LARRY, TOM CHRISTIANSEN, and JON ORWANT. 2000. *Programming Perl,* third edition. O'Reilly Media.

WATTS, DUNCAN J. and STEVEN H. STROGATZ. 1998. Collective dynamics of small-world networks. *Nature,* 393(6684), 440–442. dx.doi.org/10.1038/30918.

WEISS, GEORGE H. 1983. Random walks and their applications. *American Scientist,* 71(1), 65–71. www.jstor.org/stable/27851819.

WEISS, GEORGE H. 1994. *Aspects and Applications of the Random Walk.* North Holland.

WEISSTEIN, ERIC W. Hypocycloid. *MathWorld.* www.mathworld.wolfram.com/Hypocycloid.html.

WEISSTEIN, ERIC W. Lucky number. *MathWorld.* mathworld.wolfram.com/LuckyNumber.html.

WEISSTEIN, ERIC W. Sierpinski sieve. *MathWorld.* mathworld.wolfram.com/SierpinskiSieve.html.

WEISSTEIN, ERIC W. Sphere point picking. *MathWorld.* www.mathworld.wolfram.com/SpherePointPicking.html.

WELLIN, PAUL. 2013. *Programming with Mathematica: An Introduction.* Cambridge University Press.

WICKHAM-JONES, TOM. 1994. *Computer Graphics with Mathematica.* TELOS/Springer-Verlag.

WIER, THOMAS. 2014. Is it easier to make palindromes in some languages than in others? *Quora.* www.quora.com/Is-it-easier-to-make-palindromes-in-some-languages-than-in-others (accessed 15 June 2015).

WIKIBOOKS. Strings, *Python Programming.* en.wikibooks.org/wiki/Python_Programming/Strings (accessed 25 Mar 2015).

THE WILCOX SOLAR OBSERVATORY. Complete MF time series, *The Mean Magnetic Field of the Sun.* wso.stanford.edu/#MeanField (accessed 8 Aug 2015).

ZAKI, MOHAMMED J. and WAGNER MEIRA JR. 2014. *Data Mining and Analysis: Fundamental Concepts and Algorithms.* Cambridge University Press.

Index